SHELLEY

EARL R. WASSERMAN

SHELLEY
A Critical Reading

THE JOHNS HOPKINS PRESS BALTIMORE AND LONDON

Copyright © 1971 by The Johns Hopkins Press
All rights reserved
Manufactured in the United States of America

The Johns Hopkins Press, Baltimore, Maryland 21218
The Johns Hopkins Press Ltd., London

Library of Congress Catalog Card Number 70-138036

International Standard Book Number 0-8018-1212-7

This book has been brought to publication with the
generous assistance of a grant from The Carl and Lily
Pforzheimer Foundation, Inc.

Contents

⌒

v

Preface

To commit oneself to literary interpretation is necessarily to enter the unending hermeneutic circle, with its promise of progressive revelation. Part and whole being interdependent, the full meaning of the part is contingent on its role in the totality, but the nature and significance of the totality are functions of its parts. The interpreter therefore alternates between partial comprehension of a literary datum and what it implies of the significant form of the whole made up of its component data, widening and refining his understanding of the literary text as the encompassing form and the sum of the components gradually assimilate each other. The movement from part to whole is not from one datum to another but from a given detail—a recurrent word, perhaps, an image, metaphor, character, scene—to the implicit relational principle significantly governing the whole and, in turn, defining the particular functions of the details. The factors generate the inclusive relational laws, and those laws assign the parts their duties, in order that parts and organizational principles, like the signifying words and organizational syntax of a sentence, may constitute meaning. The fundamental requirement of interpretation is always the determination of context, that is, the principle by which the parts perform their constitutive function; and our interpretive disagreements are usually disagreements over what the relevant context is, over whether we have the right framework for putting the work together organically. Shelley's *The Sensitive Plant* means

one thing if we read it for its narrative structure and quite another in the
context of the organization mapped out by its ancillary imagery. But as
we have learned from the fact that a literary work may yield more than
one apparently adequate interpretation of its components, the hermeneutic
circle *per se* tends to be self-confirming, since it reads back into the parts
the form of the whole it has derived from them. To achieve greater precision, therefore, it is customary to choose among the syntactical systems
possibly applicable the one that conforms most nearly to the author's
habits of mind as evidenced in his other statements.

Of the poetic interpretations that make up this book, those previously
published as discrete, but now set into a comprehensive organization, were
composed on these principles. In *Adonais* the images of light and moisture,
for example, are found to play upon each other in particular patterns that
generate a significant inclusive relationship between life and immortal
spirit; that relationship in turn clarifies the role of other images and actions
in the poem; and other poems and statements by Shelley are found to
confirm that syntactic principle by conformity. But an explicatory procedure directed so narrowly toward a single text, I have come to believe,
neglects a larger operative context. Even though it turns to other expressions by the author for direction and confirmation, it insufficiently regards
the participation of the individual poem in the inclusive organizational
principles of his "mind"—by which I mean no metaphysical absolute but
whatever mental structure is formulated by the total body of his available
works. Mere reference to his other statements and practices is an inadequate extratextual guide to and verification of context. There is a
larger hermeneutic circle that passes back and forth between the interpretation of the single text and the mental organization evident only
through the interpretation of the inclusive available corpus. For that
literary whole constructs and incorporates a coherent mind which defines
the context of the individual work. Explication of a single work and explications of all the works—or at least a sufficiently representative number
of them—presuppose each other.

Such a theory of the relation of poem to corpus does not assume the
identical behavior of all the poems: Shelley's poems obviously differ from
each other in their significant organizational laws. Nor, while insisting
that, in a radical sense, the poetic mind as defined does not change, does
the theory assume that the poet cannot "change his mind" or even that
his poems may not contradict each other. But it does assume a radical
character of mind that is constant and unfolds in coherently related patterns. Shelley's uncertainty of utopia in *Julian and Maddalo* is contra-
dicted by the utopianism of his subsequent *Prometheus Unbound*, but the
mental network on which the two poems rest is the same. This difference
of stance within a coherent mental structure is not to be confused with a
chronological transformation of that mental structure. There is some
semblance of chronology in the arrangement of the following chapters:

they begin with *Alastor* and *Julian and Maddalo*, which are relatively early, and end with *Epipsychidion* and *Adonais*, which are relatively late. But my intention is not a study of temporal change or development. I have, instead, assumed that, synchronically, Shelley's poetic corpus forms a coherent design and have arranged the individual analyses in that order which appears most logical and convenient—that is, in the order that best allows me simultaneously to unfold the structure of his mind and to explicate the poem in the context of that structure, regardless of the date of the poem's composition.

At the center of the mind in Shelley's collective works are a denial of any self-evident truths that may serve as constructive first principles and a consequent indecision between contradictory desires for worldly perfection and an ideal postmortal eternity. Therefore, the first section of this book is devoted to those poems that are most fully governed by this kind of skepticism and are least metaphysical. The next section, drawing on both Shelley's prose and explications of his relevant poems, elaborates the structure of his metaphysics—principally his conceptions of existence, reality, selfhood, and causation, and their relation to transcendence—and his consequent poetics. In this expanded context, I then read *Prometheus Unbound* and *Hellas*, the major poems expressive of his impulse toward utopianism, and then *Epipsychidion* and *Adonais*, the major expressions of his impulse toward a postmortal transcendence. My objective is still the interpretation of the individual poem, not an anatomy of the Shelleyan "mind" or analysis of anything that cuts across or lies behind the collective works, for my conviction is that the end of the critical act is the fullest possible experience of the discrete work of art and that all other critical activities are only heuristic. What is gained, I believe, by simultaneously interpreting the single poem and organizing the structure of the poet's mind implicit in his total works is not only a greater refinement of the relevant context but also the exclusion of irrelevant and distorting ones. It makes a great deal of difference, for example, whether we assume that the *Hymn to Intellectual Beauty* and *Ode to the West Wind* share the same particular frame of reference or whether we recognize that the former is concerned with the relation of some transcendent perfection to our mutable world and that the latter confines itself to causation within the temporal world. *Prometheus Unbound* becomes considerably different if we assume that its dimensions include transcendent being or if, locating it properly in the map of Shelley's poetic mind, we recognize it as limited to the world of existence. Such poems as *Mont Blanc, Prometheus Unbound, Epipsychidion,* and even *Adonais* gain their special tonality only if, in the context of their comprehensive poetic mind, we perceive the skeptical quality in them, and nearly all the poems become richer when we recognize in them their related but variant strategies for embodying or surmounting Shelley's skepticism.

Acknowledgments

                    In the preparation of this book I have been aided by a Guggenheim Fellowship, a travel grant from the American Council of Learned Societies, and a visiting residency at The Ohio State University for a quarter. For the last of these and for his interest and intellectual companionship I am especially indebted to Professor Albert J. Kuhn. The Bodleian Library and the Delegates of the Clarendon Press have kindly granted me permission to quote from the Bodleian Shelley MSS; and the Pierpont Morgan Library has allowed me use of its Shelley MSS. I want particularly to express my debt to Dr. Donald H. Reiman, of the Carl H. Pforzheimer Library, for his unfailing kindness and his readiness to draw on his rich knowledge of Shelley to answer my too-frequent questions. I am conscious (especially in its archaic sense of awareness of wrongdoing) that I have failed to confess in my footnotes my debts to many, if not all, who have written on Shelley; my defense is that the book is already sufficiently cluttered and that the reader would not be illuminated by such a roster, and my reason is that I can no longer distinguish between *tuum* and *suum*, much less between *meum* and *tuum*.

In somewhat different form and without the encompassing context of this book, the chapters on *Mont Blanc*, *The Sensitive Plant*, and *Adonais* appeared in my *The Subtler Language* (Baltimore: The Johns Hopkins Press, 1959) and the chapters on *Prometheus Unbound* in my *Shelley's*

"Prometheus Unbound" (Baltimore: The Johns Hopkins Press, 1965). The chapter on *A Defence of Poetry*, also in slightly different form, appeared as "Shelley's Last Poetics: A Reconsideration," in *From Sensibility to Romanticism*, edited by Frederick W. Hilles and Harold Bloom (New York, 1965), and the editors of the Oxford University Press have graciously permitted its incorporation.

Abbreviations

HARVARD NOTEBOOK *The Shelley Notebook in the Harvard College Library,* ed. George E. Woodberry, Cambridge, Mass., 1929.

HUNTINGTON NOTEBOOKS *Note Books of Percy Bysshe Shelley, from the Originals in the Library of W. K. Bixby,* ed. H. Buxton Forman, 3 vols., St. Louis, Mo., 1911.

JULIAN *The Complete Works of Percy Bysshe Shelley,* ed. Roger Ingpen and Walter E. Peck, 10 vols., New York, 1965.

LETTERS *The Letters of Percy Bysshe Shelley,* ed. Frederick L. Jones, 2 vols., Oxford, 1964.

MS Bodleian MS Shelley adds. (e.g., MS e. 6 = Bodleian MS Shelley adds. e. 6). All other MS references will be noted in full.

REIMAN Donald H. Reiman, *Shelley's "The Triumph of Life": A Critical Study, Based on a Text Newly Edited from the Bodleian Manuscript* (Illinois Studies in Language and Literature, 55; Urbana, Ill., 1965).

ZILLMAN *Shelley's "Prometheus Unbound": A Variorum Edition,* ed. Lawrence John Zillman, Seattle, Wash., 1959.

⟨ ⟩ Manuscript cancellation.

All translations from the Greek and Latin classics are from the Loeb Classical Library.

Part I Skepticism

1 The Poetry of Skepticism

Alastor

Hymns of Pan and Apollo

∽

In the labyrinthine confusion of Shelley's early intellectual probings two convictions persist unequivocally: his denial of a creative and superintending deity (together with a rejection of institutional Christianity and the doctrine of original sin) and his persuasion that human life is perfectible. After a brief and unsuccessful struggle to demonstrate to Thomas Jefferson Hogg a creative Cause, he conceded that the universe has existed from eternity and is governed by the indwelling Spirit of Nature. This pantheistic Spirit is the "beneficent actuating principle," not because it has will and chooses good rather than evil, but because it is "*necessarily* beneficent," fulfilling itself in accordance with ineluctable causal laws.[1] Consequently, were man to withdraw the obstacles, such as Christianity and monarchy, with which he has thwarted this Spirit and were he to submit to it as passively as nature does, his "present potence will become omnipotence," and "human powers whose progression in improvement has been so great since the remotest tradition" will develop interminably toward perfection.[2] The vision of this youthful heir of the French Revolution is as splendidly optimistic as his denunciation of Christianity is vehement.

But from the beginning he also insisted on a further doctrine that he could not easily fit into his atheistic perfectibilism, or the Godwinian

[1] To Hogg, 3 January 1811 (*Letters*, I, 35).
[2] To Elizabeth Hitchener, 19 October 1811 (*Letters*, I, 152).

3

theory of an unending progress toward perfection.[3] His early reason for being reluctant to abandon the notion of "some vast intellect" that "animates Infinity" and is the "First Cause" was, he confessed, that such disbelief annihilates "the strongest argument in support of the existence of a future state."[4] "Do we not exist after the tomb?" he persists in asking his correspondents, as though pleading that they supply the explanation for his faith; for by finally denying a superintending intelligent deity and placing all his confidence in the mindless Spirit of Nature and its inherent laws of necessity whereby events must succeed each other in a fixed causal sequence,[5] he abandoned the principal support for immortality. "I have considered it in every possible light & reason tells me that death is the boundary of the life of man. Yet I feel, I believe the direct contrary."[6] Having grounded on rational credibility both his rejection of Christianity, with its anthropomorphic God, and his doctrine of the Spirit of Nature that necessarily drives to perfection, Shelley could account for his conviction of immortality only on the basis of feeling and imagination.[7] I "feel" that we do not end in annihilation, he writes Elizabeth Hitchener; and he adds, the underscoring revealing the degree of his desperation, "can *you* PROVE it?"[8]

Shelley's two aspirations, then, are unrelated and have different roots. On the one side, he has rational confidence in a Spirit of Nature that, operating in the same manner on nature and man, can impel them interminably toward perfection; on the other, he aspires to a perfect eternal afterlife, sanctioned not by divine revelation and a transcendent deity but only by his feeling and wishes. They not only are unrelated doctrines but also devalue each other, since perfection in either realm renders the other pointless; and they can be brought together only by the kind of poetic forcing that he undertakes in his unguardedly optimistic *Queen Mab*. The

---

[3] William Godwin, *Enquiry Concerning Political Justice*, ed. F. E. L. Priestley (London, 1946), I, p. 93: "By perfectible, it is not meant that [man] is capable of being brought to perfection. But the word seems sufficiently adapted to express the faculty of being continually made better and receiving perpetual improvement. . . ."
[4] To Hogg, 3 January 1811 (*Letters*, I, 35).
[5] *Queen Mab*, VI. 198n. ("Necessity! thou mother of the world!"): "He who asserts the doctrine of Necessity means that, contemplating the events which compose the moral and material universe, he beholds only an immense and uninterrupted chain of causes and effects, no one of which could occupy any other place than it does occupy, or act in any other place than it does act. The idea of necessity is obtained by our experience of the connection between objects, the uniformity of the operations of nature, the constant conjunction of similar events, and the consequent inference of one from the other. Mankind are therefore agreed in the admission of necessity, if they admit that these two circumstances take place in voluntary action. Motive is, to voluntary action in the human mind, what cause is to effect in the material universe," etc. Cf. Godwin, *Political Justice*, I, pp. 363ff.
[6] To Elizabeth Hitchener, 16 October 1811 (*Letters*, I, 150).
[7] To Elizabeth Hitchener, 16 October 1811 and 24 November 1811 (*Letters*, I, 150, 192).
[8] 10 December 1811 (*Letters*, I, 201).

subject there is earthly, human perfectibility through man's passive "coalescing" with "changeless nature," whose Spirit is the "all-sufficing Power," the "mother of the world";[9] and yet, however incompatibly, Shelley cannot refrain from also contemplating the even more glorious prospect of death, which "leads to azure isles and beaming skies / And happy regions of eternal hope," the "sempiternal heritage" to which the soul aspires.[10] This is the naively optimistic Shelley we have customarily resisted, Matthew Arnold's "beautiful and ineffectual angel, beating in the void his luminous wings in vain." But there is another Shelley, who becomes a poet when his two aspirations, so imperfectly held together in *Queen Mab* and his early letters, begin to fall apart into an opposition. Even in 1811 he was conscious that his doctrine of perfectibility depends upon man's blinding himself to his own nature and avoiding analysis of his own mind:

We look around us—we find that we exist, we find ourselves reasoning upon the mystery which involves our being—we see virtue & vice, we see light & darkness, each are separate, distinct; the line which divides them is glaringly perceptible; yet how racking it is to the soul, when enquiring into its own operations, to find that perfect virtue is very far from attainable, to find reason tainted by feeling, to see the mind when analysed exhibit a picture of irreconcileable inconsistencies, even when perhaps a moment before, it imagined that it had grasped the fleeting Phantom of virtue.[11]

Underneath Shelley's apparently unqualified optimism about an afterlife and the perfectibility of human life there is a dark uncertainty that surfaces in moments of despondency: "How little philosophy & affection consort with this turbid scene—this dark scheme of things finishing in unfruitful death."[12] When that kind of uncertainty enters functionally into his poetry, his adolescence is over and his true poetic career begins.

Whereas the optimistic utopianism of *Queen Mab* had been based on Shelley's confidence in the omnipresence and constancy of the morally neutral, "*necessarily* beneficent" Spirit of Nature, almost all the poems in the *Alastor* volume of 1816 revolve about the theme of man's transience and nature's inconstancy, and they consequently meditate on the possibility that there is meaning in death rather than in the world of life. No dark personal experience, no sudden depression of spirits, and certainly no mere concession to a faddish *Weltschmerz* will adequately explain his abrupt change of mood, for underlying it are the inherent antinomy and instability of his premises. The only enduring principle in the world that he now admits is not the Spirit of Nature but mutability: only transience

---

[9] *Queen Mab*, VI. 42, 197–98.
[10] *Ibid.*, IX. 161–63; I. 149.
[11] To Elizabeth Hitchener, 20 June 1811 (*Letters*, I, 109).
[12] To Mary Godwin, 4 November 1814 (*Letters*, I, 419).

is not transitory.[13] The contradictory alternations of spring and autumn, morning and midnight, frown and smile, are reconcilable only by "the frost that binds the dead," for "Whatever moves, or toils, or grieves, hath its appointed sleep," nature in its recurrent pauses and man in his grave.[14] Shelley was soon to repeat approximately the same words in *Mont Blanc,* but there, in an effort to make coherent sense of mortal existence, he envisions a transcendent constant behind these apparent cessations and vacancies. Meanwhile, however, the brief poems of the *Alastor* volume mourn both man's transitoriness and nature's instability, so that no hopes can be built either "On the false earth's inconstancy" or on men, who are but "clouds that veil the midnight moon" or fickle flames of life or "forgotten lyres" responding variously to each varying wind.[15]

Such inconstancy, both subjective and objective, vitiates all earthly values. Although Nature's active spirits minister to man[16] and although the sublime and novel in "the boundless realm of unending change" are stirring experiences,[17] the principle of mutability has swollen to such predominance in Shelley's mind that it forbids the utopian vision of the brotherhood of man and nature promulgated in *Queen Mab* and replaces it with a starkly realistic portrait of man as solitary, alienated, inconsistent, and negligible—a "lonely and sea-girt isle," an abandoned and forgotten wind-lyre. Even Dante's sonnet to Cavalcanti that Shelley chose to translate and include in the *Alastor* volume is a dream of escape from chance and the world's vicissitudes;[18] and the sonnet to Wordsworth ("Poet of Nature") not only imitates Cavalcanti's lament over Dante's moral inconstancy and loss of "true integrity"[19] but adds the irony that turncoat Wordsworth, who has deserted truth and liberty, had himself once mourned

That things depart which never may return:
Childhood and youth, friendship and love's first glow,
Have fled like sweet dreams. . . .

Conviction that the world is incorrigibly deficient has withered Shelley's utopian zeal and redirected his aspirations to the "secret things of the grave": Silence and Twilight, though "unbeloved of men" because they put out the world of life, cast such hushed beauty as to engender hope

---

[13] "Mutability" ("We are as clouds").
[14] "Stanzas, April 1814."
[15] "Mutability."
[16] "Oh! there are spirits."
[17] "On Death."
[18] "Guido, I would that Lappo, thou, and I."
[19] Shelley also translated Cavalcanti's sonnet ("Returning from its daily quest") but did not publish it.

that death did hide from human sight
Sweet secrets, or beside its breathless sleep
That loveliest dreams perpetual watch did keep.[20]

The most nearly optimistic of these 1816 verses, "On Death," imagines a continuation in the grave of all but the physical body and the senses. At the regrettable cost of

All that is great and all that is strange
In the boundless realm of unending change,

there will be a postmortal "sleep in the light of a wondrous day," or, in the manuscript version,

the calm of eternal day,
For all in this world we can surely know
Is a little delight and a little woe.[21]

Thus, instead of praying to be the trumpet of a prophecy that will herald mankind's moral springtime, Shelley can only urge stoic endurance of an absurd world of mixed beauty and darkness:

O man! hold thee on in courage of soul
Through the stormy shades of thy worldly way.

His despair of the world, moreover, has become compounded by the appearance, even this early, of a skeptical empiricism that will evolve ultimately into the idealism that he was to call the "intellectual philosophy." As empiricist, he accepted the fact that the world must be defined in terms of sensations and their structures, but as a student of Hume's skepticism he had to confess the absence of any evidence that mental images correspond to an extramental reality. We are assured of our sensations but not of the outward world they seem to report; or, as he aphorized it in the manuscript of "On Death,"

All we behold, we feel that we know;
All we perceive, we know that we feel.[22]

"We *feel* that we know" nicely puns on the sensational basis of knowledge and the uncertainty that it is knowledge of external fact. When Shelley

---

[20] "A Summer-Evening Churchyard."
[21] *The Esdaile Notebook,* ed. Kenneth N. Cameron (New York, 1964), p. 79.
[22] *Ibid.*

revised these lines for the 1816 volume he replaced the wit with an efficiently connotative metaphor:

This world is the nurse of all we know,
This world is the mother of all we feel.

Our sensations are generated immediately by the world, but the world only stands *in loco parentis* to our knowledge, which she does not produce, although she acts as if she did; and, like the traditional nurse, she may well be misleading us with old wives' tales. Consequently "On Death" is ultimately an elaboration of a dilemma, not an act of resolution. Choice between a stormy, dark, inconstant world and an "eternal day" should be easy to make, but whereas the world may be only a transitory fiction of the mind, what the grave conceals is not an object of empirical experience. Although the poet is persuaded for the moment that the world is made meaningless by its unending change and the probable unreality of our knowledge of it, he can only end by confessing ignorance of the "secret things of the grave":

Who telleth a tale of unspeaking death?
Who lifteth the veil of what is to come?
Who painteth the shadows that are beneath
The wide-winding caves of the peopled tomb?

Paradoxically, it is precisely because Shelley wishes to unite "the fears and the love for that which we see" with "the hopes of what shall be" and now, unlike the author of *Queen Mab*, suspects they are irreconcilable that he is led to doubt each alternately. Much of his subsequent career will be devoted to poetic endeavors to bring about that reconciliation, or at least to speculate on the bearing of life and eternity upon each other.

More explicitly than any other, the poem "Oh! there are spirits of the air," immediately following *Alastor* in the 1816 volume and closely akin to it in theme, displays Shelley's division between the inadequacy of the temporal world and the possibly illusory, certainly tormentingly solipsistic, aspirations of the mind. Together with "On Death," it can serve as an index to a body of Shelley's poetry which has as its purpose the skeptical representation of the human dilemma but which criticism has tended to distort by demanding of it clear resolutions. At this moment in his career his faith in the Spirit of Nature will no longer hold, and in addition, his frustrated desire for community with a soul corresponding to his own stultifies life. The addressee of the poem[23] has sought in vain to

---

[23] Mary Shelley's identification of the addressee as Coleridge seems to be without support but at any rate contributes nothing to the meaning of the poem.

satisfy his desires with either the splendors of the natural world or the spirits of his fellow mortals. In vain has he searched for communion with nature's indwelling ghosts, or genii, whose "eyes as fair / As star-beams" are the windows of the luminous astral soul, or essence; and in vain has he sought the beams in the corresponding "starry eyes" of mortals, only to find they "were never meant for thine, / Another's wealth." He rejoices so long as he can hold communion with the ministering spirits of mysterious, "inexplicable" nature and they "answer" him, but ultimately they cannot value his love adequately; nor do mortals "answer thy demands." For he is not essentially of the order of nature, nor is he fulfilled by the human, which is inherently inconstant.

In a deficient and "false"—that is, inconstant—world whose "falsehood" leaves one "broken-hearted," there remains, then, only himself, a subject with the capacity of being its own object: only "Thine own soul still is true to thee," and only the mind's own thoughts and love are constant and of a scope equal to itself. Consequently, when "natural scenes or human smiles"—"faithless smiles"—can no longer wind one "in their wiles" and the inconstant world can no longer be a source of hope, the solitary mind is driven to project itself as its own narcissistic object, an ideal *doppelgänger*, a "ghastly presence" ever hovering "Beside thee like thy shadow." The motif of the elusive Other Self that walks beside one through life recurs in Shelley's poetry in various modes: for example, in *Alastor* a spirit inferior to the protagonist's vision "seemed / To stand beside him"; in *Epipsychidion* the poet is told that the visionary ideal "whom thou seekest . . . is beside thee," but he is unable to find it in realizable form;[24] in *The Triumph of Life* the ideal "Shape," obliterated from sight by the blinding light of life, nevertheless kept "its obscure tenour . . . / Beside my path, as silent as a ghost." Shelley's Hegelian Unhappy Consciousness repeatedly senses that it is attended in life by its fulfilling self, from which it has been divided and alienated—indeed, to which it has been blinded. In a poem like *Alastor* the Visionary's objective is union with that ideal projected Other Self, but the misguided, like the tyrant's slaves in *The Revolt of Islam*, are forced to see "Their own lean image everywhere," walking as a "ghastlier self beside them."[25] Similarly, the soul that is true to the subject of "Oh! there are spirits" and hangs beside him like his shadow has been changed by his disillusionment into a Byronic "foul fiend" which, at best, he must resign himself to endure in life.

At this uneasy stage Shelley is rebuffed by both his utopianism and his faith in immortality, by his confidence in the autonomous universe

---

[24] Also *Epipsychidion*, 136, where the poet laments that he had not from his birth "moved beside [Emily, his ideal vision] on this earth."
[25] *The Revolt of Islam*, 3983–84.

and his desire for a transcendent reality, by nature and mind, life and death; and he can find no solution to his dilemma. The human soul is divided against itself by its earthly and ideal affiliations, and each of the bonds frustrates the other, as Shelley intimated in a later fragment addressed to the moon, which—to use James Joyce's description of that fragment in his *Portrait of the Artist*—elaborates the "alternation of sad human ineffectualness with vast inhuman cycles of activity." Related to both heaven and earth, the moon, like divided man, is companionless, alien to each region. It climbs the heaven but is not of the same order as the wholly transcendent and immutable stars; there it devotes itself to gazing on earth but fails to see any constancy that is compatible with its heavenly station and that would justify its being constant:

> Art thou pale for weariness
> Of climbing heaven and gazing on the earth,
>   Wandering companionless
> Among the stars, that have a different birth,—
> And ever changing, like a joyless eye
> That finds no object worth its constancy?

Human experience falls short of the mind's capacities and desires; and we do not, in this world, belong wholly to the transcendent realm to which those capacities and desires are native. Trapped between our divisive desires for life and eternity, we move toward a "dark and distant shore" that "Still recedes" as we drift onward,

>   ever still
> Longing with divided will,
> But no power to seek or shun.[26]

According to "Oh! there are spirits of the air," the only thing in life commensurate with the self, the attendant visionary Other Self, is perverted by experience into a tormenting "ghastly presence." For the moment Shelley can only accept the fact that life is, as that poem's epigraph from Euripides declares, an ill-starred destiny, a future-less future. Nothing remains but to submit, with the cynicism that Shelley was to attribute to Byron, to a kind of bitter life-long paralysis, since the "mad endeavour" to dispel the attendant Self made fiendish by misery would only heap mutability on mutability:

Be as thou art. Thy settled fate,
Dark as it is, all change would aggravate.

[26] *Lines Written among the Euganean Hills*, 20–23.

ii

This is exactly the kind of dilemma Shelley explored in *Alastor, or the Spirit of Solitude,* and the ambivalence displayed by the other poems of the 1816 collection directs us toward the special mode of its title-poem. *Alastor* has suffered a good deal from its apparent inconsistency with its Preface, which, it has usually been assumed—perhaps excusably if not correctly—ought to be a summary of the poem or at least should offer clear directions for reading it. That supposed inconsistency has been compounded by a critical penchant for finding Shelley's autobiography in everything he wrote and therefore for taking all passages in *Alastor* as meant to be of equal validity, as spoken by the same voice, and as existing in a single frame of reference, despite the fact that the poem is an elegiac biography narrated by a dramatic speaker who has his own fictional identity. *Alastor* is, in fact, far more coherent than commentary on it has allowed, and much of the supposed difficulty is of the critic's making. By identifying the Narrator with Shelley or occasionally by confusing the Narrator with the Visionary, whose history he tells, the received interpretations find the poem obscure and internally inconsistent, on the assumption that it ought to arrive at some unqualified decision and leave us with moral instruction. The Visionary, it is felt, ought to be thoroughly admirable or totally wrong; he should be praised for his worthy quest of an ideal or punished for a sin against humanity, especially if we take the title to mean that, since the "Spirit of Solitude" is an *alastor,* or genius that avenges by tormenting, usually for the sin of hubris,[27] the ideal vision which the protagonist pursues beyond life is sent him as deserved punishment for spurning human love. But Shelley's use of the dialogue form for the skeptical purpose of bringing contrary views into mutual confrontation in such works as his *Refutation of Deism, Julian and Maddalo,* and "The Two Spirits," or his opposition of Apollo and Pan in their two hymns, suggests at least the possibility that the presence of both the fictional Narrator of *Alastor* and the Visionary who is the subject of his lament implies a dramatizing of sharply discriminated perspectives; and the unresolved conflict of goals and values in other poems of the volume, such as "On Death" and "Oh! there are spirits," is in harmony with the likelihood that Narrator and Visionary represent Shelley's polarized impulses.

[27] Carlos Baker (*Shelley's Major Poetry* [Princeton, 1948], p. 45) was surely right in objecting that Peacock drew a red herring across the reader's path when he explained that he had proposed the title to Shelley because "The Greek word *Alastor* is an evil genius. . . . The poem treated the spirit of solitude as a spirit of evil." The Greek word does not carry this sense, nor does the poem support this idea of evil. Despite Peacock's explanation, the possibility is not to be rejected that the title may mean "one tormented by an avenging spirit" and designates the protagonist of the poem (e.g. Aeschylus *Eumenides* 236; Sophocles *Ajax* 374. See M. C. Wier, "Shelley's 'Alastor' Again," *PMLA,* 46 [1931], 947–50).

Especially if we do not allow the Preface to govern our reading of the poem but interpret it as but one factor of the total artistic design, *Alastor* develops a skillfully controlled ambiguity whereby confidence in the adequacy of nature and aspiration to perfect self-fulfillment in afterlife undercut each other. In such an ambience the title, in the sense of a tormenting spirit, proves a morally ambivalent term.

The mode of *Alastor* is best understood in the light of Shelley's earlier experiment with the skeptical and paradoxical manner of proceeding in his *Refutation of Deism* (1814).[28] This prose dialogue between a Christian and a Deist, purporting "to show that there is no alternative between atheism and Christianity," is in the skeptical tradition of Cicero's *De natura deorum* and Hume's *Dialogues concerning Natural Religion*, which doubtless supplied Shelley with many of his arguments and taught him its ironic strategy. That is, his *Refutation* belongs to that dialogue form of which Dryden has given us the most succinct definition in describing his own *Essay of Dramatic Poesy*:

> . . . my whole discourse was sceptical, according to that way of reasoning which was used by Socrates, Plato, and all the Academics of old, which Tully and the best of the Ancients followed. . . . it is a dialogue sustained by persons of several opinions, all of them left doubtful, to be determined by the readers in general. . . .[29]

As Dryden implies, skepticism here does not refer to distrust of reason, nor is its end the Pyrrhonic quietude resulting from a suspension of judgment; rather, it designates a methodical equipoise of arguments whereby irresolvably conflicting positions are deployed against each other without excluding the possibility of either, for the purpose of an open-ended inquiry into truth.[30] "The main basic principle of the Skeptic system," according to Sextus Empiricus, "is that of opposing to every proposition an equal proposition; for we believe that as a consequence of this we end by ceasing to dogmatize."[31] Despite whatever biases we may be tempted to read into Shelley's *Refutation* as a consequence of our knowledge of his preferences at this or at a subsequent time, the work itself leads to no single tenable conclusion, despite the Deist's admission of defeat. It only exposes the questionable implications of whatever position we choose to take. For Shelley was convinced that

> Philosophy, impatient as it may be to build, has much work yet remaining, as pioneer for the overgrowth of ages. It makes one step towards this object; it destroys error, and the roots of error. It leaves, what is too often the duty of

[28] In his *The Deep Truth* (Lincoln, Neb., 1954), C. E. Pulos has skillfully interpreted the *Refutation* and demonstrated the skeptical basis of Shelley's thought.
[29] "Defence of An Essay of Dramatic Poesy," in *Essays of John Dryden*, ed. W. P. Ker, I, p. 124.
[30] For the distinction between philosophic skepticism and skepticism as a method of inquiry, see Philip Harth, *Contexts of Dryden's Thought* (Chicago, 1968), chapter I.
[31] *Outlines of Pyrrhonism* i. 12.

the reformer in political and ethical questions to leave, a vacancy. It reduces the mind to that freedom in which it would have acted, but for the misuse of words and signs, the instruments of its own creation.[32]

The arguments of *A Refutation of Deism* are thoroughly conventional; Shelley's contribution is the Humean artistry with which he has marshalled them dramatically into a dilemma that tosses the mind back and forth between its horns. The two disputants adequately damage each other—and themselves. The Deist paraphrases Scripture and recounts subsequent Christian history in a fashion that renders Christian revelation immoral and contrary to reason. In addition, Shelley employs an irony whereby even the Christian, while conscientiously pursuing his own argument, unconsciously makes Christian morality suspect:

Friendship, patriotism and magnanimity; the heart that is quick in sensibility, the hand that is inflexible in execution; genius, learning and courage, are qualities which have engaged the admiration of mankind, but which we are taught by Christianity to consider as splendid and delusive vices. (29)[33]

Or, to take another example, the Christian unguardedly phrases his defense of the doctrine of divine punishment of infidels in such a manner as to paint a remorselessly sadistic Deity:

I dare not think that the God in whom I trust for salvation would terrify his creatures with menaces of punishment, which he does not intend to inflict. The ingratitude of incredulity is, perhaps, the only sin to which the Almighty cannot extend his mercy without compromising his justice. (31)

On the other hand, the Christian is a philosophic skeptic who has been led to fideism by his rejection of the validity of human reason and the senses. Consequently, his method for countering the Deist's rational and natural theology is to demonstrate that such arguments as those from design and cause fail to prove the existence of a Deity and therefore lead to atheism. Only irrational faith can sustain religion, despite the Deist's argument that belief is an involuntary passion and therefore cannot be subject to reward or punishment. Since both disputants are committed to closing their minds to the possibility of atheism, the argument ends with the Deist's tentative admission of defeat: there probably is no rational ground for religion, which can be sanctioned only by faith in supernatural revelation.

But the successful refutation of deism, instead of settling anything, only raises the real problem: although no atheist is present to argue his cause, the real contest is implicitly between fideistic religion and rational atheism. The Deist, arguing for a rational theology, must concede defeat

---

[32] *On Life* (Julian, VI, 195).
[33] This and the subsequent references to *A Refutation of Deism* are to pages in Julian, VI.

so that there may be no "alternative" between Christianity and atheism, no means of reconciling this antinomy of religion and reason. Indeed, the absence of any atheist to argue his own position is a strategic irony that makes atheism all the more insidiously compelling, for the antirationalistic Christian, in order to show that reason leads irresistibly to atheism, poses momentarily as a rationalist and succeeds splendidly in demonstrating how reasonable atheism is. The Christian has advanced the absent atheist's most persuasive arguments. Reasonably considered, for example, the universe has existed from eternity and requires no Creator or divine Governor, and "In the language of reason, the words God and Universe are synonymous" (47, 56). There is an additional way of reading the Deist's final words, unintended by him, when he promises the Christian he will consider whether the argument "which you have advanced in favour of Atheism" should appear incontrovertible. Moreover, just as the Christian has unintentionally phrased Christian doctrine in a fashion that makes it repellent and has given a convincing demonstration of the reasonableness of atheism, the Deist chooses to condemn the hypothetical atheist in the following ambivalent terms:

His private judgment is his criterion of right and wrong. He dreads no judge but his own conscience, he fears no hell but the loss of his self-esteem. He is not to be restrained by punishments, for death is divested of its terror, and whatever enters into his heart, to conceive, that will he not scruple to execute. (43–44)

The reader of the *Refutation*, then, is left with only a dilemma, not a conclusion. If he is a rationalist, he is an atheist. Yet, the atheistic case has been expounded only by the skeptical Christian for the purpose of repudiating reason; religion has been assumed by Christian and Deist as the agreed ground of their dispute, and the possibility of atheism is not part of the dramatic exchange; and neither has disputed the Christian's statement that "If the Christian Religion is false, I see not upon what foundation our belief in a moral governor of the universe, or our hopes of immortality can rest" (30). On the other hand, if the reader is a Christian, he must accept on faith alone an unreasonable revelation and its unattractive morality. But there is no reconciliation of religion and reason, such as deism, and no common touchstone for preferring atheism to Christianity, since they have contradictory foundations. The Deist's final words are only deceptively conclusive:

I am willing to promise that if, after mature deliberation, the arguments which you have advanced in favour of Atheism should appear incontrovertible, I will endeavour to adopt so much of the Christian scheme as is consistent with my persuasion of the goodness, unity and majesty of God. (57)

The *Refutation* asserts nothing and intimates nothing, but invites the reader to this "mature deliberation" of the quandary in which he finds himself at its close. If the argument for atheism proves incontrovertible, he may find himself "in favour of" it, or he may equally well reject it for irrational faith in some features of Christianity. Whether anything in the Christian scheme is actually consistent with the goodness, unity, and majesty of God is still open to question, but the subsequent development of Shelley's thought also should be sufficient evidence of the possibility of a "modest creed" that tentatively assumes, on the basis of faith, some kind of beneficent divinity, largely for the purpose of supporting confidence in immortality.

Shelley's seizure here on irreconcilable polarities is a fundamental characteristic of his bent of mind; and his unresolved, skeptical way of proceeding in this prose dialogue, in accordance with the established ironic conventions of that genre, is the normative structure which he then shaped into a variety of complex poetic modes in *Alastor* and other poems that similarly involve a dramatic conflict of characters. These skeptical poetic modes, and their later transformations, distinguish his particular genius. The radical form is the dialogue, but the skeptical inquiry can also take the shape of a biography related by an opposing narrator.

iii

Assuming that the difference between the two characters in *Alastor* is crucial, it is especially necessary to define the Narrator with care since, although implicit throughout, he is immediately before us only briefly. The muse he chooses to invoke is not a visionary Mind or a perfected reflection of his own soul or a transcendent Intellectual Beauty, but the "Mother of this unfathomable world" (18); and, like the Prometheus of Shelley's lyric drama, he identifies himself as of the brotherhood of her other children—earth, ocean, and air—whom he sets admiringly in a context, not of eternal immutability or of absolute being, but of time's diurnal and seasonal flux and corresponding variety—of

... dewy morn, and odorous noon, and even,
With sunset and its gorgeous ministers,
And solemn midnight's tingling silentness, (5–7)

of "autumn's hollow sighs," winter's snow, and "spring's voluptuous pantings." The Narrator is, in other words, the same as the author of *Queen Mab*, who conceived of man and nature as of essentially the same category because both are imbued with, and defined by, the "Soul of the Universe," the necessarily beneficent shaping and activating power that endows everything with its characterizing soul and can impel all things toward their perfection. Therefore he differs radically from that aspect of Shelley's mind soon to address a prayer to the transcendent and immutable Intellectual Beauty, whose shadow visits the human mind at uncertain moments—and just as radically from the Visionary of *Alastor*, who pursues an ideal unobtainable in the world. The dominant motif of the Narrator's invocation is love equally reciprocated, since he holds that as offspring of the same Mother of the world, nature and man are "beloved brethren" (16), equal to each other. Filled as all natural objects are with "natural piety" to the Great Mother who bore him (3) and limiting his love to her—"Thee ever, and thee only" (20)—he can both receive nature's love and "recompense the boon with mine" (4), unlike the discontented poet of "Oh! there are spirits," whose love nature cast away "like a worthless boon." Consequently the equal exchange of love between Narrator and nature is of the same order as that within nature itself, where, according to the picture he paints, parasite blossoms "twine their tendrils with the wedded boughs / Uniting their close union," like infants' eyes that fold their beams around "the hearts of those that love" (439–45). As the metaphor suggests by translating vegetation into human terms, the reciprocal love-fulfillment that men only aspire to among themselves is a fact in nature, and the Narrator conceives of himself as a participating member of this realm of "meeting boughs and implicated leaves" (426) and "mingling shade" (422), where caves "respond" to the sound of the forest (425) and the immense oak "embraces" the light beech (433).

Like the "passive things" of *Queen Mab* that "unconsciously" fulfill the laws of nature's Spirit, the Narrator in his role of poet offers himself as an aeolian lyre to be moved by the inspiring breath of the "Great Parent," so that his song will modulate with her moving presence in all other earthly things, human and natural:

> . . . with murmurs of the air,
> And motions of the forests and the sea,
> And voice of living beings, and woven hymns
> Of night and day, and the deep heart of man.[34]   (46–49)

It is appropriate to his character, therefore, that his invocation should echo so many phrases in Wordsworth's pantheistic poems[35]—and notably ironic that he should invoke Nature to aid his singing of one who had found her inadequate. Far from being a troubled solitary tormented by unsatisfied dreams, he conceives of himself as a serene and equal member of the entire earthly community; and although, like the Visionary, he has been driven by "obstinate questionings" to seek out the mystery of "what we are" (26–29), he has sought the answer only in Nature's "inmost sanc-

---

[34] Cf. Wordsworth's *Lines Composed a Few Miles above Tintern Abbey*, 95–99, where the analogous passage describes the presence of the pantheistic spirit.
[35] For these echoes, see Paul Mueschke and Earl L. Griggs, "Wordsworth as the Prototype of the Poet in Shelley's *Alastor*," *PMLA*, 49 (1934), 235–39.

tuary" (38), not beyond her bounds. To understand Nature's mystery is, in his limited view, to understand man's. Even his comparison of his quest to that of an alchemist, and his extension of this metaphor in "mixing" speech and looks with love and "uniting" tears with kisses to perform natural magic (31–37), reveal that his inquiry is only into the mystery of "what we are" as creatures of the physical world.

Clearly the epigraph of the poem from Augustine's *Confessions* cannot apply to him: *Nondum amabam, et amare amabam, quaerebam quid amarem, amans amare.*[36] For *his* love does not lack an object. Rather, he is the norm against which the Visionary's love can be defined and measured, just as the somewhat distracting Preface introduces an additional standard—those who are solitary because they are entirely without love—against which to define and measure the Visionary's solitude.[37] Like the flowers of *The Sensitive Plant*, each of which

> was interpenetrated
> With the light and the odour its neighbour shed,
> Like young lovers whom youth and love make dear,
> Wrapped and filled by their mutual atmosphere,

the Narrator is securely reconciled to the world and fulfilled by it because his sole deity and sole object of love is that "great Mother" who is the World Spirit. He is the one capable of conceiving of an earthly utopia and of experiencing the Sensitive Plant's world-garden as an "undefiled Paradise."

Consequently, as representative of a human category, the Narrator falls between those "selfish, blind, and torpid" solitaries of the Preface who "keep aloof from sympathies with their kind" because they have no desire for community with the human spirit, and the Visionary, who is solitary because, finding the world, both natural and human, to be inferior to his desires, he is lured by love of some supposedly greater spirit than the "Mother of this unfathomable world." The question Shelley confronted and the categories he elaborated by adding the Preface are approximately those of Keats in *The Fall of Hyperion*, which also explores the disparity between man's dreams and his mortal existence. The loveless solitaries of Shelley's Preface (who play no part in the poem itself and only define the Visionary by contrast) are Keats's thoughtless ones who sleep away their days; his Visionary is Keats's dreamer, or fanatic, who weaves his dreams

---

[36] "Not yet did I love, yet I loved to love; I sought something to love, being in love with love" (*Confessions*, III. i). The Latin passage greatly impressed Shelley: he included it in the "Advertisement" of some poems of 1810 in *The Esdaile Notebook* (ed. cit., p. 115) and jotted it down in a notebook, perhaps in 1814 (*The Journals of Claire Clairmont*, ed. Marion K. Stocking [Cambridge, Mass., 1969], p. 61).

[37] In the poem, solitude is to be understood as divorce from both man and external nature, not from man alone.

into an imaginary paradise for a sect and "venoms all his days"; and his
Narrator is approximately Keats's humanitarian, who seeks no wonder but
the human face. But whereas Keats evolved in the character of the poet
an existential union of humanitarian and dreamer on the assumption of
a causal relationship between life and afterlife, Shelley, essentialist and
not existentialist, has no means of reconciliation and can only display the
tension between dream and reality, between the solitude and possible
futility of vision and the inadequacy of human community.

By 1815, according to Mary, the ardor of Shelley's utopian hopes had
been checked, and he turned "his eyes inward," inclined "rather to brood
over the thoughts and emotions of his own soul, than to glance abroad,
and to make, as in *Queen Mab*, the whole universe the object and subject
of his song."[38] The fictional Narrator contemplating the career of the
Visionary is, in effect, the extroverted, utopian Shelley now turning his
eyes inward to explore his interior life—and, since both Narrator and
Visionary are poets, the Narrator also represents one kind of poetry contemplating another. That the psychological depth Shelley is probing is
dim and that the validity of what he sees is uncertain are confessed by his
refusal to let the Visionary speak for himself; a song inspired by the Great
Mother of the world will report the realm of vision only in the limited
perspective, dimensions, and assumptions of quotidian experience.

If the equivalent of the Narrator is the contented, perfectly gratified
flowers of *The Sensitive Plant*, the Visionary's equivalent is the Sensitive
Plant itself, which, in a realm where "none wanted but it," received "more
than all" and yet "loved more than . . . could belong to the giver," loving
"even like Love"—*amans amare*. Like St. Augustine, the Visionary is compelled by a desire that, by virtue of its infinitude, can have no immediately
attainable object; and just as Augustine's love could be satisfied only by
the infinite and perfect God, so the Visionary seeks an Absolute which
will match his mind's perfect conceptions and ideals and, to use the language of "Oh! there are spirits," alone can answer his demands. Unlike the
Narrator, who can boast that the creations of nature are his "kindred"
(15), the Visionary, molded by his own visions, by nature's best impulses,
and by the true, good, and beautiful that philosophers have taught, early
left his "alienated home" (76), an exile without kindred but filled with
an insatiable need for some essence with which he can identify himself.

His first search for fulfillment is, like the Narrator's, in the realm of
the "Great Parent," whose essential meaning he seeks, even by following
her "most secret steps" (81). His boundless desire, his compulsion to press
beyond finite limits is evident in his journeys into "undiscovered lands" to
seek out "strange," hitherto unknown truths (77). Momentarily he, too,
is of the family of creatures, in harmony with dove, squirrel, and antelope.
But at this point his similarity to the Narrator ends. Still driven by desire,

[38] Mary Shelley's note on *Alastor* (Julian, I, 198).

he visits lands of ancient culture to pore over zodiacs and hieroglyphs, "memorials / Of the world's youth" (121–22), which, before Champollion, were thought to be mystical forms hiding transcendent truths of the highest order, early revealed to man but lost when their secret key was forgotten. His search into nature's inmost sanctuary, into the secret fountains of human thought, and over far-distant lands brought him "joy and exultation" (144); for to this point, to use again the language of "Oh! there are spirits," with the voice

Of these inexplicable things,
    Thou didst hold commune, and rejoice
When they did answer thee

—or, in the language of the Preface of *Alastor*, his desires were directed toward objects "infinite and unmeasured," and he was adequate to himself, self-possessed. But, being objects, they cease ultimately to suffice. His mind requires an infinite subject as its object, an "intelligence similar to itself"; and, having ignored the love of finite mortals, including that of the Arab maiden (129–39), who is presumably among human love's "choicest gifts" (205), in a dream he "images to himself the Being whom he loves," a maiden who is "a dream of hopes" (150).

Because the poem tells us that the "spirit of sweet human love" sent this dream-vision "to the sleep of him who spurned / Her choicest gifts" (203–5), it has been customary to link this fact with the tormenting "Spirit of Solitude" of the poem's subtitle; but actually nothing in the text indicates that the vision is punitive, however tormenting its consequences. The words ask merely for a psychological rendering: the spirit of human love is the desire inherent in any human mind, and when the mind refuses to limit itself to any finite being it has no choice but to envision its own object in a dream, not of actual reality, but of "hopes"— an object that is only potential. *Quaerebam quid amarem, amans amare*: I sought something that I might love, loving to love. The act is reflexive and has no completing object but itself, as though "to love" were an intransitive verb. But could the Visionary gain access to the subjective goal of his dreams, his hope is that he would have access to the innermost mystery of all, beside which the mysteries of nature's sanctuary and man's hieroglyphs would pale.

Whereas the Narrator's limited desires make the world compatible with him, the Visionary's quest hastens his departure from it because, according to the quotation that closes the Preface of the poem,

The good die first,
And those whose hearts are dry as summer's dust,
Burn to the socket.

The lines are from Wordsworth's *Excursion* (I. 500–2), which Shelley read in mid-September 1814, only a few months after it first appeared and about a year before he composed *Alastor*.[39] Mary recorded that they were "much disappointed" and that Wordsworth is "a slave," while Claire Clairmont found "the Story of Margaret very beautiful." No doubt these represent faithfully the mixed opinion of the Shelley household: admiration for Wordsworth's poetic powers and contempt for the man and his moral themes. Now, solitude is also the central subject of the *Excursion*; and the lines Shelley borrowed to introduce the story of the Visionary also introduce Wordsworth's story of Margaret and are spoken by the Wanderer, who narrates Margaret's brief and tragic career. The framing structure of the two narratives is the same: in place of Wordsworth's Wanderer, a disciple of nature who tells Margaret's story and laments her early death, there is Shelley's Narrator, who tells of the Visionary and might well subscribe to Wordsworth's claim that the external world and the individual mind are exquisitely "fitted" to each other. Fallen upon hard times, Margaret's husband left her the sum paid for his enlistment and disappeared to join a troop of soldiers in a distant land. For loss of him, Margaret grows negligent of home and children, gradually abandoning all concern with life itself. Single-thoughted, she can rouse herself only to search for news of her husband, "knowing this / Only, that what I seek I cannot find," and with this "one torturing hope... / Fast rooted at her heart," she pines away to the premature death of the good.

The relation of the two poems, then, is polemical, and by quoting Wordsworth's lines in his Preface Shelley has in effect corrected the theme of the most recent major poem by England's major poet, just as he was later to oppose with the "visionary rhyme" of his *Witch of Atlas* Wordsworth's anti-visionary *Peter Bell*,[40] so earth-bound that Wordsworth's laurels "their roots to Hell / Might pierce, and their wide branches blot the spheres / Of Heaven." To Shelley, Wordsworth has not set his sights high enough and has defined man's spirit too mundanely, too humanly: the truly good who are soonest taken out of life are not those with unwavering and devoted hope for, and faith in, an absent human love, but those who aspire to a vision that is absent because it can have no existence on earth. If Wordsworth resolved his fear of vision by binding the imagination to earth and the human and by eschewing transcendent flight in his "sky-canoe," Shelley, to whom this appeared timidity of spirit, sustained his incertitude by skeptically and ambivalently setting his Wordsworthian

---

[39] *Mary Shelley's Journal*, ed. F. L. Jones (Norman, Oklahoma, 1957), entries for 14–16 September 1814; *Journals of Claire Clairmont*, ed. Stocking, entry for 15 September 1814.
[40] Which, in turn, is a reply to Coleridge's "visionary" *Rime of the Ancient Mariner* and is intended, according to Wordsworth, to show that the imagination "does not require for its exercise the intervention of supernatural agency."

Narrator against the pure Visionary. Shelley's dedication to reform is as much literary as political, a fact that will become philosophically explicit in the *Defence of Poetry*; and his tacit transformation of Wordsworth's story of Margaret is the earliest of those corrective poetic "reformations" that will later reappear as the central modes of *Prometheus Unbound* and *Hellas*.

iv

Shelley's fragmentary verses, "Yet look on me," [41] are but a slight attempt at a lyric in the tradition of courtly love and its aloof lady, but the organizing metaphor reveals how persistently the relation of the desired ideal to the self was formulated in Shelley's mind as a self-reflection. Because the poem is concerned with the love of one human being for another and therefore, unlike *Alastor*, assumes the real existence of the adored lady, it represents the lover as her mirror and in that sense displays the relation of the two in the ontological perspective of the ideal. By look-ing in her lover's eyes, the lady feeds on the love within them, which is "but the reflected ray" of her own "beauty from [his] spirit thrown"; and her voice is his "heart's echo." The lady is totally sustained and fulfilled by her own reflection, "Like one before a mirror" who is careless of every-thing but what is "imaged there," while the lover wears out his life amorously watching her and thus serving as her reflection. His nature is determined by what he reflects, while the lady sees only herself in him. Then, were the ideal a human reality it would be an absolute completed by its reflection in another human soul, the character of which would be wholly contingent upon the absolute it mirrors. But "Yet look on me" is a love lyric, not a visionary quest; if, on the other hand, the ideal exceeds the possibilities of human reality and thus has no demonstrable self-existence, the metaphor necessarily reverses itself, and the ideal becomes for Shelley a visionary, or imaginary, reflection contingent upon the human soul-within-the-soul that it mirrors.

With no a priori God or institution to declare the nature of perfec-tion and with no Christ to serve as divinely authoritative model of it, Shelley was thrust back on "the visitations of the divinity in Man" [42] as the only absolute to aspire to. What might otherwise have been a Chris-tian journey of the mind to God becomes an atheistic journey of the soul to the divine soul within it, projected as its own object. Absolute values originate within man, for, as Julian says in *Julian and Maddalo*, "Where is the love, beauty, and truth we seek / But in our mind?" The value

[41] Huntington Notebooks, II, 4–8. Mary Shelley, on publishing the poem in the 1839 edition, dates it 1817, speculatively.
[42] *Defence of Poetry* (Julian, VII, 137).

system therefore is reflexive, requiring that one both project those values from within and strive to identify himself with them: "Whoever has maintained with his own heart the strictest correspondence of confidence, who dares to examine and to estimate every imagination which suggests itself to his mind, who is that which he designs to become, and only aspires to that which the *divinity of his own nature* shall consider and approve—he, has already seen God." For "that those who are pure in heart shall see God, and that virtue is its own reward, may be considered as equivalent assertions."[43] Consequently, for Shelley the perfect object of love is a visionary mirror-image of one's inmost soul, an idealized reflection that would complete the self by fulfilling its desire. In this mutable world only "Thine own soul still is true to thee." Of this view Shelley's most famous expression is, of course, his essay *On Love*, admittedly born of his own disappointing failure to find this fulfillment in the finite world and directed, he confesses, toward the "unattainable" goal of love:

We are born into the world, and there is something within us which, from the instant that we live and move thirsts after its likeness. . . . this propensity developes itself with the developement of our nature. We dimly see within our intellectual nature a miniature as it were of our entire self, yet deprived of all that we condemn or despise, the ideal prototype of everything excellent or lovely that we are capable of conceiving as belonging to the nature of man. Not only the portrait of our external being, but an assemblage of the minutest particulars of which our nature is composed; a mirror whose surface reflects only the forms of purity and brightness; a soul within our soul that describes a circle around its proper Paradise which pain, and sorrow, and evil dare not overleap. To this we eagerly refer all sensations, thirsting that they should resemble or correspond with it.[44]

To discover the "anti-type" of this soul within the soul is "the invisible and unattainable point to which Love tends; and to attain which, it urges forth the powers of man to arrest the faintest shadow of that without the possession of which there is no rest or respite to the heart over which it rules." Correspondingly, in *Alastor* the lady of the Visionary's dream, sent by the spirit of human love, is a replication of his inmost soul. Like him, she is a poet; her voice echoes his internal voice, like that of "his own soul / Heard in the calm of thought" (153–54), and hers is a "pure mind" (162):

Knowledge and truth and virtue were her theme,
And lofty hopes of divine liberty,
Thoughts the most dear to him, and poesy,
Herself a poet. (158–61)

---

[43] *Essay on Christianity* (Julian, VI, 231–32; itals. added).
[44] I have transcribed the text as it appears in MS e. 11, pp. 4–6.

"How many a one," Shelley elsewhere exclaims, "though none be near to love, / Loves then the shade of his own soul, half seen / In any mirror."[45]

The growing physicality of the Visionary's dream-lady and her sexual union with him in his dream have unnecessarily troubled those who apparently feel that as an ideal she ought to be all spirit and that Shelley's bad faith made him lose control of his high spiritual purpose when, in his imagination, the lady's "glowing limbs" began to appear beneath her veil and

> her outspread arms now bare,
Her dark locks floating in the breath of night,
Her beamy bending eyes, her parted lips
Outstretched, and pale, and quivering eagerly. (177–80)

The lady, however, is not to be understood as a spirit distinct from the Visionary, a soul to his flesh, but as the union of all that he yearns for in his intellect, his imagination—and, the Preface adds, in his senses. She is created out of the desires of his total nature. "If we reason," Shelley wrote in his essay On Love, "we would be understood; if we imagine, we would that the airy children of our brain were born anew within another's; if we feel, we would that another's nerves should vibrate to our own, that the beams of their eyes should kindle at once and mix and melt into our own, that lips of motionless ice should not reply to lips quivering and burning with the heart's best blood." The unattainable point to which love tends is the meeting not only with "an understanding capable of clearly estimating the deductions of our own" and with "an imagination which should enter into and seize upon the subtle and delicate peculiarities which we have delighted to cherish and unfold in secret" but also "with a frame whose nerves, like the chord of two exquisite lyres strung to the accompaniment of one delightful voice, vibrate with the vibrations of our own." Although Shelley held that love is "the universal thirst for a communion not merely of the senses, but of our whole nature, intellectual, imaginative and sensitive" and that sexual gratification is but a "small part" of the sentiment of love,[46] he nevertheless acknowledged that erotic fulfillment is the consummation and collective center of all other sympathies:

all sympathies [must] be harmoniously blended, and the moments of [sexual] abandonment [must] be prepared by the entire consent of all the conscious portions of our being; the perfection of intercourse consisting, not perhaps in a total annihilation of the instinctive sense, but in the reducing it to as minute

---

[45] Prince Athanase, 251–53.
[46] Discourse on the Manners of the Ancients (Julian, VII, 228).

a proportion as possible compared with those higher faculties of our nature, from which it derives a value.[47]

The eroticism of the Visionary's dream, then, is not a mere symbol of spiritual union or even synecdochic of it, and certainly not a dishonest substitute for it; it takes cognizance of the fact that the senses are part of the psyche and that sexual union is truly consummated only when all other aspects of the psyche are blended in sympathy. All of this is to be presupposed when we are told that the Visionary

> reared his shuddering limbs, and quelled
> His gasping breath, and spread his arms to meet
> Her panting bosom. . . . she drew back a while,
> Then, yielding to the irresistible joy,
> With frantic gesture and short breathless cry
> Folded his frame in her dissolving arms.
> Now blackness veiled his dizzy eyes, and night
> Involved and swallowed up the vision; sleep,
> Like a dark flood suspended in its course,
> Rolled back its impulse on his vacant brain.   (182–91)

This orgasmic merging with the perfect and mirrored Other until the finite self is absorbed into the infinite ("in her dissolving arms") not only defines the absoluteness of the Visionary's love but also distinguishes it from the Narrator's, which precludes the possibility of sexual fulfillment and the oneness that it consummates. The Narrator's reciprocated love for his "brothers" of nature is a mutual exchange, not a union, and his love of the World Mother is a devotion to his source, with which he can merge only in the extinction that completes the circle of man's animate life: in nature's endless cycle of death and birth, the Great Mother's "cradle" is man's "sepulchre" (430). His is a love of mother and brothers, not what is implicit in the Visionary and will appear explicitly in *Laon and Cythna* and later poems as incestuous love of a sister, of a Laon for a Laone, as Cythna calls herself at one point. For Cythna is to Laon like "mine own shadow," a "second self, far dearer"—Shelley first wrote, "far purer"[48]— "and more fair."[49] Although Cythna is a real being and not a vision, she is only lightly tied to reality, moving "upon this earth a shape of brightness, / A power, that from its objects scarcely drew / One impulse of her being." To Laon she seemed to stand "Beside me... / Like the bright

---

[47] MS e. 6, p. 49; published in James A. Notopoulos, *The Platonism of Shelley* (Durham, N.C., 1949), p. 410.
[48] MS e. 19, p. 67.
[49] *The Revolt of Islam*, 874–75. In the dedication of *Queen Mab*, Shelley addresses Harriet as "my purer mind." See also *Letters*, I, 95, 189.

shade of some immortal dream."[50] This "purest being," like the visionary lady of *Alastor*, is an idealization of the speaker, who holds communion with her, finds "Hers too were all my thoughts," and sees "in hers mine own mind,"[51] just as Byron's Astarte, born of the same blood as Manfred, is the perfect form of the star that rules his destiny.[52]

In itself the vivid description of the sexual union in *Alastor* may seem open to the charge of being Shelley's projection of auto-eroticism, especially since Shelley elsewhere took explicit cognizance of "the facility with which certain phenomena connected with sleep at the age of puberty associate themselves with those images which are the objects of our waking desires; and even that in some persons of an exalted state of sensibility a similar process may take place in reverie. . . ."[53] It would be blindness to deny the auto-eroticism of the dream, but as a visionary fulfillment of a desire for a perfect Other Self it points more importantly to the pervasive vacancy felt not only by Shelley but also by others of his era.

v

The divine sanctions for established institutions had reached their ultimate dissolution in the French Revolution. Instead of being accepted as the dictates of God, the structures and laws of church, state, and society were recognized as the work and responsibility of man, and the Revolution, as the dramatic assertion of man's authority for his own civilization, opened up giddying possibilities centered in the capacities of man's own nature.[54] In 1791 Volney could exclaim in his *The Ruins: or Meditations on the Revolutions of Empire*, "Now may I live! for after this there is nothing which I am not daring enough to hope"; and years after the Revolution, Southey could recall "what a visionary world seemed to open upon those who were just entering it. Old things seemed passing away. . . ."[55] For many, the millennium promised by the Book of Revelation was at hand, and they could behold prophetically, as Wordsworth did,

Glory—beyond all glory ever seen,
Confusion infinite of heaven and earth,
Dazzling the soul.[56]

[50] *The Revolt of Islam*, 865–72.
[51] *Ibid.*, 946–48.
[52] *Manfred*, I. i. 185–91; II. ii. 105–17.
[53] MS e. 6, p. 52; Notopoulos, *Platonism of Shelley*, p. 411.
[54] For the unrestrained optimism to which the French Revolution and its ideology gave birth, see M. Ray Adams, *Studies in the Literary Background of English Radicalism* (Lancaster, Pa., 1947), and M. H. Abrams, "English Romanticism: the Spirit of the Age," in *Romanticism Reconsidered*, ed. Northrop Frye (N.Y., 1963).
[55] *Correspondence of Robert Southey with Caroline Bowles*, ed. Edward Dowden (Dublin, 1881), p. 52.
[56] *Excursion*, III. 720–22.

Even more symptomatic of the new temper was the perfectibilism of men like Condorcet, Godwin, and Shelley that encouraged faith in an improvement that asymptotically approaches perfection at the infinite extension of time. This, however, is aspiration with no definable goal, or with a goal that can be defined only in terms of infinity. Even Shelley acknowledged that "such a degree of unmingled good was expected as it was impossible to realise," and the failure to achieve perfection immediately, he insisted, unnecessarily led to despondency.[57] The exhilaration engendered by the French Revolution therefore tended to incite men's minds toward two different goals: toward an immediate millenarian reform of the world, and toward an infinite perfection at the end of infinite time. While the first involves collective society, the second tends to become a quest by the individual self. Like many of his contemporaries and predecessors who refused despair, Shelley oscillated between these goals, now writing a *Queen Mab*, *Revolt of Islam*, *Prometheus Unbound*, or *Hellas*, and now an *Alastor*, *Epipsychidion*, or *Adonais*. However mutually exclusive and irreconcilable may be the directions of Shelley's two kinds of poetry, social and personal, they have a common source in an unqualified aspiration to perfection that is part of the spirit of the age. The self-dependent perfectibilitarian assumes the infinite possibility of the self, rather than of society, and aspires to an absolute that he can imagine but cannot define and that cannot be realized in the finite world. Consequently, stripped of—or emancipated from—those authorized systems and conventional institutions that had regulated human life and determined its purposes, a whole class of Romantics experienced, not the exhilaration of expanded goals, of standing on a peak in Darien, but that neurotic freedom of having no basis on which to limit and thereby define their goals. "I cannot rest," declares Byron's Manfred, whose "aspirations / Have been beyond the dwellers of the earth"; "I know not what I ask, nor what I seek."[58] I desired, says the speaker of Shelley's "The Zucca," "More in this world than any understand," something not contained in "this low sphere": "I loved, I know not what—."[59] In the past, says Ione in *Prometheus Unbound*, "I always knew what I desired . . . / Nor ever found delight to wish in vain." But when Panthea has a dream-vision of the future transfigured Prometheus, her sister Oceanid sympathetically but subconsciously experiences this anticipated absolute perfection and adds,

Canst thou divine what troubles me tonight? . . .
. . . now I cannot tell thee what I seek;
I know not; something sweet, since it is sweet
Even to desire. . . .[60]

[57] Preface to *The Revolt of Islam*.
[58] *Manfred*, II. iv. 58–59, 131–32.
[59] "The Zucca," 3–4, 20.
[60] *Prometheus Unbound*, II. i. 94–99.

Liberated into infinite possibility with nothing to check or channel normal human aspirations, the Romantic, like Ione, often found himself in troubled possession of only those passionate longings, *Sehnsucht*, love-without-an-object, or infinite subject with only finite immediate objects, which the Preface to *Alastor* declares to be "one of the most interesting situations of the human mind" and which the epigraph from Augustine describes.

It was, for example, the situation of Keats's Endymion, who turned away from nature and his societal duties because he aspired to his vision of the moon-goddess Cynthia, the "known unknown" and "completed form of all completeness," and whose dream of union with her is as erotic as that of Shelley's Visionary. In a related way it was Wordsworth's experience when, anticipating still to ascend the Alps at Simplon Pass, with "hopes that pointed to the clouds," he learned in disappointment that he had already crossed the peak and had to descend. For in the disparity between the finite world and his mind's ascending expectations the inadequate world of the senses suddenly dropped out, as it does at the end of Shelley's *Epipsychidion*, and there flashed on Wordsworth's mind the invisible world of his own imagination, self meeting Self, to reveal that one's kinship is with infinity:

Our destiny, our being's heart and home,
Is with infinitude, and only there;
With hope it is, hope that can never die,
Effort, and expectation, and desire,
And something evermore about to be.[61]

Or, even more strikingly, it was the situation of the hero of Chateaubriand's *René* (1802), who, exactly like Shelley's figure, found no adequate value in the historical past, in nature, or in society because he instinctively sought some "unknown good" and, Actaeon-like, was pursued by that instinct. As the priestly commentator on René's story says, solitude only redoubles the powers of the soul and at the same time deprives it of any object on which to exercise itself. "I probed my heart to discover what it was I desired," says René; "I could not tell." Others recognize him as the prey to an imagination that drives him to overreach all attainable limits. Every object being bounded and therefore valueless, and "the world offering nothing worthy of him," he lacks what is needed "to fill up the abyss of my existence." Without parents, friends, or an earthly lover, like the protagonist of *Alastor* he is pressed by his desires now to envision the "ideal object of a *future* passion," or what Shelley called "a dream of hopes": "I embraced her in the winds; I believed I heard her in the moanings of the river; everything became this phantom of my imagination, even the stars in the sky and the very principle of life in the universe." But although his tormenting, demonic vision ("le démon de mon coeur"),

[61] *Prelude*, VI. 604–8.

like that of the speaker of *Epipsychidion*, pervades all objects of his experience, she is not realizable, and he can only aspire to fulfillment in
death: "a voice from Heaven seemed to say to me: 'Man, the season of
your passage has not come; wait till the wind of death rises, then you
will take flight towards the unknown regions that your heart desires.' Rise
quickly, desired storm, which will bear René to the spaciousness of another life!... O God! if only you had granted me a woman commensurate
with my desires." Life goaded on by unobtainable wants therefore takes
on for René, who calls himself a "mere traveller," the pattern, not of
purposeful quest, but of aimless, solitary wanderings, as it does for
Shelley's Visionary, or for the speaker of *Epipsychidion*, or Byron's Childe
Harold, or Senancour's Obermann, the undirected roving being the expression of the inadequacy of the world or, in the words of Shelley's *On
Love*, of the fact that without possession of the soul's visionary ideal "there
is no rest nor respite to the heart over which it rules."

Actually, René, who had felt cowed before his father and whose
birth had been his mother's death, does have one worldly love, one to
whom he is bound by consonance of feelings and who is like himself in
spirit. His sister, capable of reading even the recesses of his heart, is, in
the manner of Manfred's Astarte and the many beloved sisters of Shelley's
poetry, a mode of the self, the self made perfect: "Amélie had received
from nature something divine; her soul had the same innocent graces as
her body; her feelings were infinitely gentle;... her heart, her thought,
and her voice all sighed in harmony." In the language of Shelley's Preface,
she is an intelligence similar to René, a vision in which the imagination
"unites all of wonderful, or wise, or beautiful, which the poet, the philosopher, or the lover could depicture." But unless this kind of desire
remains merely visionary, it can fulfill itself in the living world only as
narcissism or as forbidden incest; and René is horrified when he learns
that his sister has incestuous desire for him, a revelation that allows him
to see, as in a mirror, the desire he conceals from himself.

vi

Except for the real existence of Amélie, René's story is essentially
that of Shelley's hero, whose life, after his aimless solitary wanderings, is
an allegorical voyage to his vision in death. Seeing a swan, the Visionary
envies its fulfillment by life. Unlike the alienated, homeless, and wandering Visionary, it has a home in the world and a mate, while his mate is
but a figure of his dream. Like Keats's nightingale and unlike the Visionary, the swan was not born *for* death; all that belongs exclusively to nature
is completed by nature. The Narrator, then, a worshipper of the Earth
Mother only, believes he is of the same order as the swan; but the Vision-

ary defines man in terms of his mortality, and earth's dawn therefore only sheds "the mockery of its vital hues / Upon his cheek of death" (238–39). Why, then, he asks, should he, with "Spirit more vast" than the swan's and "frame more attuned / To beauty," linger in the world,

> . . . wasting these surpassing powers
> In the deaf air, to the blind earth, and heaven
> That echoes not my thoughts? (288–90)

The bird's desires are answered by the world because they are lesser than the Visionary's, whose nature exceeds what the world can supply. The swan traditionally sings only at death and only to lament leaving life. Like the Narrator, it is an elegist; but the Visionary-Poet, gifted "With voice far sweeter" than the swan's "dying notes," must sing of what transcends the world. The sight of the bird "voyaging" to its worldly home and to its mate stirs the poet's desire for his home and mate, but for that purpose he must embark on his allegorical voyage to "meet lone Death on the drear ocean's waste" (305). Yet, although life is inadequate to him, his hope to meet his vision in death is fraught with uncertainties and ironies that preclude any clear conclusion to the poem: his is a "desperate hope," the hope of hopelessness, and sleep, in which he had received his vision,

> he knew, kept most relentlessly
> Its precious charge, and silent death exposed,
> Faithless perhaps as sleep, a shadowy lure,
> With doubtful smile mocking its own strange charms. (292–95)

"I hope," Shelley had written in 1814, "but my hopes are not unmixed with fear for what will befal this inestimable spirit when we die."[62]

Because the Visionary's thirst is for union with his own soul's ideal mirror-image, the perfect subject standing as coveted object to the imperfect subject, a dialectic of the symbol of reflection is threaded through all his experiences. For the mirror-image is but a metaphoric extension of the fact that the dream-lady's voice "was like the voice of his own soul / Heard in the calm of thought" (153–54) and that the "Two starry eyes" that seem to beckon him and are Shelley's recurrent symbols for the soul are eyes "hung in the gloom of [his own] thought" (489–92). Like Keats's Endymion, who, awakening from his visionary experience of the "completed form of all completeness," found that "all the pleasant hues / Of heaven and earth had faded" and that now "deepest shades / Were deepest dungeons," Shelley's Visionary, after his erotic dream-union with

[62] Julian, VI, 361.

the ideal lady, awakens to a physical world, cold and garish, from which the "hues of heaven" have vanished. The "mystery and the majesty of Earth" (199) felt by him as a mere creature of nature have fled, now that he knows the potential relation of his self to some transcendence. The ideal vision has demeaned the Narrator's world of nature, for in contrast to the infinitude and perfection of the vision, the hills are now seen as "clear" and the valley is "distinct," finite.[63] Consequently, whereas he had seen his own soul reflected infinitely in dream, he now looks on the "empty" finite world "as vacantly / As ocean's moon looks on the moon in heaven" (201–2). Having experienced in dream the mirror-image of his own soul and desiring union with it, he now knows that as an element of nature he is not reflected by the world but is only a vacant object that reflects mechanically and meaninglessly the outward world to itself, not a spiritual subject with a life of its own. Passive sensory perception of the finite world is not an act of knowledge, not a union of world and mind, despite the Narrator's claim, but only a mindless mirroring.

Nor is anything in life a meaningful reflection to the Visionary. In his voyage to his vision in death, his boat, symbolic of his worldly self, enters the whirlpool of life's wild turmoil,[64] and there in its midst a pool of "tremendous" calm distorts the clouds it reflects and, "treacherous," threatens to suck the Visionary down to death (385–86). The deceptive placidity at the center of the merely disordered activity of life—in effect, the placidity the Narrator thinks is his accord with nature—falsifies the world, and to succumb to it is to be swallowed in meaningless extinction. The Visionary's way, instead, is to be swept to the topmost height of the world's boundaries as the whirlpool of life's stream carries his boat upward "Stair above stair." There, at the utmost summit of life's domain, above its mad motion but short of the "abyss" of death into which the river pours, the water forms a stream of truly "glassy quiet" (393), unlike the deceptive calm in the midst of the whirlpool below. In this mirror, nature can reveal the self-fulfillment possible to it but not possible to man: in their "pensive task," the flowers "For ever gaze on their own drooping eyes, / Reflected in the crystal calm" (406–8), like the narcissi of *The Sensitive Plant* that "gaze on their eyes in the stream's recess, / Till they die of their own dear loveliness"; and the Visionary's symbolic distinction of himself from this order of being is his rejection of a sudden longing to deck his hair with these flowers and his return to his own solitude, his isolation from the world of nature. But when the Visionary himself, at this uttermost limit of the world, then gazes into a well that reflects all the overhanging natural scene,

[63] Cf. the "cold glare" of the chariot of Life in *The Triumph of Life*, 77.
[64] Cf. *The Revolt of Islam*, 2589–90: "while the stream / Of life, our bark doth on its whirlpools bear." For a similar use of ship as the worldly self, see *Lines Written among the Euganean Hills*.

His eyes beheld
Their own wan light through the reflected lines
Of his thin hair, distinct in the dark depth
Of that still fountain; as the human heart,
Gazing in dreams over the gloomy grave,
Sees its own treacherous likeness there. (469–74)

At the spiritual summit of life the mirrored image of the human self is unlike that of nature, for it does not fulfill reflexively. The calm at the center of life's whirlpool was also "treacherous" (386), but only because passive submission to nature's apparent tranquillity leads to empty annihilation; man's mirror-image in nature is treacherous because it lures him actively to merge with it in death—which may be only extinction. Shelley was repeatedly to be a poet of two parallel realities, often related as an image is related to its watery reflection: one that seems and one that is; one finite, the other infinite; one perceived by the senses, the other apprehended by imagination; one existent in life, the other in death. If all that man believes and hopes is a reality beyond the grave, life does not differ from the world of death in form; rather, life is a veil on which are painted shapes that "mimic" the world of the grave.[65] Whatever else Shelley may have intended in *Prometheus Unbound* by his account of the Magus Zoroaster as the only son of Earth who has ever met his own image walking in the garden—which, significantly, echoes Adam and Eve's hearing "the voice of the Lord God walking in the garden" just prior to their being expelled from Eden[66]—it is clear that he designated two coexistent worlds that mirror each other, one sensory, the other spiritual:

For know there are two worlds of life and death:
One that which thou beholdest; but the other
Is underneath the grave, where do inhabit
The shadows of all forms that think and live
Till death unite them and they part no more.

There, underneath the grave, all creations of the imagination, such as the Visionary's dream-projection of his own perfected self, or what Prince Athanase calls one's sought-for "shade of his own soul, half seen / In any mirror," are real:

Dreams and the light imaginings of men,
And all that faith creates or love desires,
Terrible, strange, sublime and beauteous shapes.[67]

[65] "Lift not the Painted Veil."
[66] Gen. 3:8.
[67] *Prometheus Unbound*, I. 195–202.

Shelley's compulsive yearning for the union of his finite self and its ideal double during life, dramatized in his Visionary, was at work when, after the line, "For know there are two worlds of life and death," he added (but then deleted), "Which thou"—that is, Prometheus as the perfected universal Mind—"henceforth art doomed to interweave."[68] The idea of the double self was no idle fancy. Shortly before his death, according to Mary's report, Shelley frequently had visions of himself, in one of which "he had seen the figure of himself which met him as he walked on the terrace & said to him—'How long do you mean to be content[?]' "[69] This might well have been said to the Narrator of *Alastor* by the Visionary or, better, to the Visionary by his reflected vision, whose eyes "seemed with their serene and azure smiles / To beckon him" (491–92).

Having been tempted beyond the grave by his own reflection, the Visionary, like many of Shelley's questing heroes, is dimly conscious that the Spirit he seeks attends him even in life, standing "beside him," but not in realizable form,

> clothed in no bright robes
> Of shadowy silver or enshrining light,
> Borrowed from aught the visible world affords
> Of grace, or majesty, or mystery,   (480–83)

but diffused mysteriously throughout nature. This is also the attendant Spirit who stands unbeheld "beside" the speaker of *Epipsychidion* and is known to him only in the sounds, odors, and motions of all the elements of nature; or as the experience is described in *Alastor*,

> But, undulating woods, and silent well,
> And leaping rivulet, and evening gloom
> Now deepening the dark shades, for speech assuming,
> Held commune with him, as if he and it
> Were all that was.[70]   (484–88)

This is not any Spirit of Nature but the unrealizable presence of the mind's vision investing all that one experiences, like the object of the "soul's idolatry" whom, "seen nowhere, I feel everywhere."[71] But the mere sense of the dream-lady's unknowable presence in the world is inadequate for the mind; and the Visionary and her diffused attendance prove not to be "all that was"; for the lure of the grave is too great. When the poet

[68] *Shelley's "Prometheus Unbound": A Variorum Edition*, ed. Lawrence John Zillman (Seattle, Wash., 1959), p. 143.
[69] Mary to Maria Gisborne, 15 August 1822 (*Letters of Mary W. Shelley*, ed. F. L. Jones [Norman, Okla., 1944], I, 180). Thomas Medwin tells a variant of this episode (*Life of Percy Bysshe Shelley*, ed. H. B. Forman [London, 1913], p. 405). See above, pp. 9–10.
[70] See pp. 27–28 above for the similar theme in *René*.
[71] "The Zucca," 22–23 (1824 variant, from MS e. 17, p. 196).

now raises his glance *above* the world of nature because of "intense pen-
siveness"—unlike the self-completing flowers that *drooped* in their pensive-
ness to see their reflected eyes—two "starry eyes" shine "within his soul"
(493) beckoning him to an afterlife. Or, we are asked to consider, are
those smiling eyes also a delusion? For even as the poet tempts us to hope
the Visionary will meet those eyes in death, we find that the last thing
the dying Visionary observes is not two starry eyes hung in the gloom of
thought, but "two lessening points of light" that "alone / Gleamed
through the darkness" (654–55), the two remaining points of the horned
moon, whose sinking is symbolic of his physical extinction.

   The fact that, unlike nature, man's spirit is not complementarily returned to him as a reflection in water but lures him to pursue it leads to
Shelley's characteristic skeptical use of the ambiguous image, which is a
kind of imagistic analogue of the unresolved skeptical dialogue. There
being no assured ground of truth, everything is relative to the perspective
in which it is viewed, and the same object of experience changes its meaning and value proportionately as it is seen by natural or by spiritual man,
as it is seen in the context of time or of eternity, this world or afterlife;
and one can only weigh the consequent forms of an image as they stand
in ironic opposition to each other. Boldly reversing expected values and
emotive terms, the Visionary measures the worth of nature's splendors and
thus of man as a natural creature:

   Does the bright arch of rainbow clouds,
And pendent mountains seen in the calm lake,
Lead only to a black and watery depth?   (213–15)

For Death loves the "slimy caverns of the populous deep" (307). Perhaps,
then, the calm self-reflection of nature, whereby it completes itself, also
points to the meaningless extinction of all that belongs to nature, unlike
the treacherous watery reflection of the Visionary's eyes, which tempted
him to self-completion in the grave. Perhaps nature's aspiring mountain
height, unlike the perilous height the Visionary attains at the world's rim,
is reflected only to point down to nature's death; and perhaps the su-
pernally beautiful rainbow merely dissolves into the hideous watery depth
from which it arose. Nature's beauty and sublimity may end in grisly
death. On the other hand, the Visionary considers an ironic mockery of
nature's resplendent structure: could it be that, instead of nature's brilliant
blue vault of heaven hung with rainbow clouds, her anti-world, "death's
blue vault" of the tomb, hung with bluish "loathliest vapours" rising from
the corpse,

Where every shade which the foul grave exhales
Hides its dead eye from the detested day,
Conducts, O Sleep, to thy delightful realms?   (216–19)

Glorious nature may end in black death; but for that which is also spirit, loathsome death may be the gate to the glorious realm of visionary ful-fillment.

Yet, all this may be illusion. Death may be "Faithless perhaps as sleep, a shadowy lure, / With doubtful smile mocking its own strange charms" (294–95). The Visionary is led on his journey to death by a hope that "stung / His brain even like despair" (221–22), and we are never to know whether hope or despair was justified. The Narrator, our only source of information, knows only the domain of the Mother of this unfathomable world.

vii

The Visionary's career, however, while the major subject of *Alastor*, is not the total poem, which we misread and severely limit if we fail to take into account the function of the Narrator.[72] The Narrator is a subtly operative factor not only because he distances the Visionary from us psy-chologically and prevents his self-torment from lapsing into René's senti-mentalism but also because the Narrator (poet of the natural world) and his subject (poet of the ideal) can ironically play against each other in the skeptical and ironic manner of the Christian and Deist in *A Refuta-tion of Deism*. Despite the Narrator's admiration for the Visionary, the disparity between one's exclusive devotion to the Spirit of Nature and the other's aspiration to a transcendent Self so directs the course of the poem that, while the Visionary's dream eventually becomes as much doubtful as hopeful, the Narrator ultimately undermines his own values without wholly destroying them. Poet-Narrator and Poet-Visionary dis-cipline each other like the Yeatsian self and anti-self to prevent deception and to load either position with risks. For if the Visionary represents Shelley's yearning for the ideal Self, the Narrator is the contrary, mun-dane half of the skeptical Shelleyan self. As in the conflict of reason and faith in *A Refutation of Deism*, whatever is advanced in the poem is also withdrawn or gravely qualified, statement is met by counterstatement, and much of the art of the poem lies in the appearance of similar image pat-terns that reflect ironically on each other. Skeptically uncertain of both the value of human life and the probability of afterlife, Shelley can only test tentatively by watching the esthetic consequence of placing the same image or ironically similar images in opposing contexts.

Significantly different though the consequences are, Narrator and Visionary differ in degree rather than in kind, and the very similarity of

72 There is at least a general structural analogy between *Alastor*, which opens and closes with the commentary of the Narrator, and Chateaubriand's *René*, which en-folds René's confessions in an account of a priest and the Indian Chactas, who urge him to abandon his discontent and useless reverie and to find happiness in following the common paths.

the early careers of these two poets is the ironic means of setting them at odds with each other. Visionary is to Narrator as he also is to the swan, which, though its dying song is less sweet than his voice and its spirit less vast, has a mate and a home in the world to which it voyages in its flight.[73] Both Narrator and Visionary seek an object worthy of each one's love, but whereas the former is content with the reciprocal love between him and earth, ocean, and air, the latter finds that in response to his mind the air is deaf, the earth blind, and heaven "echoes not my thoughts" (289–90), just as the subject of "Oh! there are spirits" found that nature scorned his love. Similarly, the Narrator glories in his brotherhood with the other creations of nature; but when maidens, despite his disregard of them, call the Visionary "Brother, and friend" they call him by "false names," not because they are wholly wrong but because, being taught by "nature" alone, they can interpret only "*half* the woe / That wasted him" (266–69). Nature can teach only equal desire among her offspring, only their brotherhood and friendship, not the desire of the soul for union with its own transcendent perfection. That man is a child of the World Mother is a half-truth; the other half is that he is akin to something which exceeds nature and which he can only envision during life. The cottagers, whom the Visionary equally disregards as he pursues his dream, also can minister only to his "human" wants with their "human charity" (254–56).

Narrator and Visionary, too, have an "incommunicable dream" (39) that determines the course of each one's life. The former has sought the mystery of existence in Nature, watching the darkness of her "steps" (21), and although, like all who attempt to unveil the Isiac Great Mother, he has been unable to bare her inmost shrine, a light from dreams, phantasms, and deep thought has "shone" within him (41), leading him to a life of serenity by teaching him to submit passively to the breath of the Earth Mother. The Visionary, however, filled with a more glorious, though possibly illusory, degree of desire, graduates beyond his similar pursuit of Nature's "secret steps" (81) and the mystery hidden in records of human thought until he, too, experiences a dream vision as a "light / That shone within his soul" (493). But this is a vision of his own mind's ideal, which the world cannot supply, and instead of being led by it to a life of serenity, he is driven on his life-voyage of quest beyond the grave. From the limited, worldly view of the Narrator, who is content with a lesser inner light, the Visionary is not without greatness but rather, like

[73] A similar use of the image appears in Chateaubriand's *René*: "I often watched birds of passage flying overhead. I imagined the unknown shores and far-off regions to which they were bound. How I wished to be on their wings. A secret instinct tormented me; I felt I was only a voyager myself; but a voice from heaven seemed to tell me: 'Man, your season for migration has not yet arrived; wait for the death-wind to arise, then you will spread your wing towards those unknown regions that your heart yearns for.'"

the subject of "Oh! there are spirits," suffers from a glorious self-destructive
excess of virtue, so that he is one of the "luminaries of the world," a "surpassing Spirit" whose light, ironically, adorned the very world he spurned.

Although it is necessary to be aware that the entire poem is inspired
by the Earth Mother, throughout the account of the Visionary's quest
the Narrator's voice is largely sublimated or intrudes only occasionally,
despite the fact that the luxuriant descriptions of the natural scene, especially of the perfect unions within itself, are consonant with the Narrator,
not the Visionary, who devotes himself mainly to holding "mute confer-
ence / With his still soul" (223–24). But after the Visionary's death
has been recounted and he passes out of range, the pure voice of the
Narrator can be heard again in the final lament as it was in the opening
invocation—and, like that of the Christian in the *Refutation of Deism,* it
now proves a voice that either betrays his own narrowness or tends unconsciously to refute him. The very fact that he now laments the loss of
the human life that the Visionary had intentionally evaded as meaningless
points to the disparity of the two views and to his own earth-bound perspective. He grieves that the Visionary can no longer know the things of
nature that had been to him "purest ministers" (698), a ministry that the
Visionary, who refrained from adorning himself with flowers because his
more aspiring solitude alienated him from the natural order (412–15),
had found inadequate while instead it was the impulse of his vision that
"performed its ministry" (417).

Superficially the close of the poem appears to be the expected, conventional elegiac lament over the Visionary's death. Actually, the Narrator
has no choice but to phrase his lament as a wish for endless life on earth,
for if the world satisfies him totally, it is an end in itself, and he could
leave it, like Keats's Godwinian perfectibilist, only as Eve left Paradise.
Yet, the Narrator's wish, though sincere, shapes itself in shocking, even
horrifying images that, with unintended irony, defeat its intent, just as the
Christian of the *Refutation of Deism* undermines Christianity in the very
act of supporting it. As the Narrator identified himself with alchemy in
his invocation, so his wishes for eternal earthly existence are expressed in
terms of the alchemical search for the elixir of life, in accordance with his
belief that the only mystery of existence resides in physical nature. Recalling Medea's magical rejuvenation of the dying Aeson, he calls upon
only a minor detail of Ovid's myth,[74] the fact that the dead branch with
which Medea stirred the vital potion suddenly bloomed and bore fruit
and that flowers sprang up where the potion dropped on the earth:

O, for Medea's wondrous alchemy,
Which wheresoe'er it fell made the earth gleam
With bright flowers, and the wintry boughs exhale
From vernal blooms fresh fragrance!   (672–75)

[74] *Metamorphoses* vii. 275 seq.

Far from identifying the mind of man with an immutable spirit transcending nature, this brother of earth, ocean, and air recognizes only the
vegetative character of life. The other expression of his wish invokes an
even more obvious example of eternal life on earth, the Wandering Jew.
But the choice is patently inappropriate, and something horribly paradoxical happens, unintended by the Narrator, when he formulates his wish:

> O, that God,
> Profuse of poisons, would concede the chalice
> Which but one living man has drained, who now,
> Vessel of deathless wrath,[75] a slave that feels
> No proud exemption in the blighting curse
> He bears, over the world wanders for ever,
> Lone as incarnate death! (675–81)

Unexpectedly, earthly life without end reveals itself as the solitude of
"incarnate death," a boon, ironically, from God's chalice, from which the
Christian expects the eucharistic gift of *spiritual* immortality after death.
In his youthful St. Irvyne and The Wandering Jew Shelley had already
treated the traditional theme of the curse of eternal wandering on earth;
and he also had before him the example of Godwin's St. Leon, who, given
the alchemical secret of life, makes himself immoral, only to find himself
cursed with solitude, cut off from human society, even from his own
family. Compelled by curiosity, the comparable figure in Shelley's St.
Irvyne (1811) discovers the elixir of life by "unveiling the latent mysteries
of nature" and gains "endless existence . . . a dateless and hopeless eternity
of horror."[76] As Shelley wrote of the "blighting curse" of endless life at
about the time of St. Irvyne: "For the immoral 'never to be able to die,
never to escape from some shrine as chilling as the clay-formed dungeon
which now it inhabits['] is the future punishment which I believe in."[77]
In the very act of wishing for an eternity of the life his Earth Mother
gives, the Narrator of Alastor has made man subhuman and life either
nugatory or a burden, if not a curse; and we are being asked to consider
whether our merely physical existence may not be a solitude as total as the
Visionary's, whether the tormenting Spirit of Solitude of the poem's title
may not threaten the Narrator also.

Indeed, when the Narrator describes the Visionary's dead body, he
unwittingly subverts his own supposed values:

Even as a vapour fed with golden beams
That ministered on sunlight, ere the west
Eclipses it, was now that wondrous frame—

[75] For this phrase, see Romans 9: 22–23.
[76] Julian, V, 180, 199.
[77] To Hogg, 3 [January] 1811 (Letters, I, 35).

No sense, no motion, no divinity—
A fragile lute, on whose harmonious strings
The breath of heaven did wander.   (663–68)

And he unintentionally stamps an interpretation on this when he transforms this metaphor into the literal fact that the decaying corpse will be
"divinest lineaments, / Worn by the senseless wind" (704–5). For in his
opening invocation the Narrator had prayed that the inspiring breath of
the Great Mother sweep over him,

> moveless as a long-forgotten lyre
Suspended in the solitary dome
Of some mysterious and deserted fane.   (42–44)

His later management of the same image reveals that for man to be but
a passive lyre totally submissive to the forces of nature is actually to be a
corpse, senseless, motionless, soulless, and gradually eroded by nature's
forces. Now the Narrator's original comparison of himself as poet to the
"long-forgotten" lyre in the "solitary" dome of a "deserted" fane, so casually
brushed over in a first reading of the invocation, gains its full ironic
horror in retrospect: despite his belief that he is of the community of
nature, he is, as merely a child of the World Mother, just as solitary as
the Visionary, as alone as the incarnate death of the Wandering Jew. In
a similar way the image of the forgotten lyre appeared elsewhere in the
Alastor volume to symbolize the meaningless solitude of our earthly subjection to mutability and death: we are

> like forgotten lyres, whose dissonant strings
Give various response to each varying blast,
To whose frail frame no second motion brings
One mood or modulation like the last.[78]

What the Narrator had originally intended as an image of fully meaningful life has ironically proved an image of meaningless death.

viii

In the process of the poem, then, the Narrator's faith in the Spirit
of Nature either ironically undermines itself or is gradually eroded as a
consequence of the opposing presence of the Visionary until any hypothetical value becomes equivocal; for the art of the poem is, at nearly every
point, its protean evasion of any effort to pin it down into an assertion.
If we recognize this purposeful ambiguity, together with the fact that the
poem is spoken by a narrator of a certain character, much in the poem
that has the appearance of being inconsistent or contradictory proves centrally functional.

[78] "Mutability," 5–8.

It would seem congruent with the stance of the poem to conceive of the Narrator, and not Shelley, as the one who, as putative author, elected to entitle the work "Alastor," the avenging spirit of solitude, and recorded in the Preface that the Visionary's "self-centred seclusion was avenged by the furies of an irresistible passion pursuing him to speedy ruin."[79] A yearning for union with one's ideal self as Other and the pursuit of that ideal beyond the limits of life could receive no other interpretation in the Narrator's exclusively extroverted, world-oriented perspective. But the presence of the Visionary exerts considerable pressure against that perspective, and that pressure generates a series of ambiguities—not inconsistencies—that make both perspectives equally doubtful, or equally probable. If, for example, the Visionary's passion for the "bright shadow" of his "lovely dream" (233) is, paradoxically, like a tormenting "fierce fiend of a distempered dream" (225) that drives him in agony on his life-journey and causes him to flee (232, 237), he is merely being driven from the world that the Narrator finds gratifying, and life becomes a "weary waste of hours" laden with "brooding care" (245–46). On the other hand, it is equally true that he himself "eagerly pursues" the vision (205), urged by his own impulse that seeks to fulfill its "ministry" (274, 304, 415–17), and that he is led by spirits who are "ministers / Appointed to conduct him" to his vision (330–31). He is also only following his own "eager soul" (311) in obedience to the light within it (492–93), or, what amounts to the same thing, is beckoned by the "starry eyes" of his dream figure. The first interpretation is the consequence of the Narrator's view, a lament for the wasted and tortured life of one pursued; the second is the Visionary's, a zealous pursuit, however illusory, of a good beyond the limits of an inherently inadequate and negligible world. The accounts of the Visionary's relation to his dream are contradictory only because two irreconcilable conceptions of life are in contest with each other.

But either is a valid view, depending on how the ambiguity is tilted, just as the question of whether Keats's La Belle Dame is a Circe or a visionary ideal similarly depends on whether one's perspective is mortal or immortal life. If our dream-projection of a Self equal to the perfect conception of our own self is true and promissory of our union with it in afterlife, then human existence has no meaning, and the Visionary's solitude is an expression of his spiritual grandeur; otherwise, the vision of transcendence is a treacherous illusion and leads to a tormenting discontent with life and waste of it. We cannot know whether the Visionary is led to his hasty end by "love, or dream, or god, or mightier Death" (428). Since Shelley has no ground for affirmation, no first principles from either received authority or empirical experience, his poetry is fundamentally a search for probable, not absolute, truth. Given that the goals he is testing are con-

[79] The prefaces of *Julian and Maddalo* and *Epipsychidion* are explicitly by fictional *personae*. It would seem logical that the pretended "author" of *Alastor* is also the author of its Preface.

tradictory and irreconcilable, he can prepare a ground for himself only
by the skeptic's method of lifting himself up by his own bootstraps, sustaining each position only by repudiating its opposite through ambivalence
and paradox, as though supporting the two sides of an arch by the sheer
pressure they exert against each other. As a skeptic Shelley has, in Keats's
words, "no standard law of either earth or heaven," and he can initiate his
inquiry only by means of a paradox in such a way that each side of the
contradiction remains a possibility: the poet is a passive wind-lyre, but in
another perspective that is a metaphor for a corpse; eternal earthly life
may be a good or a curse; from one point of view the Visionary zealously
pursues his vision and from the opposite view is driven by it to death. The
paradox of the contradictory faces of the same object, the equivocal image
that, like the blue vault that is either sky or tomb, yields opposing meanings depending on the perspective in which it is viewed—this will remain
an essential operative element of Shelley's poetry. Even when he later
attains greater assurance of belief it will be a tentative confidence resting
on the skillful management of various modes and extensions of the
skeptic's basic paradox.

But the presence of the Visionary results in more than ambivalent
views; it also exerts a pressure on the Narrator that complicates his sense
of values. Consequently, although the Narrator professes the total sufficiency of nature, by the end of the poem he himself has acknowledged
something that exceeds it; for, he confesses, the Visionary's "surpassing"
spirit which sought a reality transcending the world was nevertheless a
"light" that not only "adorned the world around it" (715) but even transfigured it so that upon his departure from it man and "Nature's vast
frame . . . are not as they were" (719–20). Describing the Visionary's faith
from the point of view of a sympathetic and admiring nonbeliever, the
Narrator, whose mind cannot extend beyond the mortal world, is led into
the paradox that to aspire to the improbable ideal and thereby to scorn
the world is nevertheless to cast unintentionally a glory on that world. It
is a paradox of the same order as that the good die first.

It is, then, the Narrator's voice that we hear in the prose Preface
telling us in disapproval, within the limits of his earthly perspective, that
the Visionary was "Blasted by his disappointment" and descended "to an
untimely grave"; yet, by quoting from Wordsworth's Excursion, he also
confesses with admiration that it was an excess of virtue that deprived
him of life, while the fullness of life's span is granted the worthless:

<blockquote>
The good die first,
And those whose hearts are dry as summer's dust,
Burn to the socket!
</blockquote>

While worshiping the Earth Mother alone, the Narrator has unwittingly
subverted the value of the life to which she gives birth, just as he does
when he pleads for the "incarnate death" of the Wandering Jew or when

he unintentionally reveals that the worshiper of nature is at least as solitary as the Visionary. Unconscious of undermining his own values and his content with the world, he can only admire but deplore the desire for a transcendent good, which, in his view, "strikes the luminaries of the world with sudden darkness and extinction, by awakening them to too exquisite a perception of its influences," for the "pure and tender-hearted perish through the intensity and passion of their search after its communities, when the vacancy of their spirit suddenly makes itself felt." Consequently, the Visionary's pursuit of his "dream of hopes," according to the author of the Preface, is an error, but a "generous," not a selfish, one; only a "thirst of doubtful knowledge," yet a "sacred" thirst; merely a superstition, nevertheless an "illustrious" one—and illustrious enough to make him a "luminary" whose light adorns the world while he evades it. If one side of Shelley yearns for accord with the world, the other seeks to justify solitary aspiration to an unworldly absolute as an act that, by indirection, also transforms the world.

ix

"The good die first": one who profits the world most is snatched—or released—from it soonest, while one who profits it least is given the largest measure of life to remain in it. Goodness irresistibly compels an infinite love that cannot be satisfied by the finite world and results in the luminary's "sudden extinction." To restrict one's love to a single mistress or friend, Shelley was to write in *Epipsychidion*, is to follow

> the beaten road
> Which those poor slaves with weary footsteps tread,
> Who travel to their home among the dead
> By the broad highway of the world, and so
> With one chained friend, perhaps a jealous foe,
> The dreariest and the *longest* journey go; [80]

and, contrarily, the poet of *The Triumph of Life* speaks of

> the sacred few who could not tame
> Their spirits to the Conqueror [i.e. Life], but as soon
> As they had touched the world with living flame
>
> Fled back like eagles to their native noon. . . . [81]

[80] *Epipsychidion*, 154–59 (itals. added).
[81] *The Triumph of Life*, 128–31. For "Conqueror" in line 129, Shelley first wrote "yoke" (Donald H. Reiman, *Shelley's "The Triumph of Life": A Critical Study, Based on a Text Newly Edited from the Bodleian Manuscript* [Urbana, Ill., 1965], p. 153).

The line from Wordsworth's *Excursion* must have struck Shelley as an extraordinarily compressed formulation of man's paradoxical involvement in both mortal life and afterlife, for it reappears as the epigraph of his hauntingly visionary poem, "The Two Spirits," which he left in manuscript, just short of final form. The epigraph suggests the kinship with *Alastor*,[82] and to a significant degree the poem is a translation of the human story of *Alastor* into a myth and into astronomical symbolism, so that what is represented as actually lived experiences of Narrator and Visionary is here expressed as a lyric dialogue between opposing impulses of the human soul, or, as Shelley subtitled it, "An Allegory." It can help us to understand how Shelley interpreted Wordsworth's phrase and to see better the skeptical mode of *Alastor*.

Although the original dream framework was cancelled in the manuscript,[83] the lyric dialogue between the two Spirits remains something we overhear in a vision. One Spirit, whose wings are "strong desire" for more than the world can provide, would, like the Visionary of *Alastor*, escape mortal limitations (hence the epigraph) and "float above the earth," a fiery light like the "deathless stars," which are Shelley's symbol of the soul's perfection and immortality. The other is the cowering earthbound Spirit, who urges the first to be content within the earthly "regions of the air": "It were delight to wander there." The regions of earth, he claims, are bright, and the night of death lies ahead of us with its whirlwinds of darkness, hail, lightning, and storm: death's "Shadow tracks thy flight of fire,"[84] and even now, he warns, the outer bounds of earth's air "are shaken." But the first Spirit scorns the other's safe "dull earth, slumber-bound," for the soul that dares desire without bound and aspire dangerously to transcendence has within itself a "lamp of love" which is the light of day. Moving like the deathless stars beyond earth's bound of air, and granted there also the borrowed lustre from the other heavenly bodies, he will be a light like day even when, star-like, he crosses through

[82] Mary assigned "The Two Spirits" to 1820. But since it appears in MS e. 12 (pp. 13–17) between "Mine eyes were dim," which she assigns to June 1814, and "There late was One," which she dates 1816, there is some reason to believe it may be a far earlier poem, perhaps even contemporary with the composition of *Alastor* in 1815.

[83] The original opening line was, "Two genii stood before me in a dream" (MS e. 12, p. 13).

[84] On the notebook page immediately preceding "The Two Spirits" Shelley wrote:

[. . .] once more descend
The shadows of my soul upon mankind
For to those hearts with whom they never blend
⟨My⟩ thoughts are but shadows; which the flashing mind
From the swift clouds which track its flight of fire
Cast on the gloomy world it leaves behind.   (MS e. 12, p. 12)

There is no apparent justification for Forman's connecting this fragment with Shelley's projected poem on Otho.

earth's dark cone of night, in whose "deep gloom" the earthly Spirit is bound. The timid Spirit's refrain urges relish of earth's delights because "Night is coming!" The other's answering refrain is that transcendent desire and love "make night day" because infinite love for an absolute is an eternal light to which earth's vicissitudes and its night of death are irrelevant.

One of the triumphs of the poem is its abrupt transformation from a visionary dialogue of mythic spirits into a skeptical legend and, correspondingly, its descent from an unmediated dramatic vision to a kind of indeterminate folk legend mediated by a human *ingénu*. Dream vision is replaced by consciousness of fancied beliefs without ever becoming conscious experience. As though the dialogue of Spirits had never taken place or as though it had no relation to what follows, the last two stanzas postulate a wholly human and earthly context: they report ingenuously, in the voice of the poet and without judgment or bias, alternate legends. Some men, we are informed, tell of a vast pine "frozen to ruin" on an Alpine precipice where

> the languid storm[,] pursuing
> That winged shape[,] forever flies
> Round those hoar branches, aye renewing
> Its aery fountains.

The eerie flight of the "winged shape" from the pursuing storm is but a minor, almost parenthetical feature in the description of the storm's endless whirling about the pine, and the consequence is a miracle of symbolic transformation of the winged Spirit so that the frozen pine acts as its surrogate, or so that the aspiring Spirit seems the ghost of the pine. The scene is analogous to the one the Visionary of *Alastor* finally reaches in his allegorical life-journey: at the summit, above the world on the one side and the "immeasurable void" on the other, at the highest point of life and on the verge of death,

> A pine,
> Rock-rooted, stretched athwart the vacancy
> Its swinging boughs, to each inconstant blast
> Yielding one only response. . . .[85]

The earthbound Spirit of the lyric, then, was right: the aspiring Spirit's flight "above the earth" does not transport him to the starry heavens but, ironically, raises him only to the earth's summit, perilously exposed like the ruined pine to the endless pursuit of the storm of which the earthly

[85] *Alastor*, 561–64; see also 571, 634. Byron also uses the blasted mountain pine as a symbol of man (*Manfred*, I. ii. 65–69).

Spirit had warned, a storm ever renewed in nature's perpetual cycle of mutability.

But another legend[86] tells that on nights when the heaven is clear above and the obscuring "death-dews," or miasmas that symbolize man's mortality, do not rise from the morass below to blot out the deathless stars, the sleeping traveller through the world has a visionary dream of a "silver shape like his early love"[87] and, awakening, "finds night day." Then, to surpass the limits of mortal life is to become a luminary to the world that has been spurned. The two legends are left equally possible, and Shelley sustains his skeptical stance. The passage from an unmediated visionary dialogue of opposing Spirits to ingenuously reported conflicting legends leaves the poem suspended between the human need for truth and the fantasy world of sheer possibility, a borderline area where decision is called for but where there is no ground for one, and where the poet is relieved of obligation to decide. But it is a skeptical indeterminacy with a bias, for the aspiring Spirit has the best lines and the last words. The poem closes with the legend of the winged shape that visits man's dreams and transforms his mortal night into spiritual day, and the repeated refrain, "Which makes night day," becomes in the closing line the confidence of a revelation—"He finds night day."

Yet the paradox remains for Shelley that only the striving beyond life casts a light on the limited mortal world, just as the Visionary of *Alastor* transfigured it, not despite the inadequacy of the world to his desires, but because of it. However much Shelley was inclined to the ideal world of his visions, he never fully resolved the psychomachy of the two Spirits, and on occasion he was to return, at least apparently, to the view of the earthly Spirit and the Narrator of *Alastor*, as in his sonnet "Ye hasten to the grave." What do you hope "to inherit in the grave below?" he wearily asks his restless thoughts, his heart, which yearns "to possess / All that pale Expectation feigneth fair," and his "vainly curious" mind, which would guess "Whence thou didst come, and whither thou must go, / And all that never yet was known would know."

Oh, whither hasten ye, that thus ye press,
With such swift feet life's green and pleasant path,
Seeking, alike from happiness and woe,
A refuge in the cavern of gray death?

[86] Before writing "Some say" at the opening of this stanza, Shelley wrote, "And other."
[87] Shelley first wrote, "winged shape"; in other words, it is to be identified with the luminous "plumed" Spirit that would float "above the earth." Shelley, incidentally, wrote in *Alastor* of "silver dream" (67) and "silver vision" (316); and the term "silver dreams" appears also in *Rosalind and Helen* (768), begun in 1817. The term does not occur thereafter in his poetry.

The sonnet, which reads like a protest against Keats's "Why Did I Laugh Tonight?," seems utterly without ambiguity: the world's mingled happiness and pain, says a voice like that of the mundane Spirit, is preferable to death's unknown realm, and in his interior dialogue the weary speaker chides his impetuous heart and mind for their neglect of the green and pleasant world. The Narrator of *Alastor* is right, not the Visionary. Or so it may appear until we notice the nearly submerged fact that the brain's "restless thoughts and busy purposes" that probe beyond life's verge wear "the world's livery." They are menials of the world, not masters of it or themselves, and their quest is for freedom from their servitude. The fact subtly undercuts the expressed delight in mortal life and tells us that the poet's opposing voice prevents him from speaking his protest with complete sincerity, so that his final question is, ambiguously, both exhausted complaint and sincere curiosity: "O heart, and mind, and thoughts! what thing do you / Hope to inherit in the grave below?"

Shelley never attained total conviction, and an even sharper ambivalence, approximating that of *Alastor*, produced the oscillating course of his sonnet "Lift Not the Painted Veil." What men call "life," it concedes, may be an unreality, a deception—a veil like a stage curtain on which are painted "unreal shapes" only imitative of "all we would believe." Behind that veil may be the reality of which our world is only an illusion.[88] But illusory and imperfect though human life may be, the risk is that we may hazard it for what, in our ignorance, must be uncertain and is as likely to be what we dread as what we desire. On the other side of the veil of illusions may lie all we hope for, or, if not more imperfection, perhaps nothing at all:

> . . . behind, lurk Fear
> And Hope, twin Destinies; who ever weave
> The shadows, which the world calls substance, there.[89]

The speaker is, in effect, the Narrator of *Alastor* or the earthbound soul of "The Two Spirits," and he cautions, even in admitting life's inadequacy, "Lift not the painted veil"; in the context of his skepticism it is better to reconcile oneself to the imperfect illusion of life than to neglect it for what may be an even more monstrous illusion.

Yet this same speaker tells of having known one who, like the Visionary of *Alastor*, finding nothing in the world worthy of his perfect

---

[88] Cf. Huntington Notebooks, II, 109–10:

What hast thou done then. . . . Lifted up the veil
Which between that which seems & that which is;
Hangs on the scene of life? with shapes uncertain
Confused oerwrought—tombs palaces. . . .

[89] The text is that of the 1824 *Posthumous Poems*. The 1839 text reads, "Their shadows, o'er the chasm, sightless and drear."

love and nevertheless seeking that worthy object, did lift the veil. What
he found the timid speaker could not possibly know, but that the aspirant
did raise the veil made him, paradoxically,—like the Visionary of *Alastor*
and like the aspiring soul of "The Two Spirits"—a light, a "splendour"
among the "shadows" of the world he disdained, a glory to the world
because he sought to exceed it. Yet, such spirits, glorious though they are,
are unsettling to the earthbound soul that would be content with the
world, for in the very act of seeking to satisfy the superhuman factor in
man they also release the demonic into the world. To be unable, like the
Preacher of Ecclesiastes, to find "truth" in the world and nevertheless to
strive for it beyond the world, is from one ironic perspective to be a
"splendour among shadows"; from another it is to be "a bright blot,"[90] a
blemish, "Upon this gloomy scene," which, according to the "Conclusion"
of *The Sensitive Plant*, can "endure no light." So the sonnet ends in the
version Mary published in 1824; but a draft in Shelley's hand,[91] without
altering the basic sense, casts the conclusion in another context:

I should be happier had I ne'er known
This mournful man—he was himself alone.

The solitary's aloneness, in terms of the Preface to *Alastor*, is his "self-
centred seclusion," but it is also the self-possession of a finite spirit directing
itself exclusively to the infinite perfection that fulfills it, an admirably
deplorable and splendidly mournful autonomy that both illuminates the
world and makes other mortals dissatisfied with their earthly lot.

x

It may well be that Shelley encouraged Mary to write her drama
of 1820 on Midas in order to be provided with a pretext—and context—
for composing the so-called "hymns" of Apollo and Pan that he contributed to it.[92] Ovid's tale of Midas and the singing contest between the two

[90] Shelley consistently uses "blot" in a pejorative sense.
[91] MS e. 12, pp. 22–23. The Morgan Library fair copy in Shelley's hand corresponds, with a few minor exceptions, to the version Mary published in the 1839
edition of Shelley's *Poetical Works*, which differs from the 1824 text mainly in the
line quoted in footnote 89 above. She did not make any use of the Bodleian draft.
[92] Mary was apparently responsible for supplying the titles "Hymn of Apollo" and
"Hymn of Pan" when she published the poems independently of her play in the
1824 volume of her husband's poems. The songs are without title in Shelley's working manuscript (MS e. 6, pp. 22–29) and, of course, in Mary's manuscript of the
entire play, where they are incorporated into the dramatic action. Her play, entitled
Midas, remained in manuscript until 1922, when it was published by A. Koszul.
    A hymn *of* a god is, of course, an anomaly, and the songs by the two gods are
not hymns in the customary sense of prayers. The title is appropriate only inasmuch
as, in accordance with some of the conventional features of the classical hymn, each
song is in (self-) praise of a deity and describes his domain, attributes, powers, and
history.

gods invites interpretation as the archetypal myth of the claims of two opposing orders, and a singing match lends itself as a variant form of the skeptical dialogue. The myth therefore offered Shelley a renewed challenge to explore and dramatize the irreconcilable affiliations of man's dual nature, and this time he did so with a technical virtuosity and a total artistic functionalism unparalleled in his poetry.

According to the Ovidian myth, Tmolus, a hill god, heard the contest between the two deities and adjudged Apollo's song the superior, but King Midas, a worshipper of Pan, disputed the decision and was given ass's ears by Apollo as punishment. Ovid of course represented Apollo and Pan as gods of a higher and a lower order of values, and his myth leads almost necessarily to such typical interpretations as George Sandys's: "Pan presents illiterate rusticity; Apollo is a mind imbued with the divine endowments of art and nature. . . . For there is a two fold harmony of musick; the one of divine providence, and the other of humane reason." Midas, by preferring Pan's music and electing the "vile" instead of the "excellent," denotes "the brutish and ignorant life." The myth must have appeared to Shelley the archetypal form of the dilemma that persisted in confronting him: a contest between "universal Pan" and Apollo, god of the heavens, dramatizes man's divisive desires for mortal life and for the absolute values that he can conceive of but that exceed the world's resources. As established myth it is a traditional and therefore universal statement of the oppositions of which *Alastor*, "The Two Spirits," and "Lift Not the Painted Veil" are enactments in a variety of more special modes—human history, allegory, dream vision, and popular beliefs. That Ovid's two gods, presiding over opposing realms—earth and heaven, human and divine, mutability and immutability, experience and desire—embraced all possible domains for Shelley is suggested by his representing the sum of the classical pantheon elsewhere as Jove (the overriding spirit), Love (the operative principle of the universe), Apollo, and Pan.[93]

Shelley's Apollo boasts not only of his role as source of all natural light but also of the mental realms over which he presides. As the destroyer of Python, or Error, the god of Truth[94] slays with his sunbeam-arrows "Deceit, that loves the night and fears the day"; and, as Ovid illustrated in his story of Apollo's disclosure of Venus' adultery with Mars,

All men who do, or even imagine ill
Fly me; and from the glory of my ray
Good minds, and open actions take new might.[95]

[93] *Hellas*, 232–33.
[94] For this traditional interpretation of the myth of Apollo and Python, see Sandys's Ovid.
[95] Shelley is probably also alluding indirectly to the tradition that the eagle renews its youth and regains clarity of sight by flying into the sun (cf. below, pp. 400, 489–90).

In his various roles, he is god of poetry, music, medicine, and prophecy—
"All light of art or nature."[96] He is not symbolic of an otherworld, as has
been suggested, but is god of all that the human mind is capable of conceiving, "all of wonderful, or wise, or beautiful, which the poet, the
philosopher, or the lover could depicture," however much actual experience may be at odds with those mental ideals. It is for this reason that,
transforming the sun's speech in Ovid—"I am he . . . who beholds all
things, by whom the earth beholds all things, the world's eye [*mundi
oculus*]"[97]—Shelley has Apollo sing,

I am the eye with which the Universe
Beholds itself, and knows it is divine,

just as in his "Ode to Heaven" Shelley described the sun as the "Power
which is the glass / Wherein man his nature sees." Apollo's words may
well reflect, as has been proposed, Plato's association of the sun with the
spiritual eye and with the Good, which supplies the "light" that allows
the soul's eye to see Truth.[98] But if so—and the analogy is enriching—
Apollo's words do not carry with them anything else of Plato's supposed
philosophy, such as the postulation of the real existence of a transcendent
ideal world distinct from the world of appearances. Their import is that
there is a mode of self-knowledge whereby the universe can see truly its
own divinity, a mental view from "above" in which its inherent perfection, or true potential nature, can be discerned. In one of its aspects, then,
the universe is divine and has access to a special mode of vision in which
its own divinity is evident to it. For the distinction between Shelley's
Apollo and Pan is not really one between two realms of being, one here
and now, the other "there" and hereafter; it is between the contradictory
aspects shared by both the self and the world—the one aspect perfect,
eternal, conceptual, and transcendent (in the sense that it is outside lived
experience), and the other inadequate, mutable, and experiential. Like
the Visionary of *Alastor*, like the one who lifted the veil of life, and like
the aspiring Spirit, Apollo, presiding over absolutes alone, is "superior" to
life and not engaged in it, while nevertheless transfiguring it with his
light—a splendor among shadows who makes night day.

Yet there are disturbing counterstatements in Apollo's song that
seriously qualify his tone of easy perfection and degrade it at length to
the too-insistent boastfulness with which the lyric ends: "to my song /
Victory and praise, in its own right, belong." Deceit flees Apollo's light,
but it "loves the night"—and to that night Apollo must give way. Good
minds and open actions gain their renewed power from the light of day—

96 The MS (e. 6, p. 25) shows that Shelley also tried "All light of mind or nature."
97 *Metamorphoses* iv. 226–28.
98 *Republic* 507 seq.

"Until diminished by the reign of night." And however "unwilling" Apollo's descent from his absoluteness at noon "upon the peak of Heaven," he must yield to night and leave the clouds weeping with rain and frowning with darkness where he had brought them the light of smiles:

> Then with unwilling steps, I linger down
> Into the clouds of the Atlantic even;
> For grief that I depart they weep and frown—
> What look is more delightful, than the smile
> With which I soothe them from the Western isle.[99]

In his inevitable sinking he can at best "soothe" the clouds with his twilight from a distant Hesperides, a far-off paradise of hope. Although he is the power with which the universe sees its own divinity, he does not have omnipotent sway over the universe, but must share his reign equally with night and deceit, just as he shares with Pan exactly the same number of lines of poetry in their singing contest. For man, paradoxically, the absolute exists in the context of mutability; the eternal is occasional.

On the other hand, universal Pan appropriately sings, not of the mind's ideal and abstract powers, but of lived experience and its objects— of the natural elements, creatures, and nature deities who come to hear him pipe of stars, earth, and heaven, and of the range of human events, conflict, love, death, and birth. He sings not of the earth as an abstraction or an undifferentiated entity but of the "daedal Earth." He sings of the "dancing stars," that mystic movement supposed to be the model for the human dance that traditionally attends upon Pan's pipe, not, as Apollo does, of the "pure" stars—stars as deathless and immutable spirits—and of their "eternal" bowers.[100] But his central theme is love, love as a contingent earthly experience and not as a mental concept; and this is what essentially distinguishes him from Apollo. Apollo's subjects are absolutes— Love, Truth, Beauty, Virtue, and Divinity—not the relational act of love, whereas Pan's themes are his love of Syrinx and the enraptured silence of love with which all of nature and her creatures have listened to his songs of life and the world. Apollo therefore is entirely self-contained subjectivity, the absolute ego, concentrating exclusively on defining himself and attributing everything to himself: "I arise," "I kill Deceit," "I feed the clouds," all lights are "portions of one spirit, which is mine," "I am the eye with which the Universe / Beholds itself," all harmony, prophecy, medicine "are mine." All forms of the first person singular of

[99] All quotations from the two songs are derived from Shelley's manuscript, which differs at a number of places from the text Mary published. For "Atlantic" Shelley first wrote "Hesperian" (MS e. 6, p. 25).

[100] It may be that the distinction between Apollo's pure stars in eternal bowers and Pan's dancing stars is meant to be the distinction between the fixed stars and the wandering planets.

the pronoun flood each of his stanzas. Like the Solitary who lifted life's veil, he is "himself alone," the same term with which Shelley elsewhere addressed the Absolute.[101] Pan, on the other hand, concerned centrally with the love-response of Syrinx and of his past audiences, and even preoccupied with how Apollo and Tmolus are at this moment responding to his song, is entirely oriented to a subject-object relationship that is signalled by his beginning his song not with Apollo's egotism but with a sense of community and shared experience: "From the forests and highlands / *We* come, *we* come." And he ends not with his private sorrow but with the fact that all of us share it with him: "Gods and men, we are all deluded thus." By embracing his audience he has also, unlike Apollo, implicated us, the readers. Correspondingly, the song of Apollo is cast in the present tense of universal statement, for the abstract perfections he represents are atemporal; Pan's lyric, except for his references to the immediate moment of the contest, is a narrative entirely in the past tense,[102] the dimension of that constantly vanishing time in which mutable human beings live and experience.

As a description of vital experience, Pan's song opens with rhythmic verve; yet, for all its sprightly energy, an ominous and contravening note intrudes into the center of it, just as Apollo's song makes counterstatements that undermine that god's sovereignty. For not only are Apollo and Pan irreconcilable opposites, neither the mind's ideals nor the actualities of human experience that they respectively preside over are self-sustaining. Like the Christian and Deist of *A Refutation of Deism* and the Narrator and Visionary of *Alastor*, each god repudiates the other and at the same time opens up the flaws in his own domain. Pan tells that when he sang, idyllic Tempe lay dark

In Pelion's shadow, outgrowing
    The light of the dying day,
        Speeded with my sweet pipings.

For Pan's reign begins only as Apollo's reign of sunlight declines, and although his songs of the world's beauty and of mortal life enamor worldly creatures, they also contribute to dispelling and displacing Apollo's ideal light of mind. Lived experience hastens the inevitable fading of conceptual perfection and lengthens the shadows over existence. But, as Apollo has told, at night, when the light of Apollo's day no longer nourishes good minds and open actions and no longer shows the world its divinity, Deceit returns and flourishes. Lovely and captivating though the world of human experience is, it is a world of deceit and inconstancy. Correspond-

---

[101] See below, pp. 181n., 401–2.
[102] The received text, "Where loud waves are dumb" (line 4), should read, according to Shelley's manuscript, "were dumb" (MS e. 6, p. 27); "are" is cancelled and replaced by "were."

ingly, after Pan has sung joyously of the dancing stars, the daedal earth, and the heavens, and of conflict, love, death, and birth, he abruptly "changed" the tenor of his pipings to bitter sorrow and so incorporated into the structure of his narrative the very inconstancy of which he is singing, the very Deceit that is native to his reign. What he changed to in his inconstant piping is itself a tale of the world's deceit, the product of Shelley's ingenious mythopoeia, richly reinterpreting the myth of Pan's pursuit of Syrinx and of her change into a reed in a world where all mutability is an Ovidian metamorphosis from a higher to a baser form:

> And then I changed my pipings
> Singing how down the vales of Maenalus
>   I pursued a maiden and clasped a reed.
> Gods and men,[103] we are all deluded thus!—
>   It breaks in our bosom and then we bleed.
>   They wept as I think both ye now would,
> If envy or age had not frozen your blood,
>   At the sorrow of my sweet pipings.

Pan's experience is that of the Maniac in *Julian and Maddalo* and of Shelley's Prince Athanase, who seeks the Uranian Venus but, until death, can meet only the Pandemic: what the mind pursues in the world through love proves inconstant, untrue, inferior to the mind's perfect pattern that sought to be fulfilled by an outward correspondence, and the deluded pursuing heart is pierced by what it pursues. Both Julian and Maddalo also lament the ill wrought on the Maniac by his lady's "falsehood":

>   ... it were a grief indeed
> If he had changed one unsustaining reed
> For all that such a man might else adorn.

Pan's whole story is told in the evolution of his song's internal refrains:

> Listening my sweet pipings. . . .
> Pelion's shadow . . . Speeded with my sweet pipings. . . .
> And then I changed my pipings. . . .

And at another level it is told by the course of the final refrains:

> Listening my sweet pipings. . . .
> For envy of my sweet pipings. . . .
> At the sorrow of my sweet pipings. . . .

---

[103] Pan's distinction is not between two orders of beings, but between the two natures of man, one divine and ideal, the other earthly and experiential. Both are deluded in their search in the world for fulfillment.

As Shelley wrote elsewhere, mortal man's "sweetest songs," unlike those of the skylark or of Apollo, "are those that tell of saddest thought." The unsustaining reed into which Syrinx was metamorphosed not only pierced Pan's heart, according to Shelley's myth, but also, according to the original myth, is the instrument on which he pipes his songs. To Shelley it is because the reed pierces the heart that it is the instrument for songs of sweet sorrow: to use Shelley's language, poets who "transcribe" human reality instead of creating poetry that is "wholly ideal," like Apollo's, are those who "learn in suffering what they teach in song."[104] Apollo brings grief only because of his necessary departure; the equal mixture of sweetness and sorrow is the very substance of Pan's mortal song.

Shelley gave his gods equal opportunity, granting each exactly thirty-six lines in which to assert his superiority by singing of his own domain, powers, and attributes; but each elects to shape his allotted space into a different rhythmic form, the emotional character of which corresponds to the god's special ethos. Since a choice is to be made between the two songs, there is no distinction between each song's lyric power and its thematic content: what each god declares of his own powers and domain is identical with the esthetic character of his singing, and any judge's esthetic preference is also his determination of the realm to which he has bound himself and the way in which he defines himself. Both lyrics are therefore brilliant tours de force directed toward fusing form and content; singing, song, and singer; the god's art and the character of the domain over which he presides.

The lines of Pan's song vary in number of syllables, but the preponderant tendency toward anapests imparts a vivacity and forward thrust, especially in the opening two-stress lines:

From the forests and highlands
    We come, we come;
From the river-girt islands
    Where the loud waves were dumb.

The poem, in its "inconstancy," never returns to this two-stress unit, and the basic pattern thereafter is the rapid three-stress line that lengthens out to one four-stress line toward the end of the first stanza ("Were silent as ever old Tmolus was") and two toward the end of the second, the deceleration and growing deliberateness being furthered by the increasing number of syllables and the irregularity of the meter:

    And all that did then attend and follow
Were as silent for love, as you now, Apollo.

[104] *Julian and Maddalo*, 546.

Progressively this new tempo foreshadows the third stanza, for with Pan's announcement of the change of his piping from joy to the sadness of the story of Syrinx, all six lines (quoted above) preceding the final refrain have four stresses or hesitate between four and five, slowing the reader with iambs and spondees where he anticipates more anapests, and moving with wistful solemnity. Moreover, in each of the first two stanzas the internal refrain (the fifth line) terminates the first unit of thought: for example,

> Liquid Peneus was flowing,
>   And all dark Tempe lay
> In Pelion's shadow, outgrowing
>   The light of the dying day,
>   Speeded with my sweet pipings.

But, as Milton Wilson has observed in his sensitive analysis,[105] in the third stanza the thought breaks at the end of the fourth line, and the refrain initiates the next unit instead of closing the previous one:

> I sang of the dancing stars,
>   I sang of the daedal Earth,
> And of Heaven, and the giant wars
>   And Love and Death and Birth;
>   And then I changed my pipings
> Singing how down the vales of Maenalus
>   I pursued a maiden and clasped a reed.

The consequence is not only to throw the momentum and emphasis forward upon the story of Syrinx rather than back upon Pan's vivacious songs of the universe and life; the reorganization of the rhetorical pattern, together with the shift to successive four-foot lines in the rest of the stanza, is the structural enactment of the very "change" Pan here speaks of from joyous to sorrowful song, of the "change" which is Syrinx' metamorphosis into a reed, and, at the profoundest level, of the "change" which is the inevitable inconstancy and deceit of all earthly things in the realm over which Pan presides.

Yet, the rhythm of Pan's song, modulating from sprightly joy to the disillusioned languor in which all earthly pleasure and vitality must end, is the authentic rhythm of life. Apollo's song, on the other hand, so squarely of six stanzas of six ten-syllable lines, is consistently stately and majestic, invariable in form and quality. But it is more than that: the recurrent clashes between the metrical and rhetorical emphases, the re-

---

[105] *Shelley's Later Poetry* (New York, 1959), pp. 30–37.

peated and unexpected substitution of one kind of foot for another, the occasional spondees, all tend to frustrate forward movement and require that the reader advance deliberately enough to readjust his psychological momentum to new and unanticipated rhythms. Without being unrhythmical, it is a rhythm to which the living voice has difficulty adapting itself:

The sleepless Hours who watch me as I lie,
    Curtained with star-enwoven tapestries
From the broad moonlight of the open sky,
    Fanning the busy dreams from my dim eyes
Waken me when their mother, the grey Dawn,
Tells them that Dreams and that the moon is gone.

Then I arise; and climbing Heaven's blue dome
    I walk over the mountains and the waves,
Leaving my robe upon the Ocean foam.
    My footsteps pave the clouds with fire; the caves
Are filled with my bright presence, and the air
Leaves the green Earth to my embraces bare.

Apollo's song is that of the lyre; each line measured exactly to ten syllables, it is appropriate to lyric recitative. Pan's is that of the pipe, the lines of constantly changing length being suggestive of the dancing chorus, with which his pipe was traditionally associated. Yet both rhythms are defective, each in a different way. One can at least understand why, in Mary's play, Midas prefers Pan's "sprightly" song of sweet sorrow, which "in melody outweighs" Apollo's "drowsy tune"; Apollo, she has Midas say, "put me fast asleep," but Pan's "gay notes awoke me." Pan's varying rhythm is that of experience felt in the blood and felt along the heart; Apollo's, that of the purer mind's abstract aspirations, a constant but cold ideal harmony that is lifeless and dull to Midas' "blunted sense," as Apollo calls it. For Mary was careful to point out that whereas Tmolus, the hill god who finds in Apollo's song the "wisdom, beauty, and the power divine / Of highest poetry," is an immortal, Midas is only a man. Like all mortals, Midas is foolish, incapable of appreciating highest poetry, or what Shelley elsewhere calls "poetic idealisms"; and for his devotion to the earth god, Midas, like all mortals and like everything else in Pan's song, suffers a debasing metamorphosis that symbolizes the world's inconstancy—according to Mary's play, his "soul's oppressed with the sad change" when Apollo gives him ass's ears. But his choice is really an impossible one for mortals: the lovely and vital night of life in which the heart is inevitably crossed by deceit and saddened by the incompatibility of its desires with what the false, disappointing world has to offer, or, on the other hand, the grand but unvital day of the mind's ideal conceptions of immutable truth, in the light of which the world reveals its divinity but not its humanity. In a sense, the contest between Pan and Apollo reflects the dispute between Mary and Shelley on the subject of Shelley's poetic talents and duty. She urged him to write "in a style that commanded popular favour" and to devote himself to "the delineations of human passion"; but "the bent of his mind went the other way," and he believed "he was too metaphysical and abstract—too fond of the theoretical and the ideal," too Apollonian for that kind of poetry.[106] Of Shelley's *Witch of Atlas* Mary wrote: "This poem is peculiarly characteristic of his tastes—wildly fanciful, full of brilliant imagery, and discarding human interest and passion, to revel in the fantastic ideas that his imagination suggested."[107]

In his "hymn," Apollo himself has subtly explained Midas' preference for Pan: "to my song," he sings, "Victory and praise, *in its own right*, belong." In its own right—but not as an object of vital encounter. It is of the highest worth intrinsically, independent of its effect upon any auditors, of whom, indeed, Apollo as absolute subjectivity is oblivious. Or Apollo is what Maddalo describes as "a system refutation-tight / As far as words go"; in *Julian and Maddalo* the Maniac's "wild talk will show / How vain are such aspiring theories." But the only touchstone that Pan can conceive is his effect upon an experiencing audience, since his song has no worth in its own right. Not only is his song itself a proud recounting of the audiences he has sung to and the spells he has cast upon them, each of his stanzas ends with a comment on the response of his present auditors, first Tmolus, then Apollo, and then both. Even as he sings he is troubled that he is failing to move them, and he ends each of his last two stanzas by incorporating into his song a direct address to them, explaining why they are unmoved. At the end of his first stanza he draws in Tmolus: all creatures who have heard Pan's songs

Were silent as ever old Tmolus was
    Listening my sweet pipings.

Then he tells that his past audiences, in their responses,

Were as silent for love, as you now, Apollo,
    For envy of my sweet pipings.

And at last, when he used to sing of the deceitfulness of love, his auditors would weep,

---

[106] Mary's note to *The Cenci* (Julian, II, 156, 158).
[107] Julian, IV, 78.

> as I think both ye now would
> If envy or age had not frozen your blood
>   At the sorrow of my sweet pipings.

Tmolus was once enthralled into silence by engagement in life and the love of it. But although Tmolus is immortal, he is not, like Apollo, an eternal youth outside time; bridging the immortal and the human, he endlessly ages, and therefore he, too, is subject to and illustrative of the change, the disappointing metamorphosis, the deceit, which is everywhere the subject and form of Pan's lament. Now old, Tmolus has voted for Apollo because age has frozen his blood until he is silent through indifference to life or incapacity for it; and Pan's song is of blood, not of Apollonian mind, or soul.

Apollo, on the other hand, is silent with envy, the opposite of love. As the absolute subject he has laid claim to everything—all is "mine"—and would also assume the domain of Pan, if he could. His blood is frozen because he would assume everything into his own absoluteness and so has nothing to do with life, which is the relationship of love, however disappointing. At least, tragic Pan is aware of a possession unavailable to Apollo. Life mourns that its experiences of the world have not the eternity and truth of conceptual ideals; the ideal envies what it is incapable of, human life. Keats, too, had recognized that essence cannot engage in existence unimpaired, that the ideal cannot be superimposed on reality, that divinity is no longer divine when incarnated in the world. The Titans of *Hyperion*, divine from birth, lose their "strong identity," their "real self," when they descend into the world and take on human experience. But unlike Keats, Shelley cannot conceive of an Apollo born on earth who becomes a god through enormous knowledge of life. For him the human and divine, although co-present in man, refuse to compromise their conflict and become one.

Shelley, however, is not merely unfolding the continuous conflict between the mutually exclusive ideal and human. In this singing contest he is also raising the question of the role and possibilities of poetry, for Apollo is the god of poetry, and the reed which pierced Pan's heart is the instrument on which that god pipes his songs of sweet sorrow. It was for the same reason that he made both the Visionary and the Narrator of *Alastor* poets. There are, then, two fundamental kinds of poetry: the inhuman, unvital, and possibly futile ideal and the tragic, disappointing human. Each is flawed, and option for either would be blind negligence of the other. Here and in *Alastor* Shelley has made no choice, but one purpose of his waging the unresolved contest is to learn, clear-eyed, all the pitfalls as he searches for a poetic mode and matter that will allow him, in good conscience, to take a stand without compromising his skepticism.

2   Skepticism and the Poetry of Reality

Julian and Maddalo

In 1817 Byron published his *Manfred*, the despondency of which left Shelley "dreadfully melancholy,"[1] and in April 1818, the sombre fourth canto of his *Childe Harold's Pilgrimage* appeared, which was later to impress Shelley as an expression of "contempt & desperation."[2] Shelley's ride along the desolate Lido with Byron late in August of that year therefore supplied him with a context in which to test in poetry his own insecure meliorism against the resistance of his companion's misanthropic fatalism. Like a well-trained orator, Shelley accommodated himself to his adversary for that purpose by adopting in *Julian and Maddalo: A Conversation* something of Byron's own Horatian manner of urbane poetic talk. That style also defines the poem's limited sphere, for as Shelley wrote Leigh Hunt, the familiar manner is not suited to subjects "wholly ideal" or even to topics of common life when the passion "touches the boundaries of that which is ideal."[3] That is, the poem was not to be, like *Prometheus Unbound*, which he was composing at the same time, an imaginative vision of possible human perfection, an Apollonian picture of what ideally ought to be as the mind is capable

---

[1] To Byron, 9 July 1817 (*Letters*, I, 547). Shelley was not reluctant to report to Byron Hunt's feeling that the play "administers to a diseased view of things," but added, perhaps insincerely, "I should say that some of your earlier writings had that tendency, but that 'Manfred' was free from it" (24 September 1817 [*Letters*, I, 557]).
[2] To Peacock, 17/18 December 1818 (*Letters*, II, 58).
[3] 15 August 1819 (*Letters*, II, 108).

of envisioning and desiring it; nor, unlike the *Hymn to Intellectual Beauty*, was it to peer into the mysteries surrounding and interpenetrating the human world, or to speculate on the glories beyond the grave. It would represent, instead, the views of two human beings on the situation in which man finds himself in common life, and it would be all the more real and non-visionary for being based on a lived experience instead of an imaginary construct. "You will find the little piece, I think," he wrote Hunt, "in some degree consistent with your own ideas of the manner in which Poetry ought to be written. I have employed a certain familiar style of language to express the actual way in which people talk with each other whom education and a certain refinement of sentiment have placed above the use of vulgar idioms."[4] Shelley felt strongly this difference between *Julian and Maddalo* and *Prometheus Unbound* and insisted on it. "I would not print it with 'Prometheus,'" he advised his publisher. "It would not harmonize. It is an attempt in a different style, in which I am not yet sure of myself, a *sermo pedestris* way of treating human nature quite opposed to the idealism of that drama."[5] On the other hand, in wishing it printed with *Prince Athanase*, he intimated its thematic relation to the somewhat Byronic hero of that fragment: a noble, Manfred-like figure inspired by all virtuous principles but goaded by the maddening fiends of an inward discontent.

The opening of the poem, we know, reflects a real event. In life Julian was Shelley, Maddalo was Byron. The ride on the Lido actually took place, and the two poets, having dealt with the future care of Byron's daughter by Claire Clairmont, discussed, among other things, the fourth canto of *Childe Harold* and the histories of Byron's "wounded feelings."[6] These are the biographical but not the literary facts: even if we were tempted to feed biography into the poem, Shelley's explicit intention that it be published anonymously obliges us to read it on the limited terms it itself dictates if we intend to keep faith with the mode of existence to which it lays claim. The poem offers itself as Julian's monologue (not Shelley's), reporting, first, his conversation with Maddalo (not Byron) as his Horatian *adversarius* and then their visit with a madman; and although our relation to Maddalo is thus mediated by Julian, as the Narrator of *Alastor* intervenes between us and the Visionary, the doctrine of neither man is allowed to overshadow that of the other, and the title assigns the two conversationists equal importance.[7] Moreover, although the poem is spoken by Julian, the Preface pretends to be written by yet a third person, someone (not Shelley) who addresses us in the first person, is ac-

---

[4] *Ibid.*
[5] To Ollier, 14 May 1820 (*Letters*, II, 196).
[6] To Mary Shelley, 23 August 1818 (*Letters*, II, 36).
[7] Indeed, in Mary's transcript of the poem (MS e. 12, p. 177) and in her table of contents in the Harvard Notebook the poem is entitled *Maddalo and Julian*.

quainted with Julian and Maddalo, and ostensibly is responsible for making Julian's poetic report available to us. Despite our normal expectations, the function of the Preface and its anonymous intervening "author" is not so much to guide our understanding of the poem as it is to intrude a psychic distance between us and the speakers and thus obstruct our sympathetic identification with either. Our first view of them is through another's uncommitted, impartial, almost indifferent mind.

To him Count Maddalo is of "consummate genius," capable of being the redeemer of his country—that is, of corrupt Italy—but, because of the disparity between his own "extraordinary mind" and the "dwarfish intellects" surrounding him, he is unable to find any object worthy of his concern and so is convinced of the "nothingness of human life."[8] Or, as Byron himself was later to describe his Maddalo nature,

They accuse me . . . of . . .
A tendency to under-rate and scoff
    At human power and virtue, and all that. . . .
I say no more than hath been said in Dante's
Verse, and by Solomon and by Cervantes;

By Swift, by Machiavel, by Rochefoucault,
    By Fénelon, by Luther, and by Plato;
By Tillotson, and Wesley, and Rousseau,
    Who knew this life was not worth a potato. . . .

Must I restrain me, through the fear of strife,
From holding up the nothingness of life?[9]

To this extent Maddalo's attitude is not essentially different from the one Shelley entertained when he described the Visionary of *Alastor* or, in "Lift Not the Painted Veil," the one who, searching in the world for an object to love, found nothing "the which he could approve" and moved among men, a disturbing "splendour among shadows." However vigorously Shelley protested Byron's misanthropy, there is a kinship between Byronism and Shelley's disposition on those occasions when he himself sought more than the world can satisfy; and the reason his thought repeatedly returned to Byron with both admiration and annoyance was his uncom-

---

[8] Preface. The model, of course, is the Byron Shelley found in Venice who, associating with the most depraved in that city, "is heartily & deeply discontented with himself." "Contemplating in the distorted mirror of his own thoughts, the nature & the destiny of man, what can he behold but objects of contempt & despair?" (Shelley to Peacock, 17/18 December 1818 [*Letters*, II, 58]).

[9] *Don Juan*, VII. iii–vi. Perhaps Bryon's most explicit statement of the Maddalo view is his description of the protagonist of his *Cain* as motivated by "the inadequacy of his state to his conceptions" (Byron to Murray, 3 November 1821).

fortable awareness that Byron represented an opposing aspect within his own mind. If the Visionary and his vision are the two egos of the Hegelian Unhappy Consciousness, Julian and Maddalo are the Yeatsian self and the antithetical self which we assume to impose discipline upon ourselves. Maddalo, however, significantly differs from the visionaries of *Alastor* and the sonnet in cynically resigning himself to the emptiness of life, in not pursuing his own fulfillment beyond the grave, and in not seeking to achieve in afterlife a self-consciousness which is identical with the Absolute. Shelley is determined in this poem to confine his speculations within the boundaries and data of human existence. Maddalo, according to his own creed at least, is to be classed among those who, in terms of the categories of the Preface to *Alastor*, "loving nothing on this earth, and cherishing no hopes beyond, yet keep aloof from sympathies with their kind, rejoicing neither in human joy nor mourning with human grief.... They are morally dead. They are neither friends, nor lovers, nor fathers, nor citizens of the world, nor benefactors of their country." The poem will ironically reveal that his humanitarian actions in fact belie his creed and make its authenticity suspect; his contempt for life, of course, arises not from meanness of mind but, on the contrary, from his "extraordinary mind," which finds no worldly object worthy of it. Others appear mean to him because he is incomparably greater. In brief, it is his intention to be what the Visionary of *Alastor* would have been had he abandoned in despair his aspiration to intercourse with "all of wonderful, or wise, or beautiful, which the poet, the philosopher, or the lover could depicture" and had resigned himself to the nothingness and futility of human life. But the author of the Preface sees more inward discontent in Maddalo than the poem will divulge: his proud ambition, lacking worthy objects, "preys upon itself," and his impatient feelings "consume him."

Julian, on the other hand, is seen by the author of the Preface as a meliorist who, without denying the reality of evil, is confident of "the power of man over his mind" and hence of man's power to suppress evil and make the good better. His belief is that man can be what the Preface-writer asserts the more powerful but disillusioned Maddalo is capable of being, the "redeemer of his country." Indeed, because Julian recognizes no governing deity outside the human mind, he is a "complete infidel"; or, as the poem will express it, his faith that "we have power over ourselves to do / And suffer" and so have something nobler to do than live and die *is* his religion as it was the religion of "those kings of old philosophy / Who reigned before Religion made men blind" (185–91). Yet, despite his optimism—or, better, because of it—he is "rather serious," whereas Maddalo's despairing resignation to the nullity of life releases him to be, at least outwardly, "cheerful, frank, and witty." Maddalo scoffs at Julian's atheism, but his own religious position "is not exactly known"; the implication, without introducing the mysteries of religion into the poem, hints darkly at his Byronic acceptance of a Providence that for its own unknowable reasons has maliciously left man powerless and made life absurd. Shelley, of course, was in a satiric mood when he wrote, "Julian, in spite of his heterodox opinions, is conjectured by his friends to possess some good qualities. How far this is possible the pious reader will determine." But as this is addressed to us by the anonymous author of the Preface, not by Shelley or Julian, the irony asks us to consider, as the unresolved irony at the end of A Refutation of Deism does, whether indeed it *is* possible and what our decision does to the definition of our piety on one side or to our estimate of human nature on the other. By formulating the dilemma and declining opinion on this point, the Preface makes the first of a series of strategic moves to transfer the moral burden to the reader and to incite him to come to a decision. This will emerge as the total rhetorical strategy of the poem.

The whole thrust of the poem will eventually press for an interpretation of the Maniac, since both Julian and Maddalo expect this figure, to whom the last two-thirds of the poem is devoted, to be exemplary proof of their opposing conceptions of the human condition. Because the poem is made to seem to hang on the interpretation of the Maniac for its meaning, we especially want guidance on that score from the author of the Preface—and it is the one subject from which he totally withdraws: "Of the Maniac I can give no information.... His story, told at length, might be like many other stories of the same kind: the unconnected exclamations of his agony will perhaps be found a sufficient comment for the text of every heart." *We*, the readers, then, are in the end the text to be read and understood, and the wild ramblings of the Maniac do not decide the case between Julian and Maddalo but serve as a gloss in aid of our interpreting ourselves. We all suffer the human state, and—to use the language of the Preface to *The Cenci*—whatever we sympathize with or are averse to in the Maniac's cries will be our personal explanation of that state. In sum, the detachment and impartiality of the Preface induce us to enter the poem with an open and questioning mind, prepared to take on ourselves the task of arriving at an evaluative decision. We would fall victim to the biographical fallacy if we should assume that because, outside the poem, Julian represents Shelley, the poem must necessarily validate his beliefs. The mode of the poem is a transformation of the skeptical method of proceeding in A Refutation of Deism, and its purpose with respect to the reader is the effect that Julian attributes to Maddalo's companionship: not to dictate a truth or impose a conclusion but, through the unresolved dialectic of friendly controversy, to "make me know myself" (561).[10]

[10] The MS (e. 11, p. 104) is more universal: "make one know oneself."

ii

Loosely modeled on the Horatian *sermo*, the poem opens brilliantly with a series of emblems that both define the two characters and hint at two views of life by hesitating between optimistic delight and despondency in such a fashion that neither mood wholly sustains itself. Even the autumnal scene against which the first meeting takes place conspires with the two speakers by being ambiguously "cheerful" and "cold" (34).

Julian is exhilarated by the ride along the barren, uninhabited Lido under skies equally "bare, / Stripped to their depths" (23–24), because in "waste / And solitary places"

> we taste
> The pleasure of believing what we see
> Is boundless, as we wish our souls to be.[11]   (15–17)

This experience of the extramental as spatially unlimited corresponds at the lowest phenomenological level to Shelley's recurrent yearning that the finite, empirical self encounter the infinite self as its Other and unite with it, healing the Unhappy Consciousness. As the object of consciousness, the scene is experienced as infinite because uninterrupted by finite particulars; but since consciousness and its object are here different in kind, the consciousness returns upon itself to become reflexively aware of its own freedom, infinitude, and unlimited capability. This awareness corresponds to what Wordsworth attributed to anyone who, in a kind of revival of his childhood,

> feels that, be his mind however great
> In aspiration, the universe in which
> He lives is equal to his mind, that each

[11] Byron ended Canto IV of *Childe Harold* with a similar soul-expanding description which may well have been the "stanzas of great energy" he recited to Shelley on the Lido (Shelley to Mary, 23 August 1818 [*Letters*, II, 37]):

> There is a pleasure in the pathless woods,
> There is a rapture on the lonely shore,
> There is society, where none intrudes,
> By the deep Sea, and music in its roar:
> I love not Man the less, but Nature more,
> From these our interviews, in which I steal
> From all I may be, or have been before,
> To mingle with the Universe, and feel
> What I can ne'er express, yet cannot all conceal.   (*Childe Harold*, IV, clxxviii)

Then, after the ensuing famous address to Ocean, Byron pictured the sea as

> boundless, endless, and sublime,
> The image of eternity, the throne
> Of the Invisible. . . .   (*Ibid.*, clxxxiii)

Is worthy of the other; if the one
Be insatiate, the other is inexhaustible.[12]

The infinitude experienced on the Lido by Julian, however, is not merely spatial, for the result of the soul's union with its perfect prototype that Shelley aspires to in poems like *Alastor* and *Epipsychidion* is the soul's unrestricted potency, the very power that Julian claims for it and Maddalo denies. Infinite space therefore translates into spontaneous force: the unbounded scene transmits its own energetic "delight" and "merriment" (25, 27) that are subjectively echoed in Julian's and Maddalo's thoughts by "laughter" and "glee" (29, 30), Shelley's customary image of unrestricted freedom.[13] Julian is like the Visionary of *Alastor* before the evolution of his *self*-consciousness, when, according to the Preface of that poem, he was still content with the "magnificence and beauty of the external world" and had not yet yearned for an intelligence commensurate with his own. "So long as it is possible for his desires to point towards objects thus infinite and unmeasured, he is joyous and tranquil, and self-possessed"—the self-sufficiency, that is, of the ego conscious of the sensible object as infinite, not the absolute self-possession of fulfilling self-consciousness.

But Julian is not merely an asocial visionary who gratifies himself by measuring his mind and its powers with the experience of unlimited external space and force. That way can lead only to the hope of perfect completion in afterlife. His fundamental concern is to be a humanitarian, to make the moral world better, and thus to know other minds as corresponding to the perfect desires of his own; as the Preface to *Alastor* tells us, when desires are no longer satisfied by directing themselves toward the "infinite and unmeasured" external world, the mind "thirsts for intercourse with an intelligence similar to itself." Consciousness completes itself, not in its sensible object, but in another consciousness—that is, in self-consciousness. Consequently, even greater than Julian's delight in boundless space is his love of companionship "with a remembered friend." If the mind's delight in barren, "uninhabited" space is the experiential evidence of its own boundlessness, the central question the poem poses is whether the unlimited mind can complete itself as subject by meeting, as object, its real human equivalent and see itself reflected in its Other— hence the significance of the term "friend" given to Maddalo—or whether the mind's ideal concepts and the facts of human actuality are unalterably incompatible.

We have already noted that the disillusioned and misanthropic Byron who is the model for Maddalo corresponds in many ways to a recurrent figure in Shelley's poetry because Shelley recognized in him the enviably

---

[12] *The Prelude*, ed. de Selincourt, 2d ed., p. 576.
[13] Cf., for example, *Prometheus Unbound*, IV. 332–34.

heroic but negating side of himself that he yearned to convert to his own ends. In many ways, both in form and theme, *Prometheus Unbound* is a reply to *Manfred*; Byron appears as a tragically admirable figure in *Lines Written among the Euganean Hills* and in *Adonais*; the optimistic epigraph of the *Ode to Liberty* derives from *Childe Harold*; and it was probably in recollection of the fact that the epigraph of *Manfred* is Hamlet's explanation of his father's ghost—

There are more things in heaven and earth, Horatio,
Than are dreamt of in your philosophy—

that Shelley, rejecting all theologies, jotted in one of his notebooks his corrective version:

There is more on earth than we
Dream of in our philosophy.[14]

Julian and Maddalo are Shelley's divided and conflicting selves skeptically confronting each other, as they do in *Alastor*; and the poem, in effect, is Shelley's debate with himself. Count Maddalo is noticeably the more masterful of the two, superior in rank and firm in his convictions. But it would be inadequate merely to exorcise him and dispel the pessimism he introduces, for Julian is confident of the greatness of Maddalo's "eagle spirit," not of his own; it is Maddalo who is capable of being "the redeemer of his degraded country" despite his conviction that man is impotent. Ideally, he must, instead, be reckoned with and reconciled with his "friend" Julian, who argues a doctrine of goodness and has confidence in man's power. Ideally, the doctrine to be refuted is the one with which the Furies taunt Prometheus:

The good want power, but to weep barren tears.
The powerful goodness want: worse need for them.[15]

But instead of striving toward that reconciliation, the poem of "sad reality" will reach out to the opposite goal: the reader's attainment of self-knowledge through the poem's skeptical manner of proceeding, which reveals that the human self is divided and contradictory, infinite but finite, free but limited.

There can be no doubt about the views of Julian, self-dependent atheist and humanitarian optimist, when he and Maddalo, like Milton's

[14] MS e. 6, p. 5. The next line of this fragment, "I sung of One who seemed to be," may echo *Childe Harold's Pilgrimage*, III. iii. 1: "In my youth's summer I did sing of One."
[15] *Prometheus Unbound*, I. 625–26.

fallen angels (an identification both disputants could agree upon for opposite reasons) and presumably equally lost in "wand'ring mazes," debated "Concerning God, freewill, and destiny,"

Of all that earth has been or yet may be,
All that vain men imagine or believe,
Or hope can paint or suffering may achieve.[16]   (42–45)

Unlike world-wounded Maddalo or the Maniac, Julian, delighting in the infinity of space and therefore the infinity of his perceptual mind, is still in the State of Innocence, only vaguely aware of the State of Experience. Consequently, his optimistic emblem of life is the gorgeous sunset-flooded world at the moment when "the glow / Of Heaven descends" upon the land (55–56), the various modes of that emblem being the Alps, "an heaven-sustaining bulwark" (69), the Euganean Hills against the setting sun, "towering as from waves of flame" as though the earth itself were the "vaporous sun" (82–83), the water "Paved with the image of the sky" (67), and the temples and palaces of Venice "Like fabrics of enchantment piled to Heaven" (92). Earth towers to Heaven, and Heaven's glow suffuses the land.

    Yet, Julian has, in fact, expressed much less than an optimistic conviction of a heaven on earth. The presence of Maddalo has a disturbing gravitational pull on him. That the world we see is infinite is only his momentary belief, not necessarily a truth, and that our souls are equally unlimited is but a "wish." Besides, however glorious Venice and the hills appear, he recognizes that Italy is the "Paradise of exiles," of alien spirits like Byron and Shelley; and since Paradise is the earthly perfection from which man was originally exiled, the paradox in the phrase nicely equivocates between hope of a utopian world and the irreparable disparity between man's perfect conceptions and the recalcitrance of his human condition. The English exile in paradisiacal Italy was for Shelley the type of all mankind. Moreover, there is considerable irony in the fact that the scene has been felt as infinite only because it is a solitary, uninhabited waste. What seems infinite is really an emptiness, the vacancy that leads Shelley in such poems as *Mont Blanc* and *The Sensitive Plant* to consider such a world ontologically absurd. An unsettling note therefore creeps in, threatening that Julian's feeling of the soul's boundless power

---

[16] Cf. *Paradise Lost*, II. 559–64:

Of Providence, Foreknowledge, Will, and Fate,
Fixt Fate, free will, foreknowledge absolute, . . .
Of good and evil much they argu'd then,
Of happiness and final misery,
Passion and Apathy, and glory and shame. . . .

will be spoiled when its object is not empty space but human society: "we came / Homeward, which always makes the spirit tame" (32–33), tempering one's mind to the finitude and weakness of other minds. It was only with "solitude" that the waves' sounds of "delight" had harmonized. The friends' original cheerfulness, corresponding to limitless nature's glee, is therefore modulated into an intermittent raillery that "mocks itself" because it cannot banish the growing despondency, just as Maddalo's ambition is self-reflexive, preying on itself because it has no other object. The suspicion now is that the "world" is narrowly limited and that man, however infinite his desires, is impotent.

The ensuing talk of "God, freewill, and destiny" (42) consequently takes place in the context of irrepressible under-consciousness of an imperfect and alien world, an atmosphere that should warn us that the poem can attain no optimistic conclusion. Hence the relevance of the allusion to the fallen angels in Hell—"this Hell" (260), as Maddalo calls our madhouse world in contradistinction to Julian's Paradise of exiles. The discussion proves "forlorn, / Yet pleasing," like that of Milton's fallen angels, which "with a pleasing sorcery could charm / Pain for a while or anguish."[17] The discourse of Milton's fallen angels had the power either to "excite / Fallacious hope" or to "arm th'obdurate breast / With stubborn patience":[18] of these consequences the first is echoed by the friends' discussion of "All that vain men imagine or believe" (44), which supports Maddalo's cynicism and casts doubt on Julian's optimism, and the second is echoed by their descant on all that "hope can paint or suffering may achieve" (45), which sustains Julian's faith. Insofar as the Miltonic allusion is operative, Julian, arguing "against despondency" and urging that it is "wise to make the best of ill" (47–48), is the spiritual analogue of materialistic Mammon, who advised the fallen angels to "seek / Our own good from ourselves, and from our own / Live to ourselves. . . . / Free, and to none accountable, preferring / Hard liberty before the easy yoke / Of servile Pomp."[19] Hell, like Italy, can be the "Paradise of exiles." Maddalo, on the other hand, is blinded by the Satanic pride of his own greatness and yet holds to Belial's policy:

Shall we then live thus vile, the race of Heaven
Thus trampl'd, thus expell'd to suffer here
Chains and these Torments? better these than worse
By my advice; since fate inevitable
Subdues us. . . .[20]

[17] Paradise Lost, II. 566–67.
[18] Ibid., 568–69.
[19] Ibid., 252–57.
[20] Ibid., 194–98.

iii

The major unifying control over the poem is its atmospheric symbolism, progressing by stages from the cold but cheerful day to the dark
raging storm against which the Maniac is set, and carrying us unrelent-
ingly into the wild turmoil at the heart of man's discontent. The quality
of each successive natural setting is a different interpretation of the world.
It is the paradoxical management of imagery of light and darkness that
subtly governs the moods and themes of the poem's opening passages. To
Julian the blazing sunset is a sign of a possible heaven on earth; but
against the sinking sun Maddalo, a spirit of darkness, takes the "darker"
view of the human state because of his somewhat admirable and justifiable
Satan-like pride:

The sense that he was greater than his kind
Had struck, methinks, his eagle spirit blind
By gazing on its own exceeding light.   (50–52)

Putting aside the consequent misanthropy, the same could be said also of
the Visionary of *Alastor*, who also pursued a light projected from his own
mind and could find nothing in the world worthy of himself, or of the
subject of "Lift Not the Painted Veil," whose exceeding splendor was a
"blot" upon the world. Not a defect, but an excess of a virtue has led to
a fault: the eagle, traditionally exceptional for withstanding the blaze of
the sun, is blinded by his inner and greater light. The wide disparity
between the light within himself and what, self-blinded, he sees as the
dark condition of man in the world has led Maddalo to despair that man
can ever be "in deed" what he is "in desire" (176).

We can better understand what Maddalo represents and why Byron
and his poetry reappear so frequently and obsessively in Shelley's thought
if we recognize that, together with the visionaries of *Alastor* and the
sonnet, Byronic Maddalo is one of Shelley's archetypes. In the *Letter to
Maria Gisborne* Coleridge, for example, is also

he who sits obscure
In the exceeding lustre and the pure
Intense irradiation of a mind,
Which with its own internal lightning blind,
Flags wearily through darkness[21] and despair—
A cloud-encircled meteor of the air,
A hooded[22] eagle among blinking owls.[23]   (202–8)

[21] The autograph MS (e. 9, pp. 97–115), from which the text presumably was
published, reads "terror."
[22] Shelley first wrote, "blinded."
[23] A rejected stanza for *Adonais* reads, "And then came a Shape half concealed /
In darkness of his own exceeding light" (MS e. 9, p. 29).

And in *The Triumph of Life* Rousseau assumes this Byronic role, saying,

> I was overcome
> By my own heart alone, which neither age
>
> Nor tears nor infamy nor now the tomb
> Could temper to its object.   (240–43)

Such Byronic supermen, finding no worthy object, destroy themselves with their own greatness and are to be distinguished from the luminaries destroyed by the world, conquered, that is, by life "in the battle / Life and they did wage"(239–40)—the fate against which Maddalo warns Julian, the sanguine activist. The so-called[24] wise and great—kings, priests, and philosophers —have not learned from all their lore "to know themselves":

> their might
> Could not repress the mutiny within,
>   And for the morn of truth they feigned, deep night
>
> Caught them ere evening. . . .   (212–15)

We shall be better able to grasp the full meaning of such self-knowledge when we turn to *The Cenci*, but for the moment it is sufficient to understand that these men of power actively entered into the struggle with life, sought to transform it, and were defeated by it because they failed to understand the true nature of the human soul and the true relation of evil to it. On the other hand, the self-blinded luminaries—the visionaries, Byrons, Rousseaus, and Coleridges—could not temper their hearts to their hearts' objects,[25] that is, their boundless expectations and desires to man as he is. They therefore impatiently and misanthropically withdrew from life, admirable for their blazing ideals, lamentable for their self-destructive withdrawal and self-reflexive lives. They are, according to the Preface to *Alastor*, the "luminaries of the world" who are struck with "sudden darkness and extinction" by "too exquisite a perception of the influence" of the ideal "Power." Shelley could not accept the poet who wrote, "I have not loved the world, nor the world me"; but he also could not get Byron out of his mind because of the grand ideals for which Byron scorned mankind, ideals and powers that might have made him, like Maddalo, the redeemer of his degraded country. There is, besides, as we have noted, a good deal of Byron in Shelley's temperament, and much of his fascinated opposition to Byron is an act of self-correction.

[24] A cancellation in the MS reads, "Such were they called" (Reiman, p. 165).
[25] In "temper to its object" (243) I take the antecedent of "its" to be "my heart" (241).

The same ambiguity applies to Shelley's attitude toward Byronic poetry. The "great bards of old,"[26] Rousseau reports in *The Triumph of Life*,

> who inly quelled
>
> The passions which they sung, as by their strain
>   May well be known: their living melody
> Tempers its own contagion to the vein
>
>   Of those who are infected with it.   (274–78)

By quelling the passions of which they sang and tempering their songs to the condition of their audience, they were curative, like those who can patiently temper their hearts' desires and ideals to the world as it is. But I, says Rousseau,

> Have suffered what I wrote, or viler pain!—
>   And so my words were seeds of misery—
> Even as the deeds of others.   (279–81)

The speaker in *The Triumph* will correct him, since Rousseau has not been, like tyrants, a mere destroyer; and Rousseau will confess that he has been "one of those who have created, even / If it be but a world of agony" (294–95). Nevertheless, the charge remains, as Shelley wrote elsewhere, that Rousseau "gave licence by his writings, to passions that only incapacitate and contract the human heart."[27] Maddalo is what Rousseau laments having been, for he also holds that

>   Most wretched men
> Are cradled into poetry by wrong,
> They learn in suffering what they teach in song.[28]   (544–46)

Admirable though the idealistic premises are on which it is based, that poetry is vicious which records only misanthropy and despair and wails that the world is wrong. It fulfills neither of the two major functions of poetry that Shelley recognized: to teach us "to know ourselves" and to induce us to love and aspire to "poetic idealisms." Like Keats's savage and

[26] The MS shows Shelley had in mind "Homer & his brethren" (Reiman, p. 173).
[27] *Proposals for an Association* (Julian, V, 265).
[28] With Rousseau's speech, "I / Have suffered what I wrote, or viler pain," etc., compare one of the draft versions of Maddalo's words: "It is because they act the parts themselves / And learn through suffering what they speak in song" (MS e. 11, p. 159).

fanatic who only dream of heaven and eschew the world, the idealistic misanthrope only vexes the world. We may now better understand why the solitary visionary of "Lift Not the Painted Veil," who could approve of nothing in the world, was, paradoxically, a "bright blot" upon our gloomy scene.

iv

It is effectively startling that the description of Maddalo blinded by his own excessive light is abruptly followed by a picture of the setting sun:

Meanwhile the sun paused ere it should alight,
Over the horizon of the mountains;—Oh,
How beautiful is sunset, when the glow
Of Heaven descends upon a land like thee,
Thou Paradise of exiles, Italy!   (53–57)

Ironically juxtaposed are an ideal light turned blindingly inward upon itself and an ideal light that sheds itself on the world and transfigures it. For Shelley has set the two views of life in sharp opposition: the dark vision because Maddalo's mind has dazzled his eye with its own brilliant ideals; and Julian's vision, which, seeking to know the world for what it is, sees it, with all its threatening ills and limitations, as capable of being filled with a light from heaven.

But even the sunset is as equivocal in significance as most other things in the poem and is of the order of Shelley's recurrent skeptically ambiguous image. If, on the one hand, it intimates a heaven on earth in opposition to Maddalo's self-blinding light, on the other it signals the inevitable vanishing of light and the coming of the "night of death" (127) that makes life meaningless no matter how nearly perfect it may be made. Correspondingly, Maddalo and his dark disillusionment now take control of the poem. Instead of Julian's splendid view of the fiery hills against the sun, Maddalo proposes a "better station," a better perspective in which to understand the world; and in an appropriately "funereal" gondola (88)[29] they make their way, for that purpose, toward a ghastly madhouse, also silhouetted against the setting sun, its vesper bell swinging in that radiance. As they stop, the prayer bell tolls "In strong and black relief" against the sun setting behind the belfry (106). Such, says Maddalo, is our mortal state in this madhouse world:

[29] Shelley to Peacock, 8 October 1818 (*Letters*, II, 42): "I can only compare them [the gondolas] to moths of which a coffin might have been the chrysalis. They are hung with black, & painted black, & carpeted with grey...." Byron also likens a gondola to a coffin in stanza 19 of *Beppo* (1818).

And this must be the emblem and the sign
Of what should be[30] eternal and divine!—
And like that black and dreary bell, the soul,
Hung in a heaven-illumined tower, must toll
Our thoughts and our desires to meet below
Round the rent heart and pray—as madmen do
For what? they know not,—till the night of death
As sunset that strange vision, severeth
Our memory from itself, and us from all
We sought and yet were baffled. (121–30)

Like madmen, our thoughts and desires are summoned by the idealizing soul, whose eternity and divinity are doubtful, to pray about the altar of the broken heart for what is unknowable and as hopeless as the lot of the maniacs. Maddalo's emblem of the divided human self is like Shelley's moon ("Art thou pale for weariness") which wanders companionless in the heavens among the immutable stars and devotes itself to gazing upon the earth, where it can find "no object worth its constancy." Correspondingly, the soul in its "heaven-illumined tower" is aloof from life, but the heart below is doomed to be broken by the world; and it is hopeless insanity for the world-engaged thoughts and desires to expect to gain in life what the aloof and idealistic soul calls them to, an insanity made all the more absurd by the necessity of death, which cuts us off even from our inevitably vain efforts to gain what the soul urges us to seek. As though Maddalo were right, the sun sets, and Julian's glowing and enchanting emblem vanishes. The black bell of the soul disappears, the belfry turns gray; and instead of the sense of the infinity of space and the boundless power of the soul with which the evening began, the temples and palaces of the world seem "Huddled in gloom" (137), cramped in impotence and fear.

The following day is a setting of even deeper gloom, as though man can do nothing to prevent the natural momentum toward turbulence and despair. The previous day had been sunny and cheerful, but cold; this one is "rainy, cold and dim" (141). Nevertheless, Julian strains to counteract it and returns with renewed optimism, his emblematic evidence now being a human and domestic one sheltered from nature's dreary weather: Maddalo's daughter, a "lovely child, blithe, innocent and free" (167). She is therefore evidence that nature creates man free, not enslaved; guiltless, not doomed by original sin; happy, not despairing. Her eyes, moreover, gleaming like "mirrors of Italian Heaven" (148), reflect that transcendent light which had been essential to Julian's image of a world, however

[30] That is, what we should like to think is eternal and divine. The MS (e. 11, p. 80) shows "we deem" and "would deem" for "should be."

"bleak" (153), capable of perfection, of being a Paradise of exiles.[31] For, having originally drawn his confidence from his own experience of uninhabited nature's infinitude, Julian has now transferred his faith, without nature's mediation, to the universal capacity of mind: in place of the earlier heaven-reflecting sea he has substituted the child's heaven-reflecting eyes, which "gleam / With such deep meaning as we never see / But in the human countenance" (148–50). He can now hold, therefore, that it must be

> our will
> That thus enchains us to permitted ill—
> We might be otherwise—we might be all
> We dream of happy, high, majestical.
> Where is the love, beauty, and truth we seek
> But in our mind? and if we were not weak
> Should we be less in deed than in desire?   (170–76)

We all become chained madmen when we *allow* ourselves to be enchained. Julian's faith is that we are free agents, able to break "the chains... which our spirit bind" (181) and not necessarily bound with "madmen's chains" (260), doomed, like the Maniac, "To drag life on, which like a heavy chain / Lengthens behind with many a link of pain" (302–3). The chains binding madmen are the same as those that bind Prometheus to the rock and that he breaks by reassuming his autonomy.

This is the only real point of difference between Julian and Maddalo. Both believe that all love, beauty, and truth[32] reside in the human mind, and, according to Julian's atheistic creed, there only—that is, not in any transcendent deity. Both agree there is a wide gulf between the soul's ideals and human actuality, or, in the historico-political terms Shelley used in the Preface to his *Revolt of Islam*, "a defect of correspondence between the knowledge existing in society and the improvement or gradual abolition of political institutions." From Maddalo's point of view, despite the evidence of his child, men simply are doomed by their mortal state to be

---

[31] In the MS (p. 82), on comparing the child's eyes to the moon, Shelley added of the moon, "loveliest of insensate things." This Wordsworthian phrase, together with Shelley's reference to the child as the toy made by "sweet Nature" and to himself as having nursed her, suggests that the model is the child in Wordsworth's "Three Years She Grew," who, nursed by Nature as "law and impulse," gains "the silence and the calm / Of mute insensate things," and experiences only "vital feelings of delight." Cf. also "A lovelier toy sweet Nature never made" (144) with Wordsworth's "Then Nature said, 'A lovelier flower / On earth was never sown.'" Shelley's picture of Maddalo's daughter, that is, is informed by the Wordsworthian doctrine that the world of nature is beneficent, working only to fulfill the human spirit's free potentiality for perfection.

[32] MS variants read, "The image of perfection" (p. 83) and "The patterns by which" (p. 84).

too weak ever to be in fact commensurate with the patterns of perfection in their minds. They are "teachless" (164), incorrigible, and constitutionally "passive" (161), acted upon but incapable of corrective action; and madness is the inevitable result of expecting them to correspond to the mind's desires. Julian's reply is that madness results, not from the impossibility of making the world match the soul's wishes, but from pride, the very flaw he and the author of the Preface find in Maddalo—pride defined as the *impatient* insistence that the world answer one's perhaps too-brilliant demands, that love be *immediately* reciprocated without one's persistent, suffering effort to "seek a 'soul of goodness' in things ill / Or in himself or others" (204–5). Once scorned, such impatient men, says Julian, "die / Some living death" (210), the very phrase with which the Maniac will describe his life of agony (415), as though confirming Julian instead of Maddalo, who had chosen him as proof of his thesis. The essential question, then, is whether it is the decree of destiny that the heart be broken or whether, there being no other deity, one can attain in the world one's ideal desires by a patient act of will; whether madness arises from the vain expectation that man's stubborn, "teachless nature," as Maddalo believes it to be, will answer the perfection of the mind or from the disappointed love that will follow if one does not patiently exert his will to *make* the world answer the mind. Indeed, the question is whether Julian or Maddalo is on the path to madness.

We are, in other words, once again encountering Shelley's divided and unreconciled aspirations. On the one side is the poet who wrote *Queen Mab, The Revolt of Islam,* and *Prometheus Unbound,* on the other the author of *Alastor* and *Prince Athanase.* The manuscript of *Julian and Maddalo* shows that when the two friends discussed the poetic quality of the Maniac's lamentations Julian asserted that "such passion gave such language high / As writers who transcribe call poetry" and Maddalo replies that "Poets . . . are men whose muse is wrong; / They learn by suffering what they teach in song."[33] Julian, that is, has denied that all poetry is of this sort: only poetry that merely "transcribes," or reports indifferently, the realities of human experience as it now is deals with suffering and despair. Part of the occasion for the composition of *Julian and Maddalo,* we recall, was Byron's account of the "history of his wounded feelings," like those of the Maniac. If Maddalo were right in his definition of poetry, Shelley could compose only works like *Alastor,* which, although not misanthropic and disillusioned in the Byronic and Rousseauistic manner, eschews in the figure of the Visionary the human world for a postmortal realization of the mind's desires. But what Shelley is searching for is justification for a *Prometheus Unbound,* which does not transcribe the gloom of human suffering but encourages the worldly real-

[33] MS e. 11, p. 109. The sense is that the name of the muse is "Wrong."

ization of "all / We dream of happy, high, majestical." Indeed, Shelley was composing the second act of *Prometheus Unbound* at the very time he paused to write *Julian and Maddalo*, and the force interrupting that apparently confident "ideal" work was Shelley's persistent skeptical incertitude that demanded he once again examine in a kind of impartial interior dialogue about actuality his grounds for visionary optimism. The result is a poetic psychomachy that, without gaining any clear victory, uncovers for honest conscious confrontation the subliminal conflict in the poet's mind and reassures that, since at least the psychic battle has been frankly waged, the optimism of *Prometheus Unbound* is in good faith.

What Shelley succeeded in creating in *Julian and Maddalo* was a way of presenting "sad reality"—or, in another of his phrases, "dreadful" reality[34]—which, while still "quite opposite to the idealism" of *Prometheus Unbound*, is nevertheless not a melancholy, misanthropic, Byronic transcription of it. Poetic transcription of human reality merely spreads its own despair, inspired by the muse called "Wrong." But reality may also be represented by an unresolved opposition of the optimistic and pessimistic interpretations of it in the dramatic form of *Julian and Maddalo*. Each of the opposing views is skeptically undermined in the very act of being advanced, for profound insight into man as he is—true self-knowledge—tempers disillusionment with the possibility of hope and informs optimism of the force of the gale against which it must make its way, instead of teaching superficial despair. Having no first principles, the skeptic can understand essential human nature and the foundation on which to build only by watching first the abrasive interaction of opposing doctrines. Shelley interrupted the composition of *Prometheus Unbound* to grapple with reality and earn for himself—at the price of much self-searching and many concessions—a hard-won and insecurely held footing in the actual human condition on which to sustain the idealisms of which he had been writing in his lyric drama.

v

Although Julian and Maddalo each expects that the Maniac whom they are to visit will be the proof of his theory, it is undeniable that he supplies no resolution to their disagreement—and that, indeed, is the point.[35] He is enigmatic, but he embodies no secret that would unriddle

---

[34] To Ollier, 15 December 1819 (*Letters*, II, 164).

[35] The absence of any apparent solution in the poem to the question it raises has usually led to the conclusion, characteristic of the most extreme form of the intentional fallacy, that Shelley altered his course in mid-poem when he introduced the figure of the Maniac. N. I. White (*Shelley* [New York, 1940], II, 42) reported sympathetically that "This desertion of the assumed initial purpose of the poem has been accepted as a more or less characteristic structural weakness. . . . The Madman's story is a story of love and tears, a subject with which the conversation of Julian

the poem, for, like the early dialogue on deism, the poem is the honest presentation of a skeptical incertitude, not a solution. Only the reader, whose heart is the text the Maniac's ravings annotate, can come to a decision of his own, and even that will be a decision under the pressure of all the conflicting evidence. The sullen rain that succeeded the initial setting of cold cheerfulness has developed into a tumultuous, hissing storm (212, 295–97) enacting outwardly the wild raging of the Maniac's mind; and from that storm the poem will not return, for we are being led into the center of the human state so that we may be made to know ourselves, not supplied with a facile answer.

Because the Maniac, like Julian, has always "talked Utopia," Maddalo expects "his wild talk" to show Julian "How vain are such aspiring theories" once the heart encounters reality, admirable though utopian theories are as abstract, "refutation-tight" systems. Julian, on the other hand, expects the Maniac to give evidence that he lacks an adequate moral theory and that the mad are those, "by nature proud,"

Who patient in all else demand but this—
To love and be beloved with gentleness;
And being scorned, what wonder if they die
Some living death? (207–10)

That is, he expects the Maniac to be like Maddalo.[36] And each is right—or wrong. By means of ambiguity Shelley has drawn the Maniac as both a utopian theorist like Julian and an impatient idealist like Maddalo; and

---

and Maddalo is totally unconnected." Carlos Baker (*Shelley's Major Poetry*, p. 126) reversed the emphasis but with the same results: "There is a strong likelihood that Shelley invented most of the remainder of part one of *Julian and Maddalo* in order to ease his way into the lament of the maniac."

G. M. Matthews ("'Julian and Maddalo': The Draft and the Meaning," *Studia Neophilologica*, 35 [1963], 57–84) has effectively answered these objections, recognizing that the poem requires no further conclusion and showing, on the basis of the manuscript, that the beginning and end of the poem were conceived of as a unit. I do not, however, agree with his claim that the reason why "the main question at issue, whether man is master of his own fate, is left without a categorical answer" is that "the problem is one which can only be solved in practice." True, Maddalo insists on the disparity between irrefutable theory and the destined facts of life, and Julian demands the test of action; but the dispute is the irresolvable one between two concepts of man, not the resolvable one between theory and practice. It would be an entirely futile poem if it were one that could be rendered irrelevant by an act. At the end of the poem we are still left with the question of whether, given man's nature, the practice is possible.

[36] Shelley drew the name "Maddalo" from a minor figure in the actual history of Tasso's insanity, about which he intended to compose a drama in which one of the characters was to be the historical Maddalo (MS e. 11, pp. 162–69; see also Matthews, "'Julian and Maddalo'"). But he would have had to be remarkably inattentive to language had he been insensitive to the relation of the name to madness, especially since there is no other apparent reason for his choice. His original intention, as his

it is suggestive of Shelley's success that some biographical critics have
seen the Maniac as Shelley, others as Byron.[37] Aspects of Byron's and
Shelley's experiences unquestionably are drawn on, and no doubt Shelley's
study of Tasso's life and madness left its mark; but it is only in this composite sense that the Maniac, like Julian and Maddalo, "is also in some
degree a painting from nature, but, with respect to time & place, ideal,"
as Shelley informed Hunt.[38]

Although the most explicit and extended explanation offered in the
poem for the Maniac's disorders is the inconstancy of his lady's love, that
inconstancy is synecdochic, as elsewhere in Shelley's poetry, of the falsehood in human nature;[39] and we would be misled if we were to try to
piece together a specific biography on the basis of his rantings. Some, we
are told, speculate that his madness resulted from loss of wealth, others
from tyranny of some unidentified sort, so that he seemed hurt "To hear
but of the oppression of the strong" (239). The fickleness of his lady is
an explicit fact but not necessarily the exclusive cause. Even Julian and
Maddalo confess they do not know the specific source of his madness.
By means of this incertitude Shelley was able to draw the Maniac as a
composite type representative of what any of the world's inconstancies
does to the aspiring mind; and the lack of rational connection among his
ravings is an admissible psychological disorder that provided Shelley with
a convenient device for jumbling together in one figure the various modes

---

manuscript shows (e. 11, p. 78), to have Maddalo address Julian as "Yorick," the
imposed upon, foolishly sentimental jester of Sterne's novels, indicates that he meant
names to be suggestive. That "Julian," as some have proposed, is meant to suggest
Julian the Apostate seems likely.

Shelley, moreover, was inclined to think of Byron's pessimism and misanthropy
as a kind of madness. Lord Byron is "as mad as the winds," he wrote Peacock (17
July 1816 [Letters, I, 491]); and the spirit in which the fourth Canto of Childe
Harold is composed is, "if insane, the most wicked & mischievous insanity that ever
was given forth" (17/18 December 1818 [Letters, II, 58]).

[37] Byron: G. Wilson Knight, Lord Byron: Christian Virtues (London, 1952); J. E.
Saveson, "Shelley's Julian and Maddalo," Keats-Shelley Journal, 10 (1961), 53–58.
Shelley: H. S. Salt, "A Study of Shelley's Julian and Maddalo," The Shelley Society
Papers (1881), II, p. 326; Edward Dowden, The Life of Shelley (London, 1886);
John H. Smith, "Shelley and Claire Clairmont," PMLA, 54 (1939), 785–814;
White, Shelley (1940); Ivan Roe, Shelley: the Last Phase (New York, 1955).

[38] 15 August 1819 (Letters, II, 108).

[39] It is evident that the "falsehood," or the opposite of "truth," against which the
Maniac inveighs is inconstancy in general, or the mutability that is in the nature
of the world and that prevents it from corresponding to the mind's ideals. For example, in "The Zucca" Shelley wrote that the passage of summer into winter, leaving the earth bare, is evidence of "the falsehood of the flattering Hour," who had
brought the merely transitory beauty of summer. In that poem, too, the tension is
between the poet's desire for "More in this world than any understand" and the
world's "falsehood," the "instability of all but weeping." Falsehood is also equated
with inconstancy in "Oh! there are spirits of the air." In Julian and Maddalo the
inconstancy of the Maniac's lady is the type of all the world's "falsehoods," especially
since it is love that should make the world conform to the mind's desires.

in which life's falsehoods manifest themselves. The Maniac's vows, for example, that he will never sanction tyranny or be moved by ambition or avarice, while supporting two of the speculations on the cause of his misfortune, can hardly have any bearing on his lady's infidelity; they only express his refusal to respond in kind to any of reality's assorted "falsehoods." One would be equally misguided to attempt a biographical identification of the various ladies in the Maniac's rantings. His "spirit's mate" whom he invokes (337) is no particular person but the frequent Shelleyan figure who serves as the projection of the idealizing mind, the perfect fulfillment of oneself, like the ideal spirit the Visionary of *Alastor* pursues. The manuscript shows that she was originally addressed as "Sister, my beloved mate / And yoke fellow of youth"[40]—that is, in accordance with Shelley's recurrent use of the sister-bride figure, the ideal counterpart of the self, like Laon's sister-bride Cythna. Similarly, "Death's dedicated bride" who has deserted the Maniac for her "paramour" Death is not to be searched out as a real person who played a part in his life; addressed as "Thou mockery which art sitting by my side" (385),[41] she is the phantom attendant upon everyone's mind and represents the falsehood and inconstancy that mortality makes not only of one's own life but especially of the lives of those in whom one would find the constancy of love. All those we love are Death's dedicated brides and must desert us for their "ghastly paramour."

Maddened by inconstancy itself, the Maniac accepts not only Maddalo's conviction that man is doomed by an ineluctable force outside himself to be heart-broken by the world and cannot be master of himself, but also Julian's conviction that suffering is a "wilful ill." "What Power delights to torture us?" the Maniac asks. "I know / That to myself I do not wholly owe / What now I suffer—"; but then he adds, "though in part I may" (320–22). He is not, therefore, wholly of Julian's faith that the human will is free and limitless, nor of Maddalo's that the human tragedy is destined and man impotent. He confesses that, like Maddalo, he is called proud by others, impatiently reacting to wrongs done him; yet, he thinks himself, like Julian, humble, though shattered by his patient endurance of his agonies. Although he adheres to his utopian "creed," before his madness he was, like Maddalo, "a humourist in his way" (244), with all that implies of Byronic cynicism. Fundamentally, he is one whose understanding has convinced him of his utopian faith—or, in Maddalo's terms, "theory"—but whose heart has been wounded by the world. He would seem, then, to validate Maddalo's claim that madness arises from any expectation that the world can accord with the love and truth in the mind. But on the other hand, since he gives no evidence of having exerted

[40] MS e. 11, p. 96.
[41] Cf. Shelley's other visionary ladies who move "beside" one in life; see pp. 9–10, 32, 164, 428–32.

himself to make the world other than it is, he also illustrates Julian's argument that "it is our will / That thus enchains us to permitted ill." The Maniac can only weakly lament that the world did not prove equal to his ideals, not that it resisted his will; his creed is right, the facts of the world are at fault:

> ... if love and tenderness and truth
> Had overlived hope's momentary youth,
> My creed should have redeemed me from repenting;
> But loathed scorn and outrage unrelenting
> Met love excited by far other seeming
> Until the end was gained. ...   (330–35)

Having demanded, in Julian's words, to "love and be beloved with gentleness" and having been "scorned" (209), he lives a "living death" of madness; and this, according to Julian, is not "destiny, / But man's own wilful ill." Yet, the Maniac's life-decision is Julian's, for he would, in theory, separate heart from mind, enduring stoically the broken heart and preserving the perfect concepts and ideals of his understanding:

> There is but one road
> To peace and that is truth, which follow ye!
> Love sometimes leads astray to misery.
> Yet think not though subdued—and I may well
> Say that I am subdued—that the full Hell
> Within me would infect the untainted breast
> Of sacred nature with its own unrest;
> As some perverted beings think to find
> In scorn or hate a medicine for the mind
> Which scorn or hate have wounded—O how vain!
> The dagger heals not but may rend again. ...
> Believe that I am ever still the same
> In creed as in resolve, and what may tame
> My heart, must leave the understanding free,
> Or all would sink in this keen agony.   (347–61)

This is also Julian's creed: the patient endurance of ills and the preservation of the ideals whose pattern is in the mind, but without the scorn with which Maddalo has responded, at least in theory, to the world's falsehood. To his false lady the Maniac replies, "I give thee tears for scorn and love for hate" (496),[42] a Christian doctrine that hardly consorts with Maddalo's theoretical misanthropy. And yet, the Maniac is not consistent

---

[42] Approximately the same words will reappear in *Hellas* (737), where they signal patient endurance of ill for the sake of good.

with himself and has not stoically separated heart and understanding: he confesses that the wounds his heart has suffered have blotted "all things fair / And wise and good which time had written" on his brain (480–81), which is also an adequate way of accounting for Maddalo's misanthropy. The Maniac's intended stoicism has proved false or ineffective.

The Maniac, in short, is drawn ambiguously, so that both Julian and Maddalo may claim him as proof of their opposite theories. On only one conclusion can they agree, since it is the only fact shared by both their doctrines: the Maniac can tolerate only truth and cannot accommodate himself to the world's falsehood. We have noted earlier that Julian's delight in the company of his "friend" Maddalo is expressive of the mind's "thirst for intercourse with an intelligence similar to itself," hence of the desire of the self to complete itself in absolute self-consciousness; and it is the betrayal by a "dear friend" (527) that has left the Maniac an incomplete, deranged self in whom desire clashes with experience. The "deadly change" in the one he loved

> fixed a blot
> Of falsehood on his mind which flourished not
> But in the light of all-beholding truth. (529–31)

This is the one fact that remains, even when, moved by the Maniac's ambiguous evidence, the disputants' "argument was quite forgot," warning us that there is no easy or simple solution to their difference. The Maniac's is the essential human condition, even as it had been defined by the poem's epigraph from Pan's speech in Virgil's tenth Eclogue:

> The meadows with fresh streams, the bees with thyme,
> The goats with the green leaves of budding Spring,
> Are saturated not—nor Love with tears.

Virgil's Gallus, like the Maniac, has given himself to madness ("Galle, quid insanis?") and laments extravagantly because his faithless Lycoris[43] has deserted him for another; and, significantly, it is Pan, god of the mortal world, not an Apollonian god of transcendence, who advises him of this necessary disparity between the grief of experience and the love in the mind. Everyone and everything is endowed with infinite desires, to which the world is inadequate; and no amount of earthly experience can ever equal the soul's conceptions. But whether it is destined that the heart meet falsehood in the world or whether that falsehood springs only from man's own willful passivity remains to the end of Shelley's poem an open question. In either case, mad grief is not the answer.

---

[43] According to Shelley's notebook translation, "unworthy love" (Julian, IV, 287).

vi

Ironically, even Julian, with all his theoretical faith that man has strength to break the "madman's chains" that bind him, ultimately casts doubt on the practicability of his own utopian creed, in the same manner that the Christian of *A Refutation of Deism* unwittingly makes suspect the religion he is defending. Agreeing with the Preface-writer's analysis of Maddalo's pride as "the concentered and impatient feelings which consume him," Julian is confident that only the impatience of pride leads to the madness of expecting the unregenerated world to correspond immediately to the mind's ideals (206–10). He therefore plans "by patience" to reclaim the Maniac from his "dark estate" (572–74). But in fact he unconsciously contributes evidence to Maddalo's thesis that an unbridgeable gulf separates the perfect theory of the understanding from the call of the heart, just as Maddalo contradicts his own misanthropy by his charity to the Maniac. The poem at the end returns to its opening, and Julian has learned nothing. He still would like to remain in Venice because of his delight in "the lone sea" (550), with its intimation of outer and inner infinitude, and because of Maddalo's friendship; and instead of patiently and therefore willfully curing the Maniac, he returns to London, mainly for the passive, self-indulging purpose of dispelling his gloomy thoughts of him. His humanitarian plan to restore the Maniac "with patience and kind care" (229), he confesses, is only one of those utopian "dreams of baseless good" that "Oft come and go in crowds or solitude / And leave no trace" (578–80), an unrealistic theory, however "refutation-proof," that fails to take human nature into account. With inverse irony, it was misanthropic Maddalo, self-consumed by impatient feelings but "patient" in "social life," who had so humanely provided for the Maniac because of the "claim" all men have on each other. Julian may be right to believe that our own will enchains us to permitted ill, but he himself gives testimony to Maddalo's persuasion that we are incorrigibly weak—"and we aspire / How vainly to be strong." Julian's feeble rationalization of his leaving Venice is that he is not "an unconnected man" (547), that is, that he has a family in England who have claims on him; and he stands self-convicted by the irony of his phrase. Because of his self-satisfying impatience he is as much an "unconnected" man as would follow from Maddalo's theoretical policy of voluntary withdrawal from mankind.

Maddalo, capable of being the redeemer of his country, is so disillusioned as to scorn the possibility of such redemption; potentially strong, he denies that man has strength. Julian, persuaded of man's power to reform the world, is too weak to redeem even the Maniac. Perhaps the Furies who torture Prometheus are right: men

... dare not devise good for man's estate,
And yet they know not that they do not dare.
The good want power, but to weep barren tears.[44]

In the farthest reaches of his reference Shelley is depicting in the characters of Julian and Maddalo the two kinds of paralysis that prevented his generation from pursuing the ideals of the French Revolution: the impatient believe pessimistically that the momentary failure of the Revolution proves its goals are visionary and unobtainable; the optimists lack the will to act.

It is an integral fulfillment of the poem, then, that it ultimately trail off anticlimatically in a kind of meaningless and prosaic indifference, without resolution. When Julian returns years later, he questions Maddalo's daughter, now a woman. The Maniac's fickle lady later rejoined him, she reports,—"but after all / She left him" (605–6). There is no false, superimposed happy ending. The Maniac's lady is not constant even in her desertion; and inconstancy is doubly proved to be the prosaic fact of life. And then?

"How did it end?" "And was not this enough?
They met—they parted"—"Child, is there no more?"

The flat, monosyllabic inconclusiveness is the proper conclusion, for the whole skeptical drift of the poem is to thrust on the reader the burden of weighing the alternative views of life. "The Julian & Maddalo & the accompanying poems," Shelley wrote his publisher, "are all my saddest verses raked up into one heap"; and the subject of the poem is drawn from a "dreadful" reality.[45]

And yet, even as we think the poem is ending in sad and bewildering indecision, we become conscious that at the border of our attention stands Maddalo's daughter as she had stood before us earlier, in her childhood, Julian's evidence of man's innate freedom, innocence, and happiness. Now grown to womanhood, she has not been broken by the world and still could be the living refutation of Maddalo's gloom and the basis for hope:

A woman; such as it has been my doom
To meet with few,—a wonder of this earth,
Where there is little of transcendent worth,—
Like one of Shakespeare's women. (589–92)

---

[44] *Prometheus Unbound*, I. 623–25.
[45] To Ollier, 15 December 1819, and 10 November 1820 (*Letters*, II, 164, 246).

That this perfect human being is the daughter of misanthropic Maddalo
is more than an irony. In addition to Julian's and Maddalo's abstract dispute over human potentialities, there is a finely spun thread of human
history in the poem that raises the father-child relationship to the level
of temporal symbolism. When, in *Hellas*, for example, the Turkish sultan
wishes to see the phantom of his ancestor, he is told he would commune
with "That portion of thyself which was ere thou / Didst start for this
brief race"; and in *Prometheus Unbound* the representation of Demogorgon as Jupiter's child is symbolic of the relation of the past to the future
to which it gives birth. The question of whether the French Revolution
had to lead to the Reign of Terror and whether the tyranny of the *ancien
régime* had to lead to Napoleonic tyranny—or, on the other hand, whether
the enervating disillusionment of Shelley's generation over the failure of
the Revolution could be displaced by optimistic meliorism—was never far
from the mind of Shelley, who could hardly have helped having as his
model the wide difference between his own father and himself. Maddalo's
pessimistic model is the madhouse, "such a one / As age to age might
add, for uses vile" (99–100), history being to him a progressive accumulation of various modes of wrongs and horrors; yet his own daughter is
evidence that an age of pessimism may give birth to a generation of
Edenic perfection.[46] Shelley himself had conceded in the Preface to *The
Revolt of Islam* that with the Revolution "such a degree of unmingled
good was expected as it was impossible to realise," at least without "resolute
perseverance and indefatigable hope, and long-suffering and long-believing
courage, and the systematic efforts of generations of men of intellect and
virtue"—in brief, without the attributes of his Prometheus. Out of that
failure have flowed the "gloom and misanthropy" characteristic of "the age
in which we live," which "finds relief only in the wilful exaggeration of its
own despair" and which has "tainted the literature of the age" with
Byronic "hopelessness" and "infectious gloom." However,

it has ceased to be believed that whole generations of mankind ought to consign themselves to a hopeless inheritance of ignorance and misery.... There
is a reflux in the tide of human things which bears the shipwrecked hopes
of men into a secure haven after the storms are past. Methinks, those who
now live have survived an age of despair.

[46] The historical dimension is more explicit in an unused passage in the draft of the
poem. At the end of his reply to Maddalo's fatalism—that is, after line 210 of the
published version—Julian adds (MS e. 11, p. 86),

           this is not destiny—
At least, tho all the past cd not have been
Other than it was—yet things foreseen
Reason and Love may force beneath their yoke
Warned by a fate foregone [that is, by what had happened in the past].

As bearer of the new age, Maddalo's daughter, however, is present only to our peripheral vision. The possible truths about human potentiality have so steadily oscillated and undercut each other that Shelley's contradictory views can only confront each other indecisively. Is man, like Shelley's Prince Athanase, destined to find only the Pandemic Venus of falsehood in the world? If so, the world is "teachless," utopia is impossible, and man's soul can be fulfilled only in a future life, if at all. Or is man corrigible so that, with patience, the perfect pattern in the mind may become at least a qualified actuality? If so, the world of the poem contains no one who can stand in proof of that—unless it is Maddalo's daughter, whom we nearly overlook as we concentrate on puzzling out the Maniac. The quantity of commentary seeking to demonstrate that the poem supports either Julian's view or Maddalo's and lamenting that the Maniac's speeches are insufficiently directive is proof of the poem's rhetorical success. Such commentators—like those who have tried to identify the particular historical persons who were the unnamed objects of Pope's satires —have proved good and willing readers. The poem has successfully engaged them in its own purpose: to teach them, by compelling a probe of human nature, to know themselves. How the unresolved poetry of sad reality leads to the reader's self-knowledge and what that knowledge reveals will become more evident in *The Cenci*.

3 Sad Reality and Self-Knowledge

The Cenci

Shelley's other major representation of "a sad reality," as he defined *The Cenci* in its Dedication, shares with *Julian and Maddalo* the fact that it focuses on a tragedy, is based on actual events, and is composed in "the familiar language of men"; and he was as concerned as he had been in the case of the slightly earlier poem to distinguish the nature, style, and purpose of such compositions from those of the poetry of "beautiful idealisms." His previous publications, he felt, had been "little else than visions which impersonate my own apprehensions of the beautiful and the just," "dreams of what ought to be, or may be," not the actualities with which all idealisms must ultimately reckon.[1] In *The Cenci*, however, "I lay aside the presumptuous attitude of an instructor, and am content to paint, with such colours as my own heart furnishes, that which has been." In the main, his play is scrupulously faithful to the historical document on which it is based, and in planning to publish along with the play a translation of that document,

[1] Shelley must have had in mind *Queen Mab* and *The Revolt of Islam*; certainly the *Alastor* volume does not fit this description.

It is significantly indicative of Shelley's shifting perspectives and of his search for a ground of adequate assurance that he interrupted composition of Act II of *Prometheus Unbound* to write *Julian and Maddalo* and that he wrote *The Cenci* after completing the third act of *Prometheus Unbound*, which assuredly is a dream of "what ought to be, or may be."

his purpose was to demonstrate that what he had written was indeed "matter-of-fact" and not his invention, much less an ideal vision.[2]

i

Driven by "implacable hatred towards his children," despotic Count Cenci rejoices in the deaths of two of his sons, impoverishes another desperately, and violates his daughter Beatrice. Around this last deed and, more centrally, around Beatrice's consequent part in the murder of her father, Shelley's play revolves. Any such factual summary of the drama, however, fails to suggest its dimensions. Denying the a priori validity of all institutions and their codes, Shelley located in the psychological and moral nature of individual man the source from which institutions have historically evolved. Church, state, and society are but factitious extensions of the character of men, particularly of that character as it manifests itself in the most fundamental of all human relationships—that is, with father or mother, son or daughter, brother or sister. Consequently, actual human events, especially a historical domestic tragedy like that of the Cenci, almost necessarily imply all-inclusive moral dimensions, as familial relations so consistently do in Shelley's writings. The Count's incest therefore is dramatized less as a unique man's uncontrollable lust than as the radical expression of the sadism inherent in every form of oppression. With his characteristic skeptical tendency to conceive of everything as open to ambivalent perspectives, Shelley explained that incest

is like many other *incorrect* things a very poetical circumstance. It may be the excess of love or of hate. It may be that defiance of every thing for the sake of another which clothes itself in the glory of the highest heroism, or it may be that cynical rage which confounding the good & bad in existing opinions breaks through them for the purpose of rioting in selfishness & antipathy.[3]

Incestuous desire of brother and sister motivated by love, though "incorrect," expresses the desire of the self for union with its own perfection; motivated by hate, however, it produces an Amnon, who, in Calderón's adaptation of the biblical story of incest, "is a prejudiced savage acting what he abhors & abhorring that which is the unwilling party to his crime"[4]—a description that applies exactly to Count Cenci. According to the Count's self-analysis, in youth his expression of tyranny was lust, the sensual subjugation of another for his own use; having outlived that

[2] To Byron, 26 May 1820 (*Letters*, II, 198). *The Relation of the Death of the Family of the Cenci* (Julian, II, 159–66), which Mary translated from the Italian, occupies MS e. 13. Mary published it in her second edition of the *Poetical Works of Shelley* (1839).

[3] To Maria Gisborne, 16 November 1819 (*Letters*, II, 154).

[4] *Ibid.* Calderón's *Los cabellos de Absalón* is based on 2 Sam. 13.

pleasure, the septuagenarian has graduated to those forms of oppression that destroy the foe's soul through terror (I. i. 96–117). The rape of Beatrice identifies Cenci as the human impersonation of the Jupiter of *Prometheus Unbound*, whose similar act of oppression is his destructive rape of Thetis under the tyrannic delusion that this is the nature of union; but incestuous rape, combining the Count's early and late modes of oppression, is his ultimate expression of his hate for his own children and thus is the ultimate degree of hatred itself.

Although Shelley works out his tragedy in strictly human terms, rather than through the esoteric symbolism that is the medium of his poetry of "idealisms," the Count's torture of his children represents not only a domestic but a political and religious tyranny as well, the three modes being implicated in each other. Others repeatedly refer to him as a tyrant, and his son compares him to the most severe of despots, Galeaz Visconti, Borgia, and Ezzelin (II. ii. 49). For the Count builds his vengeance on a conviction of absolute paternal power—hence the most precise exercise of his tyranny is his violation of his own child—and his model of fatherhood is his conception of God's fatherhood of man.

If, when a parent from a parent's heart
Lifts from this earth to the great Father of all
A prayer,

what more, he asks, could he wish for his "disobedient and rebellious sons" than that they die? (I. iii. 22–44). Like the God of Scripture, therefore, he consistently regards filial disobedience as the ultimate sin and the unquestionable justification for vengeance.[5] But exactly what the relation is between his fatherhood and God's is imprecise and inconstant in his mind. That his prayer for his sons' deaths has been fulfilled he takes as evidence of a special Providence granted by a God who also punishes His disobedient and rebellious sons with death, the assumption being that God acts on behalf of His human analogue as He acts for Himself. Planning to curse Beatrice, the Count asks,

With what but with a father's curse doth God
Panic-strike armed victory, and make pale
Cities in their prosperity? The world's Father
Must grant a parent's prayer against his child,
Be he who asks even what men call me.   (IV. i. 104–8)

"God!" he cries out even in his sleep, "hear, O, hear, / A father's curse! What, art Thou not our Father?" (IV. iii. 18–19). If his power derives from his domestic office as God's representative and if "the common God

---

[5] For example, III. i. 316 ("Such was God's scourge for disobedient sons"); IV. i. 90 ("A rebel to her father and her God"). Also II. ii. 32; IV. i. 109.

and Father" (IV. i. 126) is the authority for his parallel actions, he can disclaim responsibility for his deeds: "And more depends on God than me" (IV. i. 43). On the other hand, perhaps he is sovereign in his realm as God is in His, so that God "does His will, I mine!" (IV. i. 139); and if so, he can play God, declaring his wife's opposition to him to be a "blasphemy" for which she is "damned" (II. i. 162).

If at one extreme Count Cenci assumes he is an autonomous father-deity, at the other he frees himself from responsibility by assuming he is the agent of God the Father, a self-exonerating assumption Beatrice and others will also make about themselves later in the play. His soul, the Count says in serious self-justification, is only a scourge wielded by God against an inherently evil world (IV. i. 63–64). For the foundation on which he builds his tyranny and this concept of vindictive fatherhood and justifies his unprovoked actions is his acceptance of the doctrine of man's innate sinfulness, "for Adam made all so"; and he unconsciously lays bare the hypocrisy of expecting man to believe himself created to be involuntarily evil and at the same time demanding that he be, as this religion requires, "tender-hearted, meek and pitiful" (I. iii. 12–13). Had man necessarily inherited Adam's evil—a doctrine Shelley was convinced leads to despair and slavish self-contempt that correspondingly invites tyranny—then the righteous reigning power would be the avenging Devil: "I do not feel as if I were a man," the Count declares, "But like a fiend appointed to chastise / The offences of some unremembered world," some Eden of original sin (IV. i. 160–62). As Julian had said, if man *were* the "passive thing" that Maddalo claimed, "I should not see / Much harm in the religions and old saws ... / Which break a teachless nature to the yoke."[6] Consequently, as the avenging God—or Devil—of a world supposedly evil, the Count, unlike Beatrice, performs his monstrous deeds without personal provocation and so without apparent dramatic motivation. Like God, he is the fatherless father, the uncaused cause, the point behind which succession cannot be palpably traced. In Shelley's Manichaean system, in which evil is an autonomous and pressing potentiality, the Count is the original and unmotivated point at which transcendent evil enters into human reality and begins its causal sequence simply because the Count *permits* it to enter by assuming man is necessarily evil. The relation of Beatrice to her father, then, is not only filial but also temporal and causal. Given a necessitarian world in which events must act out their invariable causal succession but from which ultimate cause is inaccessibly remote, there must be a point at which ultimate cause, which is outside time, is allowed to enter the finite as the first event of a temporal sequence. That point is the "father," who is not the evil *consequence* of an evil cause, but whose nature allows evil to enter him as the first finite cause, the potential having now become actual. Thus the relation

---

[6] *Julian and Maddalo*, 160–64.

of Cenci to Beatrice is not only that of father to daughter but also of cause to effect, of past to present, and present to future. That parentage is equatable with cause is made nearly explicit when Lucretia explains her violated step-daughter's wild behavior:

Her spirit apprehends the sense of pain,
But not its cause; suffering has dried away
The source from which it sprung. . . .

Beatrice replies, the idea of parricide entering her mind for the first time, though only collaterally: "Like Parricide ... / Misery has killed its father" (III. i. 34–37). The causal relation of Cenci to Beatrice is like that of Jupiter to his "child" Demogorgon in *Prometheus Unbound,* or of Mahomet the Second to his distant descendant Mahmud in *Hellas.* It is a relationship that Shelley meant to show can be broken when he painted Count Maddalo and his daughter.

   Other characters also sustain the play's paradigm of paternity as delight in tyrannic oppression by their paying deference to "a father's holy name" that shields a "murderous persecutor" (II. ii. 72–73) and by pointedly referring to the Pope as "the Holy Father" who fears any weakening of "the paternal power, / Being, as 'twere, the shadow of his own" (II. i. 24; II. ii. 55–56). Even Beatrice accepts the identity by praying to "God, the Father of all" (I. iii. 118), the "great God, / Whose image upon earth a father is" (II. i. 16–17); and it is the basis of her "pernicious mistake" that she does so. As the Father, Count Cenci hypocritically makes an "outward show of love," with which he "mocks / His inward hate," like Jupiter raping Thetis, or like the "hypocritical Daemon" described in *Queen Mab* (VII. 135–36 n.) who announces "Himself as the God of compassion and peace, even whilst He stretches forth His blood-red hand with the sword of discord to waste the earth, having confessedly devised this scheme of desolation from eternity." Beatrice's ambiguous exclamation over her own father's hypocrisy unintentionally sheds double meaning: "Great God! that such a father should be mine!" (I. ii. 50–54). Both the tyrannical and reverentially religious senses are combined in her speaking of "father" as a "dread" name (III. i. 144); and a most complex irony and a muddled theology of fatherhood emerge when she traces what she has suffered from the Count:

                    so my hate
Became the only worship I could lift
To our great father, who in pity and love,
Armed thee [the actual murderer] ... to cut him off.   (V. ii. 126–29)

Indeed, Beatrice's words might equally well apply to the "Father of all" when she asks the Count, "Wouldst thou have honour and obedience /

Who art a torturer?" (I. iii. 148–49) or when she recounts her patient sufferings from him in the past:

What, if 'tis he who clothed us in these limbs
Who tortures them, and triumphs? . . .
I have borne much, and kissed the sacred hand
Which crushed us to the earth, and thought its stroke
Was perhaps some paternal chastisement!   (I. iii. 101–2, 111–13)

The tendency of such recurrent collocations of these two fathers is to blur all distinction between the Count and God, as when the Count's son repents his part in his father's murder: "Father! God! / Canst Thou forgive even the unforgiving, / When their full hearts break...!" (V. iii. 104–6). Since the identification of the Count's despotic fatherhood with God's is so carefully threaded through it, the drama becomes at least as much a theological as a human tragedy, or, rather, it becomes a human tragedy because of an acceptance of a theological model for moral behavior.

But the reality of that theological model is made highly suspect, especially since, as we have noted, the Count can paint himself variously as a passive agent of God, an authority parallel to God, or a power independent of God, as it suits his purpose. The consequent implication is not merely that tyrants model themselves on a vengeful God but that God is fabricated in the image of the human tyrant and that established theologies are only self-projections by which oppressors invent authority and justification for their power. Shelley's normative model is always the autonomy and divinity of the self, and therefore man's fabrication of a tyrannic God in his own image is a parodic inversion of the relation of such figures as the Visionary of *Alastor* or the speaker of *Epipsychidion* to the visions of which they are in quest. Instead of projecting the ideal absolute form of the finite self and seeking union with it in love so that the self may attain its autonomy, the slave projects—and gives away—his innate power, as Prometheus first does, and allows it to tyrannize over him in fear.

The "popular and visible symbols" of religion, Shelley was to write, merely "express power in some shape or other"; and those ultimate mysteries about which, he was convinced, mortal man must forever remain ignorant have been erected, under the name of religious truths, into "symbols of unjust power ever since they were distorted by the narrow passions of the immediate followers of Jesus." Upon the institution of Christianity, mere "names"

borrowed from the life and opinions of Jesus Christ were employed as symbols of domination and imposture; and a system of liberty and equality . . . was perverted to support oppression. . . . Such was the origin of the Catholic Church, which . . . means, being interpreted, a plan according to which the cunning and selfish few have employed the fears and hopes of the ignorant many to the establishment of their own power and the destruction of the real interests of all.[7]

An established theology is so radical a form of tyranny, he continues, that in the English Renaissance the "exposure of a certain portion of religious imposture drew with it an enquiry into political imposture."[8] It was this centrality of the imposture of religion that Shelley had in mind when he wrote in the Preface to *The Cenci* that Catholicism is "interwoven with the whole fabric" of Italian life. Protestantism he passed off as a mere cloak worn on particular days, a passport exhibited to avoid being railed at, or "a gloomy passion for penetrating the impenetrable mysteries of our being," such as the cause of life, impenetrable mysteries which religion, for its self-serving purposes, pretends to resolve by assigning them such meaningless names as "God," "Daemon," and "Heaven."[9] But Catholicism is merely the artificial apotheosis of unrestrained human conduct. It is not prescriptive: it is "not a rule for moral conduct" and "has no necessary connection with any one virtue." It is descriptive of actual human conduct in fictitious theological terms and thus permissive, so that one may combine "an undoubting persuasion of the truth of the popular religion with a cool and determined perseverance in enormous guilt." Consequently Count Cenci, Beatrice, and Orsino, the Vice of the play, repeatedly claim that in carrying out their monstrous deeds they are merely agents of God's will, swords "in the right hand of justest God" (IV. iv. 126), thereby fabricating a sanction for any evil they care to perform and releasing themselves from moral responsibility.

But it was in *The Revolt of Islam* that Shelley most explicitly defined theology as a fiction invented to authorize man's tyranny over man and to sanction punishment of those who violate its own decrees. Whatever the ultimate and unknowable cause of events may be, Shelley denies

---

[7] *Philosophical View of Reform* (Julian, VII, 5).
[8] *Queen Mab*, VI. 103–7:

The self-sufficing, the omnipotent,
The merciful, and the avenging God!
Who, prototype of human misrule, sits
High in Heaven's realm, upon a golden throne,
Even like an earthly king.

[9] *Hymn to Intellectual Beauty*, 25–31. Shelley was always conscious of the "mystery or majesty or power which the invisible world contains" (*Essay on Christianity* [Julian, VI, 229]), but as *Alastor* and *Hymn to Intellectual Beauty* make clear, he shared with Godwin and Mary Shelley dread of the pernicious consequences they described in *St. Leon* and *Frankenstein* of irrepressible curiosity about the source of life and of drawing from "charnels and coffins ... the tale / Of what we are" (*Alastor*, 24–29). Part of the purpose of this chapter on *The Cenci*, moreover, is to show that he shared the view on which much of Godwin's *Caleb Williams* is founded, that undue curiosity about the suppressed thoughts of the mind also has dangerous consequences.

that it either thinks and feels or has any concern for the consequences of its effects.[10] Physical "evil" such as plague, poison, and earthquake, and moral evils such as hate, pride, fear, and tyranny inhere as ever-present potentialities in the earthly and human state. Given the proper permissive conditions, they emerge into actuality and produce their consequences according to fixed and necessary laws; and it is superstition to believe either form of evil the arbitrary work of a deity.

What is that Power?[11] Ye mock yourselves, and give
A human heart to what ye cannot know:
As if the cause of life could think and live!
'Twere as if man's own works should feel, and show
The hopes, and fears, and thoughts from which they flow,
And he be like to them![12] Lo! Plague is free
To waste, Blight, Poison, Earthquake, Hail, and Snow,
Disease, and Want, and worse Necessity
Of hate and ill, and Pride, and Fear, and Tyranny!

What is that Power?[13] Some moon-struck sophist stood
Watching the shade from his own soul upthrown
Fill Heaven and darken Earth, and in such mood
The Form[14] he saw and worshipped was his own,
His likeness in the world's vast mirror shown;
And 'twere an innocent dream, but that a faith[15]
Nursed by fear's dew of poison, grows thereon,
And that men say, that Power has chosen Death[16]
On all who scorn its laws,[17] to wreak immortal wrath.[18]

To this projected fiction slavish man masochistically assigns an imaginary rod to scourge himself into slavery, and ministers of vengeance (priests, kings, custom, and "domestic sway" like that of Count Cenci) to oppress his "freeborn" soul.[19] Such names as "God" are each "a sign which maketh holy / All power," one form of which is lust; and an anthropomorphic theology is "The pattern whence all fraud and wrong is made, / A law to

---

[10] See for example *Queen Mab*, VI. 212–19; *The Revolt of Islam*, 3235–43; *Letter to Lord Ellenborough* (Julian, V, 288).
[11] The *Laon and Cythna* version reads, "What then is God?"
[12] Shelley first wrote, "Even as a child ... might ... / Declare that the stars are in the lake below" (MS e. 10, p. 81).
[13] *Laon and Cythna*: "What then is God?"
[14] MS: "power."
[15] Shelley deleted the next manuscript line: "Is made the footstool of a bloody throne."
[16] *Laon and Cythna*: "God has appointed death."
[17] *Ibid.*: "his will."
[18] *The Revolt of Islam*, 3235–52.
[19] *Ibid.*, 3255–58.

which mankind has been betrayed."[20] For the agents of tyranny, seeking
to reduce men to servile despair and self-contempt, have taught that there
is one teacher, God,

> who, the necessity
> Of rule and wrong had armed against mankind,
> His slave and his avenger there to be;
> That we were weak and sinful, frail and blind,
> And that the will of one was peace, and we
> Should seek for nought on earth but toil and misery.[21]

Because there consistently hovers over *The Cenci* this intimation
that theology is invented for the sake of human oppression and that the
God of Christianity may be only the imaginary projection of a Count
Cenci, there arises the ghastly horror at the end of the play when Beatrice
has momentary doubt that there is a beneficent God to join in the afterlife, and it flashes on her mind that if the traditional omnipotent and
omnipresent anthropomorphic Father *really* were to exist, he would be
nothing more than the spirit of her own tyrannical father:

> If there should be
> No God, no Heaven, no Earth in the void world;
> The wide, gray, lampless, deep unpeopled world!
> If all things then should be . . . my father's spirit,
> His eye, his voice, his touch surrounding me;
> The atmosphere and breath of my dead life!
> If sometimes, as a shape more like himself,
> Even the form which tortured me on earth
> Masked in gray hairs and wrinkles, he should come
> And wind me in his hellish arms, and fix
> His eyes on mine, and drag me down, down, down!
> For was he not alone omnipotent
> On Earth, and ever present? Even though dead,
> Does not his spirit live in all that breathe,
> And work for me and mine still the same ruin,
> Scorn, pain, despair?[22]   (V. iv. 57–72)

Beatrice's revulsion against her violation by her father and her schem-
ing his murder embody therefore a revolt against all forms of despotism
summed up in the idea of paternity and represented archetypally by

---

[20] *Ibid.*, 3280–84.
[21] *Laon and Cythna*, IX. xv.
[22] See also V. ii. 120–32.

Shelley's interpretation of the God of organized religion. But Beatrice herself accepts this myth of a punitive theology as the pattern for human conduct and commits herself to the belief that God assigns man, either individually or through the collective legal code, the duty of enforcing His system of rewards and punishments. Religion and the human legal system are different modes of the same institution imposed by man upon himself, and Beatrice depends upon both to justify her parricide:

Death! Death! Our law and our religion call thee
A punishment and a reward.

Her step-mother supports her belief:

Death must be the punishment
Of crime, or the reward of trampling down
The thorns which God has strewed upon the path
Which leads to immortality.   (III. i. 117–18, 122–25)

Beatrice therefore accepts the doctrine that man is under obligation to punish crime because God's

high Providence commits
Its glory on this earth, and their own wrongs
Into the hands of men.   (III. i. 181–83)

Because her father is a tyrant and she dares not expose her violation, she refuses to entrust her cause to the law, but the punitive law is nevertheless the justifying model on which she acts. As her step-mother explains, it is not immoral but only unlawful to take the law in one's own hands because the laws are "jealous" and "Would punish us with death and infamy / For that which it became themselves to do" (III. i. 229–31). Therefore, the reader falls into a moral trap if he believes it an intentional cosmic irony that, immediately after the murder of the Count, the Pope's legate arrives with a warrant for his death, rendering Beatrice's accomplished crime superfluous. To think, as many readers have thought, that this is cosmic irony is to assume that the Count's crimes *should* have been entrusted to the law, an assumption that contradicts the ethics upon which the drama is built. True, Beatrice's step-mother is shattered to learn that the law would have done what has already been done by forbidden means, but to Beatrice it is only a reassuring ex post facto confirmation of her acts: "Both Earth and Heaven, consenting arbiters, / Acquit our deed" (IV. iv. 24–25). However, Beatrice herself then becomes subject to the law and, although never quite abandoning her shaken trust in God, learns that "high-judging" God does not save or revenge her and that the law is only another system of tyranny that fails to carry out what she thinks is divine judgment (IV. iv. 115–29). Because she has trusted what we are to understand as man-made fictions, she comes to see

> the small justice shown by Heaven and Earth
> To me or mine; and what a tyrant thou [her judge] art,
> And what slaves these [the accused]; and what a world we make,
> The oppressor and the oppressed.   (V. iii. 72–75)

Perhaps even "the laws of Death's untrodden realm" are as unjust as those of man, which presumably are modelled on them (V. iv. 73–74). I have, she concludes, "met with much injustice in this world"; "No difference has been made by God or man" (V. iv. 80–82).[23]

What has been revealed is the moral invalidity of theology and the legal system, upon both of which Beatrice has modelled her actions; both are human creations for the purpose of oppression, and man's dependence upon them results only in enslavement and the justification of crime. Hence the irony that the play ends with the tyrannical and unjust law condemning Beatrice to death. Shelley's moral principles arises out of his understanding of the internal nature of man, instead of resting upon supposedly authorized and sanctioned extrahuman systems. Implicitly repudiating those fabricated systems, his play is directed more centrally toward a moral analysis of man's psychological constitution by throwing light on "some of the most dark and secret caverns of the human heart."[24]

ii

It is, of course, Beatrice's response to the tyrannical violation she has suffered, rather than tyranny itself, that is the central concern of the drama; and Shelley's moral analysis is essentially the analysis of that response. His other compositions can leave no doubt about his own moral judgment of her way of reacting to this oppression, and his Preface to the play is explicit enough:

Undoubtedly, no person can be truly dishonoured by the act of another; and the fit return to make to the most enormous injuries is kindness and forbearance, and a resolution to convert the injurer from his dark passions by peace and love. Revenge, retaliation, atonement, are pernicious mistakes.[25]

---

23 The inefficacy and moral inequity of the law is further expressed in I. iii. 135–36; II. ii. 4–5, 25–28.

24 *The Cenci*, Preface.

25 Cf. *Philosophical View of Reform* (Julian, VII, 334): "The maxim that criminals should be pitied and reformed, not detested and punished, alone affords a source of...." The sentence is unfinished, but its intent is clear (The Julian ed. inaccurately prints "detected" instead of "detested.")

Shelley's essay *On the Punishment of Death* (Julian, VI, 185) exactly repeats the terms of the Preface to *The Cenci* and makes it evident that tyranny and re-

Shelley is elaborating on Godwin's argument on the immorality and ineffectiveness of the punishment of wrongs: Beatrice should have acted like Justice herself, who, "when triumphant," according to Prometheus, "will weep down / Pity, not punishment, on her own wrongs, / Too much avenged by those who err"[26]—that is, by those who make Beatrice's "pernicious mistake." If Beatrice had thought and acted in this manner, Shelley explains, "she would have been wiser and better." But, he adds, "she would never have been a tragic character." In the lyric drama that had occupied his mind in recent months, Prometheus, unlike Beatrice, dispels tyranny with pity and patience, instead of revenge, and sees a mirror image of himself in Christ, "a youth / With *patient* looks nailed to a crucifix."[27] Prometheus was for that reason, Shelley is making clear, exclusively a "poetical character," suitable for poetic "idealisms," not for tragedy.[28]

Patience and all the stoic, martyr-like forbearance it requires had become fundamental elements of Shelley's doctrine of moral and political reform when, as a second-generation Romantic, he thought out the implications of the French Revolution. Unlike the previous generation which had lived through the Revolution and found it a glorious failure built on impossible or impractical ideals, Shelley located the flaw, not in its doctrines or purposes, but in the reformers' impatience, which, by precluding pity and love for the wrong-doer of the *ancien régime*, had led to bloodshed and revenge, and thence to further tyranny.[29] Exulting

---

venge like Count Cenci's and Beatrice's are to be understood as the domestic expression of the tyranny and revenge that operate also at the levels of religion and government: "It is sufficiently clear that revenge, retaliation, atonement, expiation, are rules and motives, so far from deserving a place in any enlightened system of political life, that they are the chief sources of a prodigious class of miseries in the domestic circles of society."

Shelley himself privately implied the political relevance of his domestic tragedy. At the moment when he was about to send Ollier *The Cenci* for publication, he wrote him of the Manchester Massacre, "this bloody murderous oppression of [England's] destroyers," and commented on it by quoting Beatrice's first response to her father's violation of her (III. i. 86–87): "Something must be done ... What yet I know not" (to Ollier, 6 September 1819 [*Letters*, II, 117]).

[26] *Prometheus Unbound*, I. 403–5. Cf. "Ode Written October, 1819, Before the Spaniards had Recovered their Liberty," 26–28:

Conquerors have conquered their foes alone,
Whose revenge, pride, and power they have overthrown:
Ride ye, more victorious, over your own.

But the repudiation of revenge is a ubiquitous theme in Shelley's poetry and prose.
[27] *Ibid.*, I. 584–85; itals. added.
[28] *Ibid.*, Preface.
[29] See, for example, *Philosophical View of Reform* (Julian, VII, 13–15, 41, 46, 53–55). In urging that reform, though radical, be gradual, "without such an utter overthrow as should leave us the prey of anarchy" (to Byron, 20 November 1816 [*Letters*, I, 513]), Shelley was aligning himself especially with Godwin and Mary Wollstonecraft (see her *Historical and Moral View of the Origin and Progress of the French Revolution* [London, 1794]).

in the vision of a popular revolt against oppression, one chorus of Furies
in *Prometheus Unbound* sings:

See a disenchanted nation
Springs like day from desolation;
To Truth its state is dedicate,
And Freedom leads it forth, her mate;
A legioned band of linked brothers
Whom Love calls children—

But the other chorus interrupts, the very abruptness of the intrusion performing the impatience:

                'Tis another's:
See how kindred murder kin:
'Tis the vintage-time for death and sin:
Blood, like new wine, bubbles within:
Till Despair smothers
The struggling world, which slaves and tyrants win.   (I. 567–77)

This is the moral analysis of the French Revolution that stands behind
what Shelley sees as the various pernicious consequences of impatience:
the "sanguine eagerness" of the Revolution that, too soon disappointed,
had become the hopeless "gloom and misanthropy" characteristic of the
following age and the Byronic "infectious gloom" that colors contemporary
literature;[30] the impatience of pride that leads Maddalo to cynical disdain
of a world that does not correspond to his ideals; the circumstances, self-
interest, and weakness of will that deprive Julian of the patience to restore
the Maniac; the impatience that drives Beatrice to murderous revenge
for the "paternal" hatred and oppression that have caused what she
wrongly "considers" to be "a perpetual contamination both of body and
mind." In terms of the French Revolution, which was inevitably and
persistently Shelley's assumed frame of reference, the current withdrawal
of the older generation was not merely that of the Pope in *The Cenci*,
who, because of age and fear of weakening paternal power, is resolved
in "the great war between the old and young" to maintain what he thinks
is a "blameless neutrality" (II. ii. 38–40). The stagnation also results from
the lack of patience that, on the one hand, perverted the Revolution into
the Reign of Terror and Napoleonic imperialism and, on the other, made
the first generation of Romantics, notably Wordsworth and Southey, retreat mistakenly from their hopes of radical reform. Therefore, among the
virtues that Demogorgon demands in his speech that closes *Prometheus
Unbound* are not only forgiveness of wrongs and defiance of power but

---

[30] *The Revolt of Islam*, Preface.

also Endurance and Love, seated on "its awful throne of patient power /
In the wise heart" (IV. 557–58). Soon after completing *The Cenci*
Shelley was writing Hunt of "These ... awful times" on the verge of
revolution and warned equally against "the open bigotted & pensioned
enemies of freedom" and "those who profess to advocate our own cause,
yet who pollute it with the principles of legitimate murder, under the
specious yet execrable names of revenge & retribution."[31] "I fear," he
continued,

that in England things will be carried violently by the rulers, and that they
will not have learned to yield in time to the spirit of the age. The great thing
to do is to hold the balance between popular impatience and tyrannical
obstinacy; to inculcate with fervour both the right of resistance and the duty
of forbearance.[32]

It would be difficult to surpass Shelley's faith in the power of passive
resistance:

And if then the tyrants dare
Let them ride among you there,
Slash, and stab, and maim, and hew,—
What they like, that let them do.

With folded arms and steady eyes,
And little fear, and less surprise,
Look upon them as they slay
Till their rage has died away.[33]

Shelley himself had not been innocent of the fault he condemns, and
in the Dedication of *The Cenci* he dismisses his earlier compositions of
instant reform—"dreams of what ought to be, or may be"—as the "literary
defects incidental to youth and impatience." On the other hand, he
pointedly praises Leigh Hunt as the proper recipient of the play because
he is of "exalted toleration for all who do and think evil, and yet himself
free from evil," a man of "patient and irreconcilable enmity with domestic
and political tyranny and imposture." The choice of Hunt was pregnant
with implications: he would have been prominent in the public mind as
the crusading journalist who had been imprisoned for a libelous satire on
the Prince Regent; who, Prometheus-like, had rejected an offer of release
if he would pledge to abstain from future attacks, and who had cheer-
fully, if not quite stoically, set up domestic quarters in prison for two years
until the expiration of his sentence in 1815—and then renewed his op-

---

[31] To Hunt, 3 November 1819 (*Letters*, II, 148).
[32] To Hunt, 14–18 November 1819 (*Letters*, II, 153).
[33] *Mask of Anarchy*, 340–47.

position to the Prince Regent in the *Examiner*. For Shelley means this
dedicatory praise of the resisting but patiently forbearing Hunt (which
incidentally extends the relevance of the domestic drama to the political
dimension) to define, by contrast, Beatrice's moral character and to identify her tragic fault as revengeful impatience: instead of overcoming her
violator by "kindness and forbearance," she was urged to her murderous
retaliation by an "impulse" generated by "circumstance and opinion."
Therefore, just as the consistent conflation of Count Cenci with the
Christian Father-God equates him with the Jupiter of *Prometheus Unbound*, so, in the largest frame of reference, Beatrice reacts to God-like
tyranny, not as Prometheus does, but in the manner of Satan, whom
Shelley, in the Preface to *Prometheus Unbound*, explicitly rejected as the
possible hero of a lyric drama of "idealisms." Prometheus, Satan, and
Beatrice all suffer wrongs beyond measure, but whereas the "poetical
character," Prometheus, is marked by "firm and patient opposition to
omnipotent force,"[34] never submits, and retracts his hate, "tragic" Satan,
like tragic Beatrice, is marred by plotting revenge.

Shelley's Prometheus refuses to relinquish his will to the fiction of
an omnipotent arbitrary God and counters hate with pity; because Beatrice
accepts the oppressive doctrine of paternal authority, divine and therefore
human, she progressively misdirects her will until she suddenly, "impatiently," resolves on revenge. If the ideal reformation follows necessarily
from Prometheus' retraction of his curse at the opening of his drama, the
tragedy follows just as inevitably from Beatrice's initial failure of forbearance. With the opening episode of the drama she reaches the end of
a path of endurance that had been Promethean and yet was contaminated
along the way by the errors arising from religious superstition. Like
Prometheus, who, after three thousand years of torment, can still say,
"No change, no pause, no hope! Yet I endure,"[35] Beatrice has long borne
"uncomplaining wrongs" (I. i. 47). Even when she recognized that the
wrong lay entirely in her father's evil, she exercised endurance and—as
Shelley would have man do to frustrate and blot out evil—"sought by
patience, love, and tears / To soften" her father. This failing, she resorted
to prayers to the "Father of all," and when these were not heard, "I have
still borne" (I. iii. 114–20). Yet, she has in fact abased herself, as Prometheus never does, when she "kissed the sacred hand / Which crushed
us to the earth," in the faith that she has deserved "some paternal chastisement" (I. iii. 111–13). What we are to recognize in these diverse responses to evil is a character inherently, instinctively right and virtuous
but capable of being misdirected by an overlay of false religious, and
therefore ethical, conceptions; and it is these false conceptions that weaken
her will and put an end to her patient endurance. Until now she has

[34] *Prometheus Unbound*, Preface.
[35] *Ibid.*, I. 24.

been a wall of resistance between her father and her family, as Prometheus is between Jupiter and the world. "Until this hour," says her stepmother,

> thus have you ever stood
> Between us and your father's moody wrath
> Like a protecting presence: your firm mind
> Has been our only refuge and defence.[36]   (II. i. 46–49)

What such continued firm defiance might have led to is indicated by her stepmother:

> . . . you alone stood up, and with strong words
> Checked his unnatural pride; and I could see
> The devil was rebuked that lives in him.   (II. i. 43–45)

But because Beatrice has relied on God as a power outside herself that will protect innocence, momentary insecurity in her faith and the despair that follows take away her strength of will and lead to contemplation of death as the solution of her torments: " 'Twere better not to struggle any more" (II. i. 54). This is the despair that followed the failure of the French Revolution, the Byronic hopelessness that misinterprets the human potential, holds the human character in contempt, and renders melioration impossible. Because Shelley conceived of madness as the product of the clash between experience and pure mind, Beatrice passes through stages of derangement, first when she despairs of struggling against evil (II. i. 32–79) and again when she suffers violation by her father. Shelley probably was still revising *Julian and Maddalo* shortly before he began *The Cenci* in May 1819,[37] and Beatrice's madness resulting from resignation to despair is that which, by implication, threatens Maddalo; and her later derangement, like that of the Maniac, results from the blot of "falsehood" her violation has fixed upon her pure mind: "My brain," she says, "is hurt" (III. i. 1).

On recovering from madness after the act of incest, however, Beatrice rushes through a dialectic of possibilities: something must be "endured or done" (III. i. 92). Despite evidence that in the world crime goes unpunished by any divine intervention and despite her consequent doubts, Beatrice refuses to abandon her faith in a God of rewards and punishments "and so die" (III. i. 101). The world is not hopelessly evil as, say, Maddalo would have it. Two possibilities therefore remain. "You will endure it then?" she is asked; and she impatiently concludes that her wrong "asks atonement" (III. i. 215) because she is committed to a re-

[36] Cf. Earth's mistaken lament to the "Spirits of the living and the dead" when Prometheus repents his curse against Jupiter: "Your refuge, your defence lies fallen and vanquished" (*Prometheus Unbound*, I. 311).
[37] This is the date Mary affixed to *Julian and Maddalo* on its first publication in Shelley's *Posthumous Poems* (1824).

ligion whose central article is that crime requires punishment and because she accepts the doctrine, shared by her father, that God assigns to the hands of men the punishment of wrongs (III. i. 181–84): "Endure? . . . / It seems your counsel is small profit. . . . / All must be *suddenly* resolved and done" (III. i. 167–69).

Beatrice has renounced Prometheus' patient endurance. But, it is essential to note, she has not also fallen victim to Count Cenci's Jupiter-like purpose of crushing the patiently resisting will until it wills its own slavish submission. His sexual violation of her, he knows, is a "charm" that will make her "meek and tame" (I. iii. 167) by weakening her will, but his goal is absolute tyranny over that will. Her "stubborn will," he is determined, *"by its own consent* shall stoop as low / As that which drags it down" (IV. i. 10–12), for the willful abandonment of the will is the final stage of degradation. This is the condition Prometheus would have fallen into had he consented to reveal to Jupiter his "secret." It is the state when man "on his own high will, a willing slave, / . . . has enthroned the oppression and the oppressor"[38] or when, according to Julian, "our will . . . enchains us to permitted ill."[39] To this end, in order to make Beatrice willfully relinquish her will, the Count's whole hatred is directed. Demanding her presence, he adds, ". . . yet let her understand / Her coming is *consent*" (IV. i. 101–2); for it is not sufficient to his purpose merely to tame his victim: "[I] first take what I demand, / And then extort concession" (IV. i. 170–71). To this final slavish depth she refuses to fall, and her choice is another way, the way of the French Revolution when it impatiently transformed itself into bloody revenge. Because she should have defeated the tyrant with patient, stoic endurance and pity, her choice is a "mistake," but she never becomes the "willing slave," never consents to the Count's purpose to "poison and corrupt her soul" (IV. i. 45); for, as he knows, one can be corrupted only by oneself, and "no person can be truly dishonoured by the act of another." Were she to become the willing slave of the tyrant, who is himself the type of self-corruption, were she to consent to being bent to his will (IV. i. 76), then "what she most abhors / Shall have a fascination to entrap / Her loathing will" (IV. i. 85–87) and thus reduce her to total self-contempt. Such is the corrupting self-hatred the Count hopes for her when, in accordance with Shelley's symbolism of parental relations, he prays that the child he may have begotten on Beatrice be

A hideous likeness of herself, that as
From a distorting mirror, she may see
Her image mixed with what she most abhors,
Smiling upon her from her nursing breast.   (IV. i. 146–49)

[38] *Ode to Liberty,* 244–45.
[39] *Julian and Maddalo,* 170–71. Cf. *Defence of Poetry* (Julian, VII, 126): ". . . their own will had become feeble, and yet they were its slaves, and thence the slaves of the will of others."

If the fulfillment of the self is its love-union with its perfect and infinite projection and if slavery is willful submission to the fictitious mirrored projection of one's inherent powers, then corrupting self-contempt, combining slavery and perverted love, is the fascinated but loathing entrapment in another fictitious projection which is a hideous distortion of the real self. In that sense we are to understand that even to the end of the play Beatrice, whatever her other faults, never poisons or corrupts her soul with submission or self-contempt.

iii

Despite the obvious relations between *The Cenci* and *Prometheus Unbound*, it would be misleading to read them merely as exactly opposite sides of the same moral coin. True, one is the "sad reality" of which the other is the "idealism"; one is the tragedy of which the other is the divine comedy. But they are not the contrary means to the same moral end—the warning against the wrong and the advocacy of the right. Even though Beatrice and Prometheus respond to approximately the same situation in opposite ways, the purpose of *The Cenci* is not merely, or even mainly, to present its heroine to us as a model of the conduct to be avoided. The objectives and literary modes of the two works are, in fact, quite distinct. The purpose of *Prometheus Unbound*, Shelley explained, is "to familiarise the highly refined imagination of the more select classes of poetical readers with beautiful idealisms of moral excellence" until they could "love, and admire, and trust, and hope"—and, it is important to note, "endure."[40] But it follows from Shelley's doctrines, even as they are embodied in the two plays, that the purpose of *The Cenci* cannot be the corollary, to instil in us a hatred of those who do wrong, since hatred leads only to further evil, indeed to Beatrice's own "error." In the highest form of drama, he wrote, "there is little food for censure or hatred"[41] because that would provoke the very "error" that drama should eradicate. Shelley is adequately explicit and consistent in the Preface to *The Cenci*: like *Julian and Maddalo*, that other poem drawn from "a dreadful reality," *The Cenci* has as its end that which is the "highest moral purpose aimed at in the highest species of drama [i.e. tragedy] . . . the teaching the human heart, through its sympathies and antipathies, the knowledge of itself." It gains its moral objective, not by representing to the reader's imagination "beautiful idealisms of moral excellence," to which he will consequently aspire, and certainly not by making "the exhibition subservient to what is vulgarly termed a moral purpose," but by inciting self-knowledge, "in proportion to the possession of which knowledge," the Preface continues, "every human being is wise, just, sincere, tolerant and kind." Only the very few with highly refined imaginations will be drawn

[40] *Prometheus Unbound*, Preface.
[41] *Defence of Poetry* (Julian, VII, 121).

to beautiful idealisms, Shelley acknowledges; the way to the masses is through the sad realities that will make them know themselves—"Cenci," he claimed, "is written for the multitude,"[42] "partly to please those whom my other writings displeased."[43] The distinction between Shelley's two kinds of poetry is like that drawn by the ancient allegorists, who addressed the masses at the moral level but only the initiates at the mystical.

Consequently, although Shelley has told us in the Preface what his own conception of the moral truth is and how Beatrice *should* have responded to tyrannical atrocity, his own opinions are not to be read into the drama any more than they are into *A Refutation of Deism, Alastor,* or *Julian and Maddalo*. If the purpose of *The Cenci* is self-knowledge through the operation of sympathies and antipathies, its end is a creative moral insight by the audience, an insight to which the play can only provoke and guide the audience by a true representation of human nature and its experiences. "I have endeavoured as nearly as possible," Shelley carefully explains, "to represent the characters as they probably were, and have sought to avoid the error of making them actuated by my own conceptions of right or wrong, false or true: thus under a thin veil converting names and actions of the sixteenth century into cold impersonations of my own mind." In his *Defence of Poetry*, Shelley was similarly to write:

The great instrument of moral good is the imagination; and poetry administers to the effect by acting upon the cause. . . . A Poet therefore would do ill to embody his own conceptions of right and wrong, which are usually those of his place and time, in his poetical creations, which participate in neither. By this assumption of the inferior office of interpreting the [moral] effect, in which perhaps after all he might acquit himself but imperfectly, he would resign the glory in a participation in the cause.[44]

Across the manuscript page on which this occurs he wrote that this had been "Mr. Shelley's error in the Revolt of Islam. He has attempted to cure himself in subsequent publications but, except in the tragedy of the Cenci, with little effect."[45] Obviously he was unwavering in his view that *The Cenci* has a special mode of existence, and he meant it sincerely when he wrote Hunt that "it is nothing which by any courtesy of language can be termed either moral or immoral,"[46] since his intent is not that it expound a moral doctrine but that it act on the audience as the amoral cause of a moral and virtue-making discovery. If we can properly

[42] To Charles Ollier, 6 March 1820 (*Letters*, II, 174).
[43] To Hunt, 26 May 1820 (*Letters*, II, 200). In addition to *Julian and Maddalo*, Shelley planned three other poems "drawn from dreadful or beautiful realities" (to Ollier, 15 December 1819 [*Letters*, II, 164]).
[44] Julian, VII, 118.
[45] MS e. 20, fol. 13ᵛ.
[46] To Hunt, c. 20 August 1819 (*Letters*, II, 112).

define what Shelley called the "totally different character" of *The Cenci*,[47] we should have the key to the crux of the play, that is, the means of determining the significance of our invariably mixed and uneasy response to Beatrice.

How tragedy directs the spectator to self-knowledge and self-respect, as opposed to the self-contempt that would have been Beatrice's had she willfully consented to be enslaved to evil, Shelley would later try to explain in his analysis of Greek tragedy:

The tragedies of the Athenian poets are as mirrors in which the spectator beholds himself, under a thin disguise of circumstance, stript of all but that ideal perfection and energy which every one feels to be the internal type of all that he loves, admires, and would become. The imagination is enlarged by a sympathy with pains and passions so mighty, that they distend in their conception the capacity of that by which they are conceived; the good affections are strengthened by pity, indignation, terror and sorrow; and an exalted calm is prolonged from the satiety of this high exercise of them into the tumult of familiar life: even crime is disarmed of half its horror and all its contagion by being represented as the fatal consequence of the unfathomable agencies of nature; error is thus divested of its wilfulness; men can no longer cherish it as the creation of their choice. In a drama of the highest order there is little food for censure or hatred; it teaches rather self-knowledge and self-respect. Neither the eye nor the mind can see itself, unless reflected upon that which it resembles.[48]

But although this account of evil and the will is central in Shelley's ethics, it is hardly self-explanatory, and a key speech by Orsino about the Cenci family might seem to imply, on the contrary, that self-knowledge is the source of moral error:

> . . . 'tis a trick of this same family
> To analyse their own and other minds.
> Such *self-anatomy* shall teach the will
> Dangerous secrets: for it tempts our powers,
> Knowing what must be thought, and may be done,
> Into the depth of darkest purposes:
> So Cenci fell into the pit; even I,
> Since Beatrice unveiled me to myself,
> And made me shrink from what I cannot shun,
> Show a poor figure to my own esteem,
> To which I grow half reconciled.   (II. ii. 108–18; itals. added)

If these are not inconsistent statements, they must both derive from some fundamental ethical doctrine that needs clarification if we are to understand how "self-knowledge" leads to virtue and "self-anatomy" to evil.

---

[47] To Medwin, 20 July 1820 (*Letters*, II, 219).
[48] *Defence of Poetry* (Julian, VII, 121).

Perhaps the most explicit expression of Shelley's interpretation of *nosce teipsum*, which a long classical and Christian tradition declared to be the first and greatest moral duty, appears in Cythna's sermon to the sailors in the tyrant's employ in *The Revolt of Islam*. Cythna urges them to recognize that their past sins cannot affect their radical nature and require neither remorse nor expiation:

Speak! Are your hands in slaughter's sanguine hue
Stained freshly? have your hearts in guile grown old?
Know yourselves thus! ye shall be pure as dew. . . .

Disguise it not—we have one human heart—
All mortal thoughts confess a common home:
Blush not for what may to thyself impart
Stains of inevitable crime: the doom
Is this, which has, or may, or must become
Thine, and all humankind's.[49]

No self is inherently different from another. We are born neither saint nor sinner, but, like Maddalo's daughter, "blithe, innocent and free." For Shelley, as for such Lockean empiricists as Godwin, the human character is morally neutral.[50] But Shelley is not only rejecting the doctrine of original sin and the division into the elect and the damned, he is also denying that by an act one may radically transform his innate moral nature. Animated by the "subtle, pure, and inmost spirit of life" (III. i. 23), man has only the potentiality for either moral or immoral actions. He may commit wrongs, but nothing in his character obliges him to do so, nor does such a deed stamp itself on the soul ineradicably. This would seem to confirm Mary's facile statement that Shelley believed that "evil is not inherent in the system of creation, but an accident that might be expelled" and that "mankind had only to will that there should be no evil, and there would be none."[51] Yet, without falsifying, she vastly oversimplified his position, and "only" and "none" reduce to a naive optimism

---

[49] *The Revolt of Islam*, 3357–66; itals. added. The MS (e. 10, p. 113) is somewhat clearer: ". . . it is the doom / Which has been, or may be, or must become / . . . ."
[50] Godwin, *Political Justice*, III, p. 141: ". . . we are neither virtuous nor vicious as we first come into existence." Cf. Mary Wollstonecraft, *An Historical and Moral View of the Origin and Progress of the French Revolution* (London, 1794), pp. 17–18: "We must get entirely clear of all the notions drawn from the wild traditions of original sin . . . on which priests have erected their tremendous structures of imposition, to persuade us, that we are naturally inclined to evil. . . . One principle of action is sufficient—Respect thyself—whether it be termed fear of God—religion; love of justice—morality; or, self-love—the desire of happiness." Her doctrine, together with the terms in which she expresses it, is especially relevant to the close of Shelley's *Hymn to Intellectual Beauty*.
[51] Note to *Prometheus Unbound* (Julian, II, 269).

the heavy and difficult responsibility he actually assigned to the will and the gravity with which he viewed the ever-present dynamic threat of evil. Indeed, Shelley explicitly feared that a too simplistic and optimistic doctrine, such as Mary seems to imply, would not banish evil but would leave man exposed to it: "If the [French] Revolution had been in every respect prosperous, then misrule and superstition would lose half their claims to our abhorrence, as fetters which the captive can unlock with the slightest motion of his fingers, and which do not eat with poisonous rust into the soul."[52] What we require at this point is a full understanding of Shelley's special conception of the origin and nature of evil that he developed as an extension and sophistication of Godwin's.

From the fact that man is not innately evil it does not follow for Shelley that he is innately good; rather, he is continuously *capable* of evil. This openness to wrong Shelley conceived of as a constitutional imperfection, which explains, for example, the delight in tragic drama:

... from an inexplicable defect of harmony in the constitution of human nature, the pain of the inferior is frequently connected with the pleasures of the superior portions of our being. Sorrow, terror, anguish, despair itself, are often the chosen expressions of an approximation to the highest good. Our sympathy in tragic fiction depends on this principle; tragedy delights by affording a shadow of the pleasure which exists in pain.[53]

But by a similar token man is also potentially good:

Not that this highest species of pleasure is necessarily linked with pain. The delight of love and friendship, the ecstasy of the admiration of nature, the joy of the perception and still more of the creation of poetry is often wholly unalloyed.[54]

The defect makes evil possible, not inevitable; it is a necessary but not a sufficient cause. We are therefore to accept Count Cenci as correct in his analysis of human nature:

All men delight in sensual luxury,
All men enjoy revenge; and most exult
Over the tortures they can never feel—
Flattering their secret peace with others' pain.[55]   (I. i. 77–80)

---

[52] *The Revolt of Islam*, Preface.
[53] *Defence of Poetry* (Julian, VII, 132–33).
[54] *Ibid.*
[55] *Speculations on Morals* (Julian, VII, 73): "The immediate emotions of [Man's] nature, especially in its most inartificial state, prompt him to inflict pain, and to arrogate dominion. He desires to heap superfluities to his own store, although others perish with famine. He is propelled to guard against the smallest invasion of his own liberty, though he reduces others to a condition of the most pitiless servitude. He is revengeful, proud and selfish." It is important to note that Shelley is describing man's natural emotions that, if yielded to, result in evil, not man's evil nature.

These delights, like the tragic pleasure in sorrow, terror, anguish, and despair, are among the flaws in the human constitution that leave it open to evil, which, as Mary wrote, has its origin outside "the system of creation." Since all human hearts naturally find pleasure in these experiences, as Cythna explains to the sailors, capacities for such pleasures are not marks of the individual's innate and shameful evil. True, they "*may* to thyself impart / Stains of inevitable crime"—that is, stains which then, by the necessary law of cause and effect, must result in crime—but only if a failure of will allows those delights to act as motives to action.

Correspondingly, in Shelley's moral anatomy the will is neither innately good nor innately corrupt, nor is it even defective; but it may be weak. Before writing that man's thoughts "may" impart stains of "inevitable crime," Shelley wrote, "Stains of unwilling crime,"[56] that is, unwilled and therefore originating elsewhere than in the will. According to this construction, then, man can neither will evil nor generate it in himself; the imperfection of his organization makes him available to its persistent and pressing potentiality, which becomes actual if his will is too weak or misguided to suppress it. He may thus become a link in a causal chain of evil because his mistake of judgment has made possible the continuation of the sequence. As Godwin wrote, men "never choose evil as apprehended to be evil," and "vice is nothing more than error and mistake reduced into practice, and adopted as the principle of our conduct."[57] Hence Shelley's statement that through proper tragic representation "error is thus divested of its wilfulness; men can no longer cherish it as the creation of their choice." Men choose evil by unwilling mistake, but the choice does not create the evil.

Instead, crime is "the fatal consequence of the unfathomable agencies of nature," of some unknowable ultimate cause that men have made a fictitious instrument of tyranny by anthropomorphizing it with such names as "Devil" or "Demon." In Mary's terms, evil is not an essence but an "accident" of the system of creation and therefore can be expelled; although it is always a real and existent potentiality, they are deluded, Mary added, who consider "evil a *necessary* portion of humanity."[58] Denial that man's will is the source of evil accords with Shelley's Manichaean conviction, fully outlined in Canto I of The Revolt of Islam, that there is an ultimate cause of evil outside the human mind, as there is also an ultimate and independent transcendent source of good; and his skepticism and his repudiation of all theologies compel him to insist that those ultimate sources are unknowable to man. Proposing, for example, in a note to Hellas (197n.) that man will advance to "a progressive state of more or less exalted existence," he commented,

[56] MS e. 10, p. 113.
[57] Godwin, Political Justice, III, p. 247.
[58] Note to Prometheus Unbound (Julian, II, 269); itals. added.

Let it not be supposed that I mean to dogmatise upon a subject, concerning which all men are equally ignorant, or that I think the Gordian knot of the origin of evil can be disentangled by that or any similar assertions. The received hypothesis of a Being resembling men in the moral attributes of His nature, having called us out of non-existence, and after inflicting on us the misery of the commission of error, should superadd that of the punishment and the privations consequent upon it, still would remain inexplicable and incredible. That there is a true solution of the riddle, and that in our present state that solution is unattainable by us, are propositions which may be regarded as equally certain.

There are, then, three factors in Shelley's conception of evil: its unknowable ultimate cause outside the "system of creation"; a flaw in man's constitution through which it may enter; and the will, which, because of its weakness or through an error of judgment, may fail to maintain its guard over that flaw. To these must be added the physical and moral Necessitarianism that Shelley shared with Godwin, whereby motive is to moral action as what we call cause is to physical effect, and whereby motive and cause are succeeded by their *necessary* and determined consequences. The will has no capricious, arbitrary freedom; once a motive is allowed, its invariable result will follow. "The word liberty, as applied to mind, is analogous to the word chance, as applied to matter: they spring from an ignorance of the certainty of the conjunction of antecedents and consequents."[59] Evil enters the flaw in the human character whenever the conditions are proper, and it proceeds by as fixed a law as that whereby the potentiality in poison, a natural evil, kills when it is made actual. It is for this reason that man cannot blame himself for those thoughts which may, but need not, impart crime, any more than the possessor of poison can be blamed for its power to kill. It is, regrettably, natural to enjoy revenge; it is a moral error, and therefore evil, to accede to that pleasure by taking revenge against a wrong, just as it is suicidal to drink poison. In brief, Shelley conceives of moral evil as one thinks of physical cause and effect, action and reaction: if one allows himself to receive an evil effect, it will become in turn an evil motive for a further evil consequence.[60] This, for example, Shelley understood to be the theme of Mary's *Frankenstein*, a work intelligible only to those "accustomed to reason deeply" on the "origin and tendency" of human feelings. The Monster's "crimes and malevolence" are not

the offspring of any unaccountable propensity to evil, but flow irresistibly from certain causes fully adequate to their production. They are the children, as it were, of Necessity and Human Nature. . . . Treat a person ill, and he will become wicked. Requite affection with scorn;—let one being be selected, for whatever cause, as the refuse of his kind—divide him, a social being, from

[59] *Queen Mab*, VI. 198n. This long note is Shelley's fullest essay on Necessity.
[60] Cf. ". . . . ill must come of ill" (I. iii. 151).

society, and you impose upon him the irresistible obligations—malevolence and
selfishness. It is thus that, too often in society, those who are best qualified to
be its benefactors and its ornaments are branded by some accident with scorn,
and changed, by neglect and solitude of heart, into a scourge and a curse.[61]

The explanation might equally well have been applied by Shelley to his
histories of Maddalo and the Maniac, for the moral assumptions underlying his poem and his wife's novel are essentially the same. That malevolence and selfishness are the "irresistible obligations" of being scorned
does not, however, mean in the larger context of Shelley's ethics that the
consequences of these irresistible responses cannot be shunned; they follow
ineluctably from their cause, but the will can prevent their becoming
causal in turn. "Men, having been injured," Shelley wrote, "desire to
injure in return. This is falsely called an universal law of human nature;
it is a law from which many are exempt, and all in proportion to their
virtue and cultivation."[62] This does not deny it is a "law"—that is, when
considered in itself and independently of all other factors, a necessary
causal sequence resulting from our defective constitution. It only denies
that we need participate in the sequence if our will exempts us from it.
In terms of Orsino's speech, revenge for wrong is "what *must* be thought
and *may* be done"—but it *need* not be done.

The moral function of the will, it follows, is not the doing of good—
Shelley will assign to the imagination the apprehension of the good and
the transmission of the impulse to act upon it, and the moral purpose of
Prometheus Unbound will be based upon that doctrine. Rather, the whole
duty of the will is to shun evil, to exert the moral effort of refusing to be
a link in its otherwise inevitable chain:

. . . the dark fiend who with his iron pen
Dipped in scorn's fiery poison, makes his fame
Enduring there [in men's minds], would o'er the heads of men
Pass harmless, if they scorned to make their hearts his den.[63]

The moral problem is how and at what point to break the chain of evil.
The task of the individual cannot be to cease *doing* evil, since his evil act
will follow irresistibly from the unchecked presence in him of the sufficient cause, or, in moral terms, motive. His task must be to fend off the
effect of evil done to him because otherwise that effect will be an irresistible motive to further consequences; and impatience is to be defined as the
will's feebleness to persist in the difficult task of resisting the formation
of that motive. Count Cenci's rape of his daughter is, of course, an evil

[61] Shelley's review of *Frankenstein* (Julian, VI, 264).
[62] *Philosophical View of Reform* (Julian, VII, 55).
[63] *The Revolt of Islam*, 3375–78.

deed, but it achieves its evil effect only because Beatrice mistakenly allows herself to believe it dishonors her and demands revenge, instead of recognizing that "no person can be truly dishonoured by the act of another." The doctrine, like much else in the play, is Godwinian and echoes Falkland's rationale for refusing to duel when his honor, like Beatrice's, has, according to common opinion, been affronted:

Can that circumstance dishonour me? No: I can only be dishonoured by perpetrating an unjust action. My honour is in my own keeping, beyond the reach of all mankind. Strike! I am passive. No injury that you can inflict, shall provoke me to expose you or myself to unnecessary evil. I refuse that; but I am not therefore pusillanimous; when I refuse any danger or suffering by which the general good may be promoted, then brand me for a coward![64]

Since Shelley's ethics directs itself against one's accepting the effect of an evil deed rather than against the evil doing, he consistently inveighs more against the slave than against the tyrant, for only the slave's submission allows the tyrant to tyrannize. "How," Shelley asked, "should slaves produce any thing but tyranny—even as the seed produces the plant [?]"[65] Surely, says Asia, Jupiter, who spreads only evil, seems like a slave: "Declare / Who is his master? Is he too a slave?" And Demogorgon replies that "All spirits are enslaved which serve things evil."[66] The chain of willfully willing slaves—that is, those who paralyze their own will to resist the reception of evil—reaches back to the ultimate Master, the unfathomable cause which is "imageless" and therefore unknowable to us "in our present state." Because that unfathomable cause is outside the realm of existence, Mary was correct to report that "evil is not inherent in the system of creation, but an accident that might be expelled." Man has "only"—with the greatest exertion of his powers—to set his will as a barrier against the admission of that evil, and "there would be none." But it would nevertheless continuously press to enter into actuality.

But if, in this reversal of the temporal sequence—a reversal that directs moral energy against the motive for an act instead of against the act itself—the slave is responsible for his own tyrant, who would otherwise be impotent, what causes one to be a slave? What is the error of errors responsible for every moral mistake and for the paralysis of the will to resist? If that cause can be discovered, we shall have learned how to make the course of evil pass harmless "o'er the heads of men." Shelley's answer, which carries us to the center of his ethics, is self-contempt. Because self-contempt falsely defines human nature, it is the opposite of self-knowledge; it induces, especially through the doctrine of original sin, the delusion that evil is part of one's own soul; it dispels all hope; and it

[64] *Caleb Williams*, chap. 12.
[65] To Mary Shelley, 8 August 1821 (*Letters*, II, 325).
[66] *Prometheus Unbound*, II. iv. 108–10.

destroys the power of the will. The "self-despising" are the "slaves of Heaven,"[67] and it is through self-contempt that man "on his own high will, a willing slave," enthrones "the oppression and the oppressor." The first object hatred chooses, as Count Cenci illustrates, is not another but one's self, and Shelley's emblem of hate is the amphisbaenic snake, which, armed with the sting of self-contempt, first crushes one's own heart and then with its other end lashes out at others:

> ... Hate—that shapeless fiendly thing
> Of many names, all evil, some divine,
> Whom self-contempt arms with a mortal sting;
> Which, when the heart its snaky folds entwine
> Is wasted quite, and when it doth repine
> To gorge such bitter prey, on all beside
> It turns with ninefold rage, as with its twine
> When Amphisbaena some fair bird has tied,
> Soon o'er the putrid mass he threats on every side.[68]

Masochism precedes and begets sadism; insecurity begets aggression. Self-hatred, or the belief that one's own nature is evil, makes one the slavish, will-less recipient of evil and thus necessarily the doer of evil to others. Hence the essential importance of Count Cenci's determination that Beatrice's will, "by its own consent shall stoop as low / As that which drags it down," so that "what she most abhors / Shall have a fascination to entrap / Her loathing will." And hence, too, the equal importance of her refusal to fall to that depth. Therefore the first principle of Shelley's moral solution is, in the words of Cythna's sermon to the sailors,

> Reproach not thine own soul, but *know thyself*,
> Nor hate another's crime, nor loathe thine own.[69]

For self-reproach is self-contempt, the poison used by the "dark fiend," or unfathomable cause of evil, to include us among its effects and, thus, among its agents. Self-knowledge therefore is the opposite of self-reproach; it is the knowledge that human nature is not inherently evil, that evil is not the "creation" of the will, that it arises from a continuously potential transcendent force, and that man, flawed as he is, is always free to shun it. Consequently, in proportion as one has this self-respect, he is "wise, just, sincere, tolerant, and kind."

The "self-anatomy" of which Orsino speaks must, then, be different from the self-knowledge which the *Cenci* is designed to provoke in its

[67] *Ibid.*, I. 429.
[68] *The Revolt of Islam*, 3379–87.
[69] *Ibid.*, 3388–89; itals. added.

audience, since self-anatomy teaches the will "Dangerous secrets," informing it of what it should not know. By revealing, as Orsino says, what *must* be thought and *may* be done, it tempts our powers into "the depth of darkest purposes." Because of the defect in the human constitution, at some level of his mind man must, if incited, feel such emotions as revenge and sensuality; but self-knowledge reveals that the will, by stoically sublimating them, can prevent their entering consciousness, where they would act as irresistible motives. Self-anatomy—Shelley's substitute for the vainglorious or forbidden knowledge which is the traditional opposite of self-knowledge—teaches what may be done as a consequence of these necessary thoughts and leads to self-contempt by luring one to reconcile himself with these thoughts and hence to carry them out. Self-knowledge, then, is not introspection; it is only the true understanding of universal human nature. Self-anatomy, on the contrary, is the introversion of the individual mind in order to examine all that is deposited there by experience, and it results in the mind's becoming adjusted and reconciled to what it finds. Shelley's stoicism is in exact contradiction to all theories that psychoanalysis is cathartic.

Even early, in his more rationalistic phase, Shelley was conscious of the danger of self-anatomy that results from rationalism. Because reasoning is a critical examination of the processes of intellect, its by-product is to lay bare the mind's defects and the potentialities of the "error" of evil. Reason, therefore, paradoxically "sanctions an aberration from reason":

I admit it, or rather on some subjects I conceive it to *command* a dereliction of itself. What I mean by this, is an habitual analysis of our own thoughts; it is this habit, acquired by length of solitary labour, never then to be shaken off which induces gloom, which deprives the being thus affected of any anticipation or retrospection of happiness and leaves him eagerly in pursuit of virtue, yet (apparent paradox!) pursuing it without the weakest stimulus. It is this then against which I intended to caution you, this is the tree [of] which it is dangerous to eat, but which I have fed upon to satiety. We look around us—we find that we exist, we find ourselves reasoning upon the mystery which involves our being—we see virtue & vice, we see light & darkness, each are seperate, distinct; the line which divides them is glaringly perceptible; yet how racking it is to the soul, when enquiring into its own operations, to find that perfect virtue is very far from attainable, to find reason tainted by feeling, to see the mind when analysed exhibit a picture of irreconcileable inconsistencies, even when perhaps a moment before, it imagined that it had grasped the fleeting Phantom of virtue.[70]

Self-analysis makes available what otherwise is concealed from our consciousness; it proffers the fruit which is knowledge of evil if we eat of it. Psychic sickness is prevented by the willfull sublimation of potentially evil

[70] To Elizabeth Hitchener, 20 June 1811 (*Letters*, I, 109).

thoughts and by intentional ignorance of the subconscious, not by expression of it. What self-anatomy discovers is not merely the unimpaired organs but also the quiescent viruses that surround them and that can, by this self-anatomy, be activated to enter them. This is the kind of relationship between the subconscious and the conscious that Shelley intends when the Furies sent to break Prometheus' endurance ask the Titan:

Thou think'st we will live through thee, one by one,
Like animal life, and though we can obscure not
The soul which burns within, that we will dwell
Beside it, like a vain loud multitude
Vexing the self-content of wisest men:
That we will be dread thought beneath thy brain,
And foul desire round thine astonished heart,
And blood within thy labyrinthine veins
Crawling like agony?[71]

Or, as Beatrice describes the subliminal when she is in process of resolving on the parricide:

What is this undistinguishable mist
Of thoughts, which rise, like shadow after shadow,
Darkening each other?[72]   (III. i. 170–72)

She is aware that "worse have been conceived / Than ever there was found a heart to do" (III. i. 53–54), but she has not the will to make Prometheus' defiant reply to the taunting Furies. Conceding that the unavoidable subliminal thoughts and desires that the Furies personify do dwell *beside* his soul, *beneath* his brain, and *around* his heart without obscuring his soul, he can defy them:

Yet am I king over myself, and rule
The torturing and conflicting throngs within,
As Jove rules you when Hell grows mutinous.[73]

Shelley is in accord with modern psychotherapy in believing that verbalizing the thoughts beneath the brain draws them into the conscious mind, but he runs counter to it in holding that the consequence is the transformation of potential into actual causes of evil actions. As he wrote in *Prometheus Unbound*, thoughts unformulated by language are "senseless and shapeless"—impalpable and subliminal, or, in Beatrice's words,

71 *Prometheus Unbound*, I. 483–91.
72 See also III. i. 29–31.
73 *Ibid.*, I. 492–94.

an "undistinguishable mist." Prometheus' gift of speech to man "created" thought, that is, gave it a form so that it is evident to the conscious mind.[74] Hence Orsino goads Beatrice's brother Giacomo into internally verbalizing his thought of revenge against his father for the ills he has suffered. Were the Count, "our murderous persecutor," says Giacomo, not "shielded by a father's holy name," then "I would—."[75] But he checks the thought by refusing to put it into words. Orsino distracts by denying the sanctity and power of words; neglecting their power to form motives for deeds, he claims their efficacy is limited to the power they borrow from the deeds and agents they actually designate:

Words are but holy as the deeds they cover. . . .
A father who is all a tyrant seems,
Were the profaner for his sacred name.   (II. ii. 75, 80–81)

Therefore, "Fear not to speak your thought." But Giacomo still protests:

Ask me not what I think; the unwilling brain
Feigns often what it would not; and we trust
Imagination with such phantasies
As the tongue dares not fashion into words,
Which have no words, their horror makes them dim
To the mind's eye.—My heart denies itself
To think what you demand.   (II. ii. 82–88)

"Dim" to the mind's eye—senseless and shapeless, "undistinguishable mist / Of thoughts." But the function of language, whether spoken or tacit, is to give shape and sensory qualities to the unwilled "phantasies" and thus to translate them to the conscious mind, where they become irresistible motives.[76] But Orsino has succeeded, for Giacomo confesses that he is already suspect to himself and, implicitly recognizing conscious thought to be irresistible motive, that his thoughts are "a murderer"; and he promises, ". . . all I dare / Speak to my soul that will I trust with thee" (II. ii. 97–98). Even when he is resolved to murder his father, Giacomo,

[74] Ibid., II. iv. 72–73; IV. 416–17.
[75] Cf. Beatrice's similar conviction that "father" is a "dread name" (III. i. 144).
[76] This of course does not mean that words function only to incite evil. The opposite of the dark thoughts beneath the brain is the imagination (in a sense different from Giacomo's use of that word as the repository of phantasms); and the imagination's apprehension of the Good, True, and Beautiful must also be embodied in language. Re-interpreting the Incarnation and substituting the divinity in man for the Christianity of the characters of The Cenci, Shelley wrote in his Preface that Imagination "is as the immortal God which should assume flesh for the redemption of mortal passion. It is thus that the most remote and the most familiar imagery may alike be fit for dramatic purposes when employed in the illustration of strong feeling, which raises what is low, and levels to the apprehension that which is lofty, casting over all the shadow of its own greatness." The allusion is to Ezek. 21: 26.

conscious of the power of language to shape what must be thought into ineluctable cause, confesses that the "word parricide...haunts me like fear"; and Orsino's reply, however rational, is an intentional evasion of the psychological force of words: "It must be fear itself, for the bare word / Is hollow mockery" (III. i. 340–43).

Beatrice undergoes a similar psychological process. Immediately after her violation by her father, her step-mother begs her not to conceal from her the nature of her sufferings, but for the moment Beatrice has the will to suppress the unformed subliminal thoughts that are the inevitable response to injury:

What are the words which you would have me speak?
I, who can feign no image in my mind
Of that which has transformed me: I, whose thought
Is like a ghost shrouded and folded up
In its own formless horror: of all words,
That minister to mortal intercourse,
Which wouldst thou hear? For there is none to tell
My misery: if another ever knew
Aught like to it, she died as I will die,
And left it, as I must, without a name.   (III. i. 107–16)

With the psychoanalyst's goading questions and leading hints, however, Orsino at length guides Beatrice into verbalizing her undistinguishable mist of thoughts and so into anatomizing her inner responses to her father's deeds: "You will endure it then?"; "Should the offender live?"; "Then..." (III. i. 167, 172, 206). But language is not the only means of making the subconscious conscious. When Panthea asks Prometheus to tell of the tyrannical "strife, deceit, and fear" that rushed in and made capital of the revolutionary zeal for "Truth, Liberty, and Love," he protests, "There are two woes: / To speak and to behold."[77] Since, according to Shelley, the mind cannot see itself except as reflected by another,[78] our mirror image may give us self-knowledge—the self-knowledge the audience is to gain by seeing its own reflection in Beatrice—or, like the verbalizing of our subconscious, it may make us viciously aware of what should remain suppressed. Orsino therefore can visibly reflect Giacomo's subconscious until by that means Giamoco anatomizes himself and becomes reconciled to his dark thoughts. At length he cries out to Orsino:

                    O, had I never
Found in thy smooth and ready countenance
The mirror of my darkest thoughts; hadst thou

77 Prometheus Unbound, I. 646–54.
78 Defence of Poetry (Julian, VII, 121).

Never with hints and questions made me look
Upon the monster of my thoughts, until
It grew familiar to desire. . . .   (V. i. 19–24)

iv

Although Orsino may appear to be a negligible character or a dramatic
supernumerary, as the instigator of all the revenge against the Count he
is indispensable to the moral plot; indeed, his very lack of involvement in
the dramatic action, which has led some readers to consider him irrelevant
to the drama, actually defines the nature of his involvement in the moral
events. It is his function, while remaining disengaged from the action, to
motivate Beatrice and Giacomo by stirring them to self-anatomy. He is
therefore representative of those who would mediate between innocence
and evil, fancying it possible to compromise with evil and remain innocent
by effecting an evil act without being involved in it. To his mind evil is
not all bad, or at least not as bad as it is reported to be. He believes, for
example, that the Count's evil is exaggerated and pardonable:

Old men are testy and will have their way;
A man may stab his enemy, or his vassal,
And live a free life as to wine or women,
And with a peevish temper may return
To a dull home, and rate his wife and children;
Daughters and wives call this foul tyranny.   (I. ii. 74–79)

Sincerely in love with Beatrice, whom as a prelate he cannot marry, and
equally in love with the wealth that can be his only as long as he is in
the church, he hopes to have both by motivating Beatrice and Giacomo
to murder their father. His means, he confesses, are "devices," deceptive
schemes, that he fancies will bring the Count's family little suffering
(I. ii. 80–82), as though he were the stock Terentian comic hero determined to use deception to gain the girl of his choice without offending
his father and losing his inheritance. Possessing, as Beatrice recognizes, a
"sly, equivocating vein," he is a "casuist" in Shelley's sense of the word—
that is, one who would use evil for an end that he takes to be a good,
hoping to "take the profit" and yet "omit the sin" (II. ii. 122–23). Like
the Deist of Shelley's *Refutation*, who would reconcile Christianity and
reason, he is the opposite of the skeptic, who removes error by distinguishing irreconcilable polarities.

   As the instigator of crime, he too must peer beneath his conscious
mind, and it is the eyes of Beatrice, who shares with her family that
tendency to probing analysis, that, he finds,

> anatomize me nerve by nerve
> And lay me bare, and make me blush to see
> My hidden thoughts.   (I. ii. 85–87)

Were he able to observe Cythna's injunction to the sailors to "Blush not for what may to thyself impart / Stains of inevitable crime," he would have gained the self-knowledge that all men experience such thoughts, that they do not stain the soul, and that they may be kept hidden; but his blush is the first step toward self-contempt and self-anatomy. Thinking to tread the line between good and evil, Orsino has neither the will to "shun" what his self-anatomy reveals nor the completely evil intent that would reconcile him to it; he can only "shrink" from it in self-dislike and incite others to act. What he sees is

> a poor figure to my own esteem,
> To which I grow *half* reconciled. I'll do
> As little mischief as I can; that thought
> Shall fee the accuser conscience.   (II. ii. 116–20; itals. added)

He is conscious of the "dark fiend," or "unfathomable" agency, pressing to be released into being:

> Some unbeheld divinity doth ever,
> When dread events are near, stir up men's minds
> To black suggestions.   (II. ii. 155–57)

But instead of scorning it so that it will "pass harmless" or, on the other hand, willfully enslaving himself to it, he foolishly hopes to master it like a tyrant and use it for his own ends as an agent on others without himself becoming evil:

> he prospers best,
> Not who becomes the instrument of ill,
> But who can flatter the dark spirit, that makes
> Its empire and its prey of other hearts
> Till it become his slave . . . as I will do.   (II. ii. 157–61)

According to Shelley's ethical classification of literary genres, whereas Prometheus is the character for poetic idealism, which can be equated with "lyrical" drama, and Beatrice for realistic tragedy, Orsino is the spirit of modern comedy, a spirit Shelley considered "withering and perverting,"[79] a "monster for which the corruption of society for ever brings

---

[79] Thomas Love Peacock, *Memoirs of Percy Bysshe Shelley* in *Works*, ed. H. F. B. Brett-Smith and C. E. Jones (London, 1934), VIII, p. 81.

forth new food, which it devours in secret."[80] "I see the purpose of this comedy," he said of Sheridan's *School for Scandal*. "It is to associate virtue with bottles and glasses, and villainy with books,"[81] just as Restoration comedy, to which he particularly objected on moral grounds,[82] can be characterized by its application of vicious means to what it pretends are virtuous ends. Conceiving of the world as a stage and himself as an actor, Orsino confesses at the close of the play, when he has learned that evil means necessarily produce evil ends:

I thought to act a solemn comedy
Upon the painted scene of this new world,
And to attain my own peculiar ends
By some such plot of mingled good and ill
As others weave; but there arose a Power
Which grasped and snapped the threads of my device
And turned it to a net of ruin.   (V. i. 77–83)

One cannot enslave the tyrant evil or remain only half reconciled to the evil potentialities uncovered by self-anatomy. Orsino ends by discovering that he himself is evil's slave, unable to hide from himself and filled with contempt for what he sees within. His effort to assimilate bad to good— his "casuistry"—has failed.

Self-knowledge, self-anatomy, and casuistry are, then, related terms in Shelley's vocabulary and designate various relationships between moral purity and pernicious error, that is, between moral essence and moral accident. Tragedy can teach self-knowledge and self-respect because it is a mirror "in which the spectator beholds himself, under a thin disguise of circumstance, stript of all but that ideal perfection and energy which every one feels to be the internal type of all that he loves, admires, and would become." It acts, that is, by differentiating the disguise from the essential self. Shelley's tragedy therefore is not rooted in the flaw in character—all human constitutions are flawed—but in the "moral error," as he called it,[83] of believing the "mask" of circumstances to be essential, a "pernicious error" (which, incidentally, is an accurate translation of Aristotle's *hamartia*). Such circumstances are Giacomo's poverty, insofar as it is unendurable to him because he has been reared in luxury (II. ii. 6–17), and Beatrice's regard for her reputation because she has been taught to prize the world's opinion. The conflicting forces of Beatrice's tragedy, then, are analogous to those debated in *Julian and Maddalo*: in the poem, the perfections which the mind is impelled to conceive conflict with the

[80] *Defence of Poetry* (Julian, VII, 122).
[81] Peacock, *Memoirs of Percy Bysshe Shelley*.
[82] *Defence of Poetry* (Julian, VII, 122).
[83] To Hunt, 1 May 1820 (*Letters*, II, 190).

"falsehood," distortions, and limitations which tend to be generated in the world; in the tragedy, the native purity of the human spirit confronts the accidental evil to which the human constitution is susceptible. The works are to be read in the same way, in terms of two independent forces meeting in conflict, and the author conceals his "own conceptions of right or wrong, false or true," in order that we, readers or spectators, may know ourselves by seeing ourselves reflected in the unresolved conflict. In *Julian and Maddalo*, the two conversationalists debate opposing interpretations of the conflict without resolution; in *The Cenci*, the conflict is dramatized in Beatrice, as it was in the character of the Maniac. But in each case the moral burden of interpretation, which results in our self-knowledge, is thrust on us as readers or spectators.

Self-anatomy, on the other hand, being the admission into consciousness of the pressures toward evil, involves casuistry—that is, the fiction of reconciling evil with moral principles because of one's own peculiar circumstances on the assumption, as the casuistic aphorism runs, that "circumstances alter cases." Self-anatomy and casuistry, in other words, are one's sophistical justification for claiming wrong is not really evil and is compatible with good. Orsino's justification is that the wrong is possible and profitable and will do little harm; Beatrice's, that the evil done to her "everlasting soul" and "untainted fame" makes retaliation necessary (V. ii. 123–24). Self-anatomy and casuistry therefore operate on the same two unrelated elements as self-knowledge does—inherent purity and accidental evil—but instead of discovering they are unrelated, they seek to accommodate one to the other.

Shelley, however, conceived of "casuistry" as capable of resulting not only in the error of self-anatomy but also in the truth of self-knowledge: although one may sophistically attempt to reconcile an evil with good, the very speciousness and hypocrisy inherent in the attempt divulge its actual impossibility—and thus the absolute unrelatedness of innate purity and the incidental "garment" of evil. How the artistic management of casuistry can promote this self-knowledge Shelley suggested in a review of Godwin's *Mandeville*. He probably was conscious of some sort of parallelism between his drama of "sad reality" (rather than "dreams of what ought to be," such as *Prometheus Unbound*) and Godwin's *Caleb Williams*, the main title of which is *Things as They Are*,[84] "a study and delineation of things passing in the moral world" (and "no refined and abstract speculation," Godwin added in his Preface, no doubt referring to his *Political Justice*). Shelley might well, indeed, have thought of his

[84] The title of one of Shelley's poems in the youthful *Esdaile Notebook*, "A Tale of Society as it is, from facts," suggests that he had long conceived of the poetry of "sad reality" as a special category and, partly by rejecting the Byronic and Rousseau-istic literature of "transcription," had gradually developed his idea of its proper function.

play as repairing the moral inadequacies of Godwin's theme by extending it to its fullest limits. For the Falkland of Godwin's novel, which Godwin also directed toward "the modes of domestic ... despotism, by which man becomes the destroyer of man," is portrayed as an impressively noble character who, like Beatrice Cenci, was led into revenge by proud and impatient desire to preserve his own and his family's honor, which he mistakenly thought damaged by another; and to the very end the novel insists that we admire Falkland's nature. Shelley adjusted to his own terminology the ethics he shares with Godwin by inventing the concept of "sublime casuistry." The author of *Caleb Williams*, he wrote,

with that *sublime casuistry* which is the parent of toleration and forbearance, persuades us personally to love [Falkland], whilst his actions must for ever remain the theme of our astonishment and abhorrence.... [The errors] of Falkland arose from a high, though perverted conception of the majesty of human nature, from a powerful sympathy with his species, and from a temper which led him to believe that the very reputation of excellence should walk among mankind, unquestioned and undefiled.[85]

The roots of Shelley's distinctions are to be found as far back as his *Refutation of Deism*, the overt purpose of which is to demonstrate what he could now call the "pernicious casuistry" of the Deist, who sought to reconcile religion with reason. The function of Shelley's "sublime casuistry" there was to reveal that Christian fideism and atheistic reason are polar opposites, contradicting each other and sharing no common ground. But his objective in the *Refutation*—and in the succeeding poems that have been examined—was skeptical and inconclusive: the nearest approach to truth lies in the recognition of the polarized elements of man's nature, faith and reason, the desires for earthly utopia and for transcendent perfection, his participation in nature and in divinity. The purpose of the skeptical way of proceeding is both to prevent the error of casuistry by revealing that the antinomies are irreconcilable and to prevent dogmatism by showing that neither alternative is necessarily preferable or more defensible than the other. In *The Cenci*, however, Shelley has transformed his skeptical and open-ended method into positive moral analysis. The skeptical way of proceeding to a clarifying dilemma that leaves open mutually exclusive choices has become the sublime casuistry that reveals that a dilemma may be only an apparent mutual exclusion. Inherent purity of character can coexist with moral error; and, since sublime casuistry reveals that error cannot be reconciled with the purity, that purity is unaltered by the error.

Pernicious casuistry, operating on self-anatomy, reconciles one to the commission of error by persuading that the error is justified; sublime

---

[85] Review (1817) of Godwin's *Mandeville* (Julian, VI, 220); itals. added.

casuistry, by displaying the feebleness of such sophistry and leaving error unrelated to innate purity, leads the observer to that self-knowledge which is the end of tragedy. Consequently, Shelley's tragic heroine must not only engage in *pernicious* casuistry but be painted by the artist with *sublime* casuistry. What especially impressed Shelley about Beatrice Cenci's history was that, even two centuries after her death, those who heard it "never failed to incline to a romantic pity for the wrongs, and a passionate exculpation of the horrible deed to which they urged her."[86] Some paradoxical bent of mind makes men struggle to excuse an act morally repugnant to them, for they wish to believe that circumstances alter cases. Insofar as the struggle succeeds it results in self-anatomy, and hence the danger in contemplating Satan:

The character of Satan engenders in the mind a *pernicious casuistry* which leads us to weigh his faults with his wrongs, and to excuse the former because the latter exceed all measure. In the minds of those who consider that magnificent fiction with a religious feeling it engenders something worse.[87]

It is this provocation to casuistry that, for Shelley, defines Satan as potentially a "tragic" character, as opposed to the "more poetical character" of Prometheus; and the same customary response to the historical Beatrice Cenci endows her with the same tragic possibility:

It is in the restless and *anatomizing casuistry* with which men seek the justification of Beatrice, yet feel that she has done what needs justification; it is in the superstitious horror with which they contemplate alike her wrongs and their revenge, that the dramatic character of what she did and suffered, consists.[88]

This analysis more clearly reveals the opportunity for the dramatist's sublime casuistry, for it lays bare the normally unresolved conflict in the response to the historical Beatrice—the desire to exonerate her and the nagging knowledge that her deed is really indefensibly wrong, comparable to our admiration of Godwin's Falkland and our abhorrence of his actions.

The persistent difficulty that we as readers and spectators have had in interpreting Beatrice's character is evidence that Shelley has accurately analyzed our minds since critics have continuously oscillated between exonerating his heroine because of her noble bearing and intolerably horrible circumstances, and being repelled by her plotting her father's murder, her thin and cheap lies, and her ignoble effort to shift all blame for the murder onto her hirelings at the end of the play—just as the critical tradition has been to debate uneasily the precise conclusion to be

---

[86] *The Cenci*, Preface.
[87] *Prometheus Unbound*, Preface; itals. added.
[88] *The Cenci*, Preface; itals. added.

drawn from *Julian and Maddalo*. Some critics, seeking an unambiguous moral interpretation, have fallen victim to what Shelley would certainly have considered pernicious casuistry. Newman I. White, for example, resorted to criticism's traditional escape clause, that Shelley seldom could remain consistent with his own purposes:

Shelley is so sympathetic with his heroine that he can scarcely tolerate his own notion of revenge as a part of her character. Her real motive for the murder is self-protection and an almost religious mission to rid her family and the world of a dangerous monster. It is only by a narrow margin that she escapes the dramatic fault of being a flawless character.[89]

On the other hand, Carlos Baker has interpreted Shelley's intention as "to display the perhaps inevitable corruption of human saintliness by the conspiracy of social circumstances and the continued operation of a vindictive tyranny."[90] And Benjamin Kurtz, unable (as Shelley would have hoped) to reconcile Beatrice's "high arguments" with her "disingenuousness," places the blame on clumsy Shelley's "imperfect craftsmanship that failed to realize the inconsistency."[91] That we have been baffled in our efforts to make such simplistic evaluations of Beatrice is not, as has been frequently concluded, Shelley's failure or even his own confusion of objective, but the actual fulfillment of his goal. The inadequacy of all our critical impulses either to exculpate or to condemn her is evidence that Shelley's sublime casuistry has created a situation that both excites our "pernicious casuistry" and thwarts its satisfactory completion so that the dramatically activated moral ambiguity—the impossibility of ignoring or explaining away either Beatrice's faults or her noble character—may, by engendering our internal debate, cause us to know ourselves.

We tend to assume that as an audience we are to sit in judgment of Beatrice, the character on the stage before us. We are indeed, but if we engage ourselves in the world of the play we shall find it has denied us any satisfactory judgment. We, the audience, are implicated when Orsino,

---

[89] *Shelley*, II, p. 139.
[90] *Shelley's Major Poetry*, pp. 147–48.
[91] *The Pursuit of Death* (New York, 1933), p. 198. I quote these critics only to illustrate the characteristic critical uneasiness in attempts to arrive at unambiguous interpretations of Beatrice. Robert F. Whitman has adequately summarized the history of frustrated efforts at pernicious casuistry. "Most of the confusion which seems characteristic of responses to *The Cenci* centers on the figure of Beatrice, and springs from a question as to exactly how her character and role in the play are to be understood." The majority "view Beatrice as 'all but perfect,' a gentle, sensitive, generous girl, who is goaded into a single act of justifiable homicide by the brutal sadism of her monomaniac father." On the other hand, "it is difficult to reconcile a noble and upright nature with her fanatical need for self-justification after the murder of the Count..." ("Beatrice's 'Pernicious Mistake' in *The Cenci*," *PMLA*, 74 [1959], 249).

continuing a theatrical metaphor, plans to put on the disguise and mask of false innocence and pass "through the misdeeming crowd / Which judges by what seems" (V. i. 87–88); and surely we are the indirect objects of the bitter irony in Beatrice's address to the judge when her stepmother faints on hearing the accusation:

She knows not yet the uses of the world. . . .
She cannot know how well the supine slaves
Of blind authority read the truth of things
When written on a brow of guilelessness:
She sees not yet triumphant Innocence
Stand at the judgement-seat of mortal man, ,
A judge and an accuser of the wrong
Which drags it there.   (IV. iv. 177, 181–87)

As judges presiding over Beatrice's case we are to be baffled, for Shelley consistently conceived of tragedy not as a case to be tried but as a mirror in which we are made unwittingly to see and understand ourselves, since "Neither the eye nor the mind can see itself unless reflected upon that which it resembles." The principle whereby Giacomo and Orsino anatomize themselves on the stage by seeing themselves reflected in others is the same principle whereby the audience is to know itself by seeing itself reflected in Beatrice, whose ambivalence results from its frustrated effort to pass judgment on her. In his Preface Shelley defined Beatrice's tragic character not in terms of the conflict she experiences but in terms of the irresolvable conflict of sympathy and antipathy she produces in the audience. We are the ultimate objectives of The Cenci, and it is our own character that ultimately is under our scrutiny, as though we were both actors and audience. To paraphrase Shelley's account of the function of the Maniac in Julian and Maddalo, Beatrice's tortured expressions of her moral dualism are a sufficient commentary on the text of every heart in the audience—and that is the text we are actually reading.

As objective interpreters aware of Shelley's doctrines, and even as readers of the Preface that accompanies the published play, we are conscious of the moral matrix of the drama, but that is a factor in the authorial mind, not an operative element in our experience of the play: "a drama is no fit place for the enforcement of [dogmas]."[92] What, then, does the spectator learn about his own nature as a result of his struggle to understand a character engaged in pernicious casuistry in a play that does not express the author's conception of "right or wrong, true or false"? How does the spectator see his own nature by looking at Beatrice?

Shelley went to considerable pains to encourage our belief in the

92 The Cenci, Preface.

purity of Beatrice's character and was almost as insistent as Godwin was on Falkland's noble, nearly saintly nature, in spite of his vicious deeds. If there is a serious weakness in the play it is not Beatrice's ambiguity but the fact that we have to accept her purity on the testimony of other characters and with little dramatic evidence. The first thing we learn of her is, in the Cardinal's words to Count Cenci, her gentleness and her

> sweet looks, which make all things else
> Beauteous and glad, [and] might kill the fiend within you.   (I. i. 44–45)

The height of her nobility of character is her having stood as a firm bulwark between her father's hate and the others of her family. Even she, though confused by "opinion," knows at heart that her father's act leaves her guiltless: "What have I done?" she asks. "Am I not innocent? Is it my crime...?" (III. i. 69–70). Her error lies not in holding to this point but, inconsistently, in believing that the pollution of her flesh has poisoned the "subtle, pure, and inmost spirit of life" (III. i. 22–23), which, though the crime is not hers, can be cleansed, she thinks, only by the Count's death, the "punishment of crime" (III. i. 125–26). Before the murder her purity is repeatedly testified to. In her step-mother's mind, she deserves

> The peace of innocence;
> Till in your season you be called to heaven.
> Whate'er you may have suffered, you have done
> No evil.   (III. i. 119–22)

To her brother she is of such gentleness that she never trod on worm or flower without pitying it and is one "in whom / Men wondered how such loveliness and wisdom / Did not destroy each other" (III. i. 366–71). Ever her father is forced reluctantly to acknowledge her perfection and hates her for it:

> if her bright loveliness
> Was kindled to illumine this dark world;
> If nursed by Thy [God's] selectest dew of love
> Such virtues blossom in her as should make
> The peace of life....   (IV. i. 121–25)

Beatrice's own claims to innocence, although founded in part on her belief that she has been the agent of God, are also too insistent, ring too sincere, and are too consistently admitted by others to be passed off as mere casuistry. "I would pledge my soul," says the Cardinal presiding over her trial, "That she is guiltless"; "She is as pure as speechless infancy!" (V. ii. 61–62, 69). She herself warns her accusers:

                                        If thou hopest
Mercy in heaven, show justice upon earth:
Worse than a bloody hand is a hard heart.
If thou hast done murders, made thy life's path
Over the trampled laws of God and Man,
Rush not before thy Judge, and say: 'My maker,
I have done this and more; for there was one
Who was most pure and innocent on earth;
And because she endured what never any
Guilty or innocent endured before:
Because her wrongs could not be told, not thought;
Because thy [i.e. God's] hand at length did rescue her;
I with my words killed her and all her kin.'   (V. ii. 131–43)

She is, she declares,

All that which shows like innocence, and is,
Hear me, great God! I swear, most innocent. . . .[93] (V. ii. 151–52)

It is impossible to take such resolute statements as merely hardened lies
or even as casuistry, much less as self-deception, for they are spoken with
the sincerity of conviction and truth. Nor are we able to believe her
brother deceived or to be referring only to Beatrice before the murder
when at the end of the play he calls her "the one thing innocent and
pure" (V. iii. 101), or when another brother laments,

                                        To see
That perfect mirror of pure innocence
Wherein I gazed, and grew happy and good,
Shivered to dust! To see thee, Beatrice,
Who made all lovely thou didst look upon. . . .
Thee, light of life . . . dead, dark!   (V. iv. 129–34)

Despite her deeds, we are to see Beatrice not only as sincerely convinced
of her innocence but as indeed innocent in some fundamental sense, even
though she herself is incapable of understanding the reason as she searches
about for justification. The actual murderer of the Count undertook his
deed from hate and contempt for man's spirit (III. i. 234) and for gold;
his crime, therefore, was an act of will whereby he willfully enslaved
himself to evil, not an act designed to resist that enslavement. Confronted
at the trial by Beatrice's "stern yet piteous look" and her insistence on her
innocence, there is wrung from him what he himself calls "a higher

---

[93] Similarly, IV. iv. 159–60: "Our innocence is as an armed heel / To trample
accusation."

truth": "She is most innocent! . . . I will not give you that fine piece of
nature / To rend and ruin" (V. ii. 164–68). The lesser truth is that she
is guilty of wrongs she has *necessarily* been led to once she has permitted
the subliminal impulse to enter her conscious mind; the "higher" truth is
that her essential nature is innocent. As Shelley puts it in the Preface to
the play, the "necessity" consequent upon her error of acceding to "circumstances" and "opinions" has "violently thwarted" her "from her
nature." Her moral nature has not been corrupted by her acts; she has
been "thwarted"—turned aside—from it, but it persists. We misread if
we believe it a sign of her corruption that after the crime she can say,
"The spirit which doth reign within these limbs / Seems strangely un-
disturbed" (IV. iii. 63–64).

On the other hand, the crime itself, her casuistic efforts to justify herself, her equivocations (that she did not murder her father), her callous
cruelty in accusing the murderer she had hired, and her direct lies (the
denial that she had ever seen the hired murderer or that she had even
planned the crime) make her repellent; and her brother's anguished
remorse for the crime (V. i) functions to contrast with her confidence in
her purity. Yet, all this cannot blot out the impression made by the continuous and earnest insistence on her innocence. However closely her
innocence and wrongs are brought together, they refuse to accommodate
themselves to each other. Should some telling evidence be brought against
us, Beatrice says after the murder,

> we can blind
> Suspicion with such cheap astonishment,
> Or overbear it with such guiltless pride,
> As murderers cannot feign.   (IV. iv. 43–46)

Paradoxically, although she is convinced she is guiltless, she is conscious
that there is something that needs to be hidden by deception; and we
can deny neither her innocence nor her wrongs, nor can we reconcile the
two. In brief, Beatrice's "pernicious casuistry" is to us, as Orsino's is to
himself, a self-defeating failure; and our rejection of it, while we cannot
refuse the insistent claim of innocence or fail to be repelled by her patent
lies and deceptions, is the result of Shelley's "sublime casuistry," which
"persuades us personally to love [her], while [her] actions must forever
remain the theme of our astonishment and abhorrence." It is this kind of
casuistry which "is the parent of toleration and forbearance," for it teaches
us that evil is, though very real and persistently threatening, an "accident"
of human nature, not its essence, and that it can be overcome by willful
patience and endurance.

Only at the very end of the drama does Beatrice, about to be led
to execution, have a flash of insight into the moral truth (or it may be

Shelley whispering from the wings, despite his disclaimer) as she exhorts
her brother to "Err not in harsh despair," but to resort to "tears and
patience," the patience she lacked when, in weakness, she resolved on her
"speedy act" (V. iii. 114).[94] Have faith, she adds,

> that I,
> Though wrapped in a strange cloud of crime and shame,
> Lived ever holy and unstained.   (V. iv. 147–49)

The metaphor of the enwrapping cloud of crime comes from the heart of
Shelley's ethics. Beatrice means only to attack her accusers' dependence
upon appearances, but, ironically, she speaks a greater truth than she
intends when she says,

> O white innocence,
> That thou shouldst wear the mask of guilt to hide
> Thine awful and serenest countenance
> From those who know thee not![95]   (V. iii. 24–27)

For Shelley would have us learn for ourselves that the "crimes and
miseries in which she was an actor and a sufferer are as the *mask* and
the *mantle* in which circumstances clothed her for her impersonation on
the scene of the world."[96] A poet, Shelley wrote in his *Defence of Poetry*,
"considers the vices of his contemporaries as the temporary dress in which
his creations must be arrayed, and which cover without concealing the
eternal proportions of their beauty," and an "epic or dramatic personage"
wears those vices "around his soul, as he may the antient armour or the
modern uniform around his body; whilst it is easy to conceive a dress
more graceful than either."[97] But to show that evil is both hideous and
yet only a mask or mantle is also the function of tragedy, in which we
see as in a reflection our own ideal perfection "under a thin disguise of
circumstance" so that "crime is disarmed of half its horror and all its
contagion by being represented as the fatal consequence of the unfathomable agencies of nature; error is thus divested of its willfullness; men can
no longer cherish it as the creation of their choice."

[94] Her stepmother has also learned stoic patience at last: V. iii. 108–9.
[95] The opposite of this is play-acting Orsino, who, aware now of his self-corrupted
nature, would adopt for the world-audience that "judges by what seems" a deceptive
mask over "that within, / Which must remain unaltered," knowing well he can
never find "the disguise to hide me from myself" (V. i. 85–104).
[96] *The Cenci*, Preface; itals. added.
[97] *Defence of Poetry* (Julian, VII, 117). Cf. *ibid.* (p. 129): "The distorted notions
of invisible things which Dante and his rival Milton have idealised, are merely the
mask and the mantle in which these great poets walk through eternity enveloped
and disguised." For another characteristic instance of Shelley's representation of
wrong thought or action as but a mask over man's pure spirit, see *Prometheus Unbound*, III. iv. 44, 193.

v

Mary Shelley rejoiced that her husband had been persuaded to undertake the "sad reality" of the Cenci story and was convinced that his true genius lay not in "metaphysical" and "ideal" poetry like that of *Prometheus Unbound* but in "the delineations of human passion," even though "the bent of his mind went the other way":

> even when employed on subjects whose interest depended on character and incident, he would start off in another direction, and leave the delineations of human passion, which he could depict in so able a manner, for fantastic creations of his fancy, or the expression of those opinions and sentiments with regard to human nature and its destiny; a desire to diffuse which, was the master passion of his soul.[98]

Her categorical distinctions are sound, but they meander around the central fact that the stuff of his tragedy of reality is drawn from the underside of his idealisms and that, however historically real and specifically human its characters, passions, and incidents, they are the particularized foci of an assumed dimension as embracing as that of *Prometheus Unbound*. Nor does she take into consideration how dependent Shelley's "poetic idealisms" are upon his giving vent to his basic skepticism and assuring himself of man's moral capabilities in the realm of sad reality. Unlike such skeptical poems as the hymns of Pan and Apollo and *Julian and Maddalo*, *Prometheus Unbound* has an air of nearly unqualified optimism and lays down a dramatic pattern of patient endurance, forgiveness, and love whereby mankind may release the forces that will restore the utopian world. It is his hopeful substitute for the French Revolution that had failed. But the optimism of that poem is something that Shelley purchased at considerable cost. Twice he interrupted that work of "poetic idealism" to re-examine his own grounds by writing his two works of "sad reality." He was composing Act II of *Prometheus Unbound*—the act in which all the regenerative powers are released which will later free Prometheus, destroy tyrannical Jupiter, and perfect mankind—when he paused to write the "sad reality" of *Julian and Maddalo*, an indecisive debate over whether man is doomed to the disparity between his human condition and his ideals or whether man is corrigible, as *Prometheus Unbound* assumes. The inconclusive psychomachy of *Julian and Maddalo* is waged to reassure the poet that, since he has not blinded himself to the opposing facts, the optimism of *Prometheus Unbound* is in good faith. Then, after Act III of his lyric drama and before the triumphant last act, Shelley paused again to turn his theme inside out by writing the tragedy of *The Cenci*, which is related to *Prometheus Un-*

---

[98] Mary Shelley's note to *The Cenci* (Julian, II, 158).

bound as the perspective that sees the Cloud dissolving in rain is related
to the perspective in which it basks in heaven's blue smile. Whereas
Prometheus Unbound is the poetic idealism of patient suffering, forgiveness, and love, *The Cenci* probes deeply into the roots of our actual impatience, revenge, and self-contempt—in effect, into the psychological
roots of the failure of the French Revolution. Only after having explored
the tragic actuality did Shelley then have the earned confidence to add
the final celebrative act to his drama of optimism. He has not abandoned
his fundamental skeptical frame of mind; rather, instead of exposing his
incertitude, he has internalized it in order that, on that fragile basis, he
may take a stand and break free of what he called "the indolence of
scepticism."[99] In overtly skeptical poems like *Julian and Maddalo*, he explicitly engaged the actual and the ideal in indecisive debate; although
he offered *Prometheus Unbound* and *The Cenci* as independent, self-
sustaining works with confident postures, they represent, taken together,
the antinomies of the skeptical contest as it was waged in Shelley's own
mind, and in a very real sense they should be read against each other
approximately as we read his hymns of Apollo and Pan.

[99] Quoted from a draft of *The Defence of Poetry* (Bodleian MS Shelley d. 1, fol.
77ʳ) in *Shelley's Prose in the Bodleian Manuscripts*, ed. A. H. Koszul (London,
1910), p. 68n.

Part II   Speculations on Metaphysics

4 The Intellectual Philosophy

Some poets seem graced with the art of dying, if not well, at least with words that epitomize some of the compelling forces of their careers. It is moving that Keats's insight into the character of the poetic enterprise to which he had devoted his life should appear in his last known letter as a pathetic recollection of all the concentration and organizing strength that had been demanded for "the knowledge of contrast, feeling for light and shade, all that information (primitive sense) necessary for a poem." Shelley did equally well when he wrote, "Then, what is Life?" a few lines before death interrupted his composition of *The Triumph of Life*. With skepticism and its attendant paradoxes as his instruments, he made his way in *Julian and Maddalo* and then *The Cenci* to a self-knowledge that revealed a probably secure basis for human optimism: man is morally pure in essence and is endowed with faculties for resisting the pressure of moral error. But although this is the conclusion Shelley would have us arrive at through the failure of our casuistic efforts to reconcile evil with good, it does not itself explain the nature or purpose of our existence. However inherently untainted the human spirit may be and may be maintained, that does not determine whether we should seek to lift the painted veil called life—whether we should hasten to the grave, whether we should dedicate ourselves to Apollo or Pan. The "life" in which the human spirit acts is yet to be defined and evaluated: this is the metaphysical problem Shelley was constantly compelled to face because his faith in and aspiration to a perfect

131

immortality seemed to make human life illusory and absurd and individual identity a fiction. It is also a problem for which he found no single conclusive answer, although by willfully shunting aside on occasion the disabling assumption of a transcendent perfection (as the structure of *The Revolt of Islam*, for example, shows he earnestly sought to do), he ceaselessly endeavored to define life and the world inductively in order to discover their purpose. Even granting that human life is, with respect to eternal existence, an unreality, a realm where "nothing is, but all things seem, / And we the shadows of the dream," how is life in that context to be understood and carried on? The question "What is life?" was compelling enough to call from him an essay.

In *On Life*, as Mary entitled the essay when she published it,[1] Shelley surveyed his past career as a metaphysician in order to account for his rejection of both materialism and "the shocking absurdities of the popular philosophy of mind and matter," a dualism he had repudiated by 1816, when he wrote *Mont Blanc*. The "popular philosophy"—that which most men, unthinkingly and with dulled apprehensions, are inclined to assume—threatened Shelley on theological grounds because from a Lockean dualism of mind and matter it is possible to deduce a Creator Mind that governs its creation, with "fatal consequences in morals" and a "violent dogmatism concerning the source of all things," a dogmatism Shelley's philosophic skepticism cannot tolerate. Because of his early rejection of this kind of theism, Shelley admits, he was led briefly to materialism, which denies the existence of all but matter and motion, only to find that, while it disposes of a Creator, it is incompatible with man's aspiration to immortality. If all were matter and motion, any cessation of motion would leave a vacuum, and the dissolution of man's organized body would be his total extinction; but man disclaims "alliance with transience and decay" and is "incapable of imagining to himself annihilation." Always the skeptic, Shelley is not rejecting materialism in the conviction that the immortality of the human soul is a fact.[2] His concern at

---

[1] Julian, VI, 193–97. Unless otherwise noted, all quotations in this chapter will be from this essay, but the text used will be that of the Morgan Library MS (M.A. 408) since it differs in significant ways from the published version.

[2] Cf. *Essay on the Punishment of Death* (the following is from MS e. 8, p. 25, which differs from Julian, VI, 185–86): "That that within us which thinks and feels continues to think and feel after the dissolution of the body, has been the almost universal opinion of mankind, and the accurate philosophy of what I may be permitted to term the modern Academy [i.e. skepticism], by showing the prodigious depth and extent of our ignorance respecting the causes and nature of sensation renders probable the affirmative of a proposition, the negative of which it is so difficult to conceive, and the popular arguments against which, derived from what is called the atomic system [i.e. materialism], are proved to be applicable only to the relation which one object bears to another, as apprehended by the mind, and not to the existence or essence[?] of that which [above "which" Shelley wrote, "mind"] is the medium and the receptacle of objects."

The passage is also significant in translating objective annihilation into a change in the relation of thoughts. This theme becomes the central feature of *The Sensitive Plant*.

this point is not the nature of reality in the light of absolute truth but reality as it is phenomenalistically determined, reality as our minds truly experience it, even though in the aspect of eternity that reality may be only illusory: "Whatever may be [man's] true and final destination, there is a spirit within him at enmity with nothingness and dissolution." Consequently, by confining himself to human existence and disregarding its status in the context of any possible immutable eternity, Shelley set out inductively in search of an atheistic definition of reality that would take into consideration the mind's enmity with nothingness, which neither materialism nor strict dualism can account for.

Hamlet's fate, Shelley is reported to have said, was meant to represent the tragic errors to which the profoundly philosophic mind is liable because it contemplates reality as wholly subjective, that is, as a body of ideas in the mind.[3] Very nearly the first words Hamlet speaks, "Seems, Madam! Nay, it is; I know not 'seems,'" appeared to Shelley confirmation of Hamlet's solipsism. Since reality exists only in Hamlet's mind, what "seems" to him to be is all that is. "Observe, too," Shelley continues of Hamlet—

Observe, too, when Horatio tells him of this wonderful appearance [of the ghost], how philosophical his questions are, as of a man trying to realise completely, in his own mind, the image of the thing. The mysterious contradiction between reality and ideality, one of the most profound questions of ontology, is strongly shown in the beginning of this dialogue. "My father! methinks I see my father!"—"O where, my Lord?" cries Horatio, starting in terror. "In my mind's eye, Horatio." To this subject Hamlet recurs again in the conversation with his two good friends: "There is," says he, "nothing either good or bad, but thinking makes it so." And again in another place, where Osric asks "if he knows Laertes?" he replies, "I dare not confess that, lest I should compare with him in excellence; for to know a man well were to know oneself."

Then, when the ghost has charged Hamlet with his duty, Hamlet "confuses his external body with his inner self, as if he were nothing but a spirit; and when he says that he will raze out all that he learned from experience or from thought,

'And thy commandment all alone shall live
Within the book and volume of my brain':

he takes out his real tablets and writes it down."

[3] New Monthly Magazine and Literary Journal, n.s. 29, pt. ii (1830), 327–36. This posthumously published dialogue between "Shelley" and "Byron" on the subject of Hamlet purports to have been recorded by a companion of the poets. An abbreviated version, taken from The Polar Star, 5 (1830), was reprinted in Walter E. Peck's Shelley, His Life and Work (Boston, 1927), II, pp. 421–32; and the New Monthly version has been reprinted recently in Shelley's Critical Prose, ed. Bruce R. McElderry (Lincoln, Nebraska, 1967). In "Shelley's Last Poetics: a Reconsideration" (in From Sensibility to Romanticism, ed. F. W. Hilles and H. Bloom [New York, 1967]. pp. 487–511) I have offered my reasons for believing the dialogue authentic.

Apart from whatever interest we may find in this quasi-Coleridgean reading as literary interpretation, its vague Berkeleyanism has the value of showing that Shelley held up Shakespeare's play as a mirror in which to look at his own philosophic concerns. His inclination to read *Hamlet* in terms of a special ontology hints at how crucial that problem was to him and how readily he seized on the possibility of a world constituted of ideas. For Shelley's Hamlet is Shelley himself, trying vainly to transcend the human state, which bewilderingly splits reality into subject and object, thought and thing, being and seeming, until he is persuaded that the ordinary world of the senses is illusory. His definition of the ghost of Hamlet's father as "an outward and visible sign of the sudden apparitions of the mysterious world within us" and as "a great purpose coming suddenly upon a meditative mind" (that is, as a translation of mental and spiritual states into sensible qualities) suggests the symbolic externalizing of mental acts and powers in *Prometheus Unbound*—the Furies, the Spirits of the Human Mind, Panthea's dreams, and Hercules, for example. And Shelley's interest in the confusion, exchange, and interdependence of ideal and real, subjective and objective in Hamlet—the writing on the tablets, for example—recalls his account of the poetic method of *Prometheus Unbound*, a method he claimed to find preeminently in the Greeks and Dante, but also in Shakespeare: "The imagery which I have employed will be found, in many instances, to have been drawn from the operations of the human mind, or from those external actions by which they are expressed."[4] Shelley's bias, all this suggests, is toward the possibility that the "external" is in some fashion an aspect of the mind, and many of his poems operate within the framework of his own solution of "the most profound questions of ontology" and of his resolution of the "mysterious contradiction between reality and ideality."

Is there a substantive reality independent of the mind? Or is the "external" world only the mind's perceptions? Is there a sense in which all the thoughts of the mind are real existences? On these and related questions, which he inherited from eighteenth-century British philosophy, Shelley meditated earnestly throughout his life, and because his poetry frequently supposes a metaphysics unlike most men's assumptions, many of his poems have remained somewhat less than accessible. Since we ultimately become "mechanical and habitual agents" of our experiences, Shelley wrote in a deleted passage of *On Life*, "...no philosophy can at once seem and be true. A popular dogma on a high question is inevitably false." In poems like *The Sensitive Plant* he was to explore the ironic relation of the seeming reality of the "popular philosophy" to the reality that is "true."

---

4 *Prometheus Unbound*, Preface.

In 1812, when Shelley was working his way out of the materialism of Holbach's *Système de la nature*, Southey, thinking he saw in the eighteen-year-old a reflection of his own youth, claimed that Shelley should call himself a pantheist, not an atheist, and prophesied that he would graduate beyond "the Pantheistic stage of philosophy" and "in the course of a week" would become a Berkeleyan. To contribute to the fulfillment of his prophecy, he borrowed for him Charles Lloyd's copy of that philosopher's works.[5] It was not Berkeley, however, that impressed Shelley at the moment but Lloyd's marginal note *contra* Berkeley, "Mind cannot create; it can only perceive," and he at once made use of it in his *Refutation of Deism* and repeated it in *On Life*. Some years later, recalling Lloyd's pronouncement, he made clear that its special importance to him was that it counteracted the doctrine of a Creator Mind, whether in the traditional theological sense or in the sense of Berkeley's thesis that nature is the ideas the Divine Mind imprints on our minds. Lloyd's sentence, he wrote, "struck me as being the assertion of a doctrine of which even then I had long been persuaded, and on which I had founded much of my persuasions regarding the imagined cause of the Universe."[6] In a catalogue of essays he had written or intended to write, one of Shelley's pencilled jottings reads, " 'Mind cannot create, it can only perceive'—An Atheist Essay,"[7] intimating both the limited sense in which he used the word "atheism" and his antitheological reason for rebelling against the dualism of mind and world. However he was to define the "world," Shelley never wavered in rejecting a Creator after he first arrived at that decision in *The Necessity of Atheism*: "It is easier to suppose that the Universe has existed from all eternity, than to conceive a being capable of creating it."[8]

Southey's reading program was not immediately effective, and Shelley rejected Berkeley's immaterialism at first on the overly simplistic belief that it denies "the presence of matter, . . . the presence of all the forms of being with which our senses are acquainted, & it surely is somewhat inconsistent to assign real existence to what is a mere negation of all that actual world to which our senses introduce us."[9] Nevertheless, in late 1813, misreading the point of Hume's argument, he conceded that he was impressed and yet puzzled by the fact that "Hume's reasonings with

[5] *Letters*, I, 219 and note.

[6] 27 September 1819 (*Letters*, II, 122–23). Compare: "It is infinitely improbable that the cause of mind, that is, of existence, is similar to mind" (*On Life*).

[7] Bodleian MS Shelley e. 4, fol. 84ᵛ.

[8] His fullest and most explicit denial of a "*creative* Deity" is, of course, his note to *Queen Mab* on that subject. See also his much later essay *On the Devil and Devils*.

[9] To Godwin, 29 July 1812 (*Letters*, I, 316). Shelley may well have realized that he was opposing not only Southey but also Godwin, who, in his *Essay on Sepulchres* (1809), had written that he was "more inclined to the opinion of the immaterialists, than of the materialists" (pp. 5–6).

respect to the non-existence of external things" follow logically from
Locke's empiricism, which he accepted as valid.[10] In effect, Shelley's
metaphysical speculations recapitulate the course of eighteen-century empiricism and result in a special brand of idealism rooted in a persistent
epistemological skepticism.[11] The skeptical basis of his epistemology, we
have already observed, was apparent as early as *The Esdaile Notebook*,
where he asserted the undeniable reality of mental phenomena ("All we
perceive, we know that we feel") and the uncertainty that they correspond to an external reality ("All we behold, we feel that we know").[12]
Shelley remained an empiricist in the tradition of Locke and Hume, clinging to the "axiom in mental philosophy that we can think of nothing
which we have not perceived."[13] But the soft spot in Locke's empirical
ontology had been not only his dualistic distinction between primary and
secondary qualities, and hence between the perceived object and the perceiving mind, but also his pseudo-explanation of what underlies the primary qualities of objects. To say that qualities are supported by a substance which is independent of them but which cannot be experienced
in itself Shelley recognized to be meaningless, as Berkeley and Hume
had before him: "But matter deprived of qualities, is an abstraction, concerning which it is impossible to form an idea."[14] For this material substance, Berkeley substituted the divine Mind, which both sustains these
ideas, or sensible objects, by eternally perceiving them and imprints them
on our minds; and he further demonstrated that both primary and secondary qualities are properties of mind, thereby denying any reality other
than minds, human and divine, and their "ideas." Nature is the "language" with which God communicates His ideas to our minds. It would
appear that Shelley was drawing on his own atheistic rendering of
Berkeley to describe in 1816 his "extatic wonder, not unallied to madness"
upon beholding the oneness and immediacy of the scene at Mont Blanc
and experiencing the identity of his mind with the world it perceived:
"All was as much our own as if we had been the creators of such impressions in the minds of others, as now occupied our own"[15]—that is, as if he
were Berkeley's God and the scene were that God's idea, rather than the
idea as communicated to the human mind.

Just as Shelley rejected materialism because of his persuasion that
man is immortal and the world eternal, so, when he came to recognize that

---

[10] To Hogg, 26 November 1813 (*Letters*, I, 380).
[11] How firmly Shelley's thought was based on skepticism has been amply demonstrated by C. E. Pulos in his *The Deep Truth: a Study of Shelley's Scepticism*
(Lincoln, Nebraska, 1954). It is from Pulos' analysis, and not from any supposedly
fundamental Platonism, that any study of Shelley's thought must begin. Although
my conclusions differ from Mr. Pulos', I am nevertheless indebted to him.
[12] See above, pp. 7–8.
[13] *Speculations on Metaphysics* (Julian, VII, 59).
[14] *Refutation of Deism* (Julian, VI, 50).
[15] To Peacock, 22 July 1816 (*Letters*, I, 497); also in *History of a Six Weeks' Tour*
(Julian, VI, 137).

the dualism of mind and matter is not actually a phenomenal fact, he eventually arrived at Berkeley's and Hume's conclusion that we cannot separate sensible ideas from the mental act of perception and assign to them an autonomy and substantiality of which we have no experience.[16] "I confess," he wrote in *On Life*, "that I am one of those who am unable to refuse my assent to the conclusions of those philosophers who assert that nothing exists but as it is perceived. ... the solid universe of external things is 'such stuff as dreams are made of.'"[17] Similarly, one of Prometheus' gifts to mankind, Shelley tells us, was speech; and speech "created," or gave form to, "thought, / Which is the measure of the universe."[18] The last phrase is a clear adaptation of Protagoras' aphorism that "Man is the measure of all things"; and from his reading of Diogenes Laertius and Plato, among others, Shelley would have understood this to mean that man is the measure "of the existence of the things that are and of the non-existence of things that are not" and that "of the real things... their reality is a separate one for each person."[19] Existence is relative to the mind's perceptions; or, in the terms of Shelley's play, the universe is proportional to thought. The same ontological idealism reappears in Prometheus' definition of works of art, which are

> lovely apparitions, dim at first,
> Then radiant, as the mind, arising bright
> From the embrace of beauty, whence the forms
> Of which these are the phantoms, casts on them
> The gathered rays which are reality.[20]

[16] Shelley's rejection of both materialism and the dualism of mind and matter was consistent after about 1813. Occasionally, it is true, he employed the word "matter," but only as a concession to the popular vocabulary, just as Berkeley urged that "we ought to think with the learned, and speak with the vulgar." Shelley's willingness to adjust the vulgar language to his own immaterialism is suggested by the following characteristic passage in his (no doubt late) essay *On the Devil and Devils*. The Greek dualists, he writes, "accounted for evil by supposing what is called matter is eternal" and that it resisted the efforts of God to give it perfect "arrangement." This hypothesis, he explains, Christian theologians repudiated "on the ground that the eternity of matter is incompatible with the omnipotence of God." "This hypothesis [i.e. of the Greeks], though rude enough, is in no respect very absurd and contradictory. The refined speculations respecting the existence of external objects by which the idea of matter is suggested; to which Plato has the merit of first having directed the attention of the thinking part of mankind...." At this point the manuscript breaks off, but it is clear that Shelley means both to affirm the eternity of the "external" world and to claim that its materiality is a fiction. (This interpretation is based on the text as it appears in MS e. 9, not on the published transcriptions, which are inaccurate.)

[17] Cf. *Defence of Poetry* (Julian, VII, 137): "All things exist as they are perceived; at least in relation to the percipient."

[18] *Prometheus Unbound*, II. iv. 72–73.

[19] Diogenes Laertius *Lives of Eminent Philosophers* ix. 51; Plato *Theaetetus* 152a. In Cicero's *Academia* (ii. 142) Shelley would have read that "One view of the criterion [of reality] is that of Protagoras, who holds that what seems true to each person is true for each person." See also Aristotle *Metaphysics* iii. 5.

[20] *Prometheus Unbound*, III. iii. 49–53.

From some absolute beauty the mind's shapeless apparitions derive their form. But whereas man normally supposes that such phantoms of darkness reveal themselves as self-sustaining realities when the rising sun illuminates and defines them clearly, in fact it is the rays of the mind that, being cast on them, constitute their reality. Given this conclusion concerning reality, Shelley aligned himself on metaphysical questions not merely with empiricism but with that extreme skeptical form of it that might be called phenomenalism, in that its data are all the contents and experiences of the mind. Such data have at least the advantage of being incontestable, not open to skeptical doubt: "There can thus be no deception, we ourselves being the depositaries of the evidence of the subject which we consider."[21] He was to call the doctrine the "intellectual system," and some of his major pronouncements on ontology appear in a fragment that begins with the axioms of "mental philosophy."[22]

Although Shelley's phenomenalism is evident, it is fruitless to attempt to align him with any one philosopher; and any extended inferences drawn from partial similarities between him and, say, Berkeley, Hume, or Plato, almost necessarily distort his position. Rather, his thought, evolving from the implications of British empiricism, follows its own path and borrows suggestions eclectically wherever it finds a concept compatible with its own system. Actually, the only philosophic work that Shelley consistently returned to with confidence (excepting only its theism)[23] after his first encounter with it in 1812 was Sir William Drummond's *Academical Questions* (1805),[24] a study of metaphysics based on a "philosophy of mind" and devoted mainly to a skeptical destruction of materialism, or the doctrine of the external existence of what we call the universe. Although Drummond clearly leaned toward what he termed the "ideal philosophy," or the theory that what we experience as real is ideas and exists only as it is perceived, he never published the promised second volume, which was to construct his own philosophic system. Nevertheless, Shelley considered him "the most acute metaphysical critic of the age,"[25] and it is with this skeptical "critic," not with any systematically construc-

[21] *Speculations on Metaphysics* (Julian, VII, 342).
[22] *Ibid.* (p. 59).
[23] See *Queen Mab*, VII. 13n.
[24] Hogg reports Harriet Shelley's having read aloud Drummond's book (and Berkeley's *Works*) in 1813 (*Life of Shelley*, ed. Edward Dowden [London, 1906], p. 420). The book had some popularity in the Shelley circle; for Peacock's interest in it, see *Shelley and his Circle*, ed. K. N. Cameron (Cambridge, Mass., 1970), III, pp. 87, 219.
[25] To Leigh Hunt, 3 November 1819 (*Letters*, II, 142). Shelley also praised Drummond's book in his *Refutation of Deism*, the Preface to *The Revolt of Islam*, and *On Life*. Mary recorded her reading of Drummond in December 1814 (*Journal*, ed. Jones, p. 29), and Claire Clairmont reported a visit from Drummond in Rome in 1819 (*Journals*, ed. Stocking, p. 108).

tive philosopher, that he associated his own "intellectual philosophy," a term chosen to indicate its mental orientation and to distinguish it from both materialism and dualism. The manuscript of *On Life* shows that Shelley wrote of both the "intellectual philosophy" and the "intellectual system" and opposed it to the "mind-material philosophy." Similarly, Drummond had written of the "intellectual system, which I consider as founded upon the highest probability";[26] and the context, a chapter in refutation of Cartesian dualism, makes it evident that he means a metaphysics based on the reality of "intellectual phaenomena" and opposed to a matter-spirit ontology.

In Shelley's "intellectual system," then, awareness, not matter, is the stuff of which existences are formed, and their radical base is self-consciousness: "Nought is but that which feels itself to be."[27] Existence and mind are interchangeable terms in as much as mind is awareness of itself, its modifications, and its content; and Shelley can actually equate the two: "...the cause of mind, that is, of existence...." Although he never tired of repeating his Berkeleyan principle, shared by Hume and Drummond, that "nothing exists but as it is perceived," it is at this point that he and Berkeley part irreconcilably, since Shelley denies a divine Mind independent of, and in any way antecedent to, the human mind. Mary Shelley, therefore, like all who seek out Shelley's particular philosophic affiliations, was both right and wrong when, in 1840, she described the author of *On Life* as "a disciple of the Immaterial Philosophy of Berkeley."[28] That he was an immaterialist is evident, but his counter-axiom to the identification of existence with perception, "Mind cannot create, it can only perceive," removes the prop from under the divine cause and basis of Berkeley's universe. For Berkeley the universe, because its ground is the divine Mind, would continue to exist even though no human mind were to perceive it, and thereby he managed to keep distinct the human mind and the eternal sensible universe. The tree will continue as a perception of the divine Mind and thus will continue to be even when, according to the jingle, no human mind is about in the quad. But because idealism defines the universe in terms of phenomena, its inherent logic tends toward an ultimate and total fusion of subject and object, perception and percept, mind and existence; and Berkeley's God and Kant's two worlds are rather desperate efforts to hypothesize a transcendence that will keep the two apart. Even Hume maintains a kind of uncertain dualism by arguing that *if* there is an external universe we cannot know it because our knowledge of sensible reality is limited to the perceptions present to the mind. Without some autonomous transcendence or some

[26] *Academical Questions* (London, 1805), p. 135.
[27] *Hellas*, 785.
[28] Preface to *Essays, Letters from Abroad, etc.*, 1840 (Julian, V, ix).

such skeptical dualism, philosophic idealism tends to merge mind and universe totally, whether the results be the Absolutes of Fichte, Schelling, Hegel, or F. H. Bradley. In brief, unless a dualism is superimposed upon this metaphysics, it runs toward an ontological monism and tends to formulate the distinction between the One and the Many only as the difference between absolute Existence and its constituent partial modes, not as a difference in kind. Such an absolute Existence, or universal Mind, is neither a God apart from man nor an abstraction, but the unitary reality into which all apparent parts, distinctions, and relations dissolve. That Shelley's thought moved to this general position indicates that he followed in his own peculiar way the direction of eighteenth-century empiricism toward idealism and then, through the evolution of its implications for him, advanced to something like the philosophy of the post-Kantian idealists. Although he praised Drummond's *Academical Questions* as "the most clear and vigorous statement of the intellectual system" in that its destructive critique establishes a basis for phenomenalism, in fact Shelley considered his own version of the system an extensive elaboration of what is only implicit in Drummond: "Examined point by point, and word by word, the most discriminating intellects have been able to discern no train of thoughts in the process of its reasoning [i.e. of Drummond's book] which does not conduct inevitably to the conclusion which has been stated," that is, to Shelley's extension of it.[29] Mary was not wholly wrong to believe that had Shelley completed his "theory of mind" it would have been one "to which Berkeley, Coleridge, and Kant would have contributed," though we need not accept her wifely faith that it would have been "more simple, unimpugnable, and entire than the systems of these writers."[30]

Although Shelley would sustain a vague dualism with his axiom that perceptions are not mental creations, his other axiom, that nothing exists except as it is perceived and that mind and existence are therefore identical, tends toward an absolutely subsuming unity. Convinced that "the solid universe of external things" is literally "such stuff as dreams are made of," but lacking Berkeley's dualism of the divine and the human mind, he is led to a conception of experiential reality that defies all distinction between external and internal. "No distinction between mind & matter;—the intellectual system—," runs one of his manuscript notes following *On Life*. Since mind can be neither the cause nor basis of all things and can only perceive, each mind is a center to which all things in the surrounding circle of existence must be referred for their existence; but since nothing exists except in the perception, each mind is the cir-

[29] The transcriptions hitherto published have incorrectly omitted the word "its" ("its reasoning").
[30] *Ibid.* (Julian, V, xi).

cumference "within which all things are contained." Each of these is only a half-truth, for in fact the mind "is at once the centre and the circumference"; and this paradoxically monistic dualism, Shelley adds, is what essentially distinguishes the "intellectual philosophy" from both materialism and the popular dualism of mind and matter. "The difference," therefore, "is merely nominal between those two classes of thought which are vulgarly distinguished by the names of ideas and of external objects." For this reason, the "inquiry into the phenomena of mind" should not be termed "metaphysics," which Shelley assumed to mean "outside nature, or the physical"; in that sense it makes a false distinction between the phenomena of mind and what we call "the material universe." Instead, metaphysics is "the science of facts," of real existences; these facts are the data not only of our sensations and memory but also of our faith; and all these facts collectively "constitute the universe considered relatively to human identity."[31] It is a matter of indifference, then, whether we adopt the Berkeleyan and Humean position "that when speaking of the objects of thought, we indeed only describe one of the forms of thought" or the materialist position "that, speaking of thought, we only apprehend one of the operations of the universal system of beings";[32] the distinction between thought and the universe is false with respect to the mind, whose contents are the only data of our knowledge. For the "view of life presented by the most refined deductions of the intellectual philosophy is that of unity," a unity transcending that distinction of internal and external, thought and thing, subject and object, into which we fall as the result of habitual experience in our imperfect, ignorant, and illusory mortal state. To this all-subsuming unity, this total amplitude of Existence, Shelley, after the manner of the Romantics, assigned the name "Life," a term which is interchangeable with "thought."[33]

What Shelley sought by constructing his intellectual system and by refuting the dualism of thought and matter was to liberate the mind from false restrictions and thereby to expand the bounds of reality. If we define "life" as "that which we are" and the "world" as that which we "feel," then "Life and the world . . . is an astonishing thing," a singular, indivisible entity; and actually our existence and our feelings, or ourselves and what we call the "world," Shelley wrote in a sentence that could have been by Coleridge or Schelling, are subsumed in "Life," which "includes all." Only through the deception of habit, Shelley argues, only through

---

[31] *Speculations on Metaphysics* (Julian, VII, 62–63).
[32] *Ibid.* (p. 65).
[33] In *A Future State* (MS e. 11) Shelley twice writes of "the vital & intellectual principle" (singular: the published transcriptions are in error); writes of "life or thought" as interchangeable terms; and states that "Life and thought differs indeed from every thing else" (the published transcriptions, which record "differ," are again in error) and that "thought and life is. . . ."

feelings and reasonings that are the "result of a multitude of entangled thoughts, of a series of what are *called* impressions, planted by reiteration" (itals. added), are we led to the illusion of a distinction between ourselves and the world that exists by virtue of our consciousness of it: "in living we lose the apprehension of life." This is why he can maintain that any "popular dogma" about reality is inevitably false, since it arises from minds that misunderstand their own nature, having been misled by the repetition of the same "thoughts," as Berkeley and Hume also argue, to suppose those "thoughts" are independent of mind. But when we were children, Shelley writes, we

less habitually distinguished all that we saw and felt, from ourselves. They seemed, as it were, to constitute one mass. There are some persons who in this respect are always children. Those who are subject to the state called reverie[34] feel as if their nature were dissolved into the surrounding universe, or as if the surrounding universe were absorbed into their being. They are conscious of no distinction. And these are states which precede, or accompany, or follow an unusually intense and vivid apprehension of life.[35]

Obviously Shelley would have agreed with Schelling's objective idealism, toward some aspects of which his position was leading him, which elaborates the absolute "indifference" of the subject-object distinction and teaches that all philosophy consists in a recollection of the condition in

---

[34] The Morgan Library MS of *On Life* shows that Shelley intended to identify these as "Poets & Persons of a peculiar enthusiasm."

[35] The same theme also appears in two manuscript fragments apparently intended for *Epipsychidion*. In one, Shelley writes that in infancy

    every thing familiar seems to be
Wonderful, and the immortality
Of the great world, which all things must inherit
Is felt as one with the awakening spirit
Unconscious of itself, & of the strange
Distinctions, which in its proceeding change
It feels & knows, and mourns as if each were
A desolation [i.e. an isolated external object] (MS c. 4, folder 3)

The other passage (C. D. Locock, *An Examination of the Shelley Manuscripts in the Bodleian Library* [Oxford, 1903], p. 13) reads:

And we will move possessing & possest
Wherever beauty on the earth's bare[?] breast
Lies like [the] shadow of thy soul—till we
Become one being with the world we see.

The lines of the finished poem into which this last passage developed help clarify how the subsumption of the subject and object into each other constitutes both love and life:

Possessing and possessed by all that is
Within that calm circumference of bliss,
And by each other, till to love and live
Be one.... (*Epipsychidion*, 549–52)

which we were one with nature.[36] But for Shelley the special value of such a definition of existences is that it releases the mind from the limitations and the determinism imposed by the customary mechanistic dualism: the mind "is not merely impelled or organized by the adhibition of events proceeding from what has been termed the mechanism of the material universe."[37] He did not propose the intellectual philosophy as an *advance* of knowledge: operating entirely on skeptical grounds, he assumed he was merely removing the false barriers around the grounds of knowledge. Although skepticism denies the popular and therefore superficial philosophy that divides universe from mind, this denial

establishes no new truth, it gives us no additional insight into our hidden nature, neither its action nor itself. Philosophy, impatient as it may be to build, has much work yet remaining as pioneer for the overgrowth of ages. It makes one step towards this object: it destroys error and the roots of error. It leaves, what it is too often the duty of the reformer in political and ethical questions to leave, a vacancy. It reduces the mind to that freedom in which it would have acted but for the misuse of words and signs, the instruments of its own creation.[38]

This freedom is an expansion of our phenomenalist conception of the "universe," which may now be defined, within the "mental philosophy,"

[36] *Sämmtliche werke* (Stuttgart, 1856), I (4), p. 77. According to Coleridge's appropriation of Schelling's doctrine, "During the act of knowledge itself, the objective and subjective are so instantly united that we cannot determine to which the priority belongs. There is here no first and no second; both are coinstantaneous and one" (*Biographia Literaria*, chap. XII; the sentences are from the beginning of Schelling's *System of Transcendental Idealism*). Cf. *Biog. Lit.* (ed. Shawcross), I, p. 185: "... the spirit (originally the identity of object and subject) must in some sense dissolve this identity, in order to be conscious of it." Fichte also described the condition of pure thought which is the primal identity of subject and object; and F. H. Bradley, whose philosophy is at many points astonishingly like Shelley's, also postulates an original condition of immediate experience preceding the development of a consciousness of relations and therefore of distinctions.
[37] *Speculations on Metaphysics* (Julian, VII, 62). In a fictitious dialogue which could not have been written before late 1820, Shelley, referring to someone who has complained of the sophistries of his thought, wrote: "Such is your conception of the intellectual ⟨philosophy⟩ system of which Lionel [i.e. Shelley] is a disciple. The mechanical philosophy of the day which is popular because it is superficial, and intelligible because it is conversant alone with the grosser objects of our thoughts. ..." (I have simplified this heavily revised passage in MS e. 8, p. 71, without, I hope, affecting its sense. For its date, see Neville Rogers, *Shelley at Work* [Oxford, 1956], pp. 17, 257.)
   The difficulty Shelley had in speaking of the "mechanical philosophy," or, as he otherwise called it, the "popular philosophy," is evident in his having first written, "grosser objects of nature," then "grosser objects of our sensations," and finally "grosser objects of our thoughts," progressively mentalizing reality.
[38] Cf.: "...metaphysical science will be treated merely so far as a source of negative truth," that is, for "the ascertaining of what *is not true*" (*Speculations on Morals* [Julian, VII, 71]).

as the total mass of our knowledge, "including our own nature."[39] "By considering all knowledge as bounded by perception, whose operations may be indefinitely combined, we arrive at a conception of Nature, inexpressibly more magnificent, simple and true, than accord[s with] the ordinary systems of complicated and partial consideration."[40]

But in denying any valid distinction between thought and object of thought, or between the words "external" and "internal," Shelley emphasized that when speaking of the objects of thought we describe only *one* of the "forms of thought" and—what amounts to the same thing— when speaking of thought we describe only *one* of "the operations of the universal system of beings." The question remains, then, what kind of existence have those forms of thought that are not "objects of thought," that is, are not "things"?[41] Are they also to be included in the "universe" or are they to be rejected as chimeras? Shelley's answer will be arrived at, of course, not from the premises of physical science, but from those of his intellectual, or "mental," philosophy, which also recognizes that man is "pre-eminently an imaginative being. His own mind is his law; his own mind is all things to him."[42] The anchor of assurance for Shelley is the axiom that we can think of nothing we have not perceived and that therefore all thoughts must be perceptions, not fictions. Since nothing exists except as it is perceived, everything included in "life," or "existence," must be defined as thought. Thus, any so-called thing must be understood in the phenomenalist sense as "any thought upon which any other thought is employed with an apprehension of distinction." Those other thoughts of the mind that are not "things" must therefore, he concluded, be the "modes" in which thoughts grounded in perception are "combined" by the laws of the imagination and consequently are "also to be included in the catalogue of existence."[43]

By assuming without question the "Author of Nature," Berkeley had a basis in his idealism for claiming a categorical distinction not only between human minds and the sensible world, or between the spirit that knows and the ideas that are known, but also between "real things" and "chimeras." Real things are those ideas imprinted on the senses by the Author of Nature and are regular, vivid, and constant because of God's uniformity; chimeras are ideas of the mind's own compounding and lack these assuring qualities. But without a Creator, Shelley has no ground for claiming that only regular, vivid, and constant ideas are real. If the popular distinction between those "two classes of thought" called "ideas" and

[39] *Speculations on Metaphysics* (Julian, VII, 60).
[40] *Ibid.*
[41] In the Morgan Library MS, following the essay *On Life*, Shelley asked himself, "What are we to think of that portion of the universe, or that class of possible sensations of which we have no experience?"
[42] *Speculations on Metaphysics* (Julian, VII, 65).
[43] *Ibid.* (p. 59).

"external objects" is purely nominal with respect to the mind, then there is also no essential difference between regular thoughts and those ideas, such as power, or cause, which "were never objects of sensation"[44] but which the "laws of mind almost universally suggest according to the various disposition of each, a conjecture, a persuasion, or a conviction of their existence."[45] Nor is there a *fundamental* distinction even between regular thoughts and such irregular and indistinct thoughts as "hallucinations, dreams, and the ideas of madness."[46] The only valid distinction possessed by regular thoughts is their being the "most invariably subservient to the security and happiness" of earthly life as a mere practical fact, but they are not therefore generically and essentially different or more "true." "The principle of the agreement and similarity of all thoughts is that they are thoughts; the principle of their disagreement consists in the variety and irregularity of the occasions on which they arise in the mind. That in which they agree to that in which they differ is as everything to nothing."[47] Nor are such random and vague thoughts as dreams to be considered fictions, for there are no ontological criteria to distinguish them from "reality"; like all thoughts, they are grounded in perceptions and cannot be created by mind *ex nihilo*. Since the "operations" of perceptions "may be indefinitely combined" by the imagination, dreams are only "modes in which thoughts are combined" and therefore must be included in the catalogue of existence because "beyond the limits of perception and of thought nothing can exist."[48] Indeed, since man is "preeminently an imaginative being" and since imagination is the faculty which arranges, combines, and organizes his thoughts according to the laws of the mind, such combinations especially characterize his reality. The only true distinction among thoughts according to their own nature is not an ontological one of true and false, external and internal, but a distinction in terms of their "intensity, duration, connection, periods of recurrence, and utility," from the simplest combination of such thoughts to "that mass of knowledge which, including our own nature, constitutes what we call the universe."[49]

With the removal of the distinction between thought and thing, and with the translation of reality into mental experiences (which are not, however, autogenous), all other ontological categories also begin to crumble, as they tend to do in almost any system of phenomenalism or idealism; and Shelley's realm of existences inexorably evolves into an undifferentiated, immutable, and eternal unity. Time and space drop out as

[44] Hume's critique of cause is, of course, assumed here.
[45] *Ibid.*
[46] *Ibid.*
[47] *Ibid.* (p. 60). I quote, however, from Bodleian MS Shelley d. 1, fols. 112ᵛ–112ʳ (Koszul, p. 139), which differs slightly from the printed transcript.
[48] *Ibid.* (p. 59).
[49] *Ibid.* (p. 60).

objective realities, as they do for Berkeley and Hume and the subsequent idealists; for "What has thought / To do with time, or place, or circumstance?"[50] Since nothing is but as it is perceived and since we do not in fact perceive pure time or space, these supposed entities must be nothing more than the changing relations of our perceptions to each other and to our awareness of ourselves, schemata abstracted from the forms in which our disparate thoughts are arranged. The various thoughts, apprehended as distinct, upon which we employ other thoughts are "perpetually changing the mode of their existence relatively to us. To express the varieties of these modes, we say, *we move, they move*; and as this motion is continual, though not uniform, we express our conception of the diversities of its course by—*it has been, it is, it shall be.*"[51] Moreover, since there are no valid ontological distinctions among thoughts, it follows that for Shelley the individual mind is a mirror not only *upon* which all separate forms are reflected as thoughts but *in* which "'they compose one form."[52] Each mind is a single complexly organized thought.

But in fact, like the post-Kantians, Shelley does not accept even the real existence of a plurality of unitary minds. In the absence of any valid distinction between ideas and external objects, he believed he could also conclude that "the existence of distinct individual minds... is likewise found to be a delusion." Just as colors are partial modes of light, so each human mind is but a partial mode of the One Mind, which is the one absolute Existence: "The words *I, you, they* are not signs of any actual difference subsisting between the assemblage of thoughts thus indicated, but are merely marks employed to denote the different modifications of the one mind.... I am but a portion of it." This "one mind" is neither an artificial abstraction nor a deity, but is Existence itself.

At least since his rejecting the doctrine of a Creator and accepting the universe as eternal, Shelley had been inclined toward a belief that all individual minds are subsumed in a universal mind, and his impulse at all times appears to have been to dissolve individual identity in an all-encompassing unity. When in 1812 he temporarily formulated a pantheistic dualism requiring an infused animating Mind, he concluded that each human mind—"I, you, & he"—is a constituent part of the sustaining "mass of infinite intelligence";[53] and in *The Daemon of the World* he proposed that every human birth is really the awakening of a portion of the universal mind to sensory experience of the world with which it

[50] *Hellas*, 801–2.
[51] *Speculations on Metaphysics* (Julian, VII, 61). The ultimate source of this analysis is Aristotle's definition of time as the mental measure of motion (*Physics* iv. 218–24).
[52] *Prometheus Unbound*, Preface.
[53] To Elizabeth Hitchener, 2 January 1812 (*Letters*, I, 215).

coexists and which it diversifies and continuously expands by its actions, while it itself is augmented by the passions it receives from its actions:

> For birth but wakes the universal mind
> Whose mighty streams might else in silence flow
> Thro' the vast world, to individual sense
> Of outward shows, whose unexperienced shape
> New modes of passion to its frame may lend;
> Life is its state of action, and the store
> Of all events is aggregated there
> That variegate the eternal universe.[54]

Subsequently, in the context of his monistic idealism that identifies the One Mind with Existence rather than with its animating essence, he similarly holds that "The words *I* and *you* and *they* are grammatical devices invented simply for arrangement, and totally devoid of the intense and exclusive sense usually attached to them." That is, the personal pronouns are relational, not substantive, terms. The universal Mind is the same as Existence, according to the "intellectual philosophy," and all human minds are factors of it. Despite the obvious fascination the Platonic dialogues had for Shelley, it is both unnecessary and misleading in structuring his ontology to introduce Platonism, from which it differs in radical ways. Shelley's philosophic evolution followed the logical course from the empiricism that was his native heritage to skepticism and then, dodging the implicit solipsism, to an objective idealism dependent upon a nontheistic and nontranscendent Absolute; and although he educed and structured his ontology in his own special way, it shares the characteristics of almost all idealisms in such essentials as the distinctions between appearance and reality, diversity and unity, thing and idea.

A paradox, however, has developed in Shelley's system, and he was well aware of the trap toward which his philosophy was taking him. Thing and thought, external and internal, universe and mind, together

---

[54] *The Daemon of the World*, II. 539–46. Compare Drummond, *Academical Questions*, pp. 26–27: "...the Platonic doctrine, which taught the pre-existence of the immaterial soul, and according to which it was supposed, that the spiritual and incarnate effluence of universal mind, gradually awakes to reminiscence and intelligence, after its first slumber has passed in its corporeal prison." The difference between this and Shelley's statement is, of course, at least as important as the similarity.

The passage in *Queen Mab* (IX. 155–60), of which the lines quoted from *The Daemon of the World* are a redaction, differs mainly in using the word "spirit" instead of "universal mind."

It is significant that when Shelley later substituted the "intellectual philosophy" for the pantheistic dualism of *The Daemon*, the metaphor likening the universal mind to a river flowing through the world got inverted: "The everlasting universe of things / Flows through the mind" (*Mont Blanc*, 1–2).

with all modes of its thought, are one and are subsumed under an eternal and self-sustaining "Life." Time and space are unreal, so that an exhaustive spatial catalogue of thoughts and the sum total of temporal history are convertible into each other: "A catalogue of all the thoughts of the mind, and of all their possible modifications, is a cyclopaedic history of the Universe."[55] Even the discreteness of all individual minds is an illusion resulting from a failure to understand the One Mind, of which they are parts. Such, according to the "intellectual philosophy," is the constitution of what truly is, whatever may be the nature of our superficial experiences. But Shelley recognized, on the other hand, that the very existence of the individual human mind, illusory though it is, is contingent upon experience of separateness and diversity. Although those diversities of relationships among percepts and self that we call time and space are not real, nevertheless they are "essential, considered relatively to human identity, for the existence of the human mind." For, he added, "if the inequalities, produced by what has been termed the operations of the external universe [but are actually the changing modes of the existence of 'things' relatively to each other and the perceiving mind] were levelled by the perception of our being [or our 'nature,' or self-awareness] uniting, and filling up their interstices [which are responsible for our notions of] motion and mensuration, and time, and space; the elements of the human mind being thus abstracted, sensation and imagination cease." "Mind cannot be considered pure"[56] because the impurity of diversity is the necessary condition for the existence of the human mind and of individual identity. In childhood, when we did not habitually distinguish all that we saw and felt from our own existence, and when the perception of our own existence did fill the interstices between "external" perceptions, we most nearly had an apprehension of timeless, spaceless, undifferentiated Existence that is neither external nor internal; and consequently we were closest to the unitary Reality. But we were also, for that very reason, children, individual minds in only the least degree. Moreover, although Shelley translated "things" into distinct "objects of thought," like Berkeley and Hume he did not assume that this reorganized what we call the world of things: "The relations of *things* remain unchanged, by whatever system." And although all thoughts are essentially of the same order, a "specific difference between every thought of the mind, is, indeed, a necessary consequence of that law by which it perceives diversity and number."[57]

In brief, Shelley's ontology, like most idealisms, has led him into a position as ambiguous as his indecision between utopia and eternity, Pan

---

[55] *Speculations on Metaphysics* (Julian, VII, 59).
[56] *Ibid.* (p. 61).
[57] *Ibid.* (p. 60).

and Apollo. Although Existence is to be defined as the One Mind, *we* exist nevertheless as discrete minds in a spatio-temporal condition that tends to separate into thought and things. There is a veil between Existence and Seeming, and although we can construct philosophically for ourselves the undifferentiated unity that is the nature of Existence, we cannot avoid the fact that we live an illusion and cannot experience Existence directly. To exist as individual minds we must accept the illusion of diversities and their relationships that we call time, space, cause, things, thoughts, and even those interstices between them that we call vacancies; on the other hand, were we to experience Existence we would be obliterated as separate identities. Nor can the problem be solved simply by writing off appearances as mere nonexistent illusions, for, as in Bradley's philosophy, the Absolute is made up exclusively of what, when they are isolated from it, we must consider appearances. When Adonais, for example, returns to the One after death, he still bears "his *part* of the One Spirit's plastic stress": the One, paradoxically, is constituted of "parts." The "universe" (the etymological sense is functional) is also such a complex of relationships among thoughts that relationship overcomes itself as a relevant factor. Shelley's poetic explorations of Existence therefore must take into account our illusion of reality as indispensable to Existence, and he must manage the relation of the two states as ambivalently and paradoxically as he weighed against each other earthly meliorism and postmortal perfection, contraries neither of which he could abandon and neither of which he could accept with conviction. Although he aspires to escape appearances and to exist in the Absolute (in which case *he* would exist no longer), the Absolute would not exist were it not for its appearances.

In what sense, then, does the "intellectual philosophy" expand the meaning of reality? Certainly not by merely removing the distinction between thoughts and things, for, whatever name we give them, we still experience them as distinct, and since the system does not change their relationships, we still experience time, space, and individual identity, not the Absolute. We are still limited to misleading phenomena. Yet Shelley insisted that his "comprehensive and synthetical view" of the universe, as he called it, removes the false limitations upon our existence and dispels the "narrow and false conception of universal nature" implied by the popular philosophy, a false conception which is "the parent of the most fatal errors in speculation."[58] For by removing the distinction between external and internal, Shelley opened up the possibility that the mind's most nearly perfect *imaginative* configurations of phenomena may be real, although the phenomena themselves, discretely considered, are deceptive.

All that the "living world" contains—and the living world is that

[58] *Ibid.*

absolute Existence which is also, indiscriminately, life and mind—is not only "thought, passion, reason, will," but also "Imagination."[59] For Shelley, we have noted, the universe, inclusively considered, is constituted not only by our sensations and memory but also by our faith, or belief; and an isolated entry in the midst of the manuscript of the *Defence of Poetry* reads: "Things *exist as they are perceived*: our existence becomes greater in proportion to our creed: the nobility of the intellectual philosophy."[60] Although phenomena are deceptive, the structures the imagination makes of them are true in proportion to their credibility. For Shelley wishes not only to formulate a liberating phenomenalistic interpretation of Existence but also to include in his conception of the "universe" the trans-phenomenal realm of absolute Being that embraces and stands behind Existence. His atheism does not exclude what he termed the "mystery or majesty or power which the invisible world contains,"[61] and he decried the attempts of organized religion to de-mystify that realm with such mere names as "Demon, Ghost, and Heaven" for the purpose of human oppression.[62] But although he insisted that the transcendent realm of Being is unknowable because it cannot be experienced, he found in his "intellectual philosophy" a basis on which to claim that the mind can have an adequately convincing apprehension of it. For example, Shelley agreed consistently and repeatedly with Hume that we never have a sensation of cause but only of the repeated succession of the same thoughts, and he defined this succession in strictly phenomenal terms:

What cause is no philosopher has succeeded in explaining, and the triumph of the acutest metaphysicians has been confined to demonstrating it to be inexplicable. All we know of cause is that one event, or to speak more correctly, one sensation follows another attended with a conviction derived from experience that these sensations will hereafter be similarly connected. This habitual conviction is that to which we appeal when we say that one thing is the cause of another, or has the power of producing certain effects.[63]

Yet, although we experience only the repetition of the same pattern of sensations, Shelley wishes to consider a nontheistic "Power," or mysterious ultimate cause outside Existence, as one of the "modes in which thoughts are combined" by the imagination.[64] Despite his destructive skeptical demonstration, Hume would have us conduct ourselves, for obvious prac-

---

[59] *Prometheus Unbound*, II. iv. 10–11.
[60] Bodleian MS Shelley d. 1, p. 38ᵛ.
[61] *Essay on Christianity* (Julian, VI, 229). A prose fragment on the meaning of the word "atheist" (MS c. 4, fol. 8) makes it clear that for Shelley the word designates only one who denies an anthropomorphic "cause of the Universe," and not "an impious person."
[62] *Hymn to Intellectual Beauty*, 27.
[63] "On Polytheism" (Julian, VII, 151). I quote the text as it appears in MS e. 9, p. 93.
[64] *Speculations on Metaphysics* (Julian, VII, 59).

tical reasons, in accord with the notion that there *is* causation; Shelley wishes to establish its reality on the basis of confidence in the imagination's formulation of the idea of cause. In brief, skepticism alone proves inadequate for Shelley, for although it "destroys error and the roots of error," it also leaves a "vacancy" and can result in paralysis, since it arrives only at "negative truth." The ultimate function of Shelley's empirical skepticism and the probing incertitude of such poems as *Alastor* and *Julian and Maddalo*, which threaten to result in "the indolence of scepticism," is to clear the ground for a probabilism based on imagination and belief: ". . . whilst the sceptic destroys gross superstitions, let him spare to deface, as some of the French writers have defaced, the eternal truths charactered upon the imaginations of men."[65]

This does not mean that Shelley would accept as real every capricious combination organized by the imagination. Not only are thoughts limited to perceptions and their combinations according to the laws of the mind, but in *The Necessity of Atheism* and ever afterward Shelley accepted Hume's doctrine that belief is a passion, not "an act of volition."[66] It is necessary and involuntary, not capricious. In belief the mind is passive, unable to resist the persuasion of probability, which is "purely proportionate to the degrees of excitement,"[67] such as, progressively, conjecture, persuasion, and conviction.[68] As it was for the ancient skeptical probabilist Carneades, the ground of likely truth for Shelley is the degree or intensity of belief. "It is by no means indisputable," runs one of Shelley's manuscript notes, "that what is true, or rather that which the disciples of a certain mechanical & superficial philosophy call true, is the [sic] more excellent than the beautiful."[69] What the "mechanical philosophy" calls "true" is an external reality corresponding to the impressions received by the mind as it is supposedly "impelled or organized by the adhibition of events proceeding from what has been termed the mechanism of the material universe." But the "beautiful" is the imagination's most nearly perfect organization of phenomena according to the laws of the mind. A philosophy that overlooks the constitutive role of imagination and the confirming role of belief in determining the inclusive "universe" may supply

[65] *A Defence of Poetry* (Julian, VII, 132).
[66] *The Necessity of Atheism* (Julian, V, 207–9). Also *An Address, to the Irish People* (Julian, V, 222); *Declaration of Rights* (Julian, V, 274); *Queen Mab*, VII. 13n.; *A Letter to Lord Ellenborough* (Julian, V, 285); *A Refutation of Deism* (Julian, VI, 39); and *Letters*, I, 216, 248, 335.
[67] *A Letter to Lord Ellenborough* (Julian, V, 285).
[68] *Speculations on Metaphysics* (Julian, VII, 59). Hume's purpose is to depend on the "feeling" of belief as the means of distinguishing "the ideas of the judgment from the fictions of the imagination" (*Enquiry Concerning Human Understanding*, V. ii); Shelley's is to distinguish between imagination's fictions and its probable truths.
[69] MS e. 8, p. 74.

us with a reality that is true in the empirical sense, but it also supplies us with a reality that is defective.

Although Mary exaggerated in identifying Berkeley's immaterialism with Shelley's, she was no doubt right in perceiving its value to him as poet:

This theory gave unity and grandeur to his ideas, while it opened a wide field for his imagination. The creation—such as it was perceived by his mind—a unit in immensity, was slight and narrow compared with the interminable forms of thought that might exist beyond, to be perceived perhaps hereafter by his own mind; or which are perceptible to other minds that fill the universe, not of space in the material sense, but of infinity in the immaterial one.[70]

No doubt she was right also to see that the "Ode to Heaven" is an expression of a vision of the transcendent realm of Being, which is the ground of our realm of Existence—a vision made possible by the imagination's operations on the "Immaterial Philosophy."[71] In that poem, the "First Spirit" worships the *visible* external Heaven as the eternal realm within which all transitory worlds, beings, time, and actions occur—that is, as the inclusive container of reality. On the contrary, the "Second Spirit"—called in one manuscript[72] "a Remoter Voice," implying a larger vision—defines Heaven not as objective space but, subjectively and solipsistically, as "the mind's first chamber" inhabited by "its young fancies," the grave being the entrance into the mind's chamber of greater glories and "delights." But a Third Spirit—"a louder & still remoter Voice"—accusing the first two of presumption and denying this distinction between external Heaven and mind, object and subject, thereby opens up the infinity of absolute Being, in which the visible Heaven is but a transitory "globe of dew"

Filling in the morning new
Some eyed flower whose young leaves waken
On an unimagined world.

Man is "atom-born," only a "part" of the transcendent absolute Spirit that moves all things; only a part of the immanent One Mind, as Shelley wrote in *On Life*; only a part of "the one Spirit's plastic stress," as he was to write in *Adonais*. According to Mary's interpretation, Shelley considered "his individual mind as a unit divided from a mighty whole, to which it was united by restless sympathies and an eager desire for knowledge"; and on that basis "he assuredly believed that hereafter, *as now*, he would form a portion of that whole—and a portion less imperfect, less suffering,

[70] Preface to *Essays, Letters from Abroad, etc.*, 1840 (Julian, V, ix).
[71] *Ibid.*
[72] Locock, *Examination of the Shelley Manuscripts*, p. 39.

than the shackles inseparable from humanity impose on all who live beneath the moon."[73] The "intellectual philosophy" does not make the ordinary phenomenal world any less illusory, but it allows the indisputably present phenomena to serve as the means of an imaginative leap from the realm of Existence to the realm of Being on which it depends—or, in Mary's words, into that "which is veiled from our imperfect senses in the unknown realm, the mystery of which his poetic vision sought in vain to penetrate."[74] In *Mont Blanc* the legion of thoughts has the power not only to constitute the realm of Existence but also, by an imaginative act, to "float above" its "darkness."

Although the individual mind is actually part of the One Mind, which is Existence, it cannot be experienced as such in life, nor can Existence have direct knowledge of the realm of Being that embraces it. Ahasuerus, in *Hellas*, would have Mahmud "look on that which cannot change—the One, / The unborn and the undying"; nevertheless, he concedes that the "outwall" of the world of Existence, which is itself a "vision," a "thought," is "bastioned impregnably / Against the escape of boldest thoughts" to that One.[75] The paradox, then, remains: the illusory phenomena are experientially present to the human mind, while ultimate Being rests on faith, and yet the illusory phenomena, when grasped as neither subjective nor objective, are the necessary means by which the imagination can make its leap of faith, its act of necessary belief, to unknown Being. The experience of diversity is necessary for the existence of the individual human mind, but if we could overleap the outwall of the phenomenal universe to which the "intellectual philosophy" carries us, we would not merely believe but actually experience the fact that

Nothing in the world is single;
All things by a law divine
In one spirit meet and mingle.[76]

[73] Preface to *Essays* (Julian, V, x); itals. added.
[74] *Ibid.*
[75] *Hellas*, 768–75.
[76] "Love's Philosophy."

5 The Imagination's World

The Sensitive Plant

The broad, paraphrasable drift of *The Sensitive Plant* has seldom disquieted its readers, for however misty or capricious much of that poem may seem, the "Conclusion," as the final stanzas are entitled, has the air of making the meaning comfortably plain: the ideal "love, and beauty, and delight" which comprehend nature's garden and its presiding spirit are eternal. The "death" of the sensible world is no more than the eventual failure of man's perceptual faculties:

That garden sweet, that lady fair,
And all sweet shapes and odours there,
In truth have never pass'd away:
'Tis we, 'tis ours, are changed; not they.

For love, and beauty, and delight,
There is no death nor change: their might
Exceeds our organs, which endure
No light, being themselves obscure. (III. 130–37)

In some general sense, the perceptible mutable world is an illusion and the ideal world is real and eternal. With this much grasped, and with the additional assurance that comes from knowing that this bit of quasi-Platonism "places" the poem, presumably the rest of it can be dismissed as a fragile, elaborately ornamented nature fable which dances itself into

154

the attitude that the "Conclusion" explains. Shelley has adorned a tale and pointed its moral—with considerable redundancy.

Or so one could dispose of the poem if it were read in the light of what Shelley calls the "popular philosophy" and if his own paradoxical ontology were not brought to bear. The boldest hint that the poem may at every point be structuring a special conception of reality is offered by the peculiarity of its fabular form, the very feature that makes the poem seem naive and incapable of duplicity. Although it appears to be simply a flower fable with an Aesopian moral, the moral does not in fact follow from the narrative. The "Conclusion," speculating that reality, being ideal, is eternal and that it is man's senses that are mutable, is, paradoxically, counter to the whole gist of the fable, which pictures first the flourishing springtime and then the irreversible winter decay of the garden of flowers. Either Shelley has blundered into up-ending the poem at the last moment, shattering in a few dozen lines what he has built in nearly three hundred, or else what he called a "subtler language within language,"[1] a special configuration within the explicit language of the fable, makes the "Conclusion" poetically inevitable. Indeed, the consistency with which Shelley's poetry has been thought internally inconsistent—*Alastor*, we are told, is self-contradictory, Shelley changed his mind in the middle of *Julian and Maddalo*, he could not decide how to represent Beatrice in *The Cenci*, he wavered between utopia and apocalypse in *Prometheus Unbound*, the final chorus of *Hellas* undoes the entire preceding drama— all suggests that the apparent inconsistencies may be rooted and resolved in a coherently ambiguous or paradoxical vision such as we have observed in his essays on metaphysics. By virtue of its poetic genre, *The Sensitive Plant* leads the reader to anticipate that the "Conclusion" will be the logical supplement to the fable and will consist of the moral abstracted from it, not a flat contradiction of everything the fable has apparently enacted; and yet, in the paradox that the final stanzas deny the fable of nature's death and nevertheless are truly its conclusion lies the essential meaning of the poem. In the manner of the paradoxical title of the final chapter of Johnson's *Rasselas*, the "Conclusion" is that existence is never concluded, despite the wintry dis-appearance of the flowers.

The elements of the fable—the garden, the Lady, and the Sensitive Plant—are, like those of any Aesopian fable, patently allegorical and are represented in a fashion that calls for their interpretation in universal terms. The nameless garden that is both the locale and one of the major subjects of the poem is, we are told, an "undefiled Paradise" (I. 58), an analogue of Eden (II. 2); and its universality is defined by the fact that in it grow "all rare blossoms from every clime" in their springtime perfection (I. 39–40). The Garden of Eden and such other traditional modes

[1] *The Revolt of Islam*, 3112.

of the *locus amoenus* as the gardens of Adonis and Alcinous all tend toward the metaphor of the world as a paradisiacal garden; and although there are notable similarities between Shelley's poem and Spenser's description of the Garden of Adonis,[2] it is unnecessary to search out any particular source or tradition for Shelley, who thought of "this world of life" as "a garden ravaged"[3] and of the renovated world as "A garden ... in loveliness / Surpassing fabled Eden."[4] The nameless Lady who is the garden's sustaining spirit is a "Power in this sweet place, / An Eve in this Eden; a ruling Grace" (II. 1–2), and in any of these roles she is the spirit who labors to maintain the perfection of the garden. She is its "soul" (III. 18), which Shelley had defined earlier, in speculating on the souls of flowers, as "that which makes an organized being to be what it is,— without which it would not be so."[5] Consequently her death would also be the death of the flowers, just as a dryad's death is also that of the tree it inhabits. Her domain is specifically limited to the world-garden, to which she stands in the same relation as God stands to "the starry scheme" (II. 4); and Shelley had defined God as "the *existing power of existence*," "the essence of the universe,"[6] and later as "the Power which models, as they pass, all the elements of this mixed universe to the purest and most perfect shape which it belongs to their nature to assume."[7] She is not, then, Venus Genetrix but the presiding spirit who tends the flowers *as though* they were "her own infants" (II. 39) and in that sense bears the same relation to the garden that Venus, whom Mary Shelley once identified with Nature, bears to the Garden of Adonis. Among her various predecessors is the Genius of Milton's *Arcades*, who is also the "Power / Of this fair wood," nurses the trees, guards the plants from harm, and at night hears the music of the spheres which is the model for the world's motion, just as the Lady seems visited in her nightly dreams by some descended star. The Genius' maintaining the perfect Arcadian state by healing whatever "hurtful worm with cankered venom bites" is like the Lady's banishing all "obscene and unlovely forms" and the insects "whose intent, / Although they did ill, was innocent" (II. 42, 47–48), in conformity with Shelley's faith not only that the Spirit of Nature necessarily works for the greatest possible "good" but also that evil arises from ig-

[2] *Faerie Queene*, III. vi. 29ff.
[3] *Epipsychidion*, 186–87.
[4] *Queen Mab*, IV. 88–89.
[5] To Elizabeth Hitchener, 24 November 1811 (*Letters*, I, 192).
[6] To Elizabeth Hitchener, 11 June 1811 (*Letters*, I, 101).
[7] *Essay on Christianity* (Julian, VI, 235). Not only does the poem bear out this sense of the Lady's role, but also in the draft Shelley wrote at one point that she "suited to each one's feeling & form / The tendance ..." and also substituted "nature and need" for "feeling & form" (MS e. 12, p. 137). Compare Milton's description of Eve's care of the flowers, which "at her coming sprung / And toucht by her fair tendance gladlier grew" (*Paradise Lost*, VIII. 46–47).

norance, not viciousness, and enters through the defect of form.[8] The introduction of the theme of evil into the symbolism suggests even more
vividly the equation of the garden and the world. In sum, the Lady is
the ground of the most fully organized existence possible of what man
calls the world; she is the spirit of its informing form, the "might" of the
"love, and beauty, and delight" that are the ultimate substance of the
garden in its spring and summer completeness (III. 134–35).

But as the title indicates, the central subject of the poem is the Sensitive Plant, and around it everything revolves, even in the second and
third parts of the fable, where, paradoxically, it hardly appears at all.
Although a member of the garden, it is radically differentiated from all
the other flowers, especially by its participating in the world less perfectly
than the others and by its finding the garden inadequate to its desires.
What obviously distinguishes sensitive plants is that, like man, they seem
to participate in two levels of the Great Chain of Being and occupy an
"isthmus of a middle state": belonging to the botanical order, they nevertheless respond sensitively to stimuli and seem to imitate the characteristics
of animal life, as their botanical name, *mimosa*, indicates. The traditional
botanical and biological classifications were seriously under question in
the late eighteenth and early nineteenth centuries, and the sensitive plant
was one of the most frequent examples of those ambiguous border-forms
sharing both vegetable and animal characteristics.[9] Like man, therefore,
the Sensitive Plant is a native of the world-garden and yet is alien to it,
aspiring to its other order of existence; and thus it symbolically reflects
the tension, let us say, between the Narrator of *Alastor*, who seeks only
the love of the "Mother of this unfathomable world," and the Visionary,
whom the world cannot satisfy and who is drawn beyond it by the visionary complement of himself projected by his own mind. Being her-
maphroditic, the Sensitive Plant, unlike all the other flowers, is "companionless" (I. 12), unable to complement or fulfill itself in another in

[8] In his MS (e. 12, p. 187), after "whose intent, / Although they did ill was innocent," Shelley momentarily considered substituting "whose intent / Was like ours,
who do ill yet are innocent," thus intimating most pointedly the allegorical character
of the poem.

[9] *Chambers' Cyclopaedia, Supplement* (London, 1753), s.v. "sensitive plant": "This
is an herb sufficiently known to the world for its remarkable property of receding
from the touch, and giving signs, as it were of animal life." Soame Jenyns, *Works*
(Dublin, 1790), II, p. 133: "...this vegetative power ascending through an infinite variety of herbs, flowers, plants and trees to its greatest perfection in the
sensitive plant, joins there the lowest degree of animal life in the shell-fish which
adheres to the rock; and it is difficult to distinguish which possesses the greatest
share, as the one shews it only by shrinking from the finger, and the other by
opening to receive the water which surrounds it." The ambiguity of the plant's
order of existence is made use of by William Cowper in his poem, "The Poet, the
Oyster, and the Sensitive Plant." For further discussion of the sensitive plant in the
eighteenth-century discussions of biological categories, see Philip C. Ritterbush,
Overtures to Biology (New Haven, 1964).

the world-garden, where it has no compeer; and in this way it has affinities
with all of Shelley's aspiring solitaries. Again like man, the Sensitive
Plant is the special favorite of nature and receives the fullness of its
ministry. Yet its status is paradoxical in every way, for although it "Received more than all" the other flowers, it is discontent, desiring more than
the garden is capable of giving, even though, lacking bright flowers, rich
fruit, and scent, it is unable to return any of the beauty it receives from
the others.

But the Sensitive Plant which could give small fruit
Of the love which it felt from the leaf to the root,
Received more than all, it loved more than ever,
Where none wanted but it, could belong to the giver,

For the Sensitive Plant has no bright flower;
Radiance and odour are not its dower;
It loves, even like Love, its deep heart is full,
It desires what it has not, the Beautiful!   (I. 70–77)

In a world where everything else is fulfilled in a perfect reciprocity of
love and beauty, it is at least half out of place.

ii

    Like the traditional Aesopian fable, then, the poem is an allegorical
substitution of lower for higher forms of existence; and its *données* are the
world of animate nature (the garden), the presiding beneficent spirit
(the apparently human Lady), and man (the botanical-biological Sensitive
Plant), of whose ambiguous status and confused vision the poem is trying
to make sense. Operating with these three allegorical counters, the fable
is plain enough. In spring the flowers of the garden awaken from their
winter sleep into their paradisiacal form, and all, except the Sensitive
Plant, act out their perfect state of existence by interpenetrating each
other with their beauty and love, fulfilling absolutely and being absolutely
fulfilled, "Wrapped and filled by their mutual atmosphere" (I. 69). Each
is simultaneously container and contained, circumference and center. In
autumn the sustaining Lady dies and so do all the flowers, of which she
is the soul; and, contrary to nature's usual course, only hideous weeds
return when the second spring arrives. Although the "Conclusion" will
deny it, the fable represents the life of the garden as a linear process
from birth to death and extinction, not an ever-renewed circle of nature's
seasons. In terms of this thin narrative, it would seem that the elaborate
descriptions of the flowers in their perfection and decay are merely
decorative.

Yet, although the allegorical counters are lower forms substituting for higher ones, they are represented in such a way as to be associated with orders of existence even higher than those for which they stand. Thus, the flowers, standing for subhuman life, are described as human: they are like young lovers, like nymphs, like infants. The ambiguous Sensitive Plant is even more than human, for, like Shelley's Visionary, it seeks for something that transcends the natural and human world. And the Lady, "the wonder of her kind," is as companionless as the Sensitive Plant and yet seems attended by some immortal spirit from a transcendent realm. At the same time that the allegorical elements seem to diminish the orders they represent, they raise them to a level higher than their customary classification.

Moreover, although the descriptions through which the fable runs seem a thicket of baroque decorations, one of the descriptive metaphors reappears so persistently that even as the poem claims to be focusing exclusively on the garden-world it points indirectly to a higher plane of reality. The most explicit instance appears when the Lady and her domain are being defined: she is "to the flowers, did they waken or dream, / ... as God is to the starry scheme" (II. 3-4). There are, this implies, two analogous realms, in which the alternately sleeping and awakened flowers and stars are at all times presided over by the Lady and God respectively. Flowers and stars are not only analogous but also, as their other occurrences indicate, interchangeable. That flowers are the stars of earth is a commonplace that was an important, often central, symbol in Shelley's poetry after he became acquainted in 1819 with the plays of Calderón, where the star-flower analogy is so frequent that Shelley could write, "I am bathing myself in the light & odour of the flowery & starry Autos [of Calderón]."[10] But the metaphor, while seeming only descriptive, oc-

[10] To John Gisborne, c. 18 November 1820 (Letters, II, 250). For Calderón, see E. M. Wilson, "The Four Elements in the Imagery of Calderón," MLR, 31 (1936), 38-39. One of the most striking and extended instances appears in El Principe constante, II. ii, where flowers are likened to stars, the "flowers of night," and both are treated as emblems of transience and mortality. Another significant instance is the opening of El Gran teatro del mundo, where the flowers of earth, "a human heaven of dying flowers," are described as reflections of the celestial stars.

That Calderón was in Shelley's mind is further suggested by the manuscript of The Sensitive Plant, where line 58 was originally, "And in this Republic of odours and hues" (e. 12, pp. 145, 146). In a letter of 16 November 1819 to Maria Gisborne (Letters, II, 155) he quoted from La Cisma de Ingalaterra stanzas containing the phrase "un jardin, Republica de flores." Apparently the only instance of the metaphor in Shelley's poetry before 1819 is in Prince Athanase (dated 1817 by Mary): "flowers burst forth like starry beams" (248).

In her Proserpine (ed. A. Koszul, London, 1922), Mary Shelley wrote of "the starry flowers" (p. 5), the "fields ... which young Spring sprinkles with her stars" (p. 16), the "Star-eyed narcissi" (p. 20), and "Enna ... starred with flowers" (p. 41); and in her The Last Man (1826), she made the metaphor very plain: "the fire-bearing flowers of the sky, and the flowery stars of earth" (chap. iv).

curs so repeatedly in *The Sensitive Plant* and is so carefully controlled and elaborated that, especially in the context of the fable of nature's demise, it takes on ontological meaning and establishes a relationship between earth and heaven, just as the allegorical figures simultaneously diminish and exalt: the flowers are "the meteors of that sublunar Heaven" (II. 10). The lily's cup, for example, is "moonlight-coloured," and within it is its eye, a "fiery star" that gazes "through clear dew on the tender sky" (I. 33–36). In the daytime, that is, the lily is an inversion of the nighttime sky. Surrounded by its own moonlit hemisphere, the flower's star, shining through its dew, gazes on the heavens, just as at night, in the moonlit sky, stars gaze on the earth through the moist atmosphere. The metaphor persists: the river-buds are "starry" (I. 46); the flowers are stars that dart their beams as hues (I. 80–81);[11] they are "Like the lamps of the air when Night walks forth" (II. 11) and "Like stars when the moon is awakened" (III. 2); and the Lady, who is the soul of the flowers, scatters love in the garden "as stars do light" (III. 120). The garden even shapes its own overarching sky: the boughs of embowering blossoms form a "heaven of many a tangled hue" through which slants "golden and green light" (I. 41–44).

But although the flower garden and the starry sky are represented as mirror forms of each other, even to the point of being interchangeable images, they are never co-present but appear only alternately, just as the lily in the daytime is the inverse of the nighttime heaven. Remotely, this alternation is suggested when the flowers awakening in the morning to shine "smiling to Heaven" are likened to gems hidden in darkness and enkindled by mine-lamps. More explicitly, the flowers of the garden are "Like stars when the moon is awakened" (III. 2). The Lady tends the garden only "from morn to even," and during that span of time

> the meteors of that sublunar Heaven,
> Like the lamps of the air when Night walks forth,
> Laughed round her footsteps up from the Earth![12]   (II. 9–12)

---

[11]
The beams which dart from many a star
Of the flowers whose hues they [the winds] bear afar.

How intent Shelley was upon equating flowers with stars is suggested by his earlier MS version of these lines: "... many a sphere / Of the starry flowers..." (Harvard Notebook, p. 50). The Bodleian MS (e. 12) shows that he experimented with even more flower-star metaphors than he finally incorporated; and "The Question," which was written in the midst of the MS of *The Sensitive Plant* and makes direct use of some of the same material, adds more: the daisies are "those pearled Arcturi of the earth, / The constellated flower that never sets."

[12] Almost consistently Shelley uses "laughter" and "smiles" in the sense of light. Doubtless he was following the Latin practice of using *ridere* to mean "shine." See, for example, Lucretius iii. 22, iv. 1125; Horace *Odes* iv. 11. 6.

Both images seem marked by their inconstancy, alternately appearing and disappearing with the corresponding mutability of day and night, like the heavenly Apollo and earthly Pan of Shelley's hymns. Each image independently bespeaks the apparent absence of permanence and supports the fable, which tells of the annihilation of all things save the weeds of death. Yet, the star-flower metaphor tends to counteract this assumption, for a "starry scheme" is always observable somewhere, on earth in day and in the sky at night. Presumably we are to conclude either that starriness itself is mutable, alternating between sky and garden-world as day and night displace each other, or that the mutability is the observer's as his sight is suited to the darkness in which he can see the stars and to the light in which he can see the starry flowers. The images, by being metaphorically related, make it problematic whether mutability is a characteristic of reality or of experience.

Stars, however, carried a special symbolic significance for Shelley that he exploited in a number of poems. To him they are "immortal stars," "eternal," "deathless," "sacred"; they are "pure" and dwell in "eternal bowers."[13] They have a "different birth" from that of the ever-changing moon.[14] For not only did stars convey to him a spiritual significance that they derive from such traditions as astrology and the stellar origin of the human soul, he also glimpsed intimations of the eternity of transcendent Being in the fact that the stars are always present, obscured in day from earthly vision only by the diffusion of sunlight in the earth's atmosphere. The likening of the flower-world to the star-heaven suggests, then, not merely the mutable oscillation of starriness between world and sky but also, paradoxically, the immutable eternity of that starriness and therefore the possible eternity of both Existence, which is equatable with the One Mind, and the totally comprehensive and ultimate Being. For the metaphor is concerned not with the flowery character of stars but only with the starry nature of the earth's flowers and thus with the similarity of the world to heaven, which only *seems* mutable. In the flux of time, seeing alternately the starry flowers of the realm of Existence and the heavenly stars of the realm of Being, man experiences as mutable what in one of its phases, at least, only *appears* to be mutable; and the two modes of starriness, earthly and heavenly, correspond to the ambiguous botanical-biological classification of sensitive plants and to the fact that man is both a native of the world and alien to it. The region of the stars is not merely the sky, but "Heaven" (I. 64), and its presiding spirit is God (II. 4); the garden is the "sublunar heaven" (II. 10), differing from Heaven therefore only in being subject to the mutability beneath the moon. To the existence of an eternal perfection man is not totally blind,

[13] *Adonais*, 256; *The Revolt of Islam*, 3436; *The Two Spirits*, 9; *The Witch of Atlas*, 192; *Hymn of Apollo*, 21.
[14] "To the Moon."

but, being a sublunary creature, he can apprehend it only in the context of inconstancy, of alternating day and night, earth and heaven, perfect flowers and stars. The same paradox of a permanence in inconstancy is present in the fact that although the flowers alternately waken and dream and although the Lady tends them only "from morn to even," she is continuously their sustaining spirit, regardless of the flux of time (II. 3, 9); and this is likened to the relation of the immutable God to the apparently mutable stars. The flowers are to Heaven, moreover, as an infant to its mother, whose song first lulls the child to sleep but eventually awakens it, just as the sun's brightness arouses the flowers and then calls them to sleep.

The flowers (as an infant's awakening eyes
Smile on its mother, whose singing sweet
Can first lull, and at last must awaken it,)

When Heaven's blithe winds had unfolded them,
As mine-lamps enkindle a hidden gem,
Shone smiling to Heaven, and every one
Shared joy in the light of the gentle sun.　(I. 59–65)

The simile is meant to be exact: on awakening, the infant's eyes "Smile" (with its usual Shelleyan overtone of "shine") on its mother, as the awakened flowers shine "smiling to Heaven." The garden, that is, is represented as Heaven's offspring, responding in successively contrary ways to its single immutable source. Mutability, it would appear, is the observable manifestation of permanence in time, just as the one starriness alternates between garden and Heaven.

Indeed, without quite denying that the garden-world is subject to mutability, the imagery moves far toward, but just short of, trivializing the day-night alternation and the merely analogous relation of the sublunar heaven to Heaven, and toward identifying the two. In part, this is the consequence of the elaborate precision with which the mirror-relation of flower and star is carried out, as in the description of the lily as the inverted nighttime sky. When the Lady tends the flowers in the light of day, they, being stars of the sublunar heaven, shine "round her footsteps up from the Earth," just as when her heavenly counterpart, Night, walks forth in the sky the corresponding "lamps of the air" shine round her footsteps (II. 11–12). In effect, whatever may be said of Heaven may also be said of the sublunar heaven, so that the flux of day and night becomes of lesser significance. But the two realms are more than alike, as the mother-child metaphor suggests; they are also interconnected in such a fashion as to diminish their separateness. The dew, for example, mediates between the flowers and stars that otherwise are related only as alternating mirror

images. At night, the "clouds of the dew" lie "unseen" in the flowers but
sparkle "like fire" until the noonday sun [15] evaporates them and they become the flower-fragrant clouds of the sky, wandering "like spirits among
the spheres" and consequently linking the flowers with their starry counterparts (I. 86–89). Moreover, the dew inverts the temporal relation between the flowers of day and stars of night: unseen, it flashes like fire [16]
in the hidden flowers when the stars are visible but is visible in the sky
as clouds when the fiery stars are hidden in the light diffused by the
earth's moist atmosphere. Acting like stars in the extinguished flowers, the
dew carries to the hidden stars the scent of the flowers, and, compensating
for the temporal mutability of the starry flowers of day and the stars of
night, it tends to cancel out the relevance of time.

The most functional interconnection of God's starry scheme with the
Lady's apparently mutable garden-world, however, is elaborated in the
description of the spirit who seems to attend the Lady (II. 13–20).
Throughout the day she tends her "undefiled Paradise" and sustains its
perfection; but in addition, at night her dreams are "less slumber than
Paradise," a dream-Paradise that seems to descend upon her from the other
starry Heaven. Like the Sensitive Plant, she has "no companion of mortal
race," and she cannot be complemented and fulfilled as the other flowers
are, save the Sensitive Plant, by anything in the world-garden. Neither
man the Sensitive Plant nor the sustaining spirit of earthly existence has
a compeer in the mutable world, and although they exist in it they are
not completed by it. The Lady's dreams of Paradise therefore visit her as
if one of the immortal stars—a "bright Spirit" not of mortal race—had
deserted Heaven in the night, "while the stars were awake," to be her
"companion." The Lady, then, tends the starry flowers by day and seems
visited in her nightly dreams by a heavenly star from God's starry scheme
when the garden of which she is the sustaining spirit is no longer starry;
she knows Paradise in both day and night, one through direct experience,
the other in dreams. The star that descends from heaven at night to
attend the Lady exactly inverts the course of the flowers' starry dew that
mediates between the two realms by ascending in the day as odorous
clouds that attend the invisible stars.

But the bond between Heaven and the sustaining soul of earth is
drawn even tighter, for the bright Spirit from Heaven seems to attend the
Lady even by day, "Though the veil of daylight concealed him from her,"
since daylight naturally hides the eternal, ever-present stars from the senses

[15] In the MS (e. 12, p. 46) Shelley wrote, "till dawning day."
[16] Compare "dew-stars" (*Prometheus Unbound*, II. i. 168 and IV. 41); "starred
with lurid dew" (*The Sensitive Plant*, III. 61); and "starry dew" (*Adonais*, 91).
In an adjacent stanza in the MS of *The Sensitive Plant* Shelley described the wandering mist as dropping on the flowers at night "beneath the stars like a golden
star" (e. 12, pp. 46, 48).

and gives the illusion of their absence. The immortal heavenly star, only seeming to appear in nightly dream and to vanish by day when she tends the starry flowers, is properly the constant companion of the Lady, who, though she labors by day and sleeps by night, is nevertheless the constant "Power" of the garden-world. Significantly, it is only in dream that, like the Visionary of *Alastor*, she has an experience like an awareness of her transcendent companion; although still attended by the heavenly star in her awakened state, she is unconscious of him because he is unavailable to the senses, which can know starriness only as the apparently mutable starry flowers of the objective sensible world. "The phantom is beside thee whom thou seekest," the speaker of *Epipsychidion* is told when he searches for the "Being" of his dream; but in response to his "Where?" the sensible world only echoes his question.[17]

Both the immortal sky and the objective world are starry gardens; the Lady is to the starry garden as God is to the starry scheme; the immortal star from Heaven always attends the existing power of the world's existence; the world is like the child of Heaven. If it is excessive to say there is no difference between the garden in its "perfect prime" and the Heaven, at least the difference is minimized by the imagery, for behind all apparently mutable manifestations there is one constant reality. There is, therefore, but one term, the starry "Heaven," but Heaven may be experienced as an eternal transcendence or as the starry sublunary heaven of mutability. The constant is "Paradise," but the Lady experiences it in one manner by day and another in sleep. The mother's song remains the same, but her child responds by alternately sleeping and awakening. Although "the painted veil which those who live / Call Life" depicts "unreal shapes," it mimics "all we would believe,"[18] for although there appear to be two realms, one of existence and the other of absolute Being, mirror images alternating in time, they are essentially the same. The object of experience remains unchanged: the mutability resides in the child, not the song, in the flowers that respond variously to the one and persisting light of the sun, in the Lady and not in the Star that attends her. The oscillation from one extreme to another is due to the inconstancy in the experiencing subject and is epistemological, not ontological. The distinction is one that Shelley was to experiment with later in the manuscript of *The Triumph of Life*:

> "Figures ever new
> Rise on the bubble [i.e. the world], paint them how you may;
>   We have but thrown, as those before us threw,

---

[17] *Epipsychidion*, 233–34. For the recurrent Shelleyan image of the ideal self that moves "beside" one in life, see pp. 9–10, 32, 77, 428–32.
[18] "Lift not the painted veil."

"Our shadows on it as it past away."
"Or as you passed," I interrupted; "thus
One who awakes within a ship would say

That the stars move; as it appears to us
So is it not, however it may be."[19]

The ultimate "Conclusion" of *The Sensitive Plant* that the Lady and garden yet endure while " 'Tis we, 'tis ours, are changed; not they" (III. 133) has been inherent throughout in the imagery of the poem, in its subtler language, despite the seemingly contradictory surface statement made by the fable of their deaths. Although the fable seems to deal only with the question of objective existence, in another of its dimensions it has been preparing for the "Conclusion," which interprets existence in the context of subjective knowing.

In view of the use of day and night, light and darkness, in the descriptive passages of the fable to represent apparent inconstancy, the fact that the "Conclusion" is also expressed in imagery of light suggests a special significance there:

For love, and beauty, and delight,[20]
There is no death nor change: their might
Exceeds our organs, which endure
No light, being themselves obscure.   (III. 134–37)

Since star and starriness are symbolic in the poem of perfect being, the ideal condition is night: the perfection of the flowers is that in day they appear like the stars of night. Evening, therefore, is not represented as a deprivation of light but as a reality that, like the starry visitant to the Lady's dreams, "descended from heaven above" (I. 98), Evening's true home, to visit the sublunary heaven. Day, on the other hand, which divulges to man the sensible world that he usually accepts as real, is a deceptive "veil" (I. 101), a "veil of daylight" (II. 20), a diffusion of light through the atmosphere that hides Evening and her ever-present stars and conceals from the Lady the heaven-descended starry spirit that always attends her. With the coming of Evening, delight, which the "Conclusion" identifies as one of the eternal forms, "though less bright, was far more deep" (I. 100), and the depth of the experience of it is of greater value than its brilliance. The daylight diffused by the atmosphere falsely conceals from man's senses the eternal reality, although it reveals to him the transitory flowers as replicas of the eternal stars. Just as "in living we lose

[19] MS c. 4, fols. 30ᵛ–32ʳ (Reiman, pp. 168, 242).
[20] In his first attempt at this line Shelley wrote, "For love and thought there is not death" (Huntington Notebooks, I, 203).

the apprehension of life," in blinding daylight we lose the visual experience of the starlight symbolic of eternal Being. In a similar way, the visionary lady of *The Triumph of Life*, a "shape all light" that came from the "realm without a name, / Into this valley of perpetual dream," wanes like the morning star before the cold, "severe excess" of life's daylight, even though, unseen, she continues to keep her "obscure tenour" beside the speaker's path.[21] And Shelley postponed the continuation of the Witch of Atlas' story for winter nights because in the garish days of summer our *belief* is nearly limited to what we see.

With respect to the heavenly stars as symbolic of eternal Being, therefore, the "Conclusion" is to be read literally: the love, beauty, and delight that are the eternal forms constitutive of Existence are of such blazing brilliance that our senses cannot perceive them in their own blinding nature, just as we cannot see the stars in the greater glare of daylight. Paradoxically, we are so constituted that we can experience manifestations of light only in darkness. In describing the senses as "obscure" (III. 137), Shelley no doubt had reference to the traditional representation of the eye as a camera obscura, a dark chamber into which only a thin beam of light is admitted.[22] It is an index to the limitations of our nature that we are dependent on darkness for the sight of what light makes visible and that, were the eye flooded with light, it would not see at all. We cannot have direct sensory knowledge of the blinding forms but, like the camera obscura, receive only those images that the limited light impresses on our darkness, only the starriness that oscillates between earth and sky in our temporal interchange of day and night. For light, in all its Shelleyan symbolic senses, is not in our nature. Unlike all other occupants of the garden, the Sensitive Plant has "no bright flower"; "Radiance" is not its "dower" (I. 74–75).

But this reading of the "Conclusion" can explain only the fluctuation of starriness between garden-world and Heaven: because of the darkness of our senses we can see the stars only at night, and in day we see the flowers only as earthly simulacra of the nightly stars. It can, that is, explain only the fact that the forms themselves do not change, not that they do not die; it is relevant to the star-flower and day-night pattern that is elaborated indirectly in the descriptive imagery, no to the explicit fable,

---

[21] *The Triumph of Life*, 352–433.

[22] Locke had employed the metaphor for the mind at large: "... external and internal sensations are the only passages that I can find of knowledge to the understanding. These alone ... are the windows by which light is let into this *dark room*; for methinks the understanding is not much unlike a closet wholly shut from light, with only some little opening left, to let in external visible resemblances, or ideas of things without...." (*Essay Concerning Human Understanding*, II, xi, 17). Only a few pages earlier, arguing that perception distinguishes animals from inferior beings, he instanced the sensitive plant as operating only as mechanism, despite its "motion which has some resemblance to that which in animals follows upon sensation" (II, ix, 11).

which tells that the garden dies in winter and is not revived in spring and to which the "Conclusion" is offered as an answer. For there are two simultaneous time patterns in the poem: the day-night fluctuation implicit in the flower-star metaphors which has to do with the inconstancy of our perception of perfect Existence, and the seasonal movement of the fable which has to do with the question of death and extinction. The question asked by the seasonal development of the fable is whether the garden of Existence endures, and since the garden is evident to man only in daylight, the meaning of the last stanza cannot be that man is unable to see it in a flood of light. In terms of the fable, then, the statement that the might of the forms constitutive of Existence "Exceeds our organs, which endure / No light" (III. 136–37) must mean, not that our senses cannot *tolerate* light, but that they cannot long *continue* to experience the brilliant forms of Being which the garden manifests as Existence and that as the senses fade and die they mistakenly report that it is the sensory shapes manifested by the forms that vanish.[23] No doubt it was this distinction between the eternal and the imperfection of human senses that Shelley meant when he told Medwin concerning death, "My mind is tranquil. I have no fears and some hopes. In our present gross material state our faculties are clouded."

The "Conclusion" so abruptly translates into an epistemological question what the narrative had presented as ontological that we are required to consider in what sense nature can be said to die at the end of the fable and whether, indeed, the fable is, as it appears to be, an account of reality or an account of our experience of it. If it is right to identify the Sensitive Plant as man, it is significant that the speculation of the "Conclusion" distinguishes the garden and its sustaining Lady from man: "'Tis we, 'tis ours, are changed; not they." Reality only *appears* to end in annihilation because man's faculties of perception are extinguished and because man's earthy life is one

Of error, ignorance, and strife,
Where nothing is, but all things seem.   (III. 123–24)

This would seem to say, then, that the fable of nature's death is only appearance, not fact, and that our "obscure" senses do not report the true character of reality, which is symbolized as light. Now, the title of the poem implies that the subject and central point of reference is the Sensitive Plant, and although it seems inconsistent that so little of the poem is explicitly devoted to it, it is introduced at the crucial points. With the Sensitive Plant the fable begins and ends, as though its birth and death

[23] It is at least suggestive that before deciding on "their might / Exeeds our organs" Shelley wrote, "their light / Outlives our feelings" and then substituted "visions" for "feelings" (Huntington Notebooks, I, 204).

envelop and contain the story. However, the close of the fable not only violates the fact of nature but also contradicts the opening, for the poem begins with spring, when the Sensitive Plant and the other flowers "rose" from the dreams of their "wintry rest," but ends with the following spring, when, contrary to our expectation of another awakening in nature's continuous cycle, the Sensitive Plant was a "leafless wreck" and only "the mandrakes and toadstools, and docks, and darnels, / Rose like the dead from their ruined charnels" (III. 110–13). Of course the opening stanzas must be right; the senses normally report that winter is nature's sleep, not death, and that nature does revive cyclically. The garden of the second spring is filled only with the symbols of death because the description of the flowers has been subjective all along, not objective, and their state of existence has been relative to the Sensitive Plant's power of perception. *It* has changed, not they.

In the spring of its life, when its faculties of perception are purest, the Sensitive Plant has experienced the flowers as the perfect fulfillment of their forms—that is, as perfect existence—and it is significant that when autumn comes and the Lady has apparently died, the description of the fading garden begins, not with the objective facts, but with the Sensitive Plant's subjective responses: *it* "Felt the sound of the funeral chant" (III. 6). Even the one description of the Sensitive Plant's decline is presented in terms of one who is being interdicted, or banned ("forbid"), from the garden and whose eyes are blinded:

The Sensitive Plant, like one forbid,
Wept, and the tears within each lid
Of its folded leaves, which together grew,
Were changed to a blight of frozen glue.   (III. 78–81)

Correspondingly, although the flowers remain "like stars" for three days after the Lady's apparent death (III. 1–2), thereafter the metaphor, which has recurred throughout the first two parts of the fable, nearly disappears from the poem. When, however, it does return, it describes "plants, at whose names the verse feels loath" which are "starred with a lurid dew," not the lovely star-flowers of the first two parts (III. 58, 61). The metaphor, that is, has persisted, and in the sense of a light glowing in darkness the word "lurid" repeats the image of the stars of night. The object has remained unchanged: the garden is still starry. But the quality of the perception has decayed because of a decay in the perceiver, and the same image that had represented the greatest earthly beauty now represents the hideous and deathly. Similarly, just as daylight veiled the descended starry spirit that seemed, unseen, to attend the Lady, so now "meteors from spray to spray / Crept and flitted in broad noonday / Unseen." But instead of being the starry meteors of the sublunar heaven, these are "unctuous meteors"—the treacherous and misleading ignis fatuus born of the morass—and they are a "venomous blight" (III. 74–77). The garden continues to be star-like, but the image now intimates destruction and death, not because the garden is no longer a paradise and not because it is dead, but because the medium of the perception of it is dying. The poetic mode of proceeding is of a piece with Shelley's recurrent ironic transformation of his *données*, as we have already seen it in such poems as *Alastor* and *The Two Spirits*, by skeptically subjecting them to radically different perspectives. When at last the Sensitive Plant is dead, the only life in the garden is living death, the poisonous weeds that rise "like the dead from their ruined charnels" (III. 113). The flowers fail to reappear after their winter sleep only because the Sensitive Plant is dead and cannot see: man wrongly assumes that reality truly is what sensorily seems to be. In brief, that the "external" world decays, which is the theme of the fable, is the conclusion led to by the dualistic "popular philosophy," which assumes that the senses report objective fact; the "intellectual philosophy," by removing the distinction between thing and thought, opens up the possibility that the supposed transience of reality is a function of the mutability of our powers of perception. Shelley has chosen his flowers with care. All of the other flowers of the garden—snowdrop, violet, anemone, tulip, narcissus, lily, hyacinth, rose, jessamine, tuberose, water lily, and daisy—are perennials in the climates Shelley knew. Only the exotic Sensitive Plant, like man, is an annual.

iii

The poem, then, is a remarkably complex tissue of paradoxes that arise out of Shelley's persistent skeptical impulse to recognize antinomies everywhere. The "Conclusion" asserts the eternity of reality; the fable tells of nature's extinction. The fable begins with nature's ever-renewed cycle but ends with nature's final annihilation. The fable follows the course of the seasons and ends with death; but it is elaborated by a recurrent metaphor drawn from a different temporal pattern, the alternation of day and night, and this intimates the deathlessness of reality. The metaphor, moreover, implies two realms that are the same and yet different, the stars of night and the starry flowers of day, the realms of Being and Existence. The stars of night occupy "Heaven," the starry flowers the "sublunar heaven"; the Lady tends an undefiled Paradise in day and dreams of Paradise at night; and her paradisiacal dreams are of a descended star of night which also, unseen, attends her by day while she cares for the starry flowers. The Sensitive Plant is native to the garden and yet alien to it. It is even paradoxical that the titular subject of the poem appears to play so small a role in it and yet actually is its sole determinant; for the most important paradox of all is that the fable tells of the death of the objective world and the "Conclusion" attributes this bit of seeming to the destruction of the subjective faculties of perception. In these paradoxes and others related to them, all reflecting Shelley's persistent conception of man's ambiguous nature, lies the essential significance of the poem.

A partial index to the significance of these paradoxes is provided by the distinction in the "Conclusion" between true existence and seeming:

> in this life
> Of error, ignorance, and strife,
> Where nothing is, but all things seem,
> And we the shadows of the dream,
>
> It is a modest creed, and yet
> Pleasant if one considers it,
> To own that death itself must be,
> Like all the rest, a mockery.   (III. 122–29)

Like everything else we think real, death, or nonexistence, is only a seeming, since the senses can report only their own phenomena; and yet there is a true reality to which they do not have direct access. Similarly, mortal, sensory man is only the shadow of the dream, not the dream itself. The implication relates appearances to the senses and reality to dream. Moreover, if we reconsider the paradoxes of the fable we find that only the seasonal narrative of nature's eventual extinction is explicit and overt, being proffered to our literalistic mind in the same way that the world is to our senses; that narrative, then, is also of the order of a seeming which we falsely take to be true. All the other factors of the paradoxes, such as the relation of flowers to stars or the Lady's attendance by a star, enter the poem only by way of metaphor or other indirect, nonliteral means. For the poem embodies two ways of knowing: through the senses and through the imagination, corresponding to seeming and reality, or to man as shadow of the dream and the dream itself. The mode of existence of the poem is identical with that of the reality it defines. If we read the poem with our fallible senses, we "perceive" only the superficial fable telling of nature's life and death; if we read it with the imagination, we experience its nonliteral revelations that exceed the limits of sensory experience, and these intimate the eternity of the forms of reality. The two categories of experience are recurrent in Shelley's way of thought: they correspond, for example, to the distinction in *Mont Blanc* between, on the one hand, the sensation of vacancies in nature and the sensory evidence presented by "the naked countenance of earth / On which I gaze" that nature revolves, subsides, and swells, and, on the other hand, the insight into the unchanging eternal Power inaccessible to the senses but available to trance and dream, and possibly death.

As an empirical skeptic and idealist, Shelley has reversed the distinction of our "popular philosophy" between seeming, which we normally attribute to the imagination, and reality, which we assume our senses report to us. In *Mont Blanc* the "legion of wild thoughts" constitutes the so-called world by seeking to match the shadows passing over the cave of the mind with their unknowable sources: what our senses call the world is only what "seems." But the same body of wild thoughts has the power through trance and dream—in short, through the imagination—to "float above" the darkness of the mind and apprehend the eternal and immutable gleam: what the imagination gains access to is the probable reality, or an adequate ground for a "creed," or at the very least justification for a hopeful rhetorical question. But the two acts of thought are not unrelated. Shelley remains the empiricist and does not admit of any direct and certain mystical apprehension of eternal Being independent of the sensory data of Existence, illusory though they are in themselves. As sensory images, the world reveals "vacancies" and extinctions that are denied by the "imaginings" of the human mind, which is "at enmity with nothingness and dissolution." Correspondingly, the apparent and exposed subject of *The Sensitive Plant*, despite the title, is the life and death of the world-garden. But in the very act whereby the senses report these data, the poet's imagination operates on them through similes and metaphors, dreams and yearnings, to gain intimations of the eternal reality. If it is objected that this examination of the poem has devoted inordinate attention to its merely incidental features and consequently has misrepresented what it *obviously* says, the answer is that the poem, as an object, is a replica of Shelley's world, whose *obvious* appearance is an illusion but through whose apparent images the imagination can incidentally and occasionally guess at the truth. The poem, that is, is designed to be as deceptive on the surface as the superficial senses are and as true as the imagination at those incidental moments when imaging becomes imagining. Hence, for example, the apparent inconsistency that the obvious subject of the poem is the life and death of the garden and that its titular subject is the Sensitive Plant: the title is right, for what superficially seems to be the extinction of reality is the death of the powers of perceiving it.

While the sensory data of the fable, then, assert the transitoriness of the world, the imagination recurrently operates through and beyond the sensory data to make a counterstatement. Unlike the death of the Lady and her garden, the relation of the flowers to stars, and of the world of Existence to the Heaven of Being, enters the poem not as experiential fact but through the medium of simile and metaphor, which is the imagination's way of raising illusory appearance to probable truth. The Lady, who is the spirit of earthly existence, is *as if* attended by some starry spirit who is *as if* still present in daylight; and her relation to the garden is but analogous to God's relation to the eternal stars. The flowers are "*Like* lamps of the air," and only metaphorically are they earthly "meteors." Only metaphorically is the garden-world the "sublunar heaven." The "daisies and delicate bells" are "As fair as the fabulous asphodels" (I. 53–54); and this simile links the garden-world with the eternal post-mortal Elysium of Greek myth, just as the flower-star metaphor links it with the eternal Heaven. But poetic metaphors are potentially true to the imagination, and if we can find even "modest" credence in them, the poem implies, we can have faith in the one eternal reality to which they allude. Credence, we recall, Shelley did not think to be voluntary and capricious; and man is "pre-eminently an imaginative being."

Just as metaphor works through what sensorily seems to be to what is beyond the sense, so imaginative insight filters in from the desire for what is beyond the available. The earthly perfection of the spring and summer garden consists in each flower's being absolutely fulfilled, either by others or by itself in a totality of love, and the sense of total unity is further intimated by the recurrent synaesthetic confusion of light, sound, and odor. The narcissi "gaze on their eyes in the stream's recess, / Till they die of their own dear loveliness" (I. 19–20). Others are interpenetrated with each other's light and odor so that all are "Wrapped and filled by their mutual atmosphere" (I. 69). The scent of the snowdrop and violet is harmoniously mixed with the odors of the turf from which they have just sprung, "like the voice and the instrument" (I. 16). The rose totally bestows the "soul of her beauty and love" by unfolding petal upon petal (I. 32); the music of the hyacinth bells is received absolutely, for it is so intense that it is felt "like an odour within the sense" (I. 27–28). Each shares the other's joy or is self-fulfilled. From this perfect mutuality, however, the Sensitive Plant is excluded, "like one forbid." In a realm which it experiences as completely fulfilled, it is imperfect and unfulfilled, having no radiance or odor to give. And yet, curiously, although lesser than the other flowers and as incapable of attaining union with them as was the Visionary of *Alastor*, the Sensitive Plant is especially favored by nature, is served by all the beauties of sound, scent, and light as though they were its "ministering angels" (I. 94). Although it receives more beauty than all the other flowers (I. 72), it yearns for even more than the garden-world can supply. For although man is lesser than nature, he alone receives all it can offer, and yet aspires to what is beyond nature. If he is to be fulfilled, it must be in a realm commensurate with his desire, and in that power to desire lies the imagination's promise of such a realm, or state of being.

Then, just as the starry garden of day has for its counterpart the starry heaven of night, just as the Lady walks in day in her garden-Paradise and at night has dreams that are Paradise, and just as man cannot "endure," in one sense, the daylight that hides the stars of Being and, in another, the starry light of the daytime flowers of Existence, so the poem is everywhere double in its language and imagery; for each of the first of these terms belongs to empirical reality, while the second terms are the same phenomena as they exist in poetic, or imaginative, conception. Correspondingly, the ability of the Sensitive Plant to experience but not participate in all of earthly beauty and its desire for what transcends the world imply two modes of beauty, two modes of love. Although the Sensitive Plant received more than all the others, it trembles "with love's sweet want" (I. 11) in a realm where no others are in want; for it desires not merely sensible beauty, but "*the* beautiful," the ideal beauty, for the very reason that it is not endowed with it but has absolute capacity for it (I. 77). As Shelley wrote in his review of Peacock's *Rhododaphne*, "Plato says, with profound allegory, that Love is not itself beautiful, but seeks the possession of beauty; this idea seems embodied in the deformed dwarf who bids ... Anthemion [the flower] enter."[24] Because man is lesser than nature, he is, paradoxically, greater than it, for the same reason that the imaginative metaphors in Shelley's poem are subordinate to the overt narrative and are veiled beneath it, but yield a greater and more probable truth than that narrative. The very failure of man to fulfill himself in the otherwise self-fulfilling world and his aspiration to absolute Beauty are, as Keats also saw in his "Ode to a Nightingale," the testimony from the imagination that the ideal *is* a reality—that the "unattainable point to which Love tends" is a point that exists and can be attained—and that man's destiny is with it. The love of the Sensitive Plant therefore is not like that of the other flowers, a love sensorily conceived: "It loves, even like Love" itself (I. 76).

Although the starry flowers, then, are perceived in their spring and summer life as perfect beauty engaging in perfect love, these are not identical in mode with Beauty and Love; and it is to these ideals that the Sensitive Plant aspires, not despite, but because of its inadequacy in the world. But it is not, therefore, to be assumed that there are two kinds of love and beauty, the One as categorically distinct from the Many, the Uranian Venus as distinct from the Pandemic; there are, instead, two modes, or degrees, of experience. There is, ultimately, only Being, and the love and beauty the Sensitive Plant observes in the garden are those modes of Being perceived as Existence by the senses in their perfection. The dualism of the Platonic and Platonistic systems is ontological; for Shelley this apparent dualism is epistemological. Reality can be defined only in terms of subjective experience, but that experience may be merely sensory and, at best, the senses being perfect, will reveal the "beauty" of Existence, or, building on the sensory, it may be imaginative and reveal

[24] Julian, VI, 275. The reference is to *Symposium* 201. Incidentally, the use of "flower" in Greek, Latin, and English, among other languages, to mean the highest, or ideal, state of anything not only clarifies Peacock's use of the name "Anthemion" but also suggests the symbolic significance of the spring and summer state of flowers in Shelley's garden as the perfect state of existence.

the "Beauty" of Being. The ambiguity is not in the character of Being, but in that of experience: seen from below, Shelley's Cloud dissolves in rain; seen from above, it basks in heaven's blue smile.

Not only in metaphors and in unfulfilled aspirations does Shelley find imaginative intimations of the true plane of Reality behind and beyond what appears to the unstable senses, but also in the light and transient but vivid revelations of dreams. To the Lady, who is the spirit of the earthly Paradise, comes a dream-Paradise, seemingly from the starry heaven of night, and, though imperceptible to the senses, it invests her daytime existence. The garden, then, is the Paradise that can appear only briefly in the senses, not because it is inconstant, but because the senses are; the dream is the Paradise to which the imagination has access. But the use of the same name to designate the two experiences postulates that there is but one Paradise, transient to the senses but credibly eternal to transient dreams. Correspondingly, the Sensitive Plant, although the favorite of the Lady and the rest of the garden-world, is also the favorite of Night, the heavenly analogue of the Lady. Night cradles it in her embrace, and it is the earliest of the flowers to be "Up-gathered into the bosom of rest" (I. 110–13). Night and Rest grant the Sensitive Plant the favor of special insight, not despite, but because it is the "feeblest" of Nature's children. Like the Lady, the Sensitive Plant also has dreams in the night that intimate a Paradise behind the apparent Paradise of the garden, an Elysium, which is the postmortal Paradise of heroes—the realm whose flower, the fabulous asphodel, has already been linked by the imagination's metaphor-making vision with the flowers of the garden: in the silence of night

(Only over head the sweet nightingale
Ever sang more sweet as the day might fail,
And snatches of its Elysian chant
Were mixed with the dreams of the sensitive plant.) (I. 106–9)

The parentheses with which Shelley surrounded the stanza visibly separate that Elysian dream-world sung by Night's songster from the sensory world pictured by the other stanzas, so that this imaginative Paradise, like the Lady's attendant spirit, also insinuates itself into the sensory world from above ("over head") in the otherwise empty intervals between sensory experiences. It is for this reason also that evening appears on earth by descending "from heaven above" and is made manifest by the removal of "the day's veil" from "the world of sleep" (I. 98–101). For the credible reality is "the world of sleep," in which man has intimations of the Elysium that is otherwise hidden from him by his conscious senses or by the world's film of light:

Some say that gleams of a remoter world
Visit the soul in sleep,—that death is slumber,
And that its shapes the busy thoughts outnumber
Of those who wake and live.[25]

This is not to say that in *The Sensitive Plant* the senses have reported only a falsity. The Sensitive Plant is the favorite of the Lady of the daytime Paradise *and* of Night and her dreams: so long as the senses are perfect they report true Existence, the sensory and "seeming" form of Being; the more-than-sensory dreams dimly apprehend what faith is able to accept as the absolute nature of Being. Since "hallucinations, dreams, and the ideas of madness" differ in no essential way from those other thoughts "called *real*, or *external* objects," the only criterion of their relative validity is the subjective one of belief. Granting that the senses leave vivid "marks" on the mind, their evidence, although constitutive of what man normally calls "the world," is suspect because they become "obscure" and fade; on the other hand, like the other modes of the imagination, dreams are transient, irregular, and deposit only faint mental records. In accordance with Shelley's recurrent philosophic identification of the self with world, dreams are an "ocean,"

Whose waves never mark, tho' they ever impress
The light sand which paves it, consciousness.[26]   (I. 104–5)

In his "modest creed," Shelley has chosen to accept these "impressions" rather than the sensory "marks" as indicative of eternal reality.

Meanwhile, in the course of the drama of the poem an apparently casual image has been subtly urging its own symbolic meaning as attestation of the immortality of the soul, despite the mutability and mortality of the senses. In the garden, the Lady leaves, as though they were signs to be interpreted, "many an antenatal tomb, / Where butterflies dream of the life to come" (II. 53–54). Here, in the seeming world is a death that is prior to a birth, palpable evidence, even to the senses, of a life that follows death and entombment. This postmortal life, which is in fact destined for the caterpillar, is foreseen in imaginative dreams by the butterfly, the traditional symbol of the soul—just as the Lady dreams of Paradise, just as snatches of an Elysian chant enter the dreams of the

[25] *Mont Blanc*, 49–52.
[26] Cf. *Defence of Poetry* (Julian, VII, 136): Poetry "is as it were the interpenetration of a diviner nature through our own; but its footsteps are like those of a wind over a sea, which the coming calm erases, and whose traces remain only, as on the wrinkled sand which paves it." For similar instances of thought as a sea and of the mind as a sandy shore that receives transient impressions, see *Triumph of Life*, 405–7, *Unfinished Drama*, 151–4, and *Hellas*, 696–9. For the self as world, see below, Chap. 14, pt. ii.

Sensitive Plant, just as mortal men are "shadows of the dream," and just as the garden of flowers is the sublunar heaven. But it is significant that in the tomb, where it is both dead to one life and not yet born to another, it is the *butterfly*—not, as we would expect, the chrysalis—that dreams of the life to come, for the chrysalis is in essence, though not in appearance, the future butterfly. Man's mortal life, together with its most nearly perfect sensory experiences, is indeed the life to come; inherent in the shadow is the dream it reflects. The imaginative dreams that come to earthly man in his entombment in the senses divulge the pure fullness of what he is in essence. As Mary expressed it, Shelley believed that his individual mind was a unit of the Absolute and that "hereafter, *as now*, he would form a portion of that whole." Then if both the chrysalis and its future self are the butterfly, the spring and summer garden known to the senses is really identical—at least in the poet's "modest creed"—with the eternal reality. Nothing dies but the senses: the "universe" is eternal, and the a-sensory soul of man continues in another context of being.

This analysis of the poem, however, has transposed it into a key far too solemn and philosophically ponderous. The tetrameter quatrains and the frequency of the skimming anapests, the filigree quality of the descriptions, and the seeming triviality of the flower fable all suggest an attitude only lightly held. In the "Conclusion" Shelley eschews the gravity of conviction: whether the human Sensitive Plant in its separate identity or whether its inner impersonal spirit endures beyond this world and contemplates the world's decay, he "cannot say" (III. 117). Whether the Lady, when divorced from her sensible form and existing only as the "mind" which had formerly "upborne" her form (II. 6; III. 118–19), grieves over the sensible decay of the garden, he "dare not guess" (III. 122). For the senses can tell us nothing directly about a universe transcending mental phenomena. Even the poet's imaginative faith in eternal Existence and Being is not profound; it is only a "modest" and "pleasant" one—"*if* one considers it" (III. 126–27).[27] Only in the last two stanzas, the creed having been granted, does the poem rise to a sweeping pronouncement on the eternity of Existence and Being. Yet this light and provisional stance is integral to the attitude the poem must strike, for all the evidence of the poet's creed has come from the uncertain intuitions of the imagination. However unreliable the senses, they do constitute our experiential world, and the human mind "cannot be considered pure." Although Shelley would wish to believe in perfection, eternity, and immortality, they are constructs of the imagination and rest on the incertitude of faith. He is still the ambivalent skeptic, but whereas he had left ambiguous and open-ended such poems as *Alastor* and *Julian and Maddalo*, in *The Sensitive Plant* he succeeded, with the aid of the "intellectual philosophy," in

---

[27] Shelley's Latin lexicons, borrowing from Festus' second–century glossary, would have informed him that "consider" was supposedly derived from *sidus* (star).

transforming skepticism into a probabilism and, without neglecting either side of the ontological antinomy, tentatively electing one rather than the other.

iv

An obscurity yet remains: Shelley's explanation for the eternity of the garden-world of Existence is that "For love, and beauty, and delight / There is no death nor change" (III, 134). It is the might of *their* "light," not the light of the eternal flowers, that exceeds our obscure senses. Supposedly objective particulars, such as flowers, are the supposedly discrete mind's partial perceptions of absolute Existence. But Existence does not embrace Being, which includes all the unknowable mysteries outside Existence. Unitary Being is the Form of all the forms that sustain Existence, and the True, the Good, and the Beautiful are merely the partial formal names we assign it. For Shelley's purpose so, too, is any other abstract perfection, whether it is called Love, Joy, Friendship, Hope, or Liberty. On this basis, he occasionally assumed a modified Platonic ontology, conceiving of Existence as constituted, not of sensible particulars, but of the various eternal forms of Being which stand behind the mutable phenomena in which they appear to the senses. Yet, Shelley adapted this bit of quasi-Platonism to his own special vision and differs from Plato (for example, in *Parmenides* and Book V of *The Republic*) in his conception of the constitutive forms and the source of mutability. Although he treats natural particulars, such as flowers, as most nearly approximating their forms when they are in "perfect prime," or in fullest development of their inherent nature, he is concerned primarily with an ontology, not of material, but of mental forms, such as Love and Beauty, which we can perceive only in the shape of particular phenomena; and because of the subjective basis of his "intellectual philosophy," he was inclined, as we have seen, to attribute mutability to the instability of our organs of perception rather than to a world in flux. As Shelley speculates on a world that is meaningful because it is eternal and constant, he conceives, then, of three factors: Being and its unchanging forms that constitute Existence; the cyclical or transient shapes in which those forms appear to the senses; and the mutable, mortal faculties of perception, which possess or are given insight into the forms for only a moment and consequently customarily misinterpret reality. In terms of the categories in *The Republic*, the forms account for what Plato calls Being, the shapes for that which partakes of both Plato's being and nonbeing, and the senses for the illusion of nonbeing. It is for these reasons that when the conclusion is reached that the world-garden is eternal, while " 'Tis we, 'tis ours, are changed," the explanation is not that the sensible flowers persist but that the constitutive forms of Existence—love, beauty, and delight—are eternal.

The role of these constitutive forms can better be understood through an examination of one of Shelley's brief poems, for behind even some of his deceptively slight lyrics lies the special metaphysics embodied in *The Sensitive Plant*, considerably complicating their statements and functionally involving their component parts. In a posthumously published lyric that Mary entitled "Mutability," reality is first represented, as it is in the fable of *The Sensitive Plant*, in terms of the "popular," or "mechanical," philosophy: our sensible world has no constancy, and all that we perceive as beautiful and joyous is evanescent.

> The flower that smiles today
> > Tomorrow dies;
> All that we wish to stay
> > Tempts and then flies;
> What is this world's delight?
> Lightning that mocks the night,
> > Brief even as bright.

But, as in the "Conclusion" of *The Sensitive Plant*, this is exactly what the next stanza denies by substituting the constitutive forms for sensible phenomena, such as flowers, and by transferring the factor of transience to the perceiving subject:

> Virtue, how frail it is!
> > Friendship, how rare!
> Love, how it sells poor bliss
> > For proud despair!
> But these though soon they fall,[28]
> Survive their joy, and all
> > Which ours we call.

What soon "falls" is not actually the forms, Virtue, Friendship, and Love, but the phenomena, such as flowers, whereby the forms appear to our ephemeral and inadequate senses, and our personal experiences of the forms, such as our experience of human virtue and friendship. For the forms survive the transient joy which we call ours but which is really the possession of the forms constitutive of Existence—Shelley, as we shall see

---

[28] The received reading, "But we, though soon they fall," must be incorrect. Both of Shelley's manuscripts of the poem (MS e. 7, inside cover and p. 154), one a fair copy, clearly show "these," and Mary's transcript in Bodleian MS Shelley d. 7 has "these" or perhaps, as a misreading of Shelley's hand, "then." In view of the complexity of the statement Shelley is trying to make, and since he himself first wrote, "Which theirs we call" and then cancelled "theirs" for "ours," Mary can hardly be blamed for having taken on the duty of simplifying the stanza, however erroneously.

even more fully, is recurrently inclined to deny the ultimate reality of individual identity and to consider the individual a factor or passive agent of some transcendent One. Just as birth is the awakening of the universal Mind to individual sensory experience and action in order that it may receive "New modes of passion,"[29] so the momentary passions we fancy *we* experience are actually the property of the constitutive forms. Joy, hope, love, power, and life, Shelley wrote, are "not thine own" but are lent us by some Spirit, or Power, until it reclaims them.[30] It is man who is incapable of continued perfect experience and projects the inconstancy of his perceptive organs onto reality to create the illusion of transience.

According to Plato's distinction in Book V of *The Republic*, knowledge is the apprehension of Being (the forms), while the faculty of belief, or opinion, acquaints us with only mutable particulars, since they partake of both being and nonbeing. For these, as we have seen, Shelley substituted respectively imagination, or dream, as the extraordinary faculty of probable knowledge, and ordinary sensory awareness—just as in *The Sensitive Plant* dream gives insight into the eternal reality while the mutable senses reveal only momentarily a perfect reality and then falsely report its decay. Necessarily alternating between imaginative dream and awakened perception of an ephemeral reality, between his immortal and mortal nature, man can, at best, treasure those occasions when, building on the momentary perfection of his senses, he can have imaginative experience of the phenomena as the fulfillment of their forms:

Whilst skies are blue and bright,
    Whilst flowers are gay,
Whilst eyes that change ere night
    Make glad the day;
Whilst yet the calm hours creep,
Dream thou—and from thy sleep
    Then wake to weep.

[29] *Queen Mab*, IX. 155–60.
[30] MS e. 19, p. 5; see below, pp. 186–88.

6 Intellectual Beauty and the Self

Hymn to Intellectual Beauty

Lines Written among the Euganean Hills

Sometime between 1813 and 1816, Shelley revised *Queen Mab*, retitling it *The Daemon of the World* in order to emphasize the indwelling genius, or spirit, of nature. Part of the revision appeared in the *Alastor* volume of 1816, but in a section that remained in manuscript the lines we have already examined for his conception of the One Mind came to read:

For birth and life and death, and that strange state
Before the naked powers that thro the world
Wander like winds have found a human home
All tend to perfect happiness, and urge
The restless wheels of being on their way,
Whose flashing spokes, instinct with infinite life,
Bicker and burn to gain their destined goal:
For birth but wakes the universal Mind
Whose mighty streams might else in silence flow
Thro the vast world, to individual sense
Of outward shews, whose unexperienced shape
New modes of passion to its frame may lend;
Life is its state of action, and the store
Of all events is aggregated there
That variegate the eternal universe;

180

Death is a gate of dreariness and gloom,
That leads to azure isles and beaming skies
And happy regions of eternal hope.[1]

In the ensuing passage he then inserted two lines that had no source in
Queen Mab:

For, what thou art shall perish utterly,
But what is thine may never cease to be.

In 1821, however, hoping for the establishment of a republic in the Duchy
of Benevento, Shelley counseled,

　　　Man who man would be,
Must rule the empire of himself; in it
Must be supreme, establishing his throne
On vanquished will, quelling the anarchy
Of hopes and fears, being himself alone.[2]

The difference between these two views of the self is not the consequence of any radical change in Shelley's thinking; rather, it reflects
the ambiguity inherent in the concept of the One Mind, or absolute
Existence, as formulated by the "intellectual philosophy." For if each individual mind is but a portion of the One Mind, in one sense the self has
no independent existence and is only a partial medium through which
the One Mind acts and experiences; its individuality, or identity, is nugatory because the only eternal Existence is the One Mind, which employs
the individual as a passive instrument, a "human home." "I," then, am a
transitory means; "mine" is the temporary presence in me of a portion of
the eternal One, and it is for that reason, according to "The Flower that
Smiles Today," that it is a mistake to call "ours" those experiences belonging to the eternal forms. But a slight shift of perspective can invert the
relationship of "I" and "mine": if a portion of the One Mind acts in me
then "I" am that portion, the One being the sum of all such selves, and

[1] These lines were first published in 1876 by H. Buxton Forman as *The Daemon
of the World*, 532–49. For the manuscript, see *Shelley and his Circle*, ed. Cameron,
IV, pp. 564–65. For lines 533–34, *Queen Mab* reads, "Before the naked soul has
found its home"; for 539–41, "For birth but wakes the spirit to the sense."
[2] "Sonnet on the Republic of Benevento." "Being himself alone" was Shelley's
standard phrase for self-possession, or for absoluteness and autonomy. The subject
of "Lift Not the Painted Veil" who eschewed the world and sought only the ideal
that would fulfill his self was "himself alone." So, in a manuscript passage, Shelley
also described someone who was probably intended to be among Adonais' mourners
(MS e. 9, p. 23); and "Thou art still thyself alone" was the refrain of a lyric
addressed to Freedom as the Absolute of which everything is a portion (e. 7,
pp. 6–11).

what is "mine" is all that is mortal and transient in my self. Consequently, in opposition to the lines added in *The Daemon of the World*, the poet of *Epipsychidion* can pray to Emily:

To whatsoe'er of dull mortality
Is mine, remain a vestal sister still;
To the intense, the deep, the imperishable,
Not mine, but me, henceforth be thou united
Even as a bride. . . .[3]

After Adonais' death, we recall, he still bears "his part" of the "one Spirit's plastic stress." But even in life each self, as a portion of the One Mind, is potentially "himself alone," an autonomous microcosm. Shelley's thought, however, is not tightly systematic, and, depending upon his objectives, he may treat the individual mind as portion of the One Mind of Existence, or, as the passage from *Adonais* suggests, he may consider the individual self the vehicle of the mysterious transcendent Absolute. Since that Absolute is one of Shelley's divinities, each self is a transitory instrument of divinity, or each self is its own imperishable divinity, depending on whether the presence of the Absolute is considered the attribute or the essence of the self.

If we recognize these two opposing conceptions of selfhood, there is no contradiction between Shelley's contempt for self-love[4] and his approval of the Narcissus symbol. In *The Sensitive Plant*, the narcissi are admired because, gazing on their reflection in the stream, they are self-completed and "die of their own dear loveliness"; and the Visionary of *Alastor* envies the flowers fulfilled by their own reflections. Contemptible self-love, the "dark idolatry of self,"[5] is the worship of our mortal selves, not of that true self which is a portion of the transcendent Absolute and which yearns for union with its own ideal projection. Hence the ambiguity of the accusation of "self-centred seclusion" made against the Visionary in the Preface to *Alastor*: in fact the Visionary seeks the completion of that in himself which partakes of the Absolute, but from the Narrator's limited worldly perspective, this has the appearance of the dark idolatry of one's finite, mortal nature.

The conflict between Shelley's atheistic desire, expressed by his Julian, to believe that the human condition is entirely in man's power and that its model resides in his own mind, not in a body of laws imposed by an external deity, and his aspiration to a postmortal state exceeding in perfection the possibilities of life almost necessarily created this persistently ambiguous attitude toward personal identity. The reformer who viewed

---

[3] *Epipsychidion*, 389–93.
[4] For example, *Prometheus Unbound*, III. iv. 134.
[5] *The Revolt of Islam*, 3390.

all human ills as modes of slavery encouraged individual autonomy and self-possession so long as it does not lead to self-love. Each portion of the One Mind or, in other contexts, of the Absolute, is the essence of a self, and in that sense the individual is an absolute, and his freedom is his "Self-empire."[6] But as an atheistic religious theorist Shelley never contemplated a strictly personal immortality: one's portion of the eternal Absolute is a temporary attribute of the self. Consequently, when his concern was limited to human existence, independent of any transcendence, he exalted self-possession; conceived of every man as a universe, a total world, or an island, since in that domain mind is identical with existence, internal with external; and spoke of each man's own divinity. "Let us believe in a kind of optimism in which we are our own gods," he advised Maria Gisborne:

... it is best that we should think all this for the best even though it be not, because Hope, as Coleridge says is a solemn duty which we owe alike to ourselves & to the world—a worship to the spirit of good within, which requires before it sends that inspiration forth, which impresses its likeness upon all that it creates, devoted & disinterested homage.[7]

The sonnet urging the Duchy of Benevento to rebel against King Ferdinand of Naples defines a republic as a state in which everyone is king, ruling "the empire of himself." This aspiration to self-subsistence generates in Shelley's poetry a series of characteristic metaphors of perfect existence as self-enclosures and as self-perpetuating motion. In the fourth act of *Prometheus Unbound*, for example, the renovated Earth describes her perfect joy as a "vaporous exultation not to be confined," an "animation of delight / Which wraps me, like an atmosphere of light, / And bears me as a cloud is borne by its own wind."[8] Earth is folded in the light of its own joy, just as the ideal lady of *Epipsychidion* is wrapped in the atmosphere of light she herself radiates; and Wisdom's car is "Self-moving, like cloud charioted by [its own] flame."[9] This mental model of autonomy may well have been responsible for Shelley's fascination with Henry Reveley's plan to build a steamboat; at least it led him, writing jestingly on that subject, to speak of the "self-impelling steam-wheels of the mind."[10]

When, however, Shelley conceives of the individual presence of the

---

[6] *Prometheus Unbound*, II. iv. 42. Cf. *ibid.*, I. 492–93: "Yet am I king over myself, and rule / The torturing and conflicting throngs within...."
[7] 13/14 October 1819 (*Letters*, II, 125).
[8] IV. 321–24. Cf. IV. 214–18.
[9] *Prometheus Unbound*, IV. 437–39; *Epipsychidion*, 91–101; *Ode to Liberty*, 260. *The Revolt of Islam*, 938–39: "... my conceptions, gathering like a cloud / The very wind on which it rolls away." *Ibid.*, 1689: "... cloud.... / On outspread wings of its own wind upborne."
[10] *Letter to Maria Gisborne*, 108.

Absolute as an attribute rather than the essence of selfhood and denies self-sustaining identity, his characteristic metaphor is correspondingly inverted. Instead of a self-motivating cloud or a center radiating its own self-enveloping light, man is but a momentary cloud or mist suffused with a supernal and immortal sunlight that is his lent life and experiences of perfection. Christ, for example, was for Shelley a "power from the unknown God," the presence of the transcendent perfection on earth, and

> A mortal shape to him
> Was like the vapour dim
> Which the orient planet animates with light.[11]

A corpse therefore is "Like a sunless vapour, dim."[12] The transitory embodying cloud or mist—perhaps cyclically renewed—is what we call our "selves," but our real existence and our truly worthy experiences are the momentary suffusions of that cloud by emanations of light from an eternal, immutable, and perfect Absolute that lies outside Existence, outside the boundaries of the mortal and sensible world. Although that light may also radiate from the human center, it originates, not in that center, but in some transcendent extrahuman source. "A spirit not our own awakens us," Shelley wrote in a fragment probably intended for *Epipsychidion* and displaying more clearly than usual the relation of the transcendent light to the light at the human core:

> alas what are we? Clouds
> Driven by the wind in warring multitudes
> Which rain into the bosom of the earth
> And rise again—and in our death & birth
> And restless life, take as from heaven
> Hues which are not our own—but which are given
> And then withdrawn & with inconstant glance
> Flash from the Spirit to the countenance.
> There is a power, a love, a joy, a God
> Which makes in mortal hearts its brief abode,
> A Pythian exhalation which inspires
> Love, only love—⟨an expiring wind which on the wires
> Of the Soul's silent harp⟩. . . .[13]

The cloud, as this fragment suggests, may be viewed as only the inconstant medium of light or as a body whose central "Spirit" flashes

[11] *Hellas*, 211–17.
[12] *Lines Written Among the Euganean Hills*, 63.
[13] MS e. 12, pp. 159–60.

to its surrounding form; for the self-illuminating or self-moving cloud and the transiently light-suffused cloud are the earthly and the transcendent views of the same object. Contradiction arises only from our taking one view or the other exclusively. For example, the independent divinity of the self is also the subject of a section of Shelley's *Essay on Christianity*:

Whoever has maintained with his own heart the strictest correspondence of confidence, who dares to examine and to estimate every imagination which suggests itself to his mind, who is that which he designs to become, and also aspires to that which the divinity of his own nature shall consider and approve—he, has already seen God.

* * * * *

That those who are pure in heart shall see God, and that virtue is its own reward, may be considered as equivalent assertions. The former of these propositions is a metaphorical repetition of the latter.[14]

Each such man is his own god, self-completing. And yet, between these two statements Shelley also wrote:

There is a Power by which we are surrounded, like the atmosphere in which some motionless lyre is suspended, which visits with its breath our silent chords, at will. Our most imperial and stupendous qualities—those on which the majesty and the power of humanity is erected—are, relatively to the inferior portion of its mechanism, indeed active and imperial; but they are the passive slaves of some higher and more omnipresent Power. This Power is God.

Contradictory though these two passages may appear, they are but the two faces of a coherent ambiguity of which Shelley was not unaware, for he was conscious that his definition of selfhood altered radically, depending on whether his context is human society or the Absolute and immortality. Shelley was not expressing any confusion or indecision in looking forward to a time when, priests having been abolished,

> . . . human thoughts might kneel alone,
> Each before the judgement-throne
Of its own aweless soul, or of the Power unknown![15]

The "aweless soul" is a portion of the unknown Power and may be conceived of as both autonomous and contingent; as Shelley had said, he who is faithful to the divinity of his own nature has already seen God. Hence in the lines that follow Shelley builds a metaphor implying that human thoughts mirror some transcendence and generate words that obscure what

[14] Julian, VI, 231–32.
[15] *Ode to Liberty*, 231–33. Instead of "human thoughts," Shelley first wrote, "every mind" (MS e. 6, p. 100).

they reflect; and he leaves ambiguous whether the "Lord" before whom
the words are to stand in judgment is their human author or the Author:

> Oh, that the words which make the thoughts obscure
>> From which they spring, as clouds of glimmering dew
> From a white lake blot Heaven's blue portraiture,
>> Were stripped of their thin masks and various hue
> And frowns and smiles and splendours not their own,
>> Till in the nakedness of false and true
> They stand before their Lord, each to receive its due!   (234–40)

Transcendence and immanence, then, can be relatively indifferent
alternatives; or, indeed, they can be combined when the transcendent is
conceived of as visiting a self, however inconstantly. Therefore the Emily
of *Epipsychidion* not only radiates a light that enfolds her but is at the
same time wrapped in the Beauty "Which penetrates and clasps and fills
the world" (103); and in *Prometheus Unbound* the renovated Earth is
folded not only in the light radiated by its own joy but also in "heaven's
smile divine" (IV. 439).

Even apart from the logical drift of Shelley's "intellectual philosophy"
toward a denial of individual identity, no doubt his positing a transcendent
perfection in which the human mind passively participates was also the
consequence of a boyhood experience of an extraordinary spiritual visitation that he reported in the *Hymn to Intellectual Beauty* and, almost
obsessively, in various forms and with various interpretations on other
occasions. One of the fullest and most explicit statements of this conception of "lent" identity appears in a manuscript passage of early 1817
intended as an introduction to *The Revolt of Islam* (it will be referred to
hereafter as "the rejected Introduction"). Because of its central importance,
especially for its intimate bearing on the *Hymn to Intellectual Beauty*,
written shortly before it, it deserves to be quoted at length:

Frail clouds arrayed in sunlight lose the glory
Which they reflect on Earth—they burn & die
Revive & change like genius, & when hoary
They streak the sunless air, then suddenly
If the white moon shine forth, their shadows lie
Like woven pearl beneath its beams—each tone
Of the many voiced forest doth reply
To symphonies diviner than its own
Then falls & fades—like thought when power is past & gone.

The hues of Sea & Sky, & moon & Sun—
The music of the Desart & the deep

Are dark or silent—have their changes run
Thus soon? or [,] pale enthusiast [,] dost thou weep
Because all things that change & wake & sleep
Tell thine own story? like the altered glance
Of a dear friend are they?—like thoughts that keep
Their dwelling in a dying countenance
Or like the thronging shapes of some tempestuous trance.

There is a Power whose passive instrument
Our nature is—a Spirit that with motion
Invisible & swift its breath hath sent
Amongst us, like the wind on the wide Ocean
Around whose path the tumult and commotion
Throng fast—deep calm doth follow, & precedeth.
This Spirit, chained by some remote devotion
Our choice or will demandeth not nor heedeth
But for its hymns doth touch the human souls it needeth.

All that we know or seek, our loves & hopes,
Those sweet & subtle thoughts that do entwine
Swift gleamings with the shade that interlopes
Between their visitings, we may repine
To lose; but they will pass—thou must resign
⟨All that is not thine own⟩
Joy, hope & love [. . .] power & life when that which gave
The Shadow & the God, has need of thine
Abandoning thee; then no mercy crave
But bow thyself in dust, take shelter in the grave.

The lamps of mind which make this night of earth
So beautiful, were kindled thus of yore.—
All streams of mortal hope thence[?] drew their birth
Thro silent years their kindling music pour
Have thus been fed with sweetness; mighty lyres
Whose sounds awaken thoughts that sleep no more
Which that immortal Spirit which respires
In visioned rest, has breathed upon their silent wires.

It is not then presumption if I watch
In expectations mute & breathless mood
Till it descend—may not the fountain catch
Hues from the green leaves & the daylight wood
Even if blank darkness must descend & brood
Upon its waves?—each human phantasy

Hath such sweet visions in the solitude
Of thought, that human life ⟨this drear world⟩ like heaven wd. be
Could words invest such dreams with immortality.[16]

Exactly what the assumed structure of this quasi-theological myth is, the stanzas leave somewhat uncertain, and the lack of precision is symptomatic of Shelley's constantly altering mode of vision or his inability, or neglect, to develop an inclusive myth that would organize coherently those conflicting modes. Presumably there is some ineffable source from which are derived both the "Shadow" that man is and the "God" that he is lent—the shades that make up the continuity of man's cloud-like life and the sporadic gleamings that dispel the shades. As in *The Sensitive Plant* and "The Flower that Smiles Today," man falsely believes his joy, hope, love, power, and life to be truly his, whereas they are really properties of the transcendent Spirit, which then reclaims them as its own. Man is a passive instrument on which the Spirit, for some mysterious religious devotion, presumably to an even more remote divinity, performs its hymns. Man, then, both is and is not divine: he is but a medium on which divinity acts, and yet he is deified intermittently when divinity acts through him. To "see God," Shelley wrote in his *Essay on Christianity*, is to be faithful to the divinity of one's own nature; yet he added, "And those who have seen God, have, in the period[17] of their purer and more perfect nature, been harmonized by their own will to so exquisite [a] consentaneity of powers as to give forth divinest melody when the breath of universal being sweeps over their frame."[18]

It is clear that when Shelley extends his field of vision beyond mortal life he can no longer speak as the reformer outlining a program of earthly perfection, or that whenever he despairs of a durable human utopia he must seek some transcendent explanation for the mind's ability to conceive of and yearn for perfection but not to attain it. His own being, he

---

[16] MS e. 19, pp. 4–6. With a few minor errors these stanzas have been published in *Verse and Prose from the Manuscripts of Percy Bysshe Shelley*, ed. Sir John C. E. Shelley-Rolls and Roger Ingpen (London, 1934), pp. 17–21. I offer an eclectic text based on the manuscript.

Shelley's conceptions here and in his elaboration of the "intellectual philosophy" are remarkably similar to what Lady Morgan described as Hindu tenets in her novel *The Missionary* (1811), which Shelley read immediately after its publication: "That matter has no essence, independent of mental perception; and that external sensation would vanish into nothing if the divine energy for a moment subsided; that the soul differs in degree but not in kind, from the creative spirit of which it is a particle, and into which it will be finally absorbed; that nothing has a pure and absolute existence, but spirit; and that a passionate and exclusive love of Heaven is that feeling only which offers no illusion to the soul, and secures its eternal felicity" (I, p. 71). Aspects of this quasi-Berkeleyan doctrine also have bearings on *A Defence of Poetry* and *Adonais*, among others of Shelley's works.

[17] He first wrote, "moments" (Bodleian MS Shelley e. 4, fol. 11).

[18] Julian, VI, 231–32.

wrote, "overflows with unbounded love, & elevated thoughts. How little philosophy & affection consort with this turbid scene—this dark scheme of things finishing in unfruitful death."[19] Moods of this sort either express themselves in the skeptical ambivalence of *Alastor* and *Julian and Maddalo* or find their release in poems like the rejected Introduction by accounting for the mind's ideal experiences without reference to the intractable and alien world. Under the aspect of immortality, he cannot postulate, as in *Queen Mab*, merely a pure and "necessarily beneficent" spirit eternally immanent in nature—and hence a universe equatable with divinity—nor even, as in *Mont Blanc* and the *Ode to the West Wind*, a transcendent and immutable Power, or Cause, that moves the world through its eternally cyclical course. Instead, in the rejected Introduction Shelley can find consolation only by turning his back on the possibility of an earthly utopia and by denying personal identity. So intractable is mutability that life at best is but a continuous yearning for perfection only sporadically fulfilled, and consolation lies in the knowledge that as imperfect and inconstant selves we are at least momentarily lent the perfection of some eternal ideal.

The speaker of "The Zucca," like the Visionary of *Alastor*, seeks the absolute ideal, a perfection not available in the world, "desiring / More in this world than any understand":

I loved—oh, no, I mean not one of ye,
Or any earthly one, though ye are dear
As human heart to human heart may be;—
I loved, I know not what—but this low sphere
And all that it contains, contains not thee,
⟨Thou goddess of my soul's idolatry⟩
Thou, whom, seen nowhere, I feel everywhere. . . .

But, like the Spirit of the rejected Introduction, this ideal does enter into the world as intermittently as mutability permits:

By Heaven and Earth, from all whose shapes thou flowest,
Neither to be contained, delayed, nor hidden:
Making divine the loftiest and the lowest,
When for a moment thou art not forbidden
To live within the life which thou bestowest;
And leaving noblest things vacant and chidden. . . .[20]

[19] To Mary Godwin, 4 November 1814 (*Letters*, I, 419).
[20] "The Zucca," 17–30 (MS e. 17, pp. 196–97); the MS contains many additional variants.

These vacancies, which render life absurd, result from the enforced absences of the transcendent perfection, and man can do nothing to prolong its presence. Such is the view in the perspective of the transcendent. But we have observed that in the "intellectual philosophy," where the mind of man is the point of reference, Shelley assigns to the imagination the power to apprehend the Absolute and to fill the vacancies between phenomena with that apprehension, as the Sensitive Plant's parenthesis-enclosed dream of Elysium fills the lacuna in sensory experience. The contradiction lies only in the perspective: in terms of the Absolute, life can be meaningful only in irregular moments when mutability permits the transcendent to be immanent; in terms of man, life can be made meaningful by the imagination's power to transcend mutability. Either way, Shelley's purpose is to assert man's access to perfection at the same time that he takes into account man's presence in the world of inconstancy and imperfection. But, conceiving of man in the context of the impersonal immortality of the Absolute, and denying that the self is immortal or capable of action, Shelley can only trust that

⟨There is a spirit, be it God, or Love⟩
There is a Spirit, whose inconstant home
Is in the Spirit of inconstant man.
Sometimes over our Nature it will come
Like a soft cloud of ⟨splendour⟩.[21]

ii

Like many of Shelley's other speculations in prose and poetry, the *Hymn to Intellectual Beauty* springs in part from his conviction that man's mind is "at enmity with nothingness and dissolution," being incapable of "imagining to itself annihilation"—even though the senses constantly report moments of emptiness and the existence of the human mind is contingent upon there being between its experiences those "interstices" responsible for "motion and mensuration, and time, and space." In revulsion against the apparent vacuity of human existence, Shelley addresses his hymn to that Power whose passing shadow leaves the world "vacant and desolate" (17)—or, as "The Zucca" has it, whose absence leaves "noblest things vacant and chidden." In effect, the poem is Shelley's effort to locate life's worth exclusively in moments of extraordinary visitations of perfection, to come to terms with the intervening vacancies in life as a necessity imposed by sublunary mutability, and to define a possible immortality. Like the rejected Introduction, its purpose is to find in the occasional presences of the perfect Spirit that which makes mutability

[21] MS e. 12, p. 117. For another expression of such transient visitations, see Shelley's "Ye Gentle Visitations of Calm Thought."

and inconstancy tolerable—even "the altered glance / Of a dear friend" and the other untruths that drove the Maniac of *Julian and Maddalo* to madness. Although it looks forward (almost parenthetically) to the world's freedom from slavery, it is not fundamentally a poem of human reform but faces in the opposite direction, addressing itself to a godhead. Instead of seeking to overcome the world's inconstancy, it accepts it as unavoidable and considers not so much how the world may be perfected as how man is related to the transcendent ideal and to its possible eternity. That is, unlike Julian, the poet here does not consider man in his strictly earthly dimensions and endowed with mental models of perfection; he considers man as alien to the world and asks how he participates in the divine.

As Beauty, the object of the poet's prayer is ideal form, order, and harmony; but it would be misleading to define Intellectual Beauty too narrowly, for the Ideal is for Shelley unnameable and has many equivalent partial modes, such as the Good, the True, and even Freedom. There is no essential difference between the Intellectual Beauty which descended on the poet's "passive youth" (79) and that ideal Spirit "whose passive instrument / Our nature is." In the essay *On Love* and in *Julian and Maddalo*, Shelley starts with the assumption that the model of perfection resides within the self, and he represents the self as yearning for union with the mental projection of that model; even in *Alastor*, where the ideal is sent to the Visionary in a dream, the emphasis is upon the dream-lady's being a perfection of his own nature, a "second self." However, it is characteristic of Shelley's ambiguous conception of selfhood that his point of reference repeatedly alternated between the human and the transcendent, and the *Hymn* translates the internal model of perfection in those works into an extra-human divinity.

Because of the rather loose use that criticism has made of the term and because of its frequent confusion with Platonism, it is necessary to note that Intellectual Beauty, as the word "intellectual" implies, is a divinity of mind only and has no bearing on the realm governed by the immanent "Spirit of Nature" of *Queen Mab* or by the "Power" of *Mont Blanc*. Intellectual Beauty is the governing deity of the "intellectual philosophy," which identifies existence with mind and rejects all distinction between world and thought. In the *Hymn*, the "various world" (3)[22] visited by the "awful shadow" of Intellectual Beauty is the domain of mutability, not external nature. Intellectual Beauty shines only upon the "human heart and countenance," only upon "human thought or form"; and thought and human form are related as Shelley was to describe them in the *Epipsychidion* fragment: the Ideal enters a human self and then

[22] Shelley first wrote, instead, "All human (living) hearts" and then "All that has thought." The repeated cancellations in the manuscript of "heart" for "mind" make it clear that Shelley considered them equivalent terms (MS e. 16, pp. 57–61).

flashes "from the Spirit to the countenance." In subsequently translating Plato's *Symposium*, Shelley was to render Plato's "beauty" as "intellectual beauty,"[23] but this is an imposition of his own concept on Plato, not the identification of his own concept with Plato's ideal beauty. Plato's description of ideal beauty, it is true, is generally applicable to the Intellectual Beauty of the *Hymn*:

It is eternal, unproduced, indestructible; neither subject to encrease nor decay. . . . it is eternally uniform and consistent, and monoeidic with itself. All other things are beautiful through a participation of it, with this condition, that although they are subject to production and decay, it never becomes more or less, or endures any change.[24]

But there is nothing in the *Hymn* that locates the visitations of that Beauty in the *external* world or provides for an ascent to it through its presences in sensible objects.

Shelley's continued preoccupation with such unitary realities as the One Mind of the "intellectual philosophy" suggests, on the other hand, that the Intellectual Beauty worshipped in the *Hymn* is neither an abstraction nor a personified fiction like the subject of the usual eighteenth-century ode, but a self-subsisting reality. As the rejected Introduction makes clear, all that is essential in human existence derives from and returns to this transcendent source. There and in the *Hymn* only the agent, or reflection, of the divine Intellectual Beauty, only the unseen shadow of the "unseen Power," visits the realm of mutability; and both poems describe the visitation of the agent as a religious experience of the nature of a revelation and conversion, an ecstasy preceded and followed by "deep calm," no doubt reflecting the event of Shelley's Eton days. In choosing the hymn form, therefore, Shelley is not making a scrupulous adaptation of a literary convention, but, in the traditional sense of a hymn, is offering a sincere prayer to divinity as he understands it, and the religious language of the poem is the transfer of conventional Christian terminology to what Shelley would propose as the true religion.

In that religion the mutability of the world and therefore the necessary inconstancy of the visitations of the "shadow" are accepted as beyond human understanding; the reason for earthly mutability, together with the consequent imperfection of the world, is a mystery, and efforts or pretenses to explain its cause result in assigning absolute and arbitrary power to the traditional anthropomorphic fictions and therefore in the tyrannical superstitions of "Demon, Ghost, and Heaven,"[25]

---

[23] Julian, VII, 206.
[24] Shelley's translation, *ibid.*
[25] Shelley first wrote, more daringly, "Ghosts & God & Heaven" (MS e. 16, p. 58).

> Frail spells—whose uttered charm might not avail to sever,
>> From all we hear and all we see,
>> Doubt, chance, and mutability. (29–31)

In vain did the poet in his youth seek the answers to these mysteries by communicating with the dead and by calling on the "poisonous names" of Christian theology "with which our youth is fed" (53). The mystical revelation of Intellectual Beauty was also his rejection of Christianity. The *Hymn*, then, explicitly rejects the traditional theology that endows the mysteries with the power of oppression, and yet, on the other hand, it makes extensive crucial use of Christian terminology. The full sense of the poem therefore lies not only in what it presents but also in what it repudiates. For part of the poem's art consists in purging Christianity of its superstitions without destroying its abstract framework, or in revealing the irony that Christian terminology and conceptions can be transvalued by translation into the true religious framework, just as part of the meaning of *Prometheus Unbound* depends on the reader's awareness of what Aeschylean concepts are being repudiated by the adaptation. Shelley's desire to purify Scripture was evident as early as 1812, when he wrote,

I have met with some waverers between Xtianity and Deism.—I shall attempt to make them reject all the bad, and take all the good of the Jewish Books.— I have often thought that the moral sayings of Jesus Christ might be very useful if selected from the mystery and immorality which surrounds them.[26]

Parts of his *Essay on Christianity* are exercises in that kind of purification by reinterpretation.

In the context of Shelley's religion, the transient presences of the shadow of Intellectual Beauty, like the Holy Spirit, literally "consecrate" the human mind (13), are a "mystery" (12), and are acts of "grace" (11), unmerited gifts of a divinity that sanctify the passive human spirit without its "choice or will." The poet's "worship" of that divinity (81) and his vows and dedications to serve it (61) are also to be understood in their sincerely religious senses. Even the "responses" (26) that have never come from some sublimer world to explain doubt, chance, and mutability may well carry their ecclesiastical sense and ironically suggest the questions and pat "responses" of the Catechism. Not the patterns of Christian worship, but the superstitious interpretations made of them are wrong.

The poem, then, is one of those hymns of devotion that the transcendent Intellectual Beauty creates by touching the passive "human soul it needeth"; and yet, paradoxically, the poem laments the vanishing of that Beauty's shadow: "where art thou gone?" (15). The poem is the consequence of the passage of the Spirit of Beauty over the poet as a "still"

---

[26] To Elizabeth Hitchener, 27 February 1812 (*Letters*, I, 265).

and "passive" instrument, and yet the purpose of the prayer is to invoke that absent deity. The god, or at least its "shadow," is both present and absent; for poetry, as the *Defence of Poetry* will explain, is both the divine inspiration and the human artifice to preserve the experience after the moment of illumination passes. Moreover, in invoking Intellectual Beauty, Shelley does not so much pray, in accordance with the hymn convention, that the god not forsake him but rather, in his skeptical uncertainty, that the god truly be an unchanging, eternal reality, unlike the transient visits of its shadow. On the one side there is resignation to life as a "dim vast vale of tears, vacant and desolate" (17) but for momentary consecrations of the human mind by the bright shadow[27] of the divine Intellectual Beauty; on the other there is fear that the inconstancy of the shadow's visitations reflects the transitory nature of Intellectual Beauty itself. For if it does depart as its shadow does, there is no afterlife for man:

Depart not as thy shadow came,
Depart not—lest the grave should be
Like life and fear, a dark reality.   (46–48)

Man's immortality is dependent upon there being an eternal and immutable deity of perfection, not because that guarantees a power capable of granting an afterlife, but because the immortal part of a human self is only an inconstant expression of that deity. The *Hymn* is grounded on the assumption in the *Daemon of the World* that because the active presence of a portion of the "universal mind" is an attribute of the individual self and not its essence, "what thou art shall perish utterly, / But what is thine may never cease to be." "Love, Hope, and Self-esteem," the poem declares, "like clouds depart / And come, for some uncertain moments lent" (37–38)—lent, that is, and then withdrawn by Intellectual Beauty, to whom they belong, just as, according to the rejected Introduction, joy, hope, love, power, and life are only momentarily "thine" not "thee," just as, according to "The Flower that Smiles Today," the joy which "ours we call" belongs to the eternal forms, and just as, according to the *Daemon of the World*, a human birth is but the awakening of the universal mind to individual experience.

Thus the ambiguous nature of selfhood that we have observed elsewhere in Shelley is also an operative factor in the *Hymn* and generates its other ambiguities as it oscillates between the presence and absence of Intellectual Beauty. Although all that is worthy in a self is the transient

---

[27] The word "shadow" in the poem is not to be understood as a darkness but as "a diminished mode" of the light of Intellectual Beauty. E.g., *Alastor*, 233, "The bright shadow of that lovely dream"; *The Revolt of Islam*, 872, "the bright shade of some immortal dream"; *ibid.*, 4611, "A shadow, which was light"; *Hellas*, 171, "The fiery shadow of his gilt prow"; *Daemon of the World*, I. 64, "Four shapeless shadows, bright and beautiful."

presence of Intellectual Beauty's shadow, one value lent by that shadow is not esteem for the shadow or its source, but "Self-esteem." Self-esteem is relative to such visitations because the only self is the occasional presence of the shadow in the individual mortal form, which otherwise has no self, being but a medium. In this sense, self-esteem is a form of religious devotion, a worship of a momentarily immanent portion of Intellectual Beauty; and for the same reason the spirit of Intellectual Beauty inspires one to "fear himself, and love all human kind" (84). Since it visits, however inconstantly, "Each human heart and countenance," the poet can make his religious dedication both to it and to the human minds on which it shines ("thee and thine," 62).[28] To worship it in "every [human] form containing" it (82) is the same as to "love all human kind," and to worship it in those moments when it constitutes one's own selfhood is not only to "esteem" but also to "fear" oneself, in the religious sense of awful reverence and submission to divine governance.[29] The hymn that begins with a prayer to a transcendent deity ends in reverence of the self, as "thine" and "thee," attribute and essence, change places. It is for this reason that Shelley can value narcissistic self-reflection and hold up as the greatest sin self-contempt, which is not only a denial of the internal presence of a portion of the Absolute but also a sacrilege against the divinity of that self.

Love, Hope, and Self-esteem, "for some uncertain moments lent" (38), are modes of worship of the divinity when it is present in others and in oneself. A "self," then, is discontinuous and different from continuous animate existence, and, since only Intellectual Beauty—Shelley hopes—is eternal, he has not fallen into unguarded and merely enthusi-

---

[28] Although "The Zucca" differs from the *Hymn* in assuming that the Ideal, the object of the speaker's "Soul's idolatry," intermittently "lives" within the elements of external nature, it agrees that such visitations make "divine the loftiest and the lowest," and the speaker "adores" its presence and laments its absence.

[29] This is the sense, for example, in which Scripture asks us to "fear the name of the Lord." This interpretation of "To fear himself" was first made by Elizabeth Nitchie, "Shelley's 'Hymn to Intellectual Beauty,'" *PMLA*, 63 (1948), 752–53.

"To fear" is of course the meaning of *revereri*; and the *Magnum theatrum* of Laurentio Beyerlinck (Lugduni, 1678), s.v. *reverentia*, instances Aquinas: "Revereri est actus timoris, et ut debetur Deo, est actus latriae." "Maxime omnium teipsum reverere" is the form in which one of Pythagoras' Golden Verses has come down to us via Diogenes Laertius; and is translated by Thomas Stanley as "but of thy self stand most in fear" and by Nicholas Rowe as "Let reverence of thyself thy thoughts control." Christianity adapted Pythagoras' injunction to a pattern identical (but for its theology) with Shelley's. For example, Milton, *Paradise Lost*, XI. 520–25:

Therefore so abject is thir punishment,
Disfiguring not God's likeness, but thir own,
Or if his likeness, by themselves defac't
While they pervert pure Nature's healthful rules
To loathsome sickness, worthily, since they
God's Image did not reverence in themselves.

Or, *Church Government* (Columbia Milton, III, p. 260): "... he that holds himself in reverence and due esteem ... for the dignity of Gods image upon him. ..."

astic hyperbole when he writes that man would be "immortal, and omnipotent" (39) even on earth if it were continuously present in the human
mind, just as in the rejected Introduction "human life like heaven would
be / Could words invest such dreams [i.e. the occasional descents of the
"Spirit"] with immortality." The only immortality possible is not a personal eternity, but the impersonal re-assimilation of the "lent" divinity by
the eternal Mind when it "has need of thine, abandoning thee." Only if
Intellectual Beauty were itself not eternal and constant would the grave
be, "Like life and fear, a dark reality" (48), instead of an illusion. And
yet, in those ecstatic moments when man is illuminated by the light of
Intellectual Beauty, he is himself divine. Shelley's vision results in infinite humility and infinite pride.

iii

After relating the poet's youthful conversion and his dedication to
Intellectual Beauty, the *Hymn* concludes with a prayer for a tranquil
autumnal persistence of the influence of his ecstatic experience:

The day becomes more solemn and serene
        When noon is past—there is a harmony
        In autumn, and a lustre in its sky,
Which through its summer is not heard or seen,
As if it could not be, as if it had not been!
        Thus let thy power, which like the truth
        Of nature on my passive youth
Descended, to my onward life supply
        Its calm. . . .   (73–81)

In the previous year Shelley had pictured the Narrator of *Alastor* seeking
out the mystery of existence, as the poet of the *Hymn* had, in charnels,
"where black death / Keeps record of the trophies won from thee [Mother
of the world]." Although the Narrator experienced no specific conversion
but only a mild illumination, he too then sought an ongoing tranquil
passivity:

Enough from incommunicable dream,
And twilight phantasms, and deep noon-day thought,
Has shone within me, that serenely now
And moveless, as a long-forgotten lyre
Suspended in the solitary dome
Of some mysterious and deserted fane,
I wait thy breath, Great Parent. . . .[30]

---

[30] *Alastor,* 24–25, 39–45.

When we add that the rejected Introduction and the *Hymn to Intellectual Beauty* are so similar as to appear to be recastings of each other, it becomes evident that a particular psychological pattern, probably reflecting a profound personal experience, persisted in Shelley's mind and was unusually significant to him. The passive self, like an instrument, receives intermittently from some external Absolute ecstatic visitations that subside, leaving a serene tranquillity:

> a Spirit that with motion
> Invisible & swift its breath hath sent
> Amongst us, like the wind on the wide Ocean
> Around whose path the tumult and commotion
> Throng fast—deep calm doth follow, & precedeth.

These moments between vacancies are the human mind's encounters with divinity and supply the model on which to pattern human life. But while the structure of that experience was fixed in Shelley's mind he was not wholly convinced of its meaning, and his skepticism freed him to assign it different interpretations and to apply it to different contexts. For the Narrator of *Alastor*, for example, the divinity is not transcendent but immanent in Nature, and in that poem Shelley set his two fundamental psychological patterns in skeptical opposition to each other: the Narrator, who passively waits in life for the breath of the "Great Parent" to sweep over him, and the Visionary, who actively pursues beyond life the projection of the ideal that inheres in himself.

Two years after the *Hymn*, Shelley composed his *Lines Written Among the Euganean Hills*, and when it was published in the *Rosalind and Helen* volume of 1819, it appeared alongside the *Hymn*. The placement is not without meaning, for the same general design governs both poems, though with a difference of perspective and interpretation. The whole of the *Euganean Hills* is the report of a single day from the rising of the sun to its noontime height of breath-taking illumination and then to its calm autumnal descent. But although the day-long experience has the design of a visitation by Intellectual Beauty, the poem, unlike the *Hymn*, does not address itself to a transcendent divinity; it does not seek to define the relation of the individual self to that divinity and its participation in it, or to find possible grounds for "our" immortality. On the contrary, it explicitly excludes consideration of immortality as irrelevant if life is totally meaningless: if in life one can hope "To find refuge from distress / In friendship's smile, in love's caress" (32–33), that is one's only concern, and it is a matter of indifference whether friends greet and hearts meet in "the haven of the grave" (26), where

Senseless is the breast, and cold,
Which relenting love would fold;
Bloodless are the veins and chill
Which the pulse of pain did fill. . . .   (36–39)

The poem is not a repudiation of the *Hymn*; rather, it redirects the same ideological and psycho-religious pattern to a wholly world-oriented view in order to ask what it reveals about life, rather than about divinity and immortality, as though it were the *Hymn* seen from the other side.

In his single day that reaches a brilliant noon of extraordinary revelation—just as the *Hymn* represents Intellectual Beauty predominantly as light—the poet considers life in two parallel dimensions: individual existence and the history of human society, the first serving as enveloping prologue and epilogue for the second, as though within an individual mind's vision of human life an over-mind perceived the analogous course of the collective life of mankind. Space substituting for time, a single life is imaged as an aimless voyage on a sunless "sea of Misery" (2),[31] like the dark vacancy of ordinary existence pictured in the *Hymn*. But on this sea, the poet assures himself, are scattered isles, isolated and self-enclosed moments of revelation and perfect existence that give worth to an otherwise worthless endurance: extraordinary spots of time "bright, and clear, and still" (88), free from "passion, pain, and guilt" (345), and constituted of unifying friendship and love. Metaphorically, the poet's own day of illumination—which is also his poem—is one such "silent isle" (329), being, as Shelley described it, "the sudden relief of a state of deep despondency by the radiant visions disclosed by the sudden burst of an Italian sunrise in autumn, on the highest peak of those delightful mountains."[32] The poet's "island" will be his experience of the noonday sun's power to blend everything into unity, like the unifying power of friendship and love. In addition, within this personal framework the poet, stationed high in the Euganean Hills, looks out on the Lombardy plain, which also appears to him as a sea on which are the "islands" of Venice and Padua, climactic moments in mankind's history, just as his station in the hills is a temporal "island" in his own.

The model for the symbolic course of the poem and of the poet's experience is provided at the beginning by the image of the rooks that hail the rising sun. Gathering at sunrise, the black birds become gray in the mist, then gleam, "Starred with drops of golden rain" (81), and at last

[31] Donald H. Reiman, "Structure, Symbol, and Theme in 'Lines Written Among the Euganean Hills'," *PMLA*, 77 (1962), 405n., has pointed out the relevance of Shelley's lyric beginning, "Unfathomable Sea! whose waves are years, / Ocean of Time, whose waters of deep woe / Are brackish with the salt of human tears!" and "Claspest the limits of mortality." Also, "Stanzas for Epipsychidion," 64: "life's ever tumultuous Ocean." The sea-voyage of life is also, of course, central to *Alastor*.
[32] Julian, II, 5.

vanish to leave the sky bright in the sun: the black meaninglessness of life is gradually transformed and dispelled by the growing supernal light. In effect, the poem is, like the sound of those rising rooks, a "paean" (71), a joyous acclamation of Apollo, god of the sun. Correspondingly, the island of Venice, which the poet sees to the east, gradually blazes in the rising light, "Sun-girt," until

> the beams of morn lie dead
> On the towers of Venice now,
> Like its glory long ago. (211–13)

At the skirt of the gray cloud and mist that have arisen from the "sea of Misery" and that then shroud Venice, Padua is next revealed, illumined by the sun as it continues to rise. For in the successive splendor and darkening of Venice and then Padua, Shelley is tracing those scattered historical eras of mankind's cultural illumination, analogous to the successive "islands" in each man's dark ocean and like the inconstant visitations of the shadow of Intellectual Beauty. On his own "island" of special revelation he is given the historical vision to see in the present mankind's islanded moments of the past, as each free culture blazed and then was put out by the darkness of slavery, to become

Clouds which stain truth's rising day
By her sun consumed away—
Earth can spare ye. . . . (161–63)

The mist that gradually shrouds Venice as the sun rises higher is the "darker day" (117) that closed in with the fall of the city's "glory long ago" (213). In historical terms, Venice, born of the ocean of human misery and briefly illuminated from above, is gradually sinking beneath the waves like another Atlantis, drowning in the ocean of her birth (115–20) in the same manner that every mortal, whatever islands he may visit, eventually drinks "Death from the o'er-brimming deep; / And sinks down, down" (14–16).

But the climax of the poet's revelation is an event that transcends both individual history and the history of mankind, for at high noon the sun is no longer lighting up successive islands of the past. It stands overhead in an eternal present, the illuminated atmosphere filling "the overflowing sky,"

From the curved horizon's bound
To the point of Heaven's profound. (291–92)

Similarly, the poet has asked Venice to leave floating over her the memory of her visitor, Byron,

As the garment of thy sky
Clothes the world immortally;   (169–70)

and that sun-illumined dome has been contrasted with Venice's "tattered
pall of time, / Which scarce hides thy visage wan" (172–73). The black
pall on Venice's coffin, like the dark sea of misery, is to the sunlit sky as
time is to eternity. Correspondingly, the poet's moment of noon, when the
entire sky is illumined from the "horizon's bound" to "Heaven's profound," is a timeless moment, an instant in which not only is time made
one but everything in the world is merged: the natural scene—plains,
flowers, Apennines, Alps, all "living things"—and the poet's own dark
and darkening spirit are interpenetrated "By the glory of the sky" (311–
14). All things, Shelley wrote elsewhere, "seem only one / In the universal sun." [33] If, in its gradual rising, the sun has revealed man's transitory
sunlike periods of the past in Venice and Padua, the unifying noontime
radiance endows the poet with his own personal experience of perfection,
his eternal moment of absolute illumination, his insight into eternity and
into the unity of which he is a part.

When, however, he seeks to identify the interpenetrating and unifying "glory of the sky," he can only speculate. It may be the ideal forms,
"love, light, harmony, / Odour"; or perhaps the Form of forms, "the soul
of all / Which from Heaven like dew doth fall" (315–17). On the other
hand, it may be "the mind which feeds this verse / Peopling the lone
universe" in the sense in which Laon's song "Peopled with thoughts the
boundless universe," [34] poetry being the expression of the mind's creative
act of perception and perception being identical with existence. The only
universe anyone has is a "lone universe" populated by his own thoughts.
But Shelley has intentionally left ambiguous the question of what that
"mind" actually is, for he is facing the ambiguity of his conception of
selfhood and the attendant ambiguity of inspiration. Especially since the
interpenetrating glory falls "from Heaven," the mind that "feeds" the
verse is also the Absolute, the "soul of all," in which the poet's mind participates, and the poet is, for the moment of visited inspiration, a god. Just
as poets and prophets traditionally received their inspiration on mountain
tops, it is on the "highest peak" in the Euganean Hills that the poet
experiences his moment of illumination, the transfiguration of the scene,
and his historical revelation, like Gray's bard, who saw past and future
from his position on Mount Snowdon's top. Hence it is especially appropriate that the poem be a "paean," a song addressed to the god not only
of the sun but also of poetry and prophecy; and equally appropriate that
at its corresponding moment of sunlit glory Venice, together with its

[33] "To Jane: the Invitation," 68–69.
[34] The Revolt of Islam, 929.

golden sky, seem like the cave of Apollo's Delphic oracle. Venice's sunny towers seem flame-like pyramids ("obelisks of fire," 107), which traditionally symbolize eternity, and join the "dark ocean" of life (109) with the eternal sky; and the entire city is like an altar of sacrificial flames to the god, seeking "to pierce the dome of gold / Where Apollo spoke of old" (113–14).

The idealizing sunlight that interpenetrates and unifies the entire scene and momentarily removes it from time is also, then, the light of the poetic mind, and therefore just as the noon glory may indifferently be the Absolute or the poet's mind, so the poem identifies all poets with Apollonian light. Byron, already famous for his address in *Childe Harold* to the "deep and dark blue Ocean"[35] and established as the poet of the "sea of Misery," is greeted by Venice's ocean "with such emotion / That its joy grew his" (179–80) in his famous apostrophe to it. But although he is the poet of Ocean, his is a "sunlike soul" (193) that was overclouded by Venice's sin and slavery in the same manner that the rising sunlight over that city was extinguished by a mist. The love in Petrarch's urn burns, "A quenchless lamp by which the heart / Sees things unearthly" (201–3), just as the "glory of the sky" similarly transfigures the world for the poet. The two presiding images of Shelley's poem are his customary symbols of eternal spirit and incarnation in mutability, transcendent Apollonian light and the waters of human life;[36] and the poem is an exploration of their relationship. In his hymns of Apollo and Pan he finds a total division between the god of human experience and the god of light, poetry, and prophecy, but in the present poem he is working out symbolically their bearing upon each other, as though answering his own hymns. Poetry, which Shelley frequently considered as mediating between the human and the divine, is not the "sea of Life and Agony" (336) and yet derives from it, since human life is its substance: poetry therefore is the "unfailing River," which in England "winds forever" (184–85). Byron has been driven from those "ancestral streams" (176), Homer's ghost hovers still about Scamander, and Shakespeare's poetry is the Avon. *Lines Written among the Euganean Hills* is itself a "stream of song" which the poet's mortal spirit "Darkened" (312) in the sense that all of mortal existence is a darkness, until the verse was illuminated at noon by the "mind" that fed it. For whereas the passing of earthly glory is the extinction of sunlight by a mist from the sea (210–13), the poetic "mind"

---

[35] Shelley to Peacock [17 or 18] December 1818 (*Letters*, II, 58): "But that he [Byron] is a great poet, I think the address to Ocean proves." In his poem on the Euganean Hills, however, Shelley is inverting Byron's symbolism, which makes Ocean the image of eternity, not of time or human life (*Childe Harold*, IV. clxxxii–clxxxiii).

[36] Hence, for example, the poem describes a corpse as "Like a sunless vapour" (63), and bodily death as a sinking into "the o'er-brimming deep" (15).

is the Apollonian sunlight that illuminates the stream of song that is akin
to the Ocean of Misery on which all men sail; and thus

> . . . divinest Shakespeare's might
> Fills Avon and the world with light
> Like omniscient power which he
> Imaged 'mid mortality.   (196–99)

Poems are the waters of moral life made brilliant by the transcendent, in
accordance with the same water-sun symbolism that leads Shelley in
Prometheus Unbound to dramatize the fall of Jupiter by having Apollo
announce it to Oceanus beside the "Mouth of a great River in the Island
Atlantis."[37] Both the symbolic sun and the individual poetic mind therefore transfigure the world by filling it with light, since the human mind
is the mortal medium of the transcendent power. The interpenetrating
glory of the sky is, indifferently, the Absolute or the individual poet.

As we have noted, for Shelley the unitary ideal has many partial
names, just as Apollo is god of many related powers: in addition to its
ineffable noontime act, it is variously identified in the poem with truth
(161), omniscience (198), love (200), learning (256), and the poetic
mind. But since the poem ascribes the decline of the bright "islands" of
Venice and Padua to slavery, the rising sun over Padua is also, in the
poet's historical vision, "Like thought-wingèd Liberty" (207), and as such
its effect is identical with that on the poet at noon, transfiguring and
merging all into perfect unity.[38] The sun of Liberty, like the "universal
mind," is a "universal light," transforming all social differences into equality, seeming "to level plain and height" (208–9).[39] For the sun-god is also
the god of prophecy whose oracle was consulted on the future of empires,
and the poet (or is it the Absolute speaking through him as oracle?) is
endowed by the rising sun of historical revelation with the power of
prophecy. In the public domain he sees the destruction of oppression.

---

[37] *Prometheus Unbound*, III. ii. See below, p. 358.
[38] Since Liberty creates societal unity, it is essentially identical with the unifying
character of the Beautiful, which creates art. Hence in his *Ode to Liberty*, 72–75,
Shelley can write:

> For thou [i.e. Liberty] wert, and thine all-creative skill
> Peopled, with forms that mock the eternal dead
>   In marble immortality, that hill [the Acropolis]
>   Which was thine earliest throne and latest oracle.

[39] Shelley may well be echoing Isaiah 40: 4: "Every valley shall be exalted, and
every mountain and hill shall be made low . . . ," valley and mountain traditionally
being interpreted as the humble and the proud, or those of low and high degree.
See, for example, Marjorie Nicolson, *Mountain Gloom and Mountain Glory* (Ithaca,
1959), pp. 43–52. In the Preface to *The Cenci* Shelley adapted the parallel scriptural verse (Ezek. 21: 26): "exalt him that is low, and abase him that is high" (see
above, p. 113n).

Padua's mediaeval scholasticism lingers only as a treacherous will-o'-the-wisp, luminous only in the current darkness of sunless ignorance, like the darkness of the sunless sea of life:

> a meteor, whose wild way
> Is lost over the grave of day,
> It gleams betrayed and to betray.   (256–60)

But insofar as it was a true "lamp of learning," it has left scattered sparks that have become threatening flames of light around tyranny. In the private domain, however, it is not historical revelation that endows the poet with prophecy. Rather, the timeless transfiguration at noon has provided him with a personal hope of another such "isle" in "the sea of Life and Agony" (336); not a moment of breathless transfiguration, but a calm persistence like the ongoing autumnal tranquillity that is to remain after the visitation of Intellectual Beauty. The poet's hope is for another "isle" that will endure for him, another Golden Age ("the earth grow young again," 373). There, like the levelling and interpenetrating sunlight, "love which heals all strife" will circle,

> like the breath of life,
> All things in that sweet abode
> With its own mild brotherhood.   (366–69)

But the death of tyranny and the persistence of another Atlantis-like personal "isle" are prophecy and vision; the reality is a sea of Life and Agony, at best sprinkled with transient "flowering isles."

7   The Poetics of Intellectual Beauty

A Defence of Poetry

To recent analysts and historians of
critical theory Shelley's *Defence of Poetry* has proved something of an
embarrassment, if not an annoyance. The praise it has received has too
often flowed from reckless rhapsodists; and the sober, while moved by its
sincerity, customarily find its argument grievously flawed. The essay is
valuable, we are usually told, primarily for its breathless rhetoric: dis-
concertingly eclectic, it does not (or could not possibly) reconcile its
Platonism with its psychological empiricism; by attributing creation to
inspiration it becomes a defense of automatic writing; by depending upon
a single norm it collapses all arts and all poems into one and destroys
the distinction between the making of poems and other superior mental
activities; it offers unreconciled definitions of the imagination; it provides
no viable poetics for the practical critic. Running through most of the
commentaries is the assumption not only that the essay is unusable but
also that it repeatedly shifts its grounds and that its appeal, as one critic
has put it, is often "more transcendental than rational."
It is true that Shelley had extraordinary admiration for the Platonic
dialogues and that bits of them are paraphrased in the *Defence*, that the
Defence is rooted in a quasi-Platonic doctrine of inspiration, and that he
had been reading the *Ion* and had translated the *Symposium* and portions
of other dialogues shortly before and during composition of the *Defence*.
Equipped with these facts, we have tended to assimilate the essay to
Platonism and to impose upon it doctrines it does not assert, instead of

204

locating it within the structure of Shelley's own ideas. The central assumption of Shelley's poetics is, of course, the transcendent Absolute, the perfection which, in various perspectives, may be called by such various names as the True, the Good, the Beautiful, Intellectual Beauty, Liberty, or any other of the unifying modes of mental perfection. But the ambiguity of selfhood, we have noted, allows Shelley to postulate a transcendence that inconstantly visits the self or, indifferently, to identify with the self the immanent portion of that perfection. The inconsistency charged against him for constructing a poetics of creative self-expression out of a faculty psychology and yet maintaining faith in a transcendent Platonic One that is the model for all imitations is in fact nonexistent, since in the *Defence* he consistently located the form-revealing power within the individual human spirit and at the core of its concentric faculties, the senses, appetites, affections, intellect, and imagination (124).[1] For the purpose of elaborating his poetics Shelley chose to assume one of his alternatives rather than the other—namely, that the mind that "feeds this verse" is the human mind.

Each mind is essentially an equivalent particle of the Absolute, so that the distinction among individual identities is merely nominal, and since all minds, Shelley holds, perform according to the same laws, the mind of the "creator"—that is, the poet[2]—"is itself the image of all other minds" (115). The poet, then, "participates in the eternal, the infinite, and the one" (112) not because he is transported to or inspired by that transcendent One but because his internal spirit is a portion of it. Con-

---

[1] All references in this chapter to *A Defence of Poetry* are to the pages in Julian, VII.

Shelley reverses this same order—senses, affections, intellect, imagination—when he describes the *effect* of poetry on its audience: "It compels us to feel that which we perceive, and to imagine that which we know" (137).

[2] Not, as some commentators have thought, God the Creator, a concept that Shelley everywhere denies. In his vocabulary "create" means "organize," not creation *ex nihilo*; and Mary Shelley's 1831 preface to her *Frankenstein* is an adequate exposition of what Shelley means by creation: "Invention . . . does not consist in creating out of void, but out of chaos; the materials must, in the first place, be afforded; it can give form to dark, shapeless substances, but cannot bring into being the substance itself. . . . Invention consists in the capacity of seizing on the capabilities of a subject, and in the power of moulding and fashioning ideas suggested to it." Although in Shelley's inclusive system the organizing act of the poet is identical in kind with the shaping stress of the One Spirit on the universe, the *Defence* makes it unnecessary that the former be referred to the latter as a model. There is a source within the human mind that reveals to the organizing, or "creative," imagination the one "indestructible order" (112), or "eternal proportions" (117), without any necessary reference to the organization to which nature is compelled by the One; and the universal consent given to expressions of this indestructible order results, not from the fact that poetry repeats or imitates the primal act of creation by a Creator God, but from the fact that the poet's mind is the "image of all other minds."

sequently, although the *Defence* speaks of inspiration, it is to be understood as a metaphor for "instinct and intuition," as Shelley called it on one occasion (136), rather than as the inspiration from without of which the *Ion* speaks. Even in his translation of the *Ion*, Shelley attempted intermittently to transform the Platonic doctrine into the more manageable idea of intuition: "by divine influence" ($\theta\epsilon\acute{\iota}\alpha$ $\delta\upsilon\nu\acute{\alpha}\mu\epsilon\iota$), for example, becomes "from the impulse of the divinity within [the poet]."[3] Similarly, in the *Defence* Shelley writes that poetry redeems from decay the sporadic visitations of "the divinity *in* Man" (137), not the visitations of the transcendent divinity *to* man; that poetry is stamped "with the image of the divinity *in* man" (119); that the evanescent revelations are only *"as it were* the interpenetration of a diviner nature through our own" (136); and that the power which awakens the mind to transitory illuminations arises "from within" (135). Despite Shelley's representations of man elsewhere as a passive wind-lyre visited inconstantly by the divine breath[4] and as a mind illuminated by the transcendent Intellectual Beauty, or despite his prayer to be the trumpet through which the West Wind blows its prophecy, in the *Defence* he has put aside the religious question of the relation of the individual to the transcendent One and has considered the poet as autonomous, containing the inspiring force mysteriously within himself but outside the boundaries of his understanding. The relationship of this internal divinity to the conscious thoughts of the mind is like that described in an unused manuscript passage of the *Ode to Liberty*:

Within ⟨the temple⟩ a cavern of ⟨the mind of man⟩ man's inmost ⟨trackless⟩
    spirit
Is throned ⟨an Idol,⟩ so intensely fair
That the adventurous thoughts which wander near it
Worship—and as they kneel, ⟨like votaries,⟩ wear
The splendour of its presence—& the light
Penetrates their dreamlike frame

---

[3] Julian, VII, 239. "Inspired and possessed" ($\overset{\text{v}}{\epsilon}\nu\theta\epsilon o\iota \overset{\text{v}}{o}\nu\tau\epsilon\varsigma$ $\kappa\alpha\grave{\iota}$ $\kappa\alpha\tau\epsilon\chi\acute{o}\mu\epsilon\nu o\iota$) is altered to "in a state of inspiration, and, *as it were*, possessed by a spirit not their own" (238); and "inspired and put out of his senses" ($\overset{\text{v}}{\epsilon}\nu\theta\epsilon o\varsigma \ldots \kappa\alpha\grave{\iota}$ $\overset{\text{v}}{\epsilon}\kappa\phi\rho\omega\nu$), to "inspired, and, *as it were*, mad" (238). Itals. added.

[4] In the *Defence* the metaphor appears only to account for the poet's thoughts, not for the shaping or poem-forming power: "Man is an instrument over which a series of external and internal impressions are driven like the alternations of an ever-changing wind over an Aeolian lyre which move it by their motion to ever-changing melody. But there is a principle within the human being, and perhaps within all sentient beings, which acts otherwise than in a lyre and produces not melody alone but harmony, by an internal adjustment of the sounds and motions thus excited to the impressions which excite them." Contrast, for example, the Narrator of *Alastor*, who prays that, as a wind-lyre, he be inspired to poetry by the breath of the Earth Mother.

Till they become charged with the strength of flame

. . . .

They forever change & pass but it remains the same.[5]

Poets, Shelley writes in the *Defence*, are "compelled to serve the Power which is seated upon the throne of their own soul" (140), and that throne "is curtained within the invisible nature of man" (113). In its most ecstatic passages the *Defence* speaks of poets as "hierophants of an un-apprehended inspiration," but the divine inspiration these priests serve is within the human self.[6] The poet, the *Defence* adds, is "the influence which is moved not, but moves" (140); he is himself the divine Unmoved Mover.

But this does not mean that the internal inspiring power speaks the finished poem through the passive medium of the poet as the gods spoke through the sibyls. When Shelley elsewhere describes the transcendent One as Power rather than as Being, he conceives of it as "creative" in the restricted sense of a Demiurge compelling what already exists into the most nearly perfect form possible, the perfect Unity being its own model. Its "plastic stress" compels "All new successions to the forms they wear; / Torturing th' unwilling dross that checks its flight / To its own likeness."[7] The word "God" he interpreted as "the Power which models, as they pass, all the elements of this mixed universe to the purest and most perfect shape which it belongs to their nature to assume."[8] Analogously, since a portion of the One is present potentially in the human mind, this divinity within man sporadically "inspires" the imagination with momentary ap-prehensions of the one ideal form; and the imagination, acting as a form-shaping pressure, compels the mind's elemental thoughts into organic order through the mind's inherent principles of integration. The imme-diate result is an integral and noncontingent thought "containing within itself the principle of its own integrity" (109). This integral thought is a synthesis by the organizing imagination, which takes its formal model from the absolute oneness suddenly flaring within it, just as a "fading coal" flares into brilliance through the "invisible influence" of a gusting wind, or, better, as color, evolving "from within," suffuses a flower and

---

[5] MS e. 6, p. 105. A slightly inaccurate version was first published by Richard Garnett in his *Relics of Shelley* (London, 1862) as "Cancelled Passage of the Ode to Liberty."

[6] Cf. Shelley's fragment beginning, "O thou, Immortal Deity / Whose throne is in the depth of Human thought."

[7] *Adonais*, 381–85.

[8] *Essay on Christianity* (Julian, VI, 235). See also *On the Devil and Devils* (Julian, VII, 89), where he attributes to the "Greek philosophers" the belief that God at Creation "moulded the reluctant and stubborn materials ready to his hand, into the nearest arrangement possible to the perfect archetype existing in his con-templation."

then fades in proportion as the flower grows and decays (135). Everyone possesses the source of such an inward experience, and in Shelley's terminology everyone is a poet in the widest sense whenever such an experience occurs through an "excess" of the intuition of perfect form, independently of expression and regardless of the nature of the thoughts so organized. Manifest poetry, as distinct from poetic conception, is "the expression of the imagination" (109); but between conception and expression must fall the shadow of the mortal condition.

The "inspiration" Shelley speaks of, then, is exclusively the mysterious human apprehension of the perfect unitary form, not of particular forms or of content, and imagination is the mediating faculty that experiences this apprehension and transmits it to the conscious mind. Imagination is entirely an organizing force and nothing else, and Shelley's poetics everywhere resolves itself into the problems and consequences of integral form: the recurrent key words of the *Defence* are "order," "organization," "combination," "arrangement," "union," "relation," "harmony," and "rhythm" (that is, order in a temporal sequence). For Shelley the essence of the poetic conception is that it is a whole, not by virtue of some a priori formula on whose validity it must depend or of some transcendent form which it imitates, but because, under the compulsion of the internal plastic stress, it is "consistent with itself,"[9] contains "within itself the principle of its own integrity," and therefore is self-sustaining. Being self-contained, the integral thought is free of "time and place and number" and therefore, like the poet, "participates in the eternal, the infinite, and the one" (112). Thus in the verbal expression of the apprehended unity the "grammatical forms which express the moods of time, and the difference of persons, and the distinction of place" (112), although necessarily imposed by human limitations and the nature of language, are not limiting. Other tenses, persons, and places may be substituted without affecting the integrity and universality of the poem. Any breach of this formal integrity is also a diminution of universality: for this reason a mere "story," an inorganic "catalogue of detached facts, which have no other bond of connexion than time, place, circumstance, cause and effect,"[10] is a "mirror which obscures and distorts that which should be beautiful" (115), whereas a "poem," the union of whose elements is not dependent upon these merely discursive

---

[9] *A Discourse on the Manners of the Ancients* (Julian, VII, 225). Shelley offered an excellent explanation of what he meant by autonomous, self-consistent form when he attempted to clarify why the question of the relative size of a Roman temple he saw was irrelevant: ". . . it overpowers the idea of relative greatness, by establishing within itself a system of relations, destructive of your idea of its relation with other objects, on which our ideas of size depend" (to Peacock, 25 February 1819 [*Letters*, II, 80]).

[10] Since Shelley, like Hume, consistently defined cause and effect as only "a constant conjunction of events," it is essentially the same as the discursive, inorganic relationships of time and space.

relationships, transforms such distortions into an eternal and universal form by mirroring them as a "beautiful" unity. In opposition to time, place, circumstance, and cause and effect, the principles creative of organic wholeness are the mind's associative laws of "equality, diversity,[11] unity,[12] contrast, mutual dependence" (110), all of which are modes of equality and suggest why Shelley was able on occasion to identify the One with Liberty, to attribute to despotism and superstition the inequality that results in "the extinction of the poetical principle" (126), and to think of founders of society as poets (112). The distinction among pleasure, virtue, beauty, truth, and love is simply the distinction among the various media—respectively, sensation, sentiment, art, reasoning, and human intercourse (110)—to which these associative relations of equality and mutuality are applied. These associative laws of the mind, performing the task of interweaving elemental thoughts, annihilate time, space, and circumstance, and organize groups of thoughts into a single thought, a self-sustaining approximation of the imagination's intuited perfect unity. Thus, just as the "intellectual philosophy" frees us from the chaos there would be if the mind were merely "impelled or organized by the adhibition of events proceeding from what has been termed the mechanism of the material universe," so the true poetic form "defeats the curse which binds us to be subjected to the accident of surrounding impressions" by creating a heterocosm in which everything is integral and integrated, relevant and interrelated, a "being within our being" (137)—like the poet's thoughts that worship Emily in *Epipsychidion* (243), a "world" within his "Chaos." The temporal world outside poetry is experienced as "tumult" (121), "chaos" (126, 137), and "anarchy" (125), and the thoughts of men are to the unifying imagination as "bewildered armies" to their commanding general (125). Since a poem, by virtue of form, is universal and eternal, time "for ever develops new and wonderful applications of the eternal truth which it contains" (115). And since its universality contains all potentials, it is inexhaustible to interpretation and application: "Veil after veil may be undrawn, and the inmost naked beauty of the meaning never exposed ... and after one person and one age has exhausted all its divine effluence which their peculiar relations enable them to share, another and yet another succeeds, and new relations are ever developed" (131).[13]

One might, however, counter Shelley's claim for universality by insisting on the poem's necessary ties to a particular time and culture: surely

[11] Diversity, Shelley points out in discussing the distinction between the sexes, is not to be confused with inequality (129). Cf. *Epipsychidion*, 359, where the symbolic sun and moon are described as "equal, yet unlike."

[12] In Bodleian MS Shelley d. 1, fol. 83^r, Shelley wrote, more suggestively, "flowing together" before substituting "unity."

[13] Thus the "promoters of utility" merely "copy the sketches of [the poet's] creations. They make space, and give time" by applying the eternal, universal poem to a particular time and place (132).

the data, customs, beliefs, and ideals incorporated in and expressed by a work of art are temporal and local. Shelley agrees that they are but denies that these constitute part of the definition of a poem or significantly limit it as poetry, any more than the veil with which the Witch of Atlas covers herself to make her brilliance bearable to mortals is part of her perfect nature: "... it is doubtful whether the alloy of costume, habit, &c., be not necessary to temper this planetary music for mortal ears"(117). Every poet is confined to his own time, place, and culture, and to their inherent imperfections. These are the materials with which he is constrained to realize his intuition of the One, but the organic form which these transient views and circumstantial materials embody in poetry is outside time and flux, so that its "eternal proportions" are evident through its "temporary dress" (117) or "thin disguise of circumstance" (121), just as we are expected to see the purity of Beatrice Cenci's character through the mask of her misdeeds and false beliefs. Not that Shelley is divorcing eternal poetic form from transitory content, however much he may be distinguishing them: the form "communicates" itself to the "accidental vesture," which in turn reveals the hidden form by the "manner in which it is worn" (117). Moreover, although *sub specie aeternitatis* (which is the ideal vision of poetry) the temporal materials are a clog that imagination must subdue to its own ends, poetry also has a responsibility to its own age. It is crucial to the immediate culture that "eternal proportions" be imparted to materials bearing particularly on the contemporary "condition"; and the Romans, for example, were wrong to separate their life from their poetry by creating general art bearing only on "the universal constitution of the world" (125). Although poetry as an integral thought containing the principle of its own integrity is eternally relevant, it must be continuously re-created in man's successive transient conditions; it must not only be "produced" but also "sustained," and it is in this sense that the poet "participates in the divine nature as regards providence, no less than as regards creation" (123).

Yet the fact remains that universality seems flawed if the poem is tied to imperfect, transitory conditions and values, however necessary they may be to the perfecting of the contemporary culture. Shelley's reply is to admit that the revenge motif in Homer, for example, is indeed the mistaken ideal of a semi-barbarous age, but to add that this vice of disharmony only gave temporal clothing to the "eternal proportions," or ideal relationships, that Homer shaped as "the truth and beauty of friendship, patriotism, and persevering devotion to an object" (116). Homer's works are eternal and universally relevant by virtue of their formal approximation to the intuited One, their aspiration to the order in which thoughts *should* be interwoven, not by virtue of their accidental stuff. Shelley therefore has freed himself from the trap those fall into who include in critical evaluation the ethical status of the materials (the "accidental vesture"), the poet's own moral judgments, or his overt theme, all of which belong to discourse, not poetry. Indeed, although it is frequently claimed that by identifying the One with not only the Beautiful but also the True and the Good, Shelley has confused esthetic with moral and ontological judgments, he has in fact liberated his poetics from what we usually mean by moral judgments, since the Beautiful, the True, and the Good— and even Liberty—are modes of the One resulting from the different limited perspectives in which the One is viewed; criticism in any of these contexts is only a biased and incomplete consideration of the same form. It is not that Shelley has subsumed ethics under esthetics or esthetics under ethics; the Good, True, and Beautiful are all formal and share the same formal criterion. Therefore any specific ethical theme, being limited to time, place, and circumstance, is a blemish and a misapplication of poetry, and a "Poet therefore would do ill to embody his own conceptions of right and wrong, which are usually those of his place and time, in his poetical creations, which participate in neither" (118). Men like Camillus and Regulus who lived lives of poetry, Shelley claims, did not act from specific ideas of right and wrong; their imaginations, beholding the beauty of such a "rhythm and order" of action, "created it out of itself according to its own idea" (125) for the sake of expressing that formal "beauty." Moral good, like esthetic experience, is the *effect* of form; should the poet attempt a moral aim he would be interpreting the consequence instead of participating in the cause (118), and, as we have observed in considering *The Cenci*, Shelley's ethics is directed entirely to moral motive.

However occult Shelley's definition of the poet as prophet may appear, it is rendered intelligible by his conception of the formal universality and atemporality of poetry. Above all, he specifically denies that the poet has any mystical gift for foretelling events. What he does say is that the poet "beholds the future in the present" (112): confined to the present for his materials, the poet, as "legislator," compels them to conform with the "laws" according to which they "ought to be ordered" (112), those eternal proportions which include futurity. Thus "prophet" is but the temporal term for "legislator"; the poet does not perform each of these roles in addition to the other, he "unites" them (112), for they are essentially the same, and in this sense he is the unacknowledged legislator of the world. Because the poet apprehends the eternal order that ought to be, when he clothes this extratemporal vision with time he not only beholds the present ideally ordered but apprehends the "spirit"[14] of futurity in it. Hence, the paradoxical metaphor by which the poet's thoughts are

---

[14] Shelley repeatedly identifies "spirit" with the "eternal proportions," or "indestructible order," that can be infused by the imagination in things or events. The poet-prophet foretells the "spirit" of events, not their *particular* "forms" (112); harmony is the "spirit" of the traditional "forms" of metre (114); and poetry lays bare the beauty of nature, which is the "spirit of its forms" (137).

"the germs of the flower and the fruit of latest time" (112): being eternal, his thoughts are both that out of which temporal events are spun and that in which all temporal events culminate, just as Prometheus, being eternal, is, with respect to time, both efficient and final cause, "the prophecy / Which begins and ends in thee."[15] Shelley can write that prophecy is "an attribute of poetry" (112) because futurity is a temporal attribute of eternity; and, he immediately adds, time in fact does not exist with respect to the poet's conceptions.

ii

Because Shelley founds his poetics on the organic unity of the work of art, he must attribute the apprehension of and compulsion toward unity to a divine power within the mind which acts intermittently and independently of will and consciousness. Willfully motivated and consciously controlled acts, Shelley assumes, can be only aggregative, sequential; they can, he says, produce logic, not poetry (138), a mosaic, not a painting (136). For if a work of art contains its own unifying principle, it is not a mechanical assembly of discrete finished parts, but is of the order of an organism: translation cannot produce poetry because the "plant must spring again from its seed" (114), and "a great statue or picture grows under the power of the artist as a child in the mother's womb" (136). Since a poem evolves biologically out of its indwelling genetic principle, insofar as it is poetry it is not a successive accumulation of units according to a conscious external plan nor the result of a series of decisions, but an embryonic growth, at all points, toward its organic wholeness. Milton, Shelley claims, "conceived the *Paradise Lost* as a whole before he executed it in portions" (136). It follows, then, that not only must the apprehension of the One arise within the mind independently of the will and consciousness, but composition must take place under the same circumstances. The fading insight into the One and the desire to retain it operate as the compelling motives that draw the component thoughts to their perfect form, just as the sculptor does not assemble finished segments to form a statue but causes it to grow through various embryonic stages toward its final shape without being able to account consciously for the intent of any of his steps or for the nature of the overall process. As Shelley insists, awareness and the will are not "the necessary conditions of all mental causation" (139); and, without denying that organic order is mentally caused, he finds consciousness and the will incapable of producing it, just as one is incapable of willing belief.

To reverse the coin and consider the same problem from the point of view of critical norms: by attributing to the divinity within the mind the

---

[15] *Prometheus Unbound*, I. 690–91.

impulse to organic unity, Shelley has transferred to the mysteries of religion the insoluble ultimate problem of esthetics. Without that religion Shelley's argument would run as follows in its simplest terms: since we do, with considerable agreement, experience the greatness of a work of art, and since integral form is the criterion of art, the minds of men must have an apprehension of the ideal form that all poetry aspires to. If the essential criterion of a work of art is its organic wholeness, the evident facts are that systematic poetics cannot account for our desire to experience and create organic wholeness and that although we find one work of art greater than another, poetics alone cannot account for the difference. We may point to the internal interrelationships, but there can be no demonstrable formula for determining that a group of thoughts has been so arranged and combined that they constitute one thought containing its own integrative principle. Even if there were, we would still lack a yardstick for valuing one integral unity above another. The problem remains with us and continues to beset critics for whom organic unity is both the definition and criterion of poetry. How does one measure the complexity of interrelations? At what point of integrity does the *claritas* shine through? Or at what point is the full potential of the materials realized? Even if we find the answer on psychological grounds, we have to assume an intuitive and ineffable constant in man.

Hence the normative role of the random apprehensions of the ideal unity, the sporadic flarings of Intellectual Beauty, which Shelley here defines as "the visitations of the divinity in man." Although man cannot will such visitations or define their pure revelations, the mind can and does experience them; and Shelley is attempting to account for the fact. If it seems objectionable that he has abandoned poetics to the mystery of religion, it would be more accurate to say that he has identified religion with the mysteries of poetry in its inclusive sense: "Coleridge has said that every poet was religious, the converse, that every religious man must be a poet was more true."[16] It is the very identification of sporadic, unwilled poetic conception with the divinity in man that allows Shelley to set off poetry as a uniquely human act, for if poetic conception is the apprehension of the perfect form and if that perfect form is the character of the divine, then to claim that man continuously apprehends or has access to it would be to claim that he is perfect and free from mutability. If Intellectual Beauty were always present in the human mind, "Man were immortal and omnipotent." The presence of a capacity to apprehend ideal form accounts for man's potential; the intermittence of this apprehension is accounted for by his earthly limitations and locates the special significance and overriding relevance of poetry. The One is "pure," subsuming all diversities, but the human mind "cannot be considered pure";

[16] Julian, VII, 336.

only by an unwilled, extraordinary, and inexplicable event can the human mind experience that perfection and then, through the associative laws of the imagination, compel those diversities into an approximation of that unity. Hence all the arts are "the mediators / Of that best worship love" exchanged between man and that unitary perfection of Existence which Prometheus is; Art is the "ardent intercessor" between the eternal perfection and the "promoters of utility";[17] in *Lines Written among the Euganean Hills*, poetry is the world's "unfailing River" illuminated by a transcendent light.

Shelley, however, does not claim that the mind totally lacks the principles of form unless it is "inspired." The imagination, or synthesizing power, is innate, and its natural propensity is to organize the mind's data. Although poetic conception in its ultimate sense occurs only in extraordinary moments when some invisible and inexplicable influence from within enflames the "fading coal" of the mind, the coal smolders continuously. The power behind this spark is the portion of "divinity" ever present to the synthesizing imagination, so that even in his ordinary activities man may give to his otherwise chaotic or, at any rate, discursive experience a degree of self-containing form. There is no conflict, then, between Shelley's doctrine of extraordinary "inspiration" and his postulation of a natural formal principle within the mind which, instead of merely experiencing the melodic succession of impressions, creates a harmonic organization by an "internal adjustment" of the media of expression to the impressions which excite the expression (109). In this sense a child at play is a rudimentary poet when it expresses with sound and gesture its delight in impressions, the sounds and gestures being internally adjusted to bear harmonic proportion to the pleasurable impressions (110); and language itself is poetry since, being metaphoric, it marks relationships and is created by the mind's normal synthesizing principles without benefit of the extraordinary surging of absolute form (111–12).

Indeed, Shelley provides a variety of natural grounds for the synthesizing capacity. Not only are some men, being more sensitive and delicately "organized," more susceptible to the intuition of the absolute unitary form, but also the frequent recurrence of this apprehension may produce a natural "habit of order and harmony" (139). Experience with poetic expression "enlarges the circumference of the imagination" and strengthens it "in the same manner as exercise strengthens a limb" (118). Or, at the lowest level, one may simply impose upon expressions the traditional forms of harmony (114). But poetry in its true sense requires the flaming, not the smoldering coal; an access to absolute and unitary form, not merely a harmonizing power, however strengthened or artificially aided. Shelley's theory of the nature and informative source of the

---

[17] *Prometheus Unbound*, III. iii. 54–60; *Ode to Liberty*, 249.

imagination provides for both a synthesizing act in normal mental life and an extraordinary access to the oneness which is the criterion and motive for all forms; but the difference between the smoldering and the flaming coal is so great that the two states are actually different in kind rather than in degree. In the intervals between "inspiration," the poet "becomes a man, and is abandoned to the sudden reflux of the influences under which others habitually live" (139).

There is a contradiction, we are sometimes told, between Shelley's defining poetry variously as expression (of imagination, of emotions, and of "the influence of society or nature" on the mind) and as imitation (of life and of the world).[18] Above all, it is clear that, in speaking of the child and the savage as expressing emotions, Shelley is not proposing anything so naive as Hugh Blair's theory that poetry is strong passions flowing out as emotive language or that the fundamental purpose of poetry is to communicate feeling. The most rudimentary and primitive cause for imitating or expressing impressions, Shelley is saying, is the pleasure they have imparted and the consequent desire to prolong that pleasure; and only in this sense of cause and manifestation can poetry be considered merely an "expression" of the emotions. The child expresses itself because it is delighted by the impressions, and the expression gives evidence of that delight. Moreover, even here Shelley has not confined himself to the concept of "expression": the child's expression of delight is the "reflected image," or imitation, of its pleasurable impressions (110). Although Shelley then adds that the savage "expresses the emotions produced in him by surrounding objects," he is speaking of emotion as the dominant motive and as but one of the elements of the consequent expression; for he then defines the expression as the reflection or "image of the combined effect of those objects, and of his apprehension of them" (110), and not merely of his emotional responses. In context, the main purpose of these passages is not to distinguish between imitation and expression but to prepare for the statement that the mind, having colored its impressions

---

[18] There is no evidence that Shelley ever held a Platonic conception of poetry as *imitative* of the transcendent One; and certainly it is not imitative, as some commentators have believed, of the Platonic Forms, Essences, or Ideas. The statement that the imagination "has for its objects those forms which are common to universal nature and existence itself" (109) cannot mean, as Meyer H. Abrams claims, that the imagination "intuits" the eternal Forms (*The Mirror and the Lamp* [New York, 1953], p. 130) but merely means that the elements on which it performs its synthesizing act are common and not special. Nor does Shelley say that "poetry strips the veil from the forms of the world" (*ibid.*), implying that the "objects imitated by the great poet are the eternal Forms discerned through the veil of fact and particularity" (*ibid.*, 127). What he does write is that poetry "strips the veil of familiarity from the world, and lays bare the naked and sleeping beauty, which is the spirit of its forms" (137); that is, that it reveals (not "imitates"), beneath the interference of mutability and appearance, the one perfect harmony toward which the One Spirit's plastic stress compels all entities.

"with its own light," adjusts them to form a harmony by means of the order in which it apprehends them, which differs from the random order in which they are received by the senses, "expression being subject to the laws of that from which it proceeds" (110). This is not to say that poetry does not express emotions: society produces a class of emotions, Shelley writes, in addition to those produced by nature, and hence "an augmented treasure of expressions" (110). But poetry *expresses* all the contents of the mind: emotions, thoughts, however produced, and the unifying associative laws whereby the imagination acts. Even ideal poetry, which is Shelley's central concern, can be spoken of as an "expression" of delight; for man, in the fullest development of his nature, receives the purest and most intense delight from the highest degree of form (116). To him not only "beauty in art" but even "pleasure in sensation" is constituted by the internal relations of "equality, diversity, unity, contrast, mutual dependence" because the most intense and purest pleasure is inextricably bound up with the experience of the absolute order which it is the purpose of the highest poetry to approximate (110, 111).

The truth is that "imitation" and "expression," however central to the development of eighteenth-century esthetics, as Meyer Abrams has made clear they are, are inadequate terminological instruments for analyzing Shelley's poetics and only confuse the issue by oversimplifying it and by superimposing on his poetics alien systems and expectations. Because the terms describe only the partial and complementary phases of his poetics, he uses them almost indiscriminately. For example, he can say that a poem is an imitation, a "very image" of life, but it is that image "*expressed* in its eternal truth"—that is, given the form that approximates the "unchangeable" and time-annihilating form existing in the poet's mind (115). Poetry represents, it is true, since its data derive from the objects of experience, but it "reproduces all that it represents"[19] (117) by reorganizing and combining thoughts in a beautiful and indestructible order known only to the imagination, instead of following the accidental sequences of impressions. Briefly, although poetry *imitates* external impressions and *expresses* the emotions and "internal impressions" (109), it is not poetry by virtue of either of these acts, which merely account for the relation of poetic matter to its source. Consequently, Shelley's poetics does

---

[19] That is, reconstitutes, or gives order to, all that it imitates. Cf. the statement that poetry "reproduces the common Universe" (137), which explicates Shelley's plea for "the creative faculty to imagine that which we know" (134). "As to imitation, poetry is a mimetic art. It creates, but it creates by combination and representation. Poetical abstractions are beautiful and new, not because the portions of which they are composed had no previous existence in the mind of man or nature, but because the whole produced by their combination has some intelligible and beautiful analogy with those sources of emotion and thought, and with the contemporary condition of them" (Preface to *Prometheus Unbound*). Cf. also *Proposals for an Association* (Julian, V, 267): "Do we not see that the laws of nature perpetually act by disorganization and reproduction, each alternately becoming cause and effect."

not resolve into a theory of imitation or a psychology of expression, for poetry is the imparting of a unified order to thoughts, whether externally or internally produced and however "colored" by such mental attributes as the emotions.

On the other hand, it is true, there is an "external" model for such imaginative orderings. The external world of "things," considered independently of our accidental and chaotic experiences of it, is itself organized by inherent, self-sustaining, and noncontingent relations because "nature" impresses the same footsteps "upon the various subjects of the world" (111), that is, compels everything toward its own perfect likeness.[20] But since the distinction between external and internal, world and mind, is merely nominal—the *Defence* repeats that "All things exist as they are perceived; at least in relation to the percipient" (137)—"nature" in this sense is but the one "plastic stress" or power (of which each individual human spirit is a derivative particle) considered as external instead of internal. Consequently it is consistent with Shelley's ambiguous ontology that he can conceive of the poetic act indifferently as either a creation of ideal order by a human portion of the One or as a kind of discovery of the order created by the One in "the world." Because the order created by the human portion of the One is the same as the order that truly subsists in reality beneath the veil of appearance and mutability, creation and discovery are only different ways of describing the same creative—not mimetic—act of the mind. By creating the ideal organization, the mind can "see" the order beneath the apparent reality. Poetic language, for example, is a creation of the human imagination, and yet it "marks the before unapprehended relations of things" (111); poetry transmutes forms into incarnations of its spirit, and yet it "reveals" the spirit within nature's forms (137). It is a matter of indifference whether poetry is defined as spreading over the apparent world "its own figured curtain" fashioned by the mind's internal apprehension of form or as withdrawing "life's dark veil from before the scene of things" to reveal the hidden order pressed on the world by the One (137). The superficial "familiar world" (137), which exists in our merely random impressions, is a chaos; and since the mind possesses a particle of "the one Spirit's plastic stress" which organizes the true world, it is only a shift of ontological perspective, not of esthetic premises, to say that the imagination purges "the film of familiarity" and "strips the veil of familiarity from the world and lays bare the naked and sleeping beauty" (137),[21] or to say that it "reproduces"

[20] Bodleian MS Shelley d. 1, fol. 36ᵛ (Koszul, p. 122n.), reads, "Nor are these similitudes arbitrary and conventional: but they are the vestiges of ⟨nature⟩ power over form." In a cancelled passage in the same MS (fol. 77ʳ; Koszul, p. 68n.) Shelley wrote of "that analogy & even unity in all thoughts & objects of thought, the perception of which is poetry...."

[21] It unveils "the permanent analogy of things" (115) and "lifts the veil from the hidden beauty of the world, and makes familiar objects be as if they were not familiar" (117).

(that is, reconstitutes and reorganizes) or "creates anew the universe, after it has been annihilated in our minds by the recurrence of impressions blunted by reiteration" (137).[22] To demand that Shelley choose between a mimetic and an expressive theory is to misunderstand not only his poetics but also its supporting ontology, which refuses the distinction between things and thoughts and leaves ambiguous the immanence or transcendence of the poetic mind "which feeds this verse / Peopling the lone universe."

iii

The integral thought which the imagination synthesizes into a formal approximation of the fleeting vision of the One can exist independently of expression. It becomes palpable "poetry" in the inclusive sense when it is expressed upon various media, whether words, matter, sound, color, gestures, or personal and societal conduct. It becomes poetry in the "limited" sense only when its medium is language. But although Shelley postulated a unitary—and therefore humanly unobtainable—formal ideal for all poetry, he does not dissolve all verbal poems into one and destroy the distinctions among genres, among poems, or among the parts of a poem. The One is, of course, ineffable, not only because the human intuition of it is transient, but also because it is pure form by virtue of being indivisibly one; and the human mind must work with multiplicity and diversity. But Shelley is careful to distinguish between poetry as conception and as expression, and the expression of the synthesized thought can be analyzed in terms of the integrative laws of the imagination, the kinds of thoughts synthesized, the degree of synthesis, the nature of the various media, and the degree and kind of pleasure the poem produces. Whereas our passive impressions are chaotic, all expression is "subject to the laws of that from which it proceeds" (110); and it is clear that by "laws" he means the integrative principles of association.[23] "The most astonishing combinations of poetry, the subtlest deductions of logic and mathematics, are no other than combinations which the intellect makes of sensations according to its own laws."[24] Shelley's so-called Platonic doctrine of inspirational apprehension of the One is coherently complemented by an associational psychology.

Moreover, just as the one Spirit's plastic stress can compel each mass only to that degree of form which its limited character permits, so each class of expression (or mimetic representation), such as dance, music, and

---

[22] Similarly, language must be reconstituted when the integral relations it designates are lost through familiarity and it becomes signs of atomistic "portions or classes of thoughts" (111).

[23] MS e. 8, p. 76: "Association is, however, rather the law according to which this power [i.e. the imagination] is exerted than the power itself."

[24] *Speculations on Metaphysics* (Julian, VII, 59).

verbal poetry, has its own peculiar supreme order or rhythm. In Aristotelian terms, each mode has its highest potential, which the artist attempts to actualize; in Platonic terms, the eternal idea is diminished in proportion to the limitations inherent in the medium or mode of expression. Each mode aspires to a special kind of ideal configuration, the criterion of which is the degree of pure, or disinterested, pleasure imparted by that form; and the faculty which judges the degree to which the formal pleasure afforded by a work of art approximates the intuitively apprehended highest pleasure of which its mode is capable as form is called "taste" (111)—that is, the "inspired" imagination operating as a critical instead of creative faculty. Each mode of expression is directed and limited by the "materials, instruments, and conditions" of its medium, for these "have relations among each other, which limit and interpose between conception and expression" (113). Each medium—color, marble, or sound, for example—has inherent intra-relations which must be satisfied regardless of the highest order to which it is being urged, and the criterion of excellence is the degree to which these intra-relations of the materials have been exploited or overcome. Language, therefore, despite its limitations, is the supreme material of expression because, being "arbitrarily produced by the imagination," it has "relation to thoughts alone" and therefore is "more plastic" (113) than other materials and less resistant to the impress of the imagination. But sound inheres in language (the imagination, in forming language, presumably having chosen those sounds bearing true relation to what they represent), and since sounds also "have relation both between each other and towards that which they represent" (114), verbal poetry requires not only an ideal integration of thoughts, but, organically integrated with it, both the harmony of sounds as sounds and the harmonic relation of these sounds to the thoughts. While Shelley's poetics takes into consideration the various limitations upon expression, it is everywhere motivated by aspiration to the one perfect form in which relationships become absolute unity.

Correspondingly, Shelley's poetics implies that every literary genre—tragedy, epic, comedy, and lyric, each being distinguished by the kind of thoughts it employs—has its own special supreme harmony, and that they form a hierarchy of approximations to the ideal unitary order. Consequently the "most perfect and universal form" (120), the drama, being "that form under which a greater number of modes of expression of poetry are susceptible of being combined than any other" (122), was the supreme mode when it once employed not only language and action but also music, painting, dance, and religious institutions, each of these kinds of expression being developed to its own highest order and all of them organized "into a beautiful proportion and unity one towards another" (119). In brief, the highest mode was the goal Shelley set for himself in *Prometheus Unbound* and *Hellas*, the formal unity of various kinds of formal unity.

Such a harmonious fusion of individual harmonies transcends the simpler order of the drama of action and language and, by permitting a more complex synthesis, approaches more closely the ideal form revealed to the imagination. For the same reason, the harmonizing of comedy with tragedy is greater than either of the component genres. In the farthest extension of this concept of infinite harmonies of harmonies reaching more closely to the One, Shelley considered all poems "episodes to that great poem, which all poets, like the co-operating thoughts of one great mind, have built up since the beginning of the world" (124), just as his "intellectual philosophy" led to the concept of the One Mind as the ultimate Existence. The one poem of the One Mind, of which each human mind is a portion, is outside time; in time, human minds compose its unitary episodes, which are "episodes of that cyclic poem written by Time upon the memories of men" (125).

Shelley's doctrines preclude the possibility that verbal poetry exists for the willful purpose of communication. Denied the purpose of communicating explicit ethical ideas, the poem attains its final cause, although not its final effect, simply by coming into existence; and the poetic transaction involves only the poet and his poem, not an audience. The unwilled and unconsciously motivated process of expression is compelled only by the poet's desire to prolong his apprehension of the One, to sustain the pure delight in the organically rhythmic or integrated form generated among a group of thoughts. He is therefore a nightingale that "sings to cheer its own solitude with sweet sounds" (116). Yet the audience that overhears the song is significantly affected as a consequence of experiencing approximations of the ideal order, and the ultimate effect of the poem is endless. Shelley explains this effect of the poem in terms of sympathy and love. The "great instrument of moral good is the imagination" (118) because it creates the beautiful; and the beautiful awakens the observer's sympathetic love, which is the "going out of our own nature, and an identification of ourselves with the beautiful which exists in thought, action, or person, not our own" (118). The ultimate effect of poetry, therefore, is the moral goodness of the observer because by his sympathetically identifying himself with the beautiful his own imagination attains an approximation of the ideal order and assimilates all other thoughts to that order, out of which the good arises. In brief, the *Defence of Poetry*, grounded in the "intellectual philosophy," is the poetics, not of "sad reality," but of what Shelley called "beautiful idealisms," the poetics of *Prometheus Unbound, Hellas, Epipsychidion,* and *Adonais.*

8 Power and the Cycle of Mutability

Mont Blanc

Ode to the West Wind

The Cloud

The distinction between Shelley's preoccupation with immortality and with moral reform is also a distinction between a transcendent state of being and a sublunary state of action, over which the respective presiding divinities are the One, or Being, and the Power, or ultimate cause. Both of these deities abhor the "vacancies," or moments of discontinuity, that threaten to deny immortality and render life and the world meaningless and "false": the "interstices" between thoughts that are necessary for the existence of the human mind, the "nothingness and dissolution" with which the mind is instinctively at enmity, the vacancies and desolations between the intermittent visitations of the shadow of Intellectual Beauty.[1]

One pole of Shelley's mind, the one that draws him to "the fire for which all thirst," is ontological (and hence, in terms of the "intellectual philosophy," epistemological). In such poems as *The Sensitive Plant*, it tempts him, in the face of the indisputable experience of transience, to grasp Existence and Being as eternal and "true," while rejecting the discontinuities and voids as only false appearances, errors of incomplete vision. Or, in the *Defence of Poetry* and in poems like the *Hymn to Intellectual Beauty* and *Lines Written Among the Euganean Hills*, it leads him to locate the worth of life, and perhaps even the evidence of im-

[1] Without believing in the Creation myth, Shelley used it to oppose Existence to the meaninglessness of the void: God created to fill space "when he grew weary of vacancy" (to John Gisborne, 12 January 1822 [*Letters*, II, 376]).

mortality, entirely in the extraordinary moments of total illumination. The other bent of his mind draws him to inquire into the nature of action rather than of reality, for hiatuses in the continuity of action would imply an absurd world and render life as meaningless as would the possibility of lacunae in whatever really is. Shelley seems never to have faced the question of the relation among his three points of reference, the all-subsuming One, which is Being, the One Mind, which is Existence, and the Power, or ultimate cause; and his assignment in *Prometheus Unbound* of Existence to Prometheus and Power to Demogorgon suggests that he kept them distinct, as though he were a polytheist. In any event, in the summer of 1816, he addressed to the transcendent Intellectual Beauty the question,

Why dost thou pass away and leave our state,
This dim vast vale of tears, vacant and desolate?

and in that same summer, in *Mont Blanc*, he redirected his question to the transcendent and inaccessible Power, asking what existence and worth the world would have

If to the human mind's imaginings
Silence and solitude were vacancy?

In that sense the *Hymn to Intellectual Beauty* and *Mont Blanc* are companion poems contemplating the same obsessive problem in the light of two different absolutes.

i

Mont Blanc opens, not, as we might reasonably expect, with a view of the mountain, but with a metaphoric definition of the universe in terms of the "intellectual philosophy": "The everlasting universe of things / Flows through the mind." Uncreated and eternal, the universe is a river of "things," for mind can only perceive, not create; but what is asserted of the river is that it flows through the valley of mind, for everything exists only as it is perceived and therefore only as it is present in mind. By defining the universe as constituted of things rather than of thoughts and then by predicating the existence of those things exclusively in mind, Shelley formulated a syntax which, by fusing the externalizing subject (universe of things) and the internalizing predicate (flows through the mind), denies both that "things" are mental fictions and that there is any real distinction between thing and thought. Because he is concerned with reality as determined by mind, the rapid river of the universe of things is pictured as "Now dark—now glittering"—that is, in terms of the customary distinction between clarity and obscurity by which the empirical philosophy distinguished the vividness of sensory impressions from the relative indistinctness of "ideas," or recollected impressions. If there can be any doubt that Shelley is here elaborating an ontology that denies the difference between thing and thought, it is removed by the manuscript evidence that his opening line originally began, "In daylight thoughts, bright or obscure."[2] In accordance with the "intellectual philosophy," the categories "external" and "internal" are meaningless, and the distinction between clarity and obscurity is one of degrees, not of ontological states. But since the statement that the universe of things is alternately dark and glittering implies an autonomous external reality, Shelley then counteracts that implication by repeating the same facts in the mentalistic terms of the "intellectual philosophy": the river of things is "now reflecting gloom— / Now lending splendour." Appropriately, the valley of mind is the source of the obscurity that customarily characterizes "ideas"; and the river of things flowing through that valley is the source of the clarity customarily characterizing immediate sensory impressions. But if the mind's "gloom" is *reflected* by things, the darkness cast on things is returned to the mind: nothing exists except as it is perceived. If the brightness of things is only *lent* to the mind, then the mind contains what it does not originate and does not own: mind cannot create, it can only perceive. The paradox of Shelley's ontological circle is sustained by the imagery and syntax: mind is the center to which everything must be referred, and yet the mind is also the circle within which everything is contained.

The mind Shelley has been describing, however, is not the individual mind but the One Mind, which constitutes total Existence and of which each individual mind is a portion. It is for the purpose of making this distinction that, whereas the opening lines refer to "the mind," he will later resort to the apparently tautological expression, "my *human* mind" (37), and will speak of it as his "own separate phantasy" (36). Since each human mind is also one of the "things" of the universe, it too pours its tributary stream into the universal river of the One Mind, although its stream is feeble in comparison with the mighty river of sensible "objects"; depending upon those phenomena for its content, its sound is "but half its own":

The everlasting universe of things
Flows through the mind, and rolls its rapid waves,
Now dark—now glittering—now reflecting gloom—
Now lending splendour, where from secret springs

[2] MS e. 16, p. 3. I believe his next attempt reads, "In day the stream of various thoughts," and "thoughts" is then altered to "things," as it often is in Shelley's manuscripts.

The source of human thought its tribute[3] brings
Of waters,—with a sound but half its own. . . .   (1–6)

The psychological state, approximating the subjective-objective ambiguity of reverie, that occasions this phenomenalistic definition of the
universe fades, however, when the poet then tautologically introduces an
objective brook as a likeness of the metaphoric stream of human thought.
The simile, which has no significant function except to transform the
mode of vision, by its very tautology opens the door to an abundance of
supposedly external objects that exceed the requirements of the comparison, as though the tendency to conceive of images as external were
too great for the poet to resist. The sound of the stream of human thought
is

Such as a feeble brook will oft assume
In the wild woods, among the mountains lone,
Where waterfalls around it leap for ever,
Where woods and winds contend, and a vast river
Over its rocks ceaselessly bursts and raves.   (7–11)

Only now, when this plethora of "external" imagery has broken in
upon the phenomenal reality, does the poet look outward to the Ravine
of Arve from his post at Pont Pellisier, to find it a remarkably consistent
objective correlative of his metaphor for a total universe that is indifferently things or thoughts and that is located in the One Mind. Even
superficially considered, the external scene is composed of the same
imagery and can be described in the same language that constituted the
metaphor for total Existence: the waterfall (26), the contending of woods
and winds (20–24), the "bursting" of the Arve through the ravine (18)
that replaces the ceaseless bursting of the "vast river" over the rocks, the
interplay of light and darkness (15, 18–19). The scene is indeed the same;
only the framework of conception is different, for truth is relative, not to
what is seen, but to the ontological assumption in terms of which it is
seen. As Shelley wrote in his essay On Life, whether "things" are conceived as external to the mind or as thoughts that are objects of other
thoughts, "the relations of things remain unchanged, by whatever system." Like the river of "things" flowing through the mind, the river Arve
flows through its ravine, and the validity of the "intellectual philosophy"
with which the poem opened will be threatened if these opposing per-
spectival emblems result in equally adequate accounts of the universe.
Just as the universe that metaphorically flows through mind is varyingly
dark and glittering as the mind and its sensory contents interact in im-

---

[3] Cf. Prometheus Unbound, III. iii. 155: "Indus and its tribute rivers."

pressions and ideas, so a supposedly autonomous external world is a Ravine of Arve over which sail "Fast cloud-shadows and sunbeams" (15), possessing its own physical sources of clarity and obscurity. Even the sources of these qualities are consistently analogous: in the phenomenalistic ontology, the river of sensational things lends its glitter to the mind-ravine and reflects the mind's darkness; in the external scene, it is the river Arve that bursts like a "flame of lightning" while the mountains through which it passes are "dark" (18–19). The "secret" ultimate origin of human thought is replaced in the external scene by the "secret throne" (17), or ultimate source, of the river Arve. Even the complex interdependence of the mind's darkness and the brilliance of "things"—the interdependence that defined a monism which paradoxically subsumes a dualism of subject and object—is now projected in the winds that come to hear the "mighty swinging" of the pines, "an old and solemn harmony" (23–24). For, like the lent splendor and reflected darkness, the harmony the winds hear is the swinging of the pines (mind cannot create, it can only perceive), although the swinging of the pines is the work of the winds that come to hear it (nothing exists except as it is perceived).

What stands out above all else about these two worlds, one defined by the "intellectual philosophy" and the other by a kind of materialism independent of mind, is that both are intensely dynamic and filled with the sound of movement: the river "rolls its rapid waves," bursts, and raves; waterfalls leap; winds and pines contend; caves echo the river's commotion. Moreover, in each reality the powerful motion is continuous: waterfalls leap "for ever"; the rivers "ceaselessly" burst; the winds "still come and ever came"; the Arve's motion is "ceaseless," an "unresting" sound. There would appear, then, to be no real difference in defining the universe in terms of the "intellectual philosophy" or as an external reality independent of perception. In one sense that is true: the relations of "things" remain the same. And yet there is an essential difference, for in the midst of the ceaseless activity and noise of the supposedly external world, a contradictory note appears almost casually:

> the strange sleep
> Which when the voices of the desert fail
> Wraps all in its own deep eternity.[4]   (27–29)

As in *The Sensitive Plant*, the world that presents itself to our senses, unlike the world of the "intellectual philosophy," is not a plenum, but a

---

[4] That Shelley meant to describe a vacancy is supported by some of the manuscript variants (MS e. 16, p. 4): "The sudden Death"; "The momentary death"; "The sudden pause ⟨of things⟩ which does inhabit thee"; "Which when the voices of the desart fail / And its hues wane, doth blend them all & steep / Their tumult ⟨periods?⟩ in its own eternity."

discontinuity; a pause in its activity leaves only a void despite the spirit in man at enmity with nothingness and dissolution.

We have noted that in such poems as *Alastor* and "Lift Not the Painted Veil" the irreconcilable conflict between desire for meaningful life and for the perfection of immortality—and the fundamental uncertainty of either—expressed itself in a system of ironies that cut both ways, if not quite equally. Either goal could be entertained only as it undermined the other, and only the irony of incertitude made either tenable. Self-deprived of any established religion, truth, or values, Shelley is thrown back upon comparison as a means of relative judgment, and therefore a generally pervasive similarity of alternatives is the prerequisite for discrimination. When the datum—like the subject figures of *Alastor* and the sonnet—faces in contrary directions, neither of which alone is acceptable or assured, the result is the irony that sustains incertitude. An antinomy that cannot be resolved must be sustained, like a sculptured corbel that seems suspended by its reciprocal stresses. But, as in *The Sensitive Plant* or the "Ode to Heaven," irony may also be a means of discovering the more probable truth by subjecting the same data to different modes of vision and allowing the consequences to play upon each other. The very similarity of the two opening passages we have examined in *Mont Blanc* has opened up the flaw in a reality taken as external and autonomous and has verified the plenitude and continuity of the reality made available to the mind by the "intellectual philosophy." The truncation of the simile that opens the description of the world as objective— "Thus thou, Ravine of Arve" (12)—is apposite: however similar to the universe of the "intellectual philosophy," the externality of the world is only half the truth.

The poet now once again transforms his mode of vision by turning his mind in upon itself, and since the individual mind is neither an object of its own experience nor truly independent of the One Mind, he calls upon an extraordinary state, a "trance sublime and strange" (35). To see one's own "separate fantasy" (36) is to see an illusory discreteness, there being no valid distinction among the words "*I* and *you* and *they*." The poet's trance is generated by his gazing on the ravine, and the ravine, for the purpose of ironic comparison, remains the model of the interior world as it had been of both the external and the phenomenal worlds. Just as the "Ode to Heaven" considers heaven in the three successive ontological perspectives, so after the initial metaphoric definition of the universe as both internal and external according to the "intellectual philosophy," the poet has first been drawn to a hypothetically external universe corresponding remarkably with the metaphoric one and then, eyes fixed on the "external," has a trance-like vision of it as a picture of his interior mind. Within the individual "human" mind, thought is again recognized as neither subjective nor objective, but the result of an "unremitting interchange" of the dark mind with the "clear" universe of things (39–40), as unbroken in its continuity as that of motion and sound in the phenomenal world. Thought is the product of the mind's unwilled ("passively") rendering and receiving of "fast influencings" (37–38), just as the river-universe and the ravine-mind influenced each other.

The world of the introspective trance reveals that the body of thoughts so fashioned is capable of two acts, one of which is to enter "the still cave of the witch Poesy" in the mind's interior ravine (44)— poesy in its original sense of making, or constituting. For reality is thus revealed to be the product of mind, not something given *ab extra*. The "universe" of the poem is not absolute Being, but the human world, the universe of Existence, which we normally experience not as it is, but as it seems—although, as in the case of *The Sensitive Plant*, the purpose of the poem is an ascent by means of those illusory realities to a transcendent apprehension which will show to the fullest extent the real nature and significance of the world of Existence. Given the poet's supposition of trance-like introspection, both the legion of thoughts generated by the interaction of mind and universe, and the Ravine in its synecdochic role as the universe, are, we are told, "no unbidden guest" in the mind's cave of reality-constituting Poesy (43); it is clear that it is not their native home, and there is no evidence that either enters it.[5] The double negative, "no unbidden guest," suggests both the desire for their actual presence in the mental, reality-constituting cave and their absence from it. Instead, along the walls of the cave, as in Plato's myth, pass sensory images, "Ghosts of all things that are" (46), not the things-in-themselves, which the human mind cannot know. The shadows on the cave's wall are "phantoms," "faint images,"[6] like the "unsculptured image" behind the veil of the waterfall in the supposedly external world (27); and thoughts, directing themselves to these shadows, *seek* among them the correspondents to the unknowable ravine-world outside. They search in vain, but the act of searching for the coincidence of thing-in-itself and mental image is itself constitutive of reality for the human mind. The introspective trance has confirmed that reality is neither the subjective impression nor the external thing, but the active and irresolvable mental tension between the two that is embodied in the word "Seeking." The scene of that tension is not the noisy universe but a silent ("still") cave of the mind, and to the mind the universe exists only so long as the act of seeking continues—nothing exists except as it is perceived. But the hypothesis under which this revelation has been made is the illusion that the individual human mind is indeed "separate" and not a portion of the One Mind. The "legion of wild thoughts" that constitutes reality for the individual by

[5] Shelley originally wrote that the legion of thoughts "now rest / Where thou [i.e. the Ravine-world] art surely no unbidden guest / Near the wierd[?] cave. . . ."
[6] Shelley first wrote, "Some likeness" (MS e. 16, p. 5).

seeking among the shadows the "Ghosts of all things that are" belongs to the One Mind and is lent only temporarily in the same sense that, in the rejected Introduction to *The Revolt of Islam,* all that is "not thine own" is given by some Absolute until it "has need of thine / Abandoning thee." Consequently, only till the "breast [the One Mind] / From which they [the legion of wild thoughts] fled recalls them, thou [the ravine, metaphoric of the universe] art there" in the individual mind's cave of Poesy (47–48). The poet's extraordinary act of self-examination has confirmed the ontology of the "intellectual philosophy" and has exposed the mental activity behind it.

But introspection has revealed something more. As casually as the supposedly self-subsisting external world revealed that pauses in the activities of such a world leave vacancies, thought is seen not only to constitute the universe for man but also to have the power to transcend that universe, to "float above" the "darkness" of the ravine that represents the boundaries of the human universe (42), whether the dark ravine is considered as a synecdoche for the external world or as a metaphor for the mind through which the universe of things flows. If the human universe were determined only by the structure of our sensations and postulated as external, it would be discontinuous and deficient; at the opposite extreme, our lent thoughts are not confined to the boundaries in which they constitute reality, but can transcend them. The rest of the poem will be an exploitation of these two revelations, for the exploration of the nature of reality in terms of the "intellectual philosophy" and of two hypothetical distortions of it is preparatory to the real subject of the poem.

In all three variant interpretations of reality, the region of the universe has been consistently represented by the dark Ravine of Arve; the ability of thought to float above that darkness into the transcendent is now symbolized by the dramatic gesture of the poet's raising his glance above the ravine to the snow-covered peak of Europe's highest mountain:

> I look on high;
> Has some unknown omnipotence unfurled
> The veil of life and death? or do I lie
> In dream, and does the mightier world of sleep
> Spread far around and inaccessibly
> Its circles? . . .
> Far, far above, piercing the infinite sky,
> Mont Blanc appears. . . .   (52–61)

Because this is an act of pure thought independent of the sensory world, it is an extraordinary mental event, and the validity of the experience, though not the experience itself, must remain uncertain. The skeptical poet can only report hesitantly, as he also did in "The Two Spirits," that

"Some say" such experiences "Visit the soul in sleep,—that death is slumber" (49–50) and wonder whether he dreams or, because death may be a dreaming, whether he truly sees beyond the mortal world. Whatever the extraordinary means, the ascent of his thought seems to reveal to him, beyond the ravine-world, a "remoter world" whose "shapes the busy thoughts outnumber / Of those who wake and live" (51–52) or perhaps the "mightier world" of sleep that spreads "far around and inaccessibly / Its circles" (55–57). As in *The Sensitive Plant*, the ontology of the "intellectual philosophy," by denying the distinction between external and internal, has proved a basis on which dream, or imagination, can ascend to a vision of the total amplitude of Being, a universe defined not merely by our sensations and memory but also by our faith in the revelations of imagination.

When the poet assumed that the world is a self-subsisting externality independent of mind, he found—what would not have appeared in the "intellectual philosophy"—that a pause in its activity is a "strange sleep" of emptiness; and later he will describe in such a world

The torpor of the year when feeble dreams
Visit the hidden buds, or dreamless sleep [7]
Holds every future leaf and flower;—the bound
With which from that detested trance they leap.   (88–91)

But to the human mind sleep, far from being a vacancy, is a dream of an infinite reality, perhaps related to the "remoter world" that man may conceivably enter upon death and that is reported to be even more populous with "shapes"—not merely than the external "world"—but than even the "thoughts" of man which constitute for him the everlasting universe of things. In its abhorrence of a vacuum, nature springs from its "detested trance" of inactivity, but it is, paradoxically, by means of trance that the poet has had insight into his own active mind and, by means of a trance-like vision, has experienced the "mightier world." What is meaningless emptiness in a supposedly external world is an absolute plenitude to the imagination; and Shelley, however tentatively, intends that that infinity, located at the gleaming peak of Mont Blanc, above the dark ravine-world, be included potentially in the human mind's reality. The trance which is nothing in matter and everything in mind is characteristic of the paradoxes whereby Shelley's skepticism advances to probabilism by testing a specific *donnée* in contradictory contexts.

The problem of causation, or "power," had always been of deep concern to Shelley because it is indistinguishable from the question of the

[7] The manuscript (e. 16, p. 8) shows that Shelley also tried, "The sleep of winter," "deathlike dreams," "no human dreams," and "Dreamless as death," meaning to indicate the emptiness of nature's dream-pauses, as opposed to man's dreams, which reveal an infinite reality spreading "far around and inaccessibly / Its circles."

existence and nature of a divine Creator and Governor. When, in 1811, he was attempting to sustain his temporary deism against Hogg's assault, he resorted to the traditional argument from cause: since every effect arises from a cause which in turn has a cause, there must be "a First Cause, a God."[8] When he then abandoned his belief in a Creator, the problem of course became even more acute. Influenced by Holbach and Hume, but not yet a disciple of the "intellectual philosophy," he wrote in his note to *Queen Mab* that "our idea of causation is alone derivable from the constant conjunction of objects and the consequent inference of one from the other" (VII. 13n.). But, assuming as he does in *Queen Mab* that the universe is eternal and is pervaded by the co-eternal Spirit of Nature, he does not move to Hume's extreme position that one can speak of cause only as a "notion": "there certainly is a generative power which is effected by certain instruments." Nor does he affirm or deny the materialist's position: "we cannot prove that it is inherent in these instruments; nor is the contrary hypothesis capable of demonstration. We admit that the generative power is incomprehensible." What he *is* now assured of is that "to suppose that the same effect is produced by an eternal omniscient, omnipotent being leaves the cause in the same obscurity, but renders it more incomprehensible." Exactly the same words reappear in *A Refutation of Deism* with the additional statement that all the "motions of the Universe are subjected to the rigid necessity of inevitable laws. These laws are the unknown causes of the known effects perceivable in the Universe. Their effects are the boundaries of our knowledge."[9] The most significant element in this development of Shelley's ideas is his conviction that power, or causation, cannot be attributed to an omniscient, omnipotent being but operates according to rigidly necessary laws. Whereas omniscience and omnipotence imply arbitrary will, power acts in a fixed way because it has no will. Nor is power an attribute of either the human mind or of the One Mind; it is therefore absolutely distinct from the transcendent mind-perfecting deity Shelley worshipped as Intellectual Beauty. All that the world contains, Shelley wrote, invoking the Spirit of Nature,

Are but thy passive instruments, and thou
Regard'st them all with an impartial eye,
Whose joy or pain thy nature cannot feel,
Because thou hast not human sense,
Because thou art not human mind.[10]

Shelley never abandoned these tenets, but his adoption of the "intellectual philosophy" opened up the possibility of the reality of ultimate

[8] To Hogg, 3 January 1811 (*Letters*, I, 35; also 44–45).
[9] Julian, VI, 48.
[10] *Queen Mab*, VI. 215–19.

cause and an apprehension of it in the same manner that it opened up the possibility of an infinitely extended conception of Being. He is closer to Hume's skeptical empiricism when he now writes of cause, not as a constant conjunction of objects, but as "a word expressing a certain state of the human mind with regard to the manner in which two thoughts are apprehended to be related to each other."[11] Having translated objects into thoughts, he is even more convinced that it is "infinitely improbable" that the cause of mind is "similar to mind." Now that the "universe" has been enlarged by locating all existence in mental perception and equating mind with existence so that a "catalogue of all the thoughts of the mind, and of all their possible modifications, is a cyclopaedic history of the Universe,"[12] those conceptions to which Hume had assigned the indeterminate name of "notions" have a special kind of reality. "Notions" being imaginative constructs, and man being "preeminently an imaginative being," notions are valid insofar as belief, which is involuntary, accepts them. Power, it is true, remains "unknown," "secret," because it cannot be the object of sensation, and yet the imagination formulates it and the mind credits it by conviction:

... the existence of a Power bearing the same relation to all that we perceive and are, as what we call a cause does to what we call effect, [was] never [the object] of sensation, and yet the laws of mind almost universally suggest ... a conjecture, a persuasion, or a conviction of [its] existence.... [Such thoughts as that of Power] are also to be included in the catalogue of existence; they are modes in which thoughts are combined....[13]

The imaginative apprehension of this Power and the inclusion of its manifestation in existence is the ultimate purpose of *Mont Blanc* as the poet's glance now sweeps back and forth from ravine to mountain summit, from the "remoter world" to the sensible world.

However various the hypothetical ontologies that have been applied to the ravine-world in the poem, it has consistently been pervaded, we have noted, by unceasingly vigorous motion and clamorous sound. Even when in a seeming trance the poet has a supposed vision of his own mind, the mind's interchange with the world of things is "fast" and "unremitting," and that motif of perpetual and irresistible motion will continue to the end of the poem. Yet, when reality was assumed to be only the external material world, that unbroken continuity of activity proved an incomplete truth, since nature in itself manifests periods of emptiness. The mind, not the material world, must therefore in some way be the factor responsible for the continuity of power. Meanwhile, the poem has carefully distinguished between man's empirical experience of succession and the unknowable ultimate Power itself. In the ontology of the "intellectual

[11] *On Life* (Julian, VI, 197). See also p. 150 above.
[12] *Speculations on Metaphysics* (Julian, VII, 59).
[13] *Ibid.*

philosophy," the stream of human thought derives from "secret," unknowable springs (4); and in the supposedly independent external world, Power resides on an equally "secret" throne at the mountain peak and descends into the ravine-world only in the form of its "likeness," the River Arve (16–17), whose perceptible successiveness of motion is an ironic simile for the unknowable motionless Power itself. As a "likeness," the Arve is to the unknowable ultimate Power as, in Shelley's ontology, the sensible shadows on the cave of Poesy are to the unknowable things-in-themselves that cast the shadows. When the poet later asks which of the then-current theories of the origin of mountains is true, he can gain no answer:

> Is this the scene
> Where the old Earthquake-daemon taught her young
> Ruin? Were these their toys? or did a sea
> Of fire envelop once this silent snow?
> None can reply—all seems eternal now.   (71–75)

Because these mountains are "primaeval," originating with the very beginning of time, a step behind them should lead to ultimate cause; but it is a step the senses cannot take. The primaeval mountains and the merely sensible surface of nature ("the naked countenance of earth, / On which I gaze") teach the "adverting," or outward turning, sensory mind only that "Power dwells apart.... / Remote, serene, and inaccessible" (96–100). The senses have knowledge only of the first manifestation of Power in time, which the poem calls "source," or "primaeval," not a knowledge of Power itself, not of the "secret springs" and "secret throne." And yet, the thoughts that can transcend the dark ravine-world are able, beyond the limits of sensory experience, to have visionary and imaginative apprehension of the inaccessible gleaming summit of Mont Blanc, the symbolic residence of Power. Shelley was conscious that he was standing before Europe's highest mountain, and although it had recently been ascended, he conceives of its summit as still inaccessible.

Like Intellectual Beauty, Power is experienced as a transcendent light, the light of the eternally snow-covered peak of the mountain, where, Shelley wrote in the *History of a Six Weeks' Tour*, "It is agreed by all, that the snow... perpetually augments":[14] "Mont Blanc yet gleams on high:—the power is there" (127). And, again like Intellectual Beauty, only its bright "shadow" visits the dark world of mutability. It is because the moving flow of things derives from the gleaming Power that they are appropriately represented as merely modes of light in the dark container of the ravine-world: the universe of things flowing through the

---

[14] Julian, VI, 140; also *Letters*, I, 488.

mind is "glittering" (3) and a "splendor" (4); the corresponding Arve bursts through the dark mountains "like the flame / Of lightning" (18–19), makes the caves "Shine," and, belonging to the mutable world, displays a *restless* gleam" (121); snowflakes "burn" (133); and daylight is a "glare" (131). Only the Power at the transcendent peak "gleams" purely, eternally, serenely (127); only of the "remoter world" does the human soul have "gleams" (49)—in both its senses. There are, then, two worlds, related as the light of Intellectual Beauty is to its shadows: the inaccessible world of Power, the "secret Strength of things / Which governs thought, and to the infinite dome / Of Heaven is as a law" (139–41), represented as a serene supernal light, a "gleam"; and the mutable world accessible to the senses, represented by lesser modes of light. The relation of the two is that of a pure, a-sensory Absolute to its sensible manifestations, of the visionary "gleam" to its visible modes. "The universal Being," Shelley wrote in his *Essay on Christianity*, since it must be "something eternal and supreme, neither subject to change nor to decay . . . can only be described or defined by negatives, which deny his subjection to the laws of all inferior existences. Where indefiniteness ends idolatry and anthropomorphism begin."[15] The human world the poem describes is pervaded by noisy turbulence, but the Power, source of "many sights, / And many sounds, and much of life and death," is serene and tranquil, "still and solemn" (128–29).[16] Silence is the absolute of all sounds; the mover of all things is motionless. Shelley's manuscript at one point is even more explicit: "The powers that move the world themselves are still."[17] In the transcendent region of the Power, the gleaming snow falls unceasingly, regardless of the world's endlessly mutable round of "calm darkness" on moonless nights, "lone glare of day," "sinking sun," and "star-beams" (130–34), corresponding to the alternate glitter and obscurity of the river of "things" in the ravine-world. Nor are these perpetually augmented snows, symbolizing the Power, objects of sensation; "none beholds them there" (132), for these regions are "solitudes" (137), emptiness absolutely remote from the world of man. The source of the world's "many sights" is unseen. Unlike the world's winds that contend with the pines to produce a harmony, "Winds contend / Silently there, and heap the snow with breath / Rapid and strong, but silently" (134–36); and even the lightning is innocent and "voiceless" (138), in contrast to the noisy Arve, which bursts through the mountains "like the flame / Of lightning through the tempest." Like the relation of light to the spectrum of colors, Power is the quality-less source of the sensible qualities of the world and is accessible only to vision as colors alone are accessible to sight.

As Shelley stood in the Vale of Chamouni with Mont Blanc before

[15] Julian, VI, 232.
[16] Shelley first wrote, "The solemn calm of power" (MS e. 16, p. 11).
[17] MS e. 16, p. 8.

him, his emotions compounded these two worlds, one of vigorous activity, the other of empty stillness; and in one sense the poem is an attempt to explain the metaphysical grounds of that emotional paradox. The poem, he wrote in the preface to the *History of a Six Weeks' Tour*, "was composed under the immediate impression of the deep and powerful feelings excited by the objects which it attempts to describe," and it imitates the causes "from which those feelings sprang": the "untameable wildness" of the ravine-world and the "inaccesible solemnity"[18] which the poem also associates, in the same words, with the Power. Both qualities are brought together in the union of the solemn grandeur of the poem and the wildly irregular rhyming whereby nearly every line eventually finds its companion, but without any predictable order.

On the basis of this distinction between the ravine-world and the realm above its darkness, the poem seeks the answers to two questions, one moral, the other ontological, or, in its special way, "religious." For Shelley has postulated but one Power, operating according to the same inherent principle in both the material world and the mind of man: it not only is "as a law" of the universe even "to the infinite dome / Of Heaven" but also "governs thought" (139–41). The symbolic scene that has given birth to the poem is splendidly equipped to represent the relation of the transcendent Power to the world of human experience: the gleaming and eternal snow of the mountain peak that symbolizes the inaccessible Power descends as glaciers, which melt into streams that become the river Arve in the ravine. In Shelley's conceptions, we have noted, "the overruling Spirit of the collective energy of the moral and material world" differs "both from man and from the mind of man"—a distinction, incidentally, that sharply distinguishes Power from the One Mind, or Existence. Having none of the attributes of the human mind, Power has no will and is therefore amoral, manifesting itself as it does according to the fixed laws inherent in its nature, and not by choice. It is the "*necessarily* beneficent actuating principle"; and it is beneficent because it is its nature to model "all the elements of this mixed universe to the purest and most perfect shape which it belongs to their nature to assume."[19] In that sense, the terms "good" and "evil" are irrelevant to the Power and indicate merely right and wrong human relations to it: "That is called good which produces pleasure; that is called evil which produces pain," and "we are taught by the doctrine of Necessity, that there is neither good nor evil in the universe, otherwise than as the events to which we apply these epithets have relation to our own peculiar mode of being."[20]

The glaciers, streams, and river, being successive transformations of

---

[18] Julian, VI, 88.
[19] *Essay on Christianity* (Julian, VI, 235).
[20] *Speculations on Morals* (Julian, VII, 73); *Queen Mab*, VI. 198n.

the transcendent snow, are representations of the consecutiveness whereby the motionless Power manifests itself in the realm of mutability and supply sensory evidence of the Power's necessary and amoral law. The glacier region between the summit and the ravine is hostile to man, a desert ironically "peopled by the storms alone" (67), hideous, "Ghastly, and scarred, and riven" (71). It is a "city of death" or, since "city" implies men, "not a city, but a flood of ruin" (105, 107), a region of death; and as the glaciers inexorably move into the ravine, they overthrow

The limits of the dead and living world,
Never to be reclaimed. The dwelling-place
Of insects, beasts, and birds, becomes its spoil;
Their food and their retreat for ever gone,
So much of life and joy is lost. The race
Of man flies far in dread; his work and dwelling
Vanish, like smoke before the tempest's stream,
And their place is not known.   (113–20)

However, at the very point when these last stark and monotonous monosyllables seem to signal the destruction of everything and a total emptiness, there is a sudden upsurge of superabundant life, motion, and tumult:

Below, vast caves
Shine in the rushing torrent's restless gleam,
Which from those secret chasms in tumult welling
Meet in the vale, and one majestic River,
The breath and blood of distant lands, for ever
Rolls its loud waters to the ocean-waves,
Breathes its swift vapours to the circling air.   (120–26)

The distinction between glacier and river is not one between evil and good in any absolute sense but only a distinction in terms of man's painful or pleasurable responses: the river of life flows from the glaciers of death, and both derive from the eternal transcendent snows and the amoral Power. The glaciers and the river are neither maleficent nor beneficent; they simply *are* by necessity of inherent laws, but one is not the region for man, and the other is. Man's moral obligation is to conform to the "necessarily beneficent" actuating force, and it is in this sense that

The wilderness has a mysterious tongue
Which teaches awful doubt, or faith so mild,
So solemn, so serene, that man may be,
But for such faith,[21] with nature reconciled;
Thou hast a voice, great Mountain, to repeal

[21] That is, by means of such a faith alone. The manuscript shows that Shelley also considered "With such a faith" and "In such a faith" (MS e. 16, p. 8).

Large codes of fraud and woe; not understood
By all, but which the wise, and great, and good
Interpret, or make felt, or deeply feel.   (76–83)

What the mountain's voice tells of is the inaccessible Power and its amoral necessary laws. Thereby it teaches the skeptical doubt that divulges how little of total Being is revealed to us by our senses and conscious mind; or it teaches such a faith in the necessarily beneficent Power and its laws—a faith that, unlike "Christian" faith, is mild, solemn, serene, and therefore exactly like the character of Power itself—that man will yield and adapt himself to it. The barrier to that reconciliation has been erected by man himself in the form of "Large codes of fraud and woe," products of his willful imposition upon his own free will; all these man-made enslaving laws submission to the Power will "repeal."[22]

The poet's experience with the mountain has divulged to him not only that the inaccessible Power is, paradoxically, an eternal stillness but also that its manifestations move the world of sensible qualities in an endless circle of change:

All things that move and breathe with toil and sound
Are born and die; revolve, subside, and swell.   (94–95)

The nature of the eternal unmoved mover enters into the realm of time as an endless circle of events, the most nearly perfect form that eternity can assume in mutability. The empty pauses in nature, then, are the moments of apparent discontinuity in that continuous cycle. But we have noticed that whereas the trances of external nature are vacuums that nature abhors as much as the mind of man is at enmity with nothingness, the trances of mind are visions of an unbounded world filled with shapes infinitely more numerous than even the conscious thoughts of man. For the vision of the Power is, in one sense, also a vision of nothingness—silence, stillness, and emptiness. But it is, ironically, the emptiness which is the absolute of potential fullness, the quality-less and a-sensory source of all

---

[22] Mary Shelley also transformed into a similar symbolic experience the visit of 1816 to Mont Blanc. After Frankenstein, driven by his irrepressible curiosity, probes beyond human limits and, with disastrous results, discovers the cause of life, Mary sends him to Mont Blanc for the purpose of opposing to his unnatural deed the operations of nature. At this "presence-chamber of imperial Nature," which bespeaks "a power mighty as Omnipotence" that acts through "immutable laws," the sight of the glacier filled him "with a sublime ecstasy that gave wings to the soul, and allowed it to soar from the obscure world to light and joy," above the "passing cares of life." The lesson he learns is that true freedom is identical with submission to nature's necessary laws: "If our impulses were confined to hunger, thirst, and desire, we might be nearly free; but now we are moved by every wind that blows..." (Frankenstein, Chaps. IX–X).

possible sensory qualities, the absence of which leaves the sensible world empty. Nature's silence and solitude are indeed a "vacancy" (144); the emptiness of the Power is infinite plenitude. The first is what appears to the senses; the second is apprehended by the trance-like and apparently vacant imaginings. For Shelley is here applying to the question of Power the same procedure he applied to Being and Existence in *The Sensitive Plant*, where the same data viewed sensorily displayed the annihilation of reality and viewed imaginatively revealed its eternity. The paradoxes of "vacancy" and "trance" in *Mont Blanc* reflect Shelley's recurrent skeptical technique of examining the same datum in contrary perspectives, not, as in *Alastor* or *Julian and Maddalo*, to remain in incertitude, but in order to provide a choice between the evident but absurd and the uncertain but ideal.

Were reality only the discontinuous external world or even the world that is born, dies, and revives, it would be meaningless, futile. Meaning lies in the mind's visionary apprehension of a single eternal, immutable, and amoral Power which lies behind the seemingly absurd mutability and recurrent emptiness, and of whose necessary laws the activities of the world are a manifestation. Similarly, in facing the same problem in ontological terms in *Epipsychidion*, Shelley will postulate in the heart of the ideal island a "Soul" that

Unfolds itself, and may be felt, not seen
O'er the gray rocks, blue waves, and forests green,
Filling their bare and void interstices.   (480–82)

But just as the "intellectual philosophy," by removing the distinction between thought and thing, merely formulates a conception of the experiential world that justifies faith in the imagination's visions, and just as, in *The Sensitive Plant*, the sensory experience of annihilation is the ground for imaginative experience of eternity, so the sensory world of vacancies is the basis on which the poet of *Mont Blanc* rises to his vision of the "remoter world" of the Power. Images are the stuff of the "imaginings" (143); the same thoughts, we recall, that hold "an unremitting interchange / With the clear universe of things around" and constitute the universe in Poesy's cave are the thoughts that transcend the ravine's darkness and perceive the "gleam" of Power. The objective of the poem, however, is not merely the imaginative ascent to the sensorily inaccessible realm of Power, but the application of the imagination's vision to the world of the senses, and consequently the poet's final gesture is the leap of his glance from the gleam at Mont Blanc's peak back into the ravine-world. His previous downward glance from snow-covered peak to the river revealed the spatial and temporal continuity in which the amoral Power manifests itself, according to necessary laws, in the phenomenal world.

The final downward glance directly from the summit's gleam suffuses that phenomenal world of mutability and discontinuity with the imaginative knowledge of the eternal, immutable, and infinite Power from which its activities derive. Our mutable and deficient world makes sense and can be understood only if we can bring into it our extraordinary knowledge of the transcendent Power which is not mutable or discontinuous and from which all that is partial and deficient derives. It is for this reason that, in Shelley's *Hellas*, Ahasuerus, although admitting that thought cannot have direct access to it, nevertheless bids Mahmud "look on that which cannot change—the One / The unborn and the undying" if he would understand the world (768–69). Our enmity with nothingness is put at ease by a visionary knowledge of the absolute Power behind all worldly action, or, in more appropriately religious terms, of a transcendent and absolute divine Cause that gives meaning to our limited existence in an instable and illusory world.

And yet, *Mont Blanc* does not actually end with this affirmation but with a question, for approximately the same skeptical incertitude displayed in *The Sensitive Plant* is operating here. On the one side, the empirical world is deficient and may be only an illusion that we are experiencing in a realm where "nothing is but all things seem"; on the other, the apprehension of the eternal Power came about through an "imagining," a dream, or trance, that also may be only illusory. We know only that "Some say that gleams of a remoter world / Visit the soul in sleep" (49–50), and the poet can only wonder what the nature and validity of his experience are. The assertion Shelley would like to make is evident, just as it is clear he wishes he could assert more than his "modest creed" in the "Conclusion" of *The Sensitive Plant*; but the skeptical grounds of the poem will not sustain it. The poet has experienced "imaginings" in which silence and solitude have been the qualities of the Power of absolute potentiality, not the silent and solitary vacancies the external world presents to the senses; and apprehension of this Power has filled the lacunae of the sensible world and given it its worth. But this has been an experience of trance and death-like dream and cannot be asserted as fact. A rhetorical question, because it simultaneously proposes and questions, is the only completely honest fulfillment of the poem:

And what were thou [Mont Blanc], and earth, and stars, and sea,
If to the human mind's imaginings
Silence and solitude were vacancy?   (142–44)

ii

The *Ode to the West Wind* is the full exploitation of the implicitly religious character of *Mont Blanc* and is Shelley's prayer to the divine Power corresponding to his prayer to Intellectual Beauty. The *Hymn to Intellectual Beauty* expresses his worship of the divinity of perfect Being, in which man's immortality consists and which constitutes his ideal states of mind; the *Ode* (a title interchangeable with "hymn") expresses his devotion to the Power that ceaselessly imparts activity to the entire universe, physical and mental. Always conscientious about the compatability of the poems to be included in each of his published or projected collections, Shelley appropriately added the *Ode to the West Wind* and *The Cloud* to the volume dominated by *Prometheus Unbound*, a world-oriented work that optimistically plots the release into Existence of the Power that will effect man's moral regeneration, independent both of any transcendent perfection, such as Intellectual Beauty, and of man's post-mortal destiny.

In the "eternal" snows on Mont Blanc that "perpetually augment" and in its glaciers that "perpetually move onwards" in a "progress which ceases neither day nor night,"[23] Shelley had found an apposite symbol of Cause and its chain of necessity. But just as light is precisely the right image of the transcendent Ideal in the *Hymn*, wind is the especially appropriate symbol of Power, not as ultimate cause, transcendent and unknowable, but as immediate cause in the realm of mutability. Not only is the wind nature's most universal display of strength and, like the "unseen," imageless Intellectual Beauty and its "shadow," an "unseen presence" that therefore accords with Shelley's Humean doctrine that cause cannot be experienced empirically; it is also related traditionally and etymologically to breath and spirit. The West Wind, addressed in the poem as a wild and fierce "Spirit," is the "breath of Autumn's being" both literally and in the sense that it is the soul of Autumn's active existence. But what *Mont Blanc* has divulged should make it evident that the West Wind is not merely an apt image capable of standing for something else. It is not, as some have proposed, the "outer correspondent" to a transformative inner, subjective force the poet invokes to scatter his thoughts among mankind; Shelley has not found a circumlocution for addressing his own will and creative power under the disguise of the Wind. Such a reduction assumes that, images being exaggerating metaphors, a poem must mean less than its literal imagistic assertion, and consequently translates the poem out of Shelley's ontology.[24] For Shelley's standing assumptions are that the one Power is the moving spirit of all the "energy and wisdom" within existence and governs both human thought and all the operations of nature by a uniform, impartial law of sequences; and that the human requisite for receiving that Power is a state of passivity. Since

---

[23] To Peacock, 24–25 July 1816 (*Letters*, I, 499–500); also in *History of a Six Weeks' Tour*, 1817 (Julian, VI, 140–41).

[24] Compare such interpretations as that of Carlos Baker, *Shelley's Major Poetry*, p. 201: "The use of natural phenomena as emblematic of mental states is a frequent trick of Shelley's. In several of the well-known lyrics of 1819–1820, and most notably, perhaps, in 'The West Wind,' 'The Cloud,' and 'The Skylark,' one finds him seeking in the natural world for analogies by which to reassure himself that regeneration follows destruction. . . ."

the energy flowing from the one Power acts identically in nature and mind and follows the same law of "causal" necessity, the West Wind has an ontological kinship, and not merely a metaphoric or analogical one, with the Spirit invoked to act upon the poet's thoughts. Only the medium of the one dynamic Spirit is different, and to address the spirit of Autumn's being is also to address the spirit that governs thought.

In accordance with the *topoi* of the classical hymn, the first three stanzas of the *Ode* define the domains and powers of the petitioned god by describing the wind's effect on leaf on the land, on cloud in the air, and on wave on the sea. The recurrence of the imagery of leaves in each of these stanzas therefore has more than descriptive function; it is the metaphoric evidence of the universality of the West Wind as Autumn's one spirit and explicates the line, "Wild Spirit, which art moving everywhere" (13). The dead, wind-driven autumn leaves of the first stanza persist in the metaphor of the second stanza which likens the "loose clouds" shaken by the upper wind "from the tangled boughs of Heaven and Ocean" to loose leaves shaken by the wind from the trees and carried along on its motion; and in the third stanza, the "oozy woods" beneath the water are despoiled of their "sapless foliage" because, as Shelley explained in his note, the submarine vegetation "sympathizes with that of the land in the change of seasons, and is consequently influenced by the winds which announce it." Indeed, other metaphors tend further to diminish any distinction among the three regions: in the first stanza the spring buds of earth are driven "like flocks to feed in air"; in the second, where the clouds of air are likened to leaves, the wind is a "stream," a blue "aery surge" like the "blue Mediterranean" of the third stanza; and in the third, the undersea realm is exactly like land, with flowers and woods, and populated with the sunken palaces and towers of Baiae. Consequently, wherever the poet glances—about, above, or below, land, air, or sea—the same imagistic pattern of relationships presents itself; for the wind not only is "moving everywhere" but also acts everywhere according to the same law, so that however its media differ, its effect remains constant. The simile of the second stanza likening clouds to the earth's leaves, and likening to tangled boughs the cooperation of heaven and ocean in producing the clouds, therefore has not only descriptive but also metaphysical force; and the central function of the widely debated simile of clouds and leaves is to obliterate all essential differences among the processes of the Power in its various media. Hence the appropriate reappearance of the metaphor in the last stanza, where the poet prays that the West Wind act on him, a tree of falling autumnal leaves of thought that are to be driven by the Power to quicken a new birth.[25] Just as the re-

[25] The comparison of man to a tree is frequent in Scripture and functions more as a commonplace than as a description: for example, "And he shall be like a tree planted by the rivers of water, that bringeth forth his fruit in his season; his leaf also shall not wither" (Psalms 1: 3); "For ye shall be as an oak whose leaf fadeth" (Isaiah 1: 30).

currence of the leaf imagery in the first three stanzas asserts the unity of the Power and its laws in its compulsion of all levels of nature, so the application of the same image to the poet denies any essential distinction between its actions on nature and on man, for as Shelley had learned in *Mont Blanc*, the one "secret Strength," unlike the mind's Intellectual Beauty, both "governs thought, and to the infinite dome / Of Heaven is as a law."

"All things that move and breathe with toil and sound," the external world had revealed to Shelley, "Are born and die; revolve, subside, and swell." Everything subject to the Power is in constant flux, but the Power itself is unchanging, acting without interruption or variance, even throughout those apparent pauses in nature which seem to be the vacuum that nature—and the human mind—abhors. At least since 1811, the cycle of the seasons had been one of Shelley's presiding themes, no doubt intensified in importance by his readings of ancient and modern materialists;[26] and it served especially to support his faith that the universe is uncreated and eternal. It is a recurrent metaphor in his poetry, and such poems as *The Sensitive Plant* and *Adonais*, which directly face the question of extinction and eternity, derive their overall structures from it. The inevitability of the swelling of spring out of the subsiding of winter appeared to guarantee eternal duration in the context of mutability and the fact that death in nature and even its moments of emptiness are only illusions.

Thus do the generations of the earth
Go to the grave, and issue from the womb,
Surviving still the *imperishable change*
That renovates the world; even as the leaves
Which the keen frost-wind of the waning year
Has scattered on the forest soil, and heaped
For many seasons there—though long they choke,
Loading with loathsome rottenness the land,
All germs of promise, yet when the tall trees
From which they fell, shorn of their lovely shapes,
Lie level with the earth to moulder there,
They fertilize the land they long deformed,
Till from the breathing lawn a forest springs
Of youth, integrity, and loveliness,
Like that which gave it life, to spring and die.[27]

This everlasting repetition of the fixed cycle of mutability persuaded Shelley that behind the cycle there is an immutable Power and that apparent death in nature is not extinction but the necessary condition for

[26] See I. J. Kapstein, "The Symbolism of the Wind and the Leaves in Shelley's 'Ode to the West Wind,'" *PMLA* 51 (1936), 1069–79.
[27] *Queen Mab*, V. 1–15; itals. added.

rebirth. Nothing in nature dies or is absent; it only changes. *Omnia mutantur, nihil interit.*[28]

This of course is the theme of *The Cloud*, also included in the *Prometheus Unbound* volume. Like the perpetual snow at the peak of Mont Blanc that is responsible for the glaciers, tributaries, and the Arve, the Cloud is the uniform Power from which issue into the realm of mutability the multiform effects, shade, showers, dew, hail, and snow. And just as the snow on Mont Blanc results in both the murderous glaciers and the life-giving river—or just as, in *The Sensitive Plant*, the heaven's winds and sun are like a mother's song that first lulls the flowers to sleep and then awakens them—the Cloud shades the sleep of the leaves and awakens the flowers with dew (3, 5–6), gives birth to the hail and then dissolves it in rain (9–11). However varied and even antagonistic the effects in the domain of mutability, they all flow from one immutable source.

Unlike the eternal snow of Mont Blanc, however, the Cloud is subject to mutability and therefore, but only apparently, to annihilation: "I change, but I cannot die" (76). Like Urania in *Adonais*, the Cloud is in fact "chained to Time, and cannot thence depart,"[29] for the Cloud enacts the unending cycle of change whereby eternity appears in time, even as the Moon in *Epipsychidion*, which has the same role, "ever is transformed, yet still the same."[30] When the Cloud's lightning is "dissolving in rains" and the Cloud appears to us below to be expending itself, if we could see it from above we would know its real nature as undying Cloud, calmly basking "all the while... in Heaven's blue smile" (29–30). The single two-sided image correlates in a fine paradox the apparent world of transience with the real world of perpetuity within "imperishable change" and attributes to the observer's inadequate perspective, instead of the world beheld, the notion of extinction. Even when the Cloud has dissolved and disappeared, so that we assume it has been annihilated, the visible blue dome of the sky is only its "cenotaph" (81), an empty tomb, a memorial to that which is *not* buried there, an apparent sepulchre that the undying Cloud can mock with that laughter which is Shelley's frequent symbol of intense vitality. There has been no death, even though the Cloud is not visible. The Cloud is the Power, of which the mutable cloud is the visible manifestation. At length, when it reappears it is a matter of indifference whether we say it is like "a child from the womb" or "a ghost from the tomb" (83): "birth" and "death" are but different partial names for the same point on the perpetual cycle of change. When the Cloud thus arises from its caverns of rain to reappear as cloud, it again "unbuilds" (84) its "cenotaph," cyclically undoing the "blue dome of air" built by the winds

[28] Ovid *Met.* xv. 165. Shelley quotes this in *A Refutation of Deism* (Julian, VI, 51).
[29] *Adonais*, 234.
[30] *Epipsychidion*, 284.

and sunbeams. Because of this unbroken circle of mutability, Shelley frequently writes of birth and death as one, and the fact helps explicate Asia's song in *Prometheus Unbound*, in which the progress toward the Golden Age is painted as a regression from old age to infancy and "Through Death and Birth, to a diviner day."[31] Hence Shelley's West Wind is "Destroyer and preserver" (14), not Destroyer and Creator; Shelley of course does not allow for the doctrine of a Creator or for the idea of annihilation, and the extremes of the endless circle of change are—to use the form of "destroy" employed in *The Cloud*—to "unbuild" (*destruere*) and preserve.[32] In this eternal circle of nature that denies any point of annihilation, and in the conviction that but one Power moves both mind and the universe, Shelley found grounds for optimistic faith in a moral cycle in which a period of moral decay is actually transitional to a moral revival and even generative of it:

We see in Winter that the foliage of the trees is gone, that they present to the view nothing but leafless branches—we see that the loveliness of the flower decays, though the root continues in the earth. What opinion should we form of that man who, when he walked in the freshness of the spring, beheld the fields enamelled with flowers, and the foliage bursting from the buds, should find fault with this beautiful order, and murmur his contemptible discontents because winter must come, and the landscape be robbed of its beauty for a while again? ... Do we not see that the laws of nature perpetually act by *disorganization* and *reproduction, each alternately becoming cause and effect.* The analogies that we can draw from physical to moral topics are of all others the most striking.[33]

Means are fortunately available for establishing the relation of *The Cloud* to the composition of others of Shelley's poems and consequently for determining with some precision the status of its theme in the larger structure of his conceptions. When Mary undertook in 1820 her mythological drama *Midas*, Shelley, we have seen, found it an occasion to embody in poetry once again the irresolvable conflict in him between experience and aspiration, the falsehood of existence that his Pan sings

---

[31] *Prometheus Unbound*, II. v. 98–110. Cf. *On Life* (Julian, VI, 194): "What is birth and death?" I mean to suggest that there is no grammatical error here. See also *Epipsychidion*, 380: "the star of Death and Birth,"—the one star, Venus, which only seems to be two stars of opposite extremes, morning and evening.

[32] Cf. *Hellas*, 1002–04:

> If Greece must be
> A wreck, yet shall its fragments reassemble,
> And build themselves again. . . .

[33] *Proposals for an Association* (Julian, V, 266–67); itals. added. *The Revolt of Islam*, 3649–3720, elaborates the analogy of the seasons and man's moral cycle. Autumn is the "mother" of Spring, who brings fresh flowers to Autumn's grave; and correspondingly, "while drear Winter fills the naked skies," the seeds of moral springtime are in the human heart, awaiting the workings of the law of necessity.

of and the lifelessness of immutable ideals revealed by Apollo's song. In his notebook he made a few false starts at the so-called "Hymn" of Apollo, one of which reads,

The Hours, when from their wings the dews are shaken
Whose silver sounds the dreaming flowers awaken. . . .[34]

After having completed Apollo's song and then Pan's, which directly follows it in the notebook, he then adapted the false start of Apollo's song to *The Cloud*:

From my wings are shaken the dews that waken
     The sweet buds every one.[35]

The sequence of composition is revealed by the fact that part of the working draft of *The Cloud* (stanza 5) is on the page immediately preceding Apollo's song and the next part (stanza 6) on the page following Pan's song, indicating that he composed *The Cloud* on pages left blank after the two songs were completed. In addition, at the other end of the same notebook he had written for Mary's other mythological drama, *Proserpine*, part of the song *Arethusa*, cast in a verse form rich with lyric possibilities and telling in rapid tempo of the flight of Arethusa from Alpheus:

Arethusa arose from her couch of snows
     In the Acroceraunian mountains,—
From cloud and from crag, with many a jag,[36]
     Shepherding her bright fountains.
She leapt down the rocks, with her rainbow locks
     Streaming among the streams;—
Her steps paved with green the downward ravine
     Which slopes to the western gleams;
And gliding and springing she went, ever singing
     In murmurs as soft as sleep;
The Earth seemed to love her, and Heaven smiled above her,
     As she lingered towards the deep. . . .

It becomes evident, then, that Shelley's contributions to Mary's mythological dramas are the contexts of the composition of *The Cloud*. Employing the lyric form of *Arethusa*, he wrote a poem that is a kind of supplement to Apollo's song. Moreover, if there was justification for

---

[34] MS e. 6, p. 22.
[35] One of the opening lines intended for Apollo's song was, "From my soft pillow of clouds dark and golden" (MS e. 6, p. 22). Cf. *The Cloud*, 15.
[36] Cf. *The Cloud*, 35: "As on a jag of a mountain crag." I have arranged the lines in accordance with the form in Shelley's notebook, instead of following Mary's text, which breaks into two the long line with internal rhyme.

Mary's entitling the other two lyrics the *Hymn of Apollo* and the *Hymn of Pan*, this might properly be called the *Hymn of the Cloud*, for, like the others, it is the Cloud's description of her own attributes, powers, domain, and even, in accordance with the hymnic *topoi*, her genealogy. Like Apollo, god of the sun and the heaven, and like Pan, god of the earth, the Cloud is a divinity, a power. Perhaps, indeed, it is relevant that clouds mediate between Pan's earth and Apollo's heaven. For in the songs of Apollo and Pan, Shelley had represented the two unreconciled aspects of man, his heaven-oriented but lifeless mental ideals and his earth-oriented experiences of living that prove transitory and therefore false; and he had assigned to them their corresponding rhythms. But *The Cloud* is the comforting resolution of that dilemma and provides a value, however qualified, that the other two songs deny. Whereas heavenly Apollo is god of inhuman immutability and earthly Pan is god of the human mutability that ends in extinction, the Cloud is the divinity of the unending cycle of change, "eterne in mutabilitie." Embodied in the rhythm of the joyously onrushing movement that is its theme—just as the very same versification in *Arethusa* expressed the unbroken rapid flow of the river—*The Cloud* establishes the meaningful "truth" of the world, for Pan's theme of mutability and Apollo's theme of eternity are reconciled in the eternal circle of change whereby the Power manifests itself in time.

The words of the Cloud apply equally to the world of the *Ode to the West Wind*: "I change, but I cannot die" (76), which adequately translates the theme of all of Ovid's metamorphoses, *omnia mutantur, nihil interit*. Death is only the moment of rebirth, or life and death are alternately the cause and effect of each other. The autumn wind is "Destroyer and preserver," the distinction being only apparent. Nature the Renewer (*natura novatrix*), Ovid wrote, makes up forms from other forms; what we call birth is but a beginning to be other than what one was before, and death is but cessation of a previous state.[37] The West Wind that disperses the dead leaves simultaneously conducts the seeds to their "wintry bed," where they lie, only mockingly, "like" corpses in a grave (6–8), just as each stanza of the poem's *terza rima* contains an unused, unfulfilled line that, like a seed in the grave, upon the completion, or "death," of its own stanza gives birth to the rhyme of the next:

O wild West Wind, thou breath of Autumn's being,
Thou, from whose unseen presence the leaves *dead*
Are driven like ghosts from an enchanter fleeing,

Yellow, and black, and pale, and hectic *red*,
Pestilence-stricken multitudes: O thou,
Who chariotest to their dark wintry *bed*. . . .

[37] *Metamorphoses* xv. 252–57.

In nature there is no death, but only a ceaseless round of change as the world responds mutably to the persistent and unchanging force of Power, and what appears to us the death of winter is only "the dreaming earth" (10) ready to be awakened. In fact, Shelley has so managed his imagery that the West Wind transcends its apparent role as, successively, destroyer and preserver to become the indifferent manifestation of the Power, merely fulfilling its fixed nature, while the factor of mutability resides solely in the character of its objects. Whereas the earth is "dreaming" during winter (10), to be awakened by the wind of spring, the Mediterranean "dreams" throughout the summer, to be awakened into activity by the West Wind of autumn (29), just as the Cloud both ministers to the noonday slumber of the leaves and arouses the flowers in morning. The single action of the Wind awakens one and casts the other into sleep. The cycles of sleep and awakening overlap in nature, and the West Wind is revealed to be not only destroyer and preserver but also an awakener, like its spring sister, because in fact it is the indifferent, invariable "shadow" of Power and therefore the guarantee that the sleep of "death," whenever it occurs, must be followed by rebirth. The esthetic analogue is the fact that as the three stanzas continuously describe the Wind in apparently analogous areas, the descriptions alternate sharply between terrifying sublimity and gentle beauty, like the destructive glaciers and life-giving river in *Mont Blanc*.

To this point the ode, like the classical hymn, has only identified the god and exposed his character and powers; now the poet must explain his need for divine aid. For man differs from nature in possessing a will that allows him to pervert and rechannel the course of the *"necessarily beneficent"* Power. Were the poet the passive leaf, cloud, or wave that are the unresisting objects of the Wind, there would be no need for prayer, for he could not then distort or block the necessary operations of the Power's earthly cycle (43–46). Nor, given the fact that he has will, would there be need if "even" he were as he was in boyhood, when, though not will-less as nature is, he was in complete cooperative harmony with the laws of nature and so could be the "comrade" of the Wind's "wanderings over Heaven," like the cloud that flies "with" the Wind (47–49). As we have noted, Shelley held that in childhood we are conscious of no distinction between ourselves and the surrounding universe and exist as though the two constitute one mass, giving ourselves passively to the one Power that governs the universe, so that even to "outstrip" the Wind's "skiey speed / Scarce seemed a vision" (50–51). Just as the habits of time create the illusion of a dualistic reality, so the process of mortal time chains man to the world, cuts him off from nature, and cheats him of the original freedom of childhood passivity.

There is an apparent paradox in Shelley's conception of freedom that is of a piece with his paradox of the will. Freedom is not the power of arbitrary choice but the condition of being bound to act only in accordance with one's own nature. It is "that sweet bondage which is Freedom's self";[38] all else is slavery. Only the West Wind, as symbol of the will-less Power and its inherent law of Necessity, is wholly "free," and man, even in willfully yielding his will to the Power, can at best be "only less free / Than thou, O uncontrollable" (46–47). Human freedom, then, is the willful triumph over the tyrannous will so that one may give himself to the uncontrollable, necessary workings of the Power and once again be "*as* a wave, a leaf, a cloud"—not dehumanized, but as receptive to the Power as they. Faith in that necessarily beneficent Power, we recall, will reconcile man with nature and repeal his enslaving "codes of fraud and woe." Curiously, there is a persistent critical tradition according to which the poet in the *Ode* is objectionably "weak" and prays for strength. The terms are right, but not in the sense that the critics mean. If to be strong means to have arbitrary choice and self-assertiveness, then the poem presents that kind of "strength" as the poet's flaw; what he is in need of is the difficult, strenuous "weakness" that will make him available to the laws of the Power. "Resist not the weakness" of willed passivity and submission, the Spirits advise Asia in *Prometheus Unbound*:

Such strength is in meekness
That the Eternal, the Immortal,
Must unloose through life's portal
The snake-like Doom coiled underneath his throne
    By that alone.[39]

Asia's "weakness" releases the Power that removes the tyrant Jupiter.

The poet's prayer to the West Wind, therefore, is not ultimately a weak plea that it breathe on him, but an appeal to himself to be reconciled to it so that he might receive its moving breath. As a matter of fact, it is only by means of an ironic adaptation of the "popular" anthropomorphism that Shelley can invoke the West Wind at all, for, as *Mont Blanc* makes clear, the Power is indifferent, acts as it must according to its own nature, and cannot alter itself or be altered. There is, Shelley had written in the rejected Introduction to *The Revolt of Islam*, a Spirit that sends its invisible wind-like breath among us; we are its "passive instrument," and it acts without reference to our "choice or will." Man can alienate himself from it, however, by an act of will, and the poet's prayer to the divine agent of Power is actually, therefore, a demand upon himself to return to his essential "free" character. We have already noticed that the third stanza, although parallel to the first two, differs from them in representing the West Wind of autumn as awakening the sea from its summer sleep instead of compelling nature to its wintry rest,

---

[38] *Queen Mab*, IX. 76.
[39] *Prometheus Unbound*, II. iii. 93–98.

and that it thereby transforms the Wind into the uniform and indifferent Power. But the stanza is radically transformative in several ways, and, while on the surface merely continuing the description of the operations of the Wind in external nature, it lays the ground for the human prayer in the last two stanzas and is transitional to that prayer by transferring the burden of obligation to man. "Thou," the stanza addresses the West Wind,

For whose path the Atlantic's level powers

Cleave themselves into chasms, while far below
The sea-blooms and the oozy woods which wear
The sapless foliage of the ocean, know

Thy voice, and suddenly grow gray with fear,
And tremble and despoil themselves: oh, hear!   (37–42)

Whereas the leaves and clouds of the first two stanzas receive the force of the Wind passively, the Atlantic is assigned "powers" on its surface which "Cleave themselves into chasms" in the presence of the Wind. This is not merely a wonderfully kinetic metonymy transferring the force of the Wind to an act of the waters; taken literally, the water's willfully forcing a passageway upon itself to receive the Wind anticipates the requirement that the poet willfully make himself passively available to the Power if his prayer is to be fulfilled. The "oozy woods" of the ocean, moreover, are not like the trees of the forest in the first stanza which are despoiled of their foliage by the immediate action of the Wind; they "despoil themselves" and do so, as Shelley's note explains, by "sympathy" with the vegetation of the land—that is, by reconciling and harmonizing themselves with the rest of nature—and so are "influenced by the winds." This same gradual transfer of initiative from the Power to the recipient of the Power is repeated in the preface to the personal prayer in stanza 4 and leads gradually to the distinction between passive nature and man, who must make himself passive: the leaves are borne *by* the Wind, the cloud flies *with* it, the wave *pants beneath* the Wind's power, as though sympathetically adapting itself to it, so that there is no distinction between what the wave does and what the Wind does to it.

Should the poet willfully submit himself to the Power, he would of necessity be the passive lyre over which the Spirit blows as it does over the forest, and the Spirit would "touch" him for the "hymns" it sings. Indeed, that the *Ode* is such a hymn is, paradoxically, a kind of confirmation that its prayer is answered and that the poet is the West Wind's lyre. "There is," Shelley wrote in his *Essay on Christianity*, "a Power by which we are surrounded, like the atmosphere in which some motionless lyre is suspended, which visits with its breath our silent chords, at will.... This

Power is God." But only those receive this Power who have been "harmonized *by their own will* to so exquisite [a] consentaneity of powers"— that is, to a sympathy like that of the vegetation beneath the sea with the vegetation of the land—"as to give forth divinest melody when the breath of universal being sweeps over their frame."[40] The poet's plea would then be answered: "Be thou, Spirit fierce, / My spirit! Be thou me, impetuous one!" (61–62). For what we *call* our selves is only the perishable vehicle for the breath which is momentarily lent by the divinity and which is the true and imperishable "self."

But the *Ode* of course is more than a spiritual self-examination in the guise of a prayer to a divinity; it is the cry of a poet who conceives of poetry as the agent of mankind's moral reformation. Were he the inspired poet, the Spirit to which he yields himself, as nature necessarily yields itself, would drive his "dead thoughts"—dead because, having passed into his poetry, they are no longer in the living mind—as it drives the dead leaves to "quicken," or engender, a new birth; for the world of mankind, like the natural world, is only "unawakened," not dead. The words of his poems, however, are both death and life—"Ashes and sparks" (67)— simultaneously the end and the new beginning that can set fire to the minds of men. Hence the poet's affiliation of himself with nature's autumn, for the ashes and sparks of his words correspond to nature's autumnal tone, "Sweet though in sadness," simultaneously singing a "dirge" and promising necessarily a new spring of natural and moral awakening, but with the emphasis falling on the latter. In such phrases as "a new birth" and "The trumpet of a prophecy," it is perhaps possible to find, as Harold Bloom does,[41] a promise of a millennium, an enduring perfection, a kingdom of God on earth, but nothing in the poem confirms this. Shelley's conceptions of the world's mutability run counter to it, and I believe that to see in the poem any expectation of an *eternal* "spring" is to over-read it. Shelley's prayer is not that the circle of mutability will stop but that the thoughts of men will be compelled in that path as inexorably as nature and that he himself may be the agent of the Power that drives this "autumn" of the mind into the following "spring."

The poem has already richly freighted the West Wind with functional significances: it is a feature of nature, the most universal display of strength, the ontological symbol of the Power and its laws of Necessity, the "spirit" of nature's activity, and the "spirit" than can and should be man's self. But it also lends itself to the figure of the traditional "inspired" poet-prophet, not merely in addition to these other significances, but precisely because of them. The poet-prophet, whether classical or Christian, does not speak in his own voice, but, like the sibyls, is the in-

---

[40] *Essay on Christianity* (Julian, VI, 231–32); itals. added.
[41] *Shelley's Mythmaking* (New Haven, 1959), p. 77.

strument through whom the divinity breathes as a wind. Richard Fogle is
right in saying that the prophecy to be uttered is not Shelley's own.[42] It
is the voice of his divinity, the Power, and Shelley prays to be the agent
of the afflatus: "Be through my lips to unawakened earth / The trumpet
of a prophecy" (68–69). The trumpet is both the summons to a renewed
life, like the last trump which announces a new heaven and a new earth,
and the traditional symbol of the foreseeing prophet,[43] for in Shelley's
sense the two are the same. The summons to mankind to awaken to a
new moral life is intimately bound up with inspired poetry by Shelley's
definition of prophecy. It is not the gift of peering supernaturally into the
future to see that which, of myriad possibilities, is to come about in a
scheme known otherwise only to God. In Shelley's strictly necessitarian
universe, we have noted, the present is the source of the future, and the
one who knows "Nature" can "deduce / The future from the present."[44]
The poet-prophet "beholds the future in the present," and his thoughts
are necessarily "the germs of the flower and the fruit of latest time."[45]
"Wouldst thou behold the Future?" Ahasuerus asks in Hellas; "ask and
have! / Knock and it shall be opened" (803–4). This parodies Christ's
words promising God's benevolent response to man's prayer;[46] and this
characteristically Shelleyan transformation of them into a doctrine of
necessity and choiceless inevitability is of the same order as his de-
theologizing of Christian prophecy in the Ode. Frederick Pottle is profoundly right in stating that when Shelley "invoked the breath of Autumn's being, he was not indulging in an empty figure. The breath
('spiritus') that he invoked was to him as real and as awful as the Holy
Ghost was to Milton."[47] And yet the difference between the West Wind
and the Holy Ghost that inspired the Christian prophets is at least as
significant as the similarity. For the inspiring Wind that is to blow the
prophecy through the poet's lips as through a trumpet is itself the very
Power that must compel the present to become the future and will sum-

---

[42] The Imagery of Keats and Shelley (Chapel Hill, 1949), p. 226.
[43] The biblical exegetes explained that the trumpet symbolizes the prophet because
God breathes His prophecies through him (see, for example, Cornelius à Lapide on
Rev. 8: 2). The Platonizing of this symbol of both the inspired prophet and the
inspired poet was easily effected. Filippo Picinelli (Mundus symbolicus [Coloniae,
1687]), for example, explained the emblematic value of tuba by quoting 2 Peter 1:
21 ("For the prophecy came not in old time by the will of man: but holy men of
God spake as they were moved by the Holy Ghost") and Plato's Ion ("The poet
does not sing his songs through art but by divine inspiration. For the poet is a light
and sacred thing; nor can he sing unless he is possessed by the god"). Ficino, expanding on the Platonic concept of poetic fury, explained that poets sing as though
God announced through them as through trumpets (Opera omnia, 1561, p. 634).
[44] Queen Mab, III. 100–1.
[45] Defence of Poetry (Julian, VII, 112).
[46] Mat. 7: 7–8; Luke 11: 9–10.
[47] "The Case of Shelley," PMLA, 67 (1952), 595.

mon man and the earth to awaken by leading winter into spring. It "foretells" the future awakening by actually bringing it about of necessity.

Yet, despite his apparent confidence, Shelley was right to end his
prayer with a question instead of an assertion: "O Wind, / If Winter comes,
can Spring be far behind?"[48] In part, it accords with the half-skeptical
note on which he ends so many of his poems, such as *The Sensitive Plant*
and *Mont Blanc*, and in part it is consistent with the fact that he is
petitioning a higher authority than himself; but essentially it reflects the
fact that there is no inherent guarantee that man will not continue to
deflect the operations of the Power by his will.

[48] The manuscript shows that Shelley's first intent was to make a positive declaration: "When Winter comes Spring lags not far behind" (MS e. 6, p. 137).

Part III The Poetry of Idealism
Utopia

9 Prometheus Unbound

*The Premises
and the
Mythic Mode*

∽

Any interpretation of *Prometheus Unbound* as a work of "poetic idealism" will necessarily be conditioned by a determination of the drama's area of reference, the level of reality at which it is enacted; and this in turn must be a function of what its protagonist represents. Certainly Prometheus is not Man, if we mean by that the mortal human race. Prometheus himself, avowedly the benefactor and savior of man (I. 817), specifically makes the distinction in an address to Asia after his liberation and reunion with her:

we will sit and talk of time and change,
As the world ebbs and flows, ourselves unchanged.
What can hide man from mutability?   (III. iii. 23–25)

Unlike man and the world, Prometheus is, at least at this point, not only immortal but also immutable; and Shelley's insistence that only thought, or mind, is eternal demands that we assign Prometheus his role, not in a system of allegorical abstractions, but in Shelley's metaphysics of idealism. He must be whatever Shelley's philosophy provides for as eternal and immutable. Moreover, in Act I, after his torture by the Furies, consolation is brought him by Spirits that come from the Human Mind, attributes or powers of a state of existence necessarily distinct from Prometheus'; and therefore he cannot be the Human Mind. Later he prophesies that, Jupiter being dethroned, he and Asia will be visited by the arts of the "human world," which are "mediators / Of that best worship, love, by [man] and us / Given and returned" (III. iii. 58–60).[1] Even the speech of Jupiter which is sometimes offered as evidence that Prometheus is the "soul of man" actually distinguishes him from that:

Rejoice! henceforth I am omnipotent.
All else had been subdued to me; alone
The soul of man, like an unextinguished fire,
Yet burns towards heaven with fierce reproach, and doubt,
And lamentation, and reluctant prayer,
Hurling up insurrection.... (III. i. 3–8)

But this cannot apply to Prometheus, who has already retracted his curse; who now pities, not reproaches, and therefore seems to Jupiter (as he does to Earth) to have been subdued; and who never doubted Jupiter's falseness or offered him prayer, however reluctant. Jupiter's words describe his own relation to the "soul of man" in terms of what Shelley took to be the relation of the god of traditional theologies to his fearful but rebellious human worshippers, and this is precisely the relation into which Prometheus has forever refused to enter. Finally, although the freeing of Prometheus and his reunion with Asia are paralleled by the gradual, progressive improvement of man, there is, explicitly, a significant time lag between the two, as though the continuous process of the perfection of man is in delayed sympathy with the instantaneous restoration of Prometheus, or as though one occurred in time and the other outside it.

To assume, then, that Prometheus illustrates "that man as a soul is not only indestructible, but, through high will inspired by love, is creative," as J. A. Symonds mused; to fancy with Rossetti that he is "that faculty whereby man is man, not brute"; to call him, as Mary Shelley did, "the emblem of the human race" or "the prophetic soul of humanity" or "the mind of mankind" or the "potential state" of man "insofar as it is good," as other critics have speculated; even to lean on Shelley's description of Prometheus in his Preface as "the type of the highest perfection of moral and intellectual nature, impelled by the purest and truest motives to the best and noblest ends"[2]—each of these falls short of the mark insofar as it assumes that the central subject of the drama is a mankind having autonomous reality and that Prometheus is a fictional abstraction of earthly man or of his faculties or ideals. All such interpretations allow for only one mode of existence and neglect the fact that, within the totally in-

[1] Shelley regularly defines art as mediating between two different levels of reality. See Ode to Liberty, 249–53, and cf. above, pp. 201–2.
[2] In fact, Shelley is not attempting to define his own Prometheus but is describing the potentialities in the abstract Prometheus of classical myth, or, as he has just said of Satan, the way in which the traditional character "is susceptible of being described."

clusive realm of Being, Shelley's metaphysics provides for two: human minds and the One Mind. Or, rather, such interpretations postulate that Prometheus must be a fabricated abstraction drawn by the poet from a reality called "man," instead of postulating the conclusion Shelley's "intellectual system" arrives at—that what we call "real" men are time-bound portions of the One Mind and, with respect to that unitary reality, are illusory, being only the "different modifications" of it. Individual human minds are indeed a necessary part of the play, but their actions take place off-stage and are effected by sympathy with the Promethean drama; for the human revolution and the history of human perfection that were the subject of The Revolt of Islam have here been transposed to the level of total Existence, the metaphysical reality here named "Prometheus." As such, he is not a fiction abstracted from what exists, but Existence itself. Indeed, except for Demogorgon, Prometheus is the only reality actually present in the play, and it would be short of the truth even to say that the drama takes place in his mind; he is the One Mind. But the One Mind is not to be confused with unknowable Being, the One that embraces both the universe and the mysterious reality outside it—the One to which Adonais returns on his death, which is beyond the "outwall" of "boldest thoughts,"[3] and to which, on one occasion, Shelley gave the partial name Intellectual Beauty. The limited domain of Prometheus Unbound is that unitary mode of Being that appears in thought-constituted existence.

ii

According to Shelley's doctrine of Necessity, we have observed, the distinction between good and evil has relevance only to mind, for the Power that is exerted through the universe, not being mind and not having will, acts as it must according to the necessary causal succession. But mind, having will, can make possible the initiation of an evil succession by imposing on itself a fictitious authority. All such willful impositions Shelley called "tyranny," the chief agents of which are kings, priests, and "fathers" like Count Cenci because they claim the existence of an independent authority outside man's mind which dictates arbitrary systems of thought and action. These arbitrary and tyrannical codes are not real in the sense that the uniform processive patterns of Necessity are, but are fabricated by the mind, which then abdicates to these fictions its own powers and enslaves itself to its own creation:

He who taught man to vanquish whatsoever
    Can be between the cradle and the grave
Crowned him the King of Life. Oh, vain endeavour!

[3] Hellas, 768–75.

If on his own high will, a willing slave,
He has enthroned the oppression and the oppressor.[4]

It is therefore "our will / That thus enchains us to permitted ill."[5] At the heart of this ethical doctrine is the paradox of freedom, which Shelley understands to mean, not the freedom to make arbitrary and capricious choices, as though "the will has the power of refusing to be determined by the strongest motive,"[6] but only freedom from tyranny, that is, from the artificial, mind-forged restraints that the mind allows itself to impose on itself. Man abandons his natural freedom when he "fabricates / The sword which stabs his peace" and "raiseth up / The tyrant whose delight is in his woe."[7] But true freedom does not mean freedom from the fixed processes of Necessity, to which the mind must submit itself if it is to possess its own will; for this submission is "that sweet bondage which is Freedom's self," a "weakness" or "meekness" which is strength.[8]

In accordance with these concepts Shelley has represented in Jupiter all tyrannical evils and has identified him with the conventional God of the theists. But since tyrannic power is only an efficient fiction constituted of the mind's willful abdication of its own will, Jupiter has no real and independent existence in the sense that Mind or Power does. Tyrannic evil is a lapse of the Mind, its negative mode, its reflection in a distorting mirror, and is no more independent of Prometheus, the One Mind, than that. Just as Beatrice Cenci ultimately suspects that God is a fictional projection of her father, who exploits that fiction to justify his tyranny, so "God" was created by some "moon-struck sophist" upon "Watching the shade from his own soul upthrown / Fill Heaven and darken Earth":

The Form he saw and worshipped was his own,
His likeness in the world's vast mirror shown.[9]

Consequently, although Jupiter appears in the drama as a god, he is not a being or an autonomous power, but only the dark shadow of Prometheus, an unnatural condition that mind wrongfully permits and can repeal by an act of will. "I gave all / He has," says Prometheus (I. 381–82), because Jupiter is only what Prometheus has resigned; and any institutionalizing and reifying of these abdicated mental powers is, by definition, the creation of a tyranny which then demands fearful submission of the mind to its own fiction. Unlike the traditional Jupiter, who usurped the throne of the gods and was merely aided to this end by Prometheus,

[4] Ode to Liberty, 241–45.
[5] Julian and Maddalo, 170–71.
[6] Queen Mab, VI. 198n.
[7] Ibid., III. 199–202.
[8] Ibid., IX. 76; Prometheus Unbound, II. iii. 93–94.
[9] The Revolt of Islam, 3244–48.

Shelley's Jupiter is actually enthroned by Prometheus, who gave him "wisdom, which is strength," and "clothed him with the dominion of wide Heaven" (II. iv. 44–46). Hence Prometheus can say to Jupiter, "O'er all things but thyself I gave thee power, / And my own will" (I. 273–74). Not only is Jupiter unable to govern the will of Prometheus, the One Mind; he is not even self-determining because he exists only through Prometheus' concession that he be, or, rather, because he is only an unnatural surrogate for Prometheus. He has no will simply because Prometheus has not resigned his own will to his fictional creation. It is for this reason that, upon being overcome, Jupiter leaves only a blank, a "void annihilation," and is "sunk, withdrawn, covered, drunk up / By thirsty nothing" (IV. 350–51); and Prometheus knows that when Jupiter's soul is cloven it will "Gape like a hell within" (I. 56).

When Prometheus, wishing to hear again his own evil curse against Jupiter, decides that it not be repeated by "aught resembling me" (I. 220), it is more than ideologically proper that he assigns the task of repeating it to Jupiter's Phantasm; for, although it is true that Jupiter and the now-repentant Prometheus are moral opposites, the audience is thus presented with the dramatic shock of observing the Phantasm of Jupiter in effect mindlessly cursing himself. But more is conveyed than merely the irony of the situation. The curse Prometheus had once spoken is admittedly an evil (I. 219) because it is an act of revenge, a countering of a wrong with another wrong; and if it is proper that it now be repeated by the shadow of him who is all evil, the implication is that when Prometheus first spoke it he was, in a very real sense, Jupiter. Milton Wilson has called attention to the striking similarities between Prometheus' description of the Phantasm about to repeat the curse and Prometheus' description of himself in the curse.[10] In Jupiter's Phantasm, Prometheus sees

> the curse on gestures proud and cold,
> And looks of firm defiance, and calm hate,
> And such despair as mocks itself with smiles; (I. 258–60)

and at once the Phantasm repeats Prometheus' original execration:

> Fiend, I defy thee! with a calm, fixed mind,
>   All that thou canst inflict I bid thee do;
> Foul Tyrant both of Gods and Human-kind. (I. 262–64)

Indeed, it is impossible to know whether the Phantasm reflects the real appearance of Jupiter or, like a good actor, has assumed the appearance Prometheus had when he originally spoke the curse against Jupiter. But it is necessary to go beyond Mr. Wilson's conclusions and to recognize

[10] *Shelley's Later Poetry*, pp. 63–64.

this as the actual identification of the execrating Prometheus with Jupiter, the god he made in his image. Not only does the audience watch the Phantasm uttering Prometheus' curse against him of whom it is the phantom; it also observes Prometheus facing his own former self in Jupiter's ghost, since all of Jupiter's nature—pride, coldness, defiance, calm hatred, self-mocking despair—existed in Prometheus when he cursed his oppressor, although he has dispelled these evils from himself now that he no longer hates but pities. "I am changed," he says, "so that aught evil wish / Is dead within; . . . no memory [remains] / Of what is hate" (I. 70–72);[11] and it is for this reason that only his former self, the Phantasm of Jupiter, can repeat the curse. If Prometheus intends a bitter irony by causing Jupiter's Phantasm to utter the curse against Jupiter, there is also an irony he does not intend when he thinks he has not called up "aught resembling me." The difference between Prometheus and Jupiter's Phantasm is that between Prometheus and his former moral self.

Throughout the play, as we shall see, Jupiter is presented as only a cruel parody of Prometheus, and this relationship is repeatedly underscored in Act I, where he is treated as the distorted, mocking reflection of Prometheus. Although Panthea sees Prometheus as "firm, not proud" (I. 337), Jupiter's Phantasm, who himself shows "gestures proud," calls him "proud sufferer" (I. 245); and Prometheus, speaking "with a calm, fixed mind" when he uttered the curse, addressed Jupiter as "awful image of calm power" (I. 296), while the Phantasm, repeating the curse, looks cruel, "but calm and strong, / Like one who does, not suffers wrong" (I. 238–39). In one sense it is Jupiter who fills the world with his "malignant spirit" (I. 276), but in fact it is Prometheus, who, in hate, has imprecated on "me and mine . . . / The utmost torture of thy hate" (I. 278–79). Prometheus' struggle is really a contest within himself, and his reference to Jupiter's "self-torturing solitude" (I. 295) is, ironically, actually a description of his own state as, chained to the precipice, he endures "torture and solitude, / Scorn and despair" (I. 14–15).

Given that Jupiter is the privative mode of Prometheus, we can understand why Prometheus, addressing Jupiter, describes the universe as

> those bright and rolling worlds
> Which Thou and I alone of living things
> Behold with sleepless eyes! (I. 2–4)

For if the universe is the mass of thought, then it has a continuous existence by virtue of being the unending perception by the One Mind—

---

[11] When Prometheus has heard the curse he once uttered, he repents, adding, "I wish no living thing to suffer pain" (I. 305). The reference is mainly to Jupiter, it is obvious, since the curse was directed against him; but it probably is significant that at this point in the manuscript Shelley originally added the following stage direction: "he [i.e. Prometheus] bends his head as in pain" (Zillman, p. 149n.).

and by the negation of itself that the One Mind has permitted.[12] These alone, like Berkeley's God and unlike the human mind, never cease to perceive the thought that is the universe. But as the institutional reification of Prometheus' relinquished powers, Jupiter would have the One Mind bow in total submission and abandon itself entirely to the then self-determined institution. Therefore, were it not for Prometheus' "all-enduring will" to resist, the One Mind would be deprived of itself, abandoned entirely to its own negation; and the world that exists because it is perceived would have "vanished, like thin mist / Unrolled on the morning wind" (I. 116–17).[13] Without mind there can be no thought, and thoughtlessness can be the "measure" only of a vacancy.

iii

Shelley achieves an obvious and powerful expressionistic effect by reflecting in the natural settings of the play the stages of Prometheus' moral unbinding. The slow emergence of day out of night in the wintry Caucasus, for example, is the fitting scenic expression of Prometheus' retraction of his curse; and it is appropriate, for the same reason, that the events initiating the new Promethean order begin in Act II with the first day of spring. But what we have observed of the relation between mind and universe suggests that these settings are more than mere metaphors or stage backgrounds. If nothing exists but as it is perceived and if thought is the measure of the universe, the state of the "external" world is a function of the condition of the mind. It is implicit, then, that the condition of Prometheus as the One Mind, on which the existence of the universe depends, determines the manner in which those thoughts called the "external" world are modified and that his being "bound" should necessarily involve a distortion of the world. It is presumptuous, Shelley held, to believe that there is any essential "distinction between the moral and the material universe."[14]

In his early reading of the works of the French mechanists, such as Cabanis' *Rapports du physique et du moral de l'homme* and La Mettrie's *L'Homme machine*, Shelley had been impressed by the idea of a simultaneous melioration in the physical and moral worlds, and in his eagerness to find grounds for his faith in progress he assumed a beneficent force driving toward perfection in man and nature alike. "The language spoken

---

[12] This interpretation is not, of course, obviated by the fact that Prometheus' sleepless vision derives from *Prometheus Bound* 32, and Jupiter's, from the maxim that tyrants dare not sleep (in his manuscript Shelley first wrote of Jupiter, "for a tyrant seldom sleeps, / Thou never" [Zillman, p. 133n.]) and perhaps from the opening of *Iliad* ii, which Pope translated as "the ever-wakeful Eyes of Jove."

[13] Again, the fact, but not its significance, derives from the plan of Aeschylus' Zeus to destroy the human race and replace it with another (*Prometheus Bound* 233–40).

[14] *Speculations on Metaphysics* (Julian, VII, 62).

. . . by the mythology of nearly all religions," he wrote in 1813, "seems to prove, that at some distant period man forsook the path of nature, and sacrificed the purity and happiness of his being to unnatural appetites. The date of this event, seems to have also been that of some great change in the climates of the earth, with which it has an obvious correspondence."[15] Since nature would reassume perfection by returning to the Golden Age of eternal spring, Shelley wished to believe the astronomical tradition according to which the obliquity of the earth's ecliptic, or the inclination of its axis, which is responsible for the varying seasons and the unequal lengths of day and night, is gradually disappearing.[16] "It is exceedingly probable," he felt when he still believed in the dualism of mind and universe,

that this obliquity will gradually diminish, until the equator coincides with the ecliptic; the nights and days will then become equal on the earth throughout the year, and probably the seasons also. There is no great extravagance in presuming that the progress of the perpendicularity of the poles may be as rapid as the progress of the intellect; or that there should be a perfect identity between the moral and physical improvement of the human species.[17]

Although he was soon to learn from his reading of Laplace that science had demonstrated the continuous oscillation of the earth's axis instead of its gradual return to the perpendicular,[18] apparently he was able to sustain his earlier faith on the basis of his subsequent idealism, since it denies any true phenomenal distinction between mind and world. Just as Milton had attributed to the Fall God's command that

> his Angels turn askance
> The Poles of Earth twice ten degrees and more
> From the Sun's Axle,[19]

and just as Thomas Burnet in his *Sacred Theory of the Earth* had attributed the obliquity and the consequent variety of the seasons to the

---

[15] *A Vindication of Natural Diet* (Julian, VI, 5); repeated in *Queen Mab*, VIII. 211–12n.
[16] To Thomas Hookham, early 1813 (*Letters*, I, 349): "You would very much oblige me if you would collect all possible documents on the Precession of the Equinoxes; as also anything that may throw light upon the question whether or no the position of the Earth on its poles is not yearly becoming less oblique?"
[17] *Queen Mab*, VI. 45–46n. Mary Shelley's ultimate disillusionment resulted in her Peacock-like parody of Shelley's optimism in her *The Last Man* (1826). There (chap. 4) she depicts a mad astronomer who, while all mankind is being wiped out by a universal plague, is obsessed by the conviction that "in an hundred thousand years" the "pole of the earth will coincide with the pole of the ecliptic" and "an universal spring will be produced, and earth become a paradise."
[18] *A Refutation of Deism* (Julian, VI, 49).
[19] *Paradise Lost*, X. 668–70.

cataclysm responsible for the Flood, so Shelley writes that the thunder resulting from Prometheus' curse "made rock / The orbed world" (I. 68–69) and that Earth refuses to repeat Prometheus' curse, lest Jupiter "link me to some wheel of pain / More torturing than the one whereon I roll" (I. 141–42). Since the earth's mere rotation about its own axis cannot justify the image of the torture-wheel—which, incidentally, is also the instrument with which Jupiter punished Ixion—the reference to torture (*tortus*: twisting) must be to the twisting motion resulting from the displacement of its axis from the perpendicular.

Like the Fall of Man, Prometheus' curse—which, we shall see, represents the Fall in a variety of ways—has disordered nature and introduced all physical ills, not because God or Necessity punishes both man and nature in like manner, but because the universe is the mass of thoughts, including their various modes and combinations, in the One Mind. The consequences of the physico-mental distortion are not only disease and natural cataclysm but also the extremes of the seasons described by Prometheus when, in his curse, he bade Jupiter "let alternate frost and fire / Eat into me" (I. 268–69) and by Asia when, among the ills of Jupiter's reign, she lists the "alternating shafts of frost and fire" of the "unseasonable seasons" (II. iv. 52–53). This loss of the Saturnian Age of perpetual spring as a consequence of the rocking of the earth is, moreover, precisely consonant with the Greco-Roman myth to which Shelley is committed. The Golden Age ended when Saturn was vanquished, the goddess of Justice fled, and the world came under the sway of Jupiter. Then, Ovid tells us, under the reign of Jupiter spring became but one of the four seasons, and the earth began to endure the extremes of burning heat and ice.[20]

It is, then, no stale metaphor but, in the philosophic context of the play, a richly appropriate fact that the moment initiating the restoration of Prometheus in Act II is the vernal equinox, when the obliquity is overcome and day and night are of equal length over the earth. The precession of the equinoxes, "though slow, being always in the same direction, and therefore continually accumulating, has early been remarked, and was the first of the celestial appearances that suggested the idea of an *annus magnus*."[21] But Shelley's ethics, for reasons to be examined later, requires that Prometheus' restoration be instantaneous, like that described by

[20] *Metamorphoses* i. 113–24. Dryden's translation, influenced by Ovid's commentators, brings these events into closer accord with astronomy:

Then Summer, Autumn, Winter did appear;
And Spring was but a season of the year.
The sun his annual course obliquely made,
Good days contracted, and enlarg'd the bad.
Then air with sultry heats began to glow;
The wings of winds were clogg'd with ice and snow.

[21] *Edinburgh Review*, 11 (1808), 269–70.

Shelley's friend John Frank Newton in a passage remarkably suggestive of Demogorgon's volcanic flight from beneath the earth:

It is an astronomical fact which cannot easily be disputed, that the poles of the earth were at some distant period perpendicular to its orbit, as those of the planet Jupiter are now, whose inhabitants must therefore enjoy a perpetual spring.
It was a tenet of the most ancient priests of whom we have any knowledge, the Brachmans, that still, by some portentous bursting forth of the earth's bowels, a second change will be accomplished, which shall bring back equal seasons and perpetual spring.[22]

Correspondingly, when Prometheus is at last restored, the renovation of Earth is represented in terms of a return to an eternal spring: through her "withered, old, and icy frame / The warmth of an immortal youth shoots down / Circling," and "In mild variety the seasons mild" clothe the entire world with "ever-living leaves, and fruits, and flowers" (III. iii. 88–90, 115, 123).

All efforts to chart the strict chronology of *Prometheus Unbound* have inevitably ended in frustration because, all this suggests, the various seasons and times of day, together with their sequences, are neither temporal in the usual sense nor even symbolic, but are actual conditions of the mind, to which all things are relative. It would be to no avail, for example, to ask whether an actual day passes between the morning of the vernal equinox opening Act II and the moment of Asia's reunion with Prometheus; the night that apparently intervenes is the darkness of Demogorgon's realm, the "lasting night" in which he wraps "heaven's kingless throne" (II. iv. 149). Not only were the dislocation and realignment of the earth's axis traditionally identified with the terminal points of the Platonic Great Year, which begins and ends with the vernal equinox; according to Pliny, among others, the exact moment of renewal is high noon—"Heaven's immortal noon," as Shelley names it in *Hellas*—when all the heavenly bodies are again in exact alignment.[23] Correspondingly, not only is Prometheus released with the arrival of spring, but the Hour that bears Asia to the liberated Prometheus calls attention to the fact that she will rest from the labors of her flight "at noon" (II. iv. 173) and that on this day of restoration and renewal "The sun will rise not until noon" (II. v. 10), for at that perfect moment the new Promethean age will have begun.

Furthermore, if we now ask who brought about the distortion of the world and all its "physical" confusion, we are once again driven by the workings of the drama to the conclusion that Jupiter is but the privative

[22] *The Return to Nature* (1821), in *The Pamphleteer*, 19 (1822), 506 and n. (1st ed., 1811).
[23] Pliny *Natural History* x. 2. 5. See also Albert R. Cirillo, "Noon-Midnight and the Temporal Structure of *Paradise Lost*," ELH, 29 (1962), 372–95.

mode of Prometheus, the One Mind. In his curse Prometheus calls down on himself all of Jupiter's tortures:

Rain then thy plagues upon me here,
Ghastly disease, and frenzying fear;
And let alternate frost and fire
Eat into me, and be thine ire
Lightning, and cutting hail. . . .   (I. 266–70)

These words, together with other descriptions in Act I of physical disorders, echo the defiance of Zeus by Aeschylus' Prometheus:

Therefore let the lightning's forked curl be cast upon my head and let the sky be convulsed with thunder and the wrack of savage winds; let the hurricane shake the earth from its rooted base, and let the waves of the sea mingle with their savage surge the courses of the stars in heaven.[24]

Aeschylus' play then ends with Zeus's visiting upon nature the cataclysms Prometheus had invoked. But it is a calculated aspect of Shelley's drama that he be far less exact about the agent of these events. Asia will explain that when, prior to his rebellion, Prometheus first gave Jupiter power, there came disease and the "unseasonable seasons" with "alternating shafts of frost and fire"; and she connects the two events only loosely (II. iv. 43–58). Earth places the cataclysms after Jupiter's thunder had enchained Prometheus, and she is equally vague about their immediate cause (I. 161–73). On the other hand, Earth also implies that Jupiter caused her distorted motion because of Prometheus' curse (I. 140–42); and yet Prometheus asserts that the words of his own curse, like a spell, "had power" that disrupted all nature and were themselves a "thunder" that "made rock / The orbed world" (I. 61, 68–69). But these last words derive from Aeschylus' play, where, significantly, it is not Prometheus but Zeus who makes the earth rock, in response to Prometheus' invocation of his tortures;[25] and the thunder which Shelley's Prometheus attributes to his curse is Jupiter's traditional instrument, not Prometheus'.[26] These varying accounts of the cause of nature's distortion arise, then, not from any confusion, but from the ambiguity built into the metaphysics of the poem. Nature is disordered because the One Mind is disordered, the distinction between the two being unreal. Hence the distortion is equally attributable to the One Mind's yielding up its powers, to the binding of the One Mind that necessarily results from this abdication, and to the curse of hate against the yielded powers that perpetuates the tyranny. It is a matter of indifference whether the One Mind in its state of error and hate or

[24] *Prometheus Bound* 1043–50.
[25] *Ibid.*, 1081.
[26] Contrast *Prometheus Unbound*, I. 162: ". . . his [Jupiter's] thunder chained thee here."

whether "the supreme Tyrant" be considered the cause of the destruction of nature's Golden Age, for Jupiter is but the distorted reflection of Prometheus, "the shade from his own soul upthrown" so that it fills heaven and darkens earth.

iv

The coherent dialogue in Act I between Earth and Prometheus that takes place, paradoxically, despite a total absence of communication between the speakers must also be examined in the light of Shelley's brand of idealism. Earth and her elements, notwithstanding Prometheus' plea, refuse to repeat Prometheus' curse because to do so, Earth explains, would be to employ a language intelligible not only to Prometheus but also to Jupiter, who would torture her more severely than when he first heard the curse. Earth and her components, therefore, must be able to speak two different languages, Prometheus and Jupiter only one of the two. Thereafter Earth and Prometheus exchange a series of speeches and respond to each other with what appears to the reader to be mutual understanding, even though it is explicitly stated that Earth is employing a language unintelligible to Prometheus. To him the words of the mountains, springs, air, and whirlwind are only "a sound of voices: not the voice / Which I gave forth" on uttering the curse (I. 112–13); and Earth's "inorganic voice" is but "an awful whisper . . . scarce like sound" (I. 132–33) that affects him and notifies him of her presence but does not communicate intelligible thoughts. Earth's speech works strangely on him:

Obscurely thro' my brain, like shadows dim,
Sweep awful thoughts, rapid and thick. I feel
Faint, like one mingled in entwining love;
Yet 'tis not pleasure.   (I. 146–49)

Nevertheless, even Earth is aware that she is speaking in a tongue unknown to him. Obviously the reader is being asked to entertain a complex and paradoxical dramatic hypothesis. Of course only a single language is available to Shelley and his reader, and yet the reader must accept the explicit statement that Earth's language is really different from Prometheus'. Although Prometheus questions and answers Earth as though their communication were complete, the reader must assume that Prometheus is in fact speaking a soliloquy which, quite by chance, happens to form a coherent dialogue with Earth:

Prometheus. . . .
Speak, Spirit! from thine inorganic voice
I only know that thou art moving near
And love. How cursed I him?

The Earth. How canst thou hear
Who knowest not the language of the dead?
Prometheus. Thou art a living spirit; speak as they.
The Earth. I dare not speak like life.... (I. 135–40)

Shelley's rejection of materialism and of the dualism of subject and object must have driven him to reconsider the function of language, for he could no longer assume it to be an analysis of percepts into the components and relationships obtaining among their counterparts in an outside reality. It is clear that he was frequently inclined to examine the implications of the intellectual philosophy in grammatical terms and hence to conceive of linguistic structures as imprecise, artificial expedients for organizing thoughts and as only metaphoric of the relationships that truly exist in the mind,[27] as when he found the personal pronouns to be "grammatical devices invented simply for arrangement, and totally devoid of the intense and exclusive sense usually attached to them,"[28] or concluded that the various tenses really express the changing modes of the existence of our percepts relative to ourselves.[29] As other empiricists and idealists were driven by their premises to recognize, language does not report the structure of an external universe; it is a conventional arrangement imposing an arbitrary analytical structure on thought, even though thought is not truly divisible into components.[30] Instead of reporting forms, it is formative. When properly exploited by man as a particularizing and relational system, language defines and organizes otherwise vague and chaotic thoughts:

Language is a perpetual Orphic song,
Which rules with Daedal harmony a throng
Of thoughts and forms, which else senseless and shapeless were. (IV. 415–17)

Later, in his *Defence of Poetry*, Shelley was to write that "language is arbitrarily produced by the imagination, and has relation to thoughts alone" and that it expresses the mind's relational and unifying principles,

[27] His order of a copy of Lord Monboddo's *On the Origin and Progress of Language* is evidence of his interest in linguistic theory (to Clio Rickman, 24 December 1812 [*Letters*, I, 344]). His *Speculations on Metaphysics* (Julian, VII, 63) also shows his knowledge of John Horne Tooke's philological writings.
[28] *On Life* (Julian, VI, 196).
[29] *Speculations on Metaphysics* (Julian, VII, 61).
[30] Robert L. Politzer has shown how an acceptance of Berkeley's idealism led Maupertuis into a kind of pre-Humboldtian linguistic relativism that claims that a conventional linguistic system structures knowledge ("On the Linguistic Philosophy of Maupertuis and its Relation to the History of Linguistic Relativism," *Symposium*, 17 [1963], 5–16). He also instances J. D. Michaelis' *Beantwortung der Frage von dem Einflusz der Meinungen auf die Sprache und der Sprache auf die Meinungen* (1759) and J. G. Sulzer's *Observations sur l'influence reciproque de la raison sur le langage et du langage sur la raison* (1767).

not the order of "objects and the impressions represented by them."[31]
Indeed, since the universe is constituted of our "mass of knowledge...,
including our own nature," the structure of the universe is determined for
the human mind by the way in which a linguistic system shapes (in
Shelley's terminology, "creates") our knowledge, or thought: "speech
created thought, / Which is the measure of the universe" (II. iv. 72–73).
Yet it must be understood that all this applies only to the human mind,
together with its illusions of distinct minds, distinct thoughts, time, space,
and the distinction between subject and object. Given these illusions, the
relational power of language can be employed by the imagination to weave
a "Daedal harmony," an organic order that tends to overcome the chaos
of human thoughts. But language is both a blessing and a frustration.
Even under the compulsion of the human mind's extraordinary apprehensions of perfect unity, language can never entirely overcome discreteness
and the dimensions of mutability because man cannot overcome those
illusory distinctions necessary for his existence as an individual mind.
When Shelley aspires to express the absolute unity of being, he can only
lament,

The winged words on which my soul would pierce
Into the height of Love's rare Universe,
Are chains of lead around its flight of fire,[32]

or complain, "These words inefficient and metaphorical. Most words so—
No help!"[33]

The distinction Earth draws in her paradoxical "dialogue" with Prometheus is that her language is known only to mortals and therefore not
to Prometheus, who is immortal. Hers is "the language of the dead" (I.
138), understandable only "to those who die" (I. 151); and even at the
end of the Promethean action, upon being questioned by Asia about those
"who die," she answers in words almost identical with those of her earlier
explanation (I. 148–51):

It would avail not to reply:
Thou art immortal, and this tongue is known
But to the uncommunicating dead.   (III. iii. 110–12)

Earth, then, can belong to mortality or, being potentially a "living spirit,"
to immortality; Prometheus, like his distorted shadow Jupiter, belongs to
immortality alone. The distinction is between life and death, and the key
term is "living spirit." Clearly "life" here does not refer to human ex-

[31] Julian, VII, 110, 113.
[32] Epipsychidion, 588–90.
[33] On Love.

istence: as Earth explains, "Death is the veil which those who live call life: / They sleep, and it is lifted" (III. iii. 113–14). Mortality lives a death; and what it calls death is really its removal. Instead, "life" is to be understood in the sense that Shelley assigned it in his essay on that subject, the identity of existence and perception, the unity of mind and the universe, of subject and object. As the One Mind, Prometheus can understand only the language of "life." It is also a language available to Earth because, assumed in Mind, she can be a "living spirit"; or, conceived of as divorced from Mind and subjected to the mutability and dimensions of mortality, she can appear as those thoughts illusorily considered to be "external objects." We are to understand, therefore, that in her dialogue with Prometheus Earth speaks the language of mankind, which postulates the illusory distinction between earth and mind. Dividing herself from Mind as an external thing, Earth cannot speak the curse, which is an expression of Mind, and her words appear to Prometheus only as "an awful whisper," only as obscure thoughts. Despite Prometheus' awareness of the love that, were it complete, would unite him with Earth, he is conscious of the division effected by the mortal language that separates mind from an external world: "I only know that thou art moving near / And love" (I. 136–37). The ontological division, moreover, must also be a moral one, since the distinction between metaphysics and ethics is unreal. As the mere mass of thoughts called external and falsely filtered out of "life," Earth continues to meditate Prometheus' curse "In secret joy and hope" (I. 185), erroneously believing that the Mind's hate-filled resistance will ultimately overcome Jupiter. Related to Prometheus only as "things" are supposedly related to mortal minds, Earth misunderstands the moral significance of Prometheus' retraction of the curse, just as Urania, being the spirit of earthly life, fails to understand the true significance of Adonais' postmortal existence. Divorced from Mind and therefore from moral truth, Earth can conceive of Prometheus' repentance only as defeat, and not as the removal of the impediment to Jupiter's overthrow:

Howl, Spirits of the living and the dead,
Your refuge, your defence lies fallen and vanquished.   (I. 310–11)

v

Man's works of art, according to Prometheus, are

the mediators
Of that best worship, love, by him and us
Given and returned.   (III. iii. 58–60)

Art mediates, that is, between the mutable diversity and division of the human mind on the one hand and the immutable unity of the One Mind, or absolute Existence, on the other; and the radical principle of the *Defence of Poetry*—order, arrangement, combination, relation, harmony, or rhythm—is the human means of shaping diversity into an approxima- tion of perfect unity, which is truth, beauty, and goodness. The poetic imagination is—as Shelley considered himself to be—a revolutionist and reformer, first shaking "Thought's stagnant chaos" (IV. 380), shattering false and imperfect arrangements of thought, and then striving to re- arrange the liberated elements into the formal perfection they ought to have according to a poetics which is also an ethics. In *Prometheus Un- bound* this doctrine of the workings and purpose of the plastic imagina- tion is responsible for the transformation and syncretism of the myths that constitute the body of the drama.

Peacock reports that Shelley once commented on Spenser's giant who holds the scales and wishes to "rectify the physical and moral evils which result from inequality of condition."[34] Artegall, Shelley explained, "argues with the Giant; the Giant has the best of the argument; Artegall's iron man knocks him over into the sea and drowns him. This is the usual way in which power deals with opinion." When Peacock objected that this is not the lesson Spenser intended, Shelley replied, "Perhaps not; it is the lesson which he conveys to me. I am of the Giant's faction."[35] In the giant's intention to reduce all things "unto equality," Spenser saw the impending dissolution of hierarchy and the return to chaos; from Shelley's point of view Spenser's conception of order was wrong and therefore the ordering of his myth was wrong, for what to Spenser was necessary su- periority and subordination was to republican Shelley the frustration of all possibility of perfect unity. The occasion for Peacock's note was a letter in which Shelley alluded to Artegall's giant in order, it is significant, to define the purpose of the recently completed Act I of *Prometheus Un- bound*: the act, Shelley writes, is an attempt to "cast what weight I can into the right scale of that balance which the Giant (of Arthegall) holds."[36] For egalitarian Shelley was engaged in reforming and reinter- preting the myth of god-fearing Aeschylus at least as radically as he did that of Spenser, the defender of hierarchism, and to the same end of per- fect order. Recasting that myth into the shape and proportions that, accord- ing to his imaginative vision, it ought to have as the highest unity of which its components are capable meant to Shelley not only the achieve- ment of the highest formal beauty but also—since it amounts to the same thing—the purging of error and the attainment of truth.

[34] *Letters*, II, 71n.
[35] Peacock adds that Shelley also "held that the Enchanter in the first canto [of Thomson's *Castle of Indolence*] was a true philanthropist, and the Knight of Arts and Industry in the second an oligarchical impostor overthrowing truth by power" (*ibid.*).
[36] To Peacock [23–24 January 1819] (*Letters*, II, 71).

To Shelley myth is not fanciful fable. Whatever its genesis, it is not mistaken for external fact, and therefore it is more truly real than the sensory world that man falsely believes to reside outside his mind. Since "things" actually exist for man only as thoughts, the elements organized by the poet are thoughts recognized as wholly mental and not mistaken for any independent externality. The thoughts composed by the imagination are those upon which the mind has already acted "so as to colour them with its own light,"[37] which is a reflection of the light of the perfect One. Or, as Shelley expresses the same idea in *Prometheus Unbound*, the poet does not heed objects as external "things," but first watches the "lake-reflected sun illume" them and then organizes ("creates") these transfigured thoughts into "Forms more real than living man, / Nurslings of immortality!" (I. 744–49). The elements of myth, being unmistakably mental apprehensions of "things," are pre-eminently thoughts and therefore pre-eminently the valid materials to which the poet is obliged to give the "purest and most perfect shape."

But if the constituent details of myths are especially real for Shelley, it follows that the component elements of one myth are as valid as those of any other, since they are all thoughts. Syncretic mythology had been revitalized in the eighteenth century, especially by those deists who, arguing for the common basis of all faiths, had attempted to demonstrate the interconvertibility of all myths.[38] This tradition of syncretism was part of Shelley's intellectual heritage, and his mentalistic ontology provided it with a special philosophic justification. If, then, all mythic data, from Jupiter to King Bladud, are real and valid, the various received myths are not to be thought of as discrete narratives or distinct national faiths, but only as variant efforts of the mind to apprehend the same truth. Hence, the stuff of all myths is, collectively and indiscriminately, available to the mythopoeist for his task of compelling thoughts to their most nearly perfect structure. Indeed, directly after announcing to Peacock the completion of the first act of his mythopoeic drama and directly before his idiosyncratic interpretation of Artegall's giant, Shelley wrote that he could conceive of a "great work," not of poetry but of moral and political science, "embodying the discoveries of all ages, & harmonizing the contending creeds by which mankind have been ruled." For it is Shelley's assumption that if all creeds, or their mythic embodiments, were shaped into the highest form they admit, they would be precisely translatable into each other. Despite his modest disclaimer—'Far from me is such an attempt"— the syncretism of this "great work" is at the heart of *Prometheus Unbound*.

Moreover, given Shelley's interpretation of "thought," it follows that empirical science, folk science, legends, and all literature that has been

---

[37] *Defence of Poetry* (Julian, VII, 109).
[38] See Albert J. Kuhn, "English Deism and the Development of Romantic Mythological Syncretism," *PMLA*, 71 (1956), 1094–1116.

assimilated as an operative part of human culture are also mental configurations of thoughts that recognize the mental nature of "things"; they,
at least as much as conventional myths, are also permanently real in the
sense that supposedly objective things are not. Consequently, all these
thoughts, too, are among the materials for the poet's imagination to syn-
cretize and interlock into the most nearly perfect form. *Adonais*, for example, is not merely another variant of the Venus and Adonis myth; it
recasts that myth into a new and presumably true system of interrelationships, but it also organically integrates the reformed myth with the ancient
belief that souls derive from stars, with astronomy scientific and fabular,
with the science of optics, and with various traditional metaphors and
symbols, all of them having the same kind and degree of eternal reality
because they are the mind's conceptions, rather than perceptions, of things.
Myth so inclusively defined is not an assemblage of accepted fictional
terms supporting an accretion of rich connotations, as it was for Dryden
and Pope; nor merely a fiction that reveals truth better than facts; nor an
upsurging from the unconscious. Its components are indestructible and
eternal mental possessions. Consequently, however diverse and unrelated
their traditional contexts, they ask, like all other thoughts, to be interwoven into a beautiful whole "containing within itself the principle of its
own integrity." If the structures of given myths are already beautiful and
true, Shelley held, they are integral thoughts having "the power of attracting and assimilating to their own nature all other thoughts,"[39] and thus
any conventional myth so organized is inexhaustibly capable of rendering
truths for a poet by giving its shape to them. On the other hand, since
error, ugliness, and evil are but various modes of disorder, the task of the
imagination is also to reform erroneous, misshapen myths according to the
model of the mind's extraordinary apprehensions of perfect unity.

vi

Such a conception of myth and of the function of the imagination
entails an especially ambiguous relation between the traditional form of a
legend or myth and the poet's use of it, and demands of the reader an
equally ambiguous frame of mind. When, in his *Rape of the Lock*, Pope
calls Thalestris to Belinda's aid, the mere appearance of this queen of the
Amazons tacitly attaches to Belinda an unnatural displacement in the
sexual hierarchy, a belligerent rejection of men, and the Amazonian ideal
of a self-sufficient female society, just as Pope's casting Clarissa's advice
in the form of Sarpedon's speech seriocomically elevates that advice to
heroic stature and demands of Belinda quasi-heroic deeds. Through knowledge already in the reader's mind, traditional qualities and meanings out-

[39] *Defence of Poetry* (Julian, VII, 118).

side the poem attach themselves to elements in the poem. Or, for ironic purposes, the likening of Belinda's apotheosized lock to Berenice's evokes the reader's knowledge that Catullus' Berenice sacrificed her hair that her husband might be returned to her, and the clash between that intimated fact outside the poem and Belinda's rejection of the Baron within the poem is central to what the poem is saying. In either kind of instance, the established structures of the myths upon which Pope draws operate allusively in the poem, and the reader, when called upon, must bring them to bear so that they may perform upon the text their acts of supplying, amplifying, and complicating significances. But according to the implications of Shelley's theory, the myths that appear in his poetry, however traditional, are to be understood as really having no inherited contexts at all. As either actually or potentially true-beautiful organizations of thought, they are universal and eternal forms that become limited only insofar as they are thought of as specific myths; and any particular previous appearance of the myth is not a locus for literary allusion but merely another instance of the actual or potential archetypal form.

For example, the myth of Aurora, goddess of the dawn, and her union with the beautiful mortal, Tithonus, is recognizable behind Shelley's account of the creation of works of art:

And lovely apparitions, dim at first,
Then radiant, as the mind, arising bright
From the embrace of beauty, whence the forms
Of which these are the phantoms, casts on them
The gathered rays which are reality.   (III. iii. 49–53)

Yet in the more important sense the myth is not present at all behind the symbols of dawn and light, which are themselves adequate to incorporate the meaning; and although the myth does provide an additional propriety to the word "embrace," Shelley certainly does nothing to evoke the myth as an efficient reverberating echo. The Aurora myth is not to be understood as a particular narrative generally current in Western culture; it is the mind's composition of thoughts into an integral and self-sustaining thought that, because of its beauty and truth as a composition, has here assimilated to its own form another body of thoughts—or, rather, has given its form to a body of thoughts and thus lost its own special identity. Awareness of the myth will allow the reader to recognize the patterning source; and yet the end product of this recognition is, paradoxically, that he think as though no myth were present, but only the perfect archetypal arrangement, of which the story of Aurora and Tithonus is a limited instance. Of the same order is Shelley's adaptation of the legend of King Bladud, the mythical founder of Bath, who stumbled upon the curative hot springs when, a banished leper, he followed one of his afflicted swine, and whose dramatic return after his cure enraptured his mother.[40] Hate, fear, and pain, Shelley writes, are to

> Leave Man, even as a leprous child is left,
>   Who follows a sick beast to some warm cleft
> Of rocks, through which the might of healing springs is poured;
>   Then when it wanders home with rosy smile,
>   Unconscious, and its mother fears awhile
> It is a spirit, then, weeps on her child restored.   (IV. 388–93)

Although this is Bladud's legendary history in every detail, the poet's refusal to call it into conscious attention makes present only a beautiful pattern, not a special allusion. Nor in the following speech does Shelley borrow from *King Lear* the term "thought-executing" in order to call up some functional reaction between the plot of *Lear* and the relation of Jupiter to Prometheus, whose words these are:

>   Evil minds
> Change good to their own nature. I gave all
> He [Jupiter] has; and in return he chains me here
> Years, ages, night and day . . .
> Whilst my beloved race is trampled down
> By his thought-executing ministers.
> Such is the tyrant's recompense: 'tis just:
> He who is evil can receive no good;
> And for a world bestowed, or a friend lost,
> He can feel hate, fear, shame; not gratitude:
> He but requites me for his own misdeed.
> Kindness to such is keen reproach, which breaks
> With bitter stings the light sleep of Revenge.
> Submission, thou dost know I cannot try.[41]   (I. 380–95)

An interpretation of Lear's relation to his daughters is, I think, formally present and yet otherwise inoperative; it is present for the poet—and the critic—not for the "pure" reader that the play hypothesizes, who is to experience the work as though it is autonomous, not allusive. The assumption behind the creative act is that Shakespeare formed a beautiful and true arrangement of thoughts, and Shelley is fulfilling his doctrine that such mythic orderings are always capable of attracting other truths to their shape; but he is not engaging Shakespeare's play in his text to illuminate

[40] The allusion has been pointed out by G. M. Matthews, "Shelley's Grasp upon the Actual," *Essays in Criticism*, 4 (1954), 329. The legend is recorded in full in Richard Warner's *History of Bath* (Bath, 1801).
[41] The basis of this speech, but not of its form or thematic elaboration, is *Prometheus Bound* 223–27.

it or to complicate its meaning. These are, admittedly, extreme examples of Shelley's assimilation of myths as archetypal orderings, but they are symptomatic of his mythopoeic methods and indicate the paradoxical informed ignorance they demand for the most complete reading.

We have seen, however, that Shelley conceives of the poet as not merely an assimilator of beautiful mythic forms: inasmuch as he is creative, he is a mythopoeist, not by inventing myths, but by reconstituting the imperfect ones that already exist. His creations are "beautiful and new, not because the portions of which they are composed had no previous existence in the mind of man or in nature," but because of "the whole produced by their combination." Virgil was not an imitator of Homer, Shelley wrote in an unused passage of the Preface to *Prometheus Unbound*; "the (ideal) conceptions had been new modelled within his mind, they had been born again." [42] Indeed, just as Shelley held that all human minds are portions of the One Mind, so he believed that, because of the interconnection and interdependence of all poems, each is a fragment of, or partial movement toward, "that great poem, which all poets, like the co-operating thoughts of one great mind, have built up since the beginning of the world." [43] Evidence of his respect for this position is to be found not only in his resort to traditional materials but even in his refraining from forging new links to regroup and interrelate diverse myths; for his implicit assumption is that the true and beautiful relationships of wholeness already exist potentially in the qualities of the given materials, waiting to be properly drawn out. Consequently, he rather strictly confines himself to the inherent syntactical potentials, however minor or neglected they may be in the conventional myths, and his mythopoeic art lies especially in eliciting and exploiting these potentials to form new combinations.

Although the wife assigned to Prometheus by the traditional myth and by Aeschylus was the Oceanid Hesione, Shelley had authority in Herodotus for wedding him to Asia instead; and yet the substitution did not violate or sacrifice any of Hesione's characteristics, for according to Apollodorus, Hesiod, and other theogonists, Asia also was an Oceanid, born of Tethys and Oceanus. Shelley, therefore, could then invent two sisters for Asia—Panthea and Ione—and properly substitute them for Aeschylus' chorus of Oceanids. This mythologically legitimate substitution allows him to integrate into the body of his play what in Aeschylus is a dramatically separate group of commentators on the action, yet without losing the right to use Panthea and Ione as commentators. In addition, not only Asia's oceanic origin but also her quasi-geographic name, unlike Hesione's, opened the possibility of investing her with the character and symbolic values of the sea-born Aphrodite. Like the Oceanids, Aphrodite

[42] Zillman, p. 636, where "new" inaccurately reads "now."
[43] *Defence of Poetry* (Julian, VII, 124).

was born of the seminal sea; and, striking a mean between the Cytherean and the Cyprian waters whence, according to the two different traditions, Aphrodite arose, Shelley locates Asia's sea-birth near the land of her name, Asia Minor, and describes it in the conventional terms of that of Aphrodite Anadyomene:

> The Nereids tell
> That on the day when the clear hyaline
> Was cloven at thy uprise, and thou didst stand
> Within a veined shell, which floated on
> Over the calm floor of the crystal sea,
> Among the Egean isles, and by the shores
> Which bear thy name; love . . .
> Burst from thee. . . .   (II. v. 20–28)

Similarly, at the apocalyptic climax of the play, when Asia undergoes a second spiritual birth and again radiates the light of love, she is borne to Prometheus, as she was brought ashore on her first birth, in the shell which is Venus' symbol, now transformed into a chariot which is an "ivory shell inlaid with crimson fire" (II. iv. 156–57).

Mary Shelley, of course, was right to call Asia "the same as Venus,"[44] and Asia's Venus-like character is consistently sustained throughout the drama, for she is to perform a role somewhat like that of the Venus-Lady of *The Sensitive Plant*, who tends a garden like that of Adonis. The Platonic distinction between the heavenly and earthly Venuses customary in discussions of Shelley and justified by the plot of *Prince Athanase* seems quite beside the point here. Asia's nature is to radiate love, and her separation from Prometheus is the absence of love: "Most vain all hope but love; and thou art far, / Asia!" (I. 808–9). But there are no categories or levels of love in the poem, and Asia is the love divorced from the One Mind when it is enchained by its own dark tyrannical shadow, the love that can be reunited with the One Mind when it wills its own freedom. She is the ideal condition of Existence. But Existence, or the One Mind, is also the "living" spirit in that ideally it is the identity of perceiver and perception; and Shelley is everywhere inclined to conceive of life (in this ideal sense) and love—and light—as intimately related and nearly synonymous, animation being the luminous energy and joy of love. For example, Shelley writes of "one Spirit vast," the plastic force that "With life and love makes chaos ever new"; and Beatrice Cenci laments that she is cut off "from the only world I know, / From light, and life, and love."[45] Even

---

[44] Note to *Prometheus Unbound* (Julian, II, 269). No evidence, however, has been found to support her statement that this identification had been made by other mythologists; and her identification of Asia as "Nature" is not especially helpful, although that term does apply to the traditional Venus Genetrix.

[45] *Ode to Liberty*, 88–89; *Cenci*, V. iv. 85–86.

the reanimated spring vegetation, in "diffusing" its scent and color, is spending, "in love's delight, / The beauty and the joy" of its renewed vitality.[46] Hence the love that Asia radiates "like the atmosphere / Of the sun's fire filling the living world" (II. v. 26–27) is also a life-giving power; and Shelley can remain consistent with his mythic *données* because Venus —Lucretius' *alma Venus*—is also the generative or sustaining spirit like Asia, the Venus-Lady of *The Sensitive Plant*, and the Venus Urania of *Adonais*. Just as flowers burst into bloom and grass sprang up at the touch of Aphrodite's feet when she first walked on the shores,[47] so Asia's "footsteps pave the world / With loveliness" (II. i. 68–69), and her presence generates life in the barren Indian vale of her exile,

rugged once

And desolate and frozen . . . ;
But now invested with fair flowers and herbs,
And haunted by sweet airs and sounds, which flow
Among the woods and waters, from the ether
Of her transforming presence, which would fade
If it were mingled not with thine [Prometheus']. (I. 827–33)

For life-love is as dependent upon Mind for its existence as Earth is, and presumably the spirits of Prometheus and Asia, despite their separation, remain related through the agency of Panthea and Ione. It is, then, in accord with Asia's Venus-role that in the lyric concluding Act II this "Lamp of Earth" and "Child of Light" be addressed as "Life of Life" (II. v. 48), the love which is the essence of life and therefore of Existence; and that Prometheus speak of once "drinking life" from Asia's "loved eyes" (I. 123), since love's power is traditionally located in the light of the eyes. We can take literally the belief of Shelley's Rosalind that "life was love" and can understand why it is more than merely high praise that in Lionel, who is modeled on Shelley himself, "love and life . . . were twins, / Born at one birth . . . children of one mother."[48]

It is proper, therefore, that Asia make her first appearance in the drama at the opening of Act II with the very moment of the advent of the physico-spiritual spring, the moment of renovation made possible by the One Mind's retraction of the curse. For spring, and, more particularly, the month of April that introduces spring, was sacred to Venus as goddess of generation. The reanimating spring is a property of Asia's symbolic role as a condition of Mind; and because Venus was traditionally attended and prepared by the Hour (Hora) of spring,[49] it is consonant with the general structure of the conventional myth that at the end of Act II Asia ascend

---

[46] *Adonais*, 170–71. See also *Queen Mab*, VIII. 108; "When Passion's Trance," 15; *The Magnetic Lady to Her Patient*, 21.
[47] Hesiod *Theogony* 194; Lucretius i. 7ff. Compare *Adonais*, 208–16.
[48] *Rosalind and Helen*, 765, 622–25.
[49] For example, Pindar *Nemean* viii. 1; and *Homeric Hymn to Venus*.

from Demogorgon's realm in the chariot of that Hour who is a "young spirit" with "eyes of hope" (II. iv. 159–60) and that this same vernal Hour, "most desired" and "more loved and lovely / Than all thy sisters" (III. iii. 69–70), also be appointed to convey the destined renewal to the entire earth and to mortal man and so bring the Promethean action to its fulfillment.

The Spirit of the Earth who appears in Acts III and IV also derives from the network of interconnected myths introduced into the drama by the identification of Asia with Venus. For this winged child, patronizingly addressed as "wayward" and "wanton" and marked by suggestively sexual speech, performs in the poem's special context the role of Eros, or Cupid, son of Venus. Like the mythic Eros, to whom so many different parents were assigned that his ancestry was notoriously uncertain,[50] the Spirit of the Earth knows not "whence it sprung," although it addresses the Venus-like Asia as "Mother, dearest mother" (III. iv. 23–24). Related in this manner to Asia, "Lamp of Earth," "Child of Light," and personification of Love, from whose loved eyes Prometheus once drank life, the winged Spirit of the Earth, like the Eros from whom he derives, carries a torch and thereby becomes part of the symbolic complex of eyes, light, and love. "This is my torch-bearer," says Earth to Asia,

Who let his lamp out in old time with gazing
On eyes from which he kindled it anew
With love, which is as fire, sweet daughter mine,
For such is that within thine own.   (III. iii. 148–52)

This conceit further identifies the Spirit of the Earth with Eros; for when Tibullus wrote that fierce Love lights his twin torches from Sulpicia's eyes whenever he would inflame the gods, he gave birth to a persistent motif in the descriptions of the god of love.[51] As the son of Venus-Asia, therefore, the Eros-like Spirit is a derivative portion of love-life-light that in the final acts performs as the infused spirit of earth and there replaces Earth herself in the drama. First introduced by Earth as her "torch-bearer," he is instructed to guide the Promethean company to the destined cave, just as the classical Eros, whose torch was also kindled with "love, which is as fire," lighted lovers on the way to their union; and thereafter this Spirit "guides the earth thro' heaven" (III. iv. 7). This last transformation is especially apt, since the Intelligences that, according to Plato, move the heavenly spheres were converted by Platonized Christianity into angels, and the winged, torch-bearing, Eros-like Spirit of Earth easily lends him-

---

[50] For example, Plato *Symposium* 178; *Greek Anthology* v. 177.
[51] Tibullus iv. 2. 5–6. For some instances of Tibullus' conceit, see *The Elegies of Albius Tibullus*, ed. Kirby Flower Smith (New York, 1913), pp. 488–89, and M. B. Ogle, "The Classical Origin and Tradition of Literary Conceits," *American Journal of Philology*, 34 (1913), 133–35.

self to an identification with the traditional angelic guides of the spheres. Simply by drawing out and elaborating interrelations already latent in the given myths, Shelley has shaped a coherent and proportioned structure that embodies the interdependence of the One Mind and life-giving Love, and the bond between that all-embracing Love and the love that guides and is the joyous animating spirit of the earth: "L'Amor che move il sole e l'altre stelle."

This kind of tacit adaptation and restructuring of myths—nonreferential in that their meaning and value are not dependent upon or complicated by their previous forms of existence—is also at work in Earth's description of the cave to which Prometheus and Asia are forever to retire after their reunion (III. iii. 124–75). Beside this cave, says Earth, is a temple that once bore the name of Prometheus, where

> the emulous youths
> Bore to thy [Prometheus'] honour thro' the divine gloom
> The lamp which was thine emblem.

The controlling reference, E. B. Hungerford has pointed out, is to the lampadephoria, the torch race in which youths ran from the altar of Prometheus in the Academy to the Acropolis in Athens, the victory going to the first to arrive with his torch unextinguished.[52] The rather obvious possibility of likening this torch race to the course of life had already been exploited by Thomas Taylor, who identified the burning lamp, emblem of Prometheus the Fire-Bearer, with the rational soul and added:

This custom adopted by the Athenians, of running from the altar of Prometheus to the city with burning lamps, in which he alone was victorious whose lamp remained unextinguished in the race, was intended to signify that he is the true conqueror in the race of life, whose rational part is not extinguished, or, in other words, does not become dormant in the career.[53]

By rejecting the historical fact that the race was a relay, Shelley makes the symbolism entirely his own: the emulous racers are

> even as those
> Who bear the untransmitted torch of hope
> Into the grave, across the night of life,
> As thou [Prometheus] hast borne it most triumphantly
> To this far goal of Time. (III. iii. 170–74)

[52] Pausanias i. 30. Sophocles' mention of a brazen threshold into the underworld near the altar of Prometheus in the Academy near Colonus (*Oedipus at Colonus* 54–58) may have some bearing on Shelley's location of Prometheus' cave near his temple, as Hungerford suggests (*Shores of Darkness* [Cleveland, 1963], pp. 197–98).
[53] Pausanias, *The Description of Greece*, trans. Thomas Taylor (London, 1824), III, pp. 224–25. Shelley ordered Taylor's translation shortly after its original publication in 1817 (to Ollier, 24 July and 3 August 1817 [*Letters*, I, 548–49]).

The entire account of the cave and the journey to it, however, is in fact
a conflation of many myths and symbols, for if the Promethean racers are
like those mortals who, unassisted, carry hope through life to the grave,
the "far goal" of their mortal time, and if both are like Prometheus the
Torch-Bearer,[54] who has borne hope to that timeless perfection toward
which all time moves, then all are also like the Spirit of Earth, the Eros-
like "torch-bearer" whose mother is the "Lamp of Earth," whose own lamp
is kindled with love, and who has just been commanded by Earth to run
ahead like the torch-racers and guide the Promethean company to the
temple and the cave which is to be their timeless dwelling.

In addition, Earth describes the cave near Prometheus' temple in
terms that associate it with yet another place. In the destined cave, Earth
tells Prometheus,

<blockquote>
my spirit
Was panted forth in anguish whilst thy pain
Made my heart mad, and those who did inhale it
Became mad too, and built a temple there,
And spoke, and were oracular, and lured
The erring nations round to mutual war,
And faithless faith, such as Jove kept with thee;
Which breath now rises, as amongst tall weeds
A violet's exhalation, and it fills
With a serener light and crimson air
Intense, yet soft, the rocks and woods around;
        ... and it circles round,
Like the soft waving wings of noonday dreams,
Inspiring calm and happy thoughts, like mine,
Now thou art thus restored. This cave is thine.   (III. iii. 124–47)
</blockquote>

Earth's spirit therefore was first panted forth in a place that tradition
specified as the cave at Delphi, for legend tells that the first Delphic oracle
was the infernal deity Gaia, or Earth; and Shelley's history of Prometheus'
cavern is identical with the legendary history of the Delphic cavern. According to Diodorus Siculus,[55] the shepherds who first stumbled upon the
cave were overcome by the volcanic vapors, fell into prophetic frenzy, and
hurled themselves madly into the crater. How this destructive inspiration
bears upon Shelley's ethical doctrine must be explored later, but obviously
he has related it to the condition prevailing during Prometheus' captivity,

[54] Just as the shell is Venus' traditional emblem, the torch, as Shelley says and as
the title of Aeschylus' lost play makes clear, was the emblem of Prometheus, who
had stolen fire from the gods and given it to man. See, e.g., Euripides' *The Phoenician Maidens* 1121–22, where Prometheus is described as holding a torch; and
Philostratus' *Lives of the Sophists* xx: "Prometheus, torch-bearer and fire-carrier."
[55] xvi. 26.

the state of the "external" world being relative to that of the Mind whereby it exists. The Delphic prophetess who succeeded Gaia, many classical authors reported, was Themis, goddess of justice, or social harmony and peace,[56] so that it is quite proper that with the restoration of Prometheus the crimson vapor of the volcanic cavern inspires "calm and happy thoughts." Further, while some classical authors identified Themis as the daughter of Gaia, others, including Aeschylus, considered her the same as Earth;[57] and consequently Shelley does not at all distort the basic form of the myth when he describes the history of the cave as two successive stages of Earth's spiritual history. The same legend of the discovery of the Delphic cave also determines Panthea's picture of Demogorgon's oracular-volcanic cave, and it not only does so to analogous symbolic ends but also establishes thereby an important thematic relationship between Demogorgon's cave and Prometheus'. The portal to Demogorgon's cave is

Like a volcano's meteor-breathing chasm,
Whence the oracular vapour is hurled up
Which lonely men drink wandering in their youth,
And call truth, virtue, love, genius, or joy,
That maddening wine of life. . . .   (II. iii. 3–7)

The self-destructive frenzy of the shepherds who first inhaled the volcanic vapors of the prophetic Delphic cave is not only the mad "mutual war" of earlier, uncivilized mankind when Prometheus was enchained; it is also the chaotic revolutionary frenzy of every man when in his deluding enthusiastic and impatient youth he first experiences the oracular truth.

But throughout, the Delphic cave and its legendary history, like the traditional accounts of the Promethean torch race, have been completely assimilated into Shelley's poem. To say that the story of the Delphic oracle is present in the poem either immediately or by allusion would therefore

[56] For example, Aeschylus *Eumenides* 1–3. Abbé Banier claimed that *"Themis* is accounted only an allegorical Personage whose Name in the *Hebrew* Language imports *perfect* or *upright* . . ." (*The Mythology and Fables of the Ancients* [London, 1738], II, i, 7).

[57] *Prometheus Bound* 211–13: ". . . Themis, or Gaia (she has one form but many names) had foretold to me the way in which the future was fated to come to pass. . . ."

In his translation of *Prometheus Bound* Robert Potter wrote of Themis, "As she was the second prophetic power that held her oracular seat at Delphos, she was honoured as the goddess of Truth and Justice"; and in his note to lines 211–13 (quoted above), he added, ". . . Themis could not with propriety be called Gaia, this our poet mistook for Rhea. Gaia is the earth in its primitive uncultivated state, terra inculta; Rhea is the earth in its improved state of cultivation, tellus culta: and as from this culture property arose, Justice had here her office, to assign and protect this property, suum cuique: Themis therefore, as the goddess of Justice, might well have the appelation of Rhea" (*The Tragedies of Aeschylus* [2d ed.; London, 1779], I, 9n, 23n). The two stages Potter describes correspond closely to the two stages of Earth's oracle in Shelley's account.

be rather more than the truth. In some hypothetical pre-text, we may say, torch-bearing Eros, Prometheus the Torch-Bearer, the Promethean torch race, and the legendary history of the oracle have been interconnected into a harmonious whole by means of syntactical possibilities they truly possess and then have been divested of their specific particularities so that the whole may constitute an archetypal shape for a group of the poet's thoughts. What may be said to exist truly is the beautiful potential order implicit in the connective possibilities among Eros, Prometheus, oracle, and torch race; and Shelley's lines are to be understood as an effort to embody that archetypal order, while the traditional ancient myths and rituals are but disarrayed and distorted fragments of it, or arrangements less nearly perfect than they might be. Shelley's narrative and symbols presuppose, and are sustained by, the archetypal form, and their existence is not dependent upon reference to any of its preserved embodiments.

vii

Although Shelley's drama is to be thought of, ideally, as self-sufficient and independent of the heritage of the myths it has transformed and absorbed, and as autonomous in consequence of having totally assimilated those myths, nevertheless the poem also directs the reader to be conscious of the irony resulting from the clash between certain inherited materials and Shelley's transformations of them. In other words, I am suggesting that for a total reading the poem demands the coexistence of two contradictory states of mind. At one level the reader is to accept the various formulations in the play as nonreferential embodiments of archetypal arrangements and combinations, as though only Shelley's myth exists; at the other, conscious of the prior history of the myths, he is to experience the irony directed against the erroneous, evil, partial, imperfect, and distorted orderings that Shelley is reforming. The first level applies to the poem as an autonomous product, a self-sustaining myth in its own right, a "thought containing the principle of its own integrity"; the second, to the poem as a process, a calculated maneuver on the part of the poet to rectify the errors and imperfections of the past.

To this second level the reader is directed by the play's epigraph, the nature of which would be the only contradiction to the assertion that the meaning of the drama is not dependent upon allusions to external contexts, were it not that it stands before the drama proper, as though it were an instruction in how the play, at one level, is to be experienced. When Shelley recorded in his notebook[58] the line he adopted as his epigraph, "Audisne haec, Amphiarae, sub terram abdite?," he entitled it, "To the Ghost of Aeschylus," and that notation makes unquestionable the way in which it was to be applied to the drama. The line is one of the few

[58] MS e. 11, p. 115.

known fragments of Aeschylus' *Epigoni*, and therefore it is with considerable irony that Shelley has turned it back on its own author. But since the words, as Shelley knew,[59] have been preserved only by Cicero in an anecdote concerning some Stoics, it becomes important also to be aware of its Ciceronian context. Cicero's disputation is on the subject of suffering pain and argues for self-mastery, the domination of the lower faculties by the higher, and the enduring of pain for the sake of reason and virtue. Pain is of such trifling importance, he writes, that it is eclipsed by virtue so completely as to be nowhere visible.[60] After quoting from Aeschylus' lost *Prometheus Unbound* to illustrate the suffering of pain as it was endured by Prometheus, Cicero then tells the story of Dionysius of Heraclea, who, having been taught by the Stoic master Zeno that pain is not an evil, rejected the doctrine when he found he could no longer endure physical suffering. Thereupon, Cicero records, Dionysius' fellow Stoic, Cleanthes, lamenting the moral failure, stamped upon the ground and addressed the dead Zeno by reciting Aeschylus' question that Shelley used as his epigraph: "Do you hear this, Amphiaraus, hidden away under the earth?" In the history of philosophy, moreover, Dionysius became notorious for embracing Epicureanism upon his apostasy from Stoicism and was known contemptuously as the "Turncoat," or "Renegade" (Μεταθέμενος).[61]

By borrowing the line, Shelley, a latter-day Cleanthes, is similarly lamenting that the stoically resisting Prometheus of Aeschylus' *Prometheus Bound* was to become, in his terms, the weak, hedonistic apostate of the lost sequel who could not tolerate pain for the sake of his principles and submitted at last to tyrannical Jupiter.[62] At the same time, instead of asking Stoic Zeno to hear of Epicurean Dionysius, the epigraph addresses the ghost of Aeschylus, who had allowed his Prometheus to recant, and in effect asks it to hear Shelley's entire reorganization of the myth, in which the patiently suffering Titan will resist tyranny by never weakening. Readdressing Aeschylus' line to its own author announces the ironic interplay that will take place between Shelley's drama and Aeschylus', so that while Shelley's is self-sustaining and independent of Aeschylus' for its form and significance as a work of art, it nevertheless calls upon the

[59] In his notebook, beneath the quotation, Shelley records, "Epigon. Aesch. ad Cic[?]." The reference is to *Tusculan Disputations* ii. 60.

[60] *Tusculan Disputations* ii. 66.

[61] For example, Diogenes Laertius *Lives of Eminent Philosophers* vii. 166–67.

Without indicating that he is adapting Dionysius' history, Byron made mocking use of it in a letter to R. C. Dallas, 21 January 1808, applying the anecdote to himself. Apparently it was well known to schoolboys.

[62] Preface to *Prometheus Unbound*: "... I was averse from a catastrophe so feeble as that of reconciling the Champion with the Oppressor of mankind. The moral interest of the fable, which is so powerfully sustained by the sufferings and endurance of Prometheus, would be annihilated if we could conceive of him as unsaying his high language and quailing before his successful and perfidious adversary."

reader to contemplate what is being repudiated by the ironic workings of art. Shelley's unresolved skeptical ambivalence in such poems as *Alastor* and *Julian and Maddalo*, we have seen, was convertible, with the aid of his doctrine of the imagination and the passivity of belief, into the mode of *The Sensitive Plant* and *Mont Blanc*, which tentatively elect one side of the ambiguity rather than the other, as Shelley discovers a means of raising his skepticism to a probabilism. But inherent in all these modes there has been an ironic factor: the unintentional subversion of their own positions by Julian and by the Christian of the *Refutation of Deism*; the ironic similarity of the Narrator and Visionary of *Alastor*, and the Narrator's eventual undermining of his own doctrine; the ironic reversal in "Lift not the Painted Veil"; the opposition of the fable and the symbolism of *The Sensitive Plant*; the simultaneous dissolution and permanence of the Cloud, and the similar ambivalence of many other such images. The irony in the skeptic's antinomical vision naturally leans toward something like the assertiveness of satire, and in *Prometheus Unbound* Shelley has built his drama on a satiric destruction of Aeschylus'—indeed, given his lack of first principles, he can construct only by destroying a contrary.

The general ironic relationship between the two plays is too obvious and Shelley's "borrowings" have been elaborated too frequently to justify repetition here.[63] Broadly, his procedure is to draw heavily on Aeschylus' play but to reassign the "borrowings" and re-establish them in a contrary ethical and theological context so as to transform their meanings radically. Shelley retained as part of the machinery of his drama remarkably many of Aeschylus' details, such as the temptation of Prometheus by Mercury, Prometheus' invocation of the elements, and the catastrophic effects wrought on the natural world by Prometheus' defiance, to say nothing of a host of minor details and phrases. But whereas Aeschylus' play deals with the original binding of Prometheus, Shelley adapted all these events to a much later moment in time so as to apply them to Prometheus' eventual unbinding. That is, although his play appears to be the sequel to Aeschylus' *Prometheus Bound*, by recasting a great many of Aeschylus' details and speeches he implies that had the Greek dramatist not misshapen his myth and hence enslaved Prometheus, he could have cast the very same materials into their true unifying form and thus liberated and restored the Titan. In this sense, Shelley has not so much written a counter-myth as allowed Aeschylus' version of the myth to destroy itself, in accordance with his customary hypothesis that error and ugliness, if not willfully sustained, are ultimately self-defeating.

As an example of this Actaeon-like technique of turning a myth upon itself, we may take Apollo's report of Jupiter's fall, which he likens

[63] See, among others, *Prometheus Unbound*, ed. Vida D. Scudder (Boston, 1909), pp. 121–42; and Shelley, *Poems Published in 1820*, ed. A. M. D. Hughes (2d ed.; Oxford, 1957), pp. 191–215.

to the destruction of an eagle. Although traditionally supposed to be re-markable for its ability to gaze on what is, to it, "the undazzling sun,"[64] the metaphoric eagle has now been "blinded / By the white lightning" and plummets from the sky (III. ii. 11–17). But the eagle, of course, is the bird of Jupiter and serves here, by way of the metonymy wryly mas-querading as a simile, as the god's surrogate. The lightning with which it is blinded is Jupiter's traditional weapon, and yet not only was the eagle the bearer and minister of Jupiter's lightning in the established myth but the tradition of unnatural natural history taught that the eagle was there-fore impervious to its blinding light and could not be harmed by it.[65] Shelley has not merely denied the legend of the eagle, he causes it to contradict itself because Jupiter, like all forms of evil, error, and ugliness, wields a power which is only mistakenly thought to be a fearsome weapon against others and is fundamentally suicidal. This reflexive kind of irony is the central mode of representing evil throughout the drama, and cor-respondingly the irony of turning the line from Aeschylus' *Epigoni* back on its own author is of a piece with that of asking Aeschylus to hear the play he might have made of his materials had he known the true, the good, and the beautiful. Mainly by such a series of inversions, Shelley has created the beautiful harmony that is potential in Aeschylus' materials, rather than invented the sequel.

Aeschylus' Zeus is admittedly arbitrary and tyrannical, but we are told that he is new to his reign and can be expected to soften (49–51, 189–95); Shelley seizes only on the admission of tyranny, and his phi-losophy can allow the "immedicable plague" no mitigation. According to Aeschylus' theology only Zeus, within the limitations of Necessity, can possess complete freedom (49–50); but for Shelley only mind can be free, and to grant freedom to Zeus would be precisely the means of instituting absolute tyranny (I. 273–74, II. iv. 45–49). For Aeschylus, Prometheus' sin was not only defiance of Zeus's sovereignty but also an excessive love of mankind that led him to transfer to them powers beyond their due (122–23, 29–30); for Shelley, of course, all power in this sense lies in the human spirit, which is where he locates divinity, and man's essential sin is to relinquish any of that power. Shelley assigns to man what Aeschylus assigns to the anthropomorphic deity. And for Aeschylus' arbitrary fore-dooming Necessity, which is superior to Zeus and is determined by the Fates and Furies (514–18), Shelley has substituted the inherent Necessity whereby an effect follows regularly from a given cause.

Consequently, when segments of Aeschylus' play are specifically re-peated in this quite contradictory context, blasphemy and righteousness often exchange places, and Shelley's text mocks the Aeschylean errors

---

[64] Shelley first wrote, "gazed undazzled on the sun" (MS e. 12, p. 37).
[65] E.g., Pliny *Natural History* ii. 55, x. 3; Apuleius *Florides* ii; Horace *Odes* iv. 4. 1; Ovid *Fasti* v. 732.

from which it derives. Occasionally it is sufficient for Shelley to display as true and good what Aeschylus offers as error and pride, such as Prometheus' defiant denunciation of Zeus for requiting him with imprisonment for his aid in the Titanomachy: "Such profit did the tyrant of heaven have of me and with such foul return as this did he make requital; for it is a disease that somehow inheres in tyranny to have no faith in friends."[66] Shelley sometimes modifies or alters an appropriated passage or detail,[67] for he must reject such a speech as Prometheus' answer to the Chorus' question, "Is there no end assigned thee of thine ordeal?": "Nay, none save when it seemeth good to Zeus." Although Aeschylus provides that even if Zeus does not soften and release Prometheus, the Titan is foredoomed by the decrees of Necessity, Shelley cannot leave any room for the efficacy of Zeus's tyrannical capriciousness and allows only the inherent law of Necessity. To the analogous question, "Thou knowest not the period of Jove's power?" his Prometheus therefore replies: "I know but this, that it must come" (I. 413). On still other occasions Shelley can effect an irony simply by reassigning an Aeschylean passage so that the relocation helps shape what he holds to be the truest and most beautiful arrangement of which the materials are capable. For example, Hephaestus explains to Aeschylus' Prometheus that each relief from agony will be but another torment, in an endless cycle:

... scorched by the sun's bright beams, thou shalt lose the fair bloom of thy flesh. And glad shalt thou be when spangled-robed night shall veil his brightness and when the sun shall scatter again the rime of morn. Evermore the burthen of thy present ill shall wear thee out; for thy deliverer is not yet born.[68]

Shelley reassigns this speech to Prometheus, so that what in Aeschylus is a threat to the Titan of endless pain becomes the Titan's triumphant stoic defiance of pain through faith in the inevitable workings of Necessity:

And yet to me welcome is day and night,
Whether one breaks the hoar frost of the morn,
Or starry, dim, and slow, the other climbs
The leaden-coloured east; for then they lead

[66] 223–27. Compare *Prometheus Unbound*, I. 380–94 and II. iv. 47–48.
[67] For example, by assigning to Aeschylus' cruel Hermes the beneficent character with which Aeschylus had endowed Hephaestus, Shelley has transformed him into the sympathetic Mercury who carries out Jupiter's revenge reluctantly and hates himself for his weak subservience, since Shelley's thesis is that slavery and self-contempt, or failure to value the powers of one's self, are causally related (see I. 352–60). Mercury's analogue is Cardinal Camillo of *The Cenci*, who strives for "blameless neutrality"—that is, weakly consents to the reigning oppression and strives to reconcile his beneficence to it. He admires Beatrice's character and yet reluctantly but subserviently carries out the Jupiter-like Pope's merciless, tyrannic orders.
[68] *Prometheus Bound* 23–27.

The wingless, crawling hours, one among whom
—As some dark Priest hales the reluctant victim—
Shall drag thee, cruel King, to kiss the blood
From these pale feet, which then might trample thee
If they disdained not such a prostrate slave.   (I. 44–52)

One crucial and radical transformation, however, calls for special examination. According to the conventional myth, Prometheus ultimately
revealed to Jupiter the secret that his marriage to Thetis would produce
a son who would surpass and overthrow his father, and thereby he both
prevented the marriage and bought his own release. By sacrificing his
secret knowledge of the contingent decree of Fate, Prometheus humbled
himself to Jupiter and assured Jupiter's supremacy. This sequence of
events, so abhorrent to Shelley because it represented that voluntary enslavement that he considered both the cause and guarantee of all-powerful
tyranny, he undermined by a complex system of inversions that at every
point radically reconstitute the myth without ever abandoning its traditional elements or interpolating others. Shelley's Prometheus also possesses
a secret known "to none else of living things, / Which may transfer the
sceptre of wide Heaven" (I. 372–73), a secret that Mercury urges him in
vain to clothe in words and offer up in submission to Jupiter; but Shelley's
Jupiter is already wedded to Thetis and in Act III awaits the incarnation
of their offspring. Moreover, it is significant that in Shelley's play the
substance of the secret is never specified, nor is it ever connected with
Jupiter's marriage to Thetis, even though the absence of any other dependence of the play on Aeschylus' for basic meanings would seem to require that the secret be defined explicitly. Certainly there is no other
ellipsis in the play that must be filled in by reference to Aeschylus. The
secret of Shelley's Prometheus, then, cannot be the traditional one. If it
were, certainly Jupiter could not already have wedded Thetis, and Prometheus could not be ignorant of "the period of Jove's power"; it would
come whenever Jupiter's offspring deprives him of his throne, since
Shelley's Prometheus, unlike Aeschylus', does not intend to divulge the
secret to Jupiter. More important, the traditional secret, even though Prometheus were never to reveal it, implies that Jupiter could have been
responsible for his own destruction or preservation by either marrying or
eschewing Thetis, and this would deny that the moral burden is entirely
Prometheus', to say nothing of the triviality of resting the duration of
Jupiter's tyranny upon his union with Thetis. Shelley must place the
moral burden entirely on Prometheus, and hence the "secret" has no
specific content. Prometheus' refusal has no causal relation, even indirectly,
to Jupiter's marriage, but is the general symbol of his refusal to abdicate
his will to Jupiter. For divulging the mind's "secret" is, according to
Shelley's symbolism, essentially the act everyone performs in religious

obeisance to a deity: "bend thy soul in prayer," Mercury begs when pleading that Prometheus offer up his secret,

And like a suppliant in some gorgeous fane,
Let the will kneel within thy haughty heart:
For benefits and meek submission tame
The fiercest and the mightiest.   (I. 377–80)

Prometheus has already constituted Jupiter by yielding to him power
over all things but himself and his will, and, as Prometheus adds, what
further submission remains but that "fatal word," the fateful "secret"
which symbolizes Prometheus' will (I. 396)? Jupiter is to fall, not, as the
Aeschylean myth would permit, simply because he produced an offspring
mightier than himself, but because Prometheus refuses that final abandonment of power over his own will that would be implicit in yielding up
what is secret in him. Indeed, Shelley's play in no way provides for the
possibility that Jupiter could have prevented his fall by avoiding Thetis;
the causal chain stretches back from Demogorgon to Asia and to Prometheus' repenting of his curse and his refusal to submit by revealing any
"secret." What Shelley has retained of this portion of Aeschylus' myth,
therefore, is not the traditional explanation of the course of events; he has
transformed that into a mere illusion entertained by Jupiter alone. Deprived of omnipotence by Prometheus' retention of his will, Jupiter, under
the illusion that by marriage to Thetis he can propagate his own omnipotent perpetuity, finds himself, in ironic fact, confronted by the force
that will undo him.

In effect, the conventional myth not only is being readjusted to
Shelley's philosophy but is being elaborately parodied. Fancying that his
offspring by Thetis has already been begotten and floats unbodied and
unbeheld, "Waiting the incarnation" (III. i. 46), Jupiter expects it to
be embodied when "the destined Hour" arrives (III. i. 20). It will bear,
he claims,

from Demogorgon's vacant throne
The dreadful might of ever-living limbs
Which clothed that awful spirit unbeheld   (III. i. 21–23)

to trample out man's rebellious spirit. But of course Demogorgon's throne
is not vacant—at least not in the sense that Demogorgon no longer exists—
as Jupiter in his blinding pride believes. Nor is Demogorgon an *embodied*
spirit. "I see a mighty darkness," says Panthea of Demogorgon,

Filling the seat of power, and rays of gloom
Dart round, as light from the meridian sun,

Ungazed upon and shapeless; neither limb,
Nor form, nor outline; yet we feel it is
A living Spirit.   (II. iv. 2–7)

But anthropomorphic Jupiter, whose very nature is distortion, cannot understand that Demogorgon is the unembodied eternal cause, the primal power infinitely remote from all that is embodied, not a destructible being whose might is the "might of ever-living limbs." Religious and political tyranny, perverting every truth, imagines that power rests in the embodiment, the institution, not in that which is beyond all form because it is outside Existence, or Mind, and absolutely different from it. In supposing that the unknowable Power can be incorporated in palpable human form, Jupiter not only has fallen into the ontological error of making power an attribute of existence, but in fact is fabricating that anthropomorphism on which superstitious theologies are founded; or, as Shelley described the process in his notes to *Queen Mab*,

It is probable that the word God was originally only an expression denoting the unknown cause of the known events which men perceived in the universe. By the vulgar mistake of a metaphor for a real being, of a word for a thing, it became a man, endowed with human qualities and governing the universe as an earthly monarch governs his kingdom.[69]

There is, then, no "fatal child" at all. The myth of Jupiter, Thetis, and their offspring is present only to be parodied, not to be understood as the content of Prometheus' secret. While Jupiter falsely expects the ever-living limbs of Demogorgon to incarnate the evil that he himself is, ironically it is Demogorgon himself who appears, not to "trample out the spark" of man's spirit (III. i. 24) but to descend with Jupiter into inactive potentiality. Certainly Demogorgon, who is eternal, has not been begotten or caused by Jupiter in any sense; Jupiter's "child" is his misconception. Nor has Jupiter ever been responsible for stirring Demogorgon out of potentiality into action; this has been the effect of Asia as a consequence of Prometheus' retraction of his curse. Demogorgon, then, can say to Jupiter, "I am thy child, as thou wert Saturn's child; / Mightier than thee" (III. i. 54–55) only in the sense that each has displaced his predecessor and is greater in power; and the word "child" in this sense carries an immense weight of irony in view of Jupiter's expectations. Although tyranny and falsehood "beget" their own destruction, the conventional myth, we are to understand, is wrong in predicating that, as Shelley's Jupiter assumes, they can generate their own perpetuity.

Indeed, the union of Jupiter and Thetis is not, as Jupiter believes, a fertile mingling of "Two mighty spirits" productive of a third (III. i. 43);

[69] *Queen Mab*, VI. 198n.

it is a sterile rape. In accordance with his methods of reforming the inherited myths, Shelley has called upon Jupiter's traditional character as
rapist and has transferred to him the violation of Thetis that, according
to the myth, was performed by Peleus after Jupiter had been warned to
avoid her.[70] As described by Shelley, Jupiter's rape of Thetis is to true
union what tyranny is to equality and love; and because Jupiter is but
the insubstantial, distorted reflection of Prometheus, it is presented as a
gruesome parody of the love-union of Prometheus and Asia. Knowing that
all hope is vain but love, Prometheus, in a passage that not only is implicitly sexual[71] but also has eucharistic overtones, had lamented his
division from Asia,

> who, when my being overflowed,
> Wert like a golden chalice to bright wine
> Which else had sunk into the thirsty dust.   (I. 809–11)

With acute insight into the tyrannic mentality, Shelley now has Jupiter
describe to Thetis their "mingling" through "the desire which makes thee
one with me," recalling with satisfaction that in the deed

> thou didst cry, "Insufferable might!
> "God! Spare me! I sustain not the quick flames,
> "The penetrating presence; all my being,
> "Like him whom the Numidian seps did thaw
> "Into a dew with poison, is dissolved,
> "Sinking thro' its foundations."   (III. i. 37–42)

Shelley has transferred to Thetis the fate met by Semele, who in return
for Jupiter's embrace begged that he appear to her in the full splendor of
his godhead and so was destroyed by his flames. "Her mortal body bore
not the onrush of heavenly power, and by that gift of wedlock she was
consumed."[72] Such, Shelley would have us understand, is the embrace
of tyranny's power. Moreover, in echoing Lucan's description of Sabellus'
physical dissolution by the seps's poison,[73] Thetis is crying out against the
corruptive annihilation of her body by that supreme evil beneath which,

---

[70] Ovid *Metamorphoses* xi. 229–65.
[71] In MS e. 11, p. 52, Shelley wrote, possibly but not necessarily with reference to
Prometheus Unbound: "In the human world one of the commonest expressions of
love is sexual intercourse, & in describing the deepest effects of abstract love the
author could not avoid the danger of exciting some ideas connected with this mode
of expression, & he has exposed himself to the danger of awakening ludicrous or un-
authorized images; but in obedience to an impulse. . . ." See also *A Discourse on the
Manners of the Ancient Greeks Related to the Subject of Love.* Also see above,
pp. 23–24.
[72] Ovid *Metamorphoses* iii. 308–9.
[73] Lucan *Pharsalia* ix. 762–88.

if it were omnipotent, even the earth would vanish like thin mist (I. 115–16); and yet it is this that tyrannical power, knowing "nor faith, nor love, nor law" (II. iv. 47) and ignorant of the union of equals through love, conceives of as the act "which makes thee one with me" and gives birth to a third. It is by a further misconception that Jupiter thinks Thetis the "bright image of eternity" (III. i. 36) who will bear him the power that will make his tyranny everlasting. Hence the cutting irony that Demogorgon, who will unseat him, should now appear as his "child" and announce that among his various roles *he* is Eternity (III. i. 52)—not, as Jupiter expects, unending time, but the timelessness out of which time flows.[74]

viii

To adopt the Aeschylean myth in this fashion, and yet to subvert it, is to accept the ideal potentialities of the Prometheus story and yet to reject, through irony, Aeschylus' formulation and interpretation of it. In other words, Shelley's conception of the difference between the potential Prometheus and the received myth is of a piece with his view of the difference between the life and doctrines of Christ and the Church's perversion of them for the purpose of fabricating an institutional religion presided over by a tyrannical and arbitrary deity. Consequently, just as the first three acts both echo and transform *Prometheus Bound*, one major stratum of the first act and some passages elsewhere derive in similar fashion from Scripture. Even apart from those moments when the life and figure of Christ enter into the main events of the first two acts, muted adaptations of Scripture sporadically renew the quasi-Biblical tone. The horrors brought about by Prometheus' enchainment, for example, tend to suggest the plagues visited upon the Egyptians for confining the Israelites in another kind of tyrannical bondage:

Lightning and Inundation vexed the plains;
Blue thistles bloomed in cities; foodless toads
Within voluptuous chambers panting crawled: [75]
When Plague had fallen on man, and beast, and worm,
And Famine; and black blight on herb and tree.   (I. 169–73)

Similarly, the miracle of Christ's walking on the waters, being one of those ideal orderings having "the power of attracting and assimilating to their

[74] For Demogorgon as the timeless potentiality of time, see pp. 370–73. In being described as the "image of eternity," Thetis is undoubtedly meant to represent endless duration. Note that Shelley first wrote, "Shadow of eternity" (Zillman, p. 228n.), and compare II. iv. 33–34 ("Saturn, from whose throne / Time fell, an envious shadow") and *Timaeus* 37d.
[75] Compare Exod. 8:3.

own nature all other thoughts," can give perfect form to an expression of the spiritual effect of music:

And music lifted up the listening spirit[76]
Until it walked, exempt from mortal care,
Godlike, o'er the clear billows of sweet sound,   (II. iv. 77–79)

or to the ideal conclusion of Asia's backward journey over the symbolic waters from Age through Birth to a "diviner" region where "shapes ... walk upon the sea, and chaunt melodiously!" (II. v. 108–10).

On the other hand, a scriptural phrase wrenched out of context not only rejects Christian theology but, readapted to a wholly different context, constitutes a contrary vision. Hence Asia, upon describing the creative use man has made of Prometheus' gifts, asks,

but who rains down
Evil, the immedicable plague, . . . while
Man looks on his creation like a God
And sees that it is glorious . . . ?   (II. iv. 100–2)

For Shelley there is no supernatural Creator who looked on his creation and "saw that it was good"; in his homocentric theology only man's mind can be the source of the harmony and order that "create" the universe, the arts, and sciences. "All things exist," Shelley insisted, "as they are perceived—at least in relation to the percipient. 'The mind is its own place, and of itself can make a Heaven of Hell, a Hell of Heaven.'"[77] Nor is it the Christian God of the Apocalypse who dispels the first heaven and earth and sea to create a new heaven and a new earth.[78] In Shelley's concluding act this is exclusively the creative work of the powers of the human mind; indeed, while the Jehovah-like Jupiter existed, there could not be a heaven at all, so that the mind's powers must "build a new earth and sea, / And a heaven where yet heaven could never be" (IV. 164–65). At this seemingly apocalyptic moment at the end of the play, moreover, it is not God's angel who sets a seal upon the bottomless pit into which the serpent Satan has been cast and from which he will be loosed after a thousand years;[79] Shelley's serpent is not the supernatural power of evil, but the hieroglyphic serpent of temporal change, and its suppression is the work of the human powers of "Gentleness, Virtue, Wisdom, and Endurance,"

[76] On seeing Jesus "walking on the sea," the disciples thought him a "spirit" (Matt. 14:26).
[77] *Defence of Poetry* (Julian, VII, 137).
[78] Rev. 21:1.
[79] Rev. 20:1–3, 7.

> the seals of that most firm assurance
> Which bars the pit over Destruction's strength;
> And if, with infirm hand, Eternity,
> Mother of many acts and hours, should free
> The serpent that would clasp her with his length;
> These are the spells by which to re-assume
> An empire o'er the disentangled doom.   (IV. 562–69)

But the primary function of the scriptural stratum of the play is to redefine and universalize Aeschylus' Prometheus by assimilating into his character both a modification of Milton's Satan and a strictly Shelleyan interpretation of Christ. In neither of these collations was Shelley especially original: the traditional Prometheus is clearly open to interpretation as either the suffering benefactor of mankind or the Satanic rebel against the Deity.[80] Only Shelley's brand of religion and ethics, however, could make possible the fusion of all three figures. As Shelley interpreted *Paradise Lost* in his *Defence of Poetry*, Milton subtly intended that we recognize his "Devil as a moral being...far superior to his God." Attributing to Milton his own abhorrence of explicitly didactic poetry, Shelley detected in Milton's having alleged "no superiority of moral virtue to his God over his Devil" not only a violation of "the popular creed" but also a "bold neglect of a direct moral purpose" that is "the most decisive proof of the supremacy of Milton's genius," presumably because it leaves the reader free, like the reader of *The Cenci*, to recognize with his own moral sympathies and antipathies that *Paradise Lost* "contains within itself a philosophical refutation of that system of which, by a strange and natural antithesis, it has been a chief popular support." In these terms, Milton's God, like Jupiter or Count Cenci, is a tyrant "who in the cold security of undoubted triumph inflicts the most horrible revenge upon his enemy, not from any mistaken notion of inducing him to repent of a perseverance in enmity but with the alleged design of exasperating him to deserve new torments." Satan shares with Milton's God the evils of "Implacable hate, patient cunning, and a sleepless refinement of device to inflict the extremest anguish" on his opponent, but these are venial evils in one who, like Beatrice Cenci, is subjected to enslaving torture, whereas they are indefensible in the unoppressed tyrant. Satan's moral magnificence lies in his perseverance in a "purpose which he has conceived to be excellent in spite of adversity and torture,"[81] and therefore, Shelley added in the

---

[80] See Raymond Trousson, *Le thème de Prométhée dans la littérature européenne* (Geneva, 1964). Both Alexander Ross (*Mystagogus poeticus* [London, 1647]) and d'Holbach (*Histoire critique de Jésus-Christ* [Amsterdam?, 1770?]), for example, had identified Prometheus with Christ.

[81] *Defence of Poetry* (Julian, VII, 129–30). The same passage appears also in the *Essay on the Devil and Devils* (Julian, VII, 91). Godwin had elaborated a similar interpretation of Milton's Satan in *Political Justice*, ed. F. E. L. Priestley (Toronto, 1946), I, pp. 323–24.

Preface to his lyric drama, he shares with Prometheus "courage, and majesty, and firm and patient opposition to omnipotent force." But Prometheus is the "more poetical character" because, unlike Satan, "he is susceptible of being described as exempt from the taints of ambition, envy, revenge, and a desire for personal aggrandisement." Satan therefore engenders in us the "pernicious casuistry" of seeking to justify the evil in the light of his unjustified oppression and is the model for a tragic Beatrice Cenci, who sought revenge to maintain her own dignity and the repute of her family.

Such a reading of *Paradise Lost* leaves Shelley free to identify Milton's God with tyrannic Jupiter and either to evoke Satan in Prometheus before the curse is retracted or to imply a purified Satan in Prometheus thereafter. The Prometheus who, "with a calm, fixed mind," defied Jupiter and all he could inflict (I. 262–63) is recognizable as the Satan who, with "fixt mind / And high disdain, from sense of injur'd merit," defied "what the Potent Victor in his rage / Can else inflict";[82] and Prometheus' curse on Jupiter,

Heap on thy soul, by virtue of this Curse,
Ill deeds; then be thou damned, beholding good,   (I. 292–93)

being evil, echoes by an ironic inversion God's punishment of Satan:

That with reiterated crimes he might
Heap on himself damnation, while he sought
Evil to others, and enrag'd might see
How all his malice serv'd but to bring forth
Infinite goodness.[83]

Both Prometheus and Satan refuse "To bow and sue for grace / With suppliant knee, and deify [the Deity's] power";[84] and Prometheus' determination,

Submission thou dost know I cannot try.
For what submission but that fatal word. . . .
. . . Which yet I will not yield,   (I. 395–400)

asks us to recall Satan's refusal,

                    . . . is there no place
Left for Repentance, none for Pardon left?
None left but by submission; and that word
Disdain forbids me. . . .[85]

[82] *Paradise Lost*, I. 95–98.
[83] *Paradise Lost*, I. 214–18. For this and other Miltonic echoes, see Frederick L. Jones, "Shelley and Milton," *SP*, 49 (1952), 500–4.
[84] *Paradise Lost*, I. 111–12.
[85] *Ibid*., IV. 79–82.

But Shelley's transformation of Milton's Satan and assimilation of him into Prometheus does not rest merely on verbal parallels, which primarily call upon the reader to be aware of how broadly Prometheus' role is Satan's and how heroic is their resistance to a tyrannical deity. The shock lies not only in Shelley's construction of a Satanic hero but also in the fact that the Prometheus who is the unrelenting Satanic rebel against God is also the mild and suffering Christ—but a Christ whom Shelley has purified from the perversions of Scripture.

Just as Shelley's Prometheus has transmitted wisdom and power to a fictional Jupiter who, requiting good with evil, has turned these virtuous gifts against Prometheus and man, so, in Shelley's view, institutional Christianity has appropriated the virtuous life and doctrines of Christ and, by identifying them with a terrible and dictatorial God, has turned them into a despotism. Evil minds change good to their own nature and recompense virtuous gifts by enchaining the donor.

The sublime human character of Jesus Christ was deformed by an imputed identification with a Power, who tempted, betrayed, and punished the innocent beings who were called into existence by His sole will; and for the period of a thousand years, the spirit of this most just, wise, and benevolent of men has been propitiated with myriads of hecatombs of those who approached the nearest to His innocence and wisdom, sacrificed under every aggravation of atrocity and variety of torture.[86]

"The wise, the mild, the lofty, and the just," Prometheus says to the image of Christ, "thy slaves hate for being like to thee" (I. 605–6); but the relation he is drawing between Christ and enslaved Christians is also that between himself and Jupiter, who, when Prometheus cursed him, "trembled like a slave" (II. iv. 108). By identifying Christ with a hypothetically transcendent and punitive God, the Church transformed good into evil and became its slave, hating the good it had transformed; by accepting Prometheus' virtuous gifts of mental powers and transforming them into instruments of vengeance and suppression, Jupiter has become their slave, hating both the virtuous Titan from whom he received them and the race of mankind which is "like" the Titan. Both Jupiter and organized Christianity, the great tyrants, are slaves because "All spirits are enslaved which serve things evil" (II. iv. 110).

On the basis of these analogies Shelley's first act elaborately identifies Prometheus with Christ, and throughout the drama institutional Christianity is repudiated by being ironically inverted, as Shelley has inverted the Prometheus myth of Aeschylus. The syncretic assimilation of Christ (and Satan) to Prometheus obliterates the specificity of the two myths to form the archetypal pattern, and although Christ is vividly recognizable by his description, nowhere is he specifically named, not only because "Thy name I will not speak, / It hath become a curse" (I. 603–4), but

[86] *Hellas*, 1090–91n.

also because it would limit his reference. Prometheus absorbs Christ, as he does Satan, because they are manifestations of the same pattern of truth, and when he is forced by the Furies to look at the figure of Christ on the Cross he is really seeing himself. "Nailed" to the rock (I. 20) and pierced by the "spears"[87] of the glaciers (I. 31), Prometheus is in the posture of the crucified Christ. Shelley's hero is the identity of both these pre-eminent types of superhuman and self-sacrificing resistance to evil, al-though it is part of the bitter irony of the inverted Christianity throughout the play that Shelley means the Jupiter who has crucified Prometheus to represent the God of whom the New Testament Christ is the incarnate son, and for whose redemption of man Christ endured the Crucifixion. Like the Christ he is, Prometheus "would fain / Be what it is my destiny to be, / The saviour and the strength of suffering man" (I. 815–17)—but again with the crucial difference that he would save man, not from the sinful consequences of violating God's injunctions, but from the mind-projected "god" who would tyrannize over man and crush his independent spirit. For Shelley has formed Jupiter with affinities with the jealous Old Testament God of vengeance; and it is for the purpose of an intentionally shocking repudiation of this God that Shelley has reinterpreted the open-ing of Genesis to fashion Prometheus' malediction:

Let thy malignant spirit move
In darkness over those I love.[88]   (I. 276–77)

The violent cosmic disorders that, according to Aeschylus, were wrought by Jupiter because of Prometheus' defiance[89] and the correspond-ing disruptions of nature that accompanied Christ's crucifixion easily lend themselves to Shelley's syncretic mythopoeia and its thematic motive. As the Crucifixion was attended by earthquake and the rending of rocks,[90] Prometheus' curse against his tyrant-god and his crucifixion on the moun-tain, according to Shelley, "made rock / The orbed world" (I. 68–69) and brought tempest, earthquake, and volcanic eruptions (I. 166–68). The darkness at noon during the Crucifixion[91] is represented by the "Darkness o'er the day like blood" (I. 102) attending Prometheus' utter-ance of his curse. And it is likely that the immediately preceding descrip-tion of the air's "still realm" torn by the curse and covered with darkness when the rent closed (I. 100–3) parodies in volcanic imagery the scrip-tural account of the consequences of Christ's giving up the ghost. The irony lies in the fact that the received anagogical sense of the scriptural

---

87 Cf. John 19:34.
88 Gen. 1:2: "and darkness was upon the face of the deep. And the Spirit of God moved upon the face of the waters."
89 *Prometheus Bound* 992–96, 1014–19, 1043–50, 1080–90.
90 Matt. 27:51.
91 Matt. 27:45.

verse—"And, behold, the veil of the temple was rent in twain from the top to the bottom"[92]—is that by his sacrifice Christ opened a path into heaven. Mercury, sent by Jupiter to break Prometheus' will, is far less the threatening Hermes of Aeschylus than he is the Satan who tempted Christ by promising him all the kingdoms of the world "if thou wilt fall down and worship me";[93] for in return for bending "thy soul in prayer" to Jupiter, Mercury, unlike Aeschylus' Hermes, promises that Prometheus will "dwell among the Gods the while / Lapped in voluptuous joy" (I. 425–26). Whereas Christ refused because "it is written, Thou shalt worship the Lord thy God, and him only shalt thou serve,"[94] this is precisely the authoritarian God under the name of Jupiter whom Prometheus rightly refuses to worship or serve. Christ rejected the joys of the world; Prometheus, the pleasures of a putative heaven because he would not be one of its "self-despising slaves" (I. 429). Such a heaven, Mercury admits, "seems hell" by comparison with Prometheus' self-esteem and self-mastery (I. 358).

In the light of this recurrent and generally ironic syncretism of Aeschylus' myth with that of the New Testament, we can now recognize that at the same time Shelley, as we have seen, empties of meaning the myth of Jupiter, Thetis, and their offspring, he also is mocking the Christian doctrine of the Incarnation. Not only has he, by elaborating the Jupiter myth, denied that tyranny can beget its own perpetuity, but, by fusing with the traditional myth Jupiter's expectation that his unbodied offspring will be incarnate in Demogorgon's (nonexistent) limbs, he simultaneously ridicules Christianity's belief that the godhead can be embodied (III. i. 18–24, 42–46); and no doubt Jupiter's announcement to his assembled gods, "Even now have I begotten a strange wonder, / That fatal child" (III. i. 18–19), parodies God's announcement to his assembled angels in *Paradise Lost* (V. 603–4), "This day I have begot whom I declare / My only Son."[95] To Shelley Christ is the highest form of mind in the realm of existence, not the personification of Power; and therefore he is properly reflected in Prometheus, who is the One Mind and Existence. The error of Jupiter, the disfigured shadow of Mind, is not only his belief that he himself is Power; his is also Christianity's error of believing that its fictional creation is Power and that this Power can ever be incarnate as the Son in the realm of existence. In the context of such a mesh of falsehoods, such a Son could only be conceived of as "the terror of the earth" designated by Jupiter to "trample out" man's soul, not as its savior (III. i. 19, 24).

[92] Matt. 27:51.
[93] Matt. 4:8–9.
[94] Matt. 4:10.
[95] Cf. Ps. 2: 7: "I will declare the decree: the Lord hath said unto me, Thou art my Son; this day have I begotten thee."

Unquestionably, Panthea's dream-vision of Prometheus liberated and revealing his perfection is an elaborate assimilation of Christ's Transfiguration, which made his divinity manifest to the Apostles in a vision.[96] Just as Christ's Transfiguration strengthened the three Apostles in their faith and prefigured his future state of glory and that of man after the Resurrection, so Prometheus' transfiguration, revealed to Panthea in a dream and, through her, to Asia, both implants in the Oceanids the motive and the desired goal that, by the law of Necessity, will draw them along the causal sequence of their acts and foretells Prometheus' coming state of glory after Jupiter is removed and the Titan is reunited with Asia:

>   'tis He, arrayed
> In the soft light of his own smiles, which spread
> Like radiance from the cloud-surrounded moon.
> Prometheus, it is thine! depart not yet!
> Say not those smiles that we shall meet again
> Within that bright pavilion which their beams
> Shall build o'er the waste world?   (II. i. 120–26)

During the night upon a high mountain the Apostles saw that Jesus' "face did shine as the sun, and his raiment was white as the light," the brilliance being the effulgence of the inner glory concealed beneath his human form.[97] Correspondingly, an apostolic Panthea reports that on the mountain height the

>   pale wound-worn limbs
> Fell from Prometheus, and the azure night
> Grew radiant with the glory of that form
> Which lives unchanged within . . . ,   (II. i. 62–65)

and the simile likening Jesus' brilliance to the shining of the sun dominates Panthea's further description of Prometheus: love

>   from his soft and flowing limbs,
> And passion-parted lips, and keen, faint eyes,
> Steamed forth like vaporous fire; an atmosphere
> Which wrapt me in its all-dissolving power,
> As the warm ether of the morning sun
> Wraps ere it drinks some cloud of wandering dew . . . .
> And I was thus absorb'd, until it past,
> And like the vapours when the sun sinks down,
> Gathering again in drops upon the pines,

---

[96] Matt. 17: 9; or while they were "heavy with sleep" (Luke 9: 32).
[97] Matt. 17:1–6; Mark 9:1–8; Luke 9:28–36; II Pet. 1: 16–18.

And tremulous as they, in the deep night
My being was condensed. . . .[98] (II. i. 73–86)

One detail of the Transfiguration scene of the New Testament, however, is significantly altered to strip away the theology and locate divinity in the One Mind, for Shelley could not well incorporate in his creation the bright cloud which "overshadowed" Christ in glory and from which the voice of God said, "This is my beloved Son, in whom I am well pleased." What Shelley is repudiating and what he is urging instead are made clear by his substitution: the "overpowering light" of Prometheus' "immortal shape was shadowed o'er / By love" (II. i. 71–73), an "atmosphere" that "Steamed forth like vaporous fire" and was the effluence of his inner sun-like glory. Shelley's deity is not the transcendent God of the bright cloud, but the overshadowing love that rises like a bright vapor from within Mind itself; and instead of God's acclamation of His beloved Son, the apostle Panthea hears Prometheus' voice calling on Asia, Generative Love.[99]

In the context of these transformations of the life of Christ and their absorption into the career of Prometheus we can understand more richly the dramatic function of the Spirits of the Human Mind at the end of Act I. The act is precisely balanced by the torturing Furies and Mercury the tempter on the one side and the consoling Spirits on the other, each acting on the soul of Prometheus. In accordance with the characteristic inverting irony of Shelley's drama, the Greek Furies, Zeus's agents who traditionally torture and punish evil, prove powerless to crush the virtuous Prometheus. Born of the "all-miscreative brain of Jove," the Furies are the products of the privative mode of the One Mind and are the dark impulses to evil that lurk in the "monster-teeming Hell" of the unconscious, like those that Beatrice Cenci eventually verbalizes into consciousness.

---

[98] See also II. iv. 126–27: "Prometheus shall arise / Henceforth the sun of this rejoicing world."

[99] II. i. 87–91. Later Asia's birth will also be described by Panthea in terms of a similar transfiguration:

> love, like the atmosphere
> Of the sun's fire filling the living world,
> Burst from thee, and illumined earth and heaven. (II. v. 26–28)

Since she is to be understood as the condition of Prometheus' being, when she is returned to her pristine nature during her night-journey of reunion with Prometheus, she will again undergo the same transfiguration (II. v. 11–20).

Leaning on Herschel's finding, Shelley assumed that the sun is not a burning body but is surrounded by a "shell as it were of phosphoric vapours, suspended many thousands miles in the atmosphere of that body." These vapors canopy the sun "as with a vault of etherial splendour whose internal surface may perform the same office to the processes of vital and material action on the body of the sun, as its external one does on those of the planets" (*On the Devil and Devils* [Julian, VII, 102]).

Their purpose is Count Cenci's: to reduce their victim to despair, to self-contempt, and hence to the willful relinquishment of the will. Like the "undistinguishable mist" of repressed thoughts in Beatrice's mind which, "like shadow after shadow," darken each other, the Furies lurk beside Prometheus' soul, beneath his brain, and around his heart; and they have no shape but that which falls on them as a shadow of the anticipated agony of their victim—that is, they are unformed unless accepted into the conscious mind and become the operative character of that mind. Prometheus runs that risk of consciously acknowledging them by looking at them:

Methinks I grow like what I contemplate,
And laugh and stare in loathsome sympathy.   (I. 450–51)

But, unlike Beatrice, he is "king" over himself and can "rule / The torturing and conflicting throngs within," suppressing them into the Hell of the unconscious from which they have come (I. 492–93).

Balanced against these Greek Furies, the Spirits of the Human Mind have a Christian ancestry. Making their flight from the human mind to console Prometheus after his torments by the Furies and temptations by Mercury, they perform the work of the angels who similarly "came and ministered" to Jesus in the wilderness after he overcame his temptation by Satan and who appeared to him "from heaven, strengthening him," at Gethsemane.[100] But if Shelley has transformed the Furies from potent ministers of justice into impotent agents of evil, he also rejected angels who descend from heaven: there is no transcendent deity that can arbitrarily choose to comfort the One Mind. Minds are their own spirits, their own divinity; and human minds, being the constitutive portions of the One Mind, are the only possible source of the powers that can console Prometheus, even though they must fall short of the power of Asia, or Love.

The implicit equation of Prometheus with Christ becomes part of the drama of Act I in the chorus of Furies who taunt Prometheus with a history of Christianity that is also Promethean. Removing a veil, the Furies reveal to Prometheus burning cities and the despairing ghost of Christ bewailing the havoc for which he has been innocently responsible. The "gentle" Christ who once smiled on the "sanguine earth"[101] is described and his history recounted in terms equally applicable to Prometheus, bestower of knowledge on man, so that what the Furies are presenting to Prometheus is in effect a mirror image of himself. The similarity of the

[100] Matt. 4: 11; Mark 1: 13; Luke 22: 43.
[101] According to Shelley, Christ sought to replace "the sanguinary Deity of the Jews" with "moral and humane" laws (*Letter to Lord Ellenborough* [Julian, V, 289]).

two saviors is drawn precisely: the knowledge the Titan gave man aroused a thirst that "outran" the waters of knowledge[102] and became the feverish thirst of "Hope, love, doubt, desire," which now consumes him (I. 542–45); Christ's words of "truth, peace, and pity" outlived him to become a poison that withered up these virtues, and the faith he kindled became a destructive conflagration until only the dim embers of faith remain and the virtuous survivors gather around them in dread (I. 546–59). Each virtuous gift became destructive of itself and those who received it. But of course this is the demonic version of the truth, designed to reduce Prometheus to despair, for the hope, love, doubt, and desire generated by insatiable thirst for knowledge are not evil. The Furies deceptively conceal the fact that man has been crushed, not by the gift of knowledge, but by the tyrannic use of knowledge and power by an anthropomorphic fiction, Jehovah-Jupiter; not by the words of Christ, but by the dogma of the Church into which they have been perverted. The purpose of the Furies in holding up before Prometheus an image of the crucified Christ is to persuade him of his futility because all who, like himself,

> do endure
> Deep wrongs for man, and scorn, and chains, but heap
> Thousandfold torment on themselves and him. (I. 594–96)

But Prometheus will immediately undo the Furies' falsehood by acknowledging that it is Christ's "slaves"—that is, those who serve the institution that has perverted Christ's virtuous words into an evil, authoritarian Christianity—who hate the "wise, the mild, the lofty, and the just" precisely because these are Christ's virtuous disciples.

Moreover, by dramatizing the analogy between Christ and Prometheus, the Furies have so confused the two that they create a significant ambiguity exactly like the ambiguity in Act I that makes the Phantasm of Jupiter the mirror image of Prometheus when he uttered the curse. Having revealed the ghost of Christ despairing amidst the ruined cities of men, the Furies add,

> Past ages crowd on thee, but each one remembers,
> And the future is dark, and the present is spread
> Like a pillow of thorns for thy slumberless head. (I. 561–63)

The ambiguous reference is calculated: ostensibly the words are addressed to Prometheus, but the details derive from the picture of Christ that the Furies have just painted. Christ and Prometheus are in fact one; the two myths coincide, and there is no distinction between Christ's "thorn-

[102] Ecclesiasticus 24:29: "They that eat me [Wisdom] shall yet hunger, and they that drink me, shall yet thirst."

wounded brow" (I. 598) and Prometheus' head on a pillow of thorns. Indeed, when the Furies now look at Prometheus after having tormented him with this vision of the tortured Christ, what they see in him is Christ in agony, whose "sweat was as it were great drops of blood": [103]

Drops of bloody agony flow
From his white and quivering brow.   (I. 564–65)

Appropriately, it is shortly after this echo of Christ's agony that the Spirits of the Human Mind will come to comfort Prometheus, just as the angel then strengthened Christ at Gethsemane. But it is a shocking irony that, with Prometheus brought to the height of his torture, one of the Furies appropriates the words with which Christ asked God's forgiveness of his crucifiers: "Father, forgive them; for they know not what they do." Dispassionately the Fury, Maddalo-like, thrusts at Prometheus what would be the severest taunt of all if it were true—the necessary inadequacy of man's spiritual powers:

The good want power, but to weep barren tears.
The powerful goodness want: worse need for them.
The wise want love; and those who love want wisdom;
And all best things are thus confused to ill.
Many are strong and rich, and would be just,
But live among their suffering fellow-men
As if none felt: *they know not what they do.*   (I. 625–31; itals. added)

By means of this transfer of Christ's words, Shelley denies the existence of the God whom Christ invoked, the supernatural anthropomorphic deity who may arbitrarily exercise forgiveness or, "having called us out of non-existence, and after inflicting on us the misery of the commission of error, should superadd that of the punishment and the privations consequent upon it." [104] Nor can Shelley admit either that the present inadequacy of man is inherent in his nature or that his ignorance and other deficiencies are the objects of forgiveness. Instead, to Shelley the proper response is Prometheus': the Fury's words should torture because the deficiencies are inexcusable; those not tortured by them have resigned themselves to accepting the imperfections of man's spiritual nature, and they are the ones to be pitied: "I pity those they torture not" (I. 633). Christ's words, therefore, are not the grounds for supernatural pardon; they properly belong to the agents of evil, not to a redeemer.

Prometheus can recognize in Christ a mirror image of himself, not because there is some accidentally viable analogy between the two, but,

103 Luke 22:44.
104 *Hellas,* 197n.

we are to understand, because they are different expressions of a universal truth whose pattern is always the same: to promulgate virtue without the safeguard of love is to make that virtue available to tyranny, and tyranny will pervert that virtue into the means of evil despotism. This, then, is not only the history of Prometheus and Christ, as Shelley interprets them, but also that of the political state, the most immediate and burning example for Shelley being France during the Revolution and its aftermath. Consequently, Shelley's syncretic mythopoeia provides that Prometheus, tortured with a vision of himself in Christ, also have a vision of a nation, presumably France, rebelling against slavery, only to see in horror that it then impatiently becomes the victim of a tyranny like that of Christianity and Jupiter. Shelley's myth identifies the legend of Prometheus with both political history and the course of dogmatic religion because the law that governs moral events is necessarily one and subsumes its manifest modes in state and church, the two institutions in which Shelley consistently located tyranny. Prometheus, suffering in agony like the Christ whom he has looked on, is granted by the Furies what they tauntingly call "a little respite":

See a disenchanted nation
Springs like day from desolation;
To truth its state is dedicate,
And Freedom leads it forth, her mate;
A legioned band of linked brothers
Whom Love calls children—. (I. 567–72)

The nation's moral awakening parallels Prometheus' arousing man from his vegetative, disenfranchised existence under Saturn by granting him wisdom, the birthright that had been denied (II. iv. 32–43). But another Fury breaks in to deny that this band is Love's children: " 'Tis another's." Because this accession to truth and freedom has not been bred by love, but only by impatient aspiration to truth, freedom, and equality, tyranny usurps these new powers as the evil instruments of a Reign of Terror, just as Christianity and Jupiter did:

See how kindred murder kin:
'Tis the vintage-time for death and sin:
Blood, like new wine, bubbles within:
    'Till Despair smothers
The struggling world, which slaves and tyrants win. (I. 573–77)

Or, as Prometheus will reconstruct the same vision:

Names are there, Nature's sacred watch-words, they
Were borne aloft in bright emblazonry;

The nations thronged around, and cried aloud,
As with one voice, Truth, liberty, and love!
Suddenly fierce confusion fell from heaven
Among them: there was strife, deceit, and fear:
Tyrants rushed in, and did divide the spoil.[105]   (I. 648–54)

Yet if we reconsider this process of myth-making, it is evident that Christ and Christianity are not in fact named or explicitly identified in the drama. True, it is explicit that a figure on a crucifix is displayed to Prometheus; and yet when Panthea reports to Ione that she has seen "a youth / With patient looks nailed to a crucifix" (I. 584–85), it is impossible to say unequivocally that she has seen anyone other than Prometheus, who is every patient crucified savior of man. Nor indeed is the French Revolution ever specified, even though the Furies are attempting to reduce Prometheus to the submissive hopelessness that beset those of Shelley's contemporaries who were disillusioned by its failure. The historical pattern Shelley has elaborated could equally well apply to his view of the history of Athens, Rome, Venice, or Padua.[106] In describing how contemporary Spain, for example, had moved from one tyranny into another, Shelley wrote that it has passed "through an ordeal severe in proportion to the wrongs and errors which it is kindled to erase";[107] and this might serve as well as the history of the French Revolution to explicate Prometheus' vision. True, it was with respect to the French Revolution in particular that Shelley had said that "a nation of men who had been dupes and slaves for centuries were incapable of conducting themselves with the wisdom and tranquillity of freemen so soon as some of their fetters were partially loosened."[108] But his reference is unlimited when he writes:

A Republic, however just in its principle and glorious in its object, would through violence and sudden change which must attend it, incur a great risk

---

[105] Compare *A Philosophical View of Reform* (Julian, VII, 5): "From the dissolution of the Roman Empire, that vast and successful scheme for the enslaving [of] the most civilized portion of mankind, to the epoch of the present year, have succeeded a series of schemes, on a smaller scale, operating to the same effect. Names borrowed from the life; and opinions of Jesus Christ were employed as symbols of domination and imposture; and a system of liberty and equality (for such was the system preached by that great Reformer) was perverted to support oppression.—Not his doctrines, for they are too simple and direct to be susceptible of such perversion—but the mere names. Such was the origin of the Catholic Church, which together with the several dynasties then beginning to consolidate themselves in Europe, means, being interpreted, a plan according to which the cunning and selfish few have employed the fears and hopes of the ignorant many to the establishment of their own power and the destruction of the real interests of all."
[106] See *Ode to Liberty* and *Lines Written among the Euganean Hills.*
[107] *A Philosophical View of Reform* (Julian, VII, 17).
[108] Preface to *Revolt of Islam.*

of being as rapid in its decline as in its growth. . . . A civil war, which might be engendered by the passions attending on this mode of reform, would confirm in the mass of the nation those military habits which have been already introduced by our tyrants, and with which liberty is incompatible. From the moment that a man is a soldier, he becomes a slave.[109]

Prometheus Unbound is cast in universal, not special terms, and is formed by Shelley's vision of the entire history of man's inevitable movement toward equality and freedom, from ancient Greece to the glorious future. His conception of history having been shaped by the recent sporadic eruption of revolutions for freedom throughout Europe and America, he conceived of the French Revolution as but an event in that progress, and he recognized the development that resulted in the Reign of Terror and the despotism of Napoleon as the type of all that prevents revolution from becoming freedom. Through Prometheus' vision of the merely impatient rebellion against tyranny, Shelley is observing that in all of history the release of the good in any of its forms, whether virtue, wisdom, or freedom, will, unless it is safeguarded by love, become perverted into a self-oppressive and therefore self-destructive force, just as Christianity has subverted Christ's doctrines and as Jupiter has subjugated Prometheus with Prometheus' own gifts. True revolution is rebellion governed by patient suffering and by love and benevolence; rebellion alone grows into self-destructive civil war that reinstates with its own gains what it was designed to overthrow:

If there had never been war, there could never have been tyranny in the world; tyrants take advantage of the mechanical organization of armies to establish and defend their encroachments. . . . A sentiment of confidence in brute force and in a contempt of death and danger is considered as the highest virtue, when in truth, and however indispensable, they are merely the means and the instruments, highly capable of being perverted to destroy the cause they were assumed to promote.[110]

However much the reader may be tempted to specify Shelley's references, the fact is that Shelley has consistently abstracted and syncretized archetypal patterns of religious and political history in the same manner that he has assimilated the forms or potential forms of various conventional myths by releasing them from their special particularities. Presented successively with archetypal visions of religious and political revolution, Prometheus has seen, by virtue of Shelley's myth-making processes, the two major expressions of his own inclusive archetypal history as the One Mind.

[109] *A Philosophical View of Reform* (Julian, VII, 41).
[110] *Ibid.* (Julian, VII, 53–54).

10   Prometheus Unbound

Power, Necessity,
and Love

As nearly every critic of *Prometheus
Unbound* has observed, the only dramatic struggles take place in Act I,
and all the subsequent action, including Demogorgon's explosive overthrow of Jupiter, proceeds without worthy opposition and hence without
dramatic tension. Withdrawing the curse whereby evil subsists and resolving to endure pain patiently rather than submit to evil are Prometheus'
only moral decisions, the only assertions of his will. Thereafter he does
not act, but is acted for and upon, and the course of events is determined
by other agencies. Yet by retracting his curse and stoically resisting all
temptations to weakness, Prometheus exhausts all the capacities that
Shelley assigns to the will; and the result of his utmost determinations is
to make possible the unleashing of the revolutionary and reconstitutive
forces that are external to him and that alone can advance the action in
the subsequent acts. Were Prometheus a mortal man, one might legit-
imately protest the absence of a sustained tension and the fact that after
Act I others carry out what would appear to be the protagonist's respon-
sibilities. But the events of the first three acts are not intended as heroic
human drama, and man plays only an off-stage role. As Demogorgon's
final words make clear, Shelley never thought that earthly man, in contradistinction to Prometheus, could ever be released from the strenuous
moral resoluteness made necessary by the continuous threat of resurrected
evil. The scope of the Promethean action is cosmic, not human; its end
is apocalyptic, not utopian; and its agents are all the forces that are, not
merely the moral will.

Given the metaphysical level at which the play is conducted, the
possibility of a drama of continued moral decision and a contest of an-

tagonists is precluded by the absence of a transcendent God who promulgates a moral code and punishes or rewards and by the unreality of Jupiter except as a mental contingency. Prometheus has no antagonist but himself, even though once he has objectified his distorted self as Jupiter, he must be the unwavering "barrier" to that "else all-conquering foe." The only real and autonomously existing actors in Shelley's cosmic design are the One Mind and the indifferent ultimate Power, together with its equally indifferent law of Necessity. Shelley's optimism, therefore, is not founded solely on mental capacities: perfection is the innate condition of the One Mind, not its creation. This perfection will come about because mind permits it, not because it struggles to build it, for the indwelling principle of Necessity drives to this natural end if mind will allow it to do so. Although evil, or the unnatural chain of events, is always potential, Shelley denies that it is an attribute of existence and that the mind is limited to the formulation of moral codes designed to come to terms with it. Evil is the "immedicable plague" that, once it infects, must run its course (II. iv. 101); and the infection cannot be doctored into a tolerable approximation of health because, like a cancer, "Evil minds / Change good to their own nature" (I. 380–81). It is, however, only immedicable, not irrevocable, just as Ruin, "Woundless though in heart or limb," nevertheless can be quelled (I. 787–88). On the other hand, Shelley will not admit that the effective revolutionary overthrow of evil and tyranny can be a violent, hate-filled destruction: violence begets only the means of further violence, in the same manner that the liberty released by the French Revolution became the "bewildered powers" of the next "Anarch," Napoleon.[1] The action of revenging evil, as Beatrice Cenci demonstrates, is an evil; the passion of pity removes the ground on which evil stands:

For Justice, when triumphant, will weep down
Pity, not punishment, on her own wrongs,
Too much avenged by those who err.   (I. 403–5)

All the mind needs in order to participate in the ubiquitous natural force is a faith in its existence and the submission to it that faith implies—a faith "so mild, / So solemn, so serene" that any mind may be reconciled with this natural force by means of that mild faith alone.[2] The power—not to amend, nor even to destroy—but to "repeal / Large codes of fraud and woe"[3] is everywhere and always potential, ready to act whenever it is passively admitted.

Act II, therefore, removes us from Prometheus in order to display the release of the repealing powers that are outside the One Mind, outside

[1] *Ode to Liberty*, 175.
[2] *Mont Blanc*, 77–79.
[3] *Ibid.*, 80–81.

Existence. Correspondingly, the scene changes from the desolate, barren, and wintry setting of Prometheus' self-imposed suffering to Asia's luxuriant Indian vale at the very inception of spring, the season that belongs to Venus-Asia and symbolizes the dawn of the new age. At this same moment, Panthea joins Asia and recounts two prophetic dreams that had visited her the previous night while she still attended Prometheus and experienced the spiritual winter of his mountain peak. The first proves to be a prevision of Prometheus' transfiguration, a promise of the coming restoration of the One Mind to its unclouded brilliance; for the transfiguration, like that of Christ, is not an accession to glory, but a removal of the eclipsing evil that had hidden the inherent perfection, which "lives unchanged within" (II. i. 65). As a vision of the perfection of the One Mind, the subject of Panthea's dream is the Mind's spiritual condition, not the thoughts it generates and contains; and therefore it cannot be communicated by words, the function of which is to give palpable shape to thoughts, the measure of the universe. The subject is not Existence but its ideal state. Even in her dream Panthea did not experience with her senses, but through an absorption of her soul: although Prometheus in glory commanded her to "lift thine eyes on me," she

> saw not, heard not, moved not, only felt
> His presence flow and mingle thro' my blood
> Till it became his life, and his grew mine,
> And I was thus absorb'd.... (II. i. 79–82)

Capable of being experienced only by a spiritual communion, the perfection of Existence is beyond communicable thought, and "the rays / Of thought were slowly gathered" in Panthea's mind only after her release from her spiritual absorption (II. i. 86–87). For this reason Panthea's words describing the experience are to Asia "as the air," and Asia must "feel" the vision by commanding Panthea to "lift / Thine eyes" and (eyes being the windows of the soul) by mystically seeing, beyond the "inmost depth" within them, the "soul" of the transfigured Prometheus "written" on Panthea's spirit. Like Demogorgon's realm, the purity of Existence is imageless, although the two differ in that the truths of Demogorgon's realm are totally inaccessible to mind, and the purity of the One Mind, in the unity of which all images dissolve, can be felt by spiritual communion. The former is beneath imagery, the latter beyond it.

    Panthea is unable to remember her other dream until the first has been conveyed to Asia, and the implication is that it can appear only in consequence of the first and is dependent on it. Presumably, too, its subject is something other than the perfection of the One Mind, since it is communicated by words; or, rather, it is conveyed by a process that Shelley apparently meant to represent the nature of all verbal communication. Because words, like a Kantian category, give intelligible shape to thoughts,

Panthea's verbal account of this second dream fills Asia's "own forgotten sleep / With shapes" that recall to Asia's mind thoughts analogous to Panthea's and essentially the same in meaning (II. i. 142–43). Given the premise that nothing exists except as it is perceived, presumably we experience words directly only as themselves; as communicative signs they function by giving shape to thoughts and thereby arouse in the auditor's mind similarly shaped thoughts already resident there through prior experiences. Verbal comprehension is not merely mediate but also analogous. The essential ontological difference between the two dreams is contained in the fact that whereas in the first Asia must directly experience something "beyond" the inmost depth of Panthea's eyes (II. i. 119), Panthea's words describing the second succeed in restoring to Asia's mind analogous episodes of a forgotten dream, in one of which, commanding Panthea to look on her, she saw the full meaning of the dream "in the depth" of Panthea's eyes (II. i. 161).

In contrast to the brilliant serenity of Panthea's first dream, the second is powerfully, nervously energetic, its "rude hair" roughening the "wind that lifts it" and its expression "wild and quick" (II. i. 127–29).[4] This energy is the essence of its meaning. The dream, which occurred to Panthea on Prometheus' wintry mountain, is a vision in late winter of a lightning-blasted almond tree that blossoms and then is deflowered by the frost wind, each leaf of the fallen blossoms bearing the command, "O, Follow, Follow!" The symbolism is not private, and at least from his reading of Pliny Shelley would have known that the almond tree is notable as the first of all those that bud in winter, blossoming in January and bearing fruit in March.[5] This impetuous and anticipatory characteristic of the almond tree had almost consistently been associated by the scriptural exegetes with Jeremiah 1: 11–12: "And I said, I see a rod of an almond tree. Then said the Lord unto me, Thou hast well seen: for I will hasten to perform it." As the exegetes explained the pun, the Hebrew word for "almond" is also the word for "hasten," and thus the "hastening" tree appears in Jeremiah's vision as the sign of God's promise to fulfill speedily what is prophesied. The almond tree, therefore, had long been an emblem of anticipation, since it pre-enacts and prophesies in winter the coming events of spring.[6] Implicitly repudiating the divine providence that the symbol traditionally represented, Shelley makes the image precisely appropriate to his conception of nature's processes as the ineluctable se-

---

[4] In personifying the dream Shelley is adopting a practice common in Greco-Roman mythology. See also *Prometheus Unbound*, I. 726.

[5] *Natural History* xvi. 42. See also the commentaries on Virgil *Georgics* i. 187–90, which explained that the almond tree's plentiful shedding of its leaves in winter preparatory to its bearing fruit predicts abundance in the next harvest season.

[6] See, e.g., Filippo Picinelli, *Mundus symbolicus* (Coloniae, 1687), pp. 540–41; J. Masenius, *Speculum imaginum veritatis occultae* (Coloniae, 1664), p. 1012; Alciati, *Emblemata*, No. 208. In the MS, Panthea's speech was to have begun, "I had dreams of spring" (Zillman, pp. 188n., 643).

quence of cause and effect fulfilling its own fixed requirements in all
media; and the command on the petals, "O, Follow, Follow," calls on
Panthea and Asia to submit to the course of Necessity and allow themselves to be driven and drawn by it. The budding almond tree is the
proleptic winter sign of the regenerative spring in both the natural and
moral worlds. Because it is symbolic of this irrepressible course of Necessity, the dream appears "wild and quick" in its compulsion to lead to the
new order, and even the wound the almond branch has received from
lightning cannot prevent its spring rebirth, any more than the moral
regeneration can be suppressed by the evil inflicted on the mind by
Jupiter, whose weapon lightning is.

At first glance it seems curious that Shelley chose to symbolize the
workings of Necessity in the natural world not by representing the overcoming of winter by spring, but by superimposing winter's destructiveness
upon spring's new births and by heavily weighting the description on the
side of the former rather than the latter. The winter wind blows down
the blossoms of the symbol of nature's driving compulsion to rebirth, and
the same necessitarian command is stamped by winter's hoarfrost on
spring's "new-bladed grass, / Just piercing the dark earth" (II. i. 148–49).
Even the comparison of the command on the fallen almond blossoms to
the markings on the hyacinth which "tell Apollo's written grief" (II. i. 140)
asks us to consider the grief of the sun-god of fertility when jealous
Boreas, the north wind of winter,[7] slew his favorite youth, rather than the
promise of the spring flower with which the god commemorated his loss.
The full significance of this oddly biased emphasis must be postponed for
the moment, and yet it is clearly implicit that although the almond blossoms have been blown down they will be succeeded by the fruit, that the
new-bladed grass will grow despite the frost, and that the early spring
hyacinth replaces Apollo's wintry loss. The vanishing winter, however
blasting, is not the end of nature's life but the prelude to its renewal, and
Panthea's symbolic dream of Necessity, like her flight from Prometheus'
winter to Asia's spring, is a broad promise that since winter is passing
spring cannot be far behind. The order of Panthea's two dreams, therefore,
is itself a manifestation of the necessitarian sequence: the prophetic vision
of the transfigured Prometheus imaged as the brilliant sun must first be
divulged in order to reveal, behind it, the dream of the powerful Necessity
that drives to that perfect end.

ii

It has long been obvious that the following scene, in which two
Fauns comment on the passage of the two Oceanids, Panthea and Asia,
through the forest, derives its materials from Virgil's sixth *Eclogue*; but

---

[7] In some versions of the myth the wind-god is Zephyr, but the winter wind is
obviously the one relevant to Shelley's context. For the substitution of Boreas for
Zephyr, see Servius on Virgil (*Eclogues* iii. 62).

the relevance of that *Eclogue* to Shelley's theme has remained to be considered.

At least since Servius' commentary, the sixth *Eclogue* had been identified with Epicurean atomism, for it tells that Silenus sang to the Fauns of how,

through the great void, were brought together the seeds of earth, and air, and sea, and streaming fire withal; how from these elements came all beginnings and even the young globe of the world grew into a mass.[8]

That Virgil accepted the philosophy of Epicurus seemed fully confirmed by Donatus' account of Virgil's education in that philosophy and by many similarities in his poetry to Lucretius' poem. Whatever edition of Virgil, however ancient or recent, that the early nineteenth-century reader turned to, few would have failed to explain to him unequivocally the Epicureanism of the *Eclogue*; and most glossators identified the two Fauns as Virgil and his friend Varo, and Silenus as their Epicurean tutor, Syro. Although the Epicurean philosophy, like Shelley's own, denies a divine external Creator and Governor of the world, it does not necessarily follow, it was generally thought, that Virgil also accepted the doctrine that the universe is directed by chance. The four basic texts in all traditional expositions of Virgil's thought are the Epicurean sixth *Eclogue*; the brief Epicurean passage in the second *Georgic* praising the man who, by knowing the natural causes of things, can dispel the fears of death and of a supposedly supernatural fate; the explanation in the fourth *Georgic* that the instinct of the bees is actually their participation in the infused divine mind; and Anchises' especially famous account in *Aeneid* vi of how the universe is maintained:

Principio caelum ac terras camposque liquentis
lucentemque globum lunae Titaniaque astra
spiritus intus alit, totamque infusa per artus
mens agitat molem et magno se corpore miscet.

[First, the heaven and earth, and the watery plains, the shining orb of the moon and Titan's stars, a spirit within sustains, and mind, pervading its members, sways the whole mass and mingles with its mighty frame.][9]

---

[8] *Eclogues* vi. 31–34.
[9] 724–27. On these four passages alone, Jacob Brucker, for example, based his analysis of Virgil's Epicureanism in his standard history of philosophy, *Historia critica philosophiae* ([2d ed.; Lipsiae, 1766], II, 71–75). (Brucker's work was abridged and translated by William Enfield in 1791.) But almost any commentary on Virgil, such as Joseph Trapp's or John Martyn's, will center on exactly the same passages.

The two passages concerning the world-soul were customarily ascribed to the Stoic, Platonic, and Pythagorean doctrines of an *anima mundi*, and the discrepancies between those philosophies and Epicureanism frequently embarrassed Virgil's commentators, especially since Anchises also explains to Aeneas the transmigration of the souls. Sometimes it was proposed that Virgil graduated from one philosophy to the other, but the favorite way out of the difficulty was to reconcile the obvious differences by accommodating the doctrine of the world-soul to Virgil's basic Epicureanism.

Edward Gibbon's interpretation of *Aeneid* vi can be taken as typical of those that would have come to Shelley's attention:

It is observable, that the three great poets of Rome [Virgil, Horace, and Lucretius] were all addicted to the Epicurean philosophy; a system, however, the least suited to a poet; since it banishes all the genial and active powers of nature, to substitute in their room a dreary void, blind atoms, and indolent gods. A description of the infernal shades was incompatible with the ideas of a philosopher whose disciples boasted, that he had rescued the captive world from the tyranny of religion, and the fear of a future state. These ideas Virgil was obliged to reject: but he does still more; he abandons not only the CHANCE of Epicurus, but even those gods, whom he so nobly employs in the rest of his poem, that he may offer to the reader's imagination a far more specious and splendid set of ideas [in the lines quoted above from *Aeneid* vi]. . . . The more we examine these lines, the more we shall feel the sublime poetry of them. But they have likewise an air of philosophy, and even of religion, which goes off on a nearer approach. The mind which is INFUSED into the several parts of matter, and which MINGLES ITSELF with the mighty mass, scarcely retains any property of a spiritual substance; and bears too near an affinity to the principles, which the impious Spinoza revived rather than invented.

I am not insensible, that we should be slow to suspect, and still slower to condemn. The poverty of human language, and the obscurity of human ideas, make it difficult to speak worthily of THE GREAT FIRST CAUSE. Our most religious poets, in striving to express the presence and energy of the Deity, in every part of the universe, deviate unwarily into images, which are scarcely distinguished from materialism. Thus our Ethic Poet:

All are but parts of one stupendous whole,
Whose body Nature is, and God the soul;

and several passages of Thomson require a like favourable construction. But these writers deserve that favour, by the sublime manner in which they celebrate the great Father of the Universe, and by those effusions of love and gratitude, which are inconsistent with the materialist's system. Virgil has no such claim to our indulgence. THE MIND of the UNIVERSE is rather a metaphysical than a theological being. His intellectual qualities are faintly distinguished from the powers of matter, and his moral attributes, the source of all religious worship, form no part of Virgil's creed.[10]

[10] "Critical Observations on the Design of the Sixth Book of the Aeneid" (1770), in *Miscellaneous Works* (London, 1814), IV, pp. 487–89.

Nonetheless, Gibbon insisted that Virgil is a "determined Epicurean," and, however dissatisfied he may have been, he found in the poet the consistent acceptance of a pantheistic world governed by the infused Mind and independent of any transcendent divinities. Others even held that the doctrine of the world-soul is really implicit in Epicureanism. The materialist La Mettrie, for example, was of the opinion that it is the hypothesis "de Virgile, et de tous les Epicuriens" that there is "une Ame généralement répandue par tout le corps";[11] and of the *anima mundi* Cabanis wrote:

Cette opinion fut celle des stoiciens: il paroît que Pythagore l'avoit enseignée avant eux; on pourroit même penser qu'elle n'étoit pas étrangère aux disciples d'Epicure, puisque Virgile ne fait pas difficulté de le prendre pour base du système général qu'il esquisse d'une manière si brillante, si riche et si majestueuse dans le sixième livre de l'Énéide.[12]

In sum, the recurrent practice of deducing Virgil's philosophy from a compound of the four texts—but especially from the sixth *Eclogue* and Anchises' speech in the sixth book of the *Aeneid*—had resulted in a picture of an Epicurean who, like Shelley, rejected the idea of a transcendent Creator and Presider to whom man and nature are subservient, and who substituted for Epicurus' chance an actuating and regulating world-soul. Shelley has obvious affinities with Epicurus, whom he called the most divine of philosophers[13] and whom Lucretius praised for liberating man from the tyranny of religion and the fear of death by attributing natural events to natural causes and making the threat of hell a mere superstition;[14] and with Virgil's infused spirit that sustains the universe Shelley could, with slight change, readily identify his own principle of Necessity, the immanent and self-fulfilling causal sequence that is neither a conscious guiding mind nor a teleological force, but the fixed law of the energy that effects the course of events. The relevance of Virgil's sixth *Eclogue*, therefore, is that it is a mythic form, already resident in the human mind, that gives shape to a thought approximating Shelley's atheism and immanent necessitarianism; and the scene in which Shelley introduces the Fauns dramatizes the Necessity that is the subject of Panthea's second dream. Just as Virgil's Epicurean Silenus had taught his students, the Fauns, how the world was formed by forces in nature, so Shelley's young Fauns, similarly inquiring into the principles of nature, seek to know where these powers live that, by "Demogorgon's mighty law" of Necessity, draw "All spirits on that secret way" (II. ii. 43–45).

[11] *L'Homme machine*, ed. Aram Vartanian (Princeton, N.J., 1960), p. 188.
[12] Pierre Cabanis, *Oeuvres philosophiques*, ed. C. Lehec and J. Cazeneuve (Paris, 1956), II, p. 282.
[13] See Roy R. Male and J. A. Notopoulos, "Shelley's Copy of Diogenes Laertius," *RES*, 54 (1959), 20.
[14] *De rerum natura* i. 62–79.

The setting of this scene is a dark forest through which Panthea and Asia are driven by some external compulsion and of which the Fauns, woodland deities, are natives. In these woods, they say, "We haunt within the least frequented caves / And closest coverts, and we know these wilds" (II. ii. 66–67). The peculiar character of this forest, which is the limited area of the Fauns's inquiry, is carefully defined, for there grow "cedar, pine, and yew, / And each dark tree that ever grew" (II. ii. 2–3); and this universality suggests that the forest is as inclusively the world as is the garden of *The Sensitive Plant*, where grow "all rare blossoms from every clime." Just as one of the referents of Shelley's universal garden is the universal Garden of Adonis, so his universal forest derives from the traditional interpretation of *silva*. As the commentaries on the *lucus* of *Aeneid* vi. 13 or the *silva* of vi. 131 recurrently pointed out, "silva materiam notat," for the Greek *hyle* means both wood and the basic matter of which the world is formed; or, as Shelley would have read in Thomas Taylor's *Dissertation on the Eleusinian and Bacchic Mysteries*, when Virgil in his sixth book "says that all the middle regions are covered with woods, this too plainly intimates a material nature; the word silva, as is well known, being used by ancient writers to signify matter, and implies nothing more than that the passage ... is through the medium of a material nature."[15] In his *Epipsychidion*, Shelley leaves no doubt that the "wintry forest" there represents the domain of mortal life (249–344), and, similarly, the forest of the Fauns is what man customarily designates as the world of matter.[16] Virgil's Epicurean Fauns have been appropriated to comment on the operation of the laws of Necessity in that realm.

Indeed, the "Spirits" about whom the Fauns inquire have already sung of how Necessity performs in both the natural and human worlds. One semichorus of these Spirits explains that when one nightingale in the dark woods, "Sick with sweet love," allows its song to die away, another "catches" the "languid close" to lift the song anew (II. ii. 31–32).[17] This instinctual urge that perpetuates the undulating decline and resurgence of the song,[18] like the instinct that Virgil's bees possess as their portion

---

[15] In *The Pamphleteer* (2d ed.; London, 1816), VIII, pp. 42, 462. Taylor makes the same point in his notes on Proclus (*The Philosophical and Mathematical Commentaries* [London, 1792], II, pp. 300–1n.). This definition is, of course, the reason Bacon entitled his study of natural history *Sylva sylvarum*. But, as Taylor points out, the information was in the common domain, and it was recorded, among other places, in nearly every Latin dictionary.

[16] In addition, the "gloom divine" of the forest (II. ii. 22) is clearly meant to represent the condition of mortal life: the "divine gloom" through which the Promethean racers run is explicitly equated with "the night of life" (III. iii. 169, 172), and the Spirits of Necessity sing of "the gloom to Earth given" (II. iii. 78).

[17] Shelley's terms, of course, derive from the catch-song and musical "close," or cadence. The word "bear" (II. ii. 34), meaning "sustain," also derives from its use as a musical term, as in the phrase "bear the burden."

[18] At one point in the draft of these lines Shelley wrote, "that aye renewed strain" (Zillman, p. 648).

of the active spirit infused throughout all things,[19] is the immanent working of Necessity. Just as Virgil drew an analogy between the instinctive acts of the bees and the actions of man, so Shelley's other semichorus of spirits replies by singing of Necessity in human actions. Like Panthea and Asia in their passage through the forest, the semichorus explains, men believe they are the arbitrary masters of their actions, but those who know the philosophic truth ("those who saw") are aware that it is "Demogorgon's mighty law" of Necessity that draws out of any cause its ineluctable chain of effects: the Oceanids are driven on a route that is "secret" (because Necessity, or the causative process, is not an empirical datum)

> As inland boats are driven to Ocean
> Down streams made strong with mountain-thaw:
> > And first there comes a gentle sound
> > To those in talk or slumber bound,
> And wakes the destined—soft emotion
> Attracts, impels them:[20] those who saw
> > Say from the breathing earth behind
> > There steams a plume-uplifting wind[21]
> Which drives them on their path, while they
> > Believe their own swift wings and feet
> The sweet desires within obey. (II. ii. 46–56)

As Asia awakens the slumbering Demogorgon to action in accordance with his inviolable law of process, and as Eternity must unloose the snakelike "Doom" of temporal sequence (II. iii. 95–97), so the sound awakens what is "destined" because Shelley's doctrine of causal Necessity provides that an effect is not random but is implicit in its cause, a consequence in its motive. The "relation which motive bears to voluntary action is that of cause to effect"; and it is false to "assert that the will has the power of refusing to be determined by the strongest motive."[22] To arouse motive is to arouse the whole inevitable course of "voluntary" action that it destines; and "emotion,"[23] or the principle of the relations among these successive actions, is manifest as the same attraction and repulsion ("Attracts, impels them") that is observed to govern motion in the sensible world. But the actual causative force of human action—the "plume-

[19] *Georgics* iv. 219–24.

[20] I have adopted the reading of Shelley's MS fair copy (Zillman, p. 197n.) instead of the unintelligible version in the 1820 text: "And wakes the destined soft emotion, / Attracts, impels them." I hope the interpretation that follows will justify the choice.

[21] That is, a wind that uplifts the plumes of Asia's and Panthea's wings and so drives them on their path.

[22] *Queen Mab*, VI. 198n. Shelley repeated this doctrine in his *Speculations on Morals* and *On the Devil and Devils*.

[23] For the probable pun here on "emotion," see below, pp. 338n., 454.

uplifting wind"—derives from an ultimate source infinitely remote from existence, as Shelley made clear in *Mont Blanc*: Power, the source of motion and emotion, is not an attribute of mind or of its faculty of will.

Having heard these Spirits sing of Necessity, one Faun then asks where they live, for, although the Fauns, like earthly man, are indigenous to the world of matter and inhabit its deepest recesses, they, too, have never met with their senses the causative Spirits. The second Faun's reply is an exemplary description of the way in which the invisible Necessity works in the physical world. He has heard the masters of natural philosophy—"those more skilled in spirits"—say that

> The bubbles, which the enchantment of the sun
> Sucks from the pale faint water-flowers that pave
> The oozy bottom of clear lakes and pools,
> Are the pavilions where such dwell and float
> Under the green and golden atmosphere
> Which noon-tide kindles thro' the woven leaves;
> And when these burst, and the thin fiery air,
> The which they breathed within those lucent domes,
> Ascend to flow like meteors thro' the night,
> They ride on them, and rein their headlong speed,
> And bow their burning crests, and glide in fire
> Under the waters of the earth again.   (II. ii. 71–82)

This novel description of the cycle of the will-o'-the-wisp, no doubt Shelley's invention, is founded on the fact that gases, or "fiery air," were known to be exhaled from marshy ground and to "ignite" as "meteors"; and Shelley evidently held some idiosyncratic theory that this "wandering Meteor," as he described the will-o'-the-wisp in *The Revolt of Islam*, after rising "from the morass" and shining with a "wondrous light," then returns "to its far morass."[24] Perpetually alternating as bubbles in the water and meteoric lights in the atmosphere, the "fiery air," like the nightingales' alternately surging and sinking song, represents all the cycles of nature's changes: the actuating "spirits" that dwell in the bubbles in the oozy bottom and then ride the meteors remain constant while the form that invests them undergoes a repeated sequence of alternations.[25] Like Virgil's Fauns, who were instructed in an atheistic cosmogony, Shelley's gain intimations of the presence in nature of the atheistic necessitarianism that the chorus of Spirits had already represented in nature's processes and in human actions.

In Panthea's and Asia's dreams the commands to follow, we have noted, are somewhat ambiguous. Although the conjunction of winter's

[24] *Revolt of Islam*, 2615–32.
[25] Compare *Mont Blanc*, where Necessity transforms the snow on the peak into the murderous glaciers and then into the life-giving River Arve.

blight and spring's growth clearly must represent the rebirth of spring out of the dying winter, it is on the fallen, winter-blasted almond blossoms that the command is stamped, even though the tree itself is pre-eminently the prophecy of the coming spring. Although the order to "follow" appears on the new grass of spring, it was printed there by the hoarfrost and was revealed only when the frost had melted away: the melting frost, not the burgeoning grass, demands to be followed. "Follow, O Follow" was cast on the mountain slope by the clouds "as they vanished by" (II. i. 153). The music of the pine boughs calling, "O, Follow, Follow, Follow Me!" sounds like the "farewell of ghosts" (II. i. 157–59); and the Echoes who draw the Oceanids on their path are receding voices, like dew evaporating in the morning sun (II. i. 167–76). The hastening upsurge of the new year's life is contemporaneous with the vanishing of the old year's winter, but Asia and Panthea are being compelled to follow the old order of things as it shrinks out of existence, not the new birth. Winter, together with all that it symbolizes, is not destroyed; it is forced to recede from the palpable world into its impalpable origin in the same manner that the audible Echoes drawing the Oceanids are in process of receding into the caves, their traditional native home, where they reside, inaudible.[26] Clearly "Demogorgon's mighty law" that draws Panthea and Asia is the necessitarian law of fixed and inviolable sequences, for it draws them down to Demogorgon's realm

As the fawn draws the hound,
As the lightning the vapour,
As a weak moth the taper;
Death, despair; love, sorrow;
Time both; to-day, to-morrow;
As steel obeys the spirit of the stone,
    Down, down.   (II. iii. 65–71)

But Necessity is compelling them to retreat from the sensible world, as the winter, the melting hoarfrost, the fading music, and the receding echoes are retreating, into the impalpable ultimate force behind the law of Necessity. For the retreat of the old order into its remote, inactive source is the release of the new order from its ultimate springhead into the sensible world. In the end of one is the beginning of the other. Spring, Shelley wrote in The Revolt of Islam, is the child of Autumn and wears its "mother's dying smile":

Thy mother Autumn, for whose grave thou bearest
Fresh flowers, and beams like flowers, with gentle feet,
Disturbing not the leaves which are her winding-sheet.[27]

[26] See, for example, Ovid Metamorphoses iii. 394.
[27] The Revolt of Islam, 3664–66.

To be drawn by the Spirits to the end that is the new beginning, Panthea and Asia are required not to act but to submit to Necessity by an act of will, or, as they think of it, to obey their "sweet desires." For if evil is an unnatural distortion imposed by the will, it will vanish of itself if man willfully, as though by an act of faith, submits his will to Necessity's law. "Resist not the weakness" of passive submission to Necessity, the Oceanids are urged;

> Such strength is in meekness
> That the Eternal, the Immortal,
> Must unloose through life's portal
> The snake-like Doom coiled underneath his throne
>   By that alone.   (II. iii. 93–98)

The significance of these words rests on the recognition that Demogorgon, "the Eternal, the Immortal," to whose realm Panthea and Asia are being drawn, is that ultimate and unknowable Power that is the source of the recurrent cycles in the realm of mutability but, as we are told in *Mont Blanc*, "dwells apart in its tranquillity, / Remote, serene, and inaccessible." This "secret Strength" residing on the other side of "life's portal" is Demogorgon, the Power that releases its normal processes into the realm of life when the mind bends its will into passive admission of them.

Inasmuch as ultimate cause is infinitely remote from the first palpable event in the regular temporal succession called cause and effect, Demogorgon's realm is absolutely remote not only from the universe but also from the One Mind by which the universe is constituted; and it is notable that Prometheus and Demogorgon never meet, indeed could not. Even though Asia, as the generative love which is the ideal state of the One Mind, does enter Demogorgon's domain, she learns that there its truths are "imageless" and therefore as unavailable to mind as is the imageless peak of Mont Blanc. Correspondingly, Demogorgon himself is imageless, being "Ungazed upon and shapeless" and having "neither limb, / Nor form, nor outline" (II. iv. 5–6). Since thought is the measure of the universe and since Power is distinct from that universe, Demogorgon's is "the world unknown" (II. i. 190). The distinction is not between the One Mind, which constitutes the universe, or known world, and a yet greater Mind which constitutes the "world unknown." Shelley has not slipped into a Kantian distinction between phenomenal and noumenal worlds, nor is Demogorgon a God that Shelley has been tricked into admitting while elaborating an atheistic metaphysics. There are, in Existence, only the One Mind (and its human modes) and the one universe that exists by virtue of being the object of its thought. Demogorgon cannot be mind at all because

that the basis of all things cannot be, as the popular philosophy alleges, mind, is sufficiently evident. Mind . . . cannot create, it can only perceive. It is said also to be the cause. But cause is only a word expressing a certain state of the

human mind with regard to the manner in which two thoughts are apprehended to be related to each other. . . . It is infinitely improbable that the cause
of mind, that is, of existence, is similar to mind.[28]

Consequently Prometheus is represented anthropomorphically, but Demogorgon is not. Although a "living Spirit," he has none of the attributes of
mind—neither will, nor thought, nor passion—and appears only as a
"mighty darkness" (II. iv. 7, 2; IV. 510). Since Shelley has equated mind
with "existence" and therefore has identified thought with the universe,
at the point in his manuscript where he located Demogorgon's realm in
"the world unknown," he contemplated adding, "Beyond the world of
being."[29] The route to this realm in "the depth of the deep" (II. iii. 81)
leads down through the sensible world of mortal life; through that point
of entrance and exit where Death and Life strive with each other; beyond
the barrier separating our mutable human world, where things "seem,"
from that realm where things "are"; down to "the remotest throne" (II.
iii. 54–61), the infinitely distant ultimate Power, or Cause, that "One"
whence the succession of all sensible events flows (II. iii. 79). Demogorgon is not, as some have proposed, Necessity, the "mighty law" governing
the regular events flowing from or receding to him; Necessity is Demogorgon's law and is immanent in Prometheus' reality, the "world of being," as Demogorgon is not. Nor is it adequate to interpret him as Destiny
or Revolution, as other critics have proposed, although, like all other
events, these are implicit in Power. In Shelley's words, he occupies "the
seat of power" (II. iv. 3), and Mary Shelley was right to call him "the
Primal Power of the world," although we must also recognize his isolation and absolute difference from the world. He is, in brief, infinite potentiality, needing only to be roused in order to release his force into
existence as a chain of events. Otherwise dormant in his unknowable
world, he is

Like veiled lightning asleep,
Like the spark nursed in embers,
The last look Love remembers,
Like a diamond, which shines
On the dark wealth of mines. (II. iii. 83–87)

He is the "voice unspoken" (II. i. 191), the treasured "spell" (II. iii. 88)—
the word that, on being spoken, has causal power.[30]

[28] On Life (Julian, VI, 196–97).
[29] MS e. 11, p. 111.
[30] An abandoned manuscript stanza (Zillman, p. 654) further likens this potentiality to

    a dew mist asleep
Which the winds might embolden
To climb bright & golden
The pale vault of the dawn
Till the sun rides thereon.

Since mind has no immediate access to Power, Prometheus cannot be the agent to rouse Demogorgon from his sleep; he has reached the outer limits of his reformative capacity when he withdraws the hate that has sustained Jupiter and willfully submits his will to the law of Necessity. Only Asia, generative love, serving as agency of the One Mind and acting under the compulsion of Necessity, can retreat into potentiality and awaken it. The removal of hate is only a negative act; it can only prepare the way for Love to activate Power. Asia's retreat from the world of existence into the realm of the potential, then, motivates the parallel retraction of Jupiter by Power into its own potentiality, and thus makes possible the release of the "natural" course of events, symbolized by Asia's flight from the realm of potentiality to active reunion with Prometheus.

iii

With these interpretations in hand, we can now reconsider the significance of Asia's route and, thus, the structure of Act II. We have observed that the two *loci classici* of Virgil's philosophy were understood to be the Silenus *Eclogue* and the sixth book of the *Aeneid* and that, taken together, these were generally read as forming a modified Epicureanism which denies a divine Creator and Governor and postulates an infused spirit that sustains and moves the world. Consequently, the sixth *Eclogue* was an appropriate significant form that Shelley could adapt to represent the operation of Necessity in a physico-moral world devoid of a God. Like Virgil's Fauns, who learn how the atoms came together of themselves to form the world, Shelley's Fauns have learned of the immanent Necessity which directs both the events of nature and the journey of Panthea and Asia through the forest of the sensible world. In the scene following this bucolic episode, the Oceanids then descend through a volcanic crater into Demogorgon's mysterious cave, and there Asia questions the Ultimate Cause about the ultimate truths.

In other words, this *descensus ad inferos* of the Oceanids is very like Aeneas' underworld journey in the sixth book of the *Aeneid*. Drawn to the mountain peak, Asia sees that "midway" below her it is "around / Encinctured by the dark and blooming forests" (II. iii. 24–25), just as the Sibyl had told Aeneas that between the upper air and the underworld, "tenent media omnia silvae"[31]—or, as Dryden amplified the sense, "Deep forests and impenetrable night / Possess the middle space." Beneath her is a cavern like "a volcano's meteor-breathing chasm, / Whence the oracular vapour is hurled up" (II. iii. 3–4), the analogue of which is Virgil's gate to the underworld through a cave among volcanic mountains and near the cave whose volcanic vapors inspired the Cumaean Sibyl. Thence the "Spirits" of Necessity, having "bound" Asia and Panthea and

---

[31] *Aeneid* vi. 131. The glossators noted: "per silvas, tenebras et lustra significat."

assuming the role of Aeneas' Sibyl, "guide" them to Demogorgon (II. iii. 90). In Scene 2, Panthea and Asia have experienced in the sensible world the omnipresent activity of Necessity and are now to encounter, beneath the sensible world, the Power from which the law of Necessity issues. Correspondingly the significant form provided by Virgil's sixth *Eclogue*, which offers, directly or indirectly, an antitheological explanation of the self-governed sensible world, is succeeded by that of the sixth book of the *Aeneid*, which offers an antitheological account of the *anima mundi*, one of the secrets buried in the depths and darkness beneath the earth.[32] The essential differences between Shelley's adaptation and the received interpretation of Virgil are that the *anima mundi*, unlike Demogorgon, is a mind, an intelligence; and that it is Demogorgon's law of Necessity that, like the *anima mundi*, is immanent in nature, not Demogorgon, who is outside it.

When Aeneas encounters his father, Anchises, in the underworld of *Aeneid* vi, he gains from him revelations of two distinct kinds: one explains the nature and actions of the world-soul and of the human soul; the other prophesies the future glories of his royal line, glories that are to culminate in the return of the Golden Age in the reign of Augustus. As Dryden marked these two themes in his succinct "Argument" of the book, Anchises instructs Aeneas "in those sublime mysteries of the soul of the world, and the transmigration; and shews him that glorious race of heroes which was to descend from him, and his posterity." Correspondingly, Asia's first questions to Demogorgon in the underworld have to do with the theology of creation: Who created the objective "living world"? Who created the subjective sense whereby, through our experience of nature's youthful spring and our own youthful love of another, all outside ourselves is briefly meaningful to us?[33] On the other hand, who created terror, madness, crime, remorse, lost hope, hate, self-contempt, pain, and the fear of hell? To the first two of these questions Demogor-

---

[32] *Ibid.*, 266–67.

[33]
Who made that sense which, when the winds of Spring
In rarest visitation, or the voice
Of one beloved heard in youth alone,
Fills the faint eyes with falling tears . . .
And leaves this peopled earth a solitude
When it returns no more? (II iv. 12–18)

That this sense is the love whereby the self sympathizes and unites with the nonself to form the most vivid apprehension of "life" is further clarified by comparison with the essay *On Love*: "There is eloquence in the tongueless wind, and a melody in the flowing brooks and the rustling of the reeds beside them, which by their inconceivable relation to something within the soul, awaken the spirits to a dance of breathless rapture, and bring tears of mysterious tenderness to the eyes, like . . . the voice of one beloved singing to you alone. . . . So soon as this want or power is dead, man becomes the living sepulchre of himself, and what yet survives is the mere husk of what once he was."

gon replies, "God: Almighty God" and "Merciful God." But unlike
Anchises' replies to Aeneas, Demogorgon's is really no answer at all, and
in place of the traditionally cryptic language of oracles he has substituted
words that empty themselves of all meaning. For when Asia then asks,
"Whom calledst thou God?" he replies, "I spoke but as ye speak" (II. iv.
112). Shelley's Demogorgon, who might have written the atheistic notes
to Queen Mab, has denied the validity of Asia's question. Since there is
no Creator, the only way to answer is to use the language of those who
think the question valid: If you assume the world was created, then it
was created by its creator.

Nor does Demogorgon really answer Asia's third query, not because,
like the first two, it begs the question, but because the answer is in-
expressible and incomprehensible by mind. All evil flows from tyranny;
and the answer to Asia's question is not necessarily "Jupiter," but "He
reigns," since "To know nor faith, nor love, nor law; to be / Omnipotent
but friendless is to reign," as Asia herself explains (II. iv. 47–48). "Omnipotent" is of course an ironic exaggeration, since Jupiter is but a distorted
and unreal projection of Prometheus, has no autonomous existence, and,
although raining down evil, is himself the enslaved servant of evil. The
problem is the insoluble one of causation, for every master of evil is slave
to a master of evil, ad infinitum. Jupiter is the "supreme of living things"
(II. iv. 113) only because at this moment he is master of the "world of
being," but his relation to the ultimate source of evil, the final master who
is not enslaved to yet a higher master, is that of the events of the living
world to Demogorgon. Ultimate cause, the "deep truth" which would
answer Asia's question, is "imageless" because Demogorgon and his realm,
being ontologically different from the "revolving world" and outside Existence, are imageless, a formless darkness unavailable to the senses of the
mind. Evil, then, is the eternal potentiality of tyranny in the imageless
Power and can be released into actuality as a Jupiter by the One Mind's
yielding up its faculties and objectifying them in a hypostatized institution; but evil is released into actuality as an infinite chain of tyrannies,
of which even the primaeval tyranny is an enslavement to evil, and behind that primaeval event the mind cannot see any more than the "inaccessible" Power can be seen behind the primaeval mountains in Mont
Blanc.

Like many of the other myths constitutively drawn into Prometheus
Unbound, that of Virgil's sixth book has been remolded into what Shelley's imagination conceives to be the most nearly perfect shape of which
it is capable, so that it may embody the truth that had eluded Virgil; and
as a result Shelley's adaptation, although entirely independent of its source
for its existence and meaning, ironically plays against it. Demogorgon has
in no way supplied the theology that Anchises so freely expounded, for
the idea of an oracular Anchises implies, in the context of the assumptions

of Shelley's play, superstitious faith in an external source of revelation and makes possible institutional religions, built as they are on their claims to supernatural knowledge. Demogorgon's cave is "oracular" only in the sense that everything in actuality and time flows from the infinitely distant potentiality: what will happen in time is present in, although not occasioned by, the atemporal potentiality of time. But since mind cannot have experiential knowledge of that potentiality, it can only know that there are mysteries, not what they are. Mind, therefore, cannot gain knowledge from external institutions pretending to ultimate truths, but must derive its knowledge from itself, even though that self-examination reveals, skeptically, the mind's ignorance of what lies outside Existence. Lucretius, consistently scornful of oracles, had praised some philosophers because "in making many excellent and inspired discoveries [about physical nature] they have given responses as it were from the heart's adytum, with more sanctity and far more certainty than the Pythia who speaks forth from Apollo's tripod and laurels";[34] and Asia adopts the words of this Epicurean poet in response to Demogorgon's failure to communicate oracular truths:

So much I asked before, and my heart gave
The response thou hast given; and of such truths
Each to itself must be the oracle.[35] (II. iv. 121–23)

Nor indeed is Asia's final question answered in the terms in which she poses it. In the underworld Anchises has foreknowledge of the eventual return of the Golden Age under Augustus, not because there is any inevitability in the course of history nor because his foreknowledge affects that course, but simply because he has supernatural prescience of what has been arbitrarily decreed by Fate. But when Asia, knowing only that "Prometheus shall arise / Henceforth the sun of this rejoicing world," asks when that Golden Age will be, she is answered merely, "Behold!" (II. iv. 126–28). As infinite potentiality, Demogorgon is the infinity of that which enters actuality as time, and therefore all chronological time is present to him. The Hour who will bear Asia to Prometheus and restore the Golden Age "waits" for her in an ever-present now (II. iv. 141). In the rigorously necessitarian world of Shelley's poem the answer to Asia's "When?" is "Behold!" because potentiality is ever waiting to be roused into act, and Love's quest for the Promethean Age makes that future event present.

[34] De rerum natura i. 736–39; see also Lucan Pharsalia ix. 564–65.
[35] This adaptation has been pointed out by Paul Turner, "Shelley and Lucretius," RES, n.s. 10 (1959), 275. What Lucretius meant to Shelley can be judged by his having adopted as the epigraph to Queen Mab the passage in which Lucretius announces that his poetic task is to set minds free from the knots of religious superstition. In the Preface to The Revolt of Islam he wrote that Lucretius' "doctrines are yet the basis of our metaphysical knowledge."

iv

When Demogorgon then displays to Asia the future Hours, one of whom waits for her, she at first mistakenly believes hers is a "ghastly charioteer" in a "dark chariot." This, however, proves to be the Hour with whom Demogorgon, the "terrible shadow," will ascend to "wrap in lasting night heaven's kingless throne." Only after Demogorgon has risen in the dark chariot will Asia ascend in a brilliant one guided by an Hour with "the dove-like eyes of hope." This twofold pattern recurs throughout the play in many forms, and a collation of some instances will make its significance evident. It will be recalled that in Act I, when one of the Furies sang of the "disenchanted nation" that was led forth by Freedom and called Love's children, another Fury, knowing the cruelest pain it could inflict on Prometheus, broke in to deny that these were the children of Love: " 'Tis another's: / See how kindred murder kin." Shelley means this interruption to dramatize the truth that the revolutionary overthrow of tyranny does not of itself produce the Golden Age. By itself, it merely lays the ground for another political tyranny, as the French Revolution had done: "Tyrants rushed in, and did divide the spoil" (I. 654). Correspondingly, Christ's revolution, not being succeeded by a spirit of love, permitted the ecclesiastical tyranny that enslaved the freed. Asia's first bewildered belief that she is to rise in the chariot of Revolution is man's common mistake: the revolutionary withdrawal of evil is not the work of Love but is aroused by it and must be followed immediately by it.

This simple formulation—the retraction of evil by Demogorgon upon being awakened by Love, and the immediate release and guarantee of the "natural" order of events by Love—is the heart of Shelley's millennial vision, and its model is the spring that is born in the death of autumn. It obviously accounts for the large design of his narrative: Prometheus' revolutionary withdrawal of his curse in winter is directly followed by the journey of Love to Demogorgon's realm at the very moment of spring; and Demogorgon's revolutionary flight to withdraw Jupiter is immediately followed by Love's flight to reunion with Prometheus. The same pattern explains why, when men in their rebellious, enthusiastic youth drink the oracular vapors of Demogorgon's cave and "call" it truth, virtue, and love, their maddened, Maenad-like response is a "contagion to the world" (II. iii. 10). As Shelley wrote elsewhere, the revolutionary upsurge of the spirit of liberty is a "glorious madness" that pours abroad like a "wide contagion,"[36] but it is a madness nevertheless, a mere chaotic wildness without love. The formula similarly explains why, when the primitive Gaia was priestess of the Delphic oracle, she inspired the "erring nations round to mutual war, / And faithless faith," whereas now that Asia is

---

[36] *The Revolt of Islam*, 3491–3513.

restored to the liberated Prometheus the Themis-like oracle inspires "calm and happy thoughts." The gospel that Shelley is intent on preaching demands not only that revolution be both motivated and succeeded by love but also that the succession be immediate. Hence in Act I the first of the consoling Spirits of the Human Mind, representing Revolution and flying to Prometheus on "a battle-trumpet's blast," tells that when religious and political tyranny were overthrown and the first exultant cry, "Freedom! Hope! Death! Victory!" had faded,

> one sound, above, around,
> One sound beneath, around, above,
> Was moving; 'twas the soul of love.   (I. 703–5)

Thus, despite Asia's impatience, the flight of the Hour bearing her to Prometheus takes place with the utmost speed (II. v. 6–7) because, unnatural evil having been removed, the Hour of Love must succeed the Hour of Revolution in the realm of mind with the same unrelenting haste that, as Panthea's and Asia's dreams of Necessity had revealed, takes place in the will-less physical world. What Panthea and Asia had seen was that the almond tree and the new grass of spring hasten to burgeon even before the old winter that would destroy them has faded; and Asia impatiently follows Demogorgon into the realm of Existence as immediately as the symbolic morning of her flight succeeds the symbolic night of his.

11 Prometheus Unbound

The Breathing Earth

It will be useful at this point to summarize the structure of the play's metaphysics as it has emerged in this analysis. As the One Mind, Prometheus is identical with Existence, or Life, and is limited to its scope and capabilities. Only in his possessing will can he be said to have power, and it is a power only to consent or refuse to yield control over that will to anything outside himself. He is free to resist the effort of tyranny to bend his will and free to relinquish his will to Necessity, but he has no causal power. Human minds are a mode of this absolute Existence, but since they are only portions of the One Mind and are subject to the illusions of time, space, and mutability, the reality they constitute is only appearance, a deluding "veil which those who live call life." Jupiter also is but a function of Prometheus, a feigned distortion of the One Mind projected by it upon a feigned Heaven and, in turn, disfiguring the realm of Existence by its despotism. Even though Jupiter is eventually withdrawn into Demogorgon's realm, he is to remain there as a potential condition, not an independent reality. Prometheus, Jupiter, Asia, and the human mind represent only Existence, its possible modes, and its possible factors; they can only affect events, not effect them. Within this realm, the principle governing the processes of events is Demogorgon's inviolable law of Necessity—quite independent of Prometheus' will—according to which what is called a cause must be followed by what is called a determined effect. However, these patterns of succession are the laws of the Power's manifestations within the realm of Existence, not

326

the causative Power itself. Strictly speaking, then, there are only two self-sustaining factors in the drama: Prometheus, the One Mind, or Existence; and Demogorgon, absolutely different from the One Mind and inaccessibly remote from it, and yet the mysterious source of all the energy that appears in the domain of the One Mind as the sequences of events.

In *Mont Blanc* Shelley had placed this unknowable cause where it is traditionally conceived to be, transcendently above the world, and he had symbolized it as the perpetual falling of the gleaming snow on the mountain peak. The transcendent region of the Power is the qualityless and thus inexperienceable absolute of all those sensible qualities that it evolves into in the world of human experience; and the mutating form that flows from it—snow, glacier, and river—pursues its downward course through the sensible world according to the law of Necessity. In *Adonais*, where the subject is not Existence, as it is in *Prometheus Unbound*, but the meaning of death and the postmortal existence of the human soul, the perfect One, or the Truth-Beauty-Goodness of Being from which the human soul derives and to which it returns, is also imaged transcendently as the heavenly sun and its attendant stars. Perfection is felt to be "above," as it is in the Christian cosmology; and the desired journey of the soul is an ascent, whereas the belief that death is a descent ("where all things wise and fair / Descend") is represented as arising from a mistaken theology or as true only of the material body ("Dust to the dust! but the pure spirit shall flow / Back to the burning fountain whence it came"). But in *Prometheus Unbound* the unitary perfection, or Being, which is Truth-Beauty-Goodness, although assumed in the philosophic content, is not an operative factor in the drama, which is acted out on other grounds and in other terms. Here not only does Shelley, as in *Lines Written Among The Euganean Hills*, explicitly evade the question of death and the postmortal existence of the human soul, nudging it beyond the concerns of the play with only a hint of his speculations;[1] he also is occupied with overthrowing the assumptions of conventional theologies. Consequently, he inverts the usual theological values of "above" and "below," for if the transcendent God of the theologians is an anthropomorphic projection that tyrannizes over its fabricator, then superiority of place is symbolic of tyranny over the spatially inferior. The only occupants of Shelley's spatial Heaven are Jupiter and his co-operating gods because superiority is the spatial symbol of the oppressor. Ideally, Heaven should not be occupied at all; a republic is the equality of place—"Eldest of things, divine Equality!"[2] In fashioning his Jupiter Shelley has erased all distinction between the heavenly God of Christianity and the Satanic prince of the power of air who, in consequence of ruling "on high" (I.

---

[1] For example, III. iii. 108–12.
[2] *The Revolt of Islam*, 2212.

281), can rain down plague and evil (I. 172, 266; II. iv. 100), send down his mischiefs from his "etherial tower" (I. 274–75), and cause confusion and all manners of pain to fall on man from heaven (I. 652; II. iv. 50–52).[3] Not simply because of Aeschylus' myth but also because of this symbolic significance of superior place, the punishment meted out to Prometheus is enchainment to a barren precipice in the Caucasus, where he longingly reminisces on the "o'ershadowing woods" of the ravine below, through which he had once wandered in union with Asia (I. 122). As Shelley formulates it, the history of Prometheus' restoration is his movement from bound exposure on the barren mountain height—"Black, wintry, dead, unmeasured; without herb, / Insect, or beast, or shape and sound of life"—to the freedom of the luxuriant, enclosing cave.

It is the characteristic of Shelley's imagination that he conceived many of his poems in cosmic terms, postulating in them an entire universe, together with its spiritual physics. Indeed, the cosmic scope almost necessarily follows from his theory of the relation of mind to what we call the external universe. *The Sensitive Plant,* for example, supposes a total world consisting of a universal garden, the Lady who is the existing power of its existence, and man, the sensitive plant; and the poem reveals that ideally the world-garden is a mirror image of the eternal star-covered sky. *Mont Blanc,* which defines the universe in terms of the presence of images in the mind, fashions a total metaphysical world out of the mountain and its ravine, and develops into a symbolic dynamics the evolution of the glaciers and the river from the snow on the mountain peak. Similar cosmic dimensions determine *Epipsychidion* and *Adonais,* as they do *Prometheus Unbound,* where, rejecting a world presided over from above as necessarily enslaved, Shelley has substituted a world, symbolic of the total realm of existence, whose actuating source is below, a world diffusing from its infinitely remote center. It is a world whose potentialities for perfection —and therefore its "divinity"—are inaccessibly remote, but within, not superimposed from without, just as in his *Defence of Poetry* he was to write of "the divinity in man" and to attribute the poet's momentary intuitions of perfect form not to any transcendent Idea but to submission to a power seated upon the veiled throne of the soul and arising, as he says, "from within."

ii

Behind the world-structure and spatial organization governing his drama lies Shelley's adaptation of the Renaissance conceptions of "meteorology," the science of "all natural processes that occur in the Region of Air: cloud, dew, winds, lightning, comets, rainbows, and associated

---

[3] Compare Eph. 2:2.

weather processes."[4] These diverse atmospheric events are bound together by the doctrine, rooted in classical science and still governing much of the scientific vision and vocabulary of Shelley's day, that "meteors" are "exhalations" from the surface and interior of the earth. The picture created by this science and adopted by Shelley in his drama is of a world repeatedly breathing out dew, vapor, mist, clouds, earthquakes, and volcanic eruptions. All fiery, glowing meteors are enkindled exhalations of the earth; plague is a noxious exhalation from the earth that spreads through the air by contagion; a flower's exhalation is its scent. Even the vegetation that springs from the earth may be thought of in these terms— the buried corpse "Exhales itself in flowers of gentle breath."[5] More than metaphorically, the earth is, as Shelley records in *Prometheus Unbound*, "the breathing earth" (II. ii. 52), the ultimate source of its exhalations lying immeasurably deep within itself.

But although the poem rejects a supervisory God as necessarily evil, the world Shelley pictures as dynamically exhaling and diffusing from a Power at its unimaginable center is not necessarily good. The hypothesis only provides Shelley with a cosmic metaphor for the true relation of the Power to the realm of existence and rejects the fictitious spatial relationships on which tyranny is founded; it is ethically neutral, merely describing the operations of the universe, not evaluating them. For the Power and its law of Necessity fulfill themselves indifferently, without regard to any teleology, so that in *Mont Blanc*, for example, it is merely in accordance with the neutral law of Necessity that the snow by which the Power manifests itself becomes the murderous glaciers and they in turn become the life-giving river. "We are taught by the doctrine of Necessity that there is neither good nor evil in the universe, otherwise than as the events to which we apply these epithets have relation to our own peculiar mode of being."[6] We are expected to take Jupiter at his word when, overcome by Demogorgon and finding he can beg from this Power no mercy, pity, release, or respite, he contrasts him with Prometheus, who "would not doom me thus. / Gentle, and just, and dreadless, is he not / The monarch of the world?" (III. i. 67–69). Passion, virtue, and will are exclusively the attributes of mind, and by means of them it determines and rules over the world it constitutes. But of Demogorgon, Jupiter can only ask, "What then art thou?" (III. i. 69), since no mental terms are applicable to the mysterious Cause that acts according to fixed laws, without emotion, evalua-

[4] S. K. Heninger, *A Handbook of Renaissance Meteorology* (Durham, N.C., 1960), p. 4. Despite Shelley's obvious interest in science, it is quite mistaken, as a poem like *Adonais* testifies, to believe that it prevented him from exploiting all exploded scientific theories and fantasies for the purpose of poetic conception and expression, and thus to search only among the latest scientific findings of his day for the clues to his imagery.

[5] *Adonais*, 173.

[6] *Queen Mab*, VI. 198n.

tion, purpose, or choice. What Shelley had written of Necessity applies
equally to the Power from which it derives:

> all that the wide world contains
> Are but thy passive instruments, and thou
> Regard'st them all with an impartial eye,
> Whose joy or pain thy nature cannot feel,
> Because thou hast not human sense,
> Because thou art not human mind.[7]

In the realm of amoral Demogorgon, then, both good and evil are potential, and active evil in the world can be withdrawn once again into inert
potentiality, but not destroyed, just as the Lady of *The Sensitive Plant*
merely "banished" from the world-garden the destructive insects, "whose
intent, / Although they did ill, was innocent." Jupiter can be removed
from actuality only by being suppressed into Demogorgon's center of potentiality, whence he will forever threaten to erupt again, like the "undistinguishable thoughts" that Beatrice Cenci should have suppressed.

On the cosmic scale of *Prometheus Unbound*, this ethics is embodied
in the dominant symbol of the breathing earth. Since the ethics of
Shelley's symbolism provides that the will must permit the "natural" to
diffuse itself from the central Power and must create the condition for
retracting the noxious into sleeping potentiality, the action of the play
begins, not with Prometheus' canceling or destroying the curse, but with
the request that it be shaped into palpable thought by words so that he
may "recall" it—not merely remember, but literally draw it back into
himself.[8] In accordance with the symbol of meteorological exhalations, he
had once "breathed" the vengeful curse on Jupiter (I. 59) and would now
retract, withdraw, that exhalation to its center of origin, just as in *Mont
Blanc* the Power and its laws manifest in the mountain can "repeal"
(in its etymological sense) large codes of fraud and woe, or just as Shelley
will later pray that "the pale name of PRIEST might shrink and dwindle /
Into the hell from which it first was hurled."[9] For the curse Prometheus
had "breathed" on Jupiter, like this volcanic hurling forth of the name of
priest, is represented as a volcanic exhalation that shook the mountains
and seas, split the air, and darkened the sky with glowing volcanic ash
and smoke, until "there stood / Darkness o'er the day like blood" (I.
101-2). Prometheus now wills that the evil exhaled into actuality be
withdrawn into the innocuous, dormant potentiality from which it had

---

[7] *Ibid.*, VI. 214-19.
[8] For some dissenting interpretations of "recall" (I. 59), see London *TLS*, December 16, 1955, p. 761; January 6, 1956, p. 7; January 20, 1956, p. 37.
[9] *Ode to Liberty*, 228-29.

erupted, even as Jupiter himself will, in consequence, be retracted from heaven into Demogorgon's cave. For the ethical corollary of this cosmic symbolism is that the moral atmosphere enveloping the world is not imposed from without but is the result of the breath exhaled from an inaccessibly remote and nonhuman Power within; and therefore the meteorology of exhalation perfectly symbolizes the world's moral climate, which is determined not by superimposed codes but by the manner in which the emanation of Power is received into existence. The perfect model of this ethics is the world exhaling, as was believed, its own atmosphere, the enclosing sphere of vapor, or "steam," responsible for the world's weather. Virtue is the free effluence that benignly enfolds that from whose heart it has arisen; evil, or tyranny, is an emanation that, by being received unnaturally into existence, divides itself from it and enslaves and distorts it from without. The autonomy of the symbolic sphere that diffuses from its mysterious center and thus embraces itself is radical to all of Shelley's thought and to his rejection of all imposed codes: "Each ['life and being'] is at once the centre and the circumference, the point to which all things are referred, and the line within which all things are contained."[10]

For example, as Shelley was to write in his *Ode to Liberty*, words, as exhalations of the mind, may

> make the thoughts obscure
> From which they spring, as clouds of glimmering dew
> From a white lake blot Heaven's blue portraiture. (234–36)

Similarly, because of that distortion which is hate, Earth, in accordance with the meteorological symbol, breathes forth an atmospheric plague that, in turn, infects her because it envelops her (I. 177–79). On the other hand, the transfigurations of both Asia and Prometheus are pictured as their envelopment in their own exhalations of light. From within Prometheus love "Steamed forth like vaporous fire" (II. i. 75), and he was

> arrayed
> In the soft light of his own smiles, which spread
> Like radiance from the cloud-surrounded moon. (II. i. 120–22)

At Asia's birth, and again at her spiritual rebirth, love burst from her "like the atmosphere / Of the sun's fire" (II. v. 26–27); she is shrouded in her own "atmosphere" of radiance (II. v. 54–59), and her own voice "folds" her from sight (II. v. 61–63). So, too, in the rhapsodic celebration of Act IV, Earth's joy is a "vaporous exultation" that springs from within

---

[10] *On Life* (Julian, VI, 194).

and, she says, "wraps me, like an atmosphere of light, / And bears me as a cloud is borne by its own wind" (IV. 323–24); and love, springing up "from its awful throne of patient power / In the wise heart, . . . folds over the world its healing wings" (IV. 557–61).

iii

According to this symbolic cosmology, then, the "deep" can exhale either evil or the force which removes evil; it can be either hell or the heart from which the Golden Age emanates. And hence the brilliant propriety of Shelley's electing Demogorgon as the mythic representative of what Mary Shelley called "the Primal Power of the world." In Boccaccio's De genealogia deorum, which directly or at second hand almost certainly must have been the main source of Shelley's information,[11] it is explained that the simple rustics once believed that the absolutely primal (a nemine genitum) and eternal father of all things is concealed in the bowels of the earth because they observed that all vegetation springs out of the ground, volcanoes vomit flames, caverns breathe forth winds, the earth quakes and emits bellows, and from its bowels are poured the waters. For these reasons, Boccaccio continues, the rustics believed that from the core of the earth volcanic eruptions had spewed forth the air, the seas, and the fires that became the sun, moon, and stars. Imagining, therefore, that there must be some dark, divine intelligence in the bowels of the earth, they thought it to be Demogorgon. Subsequent mythographers, of course, recognized the likelihood that Demogorgon is to be understood as the Platonic or Stoic Demiurge.[12] Shelley's representation of Power as the deep chthonian source of exhalations already had a precedent in myth, and his adaptation of Demogorgon therefore is in accord with the complex mythopoeic syncretism of the play. Moreover, according to Boccaccio, Demogorgon sent from the bowels of the earth not only its surface but also

[11] Shelley demonstrably had more information about Boccaccio's Demogorgon than was available to him in Peacock's note to his Rhododaphne, usually considered the source of his knowledge. Certainly Boccaccio's treatise must have been as accessible to him as it was to Peacock, and he could have found much of Boccaccio's account of Demogorgon summarized in the notes to a number of editions of classical works, such as Lucan's Pharsalia and Statius' Thebaid. Coleridge, incidentally, knew the Italian version of the De genealogia and in 1803 copied into his notebook a sentence from the description of Demogorgon (Notebooks, ed. K. Coburn [New York, 1957], items 1649, 1653; see also 2512, 2737).

For Joseph Harpur's early nineteenth-century interpretation of Demogorgon as the "unknown and incomprehensible energies of nature, all depending on the eternal and necessary relations and aptitudes of things," see Albert J. Kuhn, "Shelley's Demogorgon and Eternal Necessity," MLN, 74 (1959), 596–99.

[12] E.g., Lucan, Pharsalia, ed. Franciscus Oudendorpius (Leyden, 1728), I, p. 497n, where Boccaccio's account is summarized and annotated. See also Abbé Banier, The Mythology and Fables of the Ancients, II, iii, 1, where Demogorgon's name is etymologized as meaning "Genius or Intelligence of the Earth."

the heavenly bodies and the surrounding air and sky; and thus the given myth exactly accommodates itself to Shelley's recurrent symbol of a world whose defining environment arises exclusively from its own mysterious depths. Even Boccaccio's description of Demogorgon as sluggish, sleepy, and surrounded by mists and fog lends itself to Shelley's conception of the ultimate Power as a dormant potentiality which, being inaccessible to the senses, can be represented only as "a mighty darkness . . . / Ungazed upon and shapeless," having "neither limb, / Nor form, nor outline." But Boccaccio tells that he was led to descend into Demogorgon's underworld by his search for the one true God, first cause of all things, and the express purpose of his chapter on Demogorgon, father and chief of all the gods of the gentiles, was to ridicule this foolish pagan superstition and to oppose to this false earth-deity the true God of Christianity, "qui in caelis habitat." Shelley's adoption of Demogorgon not only exchanges the traditional values of height and depth, transcendence and containment, but inverts Boccaccio's Christian thesis by accepting the pagan god whose existence Boccaccio had attributed to the absence of Christian revelation and to the barbaric ignorance that deified natural forces.

Like Boccaccio's figure, Shelley's Demogorgon is represented as volcanic, a fitting image of the Primal Power: at about the time Shelley was beginning Act II he visited Vesuvius and reported it to be "after the glaciers the most impressive expression of the energies of nature I ever saw. It has not the immeasurable greatness[,] the overpowering magnificence, nor above all the radiant beauty of the glaciers, but it has all their character of tremendous & irresistible strength."[13] Not only does Demogorgon overcome Jupiter in the manner of a volcanic eruption, but as G. M. Matthews has perceptively demonstrated, the descent of Asia and Panthea to Demogorgon's realm in Act II is a journey into the crater of a volcano.[14] Looking down from a pinnacle of rock among the mountains, Panthea and Asia see Demogorgon's cave as "Like a volcano's meteor-breathing chasm" and note the "crimson foam" of the vapor rising from it (II. iii. 3, 18, 44). It is this volcanic imagery that allows Shelley to place Boccaccio's volcanic Demogorgon in the underworld of Virgil's sixth book and to send Panthea and Asia on a journey that is an ironic adaptation of Aeneas' descent to Anchises. For not only does Aeneas, like these Oceanids, pass through a dark wood, but Avernus, where the Sibyl leads Aeneas into the underworld, was notable for its sulphurous exhalations[15]

[13] To Peacock, [17 or 18] December 1818 (*Letters*, II, 62).
[14] I am greatly indebted to Mr. Matthews' "A Volcano's Voice in Shelley" (*ELH*, 24 [1957], 191–228) for directing my attention to the prevalence of the volcanic imagery in the poem. His study is, so to speak, ground-breaking, both because of its findings and, I believe, because of its critical assumptions about Shelley's poetry.
[15] *Aeneid* vi. 240–41; Lucretius, vi. 747–48.

and was associated with the surrounding volcanic region.[16] In addition, the fact that the Sibyl leads Aeneas from the prophetic cave, where she is inspired by the rising exhalations, to the underworld entrance at mephitic Avernus corresponds to Panthea's description of the vapors rising from Demogorgon's volcanic cave as "oracular" (II. iii. 4).

But the foundation on which Shelley built his volcanic symbolism is not limited to traditional meteorology, the inversion of the Christian cosmology, Boccaccio's volcanic Demogorgon, and Book vi of the *Aeneid*; the volcano was also present in an important way in the myth of Aeschylus' *Prometheus Bound*. At the height of his agonized defiance of Jove, Aeschylus' Prometheus aligns himself sympathetically with Jove's other rebellious victims:

Pity moved me, too, at the sight of the earth-born dweller of the Cilician caves curbed by violence, that destructive monster of a hundred heads, impetuous Typhon. He withstood all the gods, hissing out terror with horrid jaws, while from his eyes lightened a hideous glare, as though he would storm amain the sovereignty of Zeus. But upon him came the unsleeping bolt of Zeus, the swooping levin brand with breath of flame, which smote him, frightened, from his high-worded vauntings; for, stricken to the very heart, he was burnt to ashes and his strength blasted from him by the lightning bolt. And now, a helpless and a sprawling bulk, he lies hard by the narrows of the sea, pressed down beneath the roots of Aetna; whilst on the topmost summit Hephaestus sits and hammers the molten ore. Thence there shall one day burst forth rivers of fire, with savage jaws devouring the level fields of Sicily, land of fair fruit— such boiling rage shall Typho, although charred by the blazing levin of Zeus, send spouting forth with hot jets of appalling, fire-breathing surge.[17]

By ironically inverting Aeschylus' play and its interpretation of Prometheus and Zeus, Shelley has in effect written a counter-sequel that, by recounting Demogorgon's eruptive removal of Jupiter, assumes the fulfillment of Prometheus' prophecy, which Aeschylus of course intended only as an expression of Prometheus' sinful pride and perverted theology.

---

[16] The Delphin Virgil (Ruaeus), for example, commenting on Avernus (*Aeneid* vi. 237), notes that not only the region of Cumae but the entire coast of Campania, like much of Sicily, is everywhere hollow, as is evident from Charybdis and from Vesuvius and Aetna, the fire-breathing mountains (*montibus ignivomis*).

But Shelley's knowledge of this region was not merely literary. In the first half of December 1818, after Act I of *Prometheus Unbound* was completed but apparently before Act II was begun, he toured "the Mare Morto & the Elysian fields, the spot on which Virgil places the scenery of the 6th Aeneid," entered a Sibyl's cave ("not Virgils Sybil") on the shore of Avernus, noted that nearby "a high hill called Monte Nuovo was thrown up by Volcanic fire," and visited nearby Vesuvius, whose volcanic activity he described elaborately and with awe in a letter to Peacock ([17 or 18] December 1818, and 23–24 January 1819 [*Letters*, II, 60–64, 73–74]). Not only did he have *Aeneid* vi in mind at about the time he was to begin Act II, but he was also vividly conscious of its volcanic setting.

[17] 353ff.

Shelley is of Typhon's party, and inasmuch as he is reinterpreting the Prometheus myth as a corrective of Aeschylus, it is this allusion by Aeschylus to Typhon, whom almost every mythographer identified as the volcanic deity,[18] that acts as the basis for Shelley's network of cosmological and mythic materials embodying the image of the volcano. For Shelley has tacitly cast Demogorgon in the role of Typhon and the other volcanic giants or Titans who, like Prometheus, rebelled against Jupiter. In accordance with his consistent myth-making process, he has not fabricated a completely new myth dictated by the requirements of his theme but has fastened upon relationships already implicit among natural events and diverse myths in order to shape that myth which, in proportion as it approximates beautiful unity, embodies truth. For example, Asia's and Panthea's *descensus ad inferos* through a volcanic crater is not merely a restructuring of Aeneas' descent in a volcanic region into Hades, nor is it simply a conflation of this with the fact that Typhon lies beneath Aetna; it also embodies Boccaccio's account of his own journey, in search of the first cause of things, to Demogorgon's realm in the entrails of the earth by passing through Taenarus, the entrance to Hades, or, Boccaccio adds, through volcanic Aetna.

The established myth tells that Typhon and his fellow giants, born of Earth and sprung from its lowest depths (*emissum ima de sede terrae*),[19] succeeded briefly in driving Jupiter down from heaven by casting up bolts of fire and huge rocks; and Apollodorus adds that Typhon succeeded in imprisoning Jupiter in the Corycian cave,[20] just as Shelley's Demogorgon will imprison Jupiter in his cave. Typhon, the myth continues, was then overcome by Jupiter and flung beneath Aetna, whence, struggling to rise again, he rebelliously continues to vomit flames and rocks into the heaven and cause the earth to quake,[21] even as Prometheus was chained for his revolt and persisted in his defiance. Indeed, not only did any volcanic eruption whatsoever come to suggest renewed revolt against Jupiter, but Typhon and the other volcanic Titans like Briareus, Aegeon, and Enceladus became allegorical personifications of rebellion

---

[18] According to the scholiast on Pindar's first Pythian ode, every mountain notable for exhalations or eruptions contains Typhon. Sir William Drummond claimed that "The history of the rebellion and punishment of the Titans is nothing else than an allegorical account of volcanic eruptions" (*Herculanensia* [London, 1810], p. 47).

[19] Ovid *Metamorphoses* v. 321.

[20] *Bibliotheca* i. 6. 3.

[21] E.g., Pindar *Pythian* i; Ovid *Metamorphoses* v. 315ff. Silius Italicus, after describing the hot springs and sulphurous exhalations about the Campanian coast and connecting them with the underworld, attributes them to the panting breath of the buried Giants and adds that the Giant beneath volcanic Inarime, throwing up flames from his rebellious mouth (*rebelli ore*), seeks, if ever he is allowed to get free, to renew his war against Jupiter and the other gods. Whenever the volcanoes threaten to erupt, heaven grows pale (*Punica* xii. 113–51).

against authority, especially against that of God and monarch.[22] The volcanic giants, therefore, precisely suited Shelley's theme, and all that was needed to assimilate them to Demogorgon was to exchange the values traditionally assigned to rulers and rebels. Bacon, for instance, coming close to Shelley's application of the myth, had read the story of Jupiter and Typhon (*sive Rebellis*) as meaning that when a king becomes tyrannical and assumes absolute and arbitrary power the injured state will rise in monstrous rebellion against the oppressor.[23]

Shelley has fully detailed the volcanic quality of Demogorgon's emergence to meet Jupiter in Typhoëan combat. He is a darkly glowing cloud that

> floats
> Up from its throne, as may the lurid smoke
> Of earthquake-ruined cities o'er the sea.
> . . . watch its path among the stars
> Blackening the night!   (II. iv. 150–55)

In overwhelming Jupiter, Demogorgon hovers over him, again like a volcanic cloud, darkening his fall (III. i. 82–83). With this volcanic image in mind, we can appreciate more fully the irony of Jupiter's anticipating an incarnation of his own offspring who will preserve his tyrannous reign and finding instead Demogorgon, who will remove him from his heavenly throne. We have already observed that, as a consequence of Jupiter's perverted values, his exultant description of his union with Thetis is in fact an unintentionally repulsive parody of the union of Prometheus and Asia, a description of destructive rape, not fertile love—and that his faith that his offspring can be eternally incarnate in Demogorgon's limbs betrays his evil ignorance of both his own nature and Demogorgon's. But in addition, just as he believes Demogorgon to be his own child, he mistakes the Hour's mythic chariot bringing volcanic Demogorgon for a chariot like his own, which, according to some versions of the Jupiter

---

[22] E.g., Sandys's translation of Ovid (Oxford, 1632), pp. 190–91.

Dryden, *Astrea Redux*, 33–40:

The Vulgar gull'd into Rebellion, arm'd, . . .
Thus when the bold *Typhoeus* scal'd the Sky,
And forc'd great *Jove* from his own Heaven to fly,
(What King, what Crown from Treasons reach is free,
If *Jove* and *Heaven* can violated be?). . . .

Pope, *Dunciad*, IV. 63–67:

But soon, ah soon Rebellion will commence,
If Music meanly borrows aid from Sense:
Strong in new Arms, lo! Giant Handel stands,
Like bold Briareus, with a hundred hands;
To stir, to rouze, to shake the Soul he comes.

[23] *De sapientia veterum.* See also Natalis Comes *Mythologiae* vi. 22.

myth, was the cause of thunder and lightning. "Hear ye," he asks, "the thunder of the fiery wheels / Griding the winds?" (III. i. 47–48). There is indeed fire and thunderous sound, but it is the cleansing fire[24] and rumbling of earth's eruption from its core of Power, sent up to purge heaven, not the searing fire and thunder of punitive heaven (III. i. 66);[25] and Jupiter is right, in a sense that he does not recognize, when he asks,

> Feel'st thou not, O world,
> The earthquake of his chariot thundering up
> Olympus?   (III. i. 49–51)

It is the crowning irony, therefore, that when he realizes that Demogorgon has triumphed over him Jupiter prays,

> Let hell unlock
> Its mounded oceans of tempestuous fire,
> And whelm on them into the bottomless void
> This desolated world, and thee, and me,
> The conqueror and the conquered, and the wreck
> Of that for which they combated.   (III. i. 74–79)

---

[24] Because fire was used for medical purification and because sulphur was customarily burned to fumigate the air, Shelley, it is evident, conceived of volcanic eruption and the vapors of the associated earthquake as capable of purifying and therefore as symbolic of the cleansing revolution. "I will arise," says Laon,

> and waken
> The multitude, and like a sulphurous hill,
> Which on a sudden from its snows has shaken
> The swoon of ages, it shall burst and fill
> The world with cleansing fire: it must, it will—
> It may not be restrained! . . . (The Revolt of Islam, 784–89)

Later Cythna will promise:

> soon bright day will burst—even like a chasm
> Of fire, to burn the shrouds outworn and dead,
> Which wrap the world; a wide enthusiasm,
> To cleanse the fevered world as with an earthquake's spasm! (Ibid., 3510–13)

This last passage combines the image of the cleansing volcano with a reference to the medical practice of burning the clothes of those dead of the plague. Compare also Earth's description of the restored world: "And long blue meteors cleansing the dull night" (III. iii. 117). For the practice of fumigating with sulphur as a ritual, see the end of Odyssey xxii; and for its use to dispel the plague, see Walter G. Bell, The Great Plague in London in 1665 (London, 1951), and Charles F. Mullett, The Bubonic Plague and England (Lexington, Ky., 1956), which also reports that the infrequency of the plague in the region of Vesuvius had long been noted.

[25] Shelley would have found a symbolic battle between volcano and lightning in Aeschylus' Seven against Thebes (485ff.), where two heroes confront each other, the shield of one showing Typhon belching fire and smoke and that of the other, Zeus holding a bolt of lightning in his hand.

For a volcano has indeed erupted, though not from what Jupiter, like the theologians, thinks of as the "hell" of torments; it will withdraw the combatants into potentiality, not sink them into ruin; and the event will not destroy the wrecked world, but will free it from the harm of evil.

iv

That the single dominant image of the breathing earth symbolizes such opposite values as the volcanic disordering of the earth by Prometheus' curse and enchainment and the revolutionary eruption that removes Jupiter is the heart of Shelley's management of the image, for it allows the poem's symbolic cosmology and ethical hypothesis to coincide. Much of the theme of the poem unfolds through exploitation of the various modes of the single image of earthly exhalations: volcanoes are catastrophic, but they also can stir the lethargic earth to action and to new forms;[26] volcanic exhalations were traditionally thought to be a source of the plague, and yet their sulphurous fumes can also be conceived of as purifying, since sulphur was customarily burned to dispel the plague and since volcanic regions were thought to be free of the disease; and volcanic vapors can inspire mere frenzy or true prophecy, for the ancient prophetesses of the oracular caves uttered their prophecies in a state of madness. Violent volcanic eruption is the geological enactment of rebellion and revolution,[27] but it may overthrow evil or merely distort the earth and end the Golden Age of eternal spring. For all events of every sort in the realm of existence are consequences of the exhalations of the remote and hidden Power. As Asia and Panthea are drawn, according to the laws of Necessity, to Demogorgon's volcano—the "fatal mountain" (II. ii. 62) because it contains *in potentia* all the events that are "fated" to be—they pass through a vaporous volcanic region like the Phlegraean Fields around Avernus; and there the wings of the Oceanids are uplifted for flight, not

[26] Cf. *The Revolt of Islam*, 466–68:

> when Hope's deep source in fullest flow
>   Like earthquake did uplift the stagnant ocean
> Of human thoughts—mine shook beneath the wide emotion.

Incidentally, the word "emotion," modified as it is by the spatial word "wide," effectively plays upon its etymological meaning. The relation between volcanoes and earthquakes was, of course, thoroughly understood and generally assumed by Shelley. See also II. ii. 50–51 ("soft emotion / Attracts, impels them"); and n. 50 below.

[27] "We are surrounded here in Pisa by revolutionary volcanoes, which as yet give more light than heat; the lava has not yet reached Tuscany" (to Peacock, 21 March 1821 [*Letters*, II, 276]). Cf. also *Mask of Anarchy*, 360–63:

> And that slaughter to the Nation
> Shall steam up like inspiration,
> Eloquent, oracular;
> A volcano heard afar.

by their own will, but by the steam exhaled from the "breathing earth"[28] (II. ii. 52) by the same volcanic Power to whose throne they are being drawn. In other words, although the manifestations of the cosmic Power have multiple forms, significances, and values, they are all various modes of the single act of chthonian exhalation; and therefore this relationship exactly corresponds to the relation Shelley understood between Power and the events it effects in the realm of existence. Like the breathing earth, Power fulfills itself in a single fixed sequence in the domain of mind; but whether the series of events it projects into existence acts as cataclysm or purification depends upon the way in which mind, together with its faculty of will, receives into its domain the manifestations of Power. The dynamics of the poem's world is the precise symbol of the ethical drama; and if we add that the universe is to be defined as the mass of knowledge, no essential distinction can really be made between world and mind, science and ethics.

The opportunity to exploit the image of exhalation in different forms and contexts therefore provides Shelley with a means of elaborating the dialectic of his theme and of weaving a texture of ironies—a dialectic and an ironic texture that, somewhat like the relation of symbols to fable in *The Sensitive Plant*, cut across the unilinear dramatic progress by causing sectors of the play to interact at the level of imagery. For example, the assignment of approximately the same volcanic image to different actors in the play sustains the fact that they are all modes of the One Mind. Prometheus "breathed" forth his curse on Jupiter in a volcanic and seismic cataclysm that thundered, rocked the world, and covered the day with darkness; and, in what appears to be retaliation, his enchainment by Jupiter also produced a vast volcanic exhalation with the same consequences:

<blockquote>
the sea
Was lifted by strange tempest, and new fire
From earthquake-rifted mountains of bright snow
Shook its portentous hair[29] beneath Heaven's frown. (I. 165–68)
</blockquote>

For if it is correct to understand Jupiter as but a distorted reflection of Prometheus, Prometheus is really his own tormentor, and his volcanic curse against Jupiter is, in fact, the same as the volcanic disorder with which Jupiter tortures him. For the same reason, when Jupiter's Phantasm is called up from the depths "underneath the grave" (I. 197), it also erupts

---

[28] Shelley first wrote "steaming earth" (Zillman, p. 197n.). He may well have owed the term "breathing earth" to Silius Italicus' "tellus suspirans," which describes the volcanic fields of the Campanian coast and their vaporous exhalations (*Punica* xii. 135–36). The phrase, however, is common; for example, Wordsworth, *Excursion*, II. 363; III. 237; V. 262.

[29] The image of course derives from the etymology of "comet," the fiery meteor that was the traditional portent of disaster.

volcanically: as it appears, driven up on "direst storms" (I. 242), its sound "is of whirlwind underground, / Earthquake, and fire, and mountains cloven" (I. 231–32). When it then repeats Prometheus' curse "the Heaven / Darkens above" (I. 256–57) as it had when Prometheus originally gave volcanic utterance to the curse (I. 102). Moreover, since Prometheus represents the unitary totality of existence, it is proper that his various modes make similar volcanic and seismic defiances of Jupiter. Hence at the human level the analogue of Prometheus' volcanic curse is the distinctly Typhon-like rebellion against Jupiter's tyranny by the soul of man, which, "like unextinguished fire, / Yet burns towards heaven with fierce reproach . . . / Hurling up insurrection" (III. i. 5–8) even as the analogue in the man-made world to the noxious volcanic cataclysm is the religion-inflamed city that "Vomits smoke in the bright air" (I. 552). Like Prometheus, the Earth, since she exists in consequence of being perceived by Prometheus, also breathed a curse on Jupiter, and, she explains, "the thin air, my breath, was stained / With the contagion of a mother's hate / Breathed on her child's destroyer" (I. 177–79). The speech-breath of hate is analogous not only to the exhalation of Prometheus' curse but also to the earth's polluted, miasmal exhalations released by earthquake and spread through the air as contagious mists;[30] and just as Prometheus' curse of hate only perpetuated his imprisonment by the tyrant he cursed, so Earth's curse of hate merely infected her own enveloping atmospheric breath.

On the other hand, since the poem's spatial metaphor provides for only one central Power from which everything radiates into actuality, it is the innocent and mild forms of exhalation that tend to symbolize the natural and beneficial. The Hours, for example, originate in Demogorgon's cave "below the deep" (II. iv. 140; IV. 60) and thus in the Eternity with which Demogorgon identifies himself (III. i. 52); and, like the Echoes shrinking back into their native caves, they return to subterranean Eternity when their "time" has passed (IV. 14). For Eternity is to sequential time as Power is to all sequences in the realm of existence; and thus the Hours describe their own rising from potentiality into actuality as the removal of the "figured curtain of sleep / Which covered our being and

---

[30] The article on "plague" in Ephraim Chambers' *Cyclopaedia* may be taken as typical of the entire tradition that attributes the plague to subterranean exhalations and associates it with earthquake: "The disorder is generally supposed to be communicated by the air. . . . Mr. [Robert] Boyle attributes plague principally to the effluvia or exhalations breathed into the atmosphere, from noxious minerals. . . . The air . . . is depraved in far more places than improved, by being impregnated with subterraneous expirations . . . since morbific causes operate more effectually than curative ones, it seems more than probable, that exhalations ascending from under ground, may produce pestilential fevers, and the plague itself. . . . It is probable, peculiar kinds of venomous exhalations may sometimes be emitted, especially after earthquakes. . . ."
Lucan (vi. 90–92) attributes to the exhalations of volcanic Typhon both plague and raging madness.

darkened our birth . . . below the deep" (IV. 58–60). By assigning to Asia the characteristics of Aphrodite Anadyomene, Shelley can also picture her birth as an "uprise" from the cloven sea (II. v. 22); and Prometheus' birth from Earth's bosom is likened to her exhalation of a divine nimbus, "a cloud / Of glory" (I. 157–58). In view of these beneficent forms of exhalation in the drama, and especially in view of the curative cosmic effect of Demogorgon's volcanic eruption, we can better appreciate the reason why, at the end of the play, Earth tacitly abstracts from the legend of King Bladud and the healing springs of Bath to pattern an account of man's moral purification: evil will

> Leave Man, even as a leprous child is left,
> Who follows a sick beast to some warm cleft
> Of rocks, through which the might of healing springs is poured.   (IV. 388–90)

Like the volcanic clouds of sulphur and the curative sulphur fumes used to purge the air, the thermal springs, geologically related to volcanoes, are exhalations that "owe their origin partly to the admixture of sulphurous particles, while the water . . . creeps through beds and mines of sulphur, &c. and partly to the fumes and vapours exhaling through the pores of the earth where sulphur is. . . ."[31]

Given, then, a cosmic center of potentiality which diffuses into actuality and retracts from it, and given the premise that these exhalations are violent or gentle, beneficent or disruptive, and disruptive of good or evil, depending upon the manner in which actuality receives them, an ironic interplay can be set in motion among the occurrences of this spatial image. For example, at the very beginning of the drama Prometheus is tortured by the Jupiter-sent earthquake that wrenches the rivets in his wounds (I. 38–40); at the conclusion of the drama love radiates from Earth's center, awakens the dead to "breathe a spirit up from their obscurest bowers," and, like "a storm bursting its cloudy prison," erupts from the Demogorgon-like "lampless caves" of "unimagined being" inaccessibly remote within Thought[32] to produce an earthquake that shocks thought's chaos out of its stagnation (IV. 375–80). Similarly, Prometheus' volcanic curse on Jupiter, like the Earth's, stands in ironic juxtaposition to Demogorgon's volcanic flight to Jupiter: uttered in hate, the curse was an eruption that merely perpetuated Jupiter's reign and distorted its speaker and his Earth; Demogorgon's flight, aroused by Love, burst forth to recall

[31] Chambers' *Cyclopaedia*, art. "Bath."
[32] Shelley originally wrote that this volcanic love erupts from "the caverns of the [? depth] of thought" (Zillman, pp. 285n., 665), apparently meaning to draw a significant analogy between Power, infinitely remote within, and different from, Existence, and a mysterious source inaccessibly distant within, and different from, Mind. The analogy collapses into identity, of course, if Mind is identical with Existence.

Jupiter from actuality. And whereas the Earth's curse of hate was a self-infecting plague, upon the restoration of Prometheus Earth can prophesy that instead of the nightly miasma that is unwholesome to man and blights the flowers with mildew, the exhalations of

The dew-mists of my sunless sleep shall float
Under the stars like balm: night-folded flowers
Shall suck unwithering hues in their repose.   (III. iii. 100–2)

Because the image of exhalation and the spatial pattern it implies are radical to the cosmos assumed by the play, even the larger units of the action assume similar designs so as to evaluate and comment on each other. Thus Asia's descent into the realm of Power and her arousing of Demogorgon to an eruptive violence that topples Jupiter is the heroic version of the earlier deeds of Mercury and the Furies in Act I; for the journeys of Mercury and the Furies describe the same spatial pattern as those of Asia and Demogorgon respectively and seem a gruesome travesty of them, in the same manner that the union of Jupiter and Thetis travesties that of Prometheus and Asia. Not drawn down by the natural processes of Necessity, as Asia is, but "driven down" from Heaven by the tyrannical will of Jupiter, the messenger of the gods calls up the monsters from "the deep" (I. 462) to torture and subdue Prometheus—an anticipation of the time when Asia, Prometheus' messenger, will descend to rouse Demogorgon from the deep to rid Heaven of Jupiter. The "monster-teeming Hell" from which the Furies rise is "the all-miscreative brain of Jove" (I. 447–48), for they are fictitious distortions formed by the fictitious supreme tyrant and allowed by the One Mind to act as tormenting, but suppressed, psychological realities. Inasmuch as organized religion and political despotism are distortions of truth, this cosmic structure of a Hell from which the Furies emerge is an ugly parody of the true and natural cosmos and its workings; and consequently the Furies also, like Demogorgon, are represented as volcanic and seismic "powers" (I. 367). Ascending from the "abyss" (I. 370) like exhalations—"Like vapours steaming up behind" (I. 329)—they "climb the wind" (I. 327). Jupiter's descent to reward them with human groans and blood when, charioted on a "sulphurous cloud," he "bursts Heaven's bounds" (I. 333–34) ironically anticipates the descent on which volcanic Demogorgon will drag him. In the manner of volcanic clouds, the Furies blacken the dawn (I. 441) as they gather "in legions from the deep" (I. 462); "steaming up from Hell's wide gate," they "burthen the blasts of the atmosphere" (I. 518–19), just as the curse of hate breathed by Earth had infected her atmosphere; they "trample the sea" and "shake hills" with their screams of mirth when "cities sink howling in ruin" (I. 498–500); and Panthea complains of the volcanic thunder of their rising:

These solid mountains quiver with the sound
Even as the tremulous air; their shadows make
The space within my plumes more black than night. (I. 522–24)

Further, whereas the Furies' disfiguring eruption anticipates Demogorgon's cleansing eruption, the corrective counterpart (short of Love) to
the Furies, whom Jupiter summons to torment Prometheus, is the Spirits
of the Human Mind, whom Earth summons as consoling angels to this
tortured Christ. The Furies erupt from the hellish abyss of Jupiter's mis-
shaping brain, climb with clanging wings like steaming vapors, and call
for aid from their fellows who reside in the human mind in the form of
hatred and self-contempt and whose uprising makes "solid mountains
quiver" (I. 522). The consolatory Spirits, by contrast, ascend gently from
their "homes . . . the dim caves of human thought," rising "Like fountain-
vapours when the winds are dumb" and "Thronging in the blue air"
"Like flocks of clouds in spring's delightful weather" (I. 659–67). In accordance with Shelley's definition of the "universe," the metaphor identifies the human mind as a world that exhales these beneficent Spirits from
its obscure inmost center. Hence Earth's statement that the "homes" of
these Spirits are "the dim caves of human thought" and yet that they
"inhabit, as birds wing the wind," thought's "world-surrounding ether"
(I. 659–61), however inconsistent it has appeared to some critics, is wholly
coherent if we recognize that these Spirits are imaged as vaporous exhalations and if we assimilate the image to the poem's consistent cosmological
symbolism. The caves, like Demogorgon's cave or like that of the Echoes,
are the "homes" of human thought in the sense of source, or place of
origin; but once diffused, the Spirits inhabit the surrounding and defining
atmosphere of the mind-world, just as birds on leaving their nests inhabit
the air, or as earth's exhalations inhabit "cloudlike" the embracing atmosphere (I. 688). The mind, according to the recurrent symbol of the
self-conditioning sphere, contains a center that radiates to form the mind's
own guarding and consolatory ambience. Opposed to the volcanic Furies,
who, "steaming up from Hell's wide gate, . . . burthen the blasts of the
atmosphere," the mind's consoling Spirits wing the surrounding atmosphere not only when it is clear but even when it is laden with the mind's
dark and pestilential exhalations of evil:

And we breathe, and sicken not,
The atmosphere of human thought:
Be it dim, and dank, and grey,
Like a storm-extinguished day,
Travelled o'er by dying gleams;
    Be it bright as all between
Cloudless skies and windless streams. (I. 675–81)

Moreover, this metaphor continues, by inhabiting thought's encircling atmosphere, the Spirits of the Human Mind can "behold / Beyond that twilight realm, as in a glass, / The future" (I. 661–63). Since twilight is the atmospheric refraction of the light of the unseen sun hidden below the horizon, the Spirits, having emanated from the center of the mind-world, can perceive in its immediate and self-formed ambience, as in a mirror, the reflection of the light that must necessarily be rising; for man is a prophet in that he "beholds the future in the present" in accordance with the rigorous laws of Necessity.[33]

The prophetic cave is an obvious adjunct of the volcanic metaphor, since the oracular priestess was inspired by the vapors rising from the volcanic crevices;[34] and Shelley employs these related geological symbols in related ways. Even apart from the geological connection between volcanoes and the *fatidici specus*, there is a logical relation between the two in Shelley's symbolic system, for if volcanic Demogorgon is the primal cause that manifests itself in actuality according to the laws of Necessity, and if the future is therefore inherent in Demogorgon's realm of absolute potentiality, then the vaporous chthonian exhalations are prophetic. Moreover, Lucan, who is one of the sources for Demogorgon, also accepted the Stoic belief that a great part of total divinity (*totius Jovis*) rules the world from within it and identified this Typhon- and Demogorgon-like divinity with the omniscient source of the vapors breathed forth in the oracular caves.[35] Hence it is consistent with the world-structure framed by Shelley that Demogorgon be the source of both volcanic eruptions and oracular vapors. When, for example, Asia consults Demogorgon as an oracle and asks for those ultimate truths that reside exclusively, like Demogorgon himself, in the "unimagined" realm outside perceptible existence, he

---

[33] *Defence of Poetry* (Julian, VII, 112).

[34] Lucan, for example, describes the Delphic oracle as a huge chasm that breathes out divine truth and exhales speaking winds (*ventos loquaces*); and he compares the inspired priestess' utterance to the eruption of Aetna and to the howling of Typhon beneath his volcano (*Pharsalia* v. 82–101). Cf. also Shelley's "Fragments Connected with *Epipsychidion*":

There is a Power, a Love, a Joy, a God
Which makes in mortal hearts its brief abode,
A Phythian exhalation, which inspires
Love, only love....

[35] *Pharsalia* v. 86–96. The commentators took it that Lucan was referring specifically to Demogorgon. Not unexpectedly, this doctrine of Lucan's was associated by the commentators (e.g., Cornelius Schrevelius in his edition of *De bello civili* [Amsterdam, 1658], p. 211n.) with those lines in *Aeneid* vi which account for the Platonic or Stoic *anima mundi* and which had considerable formative influence on Shelley's presentation of Demogorgon in his Virgilian Act II (*Spiritus intus alit, totamque infusa per artus / mens agitat molem*). Banier, arguing that Demogorgon represents the earth's vegetative principle, also associates him with these lines by Virgil (*The Mythology and Fables of the Ancients*, II, iii, 1).

replies not only in the cryptic manner characteristic of oracles, but also in a volcanic metaphor:

> If the abysm
> Could vomit forth[36] its secrets. But a voice
> Is wanting, the deep truth is imageless.   (II. iv. 114–16)

Consequently, Shelley is careful to identify the volcanic with the oracular nature of Demogorgon's cave. Its mighty portal, Panthea says, is

> Like a volcano's meteor-breathing chasm,
> Whence the oracular vapour is hurled up[37]
> Which lonely men drink wandering in their youth,
> And call truth, virtue, love, genius, or joy,
> That maddening wine of life, whose dregs they drain
> To deep intoxication; and uplift,
> Like Maenads who cry loud, Evoe! Evoe!
> The voice which is contagion to the world.   (II. iii. 3–10)

This elaborate metaphor of exhalations is carefully ambivalent, since the metaphor of a universe diffusing from a center is designed to imply in itself neither good nor evil and applies equally to the Furies and the Spirits of the Human Mind. The breath exhaled into the atmosphere because of the inspiring oracular vapors is potentially a pestilential contagion to the world like the plague breathed up by Earth in her hate; or, depending on the manner in which it is received, it may be a spreading, sanguine call for the overthrow of evil. The frenzied, Maenad-like state of youth's oracular intoxication[38] may produce drunken savagery like the French Revolution or, if it is immediately succeeded by mature Love, may revoke all that is not truth, virtue, love, genius, joy. The moral determinant is not the indifferent exhalations of Power, but the intemperate circumstance of reception implied by "youth." In accordance with this pattern, Earth's volcanic cave first "panted forth" her "spirit" as oracular vapors that merely maddened and incited civil war while Jupiter determined the condition of existence; but, with the liberation of the One Mind in the next age, its exhalation inspires "calm and happy thoughts" and feeds with its rich volcanic ash the lush vegetation of nature (III. iii. 135–46).

---

[36] Vomere and evomere were the terms most frequently used by the Latin authors to describe volcanic action.

[37] The draft (Zillman, p. 201n.) reads, "breathed up," which better suits the idea of vapors. But the substitution of "hurled up" effectively fuses the image of the volcano with that of oracular cave.

[38] Compare "Youth's smooth ocean, smiling to betray" (II. v. 100) and "the self-contempt implanted / In young spirits, sense-enchanted" (I. 510–11).

v

Because actuality is symbolized by "meteorological" diffusions from an inaccessible, cavernous world-center, and potentiality by containment in a cave, the course of the Promethean drama is developed as a series of symbolic ascents and descents, diffusions and retractions. Prometheus' "recall" of the curse he had volcanically breathed on Jupiter is succeeded in the next act by the withdrawal of Asia and Panthea into the volcanic center, where all potentiality resides. By virtue of Prometheus' retraction of the exhaled curse, the Oceanids are drawn by Necessity to trace sequentiality back to its origin in Demogorgon's cave, and therefore they are led by the Echoes, not as they radiate from their resonant center as sound, but as they recede into the cave, their traditional home, where they remain as silent, or sleeping, potentials of sound. Correspondingly, Demogorgon in his containing cave is the dormant volcanic potentiality whose "rest" Asia alone can break and awaken into active cause (II. i. 193). For in a significant sense Asia, as generative Love, is not only the companion of Existence but also the earthly representative of the Power, since this "life of life" whose "footsteps pave the world / With loveliness" (II. i. 68–69) and whose "transforming presence" causes the flowers and grass to spring up (I. 827–33) is also causative, or at least is an agent that can release Cause. The love which is the generative spirit of "life" in the realm of existence and which, like Demogorgon, is eternal and unaffected by "Fate, Time, Occasion, Chance, and Change" (II. iv. 119–20) obviously has affiliations, beyond the realm of existence, with the primal Power of all such exhalations. It is for this reason that only Love, as messenger for Prometheus, can rouse the volcano from sleeping potentiality into the eruptive actuality which revokes the evil order and makes possible the release of the new. In logical sequence and in accord with the symbol of diffusion and retraction, Prometheus' recall of his volcanic curse is succeeded by Asia's withdrawal from actuality into Demogorgon's cave in order to rouse this sleeping Power behind all events to a volcanic eruption that, in subsiding, shrinks the transcendent Jupiter from actuality into the dormant center of potentiality, where he must dwell with Demogorgon "Henceforth in darkness" (III. i. 55–56). So also, Prometheus' total history, cast into these patterns of ascent and descent, is a spatial movement from the exposed height of a precipice in the Caucasus to Earth's oracular cave, like Demogorgon's, where he and Asia will be "unchanged" (III. iii. 24) and where the infinite Power will inspire these representations of perfect and absolute Existence with those happy thoughts that are their "unexhausted spirits" (III. iii. 36).

The withdrawal of Prometheus and Asia to their cave, like the descent of Asia in Act II and the revocation of Jupiter to Demogorgon's cave, is, then, a withdrawal from the mutable actuality of space and time into the containment of potentiality, which is how the play defines eternity, as Demogorgon's identification of himself as "Eternity" makes clear. Recognition of the temporal symbolism of this pattern of retreat will put into meaningful focus Asia's otherwise curious song of her withdrawal with Prometheus from human time after their transfigurations:

> We have passed Age's icy caves,
>   And Manhood's dark and tossing waves,
> And Youth's smooth ocean, smiling to betray:
>   Beyond the glassy gulfs we flee
>   Of shadow-peopled Infancy,
> Through Death and Birth, to a diviner day;
>   A paradise of vaulted bowers,
>   Lit by downward-gazing flowers.   (II. v. 98–105)

Shelley has conceived of temporal life not as a linear movement into birth and through death but, varying the circle of mutability, as a kind of cul-de-sac whose beginning, called "Death and Birth," is also its end.[39] The contradictory nature of the imagery in these lines is designed to convey this fact. Temporal life is represented as a passage inward, against the normal flow of the waters, through ocean and ever-narrowing and more forbidding waters to Age's icy caves; death is the retreat along the flow of the water and from the cul-de-sac to eternity, like the retreat of Prometheus and Asia to their cave, of the Echoes to theirs, and of Asia and Panthea to Demogorgon's. Paradoxically, although the temporal movement of life, from youth to age, is imaged as passage inward from ocean to tempestuous river and then to icy cave, the metaphor itself compels in the opposite direction; and although the chronology of life leads to the icy caves of age, the retreat from time through constantly widening expanses of water ends, like Prometheus' retreat, not in infinite space but in the enclosing "paradise of vaulted bowers, / Lit by downward-gazing flowers" (II. v. 104–5) that symbolizes the eternity of contained potentiality.[40]

This controlling pattern of a cavernous container symbolizing potentiality and of diffusions from it symbolizing actuality also defines the function of Proteus' shell, with which the Hour announces and disseminates the new age throughout the world after the reunion of Prometheus and Asia. For if the culmination of the drama is the retreat of the One Mind into the immutable eternity of the cave, it is also, inversely, through-

[39] Cf. *Epipsychidion*, 379–80: "the star of Death / And Birth." If Shelley is referring to Venus, as seems likely, the point is that the Morning Star and the Evening Star are the same.

[40] Compare the similar imagery in the description of Prometheus' cave (III. iii. 10–17).

out the human, temporal world, the diffusion of perfection from the potentiality in which it has been contained. Shelley's choice of Proteus'
"curved shell" as an analogue of the other caves of potentiality is one of
his happiest mythopoeic findings and transformations. As a sea-god,
Proteus can readily be drawn into the network of myths that includes the
sea-born Venus-Asia, daughter of Ocean, and her sister Oceanids. And
the traditional interpretation of Proteus as the shapeless and ever-changing
primal matter to whom primal nature had revealed all its secrets, including knowledge of past, present, and future, entitles him to serve as a
kind of surrogate in the realm of imaged existence for Demogorgon, the
shapeless, impalpable Cause in "unimagined" being.[41] Like Demogorgon,
whose cave exhales oracular vapors, Proteus, having knowledge of all
times, is notably the prophet; and like Demogorgon the "Primal Power,"
Proteus was addressed in Thomas Taylor's translation of the Orphic
hymn as "First-born," to whom "all things Nature first . . . consign'd."[42]
Consequently Proteus' shell is analogous at the human level to Demogorgon's cave at the level of the One Mind: each is the potentiality from
which perfection is breathed out into actuality.[43] Apparently, it was
Bacon's interpretation that most helped shape Shelley's conception of
Proteus;[44] for Bacon also rejected the idea of supernatural prophecy, and
the myth according to which Proteus divulges the future to anyone who
can hold him fast he took to represent the necessary causal sequence in
nature:

And whereas it is added in the fable that Proteus was a prophet and knew the
three times; this agrees well with the nature of matter: for if a man knew the
conditions, affections, and processes of matter, he would certainly comprehend
the sum and general issue (for I do not say that his knowledge would extend
to the parts and singularities)[45] of all things past, present, and to come.[46]

[41] For the traditional interpretations of Proteus, see A. B. Chambers, "Milton's
Proteus and Satan's Visit to the Sun," *JEGP*, 62 (1963), 280-87.
[42] *The Hymns of Orpheus* (London, 1792), p. 149. In his edition of Milton's
Paradise Lost ([London, 1750], I, 239n.) Thomas Newton interpreted Proteus as
"the first principle of things."
[43] For Shelley's interpretation of Proteus as the activating spirit of the world inhabited by man, see his *Essay on Christianity* (Julian, VI, 230): "[The God described by Christ] is neither the Proteus [n]or the Pan of the material world."
[44] *The Triumph of Life*, 269-73:

If Bacon's spirit had not leapt
Like lightning out of darkness; he compelled
The Proteus shape of Nature's as it slept

To wake and to unbar the caves that held
The treasure of the secrets of its reign.
[45] Compare *Defence of Poetry* (Julian, VII, 112): "Not that I assert poets to be
prophets in the gross sense of the word, or that they can foretell the form as surely
as they foreknow the spirit of events. . . ."
[46] *De sapientia veterum*, xiii.

Most excellently therefore did the ancients represent Proteus, him of the many shapes, to be likewise a prophet triply great; as knowing the future, the past, and the secrets of the present. For he who knows the universal passions of matter and thereby knows what is possible to be, cannot help knowing likewise what has been, what is, and what will be, according to the sums of things.[47]

It is highly appropriate, therefore, that this primal spirit of nature should have given Asia the sea shell, Venus' traditional emblem, as a nuptial gift and should have breathed into it a "voice to be accomplished" (III. iii. 67), since the original union of the One Mind and generative Love created a condition fraught with consequences that must, "according to the sums of things," be fulfilled in the manner of prophecy, now that Asia and Prometheus are reunited. The shell into which Proteus breathed his prophecy so that it contained the sounds of the sea functions like Earth's oracular cave of Power, which, upon the return of Asia to Prometheus, exhales calm perfection; and just as Demogorgon in his cave is a sleeping voice "unspoken" until roused by Asia (II. i. 191), or as the "spell" treasured for Asia in that "remotest" cave is "Like veiled lightning asleep" (II. iii. 83), so the music confined in the shell is, as latent potentiality, "like lulled music sleeping" (III. iii. 73). Like Asia when she stirred the sleeping, confined primal Power into volcanic exhalation, the vernal Hour who bore Asia from Demogorgon's cave and who symbolizes the new order of time is to "breathe into the many-folded shell, / Loosening its mighty music"[48] (III. iii. 80–81) so that the cavern-like shell may exhale into human actuality the prophecy it contains. The imprisoned "voice to be accomplished" is to be released by the Hour around the earth like a revolutionary atmospheric disturbance that it might reverberate like thunder (III. iii. 82; III. iv. 98) and shake the startled world (III. iv. 54–55), and thus correspond at the human level to the first event bringing about the new Promethean age, Demogorgon's revolutionary eruption. The revolutionary storm of the shell's music clears the earth's atmosphere, just as Demogorgon's revocation of Jupiter had purged Heaven; and the immediate succession of Demogorgon's chariot by that of Asia, or Love, is repeated in the human domain, for at once

> the impalpable thin air
> And the all-circling sunlight were transformed,
> As if the sense of love dissolved in them
> Had folded itself round the sphered world.   (III. iv. 100–3)

---

[47] *Descriptio globi intellectualis,* v.
[48] Compare the similar "many-folded mountains" (II. i. 201) within which is the entrance to Demogorgon's cave.

The gift of potentiality honoring the union of the One Mind and Love has been exhaled into the actuality of human time as an embracing and world-determining atmosphere of love, corresponding to all the many other symbolic sphere-enclosing atmospheres of the poem. The corollary of the withdrawal of the One Mind with Love into the cave of eternal and immutable perfection is the effusion of the "natural" perfection from its shell-cave throughout the world of human minds.

But although Shelley has so subtly and elaborately drawn on the myths of Venus, the Hora, and Proteus to fashion the symbolism of the prophetic shell from which the earthly millennium will flow, it is also clear that he has done so in order to adapt it to his drama as a continuous reinterpretation of Scripture. In assigning the shell to the Hour that she may breathe into it and loosen its "mighty music," Shelley has substituted the musical shell for the last trumpet, which will summon the dead to the Last Judgment so that the corruptible will put on incorruption and the mortal will put on immortality.[49] No New Jerusalem has supernaturally come down to earth "from God out of heaven," nor has immortality been divinely superadded to man; the perfection inherent as potentiality in the union of Mind and Love has come to its necessary fruition, and man's natural perfection now stands unveiled because all things have "put their evil nature off" (III. iv. 77).

vi

The image of the volcano and its analogues is especially prevalent throughout the final act, which is an exuberant celebration of the new age. Here, however, the image serves not as a pattern of dramatic action but as a symbol expressing the new cosmic joy and generative love that not only erupt with revolutionary tremors but also exhale a benign atmosphere which wraps and carries the world that has breathed it. From Demogorgon's dark cave beyond existence, love explodes like an earthquake to shake the mind-world to energy and form: "like a storm bursting its cloudy prison / With thunder, and with whirlwind," love

<blockquote>
has arisen
Out of the lampless caves of unimagined being:
    With earthquake shock and swiftness making shiver
    Thought's stagnant chaos.... (IV. 376–80)
</blockquote>

But the volcanic exhalation from the Power also embraces the world with an ambient atmosphere of joy and love, so that Earth can tell of

---

[49] I Thess. 4:16; I Cor. 15:52; Rev. 8:2ff.

The joy, the triumph, the delight, the madness!
The boundless, overflowing, bursting gladness,
The vaporous exultation [50] not to be confined!
   Ha! ha! the animation of delight
   Which wraps me, like an atmosphere of light,
And bears me as a cloud is borne by its own wind.[51]   (IV. 319–24)

And the Moon, released from her prison of ice, experiences a similar self-enveloping exhalation of generative love:

   A spirit from my heart bursts forth,
   It clothes with unexpected birth
My cold bare bosom. . . .   (IV. 359–61)

In the same manner that the purging volcanic ascent of Demogorgon made ridiculous, by contrast, the cruel lightning Jupiter flung down from heaven, the Earth can now mock the withdrawn Jupiter:

          Sceptred curse,
   Who all our green and azure universe
Threatenedst to muffle round with black destruction, sending
   A solid cloud to rain hot thunderstones,

until all things "Were stamped by thy strong hate into a lifeless mire" (IV. 338–41, 349). This image of muffling, which defines the symbolic atmospheric condition imposed from without by a supposedly transcendent power, is opposed to the metaphor of clothing, wrapping, or enfolding that defines the spiritual atmosphere exhaled from within. For, Jupiter having been removed and "Heaven's despotism" having sunk into the "void abysm" (IV. 554–55), Earth can now breathe up a volcanic thunder of laughter, a joyous exhalation, and hear its echoes rebound not only from ocean and desert but also, and more importantly, from the now-vacant sky:

   Ha! ha! the caverns of my hollow mountains,
   My cloven fire-crags, sound-exulting fountains

[50] Like the word "emotion" (see n. 26 above), this richly plays upon its etymological meaning (to spring up vigorously) so as to remove all distinction between mind and world, subject and object, and to embody Shelley's thesis "that when speaking of the objects of thought, we indeed only describe one of the forms of thought—or that, speaking of thought, we only apprehend one of the operations of the universal system of beings." See also IV. 333: "sound-exulting fountains."
[51] For the significance of this image of self-enclosure and self-generating motion, see pp. 183–85. In the Moon's reply to Earth, the line "Some Spirit is darted like a beam from thee" (IV. 327) reads in the *Mask of Anarchy* MS (Zillman, p. 662): "Some Spirit wraps thine atmosphere and thee."

Laugh with a vast and inextinguishable laughter.
    The oceans, and the deserts, and the abysses,
    And the deep air's unmeasured wildernesses,
Answer from all their clouds and billows, echoing after.[52]   (IV. 332–37)

The spirit that informs this breath and fills the vacuum left in heaven by the removal of Jupiter's hate is love; and, like all active forces, it is an exhalation that rises from the earth's core and makes its way upward through the granite, roots, clay, leaves, and flowers until it spreads upon winds and clouds to form the atmosphere embracing that from whose heart it sprang. It makes the past a vital influence upon the present, just as the winter corpse exhales itself in spring flowers, for the same power that generates thought also causes the life of nature:

It wakes a life in the forgotten dead,
They breathe a spirit up from their obscurest bowers.   (IV. 374–75)

In brief, as Demogorgon explains, shifting to an analogue of the volcano metaphor, Love "from its awful throne of patient power / ... springs / And folds over the world its healing wings" (IV. 557, 560–61); and this throne of power, so like the one from which he himself has sprung to overcome Jupiter, he locates within, in "the wise heart" (IV. 558).

    The symbolic significance of the effluence from within that becomes the enfolding atmosphere is, of course, that it expresses Shelley's rebellion against all extraneous impositions upon the mind and embodies in cosmic images his doctrine that perfectibility results from the mind's free admission of the indwelling Power. In addition to the many instances already mentioned, this symbolic design is implicit in Act III in Earth's description of Prometheus' cave, where there are "bright golden globes / Of fruit, suspended in their own green heaven" (III. iii. 139–40). It accounts for the perfected Earth's likening himself, spinning "beneath my pyramid of night, / Which points into the heavens," to

        a youth lulled in love-dreams ...
    Under the shadow of his beauty lying,
Which round his rest a watch of light and warmth doth keep.[53]   (IV. 444–49)

---

[52] Between the second and third of these lines, one manuscript (Zillman, p. 662) reads: "mouth of my ⟨volcanoes⟩." Over the canceled "volcanoes" Shelley added, "fire hills."

[53] This simile, which many readers have found confusing, rests upon Shelley's frequent identification of the human self as a world. The simile must be read as equating the dark pyramid, or cone, of Earth's night with the shadow of the youth's beauty, not with his beauty itself, which is likened to the Earth's sunlight. Just as Earth sleeps within the conical shadow it casts by turning from the sun, so the youth lies within the shadow cast by his turning, through sleep, from his own beauty. That

And the Moon informs the renovated Earth:

> Thou are folded, thou art lying
>   In the light which is undying
> Of thine own joy, and heaven's smile divine. (IV. 437–39)

However, as these last lines intimate by picturing the perfected earth wrapped not only in its own joyous light but also in the "smile" (light) of heaven, the symbol of the self-enveloping atmospheric exhalation is not quite adequate to Shelley's total theme. For his ethical doctrine also calls for some model of perfection in the realm of inaccessible Being, some image of a transcendent moral absolute as totally subsuming as the One Mind of Existence; and in itself that meteorological symbol does not provide for it. It is noticeable that in nearly every instance the perfect exhaled atmosphere is likened to an irradiation of light, and evil is likened to an eclipsing darkness or veil. The veil image admirably suits Shelley's purpose because, like the evils rained down by Jupiter or the black destruction with which he would muffle the earth, it implies a dark distortion superimposed on reality. Perfection is not an acquisition from without or a gift from above, and evil is not an inherent condition, but a mask. Perfection reveals itself when falsehood is removed from the truth it conceals and when, like the removal of Jupiter from heaven, "veil by veil, evil and error fall" (III. iii. 62) and all "such foul masks" are removed "with which ill thoughts / Hide that fair being" called man (III. iv. 44–45). Evil is like a low-lying mist that can be dissipated in the clearing air:

> Those ugly human shapes and visages . . .
> Passed floating thro' the air, and fading still
> Into the winds that scattered them; and those
> From whom they passed seemed mild and lovely forms
> After some foul disguise had fallen. . . .
> All things had put their evil nature off.[54] (III. iv. 65–77)

Just as Jupiter is a phantom-like mockery of Prometheus, what man called "life" before the new Promethean day was but a "painted veil . . . / Which mimicked, as with colours idly spread, / All men believed or hoped"; now

---

is, the sunlit heaven surrounding the pyramid of Earth's darkness is likened to the youth's beauty, which "round" (about, outside) his dark pyramid of sleep continues to give "light and warmth." When he is awake, his beauty is his own undimmed sunlit heaven; in sleep he lies under its tentlike shadow.
      Compare *The Witch of Atlas*, 60–61: ". . . she lay enfolden / In the warm shadow of her loveliness."
[54] After this line in the draft (Zillman, p. 249n.) Shelley wrote and then deleted, "Like an old garment soiled & overworn."

it has been "torn aside"—"The loathsome mask has fallen, the man remains..." (III. iv. 190–93). Even what mortal man calls "life" is really
a "veil" of death, since it is the existence of but a portion of the One
Mind under the unreal conditions of mutability; and what man calls
"death" is that sleep in which the unreal veil is removed from true life.
Consequently, all that is unreal and evil is an eclipsing darkness that cuts
the world off from light, and the result of the seismic eruption of Love
is to shake thought's stagnant chaos "Till hate, and fear, and pain, light-
vanquished shadows, fleeing, / Leave Man...a sea reflecting Love" (IV.
381–84).

The meteorological function of the irradiation of love's light from a
cosmic center to form an enfolding atmosphere is therefore to cleanse that
atmosphere of the illusory darkness of evil and error until it is transparent.
For Shelley's ultimate image of the perfect condition is not merely that
of Love springing up from its throne of power and folding over the world
its healing wings. Rather, as a consequence of the world's exhaling its own
radiant, darkness-withdrawing atmosphere of healing, perfection is the
condition in which man and the world perfectly resemble or mirror the
heaven. Earth must reflect the perfection the mind aspires to, not be
darkened by a tyrannical fiction that it fears as a real being. The symbolism of the heaven-reflecting earth is recurrent in Shelley's poetry and
frequently controls his poetic structures. Because *Adonais*, unlike *Prometheus Unbound*, is concerned with the immortality of the human soul
and assumes, in the realm of Being, a transcendent One which is Truth-
Beauty-Goodness, this transfer of the thematic center of gravity from
beneath to above curiously inverts the cosmic metaphor. Instead of the
soul's radiating a light that clears the atmosphere so that heaven may be
reflected in the soul, the transcendent One, represented as the sun, glows
more brightly as the earthly soul more perfectly mirrors it and, by thus
burning more intensely, evaporates the intervening clouds of mortal bondage:

> That Light whose smile kindles the Universe,
> That Beauty in which all things work and move,
> That Benediction which the eclipsing Curse
> Of birth can quench not, that sustaining Love
> Which through the web of being blindly wove
> By man and beast and earth and air and sea,
> Burns bright or dim, as each are mirrors of
> The fire for which all thirst; now beams on me,
> Consuming the last clouds of cold mortality.   (478–86)

But when, as in *The Sensitive Plant*, Shelley's theme is the relative perfection of mortal life, rather than absolute postmortal perfection, his basic

image is of an earth that can mirror the starry skies of the realm of Being, so that the starry flowers of the Venus-Lady's world-garden,

> the meteors of that sublunar Heaven,
> Like the lamps of the air when Night walks forth,
> Laughed round her footsteps up from the Earth!   (II. 10–12)

This is also the heaven-earth relationship implicit in Shelley's complaint in his *Ode to Liberty* that words can "make the thoughts obscure / From which they spring," for then they are like lake-born clouds that "blot Heaven's blue portraiture" that should be painted in the mirroring lake. Mind alone is the medium of those exhalations that intervene and prevent it from mirroring a heavenly perfection.

Thus in *Prometheus Unbound* when the Hour released above the earth the "prophecy" in Proteus' shell, the consequence was that the atmosphere, through an event like the transfiguration of Asia and Prometheus, became transparent:

> the impalpable thin air
> And the all-circling sunlight were transformed,
> As if the sense of love dissolved in them
> Had folded itself round the sphered world.
> My vision then grew clear, and I could see
> Into the mysteries of the universe.   (III. iv. 100–5)

This heaven to be reflected, unlike Jupiter's heaven, is not constituted by any hypothetical transcendent deity bent upon imposing himself on man. Unlike the Christian heaven, it does not assume the inherent depravity of man, the necessity of punishments and rewards, or the existence of a supreme ruler. On the contrary, like the One Mind, which contains in perfection all possible human minds, Shelley's heaven is symbolic of the absolute perfection that mind is able to conceive and become. It exists because mind is able to conceive and aspire to it, not because a deity creates and occupies it or because it has any existence apart from the mind's ideal desires. Hence in her song of spiritual perfection at the end of Act II Asia can tell of being led by Prometheus to more-than-mortal realms "where the air we breathe is love" and where this air of love, by moving in the winds and on the waves, harmonizes "this earth with what we feel above" (II. v. 95–97). The heaven of perfection exists because it is felt to be, and the end of Shelley's symbolism is such translucence of the exhaled embracing atmosphere of love and light that the earth harmonizes with, or perfectly reflects, or is precisely analogous to, the heaven felt to be by the mind. Now that heaven is "free," it "rains fresh light and dew / On the wide earth," and earth is made "like heaven" (III. iv. 154–55, 160).

How mind constitutes this heaven, as opposed to the divinity-created heaven of the theologians, is made clear in Act IV. After their mystic dance with the Hours, the Spirits of the Human Mind divide into two groups, one to remain within the sphere enfolded by the earth's atmosphere, the other to soar beyond that envelope. There the second group will build "a new earth and sea, / And a heaven where yet[55] heaven could never be" (IV. 164–65) so long as there was a merely putative heaven inhabited by Jupiter, the supervisory and punitive deity. It is not St. John's God of the Apocalypse who will create a new heaven and a new earth for man; these lines in Shelley's final act echo ironically those in the final book of Scripture, for only the spirits of the human mind can build a heaven which is a model of perfection. Taking their plan not from some deity's purpose or idea but from the now-liberated world of man himself, they will build as a transcendent ideal the absolute, or Promethean, "world for the Spirit of Wisdom to wield" (IV. 155); and beneath this ideal of the mind all that belongs to earth will assemble to mirror it (IV. 152). In this sense, the mind's vision of the full perfection of its nature and the mind's actual mortal state—"heaven and earth"—are "united now" (IV. 273).

Throughout the play this symbolic relationship between heaven and earth recurrently draws various images into patterns that bind the earthly to the transcendent. It explains, for example, why it is inadequate to describe the perfected Earth merely as wrapped in the joyous light it radiates and why Shelley felt the need to add, "and heaven's smile divine" (IV. 437–39). It makes clear why, after describing the physico-spiritual spring of the new age as descending from the winds of heaven, the poet balances this image by likening the spring to an atmospheric exhalation, a "joy which riseth up / As from the earth, clothing with golden clouds / The desert of our life" (II. i. 10–12). Somewhat more importantly, it accounts for Shelley's picture of the poet as one who

> will watch from dawn to gloom
> The lake-reflected sun illume
> The yellow bees in the ivy-bloom,
> Nor heed nor see, what things they be;
> But from these create he can
> Forms more real than living man,
> Nurslings of immortality! (I. 743–49)

The poet's concern is not with things as things: having access to a world so unencumbered by ugliness, error, and evil that it is able to mirror the absolute perfection that the mind can conceive for itself, he uses as the

---

[55] The Bodleian MS (Zillman, p. 658) reads, "till now."

elements of his poetic shaping those images thus indirectly illuminated by the mirroring world to which he is confined. But even though this accounts for the stuff of poetic creation, the passage throws its emphasis not upon those elements which the poet is constrained to use, but upon his attention to the earth's act of illuminating and transforming its component things through its capacity to resemble and thus to reflect the heavenly light. For the opposite, the imperfect mirror, symbolizes the distortion of unitary perfection into multiple hideous forms of falsehood and evil, just as Jupiter is the disfigured reflection of Prometheus. Hence at the end of the play Earth will plead that hate, fear, and pain flee like "light-vanquished shadows"[56] so as to leave man, the microcosm,

> who was a many-sided mirror,
> Which could distort to many a shape of error
> This true fair world of things, a sea reflecting love;
> Which[57] over all his kind, as the sun's heaven
> Gliding o'er ocean, smooth, serene, and even,
> Darting from starry depths radiance and life, doth move.[58]   (IV. 382–87)

As these passages intimate, then, the mortal condition closest to the ideal is that in which mutable human reality approximates, within its inherent limitations, the immutable, ideal perfection conceived by the imaginative, idealizing mind; and the central cosmic symbol of this condition is the sea, constantly changing and yet free to reflect the changeless sky: "The Sea, in storm or calm, / Heaven's ever-changing Shadow" (I. 27–28). It is the symbolism basic to *Lines Written among the Euganean Hills*, where the "stream of poetry," connected with the human "sea of Misery," is illuminated by the transcendent sunlight of Apollo, god of poetry and prophecy—the eye, Shelley adds in his hymn of Apollo, "with which the Universe / Beholds itself and knows it is divine." This basic symbolic relationship Shelley elaborated into various image patterns in *Prometheus Unbound*, and the matrix from which they derive goes far toward explaining some of the metaphoric manner of his lyric drama. When, for example, the Spirit of Earth describes the earthly perfection he has seen come into existence, he tells of two halcyons, birds whose domain is both sky and water, no longer carnivorous but feeding on night-shade, which is no longer poisonous: "and in the deep there lay / Those lovely forms imaged as in a sky" (III. iv. 82–83). In the last act, heaven and earth having been "united," the Spirits of the Human Mind explain

[56] MS e. 12, p. 54, reads, "like ⟨wind-⟩ light-vanquished ⟨vapours⟩ shadows."
[57] I take "love" to be the antecedent of "Which."
[58] Contrast the Jehovah-like picture of Jupiter in Prometheus' curse, "Let thy malignant spirit move / In darkness over those I love" (I. 276–77), which mocks Genesis 1:2: "and darkness was upon the face of the deep. And the spirit of God moved upon the face of the waters."

that the human mind is the clear reflector of its own transcendent ideal. Once "dusk, and obscene, and blind," but now no longer shrouded in darkness, it is both "an ocean / Of clear emotion" and "A heaven of serene and mighty motion" (IV. 95–98); and consequently in its double-ness it is like the Spirits of the Human Mind, who divide into two groups, one to fashion, "beyond heaven," the ideal, the other to perform a parallel work in the "world of perfect light" (IV. 168). The moment of ideal ex-perience, Shelley had written in *Queen Mab*, occurs when "the sun's highest point / Peeps like a star o'er Ocean's western edge," for then, sky and ocean having met, they are interchangeable, and "those far clouds of feathery gold / ... gleam / Like islands on a dark blue sea." At this moment "has thy fancy soared above the earth."[59]

Translated into myth, these cosmic symbols of heaven and the re-flecting sea of human existence become the sun-god Apollo and Ocean, respectively, and constitute the grounds for Scene 2 of the third act. For it is fitting, in view of the nature of the symbolism, that the withdrawal of eclipsing Jupiter from the heavens be reported by the sun-god to Ocean, father of the Oceanids and, according to Aeschylus, Prometheus' sym-pathizer, and that the setting of this dialogue between heaven and the mirroring sea be Atlantis, not merely because Plato assigned it to the sea-god Poseidon, but also because in that earthly paradise he placed the ideal commonwealth of man.[60] In effect, heaven has communicated to earth the fact that the false barrier between them has been removed; and since Ocean's domain is the "Heaven-reflecting sea" of human life (III. ii. 18), his prophecy of the coming perfection takes the form of an elaborate parallelism of sky and the surface of the sea as each is seen from beneath:

Blue Proteus and his humid nymphs shall mark
The shadow of fair ships, as mortals see
The floating bark of the light-laden moon
With that white star, its sightless pilot's crest,
Borne down the rapid sunset's ebbing sea.   (III. ii. 24–28)

[59] *Queen Mab*, II. 13–19.
[60] *Critias* 120.

12 Prometheus Unbound

The Far Goal of Time

Up to this point the analysis of the drama has been based on the premise that Prometheus personifies Shelley's concept of the One Mind, but some qualification is now required. If at the beginning of the play Prometheus were truly the One Mind as Shelley defined that concept, it would follow that he could not be represented by language. Imagery would falsify, not because Prometheus belongs to the imageless realm of Demogorgon outside sensible being, but because the supposed discreteness and diversity which we call "things" exist only in the human mind as a consequence of its necessary impurity. To adapt Demogorgon's words, unity also is imageless; and the One Mind is identical with the ineffable oneness of Existence. Even more important, were Prometheus precisely as he has here been defined, the narrative of the drama would have been impossible because the illusions of time, space, and change operate only in human minds. As the One Mind, Prometheus could have no history. The drama, then, can have been made possible only by the introduction of those unreal dimensions; and their introduction assumes that the One Mind can be less than its absolute nature—indeed, must be when human minds, its temporal portions, are distorted by evil. The absolute unity of Existence enters into time when it allows itself to be less than its own perfection, for time is merely the variable relationships made possible by the fracturing of unity into diversity. As Asia explains, it is not a reality but only the envious shadow cast by the throne of Saturn, Jupiter's predecessor and god of a Golden Age that was vapid,

mindless (II. iv. 33–34). Saturn is Father Time only in the sense that the
shadow he cast is the illusion of passing time. Permitted evil has compelled the One Mind into approximately the same illusory time-space,
subject-object world that the human mind supposes. Only after his reunion with Asia and their withdrawal to the cave can Prometheus say of
his existence,

> we will sit and talk of time and change,
> As the world ebbs and flows, ourselves unchanged.
> What can hide man from mutability?   (III. iii. 23–25)

Although, as Prometheus' transfiguration revealed, the "form" that lives
within him has been "unchanged" (II. i. 64–65), what invests that form
has undergone a history of change, just as Christ, the incarnation of the
immutable Godhead, entered into mutable human circumstances. Nor has
Shelley committed the contradiction of subjecting to change what is declared to be unchangeable: Prometheus prophesies only that, despite man's
necessary mutability, he himself will be outside time and change, not that
it is a contradiction of his nature to re-enter them.

Consequently, when Prometheus enters his cave with Asia the possibility of narrative has ended because he has passed beyond the limits
of imagery and language. Only now is he truly the One Mind, and therefore he must disappear from the play. The final act is set near the cave
of Prometheus, but neither Prometheus nor Asia reappears after their
approach to the cave at the end of Act III. Even the drama's frame of
reference has changed. Whereas the first three acts are Prometheus' story,
Act IV directs the observer's attention instead to the spectacle of the
human and cosmic analogues of the One Mind's perfection—the dances
of the Hours and Spirits of the Human Mind, and of the Spirits of the
Earth and Moon. Because Asia and Prometheus have passed into an
ineffable state, the final act is not really part of the Promethean drama
but is a commentary on it conducted on the human plane. Indeed, although Mary Shelley, in her note on the play, described the last act as
"a sort of hymn of rejoicing in the fulfillment of the prophecies with regard to Prometheus," it should more properly be thought of as belonging
to the genre of the Jonsonian wedding masque, celebrating, as it does, the
reunion of Prometheus and Asia that resolves the first three acts. Like
such a masque, it is constituted of symbolic choral dances and joyous songs
and ends with Demogorgon's speech of advice to the assembled elements
that sums up the whole moral achievement of the action.

Only an imperfect Prometheus, then, can be in time, but his task in
time has been to bear the torch of hope to "this far goal of Time" (III.
iii. 174). The goal of time for Prometheus, it is clear, is the end of time,
the end of a fiction born of error and imperfection; and so it is for man

when, having crossed the "night of life," he enters the grave. But the far goal of time on earth must be something else to man, who cannot be hidden from the dimensions of mutability. However perfected he has become, man is

Nor yet exempt, though ruling them like slaves,
From chance, and death, and mutability,
The clogs of that which else might oversoar
The loftiest star of unascended heaven,
Pinnacled dim in the intense inane.   (III. iv. 200–4)

"Nor yet"; for when he becomes entirely free of change he will no longer be man, the modified portion of the One Mind, but will be absorbed into the unity of Existence, just as Adonais is absorbed into the perfect One which is Being. However, since man now makes mutability his slave, his relation to time is thereby altered, although not severed. The two goals of time, then, do not result from any confusion by Shelley of a millennium with an apocalypse:[1] man, as man, can never transcend those relation- ships among thoughts called time, however much he may transform and subdue them. Shelley's apocalypse and millennium are the forms of per- fection at the two different levels of Existence: the timelessness of the One Mind and the nearest possible approximation to that condition in the human mind, which subsists as human mind by virtue of the illusions of diversity and change.

The relation of these two goals of time is represented symbolically by the Spirit of the Hour who introduces the new age, the mind's analogue to nature's spring season, with which the Hora is traditionally identified. After bearing Asia to Prometheus so that they may withdraw into the im- mediate perfection of their timeless eternity, she is ordered then, but only then, to bring about the corollary event, the gradual perfecting of man within time. Thereafter, the Spirit of the Hour will not fade away like other Hours that have passed but will dwell beside the cave of Prome- theus (III. iii. 83) because her perfection will attend the One Mind time- lessly. But meanwhile, after her earthly task has been performed and she has spread among mankind the prophecy contained in Proteus' shell, she interrupts her report of the gradual earthly purification she has observed to foretell how the instruments of her former temporal office will be made eternal. Since the classical Horae were assigned the task of yoking the horses of the sun each morning for its flight,[2] it is appropriate to the

[1] This supposed confusion is one of the main concerns of Milton Wilson's *Shelley's Later Poetry*.
[2] Ovid *Metamorphoses* ii. 116–21; Lucian *Dialogues of the Gods* x. 1. Hyginus catalogues the names of the Horae and of the horses of the sun in the same fable (No. 183).

details of the conventional myth that the Hour's coursers, the temporal agents of her flight, should return on the completion of their task to their "birthplace in the sun" (III. iv. 108), whose movement measures the passing of time. There, "Pasturing flowers of vegetable fire" (III. iv. 110),[3] they will be exempt from labor, never again to be the agents of passing time. Moreover, the Hour foresees, in a temple on the sun[4] will be installed her "moonlike" chariot[5] and statues of her Apollonian steeds imitating the "flight from which they find repose"—frozen, that is, in their motion—and these two symbols of the temporal succession of sun and moon, day and night, will be yoked by an "amphisbaenic snake." Now, the serpent serves elsewhere in the poem as emblematic of modes of time, and Shelley's peculiar choice here of the serpent with a head at each end and his use of it as the means of joining emblems of sun and moon require that it also be interpreted in terms of time. Joining the two poles of diurnal movement and notable for its ability to move in either direction, the amphisbaenic snake, by tautly arresting two opposing motions, serves as a kind of zodiacal sign of the dynamic capture of the perfect present. Time is obviously not at an end for man: like eternal spring, the symbol of the perfect present brought by the vernal Hour will persist on the sun, which continues to measure out time.[6] Yet its persistence will not be inert or inevitable, for the serpent represents a tension and threatens to move in either direction. There are, then, at least two different conceptions of eternity in the poem, and they are not to be confused. The symbols of the Hour's temporal role are to be fixed in the moving sun, but she herself is to attend the cave of Prometheus and Asia: presiding over the human mind will be a continuing duration of the arrested present, a *nunc stans*, but from the One Mind the illusion of time has dropped out entirely.

[3] In his account of Demogorgon, Boccaccio quoted Claudian's description of Eternity (see below, n. 27). Directly after the verses quoted by Boccaccio, Claudian had written of the return of the sun-god after he had elected to draw the Golden Age from among the four Ages secreted in Eternity's cave: the sun-god then "entered his garden which dripped dew of golden fires, his vale surrounded by a flaming stream that pours radiant light into the plants on which the horses of the Sun pasture (*quae Solis pascuntur equi*). Here he gathers flowers with which he decks the heads, the golden reins, and manes of his horses" (*De consulatu Stilichonis* ii. 467–72). Shelley had quoted Claudian's *Carmen paschale* (as his *De salvatore* was formerly entitled) in a note to *Queen Mab*.

[4] Rather like the temple of Apollo described by Ovid (*Metamorphoses* ii. 1ff.), but even more like the temple of the sun at Heliopolis as described by Strabo (*Geography* xvii. 1. 28).

[5] For the representations of the Horae as charioteers, see George M. A. Hanfmann, *The Season Sarcophagus in Dumbarton Oaks* (Cambridge, Mass., 1951), I, pp. 159–63.

[6] Compare *Queen Mab*, VIII. 53–57:

O human Spirit! spur thee to the goal
Where virtue fixes universal peace,
And midst the ebb and flow of human things,
Show somewhat stable, somewhat certain still,
A lighthouse o'er the wild of dreary waves.

Corresponding to these two forms of eternity, Prometheus and Asia disappear into the cave and vanish from the drama, and the masque-like final act is set in the adjacent forest, the *sylva* of the human world. In other words, the frame of reference of the drama has shifted radically from the One Mind of the first three acts to the purified human world, where we now view the cosmic symbols of the new Promethean age of man, the most comprehensive temporal approximations to the atemporal state of Prometheus. Each of the two cosmic dances of the masque effects a union and interpenetration celebrating and paralleling those of Prometheus and Asia; and the relation of the first set of dancers, the Hours and Spirits of the Human Mind, to the second set, the Spirits of Earth and Moon, may be recognized as the relation of the "subjective" mind to the "objective" universe. The two dances celebrate the perfection of the two worlds into which man supposes reality to be divided.

The whirling dance of the Spirits of Earth and Moon is, of course, a representation of the harmonious motions of all the heavenly bodies, of which human dance, according to tradition, is an imitation. Plato had likened the movement of the stars to a dance because they meet with each other and yet keep and repeat their own orbits;[7] and, to choose one of Shelley's favorite authors, Jonson ended his *Masque of Beauty* with a song exhorting the dancers,

Still turn and imitate the heaven
   In motion swift and even;
   And as his planets go,
   Your brighter lights do so.

Lucian, another of Shelley's favorites, not only traced human dance back to the cosmic dance but also associated it with the ancient mysteries:

Historians . . . tell you that Dance came into being contemporaneously with the primal origin of the universe, making her appearance together with Love—the love that is age-old. In fact, the concord of the heavenly spheres, the interlacing of the errant planets with the fixed stars, their rhythmic agreement and timed harmony, are proofs that Dance was primordial . . . not a single ancient mystery-cult can be found that is without dancing, since they were established, of course, by Orpheus and Musaeus, the best dancers of that time, who included it in their prescriptions as something exceptionally beautiful to be initiated with rhythm and dancing.[8]

The dance that Shelley called "the mystic measure" (IV. 129) and that Milton called the "Mystical dance" of the heavenly bodies[9] is not merely

---

[7] *Timaeus* 40c.

[8] *De saltatione* 7, 15. For a brief account of the tradition of the cosmic dance, see John C. Meagher, "The Dance and the Masques of Ben Jonson," *Journal of the Warburg and Courtauld Institutes*, 25 (1962), 258–77.

[9] *Paradise Lost*, V. 619–27.

exemplary of perfect order but expresses the divine harmony. Spiritual rather than physical, it is the work of love, not of astronomical laws.[10]

The Dance of the Hours is also a recognizable commonplace, and Shelley's usual mythopoeic processes might well lead us to suspect that, in addition to the simple design of the "subjective" and "objective" harmonies expressed by the two dances, he is complicating the texture of Act IV by transforming and assimilating mythic patterns in his presentation of the first dance. The Horae, or Hours, were generally understood as the deities of the various seasons, and their circular dance represented the harmoniously periodic movement of time. All the Horae were traditionally the attendants of Venus, but the name was associated especially with the spring, Venus' season, and was frequently used as a synonym for it in Greek. Since it was the spring Hora who, according to the myth, received the goddess when she floated ashore on a shell after her sea-birth, Shelley was consistent with the spirit and general design of the myth in having called upon the vernal Hour to conduct Asia to Prometheus in a shell-like chariot upon her spiritual rebirth, which is explicitly made analogous to her original birth out of the sea. It is further appropriate that the same Hour, thus identified with Asia and the reborn spirit of love and life, surround the earth with the new Promethean spring by releasing it from the shell given to Asia by Proteus and that she then, as an eternal spring, forever attend Prometheus and Asia as her mythic prototype attended Venus.

Moreover, Venus was also traditionally accompanied by another group, sometimes considered her daughters; these, the Charites, or Graces, were understood to express the benevolent, joyous powers surrounding the goddess' ethos and, like the Hours, were regularly associated with spring and represented in circular dance. As a consequence of these similarities, the Hours and Graces, each usually three in number, were often joined in mythology and occasionally even confused with each other. Both groups, moreover, were understood as personifications of particular virtues and delights, the Hours being identified as Irene, Dike, and Eunomia (Peace, Justice, and Law, or Order) and the Graces as Aglaia, Euphrosyne, and Thalia (Splendor, Joy, and Flourishing). Perhaps Banier best captured the general conception of the Graces when he interpreted them as "the Charms of the Mind," adding:

Among the many Divinities invented by the Ancients, none were more amiable than the *Graces*, since it was from them the Rest borrowed their Charms, Sources of every Thing agreeable and smiling in Nature. They gave to Places, Persons, Works, and to every thing in its kind, that finished Charm which crowns all its other Perfections, and is as it were the Flower of its Excellence.[11]

---

[10] See also Richard Payne Knight, "The Mystic Dance," in *Symbolic Language of Ancient Art and Mythology* (New York, 1876 [1st ed., 1818]).
[11] Banier, *Mythology and Fables of the Ancients*, II, i, 11. Pindar (*Olympian* xiv. 5–6) wrote that by the aid of the Graces all things pleasant are brought about for

The very name, Graces,—that is, favors, or benefits—reveals that these deities were thought to have as their special duty the conferring of benefits on man: they "on men all gracious gifts bestow, / Which deck the body or adorn the mind."[12] But invariably the Horae, Venus' other attendants, were also described as pre-eminently beneficent, for they

> open-handed sit upon the clouds,
> And press the liberality of heaven
> Down to the laps of thankful men.[13]

The kind of embracing cosmic harmony and universal perfection that the commingled Hours and Graces consequently tended to symbolize can be judged by a passage in Proclus' commentary on Plato's *Timaeus* in which Proclus pictures a Grace and an Hour combining their beneficent moral forces to give perfect order to each of the celestial spheres:[14]

Theologists place *Eunomia* over the inerratic sphere, who separates the multitude which it contains, and perpetually preserves every thing in its proper order: and hence celebrating *Vulcan* as the fabricator of the heavens, they conjoin him with *Aglaia*, because she gives splendour to every part of the heavens, through the variety of the stars. And again, they place *Justice*, one of the seasons, over the planetary spheres; because this deity gives assistance to the inequality of their motions, and causes them through proportion to conspire into equality and consent: but of the Graces they conjoin with this divinity *Thalia*, because she gives perfection to the ever-flourishing lives which they contain. But they place *Peace* over the sublunary region, because this divinity appeases the war of the elements; but of the Graces they associate with this divinity *Euphrosyne* because she confers a facility of natural energy on each of the elements.

These are representative interpretations of the cluster of myths that Shelley has reconstituted to fashion the Hours and Spirits of the Human Mind of Act IV; and it should also be evident that the same Spirits who come from the human mind to console Prometheus in agony in Act I take their nature from these same notably beneficent Graces, personifications of the mind's powers, whom Shelley substituted there for the Chris-

---

mortals; in *An Inscription for a Temple Dedicated to the Graces* Samuel Rogers elaborated on this theme:

From them flow all the decencies of Life;
Without them nothing pleases, Virtue's self
Admired not loved: and those on whom They smile,
Great though they be, and wise, and beautiful,
Shine forth with double lustre.

[12] Spenser, *Faerie Queene*, VI. x. 23. See also Seneca's discussion of the Graces in his *De beneficiis*; and Banier, II, i, 11.
[13] Jonson, *New Inn*, I. vi. 141–43. See also the *Homeric Hymn to Apollo* 194.
[14] I quote Thomas Taylor's translation in his edition of Pausanias' *Description of Greece* ([2d ed.; London, 1824], III, pp. 315–16) because Shelley ordered this work in 1817.

tian God's ministering angel. Like the personified Graces, the Spirits who comfort Prometheus can be recognized as Reform (or Revolution in its best sense, as the prelude to freedom and love), Self-Sacrifice, Wisdom, and Poetry; and just as the Graces are but the attendants of Venus, not Venus herself, so these Spirits from the "caves of human thought," however fair, prove inadequate without the Love that Asia symbolizes. The mental Graces having thus exercised the limits of their power in Act I, the spring Hour appears in Acts II and III to transport Asia to Prometheus—as the Hora, after receiving the newly risen Aphrodite, led her to the palace of the gods[15]—and then to disseminate the new spiritual season. Now, in the celebrative final act, Shelley at last brings together the Hours and Spirits of the Human Mind to intermingle them in a symbolic masque-like dance. The conventional similarities and interconnections of the Hours and Graces that have been mentioned are themselves a sufficient motive for Shelley's weaving together their two traditional dances. Yet this, too, is Shelley's adaptation of an established myth, for the *Homeric Hymn to Apollo* depicts a dance of the Graces and Hours, together with Aphrodite, Harmonia, and Hebe, each holding the other by the hand; Xenophon, a dance of the Graces, Hours, and Nymphs; and Apuleius, a dance of the Hours and Graces around the figure of Venus.[16] However, before we can properly examine the symbolism of Shelley's adaptation of the dance of the Hours and Graces, it will be necessary to return to his dramatization of the theme of time and eternity.

The final act opens with the funeral procession of the "past Hours" bearing "Time to his tomb in eternity" (IV. 31, 14). Since the pallbearers are the past Hours and since they are aware of the coming of new Hours, "children of a diviner day" (IV. 26), there is no reason for understanding this event to mean, as some critics have believed, that all of time is at an end. The frame of reference of this act, unlike the rest of the drama, is not the One Mind, but the time-bound human mind; and clearly Time, the "Father of many a cancelled year" (IV. 11) as distinct from the "diviner day" that fathers the new Hours, must be the order of temporality prior to the institution of the Promethean age. The necessary chain of events instituted by the reign of Jupiter has come to its end with his overthrow; hence the past years have been "cancelled," and the kind of time that is to be will differ from both past time and the timelessness of Prometheus. Since time is the perceived relationships among illusory diversities, the Time that is buried must have been constituted by the kind of relationships that subsisted while man's mind was shackled by tyranny and superstition and that thus caused time to be a swift succession of transient moments. What the Promethean order of human time is to be

[15] See the *Homeric Hymn to Aphrodite*.
[16] *Homeric Hymn to Apollo* 189–206; Xenophon *Symposium* vii. 5; Apuleius *Metamorphoses* x. 32.

is suggested by the fact that when the new Hours first appear they are observed by Ione and Panthea to be charioteers like their predecessors but, to Panthea's bewilderment, without chariots (IV. 56), for, paradoxically, they are the elements of moving time but without the means of rapid flight. They are the fondly delaying presence of that which by definition passes away. Some further sense of the kind of time Shelley is attempting to represent may be gained from an unused manuscript verse[17] which describes the new Hours as "chainless" and, unlike the past Hours, "kingless,"[18] for the intimation is that the new time is not a linked succession or series of evanescent moments, each dragging the next into the past, but a kind of free republic of independent, coexisting units.

Because the dimensions of mutability are functions of the condition of the human mind, transient time must diminish as a factor of experience in proportion as the mind grows more nearly perfect. Even as early as *Queen Mab*, Shelley had prophesied such progress of the human mind toward the fullness of its potentialities that Time, once the "conqueror" who had "ruled the world," would fall and flee.[19] Eventually the thoughts of ideally virtuous man will rise in "time-destroying infiniteness" and "gift" him

With self-enshrined eternity, that mocks
The unprevailing hoariness of age,
And man, once fleeting o'er the transient scene
Swift as an unremembered vision, stands
Immortal upon earth.[20]

But this does not mean, any more than does the burial of Time in *Prometheus Unbound*, that time is at an end and that man will experience the timelessness of Prometheus. The same temporal term acquires quite different meanings when applied to the One Mind and when applied to the human mind. What Shelley meant by *human* "time," "eternity," and "time-destroying infiniteness" he tried to make clear in a Lockean commentary on the verses just quoted from the earlier poem:

Time is our consciousness of the succession of ideas in our mind. Vivid sensation, of either pain or pleasure, makes the time seem long, as the common phrase is, because it renders us more acutely conscious of our ideas. If a mind be conscious of a hundred ideas during one minute, by the clock, and of two hundred during another, the latter of these spaces would actually occupy so much greater extent in the mind as two exceed one in quantity. If, therefore, the human mind, by any future improvement of its sensibility, should become conscious of an infinite number of ideas in a minute, that minute would be

17 MS e. 12, p. 85.
18 Compare IV. 20: "the corpse of the King of Hours!"
19 *Queen Mab*, IX. 23–37.
20 *Ibid.*, VIII. 203–11.

eternity. I do not hence infer that the actual space between the birth and death of a man will ever be prolonged; but that his sensibility is perfectible, and that the number of ideas which his mind is capable of receiving is indefinite. One man is stretched on the rack during twelve hours; another sleeps soundly in his bed: the difference of time perceived by these two persons is immense; one hardly will believe that half an hour has elapsed, the other could credit that centuries had flown during his agony. Thus, the life of a man of virtue and talent, who should die in his thirtieth year, is, with regard to his own feelings, longer than that of a miserably priest-ridden slave, who dreams out a century of dulness. The one has perpetually cultivated his mental faculties, has rendered himself master of his thoughts, can abstract and generalize amid the lethargy of every-day business;—the other can slumber over the brightest moments of his being, and is unable to remember the happiest hour of his life. Perhaps the perishing ephemeron enjoys a longer life than the tortoise.

That duration is subjective and is measured by consciousness is not, of course, Shelley's discovery, however consonant it is with the rest of his philosophic idealism. One would have found the doctrine not only in Godwin's *Political Justice*, to which he refers in the note quoted, but also in Locke and all those he influenced, including Sterne and Condillac.[21] The Time that the past Hours bury, then, is not all of chronological time, but that temporal order in which moments flee in rapid succession because of the mind's imperfect consciousness; it is the time that rules the mind instead of being ruled by it, and therefore it has significant analogies with that other tyrannical fiction, Jupiter, and belongs to his reign. The new Hours of the diviner day constitute an eternity, not in the sense of Prometheus' timelessness nor in the sense of the persistence in time of the changeless present, symbolized by the statue of the Hour's horses and chariot, but in the sense of the *indefinite* capacity of the human mind's awareness. For if the human mind is indefinitely perfectible and therefore capable of holding in a moment a quantity of ideas to which no number can be assigned, then the mental time constituted by the quantity of these ideas also becomes immeasurable, infinite. In human time "eternity" is a condition of the mind in which no fixed limits can be set on consciousness.[22]

---

[21] *Oeuvres*, ed. Thèry, III, p. 308.

[22] In the note quoted from *Queen Mab* Shelley refers the reader to Condorcet's *Esquisse d'un tableau historique des progrès de l'esprit humain*, and although Condorcet is prophesying a protraction of man's chronological life, he is helpful in clarifying Shelley's use of the word "indefinite": "Certainly man will not become immortal, but will not the interval between the first breath that he draws and the time when in the natural course of events, without disease or accident, he expires, increase indefinitely? . . . In truth, this average span of life which we suppose will increase indefinitely as time passes, may grow in conformity either with a law such that it continually approaches a limitless length but without ever reaching it, or with a law such that through the centuries it reaches a length greater than any determinate quantity that we may assign to it as its limit. In the latter case such an

Hence Shelley's interpretation and assimilation of that ideal pattern he found in the traditional interweaving dance of the Hours and Graces. Only absolute unity can be outside time, space, and mutability; but the world of mutability can tend toward that unity through the relational flowing together of its component diversities, just as the human mind's holding together an indeterminate number of discrete ideas is its way of attaining an "eternity" in time. Dance, then, corresponds to the "order," "arrangement," or "combination" of particulars that, according to Shelley, the poet effects under the compulsion of his extraordinary and ineffable apprehension of absolute unity; and the "web of the mystic measure" woven by the choral dance of the Hours and Spirits of the Human Mind (IV. 129) is the ideal rhythm unifying time and mental powers. The web is the interpenetration of the two so that "the Hours, and the spirits of might and pleasure, / Like the clouds and sunbeams, unite" (IV. 79–80) or chiastically intermingle "As the flying-fish leap / ... And mix with the sea-birds half asleep" (IV. 86–88). This intertexture of mind and time is the formation of purely mental time instead of the swiftly passing time resulting from the imperfect mind's illusion that time is an external reality. Since the most nearly perfect mental time possible is "eternal" because it has no limits, and not because it is either timelessness or the sum of time, it is represented as infinitely slow and thus as the temporal approximation of timelessness. During his torture Prometheus, being in time, had suffered its amplitude through the expanded consciousness of pain, so that the moments were "divided by keen pangs / Till they seemed years" (I. 13–14). But for the human mind in Jovian time day had passed with speed, and time lingered only in the "night of time" that symbolizes the meaningless vacancies in human life:

Once the hungry Hours were hounds
    Which chased the day like a bleeding deer,
And it limped and stumbled with many wounds
    Through the nightly dells of the desert year.   (IV. 73–76)

Now that the Hours and the virtuous powers of the mind are interpenetrated, in the still necessary cycles of human time the "day" of man's existence is protracted and his "night" overcome. Instead of hastening the day into lengthened night, the new Hours that attend the earth are

---

increase is truly indefinite in the strictest sense of the word, since there is no term on this side of which it must of necessity stop. In the former case it is equally indefinite in relation to us, if we cannot fix the limit it always approaches without ever reaching, and particularly if, knowing only that it will never stop, we are ignorant in which of the two senses the term 'indefinite' can be applied to it. Such is the present condition of our knowledge as far as the perfectibility of the human race is concerned; such is the sense in which we may call it indefinite" (*The Progress of the Human Mind*, trans. June Barraclough [London, 1955], p. 200).

Solemn and slow, and serene, and bright,
Leading the Day and outspeeding the Night,
With the powers of a world of perfect light.[23]   (IV. 166–68)

For the effect of the interwoven dance and song of the Hours and Spirits
is to

Enchant the day that too swiftly flees,
To check its flight ere the cave of Night.   (IV. 71–72)

Human time cannot stop altogether, but the powers of the mind can now
detain it indefinitely because of the infinite expansion of consciousness.
Lovers, for example, catch the Hours in their woven caresses, and Wisdom, the Siren, delays the Hours' ships of passage (IV. 105–10).[24] The
human mind rules time, its slave, and subdues it to near-irrelevance.

Thus far we have observed that Shelley has posited three different
kinds of eternity: the timelessness that is, by definition, the condition of
the One Mind, which has nothing to do with the illusion of time; the
unchanging persistence of the ideal state during time; and the boundlessness of mental duration in the free and perfectible human mind. Yet none
of these categories adequately provides for Demogorgon's identification of
himself as "Eternity" (III. i. 52), for his picture of an "Eternity" that may
free the "serpent that would clasp her with his length" (IV. 565–67), or
even for the fact that past Time is borne to his tomb in "eternity" (IV.
14). When in Act II Asia and Panthea were being drawn by Necessity
into Demogorgon's cave, the Spirits inhabiting the physical world and
symbolizing its dynamic forces sang of the perpetually repeated rise and
fall of the nightingales' song as representative of the cyclical way in which
Power manifests itself in the temporal course of natural events; and the
Fauns that inhabit the world of matter then described a similar infinitely
repeated cycle of natural events. For

All things that move and breathe with toil and sound
Are born and die; revolve, subside, and swell.

Only in the imprisoned and enslaved human mind is time a linear chain
of moments, each of which is dissipated as the next linked moment arises;
to the liberated and amplified human mind an illimitable number of non-

---

[23] Only those Hours that are driven "beyond heaven" are "Ceaseless and rapid"
(IV. 163), but their speed is not that of transience; it is to hasten the construction
of an ideal model for man by those Spirits of his mind that transcend the limitations
of human mutability, or that, unlike the thoughts confined to human existence, can
"float above" its "darkness," as Shelley expressed it in *Mont Blanc*.
[24] In MS e. 12, p. 88, after line 76, Shelley wrote: "But now like a fawn it [the
day] lingers & listens / In the net of music whose meshes are air."

linear moments are simultaneously available. In the world of nature, which freely and passively admits the Power and its law of Necessity, time both passes and is preserved, for it is a perpetually repeated circle without beginning or end.

The circle, however, is also the shape that Shelley assigns to Eternity in accordance with the ubiquitous emblem tradition that depicts Eternity as a figure holding or, more often, surrounded by, a serpent bent into a circle, with its tail in its mouth, to represent the unendingness of time. Not only is this circular serpent the "doom"—that is, all the events destined to be—that clasps Eternity (IV. 567–69); it also appears as the "snake-like Doom coiled" underneath the throne of "the Eternal, the Immortal" in Demogorgon's region outside Existence (II. iii. 95–97). Whereas the amphisbaenic snake represents the retention of the perfect present during the course of moving time, the circular serpent, tail in mouth, is the emblem of the totality of time. Because mutability is the inherent condition of the natural world, eternity in that domain is the *moving* circle, the whole possible course of events perpetually renewing and repeating itself. This circular model of time helps explain why Asia paradoxically describes life's journey from cave to ocean as a passage from age, through infancy, and beyond an entrance-exit that is both "Death and Birth." Life is a circle that ends where it begins, not a line that abandons one point for another. The same temporal circle also gives full meaning to the otherwise strange refrain of the Spirits that come from the human mind to console Prometheus at the end of Act I: "we bear the prophecy / Which begins and ends in thee!" (I. 690–91, etc.). Beginning and end meet: the serpent bites its own tail. Because knowledge of cause is foreknowledge of consequence, one may behold in the present, "as in a glass, / The future" (I. 661–63). Present contains future, and if there were no time at all, the two would be a single point; translated into sequential time, present and future are not opposite poles of a line, but the coinciding beginning and end of a circle. Consequently, while Prometheus is in time, his motive for perfection and the perfection that necessarily follows from that motive become one only in the course of the circular motion of time.[25]

Shelley's two references to the circular serpent of eternity locate it, however, not in Prometheus' realm, where eternity is the absence of time, nor in mankind's, where the models of eternity are the duration of the perfect present, the infinitude of mental awareness, and the perpetually repeated circle of the sum of time, but in Demogorgon's realm of Power,

---

[25] Compare Shelley to Leigh Hunt, 1 May 1820 (*Letters*, II, 191): "If faith is a virtue in any case[,] it is so in politics rather than religion; as having a power of producing that[,] a belief in which is at once a prophecy & a cause—."

It was traditionally with a god that one began and ended. The formula appears in Hesiod, Homer, Theocritus, Theognis, Virgil, and Horace.

outside Existence. This emblematic serpent, moreover, is dormant, motionless, not the endlessly moving circle of the sensible world, and thus it accords in its nature with the sleeping volcanic Demogorgon before he is awakened to action by Asia. Similarly, in *The Daemon of the World* Shelley had described the "vast snake Eternity" as ever lying in "charmed sleep" and had located it, too, behind the veil covering "nature's inner shrine."[26] Boccaccio had supplied Shelley with the myth that Demogorgon had Eternity as his companion[27] and was so fearsome that no one dared pronounce his name. All this, in his usual myth-making manner, Shelley adapted to his own purposes; for when Jupiter asks Demogorgon to identify himself he replies, "Eternity. Demand no direr name" (III. i. 52).[28] In the context of Shelley's play Demogorgon is entitled to the name "Eternity"—among his infinite other appropriate names—because as the Power, or absolute potentiality, he bears the relation to actuality that eternity bears to time. He is eternity because he is the infinitude of all the events that occur in time; but he also has "direr" and forbidden names because, depending upon how Power is admitted by mind into actuality, potentially can be released as a Jupiter or a revolution or any other disturbance. Correspondingly, the "snake-like Doom coiled underneath" the throne of "the Eternal, the Immortal"—it is unimportant whether we identify this figure with Demogorgon, since under any circumstance he must subsume it—is that totality of time which, self-enclosing and dormant, constitutes the last of Shelley's various conceptions of eternity. It is, for example, the "eternity," or sum total of time, in which we are told is located the tomb to which former Time has been borne by the past Hours, just as Jupiter is withdrawn from actuality to infinite potentiality. Lying thus outside Existence, the sleeping, inert circle under Eternity's throne can be aroused and unloosed through "life's portal"; uncoiled, it enters existence as sequential time and change. But on being released as moving time, its course is not random or arbitrary; the serpent of Eternity is the "Doom" in the sense of "destiny" because its determined course is inherent

---

[26] *The Daemon of the World*, 99–101. See also *The Revolt of Islam*, 1444–46: "...did my spirit wake / From sleep as many-coloured as the snake / That girds eternity?"

[27] Like innumerable other mythographers, Boccaccio, quoting Claudian, also assigns to Eternity—whom he defines as the immeasurable totality of time—the emblem of the serpent devouring his own tail, "thus in his movement tracing his own beginning.... For the end of one year is always the beginning of the next and will be thus while time lasts." Eternity herself, Boccaccio adds, gives out the periods of time and also recalls them into her bosom, just as Shelley has past Time borne to his tomb in Eternity, withdrawn from actuality into potentiality, like everything else in time. Moreover, Boccaccio places Eternity in a cave which is, he says, far off, unknown, and inaccessible (*impervia*) to the human mind and thus is like the unknowable, infinitely remote realm of Power in Shelley's philosophy.

[28] Shelley of course is adapting the fact that the ancient gods had many names, designating their different domains and powers. Similarly, Shelley assigns the ineffable transcendent One a variety of partial names.

in it, in accordance with the law of Necessity. Like Demogorgon, the serpent of Eternity is neither good nor evil: the coiled serpent is merely the morally indifferent possibility of the entrance into the world of any new sequence of events. Consequently, it can, through that "meekness" which is the willed submission of the human spirit to the natural order of things, enter the world to overthrow the unnatural Jovian regime; or, after the institution of the Promethean age, it can once again be released to introduce another sequence of temporal change.

It is supremely fitting that, as that Eternity which is the totality of possible time, Demogorgon return to the drama at its very end, like the final moral commentator in the traditional masque, to summon his audience and offer his lecture on the relation of potentiality to time. The One Mind has now been released from time, the imperfection of existence. For mankind, confined to mutable existence, the perfect moment has been arrested during the continued movement of time; in the perfected human mind, time, although still necessarily in flux, has become illimitable; and in man's sensible world the totality of time moves in its eternal circle of renewal. Finally, in Demogorgon's cave—the unknowable realm of the ultimate cause of all that man experiences as actual—the total potentiality of temporal change sleeps as a self-enclosing serpent that Shelley has ironically substituted for the serpent Satan, who is imprisoned by God's angel in the bottomless pit at the end of the Christian Scripture. But, although Demogorgon's final speech mockingly echoes the Book of Revelation (20:1–3), replacing the Devil with Mutability, Shelley has not promised an apocalypse for man, and nothing in his handling of time demands it; nor has he fatuously blinded himself to the moral stress continuously imposed upon man to sustain the highest perfection that belongs to his nature. It is inherent in the order of things that the potentiality of temporal change tend to become actual, that because of the inherent weakness of the potentiality of change to sustain itself as only potentiality,

> with infirm hand, Eternity,
> Mother of many acts and hours, should free
> The serpent that would clasp her with his length.   (IV. 565–67)

Man is continuously subject to this threat; and Demogorgon, who, after all, is the ultimate authority on the relation of the possible to the actual, calls on man for the wholehearted exercise of "Gentleness, Virtue, Wisdom, and Endurance" as the means of reassuming an "empire o'er the disentangled doom" (IV. 569) and inhibiting the inherent compulsion toward a new order of events and time.

13 Hellas

Because Greece, mother of Western culture, had long been subjugated to Turkey, the outbreak of her struggle for independence from her Moslem masters in 1821 provided Shelley with an exceptional opportunity to transpose into a human historical context the millenarian doctrines he had incorporated in the atemporal myth of *Prometheus Unbound*—to express his convictions and visions in events that were actual and immediate, rather than imaginary, abstract, and eternal. The apocalyptic restoration of Prometheus, or the One Mind, had involved the erasure of the illusion of time because that drama is pitched at the level of timeless Existence, and the alteration in the character of human time is treated there as a function of Prometheus' apocalyptic perfection. But since Shelley's optimism at the level of mankind rests, as we have seen, on his faith that human time unfolds in inevitably repetitive cycles and since for that reason no historical episode is self-determined or self-contained, his most pervasive literary task in *Hellas* was not to find an appropriate atemporal myth like that of Prometheus or, at the opposite extreme, to realize and particularize his doctrines in the specific historical events, but to elevate the current Greek revolt to its place in that universal cyclical pattern, just as for an analogous reason he had expanded the domestic history of the Cenci to inclusive political and religious dimensions.

The title of his drama therefore is not *Greece*, but, at the admirable suggestion of his friend Edward Williams, *Hellas*, the spirit of Freedom whose sun-like flag, according to one of its choruses, the Spirit of God had unfurled over chaos to give the world form. Greece is but one local habitation of the eternal Hellenic spirit, not the country to which it is limited. As it was for Hegel, history for Shelley is the universal development of Spirit, and geographical countries only house the successive stages of its evolution. It was in that sense that he wrote in his Preface, "We are all Greeks. Our laws, our literature, our religion, our arts have their root in Greece." It is in that inclusive spiritual sense also that, when in the drama Turkish Hassan reports with unconscious sympathy the self-sacrificing heroism of the Greek enemy, his Sultan comments, "Your heart is Greek, Hassan" (455). Only in a nearly trivial way is *Hellas* a propagandistic call to rally to the Greek cause; in its true scope, it centers upon the Greek revolution to validate Shelley's confidence in an imminent and ineluctable universal reformation.

We have noted earlier that Shelley's distinction between the poetry of "sad reality" and "poetic idealisms" is not only substantive and formal but also ethical. The ethical goal of proper tragic representations of things as they are, such as *Julian and Maddalo* and *The Cenci*, is to cause us to know ourselves truly, to understand our real nature, the source of evil, and our power over it; poetic idealisms like *Prometheus Unbound* presuppose an audience already in possession of that self-knowledge and incite it to love and aspire to the perfection they represent. Because that perfection resides in men's minds and not in the world as it is, its fitting representation is atemporal myth, the shape that man has agreed to give to his ideal thoughts on the assumption that it is their ideal configuration. On the other hand, because self-knowledge is an empirical act and because one can, according to Shelley, see himself only as he is reflected in another, its appropriate cause is the representation of actually lived events like the encounter of Byron and Shelley on the Lido and the tragedy of the Cenci family. This is Shelley's distinction between the persuasive moral uses of reality and idealism, or limited history and myth; but the rhetorical functions of history and myth do not define their ontological character. Aside from the uses to which they may be put, what kind of reality does each have for Shelley? and therefore how does each serve to define man's temporal moment with respect to the rest of time?

Myth offers no problem: when it is the most nearly perfect organization of man's thought—the form taken by his thoughts under pressure of the plastic force of the transcendent Unity—it is a truth outside time and applicable to any moment in it. For thought, and thought alone, is eternal and unaffected by "time, or place, or circumstance."[1] *Prometheus Unbound* is ideal human history seen in the perspective of the timeless. Because thought is eternal, what authenticates the mythic—although not

[1] *Hellas*, 795–97, 802.

necessarily the myth itself, which, like that of Aeschylus' *Prometheus Bound*, may fall short of its ideal and immutable form—is its persisting in men's minds, as the Greek myths have persisted, over an extended period of time, just as the archetypal character of certain human events, like those of the Cenci, is authenticated by their continued power over centuries to affect men's minds in the same way. Persistence in time is proof of kinship with and approximation to the atemporal, the immutable—the true. We can, then, appreciate why, on thinking that Byron's *Don Juan* may have borrowed from Thomas Hope's *Anastasius*, Shelley added that poetry has "nothing to do with the invention of facts."[2] Lacking time's confirmation, mere inventive originality runs the risk of being equivalent to inauthenticity; or perhaps it would be more nearly accurate to say that for Shelley the entirely novel, were it possible, would have to be inauthentic because it had never existed before in thought. What is poetically important about facts is only how they are organized into a thought "containing within itself the principle of its own integrity" so as to overcome time, place, and circumstance.

But history that is mere chronicle, unlike thought and myth, is "a catalogue of detached facts which have no other bond of connection than time, place, circumstance, cause, and effect"; it is "partial, and applies only to a definite period of time, and a certain combination of events which can never again recur."[3] In that sense it cannot be what Shelley termed "the very image of life expressed in its eternal truth." However, we have observed that repeatedly for him the most nearly perfect way in which immutable eternity can express itself in the domain of mutability is the perpetual cycle of change whose most obvious form is the seasons. Chronicle history therefore, although valueless in itself, participates in "eternal truth" when it is recognized not as linear but as unfolding the recurrent pattern, the inherent principle, of time. If myth is the view of time from eternity, the cyclical repetitions of universal history permit a glimpse of eternity from time. The form of *Hellas*, correspondingly, is determined by Shelley's effort to locate the Greek revolution—and even the play itself—in those recurrent historical cycles and thereby to transform merely temporal events into an eternal truth and the specific play into a universal statement.

By intention Shelley is not notably an inventive poet, and, directed by his concept of cyclically repetitive history, some of his most brilliant strokes, as we have seen especially in *Prometheus Unbound*, are in the Renaissance and neoclassic art of finding the precisely apposite in history, literature, and myth. Such a relation of poet to the past follows from his conception of all poems as "episodes to that great poem, which all poets,

[2] To Mary, 11 August 1821 (*Letters*, II, 332).
[3] *Defence of Poetry* (Julian, VII, 115).

like the co-operating thoughts of one great mind, have built up since the beginning of the world," especially since that great poem is the "cyclic poem written by Time upon the memories of men"[4]—that is, like those poems that extend the Homeric epics and link with them to form a great cycle on the inclusive history of Troy. The one true atemporal poem evolves in time as a succession of interdependent, and in that sense un-original, poems. But even apart from their relation to the One Mind's one transcendent poem that subsumes them, poems are properly born out of previous imaginative creations. Because of the circle of mutability, "all language, institution, and form require not only to be produced but to be sustained: the office and character of a poet participates in the divine nature as regards providence, no less than as regards creation."[5] One way of fulfilling that providential role is that of Virgil, who, though an imi-tator, "created anew all that he copied," that is, reorganized it into a new whole. For every great poem is available for reinterpretation and recrea-tion in that "after one person and one age has exhausted all its divine effluence which their peculiar relations enable them to share, another and yet another succeeds, and new relations are ever developed, the source of an unforeseen and unconceived delight."[6] Not only does a great work, being refined from temporality by its ideal organization, continue to have relevance to new times and circumstances; it can be sustained by being "created anew" in terms of the new circumstances that result from tem-poral differences.

Among the extant Greek tragedies, Aeschylus' *The Persians*, which Shelley "created anew" as *Hellas*, is unique because it dramatized nearly contemporary history instead of old legends, and it is therefore the proto-type of that genre. Celebrating the Greek victory of 480 B.C. over Persian Xerxes (whose father, Darius, had begun the conflict a decade before), Aeschylus' drama naturally lent itself to the current Greek struggle against Turkish Mahmud (whose ancestor Mahomet II had subjected Greece to the foreign domination she had been suffering for three and a half centuries); and Shelley exploited with subtle complexity all the analogies that Aeschylus' play held out to him, so as to extend and transform it at the same time that he assimilated it.[7] Just as he had bound himself with marked fidelity to the documents on the Cenci family because of the validity of lived events, so he kept as close as possible to the form and details of Aeschylus' play, locating his drama in the Turkish capitol of

---

[4] *Ibid.* (pp. 124, 125).
[5] *Ibid.* (p. 123).
[6] *Ibid.* (pp. 130, 131).
[7] The immediate pertinence of Aeschylus' play must have been apparent to many familiar with Greek drama: Byron was at the same time making use of its contents in his "The Isles of Greece" (*Don Juan*, canto III), which is also concerned with the Greco–Turkish war, and that lyric was eventually attended by a note which quotes from the play.

Constantinople instead of the Persian capitol of Susa, substituting the ghost of Mahomet II for Darius', assigning to Mahmud the role of Xerxes' mother, and exaggerating the few naval skirmishes with the Turks until they match the great battle with the Persians at Salamis so that the current contests on land and sea might seem to repeat the ancient ones. For Shelley is not merely hanging contemporary events on an archaic dramatic form nor merely modernizing the ancient play. As he carries out the artistic role of a sustaining providence, the whole substance and meaning of *The Persians* are to be understood as functionally operative in *Hellas*, which is also concerned with the liberation of the civilized from the tyranny of barbarians. The method is the opposite of that of *Prometheus Unbound*, where the adaptation ironically repudiates the ethical assumptions of the original myth and for that purpose reshapes its form. Instead, although Shelley ironically transforms Aeschylus' idea of supernatural prophecy, the formal absorption of *The Persians* into *Hellas* not only confirms the archetypal greatness of the original, which is thus proved ever applicable to new cultural relations; the assimilation is the literary analogue of history's cyclical repetitions, on which Shelley now based his earthly optimism. The tacit but presiding presence of Aeschylus' play in Shelley's is the presence of the earliest liberation of the Greeks in their struggle twenty-three centuries later, and the compatibility of one with the other converts transitory historical time into an approximation of an atemporal truth.

So calculated an incorporation of Aeschylus' play would seem to imply that Shelley attended to his task scrupulously; and yet he claimed his drama was written "without much care" in a moment of enthusiasm,[8] perhaps within three weeks, and in his Preface he called it "a mere improvise." These, however, are not incompatible facts, and "improvise" accurately describes *Hellas* as a recreation of *The Persians* and as a re-emergence of the original Hellenic spirit of both art and liberty. Alfieri, whose *Myrrha* Shelley urged Mary to translate and whom he recognized as a champion of liberty,[9] had set a Risorgimento model by imitating the classical drama and by founding his plots on legendary and historical themes drawn from the classical historians and from the Greek dramatists or Seneca with the intention of reviving the ancient spirit of freedom and making Italy become again what she once had been. Moreover, the *improvvisatori*, or extempore poets, had long been part of the Italian literary scene.[10] Both of these traditions met in the *improvvisatore* Tommaso Sgricci, who entered the Shelley circle in Pisa at the end of 1820, together with Prince Mavrocordato, a leader in the Greek struggle for

---

[8] To John Gisborne, 10 April 1822 (*Letters*, II, 406).
[9] Review of Hogg's *Memoirs of Prince Alexy Haimatoff* (Julian, VI, 177).
[10] See Adele Vitagliano, *Storia della poesia estemporanee* (Rome, 1905).

freedom and the dedicatee of *Hellas*.[11] Byron and others may have been somewhat contemptuous of Sgricci's performances, but Shelley and Mary were impressed: "a miracle," Mary wrote.[12] Of those they attended, one was on the death of Hector and another on Iphigenia in Tauris, "a poem," Mary reported, "as long as a Greek Tragedy, interspersed with choruses." "It was composed," she added, "on the Greek plan (indeed he followed Euripides in his arrangement and in many of his ideas)—without the division of acts and with choruses";[13] and, if Medwin is to be trusted, Shelley recognized that Sgricci even adopted Euripides' metaphors.[14] Mary also sensed in such exhibitions an immediacy, a calculated direction of the act to its effect of the moment: "God knows what this man would be if he laboured and become a poet for posterity instead of an Improvisatore for the present."[15] Moreover, like his poetic mentor Vincenzo Monti, Sgricci was zealous for Italian liberty and, according to Mary, was suspected of "carbonarism,"[16] or membership in the secret society to free Naples from France and to introduce a republican government.

An "improvise," even a "mere improvise," then, is no more spontaneously haphazard than the *commedia dell' arte*, which depends on the

[11] For a brief biographical sketch of Sgricci, see *Journals of Claire Clairmont*, ed. Stocking, pp. 470–73.

[12] In MS e. 17, pp. 5–10, 22, there appears in Mary's hand the poem which Garnett first published under the title "Orpheus" and which consists of long speeches by Orpheus' lyre interspersed with brief choruses. Although the lines are torrential and strangely unshaped, the poem is rich with metaphors characteristic of Shelley. H. Buxton Forman has suggested that Shelley may have remembered Sgricci's *Orpheus and Eurydice* and translated a fragment from memory ("The Improvvisatore Sgricci in Relation to Shelley," *Gentleman's Magazine*, 246 [1880], 122). In his *Relics of Shelley* (London, 1862) Garnett has also proposed that it might be a translation from the Italian, but his other conjecture seems far more probable—that it is Shelley's attempt at an improvisation of his own after hearing Sgricci. Between the two MS sections of "Orpheus" and hence before they were recorded, Shelley composed in Italian a long commendatory account of Sgricci's *Death of Hector* (MS e. 17, pp. 11–21).

[13] *Letters of Mary Shelley*, ed. Jones, I, p. 122. Mary later wrote: "... the plan of the tragedy was closely copied from Euripides; but the words and poetry were his own..." (*Westminster Review*, 1826; reprinted in *Journals of Claire Clairmont*, pp. 441–57).

[14] *Medwin's "Conversations of Lord Byron,"* ed. Ernest J. Lovell (Princeton, N.J., 1966), p. 137: "[Sgricci's Iphigenia] compared her brother Orestes to the sole remaining pillar on which a temple hung tottering, in the act of ruin. The idea, it is true, is from Euripides, but [Sgricci] made it his own." Medwin repeated this information in his *Life of Shelley* (ed. H. B. Forman, London, 1913, p. 266). The reference is to Euripides' *Iphigenia in Tauris* 47–58.

[15] *Letters of Mary Shelley*, I, p. 123.

[16] *Ibid.* One of his poetic improvisations, for example, was on "the future destiny of Italy; he recalled to mind that Petrarch said that neither the highest Alps nor the sea were sufficient to defend this vacillating and ancient country from foreign masters; but he said, 'I see the Alps growing and even the sea rising and becoming troubled so as to keep off our enemies'" (*Letters of Mary Shelley*, I, p. 117). Claire's journal for 1 December 1820 (p. 190) records: "Sgricci improvisava upon the future independence of Italy."

actor's rigorous training in all the conventions of his role. It is made possible by the extemporizer's intimate knowledge of a large body of literature, such as that of the Greek metaphysicians, historians, and dramatists for which Sgricci distinguished himself;[17] and through Sgricci and the contemporary classical drama of Italy it is associated in Shelley's mind with the attempt to recreate the ancient Greco-Roman spirit of republicanism. In this sense improvisation is the imagination's reconstitution and revitalization of the history, legends, and literature that well up in a state of enthusiasm from the memory's reservoir of the past; and Shelley, who thought of the Greek revolution as "the slow victory of the spirit of the past over that of the present" and wrote that the spirits of Greece "Rule the present from the past,"[18] must have seen in the extempore exhibitions of this champion of liberty the actual spontaneous resurgence of Hellenic antiquity, an act confirming his belief in time's necessary cycle, now verging on a new Hellas. Shelley, too, can assume the improvisor's role because, as his play demonstrates, his own mind is saturated with the earlier literature—among others, Aeschylus' *Persians*, Virgil's Pollio eclogue, snatches of Sophocles, of the Bible, and of Milton's *Areopagitica*, the general conventions of the Greek, especially Euripidean, tragedy—all asking, under the inspiring pressure of the rising spirit of liberty, to re-emerge in a shape relevant to the moment. The unusual number and variety of literary echoes in *Hellas* are to be taken as evidence, not of a pastiche, but of the operative presence of the ancient free spirit. *Hellas* is a palimpsest of the literature of liberty.

Despite Shelley's ingenious adaptation of Aeschylus' *Persians*, however, there had to be one fundamental difference between it and his "improvise," for whereas Aeschylus was celebrating an accomplished victory, the current struggle is still in progress. *Hellas* therefore must be not only a drama of history like the *Cenci* but also a prophecy of "idealisms" like *Prometheus Unbound*, with which it significantly shares the subtitle "A Lyrical Drama." Since for Shelley the lyric is the form in which vision and foresight express themselves, the still unresolved outcome of the war "is insusceptible of being treated otherwise than lyrically," and thus the play is a "series of lyric pictures" with which he has "wrought upon the curtain of futurity, which falls upon the unfinished scene, such figures of indistinct and visionary delineation as suggest the final triumph of the Greek cause as a portion of the cause of civilisation and social improvement."[19] In brief, while the action of the drama depicts the current battles, the choruses adopt the larger vision of universal prophecy.

The lyrics of *Hellas* have their formal authority, of course, in the choric conventions of Greek tragedy, but their burden of prophecy is au-

---

[17] *Letters of Mary Shelley*, I, pp. 122–23n.
[18] To Byron, 21 October 1821 (*Letters*, II, 358); *Hellas*, 701.
[19] *Hellas*, Preface.

thorized by *The Persians*. The internal authority there is only incidental: the ghost of Darius reports that Persian defeat is the fulfillment of old prophecies, and the chorus foresees Persia's tyranny at an end and Greek freedom imminent. More important is the authority derived from the place of *The Persians* and of its subject matter in the subsequent development of Greek culture. Although the Athenian tyrants had been expelled and a democracy established under Cleisthenes shortly before the Persian Wars, it was not until the wars were concluded that Athens felt the full pride of her democratic government and the great age of Hellenic civilization began. When, in tracing the history of freedom in his *Ode to Liberty*, Shelley writes that after vague foreshadowings "Athens arose," he means to locate in Athens at the conclusion of the Persian Wars not merely an episode of liberation but the original birth of freedom among mankind, both the prototype and the fountainhead of all subsequent human freedom and expulsions of tyranny.[20] Consequently the historical sanction for Shelley's prophecy in *Hellas* that the still indecisive war against the Turks will be followed by another great age of freedom, a "brighter Hellas," is that the near identity of current events with those of Aeschylus' drama promises that the rebirth of freedom must follow the pattern established by its original birth in the same country. Aeschylus wrote after the event, Shelley before its completion; but the relation of the Persian Wars to Athens' subsequent Great Age validates Shelley's prophesying in terms of a cyclical theory of history.

For yet another reason *The Persians* must have seemed to Shelley the archetypal expression of universal truth. To cast his story in the form of a tragedy, Aeschylus of course had to dramatize the Greek victory entirely from the point of view of the defeated Persians: messengers report to Atossa the defeat of her son at the hands of the Greeks; she calls up the ghost of her husband, Darius, who prophesies the doom of the Persian forces; Xerxes returns bewailing his failure; and the chorus of Persian counsellors comments sadly throughout on the action. The dramatic effect of this perspective undoubtedly was the Athenian audience's vengeful delight of watching their enemy sink from fear into despair, grief, and mourning, of hearing the enemy speak in amazement and disbelief of the power of Athenian freedom and democracy, of experiencing the irony of the enemy's lament that kingly power has perished and that men will no longer fear to speak their thoughts, and of being told by Darius' ghost that the Persian defeat is the gods' irresistible fulfillment of an ancient prophecy. A dramatization from the Greeks' point of view not only would have failed to constitute a tragedy but also would merely have mirrored in an art form the unmediated joyful triumph they had already experienced on the battlefield.

[20] In Shelley's many hypothetical histories beginning with creation and the emergence of Good and Evil, Athens had marked the first appearance of culture, virtue, and liberty ever since his *Revolt of Islam* (406): "Then Greece arose."

But we have already observed, especially in considering *The Cenci*, that Shelley's ethics allows no joy in triumph over evil: evil is not to be met with retribution, and the tyrant is to be pitied, not hated, for hatred is the evil effect of an evil cause and therefore the inevitable source of further evil. True, his chorus of captive Greek women begins by ambiguously wishing for Mahmud a sleep as calm and deep as that of those who have died on the battlefield and is accused of not loving Mahmud by the Indian maiden who would sacrifice all her future happiness for his peace of mind. But the chorus will eventually see the moral truth and will sing the Christian theme of "Love for hate and tears for blood" (737), and the Greek revolutionists in the drama, like martyrs, will carry out the Christian act of offering the other cheek. The failure of the French Revolution, according to Shelley, was owing to the "dreadful revenge" the oppressed took on their oppressors; and the "usurpation of Bonaparte and then the Restoration of the Bourbons were the shapes in which this reaction clothed itself...."[21] The succession of evils, otherwise necessarily endless, can be broken, as Prometheus knew and Beatrice did not, only when at some point a stoic refusal to accept its effect drives it to undermine itself: slaves produce tyrants, "even as the seed produces the plant,"[22] and the refusal to be a slave removes the causal ground from under the tyrant, who must subvert himself in frustration. In Shelley's moral terms, then, Aeschylus chose precisely the right perspective by concentrating attention exclusively on the vanquished tyrants instead of the ultimate victors, for in similarly dramatizing the Greek uprising entirely as seen by the Turks, Shelley provides himself with the opportunity to trace the growing despair of the Turkish leader and to watch the process whereby tyranny starves from lack of slaves. *Prometheus Unbound*, being a drama of "idealisms," provided no such opportunity, since the tyrant Jupiter is but a distortion of Prometheus' mind and has no real existence. But in the historical domain *The Cenci* and *Hellas* are the opposite sides of the same moral and dramatic coin: because the former adopts the perspective of the victim of oppression who takes revenge, it is a tragedy; because the latter observes the weakening of the oppressor, it can look forward with optimism. Since freedom is reborn out of the internal collapse of the spirit of tyranny, it is ideologically proper—and dramatically ironic—for Shelley's moral principles to be divulged by the Turks, however unwittingly: that tyranny is overcome not by military retaliation but by the resistance of stoic self-sacrifice, and that when it is so resisted it will, by its own momentum, rapidly complete its necessary cycle from birth to decline and death that is the temporal course of all things in the realm of mutability.

[21] *Philosophical View of Reform* (Julian, VII, 13–14).
[22] To Mary Shelley, 8 August 1821 (*Letters*, II, 325).

On the other hand, since the lyric is the medium of prophecy as drama is the medium of history, Shelley substituted for Aeschylus' chorus of Persian counsellors a chorus of Greek captive women so that the oppressed Greeks, whom the chorus represents, are shown not as reflecting upon vanquished enemies but as having knowledge of all of time's cycles and hence as being capable of prophesying the coming era of freedom. The two temporal spans are thereby separated, lest victory be dramatized as exultant and retaliatory Greek triumph over the tyrannic Turks, a reaction to an action of the same kind. The Turkish drama traces only the closing of the temporal cycle of tyranny as seen by the waning Turks, who can grasp only the immediate present; and ironically the lyrics of the Greek captives comment on the events of that fading cycle, with a seeming irrelevance that is nevertheless purposeful, by forecasting a renewal of the world's great age of freedom, a new "Hellas," in the light of their knowledge of how time moves. It was for the same purpose of representing tyranny as containing the seeds of its own destruction that in his *Philosophical View of Reform* Shelley had written, not that Greece will defeat Turkey, but that "the Turkish Empire is in its last stage of ruin, and it cannot be doubted but that the time is approaching when . . . the climate and the scenery which was the birthplace of all that is wise and beautiful will not remain for ever the spoil of wild beasts and unlettered Tartars."[23] Or, as Shelley's chorus phrases the same idea, when "Tyrants sleep," then "let Freedom wake" (30). Although the Greek chorus ultimately sings of love for hate, the current bloody struggle prevented Shelley's casting his drama in quite these terms, as he could in *Prometheus Unbound*; nevertheless his strategy of dramatizing only the growing despair of the tyrant and of assigning to Turkish drama and Greek chorus different units of time—one of the decline of oppression, the other of the rebirth of freedom—allows him to evade representing eventual triumph as military victory.

Yet, even in substituting the captive Greek women for Aeschylus' chorus of Persian elders Shelley is not actually innovating but is faithful to the Greek dramatic spirit that he is recreating as an *improvvisatore*, or that is renewing itself through him as its inspired instrument. It is highly unlikely that he was unaware that Phrynichus' lost play *The Phoenicians*, which also dealt with the Greco-Persian wars and which, in Shelley's terms, Aeschylus recreated in his *Persians*, had employed a chorus of Phoenician women, Phoenicia then being a subjugated satrapy of Persia. Certainly he was aware of the frequency with which Euripides had employed choruses of captive women, sometimes Greek and sometimes Trojan, in his tragedies of prisoners in a foreign land. If Shelley's chorus is unlike Aeschylus', at least it is markedly Euripidean. Moreover, as Shelley

---

[23] *Philosophical View of Reform* (Julian, VII, 18).

pointed out to Medwin,[24] the opening lyric of *Hellas* derives from Calderón's *Constant Prince*, which parallels Shelley's drama of conflict between Christian Greek and Mohammedan Turk in that it deals with the
contest of Christian Portuguese and Mohammedan Moors and is also set
in the conqueror's country, where the Portuguese prince is held captive.
The opening song of Calderón's chorus of captive Christian women to the
Moorish princess is clearly the model for the opening song of Shelley's
captive Greek women to Persian Mahmud, even in its moral stance. These
sources and influences in Phrynichus, Euripides, and Calderón are not, of
course, functional in our experience of *Hellas* as, let us say, Aeschylus'
Prometheus Bound is operative—or should be—in our reading of Shelley's
reformation of that dramatic myth. But they are nevertheless functional to
the thematic and artistic integrity of *Hellas* as a work of creation, as a
self-authenticating statement. Shelley's chorus, though a departure from
Aeschylus', has precedent in Greek drama, the spirit of which informs his
play, as the Hellenic spirit of freedom informs all subsequent history; and
the parallelism of Calderón's play with all his other models and subject
matter is, for him, a usable confirmation that his dramatic mode is right
and true. Such a confluence of similar or complementary precedents validates them for the poet as episodes of the "cyclic poem written by Time
upon the memories of men"; and to assimilate them is to create another
episode of "that great poem which all poets, like the co-operating thoughts
of one great mind, have built up since the beginning of the world."

ii

The two time dimensions of the play, one assigned to the Turkish
drama and the other to the Greek chorus, are clearly defined and separated
by one of the lyrics. When Destiny, the driver of the world's chariot,
hurries by—"eyeless" and therefore directed by Necessity instead of arbitrary choice—before her, we are told, flits shadowy "Ruin," the cycle
ending with the Turks, and behind her rolls bright "Renovation," the
cycle beginning with the Greeks (711–19), like the succession of Demogorgon and Asia into the world. Echoing I Kings 19, which must have
seemed to Shelley the Judaic motto of nonviolent revolution, the chorus
sings of hearing a great wind, other earthly violence like the thunder of
earthquake, the crash of falling empires, shrieks for mercy, and shouts to
kill—and then "a small still voice," which the Book of Kings tells us is
the voice of God, the voice which is not in the great wind or earthquake.
The violence of the Turks—the Ruin that flies before Destiny, or Fate—
is not the work of the divinity of Shelley's play; the stoic gentleness of the
Renovation that follows Destiny is.

For, as the Greek semichorus then sings, "Revenge and Wrong bring

---

[24] Thomas Medwin, *The Life of Percy Bysshe Shelley*, ed. H. Buxton Forman
(London, 1913), p. 353.

forth their kind, / The foul cubs like their parents are" (729–30)—the
sentiment is indeed Greek, since the lines are from Aeschylus' *Agamemnon*.[25] Wrong is the way of the Turks, and to take revenge is to adopt
their way, which only perpetuates "Ruin." The right way, the next Greek
Christian semichorus sings, is to pay "Love for hate and tears for blood"
(737), and for this Christian advice it has drawn on St. Paul's preachings
to the Greeks. On the Areopagus in Athens, near the temple of the
Parthenon dedicated to Athena, goddess of wisdom and patron deity of
the city, Paul found "an altar with this inscription, 'To the Unknown
God.'" "Whom therefore ye ignorantly worship, him declare I unto you,"
he added on this occasion of first introducing Christianity into pagan
Athens.[26] Correspondingly, the semichorus sings,

In sacred Athens, near the fane
   Of Wisdom, Pity's altar stood:
Serve not the unknown God in vain,
But pay that broken shrine again,
   Love for hate and tears for blood.   (733–37)

The admirable appropriateness of the Pauline episode in all its details to
the context of Shelley's drama and to his moral expectations of the current
Greeks operates as a kind of confirmation handed down from the moment
of the Christianizing of Athens to the present, just as the appropriateness
of Aeschylus' *Persians* is a confirmation handed down from the first birth
of Athenian freedom to its anticipated rebirth. The negative Greek truth
borrowed from Aeschylus' *Agamemnon* (to repudiate Turkish violence
and warn against Greek revenge) recurs at a later historical time in the
more exalted form of the positive Christian injunction of love in the
Pauline episode (anticipating the forbearance of the Greeks in 1821), and
the succession of the pagan and Christian morals suggests a cyclical historical progress that the play will later develop. Now these two moral
truths are to be joined and repeated in the assimilating present to constitute the ground for Shelley's hope for the future. In the lyric the Old
Testament Book of Kings, the Greek Aeschylus, Paul, and the Christian
history of Athens emerge from their successive eras in chronological order
and flow together to reconstitute the present as the circle of time renews
itself.

   The dominant structural control over *Hellas*, then, is a complex of
the various temporal modes and historical designs of freedom and oppres-

[25] 758–71. At the very time he was writing *Hellas* Shelley, in a letter to Mary,
quoted *Agamemnon* 759–60 (meaning "It is the deed of iniquity that thereafter
begets more iniquity and like its own breed"), calling it his "maxim" and adding,
"How should slaves produce any thing but tyranny—even as the seed produces the
plant" (10 August 1821 [*Letters*, II, 325]).
[26] Acts 17: 22–23.

sion, elaborated in such a fashion as to assimilate the present to all of time, or to incorporate all the past in the present. Thereby the drama, as distinct from the lyrics, dooms Turkish tyranny to follow a pre-established and recurrent historical course. Islam, Sultan Mahmud realizes, is now a "sinking empire" (459), and its tyrannic power is being carried down on "the torrent of descending time" (350). Yet this is not in fact confirmed by the messengers' various reports of the battles, which alternate indecisively between Turkish defeats and victories. Instead, the increasing gloom and despair are in Mahmud's mind, since tyranny is for Shelley a spirit, a disposition of the soul, not external events, and the guarantee of its overthrow is not the progress of the war but the waning of the internal spirit which is tyranny's source. He is not promising military victory for the Greeks but an inevitable fading of the spirit of oppression and the consequent release of the spirit of freedom, these, and not military victory or defeat, being the determinants of the future because all moral consequences are determined necessarily by their motives. Whatever may happen on the battlefield, freedom can triumph only when oppression grows dispirited. The two phases of the drama, one of the remote battles that we know of only at second hand through the messengers' reports and the other of Mahmud's spirit as we watch its decline through his own words and gestures, therefore take independent courses and touch only at points of irony.

Even as the play begins, Mahmud, like Queen Atossa at the opening of *The Persians*, dreams of disaster and starts from his sleep with cries that his capitol is being sacked. But his dream leaves "no figure upon memory's glass" (131), and he sends for the seer Ahasuerus, the Wandering Jew, to recall his forgotten vision and to interpret it. The essence of the oppressor, Mahmud is inhumanly cruel, delights in the agonies of others (241–48), and is utterly and selfishly regardless of human life, even that of his own people (118–20, 191–96). Like that other tyrant, Count Cenci, he sustains his tyranny on a conviction of the inherent evil and worthlessness of man: to him "all human sounds" are evil (186), and, like the superstitiously "religious," he would converse with spirits, as he falsely thinks Ahasuerus to be, rather than with mankind, of whom he is contemptuous (187). Theistic religion and political tyranny are built on contempt for man. But Mahmud is the decaying tyrant, filled with prophetic fear, and just as Aeschylus' audience had the ironic pleasure of hearing the enemy acknowledge that its defeat was the fulfillment of divine prophecy, it is from Mahmud that we learn the ineluctable necessity of his own decline, his growing depression being the inward manifestation of the "descending time" of which he speaks. We are enabled, that is, to learn the process of the death of tyranny and the rebirth of freedom from admissions by the tyrant himself, who is reluctant to accept his doom and yet is inwardly compelled to reject insistently and irritably all efforts to reassure him. His paradoxically reluctant insistence not only gives his expression of despair a dramatic conviction that would be weakened if it were put in the mouths of the victors as a claim; it conforms with Shelley's doctrine that oppression is defeated, not externally, but internally by the historic evolution of spirit. Greek freedom does not crush Turkish oppression with revenge; the rising spirit of liberty diffuses itself throughout the spirit of tyranny until that fades and dissipates itself. One of Shelley's notebook jottings reads, "The spring rebels not against winter but it succeeds it—the dawn rebels not against night but it disperses it."[27] Thus when his henchman Hassan reports sympathetically the heroism of the defeated Greek soldiers and paints "Their ruin in the hues of our success," Mahmud accuses, "Your heart is Greek, Hassan"; and Hassan replies, "It may be so: / A spirit not my own wrenched me within,[28] / And I have spoken words I fear and hate" (451–57). As dawn floods night, the spirit of freedom breathes through the unwilling but powerless oppressor, whose own true voice is displaced.

What impels Hassan, as a reluctant vehicle of the spirit of liberty, to dress Greek ruin in the hues of Turkish success is the bearing of the Greeks in defeat. His is the only extended description the play offers of the Greeks, and it is a picture of heroic self-sacrifice and stoic defiance: of self-destruction in preference to capture and submission, of shouted pledges of liberty in the face of death, of defiant prophecies to the enemy of the inevitable rebirth of freedom—in short, of whatever in actual battle approximates passive, self-sacrificing resistance and indefeasible hope. Here is the application of Demogorgon's final advice both "To suffer woes which Hope thinks infinite" and "to hope till Hope creates / From its own wreck the thing it contemplates"; or, better, the advice Shelley offers against tyrants in *The Mask of Anarchy*:

With folded arms and steady eyes,
And little fear, and less surprise,
Look upon them as they slay
Till their rage has died away.

Then they will return with shame
To the place from which they came,
And the blood thus shed will speak
In hot blushes on their cheek.   (344–51)

Before this Promethean kind of patient martyrdom despotism buckles, a

[27] MS e. 18, flyleaf. Shelley elaborated on this theme in MS e. 17, p. 34:

April is not a rebel to rude March
Because it weeps like Pity on the earth
Till it unlocks all its imprisoned flowers
Nor day to night though it disperses it—
Nor truth to error though it scatters it—

[28] The manuscript reads, "breathed from my lips" (e. 7, p. 75).

cause that withers when deprived of any object on which to expend itself as an effect. Because of that stoic resistance the spirit of liberty speaks irresistibly through the tyrant, and the temporal cycle of oppression must necessarily rush to its close.

Even when Mahmud is most savage—

> Are there no Grecian virgins
> Whose shrieks and spasms and tears they may enjoy?
> No infidel children to impale on spears?—

he has an unshakeable conviction that the "day of ruin" has come to him, so that his violent words seem less a wanton cruelty than a sarcasm born of futility. Never does he cease to despair; no report of victory can comfort him. The crescent moon, traditional emblem on Islam's battle flag, appears to him to be the sinking moon, "Wan emblem of an empire fading now" (340); and when Hassan reassuringly begins, "Even as that moon / Renews itself—," Mahmud completes the sentence: "Shall we be not renewed!" (347–48). But although Mahmud's metaphor implies the inexorable cycle of time, it is an intentional irony that he be incapable of understanding the full import of his own words. We are to understand in fact, as Mahmud does not, that consequences flow necessarily from their causes, and the factor of mutability will in time carry those consequences to their cyclical close. Hence the cosmic metaphors of cyclical change, like the waning and renewed moon, that make their appearance in Mahmud's speeches of despair. As an evil spirit whose insignia is the crescent moon, what he fears is the coming dawn, a "miserable dawn." The period of Turkish power was to him "a night more glorious than the day which it usurped!" (259–60); for if night is the usurpation of day, like tyrannic usurpation itself it must fade when day again suffuses it with light. Turkey had conquered Greece in the night when the emblematic "orient moon of Islam rolled in triumph" in its natural course from east to west, from Caucasus to Grecian Ceraunia (266–67). At that time the "o'ershadowing wings" of the words of the prophet Mohammed "Darkened the thrones and idols of the West," but when Mahmud looks west to Greece he sees it, in the diurnal cycle, "Now bright" (261–64). The dawn he sees is not bloody Greek victory on the field of battle, but, as the messenger reports, "shadows ... of the unborn time / Cast on the mirror of the night" (609–10), the future that must grow out of the present. It is the dawn of the spirit of freedom signalled by the spread of rebellion throughout the Eastern Mediterranean and by the fact that, in a seismic-medical pun,

> Crete and Cyprus,
> Like mountain-twins that from each other's veins
> Catch the volcano-fire and earthquake-spasm,
> Shake in the general fever.   (587–90)

Consequently the play closes with a series of reports of unqualified Turkish military victories, not defeats, for the irony is that, convinced of the inevitable dissipation of his power—the inevitable dispersal of the usurping night before the coming dawn—Mahmud senses that his victory verges on defeat, and he sinks to his lowest point of despair. His comment on the shouts of Turkish victory is, "Weak lightning before darkness!" (915); and his last words as he vanishes from the play are a bitterly ironic response to the exultation of his men, "Victory! poor slaves!" (930).

But despite the sinking of his spirit and despite his use of metaphors of time's cycles, he understands nothing of what his words imply. He may say that "Kings are like stars—they rise and set" (195) and that in paying his mercenaries he sells for defeat the gold his ancestors bought with victory (239–40), implying that Turkish tyranny is completing its temporal cycle. Hassan also speaks of Ahasuerus' having survived all the past "Cycles of generation and of ruin" (154); and Mahmud similarly acknowledges Ahasuerus wise in experience of those cycles:

Thy spirit is present in the Past, and sees
The birth of this old world through all its cycles
Of desolation and of loveliness,
And when man was not, and how man became
The monarch and the slave of this low sphere,
And all its narrow circles.   (745–50)

(It is, incidentally, fitting that the fading tyrant unknowingly get the present spin of the wheel right: first "desolation" and then the coming and inevitable "loveliness.") But actually Mahmud knows only the inconstancy of all things, thinks events are supernaturally predestined, believes that only one possessed of supernatural powers, as he thinks Ahasuerus to be, can foresee the future, and, disappointed, expects no prophecy from Ahasuerus when he learns he is merely a man, "even as we" (738). Let the future come, "Come what will!" he says fatalistically (759, 643), believing that chance or some other nonhuman power will decide what it is to be; and he thinks that Ahasuerus will come to interpret his dream only "When the omnipotent hour to which are yoked / He, I, and all things shall compel" his coming (189–90). Only after Ahasuerus has instructed him in the temporal circle of events does he face the truth that

Come what may,
The Future must become the Past, and I
As they were to whom once this present hour,
This gloomy crag of time to which I cling,
Seemed an Elysian isle of peace and joy,
Never to be attained.   (923–28)

Therefore, although Ahasuerus is invoked to recall Mahmud's dream and prophesy his future, his true function is to give meaning to Mahmud's metaphors of sun, moon, and stars by defining the place of the present in the temporal circle from fifteenth-century Mahomet II to Mahmud and, aided by that inclusive perspective, by making clear the meaning and fixed causal operations of time itself. Whereas *Prometheus Unbound* is the view of time from eternity, Ahasuerus' role is to see the immediate events of the drama from the view of all of human time and thus give the drama its largest temporal dimensions. For Ahasuerus, perhaps the mocker of Jesus, perhaps pre-Christian Enoch, perhaps even pre-adamite (150–53), and cursed with immortality, has access to all of time and is wise in its workings, able to pierce the "Present, and the Past, and the To-Come" (148).

Lacking self-knowledge, Mahmud entertains all the vulgar errors and superstitions that Shelley would overthrow, including belief in original sin and the existence of arbitrary supernatural spirits. He therefore exults in his own supposed power as a tyrant and admires Ahasuerus for his gift of endless life: "I honour thee, and would be what thou art / Were I not what I am" (751–52). But he is mistaken on both counts because he understands neither the nature and operation of time nor the nature of man as defined by time, and immortal Ahasuerus' duty is to instruct him in these matters as Demogorgon, one of whose names is "Eternity," instructs Asia. When Mahmud asserts that Ahasuerus is "raised above thy fellow-men / By thought, as I by power," Ahasuerus replies, "Thou sayest so" (739–40) in the same ironically uncommitted tone with which Demogorgon replies, "I spoke but as ye speak" when Asia asks whom he had called "God." Like Mahmud, another tyrannical governor, thinking only of temporal power, had asked, "Art thou the King of the Jews?" and Christ, like Ahasuerus, answered Pilate, "Thou sayest it."[29] Not only is there the irony of placing Christ's words in the mouth of the Jew who had mocked him; Shelley means also to deny the supernatural status of both Ahasuerus and Christ. There is neither a kingdom of this world nor a "kingdom" of heaven. As Christ was for Shelley a man who most fully developed the divine human powers and virtues in himself, so Ahasuerus is a man who has most fully developed his inherent powers of thought, not one supernaturally gifted. Mahmud's tyrannical power, then, is a fiction, and Ahasuerus' power of prophecy is available naturally to all men. Pride, says Ahasuerus, was made "for those / Who would be what they may not, or would seem / That which they are not" (764–66), for all men are defined by their mortality, and neither can they have the arbitrary power the tyrant claims nor are they denied the natural power of thought possessed by the Jew. Endless life is a curse (151) that con-

[29] Mark 15: 2. Also Mat. 27: 11; Luke 23: 3; John 18: 37.

demns one forever to the prison of mutability and illusions. Nor, blinded as Mahmud is by pride, is he right in believing that, like himself, there is an arbitrary God who holds man in contempt and that we cannot "suffer aught / Which He inflicts not in whose hand we are" (646–47). Man is a creature who can be meaningful only when he respects and accepts himself as allotted but a brief span of earthly time, as incapable of arbitrary power, and as governed, like all other earthly things, by a necessitarian, will-less Power operating for the greatest possible "good" of all, even "the worm beneath thy feet" (762).

iii

Since Mahmud's fundamental error is to misunderstand time, he believes that because Ahasuerus proves to be only a man, not a supernatural spirit, he can know only the past, not the "unborn hour," which for Mahmud, in his ignorance, is "Cradled in fear and hope." Inasmuch as Ahasuerus has lived in all of time past and will live forever, he incarnates the total historical vision available to all men; and because, as the play repeatedly demonstrates through its syncretism, history is cyclical, knowledge of the past is also knowledge of the future. Consequently, Ahasuerus' reply to the request for prophecy is, paradoxically, to call up in Mahmud's mind the ghost of his ancestor Mahomet II and a vision of the sacking of Constantinople in 1453. These are made available to Mahmud, not supernaturally, as Darius is supernaturally invoked by Atossa, but because he and Mahomet II are but interinvolved temporal factors of one subsuming thought, inseparable termini of that thought as it is translated by mutability into time.[30] Fifteenth-century Mahomet is "but the ghost" of Mahmud's own "forgotten dream" (842), that frightening dream that he could not remember as the play opened and that Ahasuerus was invoked to make present and interpret. Mahomet II, says Ahasuerus, is "That portion of thyself which was ere thou[31] / Didst start for this brief race whose crown is death" (855–56) and, as Mahmud now recognizes, the "Imperial shadow of the thing I am" (900). Though separated by centuries, they are spoken of as father and son (878) in accordance with Shelley's recurrent use of the paternal-filial relationship as cause and effect; and it is a dramatic irony that early in the play, before he is tutored in the meaning of time, Mahmud curses the earlier time when "the orient moon of Islam rolled in triumph ... / Even as a father" is cursed "by an evil child" (264–66). For Mahomet II and Mahmud are identical inasmuch as cause and ultimate effect, like birth and death, contain each other

[30] After line 804 the manuscript (e. 7, p. 116) has Ahasuerus say, "Sultan [,] thy power and that thy father wielded / Is but one thought tempered with many [...]."

[31] The manuscript (e. 7, p. 215) reads, "whose ⟨child⟩ son thou art."

and are the same point on the circle around which "the full tide of power / Ebbs to its depths" (848–49): the "seed / Unfold[s] itself even in the shape of that / Which gathers birth in its decay" (889–91).

Mahomet's victory contained Mahmud's defeat, just as Aeschylus' *Persians* implies *Hellas* and as the fourth century B.C. victory of the Greeks implies their forthcoming freedom. Then, Mahmud's frightening prophetic dream with which the drama opens was actually of Mahomet II's capture of Constantinople from the Greeks three and a half centuries before. When, starting from his sleep, Mahmud shouted in astonishment that the "breach towards the Bosphorus / Cannot be practicable yet," he was experiencing as his own loss of Constantinople his ancestor's conquest of it long before. Past conquest is identical with present defeat because the "birth" of empire is the "same" as its "mortal throes" (851–52), and Mahmud can mentally realize the ancient victory as a vividly immediate battle because he and Mahomet are portions of the same thought, not because of a supernatural revelation. Ahasuerus tells Mahmud that in the revived dream of Mahomet's bloody victory,

> The Past
> Now stands before thee like an Incarnation
> Of the To-come.   (852–54)

Consequently, in terms of the large historical perspective the ghost of Mahomet is the prophecy to that other "portion" of himself, Mahmud, that defeat inheres in the triumph of oppression and completes the cycle of time: "The coming age is shadowed on the Past / As on a glass" (805–6), or, as a cancelled manuscript passage reads, "Time itself that all resolveth / But into itself revolveth."[32]

As no more than a human being whose "spirit," by virtue of his endless earthly life, is "present in the Past," Ahasuerus is but the personification of the wisdom given by the historical perspective. With his embracing view of time he not only can see the necessary relation of the present to the past—of Mahmud to Mahomet, of the current contest to its origins in the sack of Constantinople in the fifteenth century—but also can prophesy the future because he knows the circle of time, as any man can who takes the historical view:

> Wouldst thou behold the Future?—ask and have!
> Knock and it shall be opened—look, and lo!
> The coming age is shadowed on the Past
> As on a glass.   (803–6)

Just as Shelley assigned to Ahasuerus Christ's reply to Pilate in order to

[32] MS e. 7, p. 138.

naturalize and de-mystify it, so he has assigned to Ahasuerus the words of
the Sermon on the Mount[33] precisely in order to transform Christ's promise of God's readiness to answer prayers into man's natural power of foresight, which is dependent only on a knowledge of universal history and
its pattern of endlessly cyclical repetition. It was for a similar purpose of
secularizing Christ's promise that when Asia asks when the Golden Age
will return and "Prometheus shall arise / Henceforth the sun of this
rejoicing world," Shelley has Demogorgon reply merely, "Behold!"

But ultimately Ahasuerus' knowledge of all of time and its endless
recurrences allows him to look beyond time, into eternity: "look on that
which cannot change—the One, / The unborn and the undying," he
advises Mahmud (768–69). Human thought cannot actually penetrate to
direct experience and knowledge of that One, since Ahasuerus adds that
the sky is an "outwall" which,

<blockquote>
bastioned impregnably
Against the escape of boldest thoughts, repels them
As Calpe the Atlantic clouds.   (774–76)
</blockquote>

Ultimate Being, like the transcendent Power in *Mont Blanc*, is unknowable; rather, Ahasuerus is asking that human existence in time be viewed
in the light of the transcendent, immutable, and eternal One—in brief,
from what is traditionally thought of as God's atemporal point of view.
Since for Shelley there is no anthropomorphic God but only the transcendent One into which the individual mind is reabsorbed when life's
illusory dome of many-colored glass is shattered, to adopt the perspective
of the One is to take the view of the mind when it is released from illusions—or, to use J. M. E. McTaggart's term for our experiences of an
empirically real time that is illusory in terms of the Absolute, our "mis-
perceptions." In the context of Being, time and the world itself, however
"real" to human experience, prove fictitious, and all the recurrent cycles
of time are seen as a single eternal present. Ahasuerus' definition of existence is self-consciousness—"that which feels itself to be" (785)—and
the world is not self-conscious, nor can one feel himself to be in the
future or the past. Therefore thought alone, the act of self-awareness,—
together with its animate components, "Will, Passion, Reason, Imagination"—"cannot die" (795–97), for it has no relation to time and is the
presence of the transcendent One in what we call the world. Thought is
real; but so, too, in the human domain of existence, is mutability. Thus
the un-self-conscious something we call the world is only our self-conscious
thought woven by mutability into those various patterns that are the transi-

[33] Mat. 7: 7–8: "Ask, and it shall be given you; seek, and ye shall find; knock, and
it shall be opened unto you: For every one that asketh receiveth; and he that seeketh
findeth; and to him that knocketh it shall be opened."

tory fictions of time, and place, and circumstance (802); and it is a measure of Hassan's erroneously limited understanding of time that he thinks
Ahasuerus can appear to the petitioner for prophecy only at the fit "hour
and place and circumstance" (182).

Correspondingly, every conscious present—that is, every thought—is
really eternity, containing in itself what our incomplete vision calls past
and future:

> All is contained in each.
> Dodona's forest[34] to an acorn's cup
> Is that which has been, or will be, to that
> Which is—the absent to the present.   (792–95)

In that sense also

> The Future and the Past are idle shadows
> Of thought's eternal flight—they have no being;   (783–84)

or, as Shelley expressed it in his manuscript, "The future and the past
meet in the present."[35] Similarly, when Ahasuerus, echoing the Platonic
doctrine that Time is the moving image of Eternity, urges Mahmud to
talk no longer of "the Future and the Past" but to contemplate the eternal
One (766–69), he is not denying that, however illusory time may be, it
is a real "misperception" in the realm where mutability has sway, nor is he
denying the cycles of history on which *Hellas* is based; he is demanding
that history ultimately be seen from the viewpoint of the eternity of every
moment of thought, which contains what we falsely call its past—since
that can have no real existence but in a present—and, for the same reason,
what we falsely call the future. "Did not Mahomet the Second / Win
Stamboul?" asks Mahmud in bewilderment when told that the past has
no real existence (807–8); and Ahasuerus' answer is to make Mahomet
present to Mahmud's mind. Mahomet's conquest is real only in a "now."
In 1453 it was an eternal thought that contained its "future," Mahmud's
defeat; and Mahmud's decline is an eternal present containing its "past,"
Mahomet's victory. The power of both sultans, as Shelley's manuscript
reads, is "but one thought."[36] All this of course is dizzying metaphysics,
and Shelley dramatizes it so that it will produce a "dazzling mist" in
Mahmud's mind (787). Yet, paradoxically, it is the substitution of the
natural for the traditional supernaturalism of prophecy, for Shelley means
to claim that the true "mystery or majesty or power which the invisible
world contains"[37] expresses itself in our illusorily temporal realm according to fixed and intelligible laws.

[34] Which had oracular powers.
[35] MS e. 7, p. 114.
[36] MS e. 7, p. 116.
[37] *Essay on Christianity* (Julian, VI, 229).

Shelley's impulse had always been to break free from the limits of time and to inspect human history from some transcendent, God-like position. In *Queen Mab* man's past, present, and future are seen from the farthest verge of the universe, where matter, space, and time "cease to act";[38] in *The Revolt of Islam* the "Revolution of the Golden City" is enfolded by two cantos located, beyond "Nature's remotest reign," in the Temple of the Spirit presided over by the Senate of the Great who have died; and his "progress piece," the *Ode to Liberty*, is spoken by a voice the poet hears after he has been rapt beyond the limits of the universe. This impulse is the expression of Shelley's persistent desire to reconcile his dedication to the possibility of a utopian world with his faith in immortality, to belong to the human world of mutability and yet escape into a transcendent eternity, to see as both man and God see, in time and out of it. Indeed, the idea of a poem on the Greek revolution of 1821 first presented itself to him as an elaboration on the theme and form of the Jobean "Prologue in Heaven" that introduces Goethe's *Faust* and sets that human drama in a transcendent context. It is highly unlikely that the manuscript fragment which, without textual authority, we have come to call the "Prologue to *Hellas*" was ever intended as part of the published play, which contains many passages and themes salvaged from the abandoned fragment. The "Herald of Eternity" was to assemble the three Sons of God—Christ, Mohammed, and Satan—in the Senate House, where sits Destiny, or Fate, the "shadow of God" in the same sense that past and future are the shadow cast by eternal thought. There Christ, Mohammed, and Satan,[39] ruling the present from their thrones pinnacled on the past, dispute for possession of Greece, which has already suffered the Decrees of "Ruin and degradation and despair," while God's fourth Decree now hovers before her Father's throne, ready to fulfill her task but to be speeded, prevented, or suspended, depending on the outcome of the debate. The projected poem was discarded, no doubt wisely, but the compulsion it displays to inspect time from eternity and the world from infinity, while repressed, exerts a pressure throughout *Hellas* and emerges in dramatic form as Ahasuerus, who, knowing all of time, knows that time is a fiction of eternity.

Given that relation, the larger the span of time incorporated by the play, the more, like Ahasuerus himself, it approximates the truth of eternity by more fully displaying the stress exerted by the One that prevents mutability from becoming random and brings time around full circle. (The literary analogue is that the more previous poems *Hellas* assimilates

[38] The epigraph of *The Daemon of the World* is Lucan's description of the Delphic oracle, in whom "all time is gathered together."

[39] Replacing Goethe's three archangels. Shelley's intention to adapt to the Greco-Turkish war Goethe's *Prologue*, which is itself a "recreation" of the opening of the Book of Job, is analogous of course to his ultimate decision to "recreate" Aeschylus' *Persians*, a reworking of Phrynichus' drama.

the more it approximates that atemporal "great poem which all poets, like the co-operating thoughts of one great mind, have built up since the beginning of the world.") The present state of Turkish power has no meaning independent of its origin nearly four centuries before, and so the ghost of Mahomet must appear in Mahmud's mind because past and present contain each other. The cyclical history of Greek liberty is stretched even longer when the chorus (95–100), in an appropriately Christian metaphor, traces it from its "cradle" (celebrated by Aeschylus' *Persians*), to its death (represented by the ghost of Mahomet II and the vision of conquered Constantinople), through the long funereal centuries when Greece followed its bier, to its present "resurrection" (when Aeschylus' play is being resurrected as Shelley's *Hellas*). Another choral lyric (197–238), deriving from the substance of the abandoned imitation of Goethe's "Prologue in Heaven," traces in terms of successive religious faiths a similar cycle of historical time, for the history of Greece's cultures is also the history of successive religions, and the course of religion is also the evolution of Spirit. Echoing Milton's Nativity Ode, the chorus tells of the banishment of the Greek pagan gods by the "folding-star of Bethlehem" when Christ came, a "power from the unknown God," incarnate as a vapor animated by the sun. Then with the corruption of Christianity arose the "moon" of the religion of the seventh-century Mohammed which is soon to set while the symbol of the Christian founder of Constantinople, the cross "blazoned as on Heaven's immortal noon," leads the generations on. The circle is then completed by the chorus' implied yearning for return to the Golden Age of the pagan gods.

The obvious and elaborate astronomical imagery in this lyric of successive religious faiths is not unrelated to the national conflict that is the immediate subject of *Hellas*. The crescent moon and star not only are the emblems on the Turkish flag but, according to legend, were first adopted by the Turks as their national insignia when Mahomet II wrested Constantinople from the Greeks in 1453, and hence it also represents the enslavement of the Greeks to Turkish tyranny. Correspondingly, the Greek flag of a white cross on a blue field, supposedly based on the vision of the cross of light over the noonday sun [40] that came to the eponymous conqueror of Grecian Constantinople, was first adopted on the outbreak of the Greek revolution in 1821. The emblem is rich in relevant overtones not merely because the cross carries with it, as it does in *Prometheus Unbound*, the sense of patiently resisting self-sacrifice but also because, according to the legend handed down by Eusebius, God instructed Constantine to place the emblem of his vision, together with the motto Ἐν

[40] In his manuscript (e. 7, p. 166) Shelley's line "Whilst blazoned as on Heaven's immortal noon" is followed by the cancelled "Stamped as on the Sun's eternal light," where it is evident that the reference is to Constantine's cross. The word "blazoned," a heraldic term, is designed to intimate more vividly a flag.

τούτῳ νίκη [41] (By this you conquer), on his banner to succeed in overthrowing the oppressive Roman tyrant Maxentius. The first Christian conquest of Constantinople in the fourth century, her later capture by the Mohammedans, and the imminent collapse of her power under pressure of Greek Christianity are represented respectively by Constantine's vision, the Turkish ensign, and the new Greek flag based on Constantine's vision.

But the symbolism has a further function, for by means of it Shelley is enabled not only to identify the flags with the conflicting nations they represent and thus with the contest between liberty and tyranny but also to confuse the flags with the celestial bodies imaged on them and thus to widen the dimensions of the drama, which then is enacted also in the heavens. Mahmud, for example, convinced of Turkey's impending decline, reads in the reddish sunset sky the prophetic image of his army in rout by reversing the metaphor according to which the nation equals the celestial body depicted on its flag: the

> crescent moon, emblazoned
> Upon that shattered flag of fiery cloud
> Which leads the rear of the departing day;
> Wan emblem of an empire fading now!
> See how it trembles in the blood-red air,
> And like a mighty lamp whose oil is spent
> Shrinks on the horizon's edge. . . . (337–43)

But since above the crescent moon on the "blood-red" field of the Turkish flag there is also a star, an emblem the poem has already identified with Hesperus, the "folding-star" of Christianity,

> from above,
> One star with insolent and victorious light
> Hovers above [the moon's] fall, and with keen beams . . .
> Strikes its weak form to death. (343–47)

The celestial imagery continues to be threaded throughout the play so that the contest of Greek and Turk is recurrently translated into the actions of astronomical and atmospheric bodies. The time of the drama is sunset, not long before the setting of Islam's crescent moon; Mahomet II's earlier conquests had been the triumphal procession of the "orient moon of Islam" from east to west (266–67); and when the Greek fleet surrounded the Turkish, the "abhorred cross"—Shelley first wrote, "the Grecian flag" [42]—"glimmered" on all sides and "Dried with its beams the strength in

[41] Shelley assigns this as the battle-cry of the Christian Greeks in Mahmud's vision of his ancestor's conquest of Constantinople (829).
[42] MS e. 7, p. 80.

Moslem hearts, / As the sun drinks the dew" (501–4). In battle the Moslem hordes are like clouds blown by the wind, their arms are lightning, and their march is earthquake (277–80); the warships are like vapors "Freighted with fire and whirlwind" (284–85). When the Turkish ships reverse their ensign and its emblematic moon in the traditional sign of defeat, the sympathizing moon in the sky is blotted out by the clouds, hiding "her face for grief" (636–38).

iv

The effect of this cosmic imagery is repeatedly to expand the relevance of the immediate historical events spatially in the same manner that it is expanded temporally by being fixed in the context of time's cycles. In accordance with Ahasuerus' metaphysics, the play is working throughout, especially in the Greek choruses, to relate the contest of 1821 to all of space as well as all of time until, like the setting of such poems as *Queen Mab* and the *Ode to Liberty*, it verges on releasing the event from both of these illusory dimensions. The point at which space and time meet is their simultaneous original creation, and Shelley binds that point to the Greek revolution by conceiving of creation as the primordial victory of freedom over anarchy, an anarchy that subsumes both political formlessness and material chaos:

> In the great morning of the world,
> The Spirit of God with might unfurled
> The flag of Freedom over Chaos,
>   And all its banded anarchs[43] fled,
> Like vultures frighted from Imaus,[44]
>   Before an earthquake's tread.—
> So from Time's tempestuous dawn
> Freedom's splendour burst and shone.[45]   (46–53)

---

[43] The identification of Chaos with Anarchy is of course Miltonic; see, for example, *Paradise Lost*, II. 896, 988.

[44] The line derives from Milton's comparison of Satan to "a vultur on *Imaus* bred" (*Paradise Lost*, III. 431).

[45] This stanza had its origin in Christ's speech in the so-called "Prologue to *Hellas*" (112–19):

>   [Greece] shall arise
> Victorious as the world arose from Chaos
> And as the Heavens and the Earth arrayed
> Their presence in the beauty and the light
> Of thy first smile, O Father . . . as they gather
> The spirit of thy love which paves [?]
> Their path over the abyss—till every sphere
> Shall be one living spirit—so shall Greece—   (MS e. 7, p. 28)

Opposed to the Turkish moon and like the Greek flag with its luminous, sun-drenched cross of Constantine, the battle flag of Freedom is emblazoned with the sun whose light, by divine fiat, gave the world form when "the earth was without form, and void; and darkness was upon the face of the deep. And the Spirit of God moved upon the face of the waters."[46] For the current contest against despotism is to be understood as a recurrence of the original creative war between Freedom and Chaos, and the time-span of the poem's vision now extends from the very birth of time to the present—and to the future. Just as creation was the dawning of the sun of Freedom, so the chorus will sing in a later lyric that when Slavery, the "frost of the world's prime" (676), appeared, then in a repetition of the original creative fiat,

Let there be light! said Liberty,
And like the sunrise from the sea,
Athens arose!—Around her born,
Shone like mountains in the morn
Glorious states. (682–86)

Shelley means no idle hyperbole. In Pope's *Dunciad* we are to accept the cosmic exaggeration because the destruction of culture is conceived of as a sin against God's orderly creation, not because there is a causal relation between man's "uncreating word" and the physical universe:

Lo! thy dread Empire, Chaos! is restored;
Light dies before thy uncreating word:
Thy hand, great Anarch! lets the curtain fall;
And Universal Darkness buries All.

But, always reaching out toward some ineffable Oneness that is the ultimate cause and denying the distinction between the universe and thought, Shelley, as we have noted, understands Liberty as one of the names applicable to the one organizing Power, whether its medium be the substance of space or the community of men. Therefore, after his chorus tells that the Spirit of God planted the sun-emblazoned flag of Freedom as sign of victory over the anarchs of Chaos, it traces the history of human freedom with the same image of sunlight. The dawning light that gave form to chaos and birth to time, still rising like the city-illuminating sun in *Lines Written Among the Euganean Hills*, then shone on Thermopylae and Marathon "like mountains beacon-lighted"; for these were the sites of

[46] Gen. 1: 2. The language and imagery of Shelley's stanza suggest he may also have had in mind Milton's description of creation: "Darkness profound / Cover'd th'Abyss: but on the wat'ry calm / His brooding wings the Spirit of God outspread . . ." (*Paradise Lost*, VII. 233–35).

battles against the Persians that redound to the glory of Greece in the first birth of human freedom. Through the transitional hieroglyph of the sun as a winged disk, or "winged glory," the eagle takes the place of the sun, with which it is traditionally associated, and half-alights on Philippi as the formative light continues its westward course to Milan, Florence, England, Switzerland. The disappearance of freedom is the night of time, and its eighteenth-century reappearance in America and spread to Europe is a "second sun" moving "Against the course of Heaven and doom" (66–67) —the image perhaps suggesting how man's will can redirect the course of time, cancelling the period of night.[47] In this new movement of liberty the bloodiness of the French Revolution is plague-like "sanguine steams" that, like the earth's misty exhalations, hide the sun "but quench it not" (73). Freedom again becomes the eagle "fed with morning" (76), replenishing itself with the same dawning light that gave chaos form; and her "nurslings"—Greece and other countries now in revolt—"purge their dazzled eyes...in the naked lightnings / Of truth"[48] (88–89), in accordance with the legend coming down from the *Physiologus* that the eagle's filmy eyes are cleansed by the rays of the sun. But Shelley's language and imagery here make it evident that he has "created anew" Milton's vision of English liberty in *Areopagitica*: "Methinks I see her [England] as an Eagle muing her mighty youth, and kindling her undazl'd eyes at the full midday beam; purging and unscaling her long abused sight at the fountain it self of heav'nly radiance."[49] Like Aeschylus' *Persians*, Milton's treatise on freedom—which itself alludes to Isocrates' *Areopagiticus*, a political plea addressed to the Athenian Areopagus in 355 B.C.—is a "Hellenic" truth that persists from the past and presses itself upon the present surge toward liberty through the medium of the *improvvisatore*.

Because of his identification of the creative power with the liberty that gives form to otherwise anarchic human society, it is valid for Shelley to translate the history of freedom and the Greco-Turkish contest into imagery of sun, world, moon, star, cloud, earthquake, and even to have the Greek chorus speculate on how they would behave if they were the naturally and necessarily free clouds instead of unnaturally oppressed captives (648–75). For the contest is in truth one between cosmos and chaos, and the cosmic imagery, together with the identification of freedom with creation, not only stretches the events of 1821 to their largest spatial significance but also raises the question of the ontological status of freedom

[47] Cf. *Prometheus Unbound*, IV. 167: "Leading the Day and outspeeding the Night." See above, pp. 369–70.
[48] As he frequently does, Shelley has overdetermined his image: Apollo as the sun-god slew Python, or Error, with his beams. See above, p. 47.
[49] Cf. Shelley's letter to Byron of 4 May 1821 (*Letters*, II, 289): "You felt the strength to soar beyond the arrows [of the reviewers]; the eagle was soon lost in the light in which it was nourished, and the eyes of the aimers were blinded."

and of the world, as it has already been raised of time. Within the non-lyrical drama Ahasuerus of course has partly answered the question by defining time as the illusory shadow of eternal thought and the world as thought woven into inconstant forms by mutability. Therefore, instead of a real temporal world occasionally experiencing a nominalistic freedom, Shelley postulates the eternal reality of Freedom, which manifests itself in varying degrees in the mutable illusions of space and time. Worlds are transient, the chorus sings:

Worlds on worlds are rolling ever
    From creation to decay,
Like the bubbles on a river
    Sparkling, bursting, borne away.[50]   (197–200)

But if worlds are transitory, souls are immortal, endlessly reincarnated in mutability and returned to eternity, "through birth's orient portal / And death's dark chasm hurrying to and fro" (202–3) and invested with increasingly greater purity or stain in proportion to the conduct of each previous mortal life they have led:

New shapes they still may weave,
New gods, new laws receive,
Bright or dim are they as the robes they last
    On Death's bare ribs had cast.   (207–10)

Since these souls are portions of the transcendent One, it is a matter of indifference whether Shelley declare the individual souls or the One to be the immortal reality. Correspondingly, an earlier manuscript version of the same lyric shows not only that he first wrote that Freedom is the unchanging reality but also that Freedom is the fundamental character of the One whose plastic force acts through mutability: that force is the motion of the world, the love of the angels, the pulse in the worm, the emotion in man.[51] Freedom is that Absolute which "informs the fleeting millions";

       'tis their doom
To be a portion every one
Of thee—Thou art thyself alone![52]

This seemingly idiosyncratic identification of Freedom with Spirit and therefore with Being, and the corresponding identification of the expression of Freedom not only with the world's motion and man's emotions

---

[50] Cf. "Ode to Heaven."
[51] MS e. 7, p. 10. For further discussion of this manuscript poem, see below, pp. 453–54.
[52] MS e. 7, pp. 4, 6.

but also with the original creation, are so nearly Hegelian that it would be helpful to consider the rationale in terms approximating Hegel's. Like Hegel, Shelley defines existence as self-awareness, a property of spirit alone, since only spirit can be an object to itself. Spirit unfolds, actualizes itself, as self-consciousness; and since this is a reflexive act, spirit has a self-contained existence. But such autonomous existence, such independence of everything external, is the true meaning of freedom, the condition in which spirit seeks to actualize itself. The world's motion, animal pulsation, angelic love, and human emotion are modes of the spirit's self-fulfillment relative to the various media and therefore are all states of being free. Hence, too, the highest praise Shelley can offer the individual human as an earthly incarnation of a portion of the One is, as we have noted, that "He is himself alone," since this is the relative state of the freedom of the One, which is the only reality of which it can be said in the absolute sense, "Thou art thyself alone."

Since Freedom, then, is the essence of Being, it is creative of existence, as anarchy, or tyranny, is constitutive of chaos. In his *Ode to Liberty*, again conceiving of Liberty as the analogue in the human domain of the creative Absolute, Shelley writes that the Absolute

With life and love makes chaos ever new,[53]
As Athens doth the world with thy [i.e. Liberty's] delight renew.

Because Liberty is the essence of Spirit, which is defined by its autonomous self-consciousness, its expression by the Absolute is creative of the cosmos, and correspondingly its human expression is creative of the arts— that is, of autonomous self-reflective entities that thereby become eternal, unlimited by space and time, being thoughts that contain the principle of their own integrity. Through the human spirit, Liberty's "all-creative skill" peopled the Acropolis "with forms that mock the eternal dead / In marble immortality."[54] Shelley's beginning the history of human liberty with Freedom's creative victory over chaos is therefore merely beginning with the first step in the history of the self-realization of Spirit. Ultimately, because Freedom is the essence of the Absolute, or that which is absolutely itself "alone," it subsumes all other modes of perfection, so that in *The Mask of Anarchy* Shelley can properly declare it to be synonymous with Justice, Wisdom, Peace, Love, Spirit, Patience, Gentleness—"All that can adorn and bless / Art thou."[55] Life, Hope, Truth, and Love, sings one chorus in *Hellas*, are all subject to change and revolve about their unending temporal cycle, but they would be their opposites, Death, Despair, Falsehood, and Lust, if Liberty were not the immutable reality and

[53] That is, transforms chaos into the ordered world.
[54] *Ode to Liberty*, 72–74.
[55] *Mask of Anarchy*, 259–60.

Lent not life its soul of light,
Hope its iris of delight,
Truth its prophet's robe to wear,
Love its power to give and bear. (42–45)

In this metaphysical context Greece and 1821 shrink nearly into in-
significance, and Shelley reveals that he has trapped himself once again
in his ambivalent desires for an earthly utopia and for an eternal perfection beyond the illusory. As he did in *Epipsychidion*, he so idealizes the
utopian state that he nearly refines out of the world the factors of change,
time, and space until it is almost indistinguishable from a transcendent,
unworldly state attainable only after the human soul has died out of its
mortal limitations. One side of Shelley is indeed zealous for Greek freedom and the banishment of Turkish oppression, but the ultimate unreality
of time and space reduces that to a matter approaching indifference, while
the expanding boundaries of his drama reach out to something like Hegel's
teleological philosophy of universal history. Whether Greece succeeds or
fails, Freedom exists; it exists as nothing else really does; and it would
exist even should it appear nowhere and at no time. Hence the fact that
the play treats Greece less as a place than as a spirit and appeals more to
what Shelley calls our conjectures of "the condition of that futurity towards which we are all impelled by an inextinguishable thirst for immortality" (197n.) than to our desires for a purposeful mortal existence.
The chorus that hastily traces the course of Freedom from its human birth
in 480 B.C. to its death in 1453 and to its expected resurrection in 1821
then speculates on the future of Freedom:

If Heaven should resume thee,
    To Heaven shall [Greece's] spirit ascend;
If Hell should entomb thee,
    To Hell shall her high hearts bend. (102–5)

And if—a purely rhetorical supposition that the chorus will later deny—
Freedom were to be annihilated, Greece shall be forgotten. "Greece" is
wherever Freedom is.

In fact, Shelley is more confident that the new home of Freedom will
be America than that it will reappear in Greece, and his drama closes,
not with sanguine expectations that the Greeks will be victorious, but with
hopes for the new Hellas in the West. America's Revolution and republican government, together with their effect in inspiring Europe's stirrings
for liberty—and the transitional correlation of the movement of the
heavens with the westward course of empire and learning—gave him some
justification, of course, but his reasons have less to do with actual historical
events than with the consequences of his moral symbolism and his con-

ception of time. The star which had hovered victoriously over the moon
on the Turkish flag was the "folding-star of Bethlehem," emblem of the
religion whose doctrine is "Love for hate and tears for blood," and thus
of the love that defeats tyranny and releases liberty. The symbolism is
especially appropriate, since the folding-star, Hesperus, is the evening
appearance of Venus, star of love. In the heavens the passage of time is
marked by movement in space, and now that in the midway course of
time "Darkness has dawned in the East," the chorus sings:

Let Freedom and Peace flee far
    To a sunnier strand,
And follow Love's folding-star
    To the Evening land!   (1027–30)

From the awakening night in the East, Hesperus flees westward in the
normal course of time to America, where it is now day:

Thou beacon of love! thou lamp of the free!
        Guide us far, far away,
To climes where now veiled by the ardour of day
        Thou art hidden
    From waves on which weary Noon
    Faints in her summer swoon,
    Between kingless continents sinless as Eden.   (1041–47)

Although the chorus concludes that "Greece, which was dead, is arisen!"
(1059), that resurrected and "brighter" Hellas is reached by following love's
star, for since Europe is experiencing the "sunset of hope" (1050), hope
must be dawning in the West.

    If the illusion of space is a function of the illusion of time, then the
passage of Liberty to America is but another way of expressing the temporal cycle of mutability. However, Shelley's aspiration, impelled by the
ideal postmortal "futurity towards which we are all impelled by an inextinguishable thirst for immortality," is always to transcend earthly limitations; and hence his problem here, as again in *Epipsychidion*, is how to
correlate that aspiration with the fact that those limitations must be
reckoned with, how to compromise eternity with time. His location of the
new Hellas on some cape towering threateningly over "the idle foam of
Time" is an effort to effect that compromise with a metaphor:

    If Greece must be
A wreck, yet shall its fragments reassemble,
And build themselves again impregnably
    In a diviner clime,

To Amphionic music[56] on some Cape sublime,
Which frowns above the idle foam of Time.   (1002–07)

Disassembled and reassembled in the course of Time, the Destroyer and
Preserver, Hellas is now to continue in the world of time but aloof from
its effects, as does the "Greek" spirit, whose

> foundations are
> Built below the tide of war,
> Based on the crystalline sea
> Of thought and its eternity.   (696–99)

But this is a facile vision, not an explanation, and Shelley is compelled to face more realistically the experiential facts of time and mutability and ask how they may move in the direction of a world aloof from
time. Time alone can merely bring evil and wrong to the end of their
cycle so that that sequence, personified in the drama by the Turks, may
end:

The world is weary of the past,
Oh, might it [i.e. the past] die or rest at last![57]   (1100–1)

With the cessation of the past, the world can renew its "great age," which,
like the original Golden Age, is at the beginning of time and is unravished
by it. But a manuscript fragment associated with *Hellas* makes it clear
that because of the effects of mutability Shelley does not believe that man
can ever return to exactly what once was or that Greece the country can
be restored to her original glory:

Could Arethusa to her fountain run
Or could the morning shafts of purest light
Again into the quiver of the Sun
Be gathered—could one thought from its wild flight
Return into the temple of the brain
Without a change, without a stain,
Could aught that is, ever again
Be what it once has ceased to be,
Greece might again be free.[58]

---

[56] The allusion to Amphion, whose music built a wall around previously unfortified
Thebes, is apt not only because "poets" (or musicians) are the creators of perfect
order but also because Shelley means to represent the new Hellas as more nearly
impregnable than its predecessor.
[57] Cf. *Prometheus Unbound*, IV. 9–14, where the "past Hours" bear Time, "Father
of many a cancelled year," to his tomb in eternity.
[58] MS e. 7, p. 261. The lines are part of the poem "Unfathomable Sea!"

Yet, the impossibility of a return opens up the possibility of progress, a possibility implied in the doctrine of successive reincarnations of human souls, which may progressively improve the world they leave behind on each return to the Absolute:

> New shapes they still may weave,
> New gods, new laws receive,
> Bright or dim are they as the robes they last
> On Death's bare ribs had cast. (207–10)

That "Greece, which was dead, is arisen" means not that resurrected Hellas has been restored to its prior state but, like Christ, has been raised to a higher state of being. In effect, Shelley is asking that the world begin all over again, but at a point higher above the idle foam of Time than before. Although eternity expresses itself in time as a circle, his hope is that the cycles of time may be made to spiral upward, each circle returning to the original age before mutability marred it, but making it progressively less likely that this primordial state will be touched by time.

v

The gyre of time is a recurrent motif in *Hellas*, implicit in its assimilation of a series of past historical moments and in its palimpsest-like layers of literary allusion. That spiral becomes the theme of the play's conclusion. According to the chorus' history of religions that parallels Greece's history (211–38), first there were Jove, Apollo, Pan, and Love, the "Powers of earth and air"; and these fled on the appearance of Christ, a "power from the unknown God." When Christianity then became the institutional doctrines of "Hell, Sin, and Slavery," Islam flourished but will set while Christ's cross of self-sacrificing resistance "leads generations on." This lyric, Shelley's note points out, represents the "popular notions of Christianity . . . as true in their relation to the worship they superseded, and that which in all probability they will supersede, without considering their merits in a relation more universal." Christianity is an improvement upon other institutional religions without being good or true, except relatively. But the lyric ends on a significantly ambiguous note: the original Olympian gods of earth and air had grown weak in the presence of Christianity because "killing Truth had glared on them" (234). Although Truth may be a relative good, nevertheless it is murderous and glares instead of gleaming, blinds instead of illuminating; and the expulsion of the pagan gods by Christianity is likened to the flight of

> the radiant shapes of sleep
> From one whose dreams are Paradise
> . . . when the fond wretch wakes to weep
> And Day peers forth with her blank eyes. (225–28)

Here the glare of Truth does not destroy falsehood; it banishes the radiant dreams of Paradise, which are neither true nor false, since, like the Golden Age of the spirits of earth and air, they precede that distinction, as the Paradise of Adam and Eve precedes the distinction between good and evil—"We are damned," Shelley wrote Byron, "to the knowledge of good & evil."[59] Christianity is relatively "true" with respect to things-as-they-are, the world in which one "wakes to weep," but it is irrelevant to the world of the imagination, where the distinction is not between truth and falsehood but, as we have seen, a distinction among the various degrees of unwilled belief, from "conjecture" to "persuasion" and "conviction." Shelley's yearning is for the pretemporal and paradisiacal state of imaginative faith as he described it in *The Witch of Atlas*, adapting both Milton's account of the birth of Death and the commonplace that Truth is the daughter of Time:

Before those cruel Twins, whom at one birth
    Incestuous Change bore to her father Time,
Error and Truth, had hunted from the Earth
    All those bright natures which adorned its prime,
And left us nothing to believe in. . . . (49–53)

Or, according to the chorus in *Hellas*, before

    Our hills and seas and streams,
    Dispeopled of their dreams,
Their waters turned to blood, their dew to tears,
    Wailed for the golden years. (235–38)

Although the chorus has traced the progress of religions, it has implied the paradox that the progress is also an ultimate return, a paradox that is resolved by the spiraling return to a greater Golden Age than the original. Thus the play closes with another lyric which promises that after Christianity there will once again be the "golden years" of a new Saturnian Age and the pagan gods, but purer than the first, closer to the Absolute:

Saturn and Love their long repose
    Shall burst, more bright and good
Than all [the deities] who fell, than One who rose [i.e., Christ],
    Than many unsubdued. (1090–93)

The reason America, instead of Greece, is to be the new Hellas in the ascending circles of human history is made clear by one of the concluding choruses:

[59] 21 October 1821 (*Letters*, II, 358).

Through exile, persecution, and despair,
    Rome was, and young Atlantis shall become
    The wonder, or the terror, or the tomb
Of all whose step wakes Power lulled in her savage lair:
    But Greece was as a hermit-child,
      Whose fairest thoughts and limbs were built
    To woman's growth, by dreams so mild,
      She knew not pain or guilt.   (992–99)

Ancient Greece harbored liberty during her original state of innocence, in hermit-like withdrawal from the experiences that might have taught her pain and guilt; and she was therefore too child-like and womanish to fend off the evil of oppression. However, like Rome, which was founded by the long-suffering Greek exiles, America has been settled by the European exiles who have endured persecution and despair. In the spiraling evolution of secure human freedom, triumphal defeat, not innocence, is a necessary precondition. Hence the complex paradox that while the play ends with the Turks shouting, "Victory!" which Mahmud knows to be their defeat, this same Greek chorus begins by acclaiming the "Repulse" which

Led the ten thousand from the limits of the morn
    Through many an hostile Anarchy!
At length they wept aloud, and cried, "The Sea! the Sea!"   (988–91)

The reference is to the heroic endurance of the Greek Ten Thousand whose retreat to the sea Xenophon celebrated; and Shelley means to hold up that victory-in-defeat as a model for the modern Greeks of the defeat they must endure before they can gain true freedom.

The same conception of a freedom whose foundation is the successful endurance of failure appears in a scene of Shelley's fragmentary drama, *Charles the First*, composed at approximately the time of *Hellas*. Planning to leave tyrannic England for America, John Hampden calls upon the evening star, as the chorus in *Hellas* does, to "light us to the isles of the evening land," and he petitions the New World to "Receive . . . / These exiles from the old and sinful world" (iv. 22, 35–36). The English emigrants to America, unlike the ancient Greeks, have already experienced the temporal cycle of liberty and oppression, and by virtue of that knowledge of pain and evil America is the "*young* Atlantis," the perfect republican island of the West in the state of youth, not the "hermit-child" that ancient Greece was. From their heroic passive defeats comes their greater strength to deter those who would awaken the sleeping power of oppression, that evil which ever exists but may be kept only potential.

Since time can never be called back into itself, "Greece" in the sense of the original child-like and innocent liberty can never again be free: the

place name here serves as symbol of levels of temporal Golden Ages, not
as a designation of a location. But America the country is unstained,
rather than merely purified, for she has always been "kingless" and "sin-
less" (1047). This primitive land is an Eden (1047), "Paradise islands"
in the region of Atlantis and the Fortunate Isles of the West, "like the
shapes of a dream" (1051–52); or, as Hampden describes America in
Charles the First, "floating Edens"

Where Power's poor dupes and victims yet have never
Propitiated the savage fear of kings
With purest blood of noblest hearts; whose dew
Is yet unstained with tears of those who wake
To weep each day the wrongs on which it dawns;
Whose sacred silent air owns yet no echo
Of formal blasphemies; nor impious rites. . . .   (iv. 26–32)

Like the original Golden Age and the Garden of Eden, America precedes
the distinction between truth and falsehood, good and evil: the course
from Greece to America is a full circle of time. America's human inhabitants, however, are not innocents but have grown in strength by
having endured time's cycle: those who have known "exile, persecution,
and despair" and have endured them heroically are now in an unstained
Eden, a context of innocence. Mutability has not been overcome, nor is
man yet securely above the idle foam of Time, but the power to resist and
minimize time and change has grown. Thus, although time must move in
its circles of the seasons and of birth and death, ever returning to the
pristine state, the human spirit can grow and mature both through harsh
endurance and through aspiration to the Absolute toward which it is
drawn by thirst for immortality; and the combination of that experience
and aspiration can bend the unavoidable circles of time, like a helix,
asymptotically toward the Absolute in the realm beyond life and mutability.

It is appropriate, therefore, that *Hellas* close not merely with a prophecy but with one that refashions to a higher expectation a prophecy be-
queathed by the past. The final chorus recreates Virgil's Fourth Eclogue,
the famous vision of the renewal under Augustus of the Golden Age and
the return of Astraea, or Justice—a prophecy, moreover, of a more glorious
repetition in Rome of the mythic history of her Greek predecessor, just as
Shelley is prophesying the more glorious renewal of Hellas in America.
The pattern of history remains the same, and the past will repeat itself in
another Orpheus and a new Ulysses, but at levels that more nearly resemble the unattainable Absolute outside time. Instead of Virgil's prophetic
"second Argo" that was to repeat for Rome the original Argo of her an-

cestral Greece,[60] Shelley's chorus sings of an even later one, a "loftier Argo" (1072)—and a "brighter Hellas," "fairer Tempes," and a "sunnier deep." The Sphinx's riddle of death will remain, and although time's ravages cannot be prevented, they can increasingly be impeded and deferred as Spirit unfolds itself in history: the brighter Hellas of America will

> to remoter time
> Bequeath, like sunset to the skies,
> The splendour of its prime;
> And leave, if nought so bright may live,
> All earth can take or Heaven can give.   (1084–89)

And yet it must be recognized that, as usual and as the words of that stanza imply, Shelley is honestly and skeptically aware that he has been guided by a hope and a desire, not an assurance. The obligation of the poet is "to attach himself to those ideas which exalt and ennoble humanity," guided not by proven facts but by the "presumption" that eternity, together with its perfection, "is the inheritance of every thinking being" (197n.). But the mere mortal is free to doubt. Mingled with the confident prophetic tones of the poet in the final chorus is a far less assured, more human voice, like that which ends *Prometheus Unbound*, capable only of uttering a plea that the evil of the past be not renewed in the next cycle of time:

> Oh, write no more the tale of Troy,
> If earth Death's scroll must be!
> Nor mix with Laian rage the joy
> Which dawns upon the free:
> Although a subtler Sphinx renew
> Riddles of death Thebes never knew. . . .

> Oh, cease! must hate and death return?
> Cease! must men kill and die?
> Cease! drain not to its dregs the urn
> Of bitter prophecy.   (1078–83, 1096–99)

vi

Shelley's view of history has grown vastly in intellectual sophistication since his *Lines Written Among the Euganean Hills*, where the great episodes of cultural freedom appeared as scattered and unpredictably given "islands" in the dark ocean of time. But the essential difference arises out of Shelley's ambiguous definition of man. The *Euganean Hills* as-

[60] *Eclogues* iv. 34.

sumes that man is only a vehicle inconstantly illuminated and that each such epiphany is a human or societal moment of perfection: history has no plan, and its random course is a mystery. But *Hellas* assumes that man is defined by the persistent active presence in him of the universal Spirit and that Spirit can develop through man's mastery of time's cycle. Granting the obvious differences in assumptions, Shelley's eventual teleological philosophy of history has affinities with Hegel's in proposing a progressive, not a sporadic or even apocalyptic, self-realization of Spirit, whose essence is Freedom: the collective human soul approaches more nearly, cycle by cycle of the time to which it is bound, the Absolute from which it derives, until the difference between time and the atemporal is infinitesimal. Having rejected theism and therefore all providential theories of history, Shelley assigned to the human spirit the responsibility for the infinite progress and evolution of that self-realization which is freedom. In that progress time is both help and hindrance: were there no time, the human spirit would be one with the Absolute, and yet the circular course of time sweeps away each declination into oppression and wrong and creates ever anew the Golden Age in which Spirit can be progressively unfolded. Thus free will and necessity, as in Hegel, are reconciled, for by free will the spirit evolves in self-realization, and yet that freedom depends upon the willed submission to the circle of time outside the human spirit. It is, correspondingly, significant that Shelley was one of the first in England to use the phrase "the spirit of the age." The teleology of Shelley's history provides for neither utopia nor millennium, but for the world's unceasing approach to an absolute perfection that must ever elude it; and in that way he brought into reasonable harmony the conflict that had always beset him between his aspirations to a perfect world and the perfect immortality. As in Hegel's *Philosophy of History*, each successive culture degenerates from its prime and returns to a new state of possibility, but with each return Spirit gains new strength and greater purity. The Absolute forever remains a promise of afterlife; but the world recurrently moves closer to perfection without ever actually attaining it.

In a way, this idea of cumulative progress and development had been present in Shelley's thought at least as early as *Queen Mab* when he wrote there that each human birth is but the awakening of "spirit," or the "universal mind," to outward shows so that "New modes of passion" might progressively be added to its frame; and it is also the theme of "Lines Written on Hearing the News of the Death of Napoleon," which he appropriately published as a coda to *Hellas*. Over the years Shelley had had mixed feelings about Napoleon, usually viewed him as the evil consequence of France's revolutionary impatience, condemned him as a tyrant, and lamented his tragic misuse of his extraordinary power. But in the context of a quasi-Hegelian philosophy, without minimizing Napoleon's faults and harm, he came remarkably close to the position of Hegel, who, seeing

Napoleon after the battle of Jena, felt he had seen the World-Spirit on horseback. The speaker of Shelley's poem is astonished to find Earth revolving with her usual vigor even though Napoleon is now dead. Was not that "fiery spirit" Earth's animation, and is she not merely dead limbs since his powerful ghost has fled? The submerged reference is to the traditional identification of Earth with Vesta, and of the vestal hearth-fire with Earth's central fire, the genial heat of which begets all earthly life. In his notes on the Orphic hymns, for example, Thomas Taylor had quoted Simplicius' well-known Pythagorean account of Vesta as "the fire in the middle, a demiurgic power, nourishing the whole earth from the midst, and exciting and enlivening whatever it contains of a frigid nature."[61] Correspondingly, Shelley's speaker asks Earth,

How! is not thy quick heart cold?
    What spark is alive on thy hearth?
How! is not *his* [i.e. Napoleon's] death-knell knolled?
    And livest *thou* still, Mother Earth?
Thou wert warming thy fingers old
O'er the embers covered and cold
Of that most fiery spirit, when it fled—
What, Mother, do you laugh now he is dead?

But Earth's answer is to deny that the human spirits to which she gives birth, however evil their deeds, ever truly leave her upon their deaths.[62] Of herself she is "cloudy, and sullen, and cold, / Like a frozen chaos uprolled," as Earth is in *Prometheus Unbound* without the Titan; she is a cosmos only by virtue of the human spirit that she contains. Man's spirit is the demiurge, and Earth's history therefore is the history of the progressive accumulation within her of "the spirit of the mighty dead," for these make up her central fire: "I feed on whom I fed." In accordance with Shelley's denial of a distinction between thought and thing, and his definition of the universe as the sum of man's thoughts, Earth is identical with man. Through the Earth, therefore, Spirit generates its own evolution: the spirits of the dead, constituting the genial heat, generate the new

[61] *The Hymns of Orpheus*, trans. Thomas Taylor (London, 1792), p. 221n. Also, Shelley may well have known Servius' glosses on *Aeneid* i. 292 and ii. 296, which define Vesta as the earth standing in the middle of the world and containing a fire within itself, and which offer Aetna and other fiery volcanoes as proof of Vesta, the subterranean fire. Cf. Shelley's description of Earth laughing forth "the lightning of scorn" ("Lines Written on Hearing the News of the Death of Napoleon," 20).
[62] Cf. Shelley on the fates of works of art: "The material part indeed of these works must perish, but they survive in the mind of man, & the remembrances connected with them are transmitted from generation to generation. The poet embodies them in his creation, the systems of philosophers are modelled to gentleness by their contemplation, opinion, that legislator, is infected with their influence; men become better & wiser, and the unseen seeds are perhaps thus sown which shall produce a plant more excellent even [than] that from which they fell" (to Peacock, 9 November 1818 [*Letters*, II, 53]).

life, and the progressive accumulation therefrom of the human spirits of the dead at her heart is her increasing speed, which Shelley had celebrated in the last act of *Prometheus Unbound* as symbolic evidence of the new Promethean age. "The dead," says Earth in the poem on Napoleon, "fill me ten thousandfold / Fuller of speed, and splendour, and mirth." Despite his crimes, Napoleon was another, and notable, fiery spirit whom Earth has taken to herself on his death, a fiery spirit that, though a "torrent of ruin to death from his birth," melts the metal at her heart so that others may mould it to a new shape, just as the Greek revolution of 1821, though a failure in itself, is part of that destruction of the old order that makes possible the new Hellas in the West. True, Napoleon's wrongs have left a shroud over the Earth, but it is his dynamic, revolutionary spirit that is important, making possible a reformation, and others may now weave into his shroud the hope that he failed to fulfill.

For the reason we have noted, the imagery of the poem identifies Earth with man: as a personification she has "limbs," warms her fingers, is alive, grows bold; and the spirits of mankind are her spirit. But in addition, since the universe is the sum of each individual's thoughts, each man is, according to Shelley's recurrent metaphor, a total world; and so, like the revolving Earth, during his life Napoleon's "fierce spirit *rolled*, / In terror and blood and gold," while upon his death his fiery spirit has been added to Earth's central fire. Earth is man, and man is Earth. Earth both gains her motion from the spirits of the dead and gives their "living motion" to new life. For, as in *Hellas*, the history of Earth is the history of the growth of the human spirit, and the growing momentum of her revolutions is the progress of Spirit toward the Absolute, like the spiral of time in the lyric drama. The forty lines of the poem on Napoleon's death elaborate but three rhymes, and these echoing repetitions, stanza after stanza, like the recreative echoes of earlier literatures in *Hellas*, are the formal poetic enactment of the repeated self-generated accumulation, spirit upon spirit, of which the poem speaks.

The theory of history as a progressive evolution of Spirit that bends time's circle into a spiral reaching ever closer to absolute perfection was Shelley's most optimistic and elaborate meliorism. But it is also an unstable faith. Since the difference between the ultimate earthly utopia and the transcendent Absolute toward which it moves is so infinitesimal, the anticipated perfection of mortal life shades into that of postmortal heaven. A world above the idle foam of Time too readily locates itself in eternity, and instead of his recurrent indecision between the mutually exclusive realms of Apollo and Pan, Shelley has reached the unstable center shared by the two. The consequence is the irrepressible tendency of his limitless utopia to become the transcendent life after death, of the ideal mortal existence to become indistinguishable from immortality; that transitional tendency is the force that determines the movement of *Epipsychidion*.

Part IV The Poetry of Idealism

Immortality

14 Epipsychidion

A mystic and soul-shaking visitation by a visionary perfection and a quasi-religious dedication to it such as Shelley described in his *Hymn to Intellectual Beauty* and the Dedication of *The Revolt of Islam* are, we have noted, such recurrent features of his poetry, either explicitly or implicitly, that they must be accepted as reflecting an authentic epiphanic experience profound enough to have fixed a governing psychological pattern in his mind. In *Alastor,* and again in the plan for *Prince Athanase,* he endowed with female form the visionary perfection that "can really reply to his soul,"[1] but could arrive only at the paradox that pursuit of her sheds a glory on life and yet is an evasion of life, leading to a death of dubious nature. Only on his deathbed, crushed by the failure of his search, was Prince Athanase—the Immortal—to be greeted by the Uranian Venus. In the years after *Alastor,* Shelley repeatedly returned to the effect of the secret vision of perfection on the human spirit and to the frustrations of seeking to arrive in life at the "unattainable point to which Love tends; and to attain which, it urges forth the powers of man to arrest the faintest shadow of that without the possession of which there is no rest or respite to the heart over which it rules." In "The Zucca" and "Lift not the Painted Veil," he continued to speculate on facets of the irony that in life man is drawn beyond life by an ideal desire that the world cannot satisfy; and in *The Sensitive Plant*

[1] Mary's note to *Prince Athanase,* quoted from Shelley's MS (Julian, III, 146).

417

he found some probability of immortality and perfect being in the fact that, like the hero of *Alastor*, man aspires beyond worldly beauty and loves "even like Love." Obsessed with the visionary perfection, he continuously sought various ways of discovering the meaning of the mind's visitation by it, or projection of it, or aspiration to it, even translating the pattern of the dedicatory experience of the *Hymn to Intellectual Beauty* and the Dedication of *The Revolt of Islam* into Laon's dedication to serve as agent of political freedom:

> One summer night, in commune with the hope
>   Thus deeply fed, amid those ruins gray
> I watched, beneath the dark sky's starry cope;
>   And ever from that hour upon me lay
>   The burden of this hope, and night or day,
> In vision or in dream, clove to my breast:
>   Among mankind, or when gone far away
> To the lone shores and mountains, 'twas a guest
> Which followed where I fled, and watched while I did rest.[2]

In the years that followed *Alastor* Shelley greatly ramified and clarified his metaphysics and gained mastery over his symbolism, so that when he returned once again in *Epipsychidion* to what is essentially the theme of *Alastor* and *Prince Athanase*—the search for the soul's ideal "antitype" in mortal form—he was equipped to understand it more clearly and to manage it more firmly and daringly, even though the poem ends in confession that his goal has exceeded his mortal grasp.

i

C. D. Locock's etymology of the title, *Epipsychidion*, has been so widely accepted that it would take considerable temerity to discount it, were it not that James A. Notopoulos lends some support.[3] Rejecting Buxton Forman's interpretation, "a little poem about a soul," Locock thought the title to be made up of the diminutive *-idion* and *epipsyche*, a neologism which he decided Shelley had "formed on the analogy of 'epicycle'."[4] Supported by Shelley's references in *On Love* to "a miniature ... of our entire self" and "a soul within our soul" and, in the poem, to "this soul out of my soul" (238), he concluded that the title means "a little additional soul." This etymology has been so commonly accepted that it has even become a practice to speak of Shelley's theme of the "epipsyche" as though he had actually used that nonexistent term.

[2] *The Revolt of Islam*, 793–801.
[3] *Platonism of Shelley*, pp. 278–81.
[4] *The Poems of Percy Bysshe Shelley*, ed. C. D. Locock (London, 1911), II, p. 453.

But, as Notopoulos has pointed out, the word *psychidion* does occur in Lucian;[5] and it has the sense merely of "little soul"—that is, the same *animula*, or little *anima*, to which Hadrian addressed his famous poem, the diminutive contributing only a sense of endearment. The prefix *epi-* need mean no more than "upon the subject of," and the full sense of the title is nothing more complex or subtle than "On the subject of the soul," which is what Emily represents. Although it is true that Shelley conceived of a miniature "soul within our soul" which is, according to *On Love*, "the ideal prototype of every thing excellent or lovely that we are capable of conceiving as belonging to the nature of man" and of which we seek the "antitype" in the world, there is no apparent reason for believing that the reference in the poem to the visionary ideal as "this soul out of my soul" has any direct bearing on the etymology of the title. But I believe both Notopoulos and Neville Rogers[6] are correct in thinking Shelley also meant his title to be recognized as built on the model of *epicedion, epinikion,* and especially *epithalamion.*

For *Epipsychidion* is both a poem about the soul and as nearly a song about a marriage as the subject of the human union with spiritual perfection will permit. Now, the prototypal soul-song which is also an epithalamion is the Song of Songs as it was interpreted by the Christian exegetes, and the analogy with *Epipsychidion* is more than fortuitous. The Song of Songs, or Canticles—which is also a diminutive and which Bailey's *Dictionary* explained as meaning "Spiritual Songs"—was referred to by the exegetes as "Liber Epithalamium" and was generally understood in the Christian tradition to be an allegorical "mystery" (that is, a truth transcending human intelligence) expressed figuratively in carnal terms; and doubtless it was with this sense in mind that Shelley seriocomically wrote to John Gisborne,

The Epipsychidion is a mystery—As to real flesh & blood, you know that I do not deal in those articles,—you might as well go to a ginshop [i.e. where "spirits" are sold] for a leg of mutton, as expect any thing human or earthly from me. I desired Ollier not to circulate this piece except to the Συνετοί, and even they it seems are inclined to approximate me to the circle of a servant girl & her sweetheart.—But I intend to write a Symposium of my own to set all this right.[7]

"It is to be published," he wrote Ollier, "simply for the esoteric few,"[8] that is, for the initiates, or *sunetoi,* who can understand the mystery. According to one traditional level of interpretation, moreover, the Song of

---

[5] *Navigium* 26. It also occurs in Dio Cassius (lxxvii. 16), but Shelley would have readily found it also, of course, in his copy of Scapula's Greek–Latin lexicon.
[6] Rogers, *Shelley at Work*, pp. 245–46.
[7] 22 October 1821 (*Letters*, II, 363).
[8] 16 February 1821 (*Letters*, II, 263).

Songs as an epithalamion represents the love, union, and communion between the individual soul (*anima sancta* or *fidelis*) and Christ; or, in the terms of *Epipsychidion*, between the earthly soul and its "ideal prototype" imaged as a woman, or between the soul in existence and the infinite perfection that the soul imagines, projects, or is visited by, and yearns for but cannot find in the world of existence. Both the Song of Songs and *Epipsychidion* are songs on the subject of the wedding of the soul.

In 1817 Shelley had written Tom Moore that

> The present edition of 'Laon & Cythna' is to be suppressed, & it will be republished in about a fortnight under the title of 'The Revolt of Islam,' with some alterations which consist in little else than the substitution of the words *friend* or *lover* for that of *brother* and *sister*. The truth is, that the seclusion of my habits has confined me so much within the circle of my own thoughts, that I have formed to myself a very different measure of approbation or disapprobation for actions than that which is in use among mankind; and the result of that peculiarity, contrary to my intention, revolts & shocks many who might be inclined to sympathize with me in my general views.[9]

Although he did not actually remove all the references to Cythna as both Laon's sister and lover, despite a reminder to himself in his notebook that "the sister is to be more uncertain,"[10] we must take him at his word that he found the relationship not only innocent but also expressive of the most nearly total spiritual bond between two people. That he gave the matter some thought in order to clarify and justify to himself the sense in which he meant the otherwise incestuous relationship is suggested by some jottings on the leaf directly before the manuscript of the Dedication to *The Revolt of Islam*: "Solomons Song Cap. 4—v. 9 particularly 4. v. 12 or Cap. 5 v. 2."[11] Now, the three verses referred to read: "Thou hast ravished my heart, my sister, my spouse..."; "A garden enclosed is my sister, my spouse..."; and "... it is the voice of my beloved that knocketh, saying, Open to me, my sister, my love, my dove, my undefiled...." Rather clearly Shelley was justifying himself in his own mind and validating his use of the sister-spouse relationship by noting its spiritual significance in the Song of Songs. The double relationship had the special importance to Shelley of implying coequal souls derived from a common source and again united in marriage;[12] and the same relationship appears

---

[9] 16 December 1817 (*Letters*, I, 582).

[10] MS e. 10, p. 1.

[11] MS e. 14, p. 1.

[12] We have already noted Shelley's explanation that, though "incorrect," incest may result from an excess of love; see above, p. 85. His proposals that Elizabeth Hitchener and, later, Harriet be the "sisters of his soul" in a *ménage à trois* are of course notorious. In addition to the *Revolt of Islam* the sister-and-beloved occurs in "Fragments of an Unfinished Drama," 33. The sister-spouse relationship among the pagan gods appears in Shelley's translations of the Homeric hymns ("Hymn to the Sun," 5–7; "Hymn to Venus," 39–40) and may well have been present in his mind as the mythic condition of a Golden Age, a paradisiacal state.

in *Epipsychidion* in exactly the same language. Emily is addressed as "Spouse! Sister!" (130), and on the island to which she and the poet are to escape there is a pleasure-house that—"ere crime / Had been invented," it is significant to note—some Ocean-King had "Made sacred to his sister and his spouse" (492). On that future Edenic island Emily, presently confined in a convent, is to be the "vestal sister" of all that is mortal in the poet, but the "bride" of his eternal soul (389–93), as though Shelley were playing on a nun's relations to humans as sister and to Christ as bride. Indeed, Shelley elaborates on the desire for this double, and therefore nearly totally interinvolving, relationship and its spiritual meaning:

> Emily,
> I love thee; though the world by no thin name
> Will hide that love from its unvalued shame.
> Would we two had been twins of the same mother!
> Or, that the name my heart lent to another
> Could be a sister's bond for her and thee, . . .
> Yet were one lawful and the other true,
> These names, though dear, could paint not, as is due,
> How beyond refuge I am thine.   (42–51)

But this, too, is a reconstitution of the wish of Solomon's bride: "O that thou wert as my brother, that sucked the breasts of my mother! When I should find thee without, I would kiss thee; yea, I should not be despised" (8: 1).

Seeking metaphors for Emily's beauty, Shelley compares her to the "Moon beyond the clouds" and a mirror like the sun, and, surprisingly, calls her a "Terror" (27–31)—just as Solomon's bridegroom, dazzled by the bride's beauty, asks, "Who is she that looketh forth as the morning, fair as the moon, clear as the sun, and terrible as an army with banners?" (6: 10). Shelley's words, "Thou Wonder, and thou Beauty, and thou Terror!" (29), however, even more precisely parallel Solomon's "Thou art beautiful, O my love, as Tirzah, comely as Jerusalem, terrible as an army with banners" (6: 4), where many of the commentators explained "terrible" as "dazzling" and "striking the beholder with awe." Like the garments of Solomon's bride, Emily's "light dress" sheds a "Warm fragrance" (105), and "from her lips, as from a hyacinth full / Of honey-dew, a liquid murmur drops" (83–84).[13] And like the bride, who is "a spring shut up, a fountain sealed" (4: 12), Emily is "A well of sealed and secret

[13] Song of Songs 4: 11: "Thy lips, O my spouse, drop as the honeycomb: honey and milk are under thy tongue; and the smell of thy garments is like the smell of Lebanon." Cf. also *ibid*. 2: 8–9 (". . . behold, he cometh leaping upon the mountains, skipping upon the hills. My beloved is like a roe or a young hart") and *Epipsychidion*, 75–77 ("An antelope, / In the suspended impulse of its lightness, / Were less aethereally light").

happiness" (58). The model of Shelley's opening series of metaphors for Emily is Solomon's "As the lily among thorns, so is my love among the daughters" and the bride's reply, "As the apple tree among the trees of the wood, so is my beloved among the sons" (2: 2–3). Frequently interpreted to mean spiritual perfection in the midst of worldly wickedness, these similes provide a metaphoric pattern on which Shelley could play variations to represent the embodiment of spiritual perfection in the mortal condition. Emily is the

Sweet Benediction in the eternal Curse!
Veiled Glory of this lampless Universe!
Thou Moon beyond the clouds! Thou living Form
Among the Dead! Thou Star above the storm! (25–28)

And, he asks, is she not

                              A Star
Which moves not in the moving heavens, alone?
A Smile amid dark frowns? a gentle tone
Amid rude voices? (60–63)

Finally, one of the several reasons the Song of Songs must have appeared to Shelley so apposite to his own purpose no doubt is the fact that it outlines a search in the world for a visionary perfection that corresponds to the pattern of spiritual experience and pursuit of which he had already written in *Alastor*. Solomon's bride tells that "By night on my bed I sought him whom my soul loveth; I sought him, but I found him not" (3: 1), and such exegetes as Symon Patrick explained this as meaning that men sought for Christ "and had many Dreams and Visions about Him; but could meet only with the shadows and images of Him; which signified, Him to come, but did not exhibit his very presence to them." "I will rise now," the bride continues,

and in the broad ways I will seek him whom my soul loveth: I sought him, but I found him not. The watchmen that go about the city found me: to whom I said, Saw ye him whom my soul loveth? It was but a little that I passed from them, but I found him whom my soul loveth: I held him, and would not let him go, until I had brought him into my mother's house, and into the chamber of her that conceived me.[14]   (3: 2–4)

[14] Thomas Scott's commentary on the Song of Songs (*Holy Bible*, 1818, III, p. 45) may well serve as a typical interpretation: "Here on earth the believer loves and rejoices in an unseen Saviour, and seeks his happiness from his spiritual presence; Christ manifests himself to him as he doth not unto the world: and these visits are earnest and foretastes of heavenly joy. But they are interrupted, suspended, or varied on many accounts: they are often lost by negligence or other sins, and can only be recovered by humble repentance and renewed diligence: yet the love on both sides remains unchanged, as to its principle, though varied in the expressions of it."

In its essential features this is also a summary of the first of the narrative movements of *Epipsychidion*. The poet's spirit had often met in dream and "visioned wanderings" the perfect Being (191), although she was "robed in such exceeding glory, / That I beheld her not" (199–200). Rising from his dreams, he questions every wind "Whither 'twas fled, this soul out of my soul" (238) and seeks her in many mortal forms until at last in Emily he knew "it was the Vision veiled from me / So many years" (343–44).

The Song of Songs, however, is not a structure of allusions for the first movement of *Epipsychidion*, in which all these parallel images are concentrated. Shelley's poem does not ask the reader to recall the Scriptural book, nor is its meaning dependent on or enlarged by it. Rather, the first movement of *Epipsychidion* is Shelley's own spiritual Song of Songs, a love song of the human individual to the perfect soul, a "mystery" expressed figuratively, like the Song of Songs, in terms of "real flesh & blood." It is autonomous, as though the Scriptural book had never existed, for to Shelley the Song of Songs is a beautiful mental expression, a pattern of beautiful and therefore true relationships organized by the mind according to its own laws. It is, consequently, one of those episodes of the "great poem which all poets, like the co-operating thoughts of one great mind, have built up since the beginning of the world," and it is the obligation of the poet to raise it to an even higher degree of perfection and truth or at least "to create afresh the associations" that may have become "disorganized" by time, habit, and familiarity. From Shelley's point of view, Christianity was right to read the Song of Songs as a spiritual mystery but wrong to assimilate it to a tyrannical religion, and the poet's duty is to free it from that tyranny and draw from it every beautifully true organization it permits.

There is evidence that Shelley had difficulty deciding on the precise style appropriate to his attitude toward his subject. Many abortive manuscript pages from which he then drew passages for the final poem reveal that he once contemplated veiling his seriousness in Byronic irony so that he might stand superior to and contemptuous of the ignorant, uninitiated world that would misunderstand him:

Why there is first the God in Heaven above
Who wrote a book called Nature—'tis to be
Reviewed I hear in the next Quarterly. . . .

     . . . let them stumble
Over all sorts of scandal, hear them mumble
Their Litanies of curses—some guess right
And others swear you are an Hermaphrodite. . . .[15]

---

[15] MS e. 12, pp. 68, 69.

On the other hand, the mingling of the fragment "Fiordispina" (in which the lovers are also cousins) and *Epipsychidion* on the same notebook pages and the transfer of passages from one poem to the other indicate that he also contemplated offering Emilia Viviani's story in a thoroughly sentimental narrative; and even in the poem itself he confesses that perhaps his subject deserved the high seriousness of the epic, or heroic, style.[16] His final decision lay midway among these three extremes: a highly personal exposure of ecstatic adoration in the manner of the Song of Songs. As a literary model, the Scriptural poem also released Shelley from the obligation to organize his imagery as integrally as in such poems as *The Sensitive Plant*, for the disjunctive images of the Song of Songs in praise of the beloved's beauty authorized the swift and apparently uncontrolled pageant of rhapsodic metaphors and similes for Emily that marks the opening movement.

Nevertheless, despite the appearance of a random disorder compelled by ecstatic adoration, there is some degree of coherence among Shelley's metaphors and some subtle exploitation of their symbolic potentialities that is absent from Solomon's song. Although some of the opening metaphors represent Emily in imagery of music and fragrance, the majority picture her as a celestial light, Shelley's persistent symbol of the immortal soul and of those perfections he associates with it, love and life. As pure spirit, she is a "beloved light" (63), a "Sweet Lamp" (53), a mirror like the sun (30–31), a "lodestar" like Hesper, Venus' planet (219, 222), and a "Seraph of Heaven" (21) because seraphs are of fire. Even the music with which her words are associated is "planetary," like the music of the starry spheres (86). As the diminished mode in which the transcendent appears in the domain of mutability, she is, like the "shadow" of Intellectual Beauty, an "image of some bright Eternity,"[17] a "shadow of some golden dream," a "Reflection of the eternal Moon of Love" (115–18); or she is a descended angel who had guided one of the spheres, a "Splendour" who has left pilotless the star of Venus (117–18), like the descended starry spirit who attends the Lady of *The Sensitive Plant*. As an incarnation of spiritual perfection, she embodies "light, and love, and immortality" that would be "insupportable" to the mortal beholder were she not veiled in a "radiant" womanly form (22–24), just as the light diffused through

---

16 *Epipsychidion*, 53–56:

> my moth-like Muse has burned its wings
> Or, like a dying swan who soars and sings,
> Young Love should teach Time, in his own gray style,
> All that thou art....

The manuscript shows that he wrote "heroic" before deciding on "gray" (e. 12, p. 71).

17 It is possible that Shelley is referring to a neoplatonic Aion, but it is more likely that he means an eternality, anything which is eternal.

the earth's atmosphere veils the insupportable blaze of the sun. As a transcendent perfection present in an earthly ambience, she is generally a spiritual light enclosed in darkness or immersed in moisture, Shelley's recurrent symbol of the incarnate soul. Hence she is the "Veiled Glory of this lampless Universe" (26) and a "smile"—with its regular Shelleyan connotation of light—"amid dark frowns" (62); and even the poet's dark mortal words, which "obscure" her by their effort to realize her in earthly images, are clouds that "Flash, lightning-like, with unaccustomed glow" when she looks on them (34). Or, as a light mediated by the moisture of mortality she is the "Moon beyond the clouds," a "star above the storm." Through her moist eyes the light of her soul "darkens," dimmed by the symbol of her incarnation (38), or her eyes are "wells" whose waters "leap / Under the lightnings of the soul" (88–89), so that, in a confusion of imagery, they may be thought of as "mild lights" in which "starry spirits dance," suggesting the cosmic dance of the stars (87), and as waters on which "sunbeams" play (88). The brightness of her "divinest presence" trembles through her mortal limbs, just as the moon, "inextinguishably beautiful," burns through "a cloud of dew" (77–82), for, as this symbol asserts, she is, like Christ, a "mortal shape indued / With love and life and light and deity" (112–13). Even her scent, piercing beyond the senses into the soul, is like "fiery dews," or light-filled drops of water, that melt into the center of a frozen bud (110–11).

But it does not prove sufficient even to describe her as a "Reflection of the eternal Moon of Love," or image of the transcendent; it is necessary to add that the motions of this Moon of Love move "life's dull billows," her light-love causing and governing the activities of the waters of mortal life (118–19). For she not only participates in both the divine and the human but is also the power of the divine operating on the world of mutability. In the most complex image of all, which daringly aspires to obliterate all boundaries, Emily's "glory" radiates from her to "stain" the dead, blank, cold surrounding air with a "warm shade" made of "light and motion" like the aureole surrounding the sun; this "intense Diffusion," blurring the outlines of her finiteness, flows round her, even to her finger tips, which in turn quiver with the throbbing blood as the light of morning pulsates through snowy clouds. Then, in a meeting and fusion of Emily, the immanent Soul, with the transcendent Soul, the light issuing from her and flowing about her as a God-like "Omnipresence" is "Continuously prolonged, and ending never," lost "and in that Beauty furled / Which penetrates and clasps and fills the world" (101–3). The light of the incarnate sun and that of the heavenly sun meet and dissolve into each other until all is "Scarce visible from extreme loveliness" (104).

As the incarnate soul—a spiritual light in the moisture of generation—Emily unites the perfection of the transcendent and the earthly and therefore can raise the mortal state to its most nearly ideal condition. Consequently she can weep on the poet's "flowers of thought" (384) tears of "sacred dew" (37), the traditional symbol of the divine grace given to man in his mortal state; and, just as the state of sin can become the state of grace, or as Shelley's symbol of mortality can become the symbol of mortality purified to sacred status, she will weep until human "sorrow becomes ecstasy" (39). Thus her tears, like the gift of grace, will blot from his song "All of its much mortality and wrong" (36). Made fertile by this sacred moisture of transfigured mortal sorrow, the poet's flowers of thought now need only the genial sunlight of her soul's "smile" so that they "may not die" (40). Correspondingly, in her role as the incarnate soul, combining the perfections of the earthly and divine states, Emily is the point at which mortality meets spiritual life: she is therefore a "metaphor" of spring, youth, and morning, a "Vision like incarnate April" warning "Frost the Anatomy / Into his summer grave" with her "smiles and tears"—the joys of eternity and the sorrows of the world, the light of the immortal spirit and the moisture of earthly generation.

Yet, despite the extent to which the symbolism of light and moisture dominates the lengthy opening representations of Emily, and despite the occasional functioning of the images as tightly integrated symbols, the fact remains that this Song of Songs is rhapsodically chaotic. As a light, Emily is variously related to a star, the North Star, the star of Venus, the moon, and the sun; and in a notably mixed metaphor, the wells of her eyes flash lightnings which are sunbeams and also starlight. Moreover, she serves multiple inconsistent roles because the poet cannot fix on her mode of existence, and the ecstatic confusion of the poet expresses itself in the disordered form of a Song of Songs. As a light, she is the immortal transcendent soul, a "Seraph of Heaven! too gentle to be human" (21), or, on the contrary, she is the perfection of Nature, the "Harmony of Nature's art" (30); and as a light in moisture she is both, the perfect earthly embodiment of the heavenly soul. At one moment she is transcendent; at another, an incarnation of transcendence; at another, the transcendent descended into mutability, a "Splendour" who has abandoned her guidance of the star of Venus; and yet again, a faint semblance of the transcendent, an "image," "shadow," and "reflection."[18] In one passage she is the North Star, "Which moves not in the moving heavens, alone" (60–61), sym-

---

[18] Shelley's conjunction of an "image" of some bright Eternity with a "shadow" of a golden dream, together with a "Reflection" of the Moon of Love, suggests that he had in mind the phrase "shadows and images" which are the *eidoles* and *skia* with which Plato described the relation of the Many to the Forms, explaining *eidoles* as like reflections in water. The phrase was picked up by Cicero as *imagines et umbrae* (De officiis III. xvii. 69 and *Republic* II. xxx. 53) and reappears in the titles of many seventeenth-century devotional treatises such as Jonathan Edwards' *Images or Shadows of Divine Things*, meditations on the spiritualizing of earthly things into a knowledge of things divine. The use of the word "image" in the sense of "reflection" is very common in Shelley: for example, *Epipsychidion*, 297, *Alastor*, 457–59. See also above, p. 194n.

bolizing the eternal immutability of the transcendent; but in another, she is a mortal shape indued not only with immutable "love and life and light and deity" but also with "motion which may change but cannot die" (114), that is, with the unending cycle of change which is the manner in which earthly time reflects eternity. And it seems at least inexact that in associating Emily with the moon the poet should describe that traditional symbol of inconstancy as "eternal" (118).

The truth is that in the ecstasy of his Song of Songs the poet is not in control of himself or his materials, as he himself confesses. So short of his purpose is he that at one point he can only ask Emily whether any term in his long litany of metaphors appropriately identifies her, in effect asking her to verify her own definition, and he pauses in a kind of exhaustion, admitting his failure to find in his own "world of fancies" the true metaphor (70). For the failure being enacted does not lie in the indeterminacy of Emily's nature or in the inadequacy of language or of this particular poet, but in man's paradoxical condition. What Emily is has real existence; the inability to formulate it indicates the radical "infirmity" (71) or ambiguity in human nature. Consequently the irreconcilability of the poet's mortal state with his desire of the immortal has produced a chaos of images and an inward torment as he strives unsuccessfully to find the single image that will incorporate indissolubly both the human and the divine. If a clue were needed to the psychomachy at the heart of *Epipsychidion*, Shelley supplied it by prefacing to the poem a translation of the final stanza of the first *canzone* of Dante's *Convivio* and appending to the poem an *envoi* which (though partly imitative of the contents of Dante's sonnet to Cavalcanti) has the same length as the other stanzas of the first *canzone* and a nearly identical rhyme scheme, and, like all the conclusions in the *Convivio*, is addressed to his own poem. To surround his poem in this fashion is to embrace it with a resonance that defines its central tension between the human and divine, since Dante's first *canzone* tells of his disturbance that his Thought of Beatrice in heaven, which has made him desirous of death, has been driven away by his Thought of the *donna pietosa* in life whom he met after Beatrice's death.[19]

Were he only a mortal, the poet of *Epipsychidion* confesses, he could love the human Emily, as the flowers of *The Sensitive Plant* find total fulfillment in the world, but his soul, like that of the Sensitive Plant, also desires its own perfect and transcendent prototype, which the human

---

[19] Shelley translated Dante's first *canzone* (MS e. 9, pp. 337–39) and made abstracts from the *Convivio* (MS e. 8, pp. 167–68). When he wrote Gisborne jestingly that he intended "to write a Symposium of my own" to clarify the "mystery" of *Epipsychidion*, he may have been referring to the Platonic dialogue, but it is more likely that he meant the *Convivio* (Symposium) with its prose interpretations of the *canzoni*.

Emily can only adumbrate. Because of this inherent division in the poet between his mortal and immortal natures he now envisions Emily as the transcendent perfection and now seeks to conceive of her as the perfect incarnation of it. For the mortal poet, she is "too late / Beloved" (131–32), since from his birth he should have moved beside her "on this earth, / A shadow of that substance" (136–37); as the infinite and perfect projection of his soul, she is "too soon adored" (132), for only when he will have reached the "fields of Immortality" should he worship her, a "divine presence in a place divine" (135). He himself confesses he had formerly been reconciled to the division between life's deficiency and the perfect spiritual fulfillment thereafter, having expected to see the visionary ideal of his youth "thus made perfect" only after death (41–42). Indeed, even as the incarnate divinity, Emily does not make his human existence complete, but lures him "towards sweet Death" (73), tempting him, like the Visionary of *Alastor*, beyond the limits of inadequate life, as she will again at the end of the poem. Too far advanced in mortality to begin loving the mortal Emily and too short of immortality to worship her as the immortal ideal—yet desiring both—the poet represents what Shelley recurrently took to be the human dilemma, and the ecstatic incoherence of the metaphors for Emily and the inconsistency of what she stands for arise, not from what she is, but from the irreconcilable schism in man between his finite and infinite selves. In *Mont Blanc* the vain search among mental images for correspondences to an unknown externality is an action constituting that illusion man calls the "world," but here the unsuccessful search in the poet's world of mental "fancies" for the embracing and stable image of the truly existent ideal divulges to the poet only his own "infirmity" (71), the disproportion between his human condition and his spiritual aspirations. "What have I dared?" he must ask at length; "where am I lifted? how / Shall I descend and perish not?" (124–25). He has, as Keats expressed it, seen "beyond our bourn" and is lost "in a sort of Purgatory blind" that is neither earth nor heaven.

For the poem is essentially the poet's self-examination, an inquiry into his *psychidion*, not merely the love song of P. B. Shelley to Emilia Viviani, any more than the exegetes took the Song of Songs to be merely the love song of Solomon and his dark bride. What the poet seeks in the form of Emily is not some "other," but the realization of his own interior vision, the "soul" that has fled "out of my soul" and had once been in it in his state of total self-realization, prior to the development of his Unhappy Consciousness. His search, therefore, is that of the Visionary of *Alastor*, aspiring to the "prototype" of his own conception of all that is wonderful, wise, and beautiful. As an act of self-reflection, *Epipsychidion* consequently requires two modes of a single self, the self in existence and the infinite self, under the name of "Emily"; and the knowledge that will arise out of the poem will be the product of the inevitable failure of these to coalesce, the self and the other in which it is conscious of itself. In existence, the ineradicable dualism of the two selves can, at best, be mitigated by the sister-brother relationship of similarity and adjacency. On earth the poet's spirit should have "moved beside" Emily's (136), and a mysterious voice tells him truly that the Vision he seeks is "beside thee" in the world, although not in finite form (233), just as in *Alastor* a Spirit communicating with the Visionary through natural objects "seemed to stand beside him."[20] On the other hand, the "adoration" which is the marital identity of the two selves may be possible in eternity. But "adoration" is not possible in the state that, at best, is one of "love."

If the poet and Emily are the finite and the infinite self, Shelley also, as we have observed repeatedly, had the dramatic ability to see himself through an alien vision, the skeptic's gift of adopting the role of the Yeatsian anti-self to measure himself and his actions through an opposing consciousness. Standing outside his own poem to view it as one who considers himself "deluded by no generous error" and "instigated by no sacred thirst of doubtful knowledge" as he had in the Preface of *Alastor* and through its Narrator or as he had in the character of "Byron" in *Julian and Maddalo*, Shelley wrote of the poet of *Epipsychidion* in one of the abandoned drafts of the Advertisement:

He was an accomplished & amiable person but his error was, θνητος ὠν μη θνητα φρονειν [being mortal, to think of things not mortal],[21]—his fate is an additional proof that "The tree of knowledge is not that of Life":[22]—He had framed to himself certain opinions, founded no doubt upon the truth of things, but built up to a Babel height; they fell by their own weight, & the thoughts that were their architects, became unintelligible one to the other, as men upon whom the confusion of tongues has fallen.[23]

These of course are the words of the sympathetic anti-visionary, one who stands to the poet as Shelley customarily conceived Byron to stand to him; and for that very reason they represent with faithful objectivity the condition of the poet of *Epipsychidion*, whose opinions about the soul and its love of its ideal projection are "founded no doubt upon the truth of

---

[20] *Alastor*, 479–80. Cf. also the definition of love in "Fragments of an Unfinished Drama," 51–55:

> He stood beside me,
> The embodied vision of the brightest dream,
> Which like a dawn heralds the day of life;
> The shadow of his presence made my world
> A Paradise. . . .

[21] A common classical phrase that sums up the Greek idea of *hubris*. Cf. Byron, *Manfred*, II. iv. 158–59: "He [Manfred] is convulsed—This is to be a mortal / And seek the things beyond mortality."
[22] Shelley borrowed this quotation, appropriately, from *Manfred*, I. i. 12. Again it is Byron whom he chooses as his anti-self.
[23] Bodleian MS Shelley d. 1, fol. 102ʳ–101ᵛ.

things," but who has zealously sought to overcome the irremovable fact
that direct knowledge of the infinite self is not a fruit of the tree of life,
though it may be of the tree of death, and who has vainly tried to build
a tower to heaven. He had, as Shelley wrote in another rejected preface
to the poem, "personified the τὸ καλόν"—the Beautiful—"& sought it in
every form & in every opinion fell in love with it, without being voluptuous."[24] But he had, therefore, sought "in a mortal image the likeness of
what is perhaps eternal,"[25] and the evidence is the Babel-like confusion
of thoughts and images that is the first movement of the poem. The next
movement will be the poet's more controlled, more human effort to sort out
these images, motifs, and thoughts. In the first movement, nearly all the
essential images and themes of the poem have been deposited in disarray,
and the succeeding stages will be successive efforts to draw upon that
pool of elements and organize them into a stable, meaningful, and satisfy-
ing pattern of relationships.

ii

The epistemology of Shelley's "intellectual philosophy" necessarily
has ontological implications and consequently affects the character and
significance of his metaphors. If, relative to man, the only "facts" are the
ideas in his mind, then what we call the "universe," or the "world," is
constituted of the mass of our knowledge. In that sense, the "world" consists of both the self and the sum of its experiences and has its existence
within the mind of man. However, since the mind does not create these
"ideas" but can only receive them from experience, it is equally proper to
consider the organized sum of those ideas as a world, or earth, having
real and external existence. Whether the world is assumed to be the
thoughts of the mind or whether the mind is called the "world" is a matter
of indifference; and Shelley's repeated use of the metaphor of the world
for subjective states and actions has not only poetic but also ontological
force. Recognition of this ontological ambiguity, for example, makes more
understandable Shelley's otherwise strangely intense interest in a line

from Sophocles which he translates as "Coming to many paths in the
wanderings of careful thought":

And the words οδους & πλαναι had not been used [,] as now they have been
so long [,] less in a metaphorical than an absolute sense, as to lose all outline
& distinctness, as we say "Ways & means" & wanderings for "error & confusion"
but they meant literally paths or roads such as we tread with our feet, &
wanderings such as a man makes when he loses himself in a desert, or roams
from city to city, as Œdipus the speaker of this verse was destined to wander,

[24] *Ibid.*, fol. 101ᵛ.
[25] To John Gisborne, 18 June 1822 (*Letters*, II, 434).

blind & asking Charity. What a picture does this line suggest of the mind as a wilderness of intricate paths, wide as the universe which is here made its symbol, a world within a world—which he, who seeks some knowledge with respect to what he ought to do, searches throughout, as he would search the external universe for some valued thing which was hidden from him upon its surface.

Such is the dim ghost of an imagination which now is dead for want of breathing the native air in which it was conceived & born.[26]

What Shelley is underscoring is that to the Greeks—as to the child, who, according to Shelley's theory, makes no distinction between himself and the world—the metaphoric sense of "paths" and "wanderings" was still fresh, and consequently they could feel vividly the truth which Shelley accepted, that the mind and the world are "symbols" of each other. The repetition of so-called impressions weakens the original unity of self and world until the notion develops that they are independent of each other, and analogously the repetition of metaphors converts into "signs for portions or classes of thoughts" what originally were "pictures of integral thoughts."[27] When metaphors degenerate into signs for portions or classes of thoughts, on one hand the ontological reality of the external world is lost, and the world becomes only signs, like language; on the other, segments, or inorganic classes of thought, become substitutes for the organic wholeness of the mind. In the light of the dualistic monism of Shelley's "intellectual philosophy," the poet's duty therefore is to insist on the equal reality of things and thoughts and yet to recognize their identity; and he is to treat each as an organic totality, the absolute forms of which are world and mind. It is for this reason that in the last act of *Prometheus Unbound* man's reformation is represented by the revitalized earth spinning in its orbit in a love relationship with the moon, and that in "Lines Written on Hearing the News of the Death of Napoleon" the speed of the Earth is relative to the number of human spirits she has folded to her breast, in accordance with Shelley's equation of spirit and motion. Conversely, the mourner in *Adonais* is enjoined to embrace the world with his soul—in brief, to be the world he really is, by identifying his self with the world that is the sum of his thoughts. He will then be able, like a heavenly body, to radiate his spirit's light and thereby know his own divine spirituality. These are not circuitous ways of talking about man; mind and world being symbols of each other, they are true ways of expressing the mental reality. It is on the basis of these ontological assumptions behind Shelley's recurrent world-mind metaphor that the next movement of *Epipsychidion* will proceed.

[26] Huntington Notebooks, II, 101–2; quoted by Mary in her notes to *Prometheus Unbound* (Julian, II, 270).
[27] *Defence of Poetry* (Julian, VII, 111).

The "idealized history" of the poet's life and feelings[28] that follows the opening acclamations of Emily recapitulates the biographical pattern of *Alastor*, *Hymn to Intellectual Beauty*, and related poems. In his youth the poet has a dazzling, epiphanic dream-vision of a being who unites all that the self is capable of projecting of the wonderful, wise, and beautiful. In the earlier poems, the vision had come only after the beauty of the external world and the truths captured in records of human thought proved inadequate; but in *Epipsychidion*, as in "The Zucca," the voice of the visioned being is heard by the poet in all of nature (200–9), and her spirit permeates all poetry and "that best philosophy, whose taste / Makes this cold common hell, our life, a doom / As glorious as a fiery martyrdom," a splendid but torturing self-sacrifice for a later spiritual attainment (213–15). Rising from his dream, the poet, like the Visionary of *Alastor*, is tempted to seek the ideal lady in death, but a mysterious voice tells him that "The phantom is beside thee whom thou seekest" (233). Earthly man is not unattended by his spiritual perfection, but when he asks "Where?" the world, in its necessary deficiency, can only echo his ignorance: "Where?" Yet he rashly seeks the shadow of his vision in "many mortal forms" (267) until at length he encounters the symbolic moon, sun, and star that surround him, imaged as an earth.

Sun, moon, and star were also the dominant light metaphors for Emily in the first movement, and unless the rhapsodic incoherence of imagery is persistent, we might now expect a significant and organized relationship between the original metaphors for Emily and the "idealized history" of the poet's life. The chaotic plethora of astronomical images for Emily contains the potentiality of the cosmos that now evolves, though gradually, uncertainly, and interrupted by other metaphors. As the second movement opens with the poet's vision of the ideal "Being," his mind is represented implicitly as a world, and the dream itself is enacted on a visionary earth: his youth is a "dawn" (192), sleep and dream are "caverns" that he enters (194, 217), his dreams have "air-like waves" on which the visionary lady walks (195–97); and the dream realm in which he meets her has "fairy isles," "enchanted mountains," and an "imagined shore." Life is the conical shadow of night cast by the world as it eclipses the sun (228), and upon the poet's awakening, the visionary being passes from his dream into that shadow, "like a God throned on a winged planet" (226). Clearly all these images hover in various ways about the metaphor of man as a world and just barely evade it, but as yet the mortal poet remains a "Chaos" (243). Nevertheless, "within this Chaos" is a "world" made up of and organized by the thoughts that worship the Being who is that world's deity, just as poetry, by the act of imagination that organizes thoughts into the ideal and indestructible order they ought to have,

---

[28] To John Gisborne, 18 June 1822 (*Letters*, II, 434).

"creates for us a being within our being" and "makes us the inhabitants of a world to which the familiar world is a chaos."[29] The possibility is available, therefore, that the poet's inner cosmos of loving thoughts may emerge and organize the outward disorder. Meanwhile he can only wander through a world whose partial features are modes of his mental and spiritual life. Life is a "wintry forest" (249) through which he passes, vainly "struggling through its error" (250)—the play on "error" having as its basis the ontological equation of mind and world, "a world within a world," and reflecting Shelley's analysis of Sophocles' use of "'wanderings' for 'error and confusion.'"[30] The metaphor of the poet as a wanderer through the forest of life will persist as the setting in which the cosmic imagery will fully evolve, just as in Act IV of *Prometheus Unbound* the forest near Prometheus' cave is the setting into which the symbolic earth and moon enter to perform their orbital masque.[31]

Against that setting the poet's spiritual history is recounted on two successive levels. Searching in vain among "mortal forms" for one resembling the Being he had experienced in vision, he first encounters those who are merely human, each rejected as deficient or corrupting. It is here especially that the reservoir of images collected in the first movement begins to be drawn on, for the deceptive mortals in whom he seeks "one form resembling hers" (254) are gruesome parodies and perversions of Emily in the same manner that the union of Jupiter and Thetis repeats but perverts that of Prometheus and Asia. Whereas from Emily's lips a "liquid murmur" drops like honey-dew from a hyacinth, a false one speaks "honeyed words" that betray (270). Another Pandemos has a voice like melody and breath like "faint flowers," but it is venomed melody and breath from a false mouth (256–57), and instead of Emily's animating radiance, destructive flame springs from her looks. From Emily, whose words, like honey-dew, kill the sense with passion (84–85), had also come a fragrance that, piercing the sense, entered into the soul "like fiery dews that melt / Into the bosom of a frozen bud"; but from the false Emily came

A killing air, which pierced like honey-dew
Into the core of my green heart, and lay
Upon its leaves; until, as hair grown gray
O'er a young brow, they hid its unblown prime
With ruins of unseasonable time.   (262–66)

The ideal and the merely mortal, like a Fidessa and Duessa, have an ironic similarity that can lead to a deadly mistake.

From this despair the poet is at length rescued by one who is as like

[29] *Defence of Poetry* (Julian, VII, 137).
[30] Other obvious examples of the ontological pun are "bewildered" (252) and "sphere of being" (361).
[31] For the symbolism of forest, see above, p. 314.

the lady of his vision as the moon is like the sun, and in rapid evolution of the cosmic imagery she is first proportional to the moon, then like a descended spirit of it, like the moon itself, and at last actually the moon of a symbolic universe. In other words, the astronomical imagery recapitulated from the first movement enters as secondary metaphors into a context in which the primary metaphor is the forest of life but rapidly displaces the forest metaphor to constitute a total universe of earth, sun, moon, and star. The imagery which the poet, in his ecstasy, had huddled chaotically together and tried to unite in Emily is being sorted out and distributed into a cosmos. Of those who deliver him from the false Emilys this first is

As like the glorious shape which I had dreamed
As is the Moon, whose changes ever run
Into themselves, to the eternal Sun.   (278–80)

But this attribute of eternally cyclical change the poet had earlier tried to combine in Emily as a mortal shape indued not only with the eternal and immutable but also with "motion which may change but cannot die" (114). The disorder and ultimate collapse of the first movement arose from the poet's impossible effort to fuse the mundane and the transcendent in a single image, each failure leading immediately to another; for in human nature the mundane and the transcendent are not fused into a unity but are independent of each other, pulling in opposite directions. The only possibility of harmony, therefore, lies in the poet's recognizing his divided nature and dual allegiance, in separating his human devotion to the mutable world from the divinity in him that aspires to the ideal. The Spirit of Nature and the visionary perfection which is "the ideal prototype of every thing excellent or lovely that we are capable of conceiving as belonging to the nature of man" are two and cannot be made one; but the two can perhaps be ordered into a viable harmony. The Moon-lady, "whose changes ever run / Into themselves," is the spirit of eternally repetitive cyclical change, the principle of temporal perfection in the realm of mutability as Shelley developed it in *Mont Blanc, Ode to the West Wind, The Cloud,* and *Hellas.* But the sun is unchanging and "eternal" (280), attributes assigned to Emily in the first movement when she was identified with the North Star, a "Star / Which moves not in the moving heavens, alone" (60–61)—but also, in the poet's fervid confusion, assigned there to the "eternal Moon of Love," of which Emily was supposedly a reflection (118).

The astronomical imagery as it is now separated out of its original disorder and inconsistency is precisely right for its burden of symbolism, for the moon is the sun's reflected light (362–63), just as the endless circle of change, which the Moon represents, is the way in which eternity is reflected in mutability. The symbols of mutability and its domain—the moon, the earth, and, by way of simile, even the island of the next move-ment—are consistently identified as "wandering," that is, as planets (283, 356, 459), as the "eternal" sun is not. As opposed to the unchanging Sun, the Moon "ever is transformed, yet still the same" (284), alternately "Wax-ing and waning" forever (294). The representation of the Moon-lady of mutability as making "all beautiful on which she smiles" (282) had also been implicit in the first movement but was associated with Emily and covered in obscurity. There Emily was named the "Mirror / In whom, as in the splendour of the Sun, / All shapes look glorious which thou gazest on!" (30–32), for eventually she is to be identified with the Sun; but the "mirror" that beautifies all things does so by reflecting the sun's light and therefore anticipates the symbol of the Moon of mutability that beautifies with its "borrowed" light (362). Confusedly, in the first move-ment Emily, sun-like, is a "Smile amid dark frowns" (62), but she is also the source of both the tears and smiles of generation (35–40, 122); when the confusion is untangled in the second movement, it is the Moon-lady, not Emily-Sun, who represents the mutably mixed character of mortal life, "smiling" or "frowning" as she waxes and wanes (298) and correspond-ingly making the poet's being "bright or dim" (296).

Yet although the Moon-lady is the perfect spirit of earthly existence, she is not the spirit of "life." She makes beautiful all she shines upon, but she is an icy light, a cold and unvital chastity, and her role is not, like the sun's, to penetrate the poet's "dawn" with "living light" (341–42), but only to hide him "as the Moon may hide the night / From its own dark-ness" (287–88), to negate nonexistence, but not to gift with life. For existence is not life, which is a spiritual gift, the immanent presence of divinity; and under the winter and night aegis of the Moon-lady the poet therefore belongs to neither life nor death (300–7) but to a kind of pre-vital state, which is the character of mere earthly existence vis-à-vis post-mortal spiritual "life." Rather, the Moon-lady, who ceaselessly waxes and wanes, is the spirit of the wheel of change, the endless sublunary cycle. On that wheel, as we have frequently noted, the point of death is also the point of birth, and therefore the poet will liken Hesper and Lucifer—worshipped by Evening and Morning but actually only different appear-ances of Venus—to the single "star of Death and Birth" worshipped in its partial appearances by Hope and Fear (377–81). Correspondingly, the Moon-lady of cyclical change calls upon Death and Life "Masked" like twins of one mother, identical and only apparently discrete modes of that which is single, like the morning and evening star. These, too, are "wan-dering," or planetary like the Moon and thus also belong to the realm of endless change. That they scorn the poet—"Away, he is not of our crew" (306)—announces that, unlike the rest of sublunary nature, his essence is not that of the eternal cycle of earthly renewal, of seasonal death and rebirth. Like the failure of the earth-goddess Urania to recognize the poet in *Adonais*, the repudiation by Life-and-Death threatens that no mode of earthly existence, however perfected, will fulfill the speaker's needs.

Although for a moment the poet refers to the "Heaven and Earth" of his mind and although he responds to the moon like a sea, he is still a wanderer in the wintry forest of life and, like Endymion, is led by the Cynthia-like moon-goddess to a cave of sleep. Now the mind-world metaphor reappears, and his pre-vital tranquillity under the aegis of the moon is replaced by a shattering and chaotic excess of energy. Storms shake the "ocean" of the poet's sleep, blotting out the moon of pre-vital calm and leaving his soul a "lampless sea"; he is shaken by one who is a "Tempest"; and when the moon[32] is quenched frost creeps over the waters of his soul "till from coast to coast / The moving billows of my being fell / Into a death of ice, immovable" (314–16).[33] At length, in the procession of these experiences of relationship, the "world" of the poet's being is split by cataclysmic earthquakes. The poet still remaining in his Endymion-like cave of dreams into which the moon had led him, there enters into his wintry forest the vision of Emily figured as an "incarnation" of the sun, radiating "living light" that penetrates him, whereas the moon merely brightened all between the heaven and earth of his calm mind and left him unrelated to either life or death. This energizing, life-giving spirit of the sun, like the Emily of the first movement who was

A Metaphor of Spring and Youth and Morning;
A Vision like incarnate April, warning,
With smiles and tears, Frost the Anatomy
Into his summer grave,   (120–23)

replaces the moon's spiritual night with morning (324), its pre-vital winter with spring (325–28), inert dream with life (338–42). Indeed, much of this description of Emily as an incarnation of the sun—her radiation of life and light, the light-like music of her breath, the warm odors of her hair that dissolve the dull cold air[34]—repeats descriptions of her in the first movement. Like spring-making Aphrodite or Maia, she paves her own path with flowers by radiating life from her presence, a light that penetrates the poet and brings him from his slumberous existence into life; and all earthly sounds are penetrated by the "small, still, sweet spirit" of her breathing, which spreads like radiating light (329–31).

[32] So I understand the "Planet of that hour" (313).
[33] Contrast the influence of the moon, "Under whose motions life's dull billows move" (119).
[34] Cf. the earlier echo of the Song of Songs:

Warm fragrance seems to fall from her light dress
And her loose hair; and where some heavy tress
The air of her own speed has disentwined,
The sweetness seems to satiate the faint wind.   (105–8)

The pattern of the narrative that has begun with the cataclysmic tempest and earthquake and ends with the "small, still, sweet spirit" of Emily's respiration is borrowed from I Kings 19 and, we have noted, was soon to be employed by Shelley for a different but analogous purpose in *Hellas*.[35] In his wanderings in the wilderness, the prophet Elijah, like the poet of *Epipsychidion*, entered a cave,

And, behold, the Lord passed by, and a great and strong wind rent the mountains, and brake in pieces the rocks before the Lord; but the Lord was not in the wind: and after the wind an earthquake; but the Lord was not in the earthquake: And after the earthquake, a fire; but the Lord was not in the fire: and after the fire a still small voice.

The echo defines Emily as the divine power. Divinity is not the cold, chaste, ever-fluctuating spirit who presides over an almost womb-like state of tranquil existence, nor is it in the shattering violence of tempestuous passion. It is the dynamic but steady, gentle, almost unobservable life that permeates all things, just as in *Hellas* the divine spirit is not in violent revolution but in placid patience. On hearing God's still voice, Elijah "went out, and stood in the entering in of the cave. And, behold, there came a voice unto him, and said, What doest thou here, Elijah?"; and in a similar way the vision of Emily, "this glorious One," then "Floated into the cavern where I lay, / And called my Spirit" (336–38).

The cosmic symbolism has fully emerged, and the poet is now "this passive Earth, / This world of love, this *me*" governed by the "Twin Spheres of light" (345–46). Both are required for his total cosmic being in time, calling forth from that "earth" its "fruits and flowers" and controlling its course by darting "Magnetic might into its central heart" (347–48). According to the "everlasting" laws of necessity, the mutable Moon lifts the earth's billows and folds it in sleep, the eternal Sun raises its mists and steeps it in splendor. Together, they preserve its eternal and harmonious cycle of vital change, according to which the "grave" of its "storms" is also their "cradle" (352–53)—like most of the other metaphors, one that was potential in the first movement when Emily was called "A cradle of young thoughts of wingless pleasure, / A violet-shrouded grave of Woe" (68–69), implying but not quite asserting that new pleasure is born in the death of sorrow. Like the recurrent tension between Shelley's hopes of an earthly utopia and his aspiration to postmortal perfection, the exasperating failure in the first movement to unite in Emily the perfections of the mundane and the immortal, or to fuse time and eternity, revealed the mortal's irreconcilably divided nature. The cosmic metaphor of the second movement is the poet's resigned acceptance of that fact, his recognition that he is in time and mutability; and the metaphor is an

[35] See above, p. 384.

attempt to harmonize the conflict in him. For he now concedes that the Moon of the everlasting cycle of the realm of mutability and the Sun of immutable transcendent perfection are "equal, yet unlike" (359), and are not to be made one. Ideally, neither will make an exclusive claim on the poet's "sphere" of being, the transcendent Sun not disdaining the Moon's "borrowed might," the Moon, within whose sphere all is mutable, not eclipsing the Sun's "remoter" light (362–63). Because man has two incompatible natures, the mortal "night" of Pan and the ideal "day" of Apollo, and because the impossible attempt to unite them under the regency of a single image results in chaos, the only possibility of a harmonious temporal life is to submit, like the world, to the oscillation of the extremes, the "alternate sway" of Moon and Sun (360).

But the active principle that will unify this cosmos is yet to be sought, and consequently the poet calls upon a third celestial body, the Comet of "fierce" revolutionary passion that, by extravagantly "Alternating attraction and repulsion" (371), like a wildly revolving magnet and unlike the cosmic "alternate sway" of Sun and Moon, had previously shattered the poet-world, just as, according to the speculations of Leibnitz, Whiston, Davy, and others, a passing comet had caused the cataclysmic Flood.[36] Shelley was aware that the orbits of the comets are regular and that "some astronomers have suggested the possibility of their orbits gradually becoming less elliptical until at last they might arrange themselves in orbits concentric with the planets."[37] Appropriately, the comet of disruptive passion is to become Venus,[38] the morning and evening star of the goddess of Love, and will mediate between Sun and Moon in their alternate ministrations to the dual nature of the poet's "sphere of being," joining all together in a total cosmic order:

Oh, float into our azure heaven again!
Be there Love's folding-star at thy return;
The living Sun will feed thee from its urn
Of golden fire; the Moon will veil her horn
In thy last smiles; adoring Even and Morn
Will worship thee with incense of calm breath
And lights and shadows. . . .   (373–79)

[36] Cf. *Prometheus Unbound*, IV. 314–18:
                    . . . till the blue globe
Wrapped deluge round it like a cloak . . .
                         . . . or some God
Whose throne was in a comet, passed, and cried,
"Be not!"
[37] *On the Devil and Devils* (MS e. 9, p. 84). The received text (Julian, VII, 101) is in error in omitting the word "less."
[38] Just as Demogorgon's revolutionary flight is immediately followed by Asia's.

In the realm where all must change, the violently "Alternating attraction and repulsion" of erratic passion that shatters is to become steady and cosmic Love, which, despite its apparent difference as morning and evening star, is actually the same star and thus is the unifying power that harmonizes man's destructively conflicting attractions to the Moon of sublunary mutability and the Sun of transcendent eternity. The poet's "universe" is now fully formed, and the potentialities inherent in the overzealous first movement would seem to have expended themselves in shaping the symbolic cosmos. He need no longer be divided between a love too long delayed and premature adoration.

iii

Presumably, then, the poem has reached a point of fulfillment and stasis. But it is significant that the total cosmic life the poet has attained necessarily involves passivity: "Twin Spheres of light . . . rule this passive Earth, / This world of love, this *me*" (345–46). Although the poet's cosmos symbolizes the harmonious human life, it is nevertheless limited by passive acceptance of the world as it is rather than as it may be; and it is a condition in which the poet is acted upon instead of acting, controlled by love rather than loving. However, the recurrent tendency of the poem has been to reach beyond the limitations of the world and the present, and the symbolic cosmos of the second movement constitutes only a deceptive calm and resolution. The chaotic energy released in the first movement has been channeled and controlled for a moment of passivity, but not checked; and the poem will now move in the opposite direction, toward an active and higher aspiration because of forces still present in it. From this center of comparative calm the poem will increase in passionate intensity until it has regained that ecstatic ardor with which it began, but with a better understanding of its meaning as a result of the efforts to reduce it to order. For the irresistible drive of the poem is toward breaking down all limiting barriers, and Emilia Viviani's words prefixed to the poem, which make clear the relation between the finite and the infinite self, indicate the direction of its momentum: "The soul that loves projects itself beyond creation, and creates for itself in the infinite a world all its own, very different from this dark and fearful abyss."

Having traced his "idealized history" from his past chaos to his present prayer that he be the passive earth of a harmonious universe, the poet now looks to the future that he may surpass the limits of that "universe." According to his dual nature, there are two directions in which he might move for that purpose, corresponding to Shelley's recurrent aspirations to immortality and utopia. One is indicated by the fact that even in his act of imagining himself a passive world in a harmonious universe and subject to the endless cycle of change, suddenly and almost parenthetically he oversteps the boundaries of earthly life: the circle of his own symbolic "seasons" spirals, and he prays that after the winter of his death he may "ripen to a brighter bloom" (367). The circle of time abruptly unwinds as a gyre into eternity, like the spiraling of historical time in *Hellas*.[39] The other possible direction the poet might take is elaborated in a significantly analogous passage praising the sages

> to whom this world of life
> Is as a garden ravaged, and whose strife
> Tills for the promise of a later birth
> The wilderness of this Elysian earth.   (186–89)

It is a mode of the latter that the poet chooses, the possibility of a love-union with Emily, not in a postmortal existence, but in a purified world, or rather, in the wilderness of an Elysian solitude—like the American wilderness where the new and brighter Hellas is to appear—in which he might minimize his ties to the world without leaving it, a private world within the world and "above the idle foam of Time." The social goals of *Hellas* have been replaced by analogous but strictly personal ones, and the direction of Shelley's aspirations is vividly suggested in a manuscript passage on a page following one in which *Epipsychidion* breaks off after the account of the symbolic Moon-lady (309):

> I would not be, that which another is—
> I would not be equal below above
> Anything human. I would make my bliss
> A solitude! and though my form might move
> Like a vain cloud o'er a wilderness
> Of mountains, o'er this world; I am not of
> Its shadows or its sunbeams. . . .[40]

The abandonment of the earth symbolism at this point in *Epipsychidion* and the abrupt transition to the proposed elopement with Emily to an island "solitude" of bliss are not as inconsistent a management of imagery as may superficially appear. First of all, in Shelley's system of imagery worlds are islands in space. Earlier in the poem, for example, the Moon is "Queen of Heaven's bright isles" (281); and in other poems earth is "That island in the ocean of the world,"[41] "fairest of those wandering

---

[39] Again, this development of the cycle of change was adumbrated in the first movement:

[She] lured me towards sweet Death; as Night by Day,
Winter by Spring, or Sorrow by swift Hope,
Led into light, life, peace.   (73–75)

[40] MS e. 8, p. 112. I have abstracted this text from a number of variants. The rhyme scheme makes it clear that the lines were not intended for *Epipsychidion*.

[41] *Ode to Liberty*, 19.

isles that gem / The sapphire space of interstellar air."[42] Moreover, both world and island symbolize states of the human spirit, so that Italy, being the place where the human spirit had perfectly expressed itself, is "Thou island of eternity,"[43] and its cities where freedom and learning were born are for that reason "islands."[44] Much of *Lines Written among the Euganean Hills* depends upon the symbol of islands, not as spatial, but as isolated moments of perfection, and in *Hellas* Mahmud tells of a time when "this present hour, / This gloomy crag of time to which I cling, / Seemed as Elysian isle of peace and joy."[45] Or Shelley could think of Dante as a poet of brilliant isolated passages, "those fortunate isles, laden with golden fruit, which alone could tempt any one to embark in the misty ocean of his dark and extravagant fiction."[46] The perfect spiritual existence after death also takes place on an "island": death is a dark gate that "leads to azure isles";[47] "Elysian islands bright and fortunate" are the "Calm dwellings of the free and happy dead";[48] and in an attempt at a poem in Italian probably associated with *Epipsychidion* he wrote, no doubt intending a serious anagrammatic play, that after death he would prepare as a quiet refuge (*asilo*) some island of eternity (*isola di eternita*) in the supernal Ocean to receive his loved one.[49] As many of these passages indicate, Shelley tended to associate these symbolic islands with the utopian Fortunate Isles, the Islands of the Blest, and Atlantis; he also associated the image of the island with the circle of fulfilled being and total containment that allowed one, in ideal self-realization, to be "himself alone."

Correspondingly, the island of *Epipsychidion* is in the world, and yet not quite of it, "an isle 'twixt Heaven, Air, Earth, and Sea, / Cradled, and

---

[42] "Prologue to *Hellas*," 18–19. Cf. *Hellas*, 770–71: heavenly bodies are "isles of life or light that gem / The sapphire floods of interstellar air."

[43] *Ode to Liberty*, 206.

[44] *Lines Written among the Euganean Hills*. America as a land of freedom has "isles" like "floating Edens" (*Charles the First*, iv. 22).

[45] 925–27. Cf. *Prometheus Unbound*, IV. 108: "The azure isles / Where sweet Wisdom smiles"; *ibid.*, IV. 121: "and the islets [of time] were few / Where the bud-blighted flowers of happiness grew." On the contrary, isolated man is "a lonely and sea-girt isle" ("The pale, the cold, and the moony smile," 3).

[46] *A Discourse on the Manners of the Ancients* (Julian, VII, 224). A cancelled passage of *A Defence of Poetry* (Bodleian MS Shelley d. 1, fol. 39ᵛ) reads, "The words which Poets build are paradise-islands amid the waves of life." Shelley writes Maria Gisborne of his reading of Calderón without her aid: "I have been lately voyaging in a sea without my pilot ... I have yet sailed in a kind of way from island to island. ..." (16 November 1819 [*Letters*, II, 154]).

[47] *Queen Mab*, IX. 161–63.

[48] *The Revolt of Islam*, 4726–27.

[49] MS e. 20, fols. 25ᵛ, 26ʳ. The poem, incidentally, seems modelled on Christ's words in John 14: 1–3: "Let not your heart be troubled. ... I go to prepare a place for you. And if I go and prepare a place for you, I will come again, and receive you unto myself; that where I am, there ye may be also."

hung in clear tranquillity" (457–58), so that it is both an island of the sea and a star of heaven; and, as this implies, it is like another "island," "that wandering Eden Lucifer, / Washed by the soft blue Oceans of young air" (459–60), the star of Love. Miraculously free of famine, blight, pestilence, war, and earthquake, it is the heaven that earth may be even while it is subject to the endless cycle of mutability. This border-status— an earthly island exhibiting the characteristics of heaven—is manifest not only by its being like the star of Venus, but also by its harmony with the air above it, as though the poet were at the same time describing a star under the metaphor of a sea-girt island: the "winds wandering along the shore / Undulate with the undulating tide" (433–34), "the living winds... flow / Like waves above the living waves below" (517), and the exhalations that cover its beauty both rise from the sea and fall from the sky (470–71).

Yet, although the island mirrors or parallels a superior perfection, it clearly belongs to the realm of mutability, but a perfectly ordered mutability as opposed to the chaotic contest of contraries. The lovers, for example, are to be ministered on their journey by the harmonious, peaceful cycle of day and night, storm and calm, "Treading each other's heels, unheededly" (418–21). With the island this motif of the endless cycle of mutability, which is the way eternity appears in time, reaches its fulfillment. It had appeared frequently in the first movement when, for example, Emily was described as the incarnation of motion which, like Shelley's Cloud, "may change but cannot die" (114); and, more coherently, in the second movement it became the essential nature of the Moon governing the mortal half of the poet's cosmos, for her "changes ever run / Into themselves" (279–80), and she "ever is transformed, yet still the same" (284). This now becomes the temporal attribute of the paradise isle, whose fields and woods "ever renew / Their green and golden immortality" (468–69). In the dimension of time, "immortality" is change that cancels itself by forever repeating its circle, ever restoring the perfect condition, unlike the atemporal immortality whose paradoxically dynamic stasis Shelley will symbolize as a flame that "cannot pass away" and is "ever still / Burning, yet ever inconsumable" (583, 578–79). But, like the historical spiral of *Hellas* which is to reach a peak "above the idle foam of Time," the island's "immortal" cycle is to be improved upon by the poet and Emily, who will raise time to its highest form, not by dispelling it, but by using the necessarily fixed sequence of the temporal circle to foresee the future, to recover the past, and to possess the endless cycle formed by the present. By this means they would capture in each moment the sum total of time and disengage the present from sequentiality: on the island will be books and music

and all
Those instruments with which high Spirits call
The future from its cradle, and the past
Out of its grave, and make the present last
In thoughts and joys which sleep, but cannot die,
Folded within their own eternity.   (519–24)

Beyond the temporal circle there is an earthly perfection in which eternity persists in the ambience of mutability. It was with reference to this island paradise that Shelley wrote in one of the rejected prefaces:

Those who know the world as it is, will collect from the following poem that the only refuge from the consequences of such feelings & opinions as are expressed was that which the writer sought: those who know the world as it should be may hope that the tendencies of such high emotions shall yet, in that world (if such there be) receive their consummation.—For the love of woman which these verses express was but the form of that universal Love which Plato taught.[50]

The transition from the earth symbolism of the second movement to the island symbolism of the third, therefore, is the passage from a merely acceptable harmony to a possible earthly perfection, a private utopia which would combine the world in which the poet may love and the "fields of immortality" in which he may adore. The former symbol implies the self as a world passively receiving a governance and order from a remote Moon and ever remoter Sun; the latter, a self actively united with his own soul's image of perfection as a consequence of the paradisiacal island, the "world as it should be." Correspondingly, in his heaven upon earth Emily is to remain, as she was, the "vestal sister" of the "dull mortality" that is the poet's attribute, the "mine," but is also to pass over into more integral union by becoming the "bride" of his essence, the "me." The poet's failure in the first movement to grasp firmly any single image containing Emily as both human and ideal was momentarily resolved by dividing his two natures and organizing them into a world that diurnally alternates between his sublunary and his ideal needs; but the calm, passive inadequacy of that resolution leaves a pressure urging a reversion to unite once again the human and ideal in Emily as simultaneously sister and bride—not, as in the first movement, in the world as it is, but in a world that might be, a brighter Hellas.

Thus the island-world of the elopement is the fulfillment of the "promise of a later birth" for which over the ages man has tilled the "wilderness of this Elysian earth," not because of unilinear progress but because the completion of the circle of mutability is the return to the

[50] Bodleian MS Shelley d. 1, fol. 101^v.

original Golden Age, just as the evening star is also the morning star, and as Death and Birth are the same star. As Asia's song, "My soul is an enchanted boat," paints progressive perfection as a retreat from age to childhood and then through death-and-birth to a "diviner day," and as historical progress in *Hellas* is the passage of Freedom to the pre-cultural innocence of America, so the perfection of the island is a regression in time to man's original state. It is an "Elysian isle" (539) like an "Eden" (417), like the star of Venus, the "Eden" of heaven (459), like the "wreck of Paradise" (423) and therefore immediately available for restoration—just as, according to the *Defence of Poetry*, after the Dark Ages the "familiar appearance and proceedings of life became wonderful and heavenly; and a paradise was created as out of the wrecks of Eden."[51] Not only had the island's pleasure-house been built by some Ocean King for his sister and his spouse, as, in a renewal of the past, Emily is to be to the poet; it had been built "ere crime / Had been invented, in the world's young prime" (489), and the island's "pastoral people" still "Draw the last spirit of the age of gold" (426–28). Like the Saturnian condition of belief that Shelley described in *The Witch of Atlas*, it represents a state before the distinction between truth and error became relevant. Even the island's odors, colors, and sounds seem like "echoes of an antenatal dream" (456), a pre-worldly state in which imagined existence is real. The personal pattern Shelley has elaborated here is approximately the one he constructed for society in *Hellas*: those who have suffered the vicissitudes of the present world and the tension between desire and harsh reality translate themselves to a pristine realm that has no history of crime, suffering, or error and there renew the Golden Age at a level approximating transcendent perfection.

iv

One of the most recurrent clusters of terms in the poem is "pierce," "penetrate," and "dart," and related to these terms in different ways are also the motifs of diffusion and escape. For the main thrust of the poem is simultaneously toward the deepest, most intimate of unions and the breaking down of confining barriers. The fragrance of Emily's hair is felt, beyond the senses, in the soul, "like fiery dews that melt / Into the bosom of a frozen bud" (109–11); the glowing beauty of Emily as the Sun penetrates the poet "with living light" (342); the symbolic Sun and Moon "dart" magnetic might into the heart of the poet-earth (347); the island's flowers "dart their arrowy odour through the brain" (451), its music is experienced as a "soul within the soul" (455), and Emily's glances are words that "dart" into the heart (562). It is of more than descriptive significance that on the island the tracks of animals "Pierce into glades, caverns, and bowers, and halls / Built round with ivy" (441–42). This

[51] *Defence of Poetry* (Julian, VII, 128).

recurrent theme of absolute inwardness is a factor of the dialectic of love as total union, and therefore the same term appears ironically *in malo*. From the features of the false, Pandemic Emily destructive flames darted into the poet's "vitals," and from her "living" body a "killing air" "pierced" the core of his heart like blighting honey-dew (259–66).

But the power to pierce and penetrate to the heart of another would be frustrated by any confinement within the circle of the self or within other limiting conditions. Therefore the love which experiences another as a penetration to the soul is also a lightning which "pierces" its "continents," or constraining container (400), and leads the poet at the end of the poem to seek to "pierce / Into the height of Love's rare Universe" (588–89) in accordance with Emilia Viviani's Italian epigraph, which declares that the soul that loves darts beyond creation to create in the infinite a world of its own—of which the island paradise is a terrestrial model. Emily's physical confinement to the convent is therefore a model of all the limitations the poem seeks to overcome, and the poet's proposal that they take flight to the island extends Emily's escape from the convent into an escape from all the constraints the world imposes to prevent a totally liberated life. At the opening of the poem the immortal mind is conceived as victim of the mortal body and the world, for although Emily's heart, winged with thought, "over-soared this low and worldly shade," its vain bodily endeavor to beat against the "unfeeling bars" of the convent shattered those thoughts (14–17); but in the invitation to the journey love is found to be unconstrainable, overleaping all "fence," "Piercing its continents," and—in a momentary intimation that even the island paradise will not prove adequate—bursting death's charnel to

> make free
> The limbs in chains, the heart in agony,
> The soul in dust and chaos. (405–7)

The cognate of this theme of escape and the converse of penetration is the motif of diffusion, which, like most of the motifs of the poem, has appeared in the first movement, charged with the possibility of eventually unfolding its significance. There Emily is a light radiated "lightning-like" through the obscuring cloud of the poet's words (34), a brightness that trembles through her limbs like moonlight through a cloud (77–81), an "intense Diffusion" of light that, like the sun's, pervades her surrounding atmosphere and obscures her confining outlines (91–104); and the same image is inherent in almost all the other representations of her as light. As the Sun of the poet's universe in the second movement, she radiates life through the earth (325–26), and in the heart of the island paradise is buried a soul that, like a radiating lamp, "Unfolds itself" over its surface (477–82).

Taken together, the images of radiation from a center and penetration to a center define the features of a circle, the paradoxical nature of which frequently aided Shelley in his efforts to figure forth the unity of a duality as it had aided the theologians in defining the paradoxical nature of God. It explained, for example, the paradoxical relation of poetry to knowledge: poetry "is at once the centre and circumference of knowledge; it is that which comprehends all science, and that to which all science must be referred."[52] But perhaps the most obvious example is Shelley's solution of the indifference of the distinction between thought and thing by describing the mind as both the center to which all things are referred and the circumference within which all are contained. Translated into other terms, this is an ontological monism effected by the identity of possessing and being possessed, a confusion of mutuality; and for Shelley that is another way of describing the simultaneously centrifugal and centripetal movements of love, of which his most splendid expression is his picture of the flowers of *The Sensitive Plant*, each "interpenetrated / With the light and the odour its neighbour shed, ... / Wrapped and filled by their mutual atmosphere." By piercing the earth with life, Emily, like Venus or Flora, is embowered in its resulting flowers. A sun-like circle radiating from a center, she penetrates another sphere with life that then unfolds itself as from a center and embraces her in it:

And from her presence life was radiated
Through the gray earth and branches bare and dead;
So that her way was paved and roofed above
With flowers as soft as thoughts of budding love.   (325–28)

The music of her respiration not only spreads about her like light but also penetrates every other sound (329–31); and the transcendent Beauty not only "penetrates" and "fills" the world but also "clasps" it, so that the world both possesses and is possessed by it (102–3).

Now, it is evident that the impulse of the last movement of the poem is toward a fulfillment of the love relationship in an indissoluble identity of the lovers. In the first movement, Emily, although the object of an ecstatic confusion of love and adoration, stands apart from the poet, unrelated to him despite his frantic efforts to unify his ties to the mortal and the divine: "See where she stands!" (112). She is the *object* of his adoration, and he can only pray for some binding relationship with her. Relationship then evolves in the symbolism of the poet as an earth governed by Sun and Moon, but it is only a love relationship to the remote, not a union; and his hope to be governed alternately by sublunary love and ideal adoration, which are "equal, yet unlike" (359), is but an extension

[52] *Defence of Poetry* (Julian, VII, 135).

of his conception of himself and Emily in the first movement as unlike notes of music formed "For one another, though dissimilar" and maintaining a "difference without discord" (142–44). Clearly the drive now becomes to transform relationship into identity, to dissolve the poet and Emily into one being. Like most of the themes, the passage from harmonious relationship to identity had also been forecast in the first movement when the poet had corrected himself, "I am not thine: I am a part of thee" (52). It is there in the knowledge that even

The spirit of the worm beneath the sod
In love and worship blends itself with God, (128–29)

although the poet in the next lines laments that it is too late in life for him to love and too soon before death to worship. And it is there in the poet's wish that his wife and Emily could share the name of "wife," a "sister's bond for her and thee, / Blending two beams of one eternity!" (46–48).

As an earth, the poet passively submitted to governance, but total union demands a reciprocal relationship that is consummated in mutual blending; and consequently the last movement is dominated by images of equal giving and receiving. Even the Elysian character of the island is manifested by this relationship, the skies bending to touch the mountains, their "paramour" (544–45), the seas "Kissing the sifted sands, and caverns hoar" (430–32), the shore trembling and sparkling with ecstasy on receiving the "faint kisses of the sea" (546–48). That Shelley meant nature's kisses to imply a blending into a single identity is evident in a poem of his which, characteristically, transforms Anacreon's drinking song, "The thirsty earth drinks up the rain,"[53] into "Love's Philosophy":

The fountains mingle with the river
And the rivers with the Ocean,
The winds of Heaven mix for ever
With a sweet emotion;
Nothing in the world is single;
All things by a law divine
In one another's being mingle.[54]
Why not I with thine?

See the mountains kiss high Heaven
And the waves clasp one another;
No sister-flower would be forgiven
If it disdained to kiss its brother;

[53] Ode xix.
[54] The Stacey MS reads: "In one spirit meet and mingle."

And the sunlight clasps the earth
And the moonbeams kiss the sea:
What are all these kissings worth,
If thou kiss not me?

Leigh Hunt, who may have supplied the title, probably was wrong, on publishing this Anacreontic,[55] to assume that Love is the singer, but no doubt he had insight into Shelley's mind when he described the song as "elemental, Platonical; a meeting of divineness with humanity"—an effort, like the third movement of *Epipsychidion*, to capture on earth the perfection of transcendent unity. The same interinvolvement is displayed by the island, where "the Earth and Ocean seem / To sleep in one another's arms" (509–10), where the ivy and vine "interknit" (500), and where motion, odor, beam, and tone join the island's "deep music" in "unison" (453–54), as opposed to that mere harmony of dissimilar notes, that music of "difference without discord" which, in the first movement, the poet had hoped would be his relation to Emily (142–44).

The island therefore displays the same mutual blending in love that, with all its sexual overtones, will identify the poet and Emily with each other:

Our breath shall intermix, our bosoms bound
And our veins beat together; and our lips
With other eloquence than words, eclipse
The soul that burns between them, and the wells
Which boil under our being's inmost cells,
The fountains of our deepest life, shall be
Confused in Passion's golden purity,
As mountain-springs under the morning sun.
We shall become the same. . . .   (565–73)

But the basis of their ultimate identity is their mutual giving and receiving of each other that fulfills the recurrent images of diffusion from a center and penetration to it, an identity of two circles radiating outward to each other and receiving the other within its circumference so that, like the transcendent Beauty, each "penetrates and clasps and fills" the world of the other (103). The verbal model for this simultaneous giving and receiving in unifying love had been constructed in the first movement when Emily, a Dantesque Beatrice, was described as a "lovely soul formed to be blessed and bless" (57), and it is activated in the third movement when the island is likened to a bride glowing "at once" with "love and loveliness" (474–75), where Emily, also as a bride, is to be "united" with the

55 *Indicator* for 22 December 1819, p. 88.

poet in a union whose evidence is that she is "delighting and delighted" (392–93). But most significantly the ultimate consummation of these two bridal images is the identity of the poet and Emily not only with each other but also with their island paradise:

Possessing and possessed by all that is
Within that calm circumference of bliss,
And by each other, till to love and live
Be one.[56]   (549–52)

The lovers, interassimilated by mutual giving and receiving, are also to be absorbed into the circle of their island of bliss, and the island is to be absorbed within their circumference.

The climax of the advance of the lovers toward perfect existence on the island, then, is as much their regression to the original human state as the island itself is a return to the Golden Age. If the lovers and their island-world possess and are possessed by each other until existence is this perfect unity of outward and inward being, the lovers will be in that state which, according to Shelley's attempt to define "life," characterizes child-hood and reverie, when what we see and feel seems "one mass" with ourselves, and the self and the surrounding universe seem absorbed into each other.[57] It is the original human state of infancy as Shelley also described it in some lines associated with *Epipsychidion*,

When every thing familiar seemed to be
Wonderful, and the immortality
Of the great world, which all things must inherit
Is felt as one with the awakening spirit
Unconscious of itself, & of the strange
Distinctions, which in its proceeding change
It feels & knows, and mourns, as if each were
A desolation.[58]

It is because the distinction between internal and external, or between self and world, is unreal that the island is elaborately humanized so that in being like a "bride / Glowing at once with love and loveliness" it is analogous to Emily, who is to be the bride of the poet's soul, "delighting and delighted." The island, too, has a soul burning in its heart; all the

---

[56] Bodleian MS Shelley d. 1, which shows a number of efforts at these lines, is at one point helpfully more explicit: "... till we / Become one being with the world we see" (fol. 97ʳ). The manuscript also shows that Shelley speculated on describing the beauty of the island with which they are to unite as like the "shadow" or "reflex" "of thy [Emily's] soul."
[57] See above, p. 142.
[58] MS c. 4, fols. 10–11.

elements of nature in it are in a love relation to each other; and both the prelapsarian island and the lovers are to be in the pre-cultural state before division and distinctions become relevant. The island displays the acts of love, and the union of the lovers with it is of the same order as their union with each other. For the island is but the "internal" conceived of as "external," just as Emily is the finite self projected as perfect and infinite, like that interior island in the essay *On Love* which is the "soul within our soul that describes a circle around its proper Paradise which pain, and sorrow, and evil dare not overleap." The perfection of mortal life is the identity, through love, of the self and its own visionary perfection in another and of both with their corresponding externality which is the island, until loving is identical with being.[59]

So it is ideally to be in life. After life, the poet proposes,

Let us become the overhanging day,
The living soul of this Elysian isle,
Conscious,[60] inseparable, one.   (538–40)

But we have already been told that

. . . like a buried lamp, a Soul no less
Burns in the heart of this delicious isle,
An atom of th'Eternal, whose own smile
Unfolds itself, and may be felt, not seen
O'er the gray rocks, blue waves, and forests green,
Filling their bare and void interstices.   (477–82)

A consideration of this apparent paradox will help clarify a structure that stands behind some of the important imagery of this and others of Shelley's poems. That the island has a "Soul" suggests some version of the *anima mundi*, or demiurge, but that the island's soul is an "atom of th'Eternal" indicates a peculiarly Shelleyan attempt to relate the world to the transcendent. In his notebooks Shelley made a number of starts at a passage that may have been intended as part of the so-called "Prologue to *Hellas*." The following is an eclectic and composite version:

A spark ⟨star⟩ of Heaven ⟨of inextinguishable splendour⟩
    has fallen upon ⟨through⟩ ⟨to the abyss⟩ the earth
A quenchless atom of immortal light
A living spark of Night ⟨A lamp of Heaven⟩
A sphereless star, shook from the constellations
Which gem the throne of God.
A burning monad of eternal flame
A living atom of eternal light

[59] Cf. *The Revolt of Islam*, 3304: "To live, as if to love and live were one."
[60] No doubt in its Latin sense of mutually sharing knowledge or awareness.

Into the Earth's deep heart it past
And like a seed
Secret as a thought
To the central heart
To the heart of Earth—to the well
Whence[?] its pulses flow & beat ⟨leap⟩—
Unextinct in that cold source
It burns—⟨even as a Soul of Power⟩ and on every course
Guides the sphere which is its prison
As a ray of the eternal
Like an Angel's spirit pent
In a form of mortal birth
Till, as a Spirit half unrisen
Shatters its charnel—it has rent
In the rapture of its mirth
The thin & painted garment of the Earth
A desolation ruining[?] its chaos—a fierce breath
Consuming all the forms of living death
Cities & towers & temples
A Spirit of Life. . . .[61]

The passage, apparently representing revolution as rather like a volcanic eruption, depicts the source of the cleansing eruption as a power, like Demogorgon, at the center of the earth, but, unlike Demogorgon, it also guides the earth in its regular orbit and was itself originally a starry fragment of some immortal heavenly perfection. This symbolic pattern had the attraction to Shelley of postulating the presence of an atom of the transcendent in earthly life, and so of resolving the dichotomy that pulled him in opposite directions; according to this symbolism, the world in essence is a star fallen from the immortal heavenly light, a spark which, like the light of the human soul shining through its bodily "atmosphere," then radiates through its imprisoning matter, just as the heavenly light from which it derives radiates without encumbrance. This symbolism explains, for example, why the Lady of *The Sensitive Plant* seems attended by a starry spirit who has deserted heaven, why flowers are so repeatedly pictured as stars, and why, upon becoming a star after death, Adonais has returned to the burning fountain whence he came. Divested of its element of transcendence and translated into purely mundane terms, it provides the Vesta symbolism of "Lines Written upon Hearing the News of the Death of Napoleon." And it supplies an ontological base in *Epipsychidion* for likening the brightness of the island to that of the star of Venus, "Washed by the soft blue Oceans of young air" (459–60).

[61] MS e. 7, pp. 259–60; MS e. 20, fols. 12ᵛ, 28ᵛ.

Although the manuscript verse identifies the spark in earth's heart as cleansing revolution, as the power that guides the world, and as the "Spirit of Life," its meaning cannot actually be limited: the "atom of eternal light" is, for Shelley, whatever it is that derives from transcendent and eternal perfection, and any single term must necessarily be inadequate. For example, in Shelley's so-called "Unfinished Drama" one speech built on a similar symbolism is assigned to a Demogorgon-like "Spirit" attended by "Earthquake & lightning," but the manuscript shows that it was first assigned to "Love" as another name for the central spirit of the earth:

Within the silent centre of the earth
My mansion is, in which I lived insphered
From the beginning ⟨. . . is the spirit of life⟩
                         and around my sleep
Have woven all the wondrous imagery
Of this dim spot which mortals call the world—
Infinite depths of unknown elements
Massed into an impenetrable mask
For my dread countenance, for which the tongue
Of living ⟨mortal⟩ man has never sought[?] a name
Sheets of immeasurable fire, & veins
Of gold and stone & adamantine iron
And as a veil in which I walk through Heaven
I have wrought mountains seas, & waves & clouds
And lastly light whose interfusion dawns
The purple depths of interstellar air
In the dark spaces. . . .[62]

Then in the subsequent fragment of the play, which takes place on a mysterious "Enchanted Isle" and promises to treat a theme like that of *Alastor* and *Epipsychidion*, the central event is a version of the symbolism of the descended star, which the first of these manuscript passages describes as "like a seed":

I dreamed a star came down from Heaven
And lay amid the plants of lower India
Which I had given a shelter from the frost
Within my chamber. There the meteor lay
Panting forth light among the leaves and flowers
As if it lived, and was outworn with speed
Or that it loved, and passion made the pulse

[62] MS e. 18, p. 150. This also is an eclectic text.

Of its bright life throb like an anxious heart
Till it diffused itself, and all the chamber
And walls seemed melted into emerald fire
That burned not, in the midst of which appeared
⟨And yet it had no shape⟩
A spirit ⟨shadow⟩ like a child ⟨cherub⟩ and laughed aloud
A thrilling peal of such sweet merriment
As made the blood to tingle in my warm feet
Then bent over a flower pot and murmuring
Low unintelligible melodies,
Placed something in the mould like melon-seeds,
And slowly faded, and in place of it
A soft hand issued from the veil of fire,
Holding a cup like a magnolia flower
And poured upon the earth within the vase
The element with which it overflowed,
Brighter than morning light. . . .[63]

Awakening from her dream, the Lady finds a splendid new plant with a "golden eye" that "Gazed like a star into the morning light." Although the fragment fails to complete the symbolism, it is evident that the pattern is identical with that of the other passages: a star, which identifies light with life, love, motion, and the pulsation of the human heart, falls into the earth like a seed and, evolving into a flower, radiates light, like the starry flowers of *The Sensitive Plant*.

Shelley's indiscriminate identification of what, in *Epipsychidion*, he calls the "atom of th'Eternal" in the island's heart with power, revolution, light, love, and motion—indeed with something for which the tongue of mortal man has no name—is made yet more intelligible by the fragmentary manuscript lyric that eventually developed into the first stanza of the chorus "Worlds on worlds are rolling ever" in *Hellas*. The "Spirit" addressed seems to be "Freedom," but if so, it is also identical with divinity and the Absolute of which all things are portions:

Mid the Angels thou art love
In the ⟨Sun⟩ ⟨world⟩ stars and dust thou art motion
In the worm thy pulses move
And in man thou art the emotion
With which his ⟨tameless⟩ panting heart
⟨Burst its icy zone⟩[64]

[63] MS e. 18, pp. 141, 136–38.
[64] MS e. 7, pp. 10–11. For "Freedom," or "Liberty," as one of the names of the one organizing Power, see above, pp. 398–403.

Shelley's characteristic pun here on "emotion"[65] as an outward movement is calculated to identify as but different manifestations of the one central spirit the power that guides the earth's motion, the pulsation of life, passion, revolution, love, and all the symbols of radiation and eruption from a center, so that, for example, the speed of the earth in the last act of *Prometheus Unbound* and "Lines Written on Hearing the News of the Death of Napoleon" is another expression of love and life. It is because of the integral involvement of the pun in the whole symbolic complex of a dynamic divine force in the center of the world and in the heart of man that he could define love as "a *going out* of our own nature"[66] and could write that

The winds of Heaven mix for ever
With a sweet *emotion*;
Nothing in the world is single.

The symbolism of a spark of divinity imprisoned in the globe of a world, through which it radiates, rises, or erupts is implicit in *Epipsychidion* in the metaphor of the poet's worshipful thoughts of Emily as a "world" within the "Chaos" of himself (243) and in the description of Love as able to burst Death's charnel (405). It explains why the evidence of the perfection of the island's pleasure-house is that it seems to have assumed its form in the heart of the earth and then grew "Out of the mountains, from the living stone, / Lifting itself in caverns light and high" (496–97) and so is "Titanic," that is, suggests the mountain Titans, who sprang from earth's lowest depths. But the most overwhelming image of diffusion and radiance appears in the description of Emily in the rhapsodic first movement:

The glory of her being, issuing thence,
Stains the dead, blank, cold air with a warm shade
Of unentangled intermixture, made
By Love, of light and motion: one intense
Diffusion, one serene Omnipresence,
Whose flowing outlines mingle in their flowing,
Around her cheeks and utmost fingers glowing
With the unintermitted blood, which there
Quivers, (as in a fleece of snow-like air
The crimson pulse of living morning quiver,)
Continuously prolonged, and ending never. . . .   (91–101)

---

[65] Cf. *The Revolt of Islam*, 468, 4593; *Ode to Naples*, 37; *Lines Written among the Euganean Hills*, 179; *Prometheus Unbound*, II. ii. 50; IV. 45, 97. See above, pp. 315, 338n.
[66] *Defence of Poetry* (Julian, VII, 118); itals. added.

Emily is a world from whose center love radiates light and motion, and her radiance enfolds her in its own warm atmosphere, which dispels "the dead, blank, cold air" of mortality. The image behind this symbolism of perfect being wrapped and self-contained in its own diffused radiance is, of course, the sun, just as elsewhere Shelley likened liberty to "Heaven's Sun girt by the exhalation / Of its own glorious light"[67] or wrote that

At the creation of the Earth
Pleasure, that divinest birth,
From the soil of Heaven did rise
Wrapt in sweet wild melodies
Like an exhalation. . . .
Her life-breathing limbs did flow
In the harmony divine
Of an ever-lengthening line
Which enwrapt her perfect form
With a beauty clear and warm.[68]

But the picture of Emily as a world similar to the sun constitutes only half of the symbolism of her perfection. It reveals only the divinity of her mortal state, not its relation to the transcendent divinity, the Eternal, of which the "quenchless atom of immortal light" at the heart of the macrocosm and the human microcosm is a fragment. Consequently, to his picture of her radiance Shelley adds that the diffused rays of her beauty are

Continuously prolonged, and ending never,
Till they are lost, and in that Beauty furled
Which penetrates and clasps and fills the world.   (101–3)

Like neighboring suns, the divinity in the microcosm and the transcendent divinity from which it derives radiate atmospheres of light that are lost in each other, the transcendent Beauty enfolding to itself the radiance of that which it has given—a gesture just short of what in *Adonais* is termed the flowing of a "portion of the Eternal" back to "the burning fountain whence it came," just short, that is, of death and eternity.

This is the complex of symbols that the last movement of the poem then rearranges and transmutes into a postmortal relationship between the two lovers and the island. The Edenic island, the earthly "circumference of bliss," is a world in itself, having at its heart a "Soul," a burning "atom of th'Eternal" which "Unfolds" a light that "may be felt, not seen," over the features of the island and, like Emily's radiated glory which is "one

[67] *Ode to Liberty*, 159–60.
[68] "The Birth of Pleasure."

serene Omnipresence," fills "their bare and void interstices," removing all the meaningless vacancies that would remain if the world were only its disparate visible components (477–82). The island represents the perfect condition of divinity in the context of mutability and mortality, and as a derivative atom of the Eternal it bears the same relation to the unencumbered Eternal that, in the second movement, the "borrowed" light of the Moon of mutability and mortality bears to the unchanging Sun. Yet, although the island has its own soul, on their death the poet and Emily, made one, are to become "the overhanging day, / The living soul of this Elysian isle" (538–39), for death will be their return to the burning fountain, the transcendent light, whence both they and the island's soul had come. The image reverses the corresponding structure in the first movement: whereas Emily, a mortal incarnation of divinity, was a little world whose radiant beauty blended with the radiance of the ideal Beauty, Emily and the poet will return after death to the "overhanging" eternal Soul, an "atom" of which is the soul of their island-world.

So they are to be after death, when they will be "Conscious, inseparable, one." But until then there is the "meanwhile" of life, during which they must remain "two" who are "together" (541), just as the poet had earlier wished to move in life "beside" the earthly Emily. The most intimate relationship they can attain in life is only the mutuality of possessing and being possessed by each other and their island circumference of bliss, while yet remaining distinct. For, however Elysian, the island is carefully defined as the context of eternal mutability, not eternity. Even Emily and the poet will there be caught up in that endless circle, of which the alternation of moisture and fire reflects the alternate influences of mortality and eternity: to them sleep will be "the fresh dew of languid love, the rain / Whose drops quench kisses till they burn again" (558–59). But in addition to the poet's impulse to speculate on the postmortal oneness of himself and his visionary ideal, pressures have been at work throughout the poem to prevent the fulfillment of that unity in the earthly "meanwhile."

Throughout the poem a flower and vegetation metaphor has moved like a lesser motif that the poet applies equally to his poem and to himself. For in addressing his song in both his prefatory and supplementary stanzas, Shelley is not merely following a literary convention: his song is himself, and the test of his self-fulfillment is the degree of his poem's completion and perfection. With the Renaissance, and especially with Dante's promulgation of the doctrine of love, Shelley wrote in his *Defence of Poetry*, "earth became peopled by the inhabitants of a diviner world. The familiar appearance and proceedings of life became wonderful and heavenly; and a paradise was created as out of the wrecks of Eden. And as this creation itself is poetry, so its creators were poets; and language was the instrument of their art: 'Galeotto fù il libro, e chi lo scrisse'"[69]— Galeotto was the book and he who wrote it. Life and language are both poetry, and the poet writes himself. Something more than a literary concern compels Shelley in *Epipsychidion* to occupy himself directly with the life of his poem. It is his failure to find in his "world of fancies" the image for Emily that divulges to him the "infirmity" of his mortal nature (69–71), and it is with the poem's "winged words" that his "soul would pierce / Into the height of Love's rare Universe," though they prove "chains of lead" (588–90). It is no accident, then, that in offering his poem to Emily as "votive wreaths of withered memory" (4) he echoes the opening of Dante's *Vita Nuova*, in which Dante presents his Memory under the metaphor of a book which he is annotating.[70] Shelley's flowers of poetry,[71] then, are his own "withered memory" (4), a thornless and "faded blossom" for his "adored Nightingale" (9–12). When he prays to her to "blot from this sad song / All of its much mortality and wrong" and to water it with her tears of "sacred dew" and shed on it the sunlight of her "smile" so that "it may not die" (35–40), the superficial sense is that his poem is to be purified so that it may endure. But the echo of the fifty-first Psalm—". . . according unto the multitude of thy tender mercies blot out my transgressions. Wash me throughly from mine iniquity, and cleanse me from my sin"—carries an overtone suggesting that the poet is also the subject; and to divest him of his "mortality" and limitations is to translate him to an afterlife. The first movement is then rounded off with a coda on love which applies the vegetation motif to the earth: love is

> the eternal law
> By which those live, to whom this world of life
> Is as a garden ravaged, and whose strife
> Tills for the promise of a later birth
> The wilderness of this Elysian earth. (185–89)

The metaphor is appropriate since it logically foreshadows the poet's efforts in the next two movements to create for himself an Elysian earth of love. And yet, although the reference is clearly to some brighter earthly "Hellas," the metaphor carries with it some degree of ambiguity that leaves open the question of whether the promised later birth is earthly or heavenly. In the second movement the poet is identified with a flower blighted by the false Emily and with an earth of which the symbolic Sun and Moon will "into birth / Awaken all its fruits and flowers" (346–47).

[69] *Defence of Poetry* (Julian, VII, 128). The quotation is from *Inferno*, V. 137; Shelley has, of course, quite wrenched it out of context.
[70] In his Advertisement Shelley alludes to the *Vita Nuova* and quotes from it.
[71] Shelley is calling upon the traditional designation of poetry as "flowers," and the term identifies him with his own poems. Cf. *Adonais*, 16–17, where Keats's "fading melodies" are "like flowers."

The metaphor of a later birth that, in the first movement, represented a renewed earth is here assigned to the poet himself when the recurrent cycles of change that sustain the symbolism of the poet-earth suddenly become the spiral of his advance through his "seasons" to his ripening "to a brighter bloom" after the winter of his death (364–67), a spiralling aspiration that both defines the limitations of the conditions that movement symbolizes and foreshadows its rejection. Whereas the first coda looked forward to a "later birth" of the world, the same imagery, now applied to the poet, looks forward to a postmortal "brighter bloom" and promises that the earthly island paradise of the third movement will also prove inadequate. Finally, the coda of the second movement promises far more than the island theme that follows it, for, returning to the metaphor of his poem as a faded flower and fulfilling all the implications in the previous vegetation metaphors of a postmortal perfection, the poet asks the lady not to scorn his poem,

> these flowers of thought, the fading birth
> Which from its heart of hearts that plant puts forth
> Whose fruit, made perfect by thy sunny eyes,
> Will be as of the trees of Paradise.   (384–87)

The "flowers" of poetry are what mortal life is, a "fading birth," an entrance into the process of dying; the "votive wreaths of withered memory," the "faded blossom" the poet offers Emily, is really the promise of his later fruit, the world "beyond the grave." The next movement will be an effort to realize a Paradise, but the fruit which the poet's heart of hearts will bear requires first the death of his "flowers of thought."

This tug of death has been unrelenting throughout the poem and repeatedly pulls its frame of reference beyond the limits of a mortal existence, however Elysian, as it did that of *Alastor*. The poet's youthful dream-vision of his own ideal, which he had not expected to realize until after his death and which he might properly worship only in the "fields of Immortality" had "lured him towards sweet Death," and as he passed from dream to awareness of the world, he would have followed it "though the grave between / Yawned like a gulf" (230–31). Indeed, that the impulse giving rise to the poem could complete itself only in death was foredoomed when the poet, springing toward the "lodestar"[72] of his desire, likened himself to a moth, which instinctively seeks a "radiant death, a fiery sepulchre" (223), and mistakes Love's setting star, which leads to postmortal union with the infinite, for the finite "lamp of earthly flame" (223–24). It is implicit in the metaphor that only in death can the poet

[72] Apparently Shelley conceived of a lodestar not only as a guide but also as a magnetic attraction. For example, *The Revolt of Islam*, 847–49: "whose eyes / Were lodestars of delight, which drew me home / When I might wander forth."

attain his unearthly goal.[73] Adherence to that "best philosophy," love, makes "this cold common hell, our life, a doom / As glorious as a fiery martyrdom" (214-15), a self-sacrificing endurance for ideals to be fulfilled only in death. Even the invitation to the voyage begins with a praise of love's power to liberate, even to liberate the soul from the dust in death's charnel and thus from all earthly constraints. Under pressure of his aspiration to absolute identity with his vision of perfection, the poet pushes the relationship of interpossession beyond the limits it will bear. Still "two" and "together" in the Edenic island of the world,

Our breath shall intermix, our bosoms bound,
And our veins beat together; and our lips
With other eloquence than words, eclipse
The soul that burns between them, and the wells
Which boil under our being's inmost cells,
The fountains of our deepest life, shall be
Confused in Passion's golden purity,
As mountain-springs under the morning sun.[74]   (565-72)

But in such union they would no longer be two: "We shall become the same, we shall be one / Spirit within two frames." Indeed, "wherefore two?"—and the poem then rushes on desperately and as disjointedly as in the first movement, while identity struggles to displace duality:

One hope within two wills, one will beneath
Two overshadowing minds, one life, one death,
One Heaven, one Hell, one immortality,
And one annihilation.   (584-87)

[73] Shelley drew out the dialectic inherent in this metaphor more fully in "The Woodman and the Nightingale," where he heaped three levels upon each other: the endless wheel of change that is the law of earth; man's spiral course from the finite to the infinite, symbolized by the death of the caterpillar which is the birth of the moth; and the impossibility of possessing the infinite in the finite. The following is an eclectic text of lines 24-32:

. . . every silver moth fresh from the ⟨antenatal⟩ grave

Which is its cradle—ever from below
Aspired like one who loves too fair, too far,
To be consumed within the ⟨eternal⟩ purest glow

Of one ⟨inaccessible⟩ ⟨eternal⟩ serene and unapproached star
As if it were a lamp of earthly light;
Unconscious, as some human ⟨aspirers⟩ lovers are,

Itself how low, how high beyond all height
The Heaven where it would perish! . . .   (MS e. 8, pp. 85-86)
[74] In his "Follow to the Deep Wood's Weeds," Shelley made the sexual meaning of such intermingling rather more explicit.

The lovers, become one, are to be like the traditional symbol of the eternal soul pointing to its heavenly home:

One passion in twin-hearts, which grows and grew,
Till like two meteors of expanding flame,
Those spheres instinct with it become the same,
Touch, mingle, are transfigured; ever still
Burning, yet ever inconsumable: . . .
Like flames . . .
Which point to Heaven and cannot pass away.   (575–83)

What has happened is that in the very act of describing the human interpossession of himself and Emily in the world the poet exceeds the possible earthly limits until, without his intending it, the mortal context has dropped out, and he is actually describing the identity possible only in afterlife. It "is not easy for spirits cased in flesh and blood," Shelley confessed on writing of the relation of Emilia Viviani to *Epipsychidion*, to avoid the error of "seeking in a mortal image the likeness of what is perhaps eternal"[75] (the emphasis on "error" should not distract from the force of "perhaps"); but in the poem the error insists on correcting itself. In a passage of Emilia Viviani's essay on Love which Shelley did not include in his preface, she had foreseen the course of the poem: "The universe, the vast universe, no longer capable of bounding the lover's ideas and affections, vanishes before his sight. The soul of him who loves disdains restraint—nothing can restrain it."[76] The poet had projected an eventual afterlife in which he and Emily would be "Conscious, inseparable, one," but that proves to be the irresistible objective of his love here and now; and the consequence of that aspiration is that earthly dimensions dissolve away. Meaning to depict only their perfect relationship on the paradisiacal island of the human "meanwhile," he suddenly is aware that his "soul would pierce / Into the height of Love's rare Universe" (588–89); for of the alternate futures that the poem has held out, the "promise" of an Elysian earth has succumbed to the winter of death in which the soul will "ripen to a brighter bloom." A personal millennium turns out to be a future immortality. The rhapsodic disorder of the first movement had been subjected to a control in the next two movements, which strove to create a harmonious love-relationship in the world; but the poem closes with the same desperate and ecstatic confusion, for here, as in the opening, the poet is aspiring to an identity of the finite and the infinite that is not possible in life.

Emilia Viviani's epigraph has proved right: the soul that loves cannot be content with an earthly circumference of bliss; it "projects itself

---

[75] To John Gisborne, 18 June 1822 (*Letters*, II, 434).
[76] Medwin, *Life of Shelley*, ed. Forman, p. 282.

beyond creation and creates for itself in the infinite a world of its own," and not only the poet's words but also his mortality are the chains of lead that prevent his flight to it. "Love's very pain is sweet," the poem's *envoi* tells us,

But its reward is in the world divine
Which, *if not here*, it builds beyond the grave.   (597–98; itals. added)

Shelley has not quite despaired of a "brighter Hellas": the "world divine" may yet be "here." But it is evident that his faith in utopia has grown slight and nearly untenable, and his hope, like Emilia Viviani's, is obviously directed toward death. These last words, however, are not spoken by the poet; they are a chorus sung by his "Weak Verses," whom he addresses, together with all their "sisters" whom they call from "Oblivion's cave." Like the goddess Urania in *Adonais*, who is "chained to Time, and cannot thence depart," poetry belongs to the limited realm of mortality and cannot enter the "height of Love's rare Universe"[77] any more than can the earthly poet, who is also his poem. Yet, he will eventually slough off his worldliness, whereas his poems, at best, will persist in the domain of mortal man, singing their uncertain burden of love's reward: "So shall ye live" in the world, says the poet to his Verses, "when I am there" (599). Just as Shelley, despite the clear drift of his poem, has left open the slight, doubtful possibility of utopia, so it is probable that, with characteristic uncertainty of immortality also, he intended the meaning of "there" to be ambiguous: it could mean merely *"in* the grave," but its nearest reference is "beyond the grave" (598), where one may project a "world divine." The whole burden of all his poems, with all their striving after the ideal, Shelley realizes as he looks back over his career, has really been that love needs a perfect world, which, if it is impossible here—and the ultimate transfiguration of the island paradise into a postmortal state makes that likely—it "creates for itself in the infinite" ("nell' infinito un Mondo tutto per essa").

---

[77] Cf. *Lines Written among the Euganean Hills*, where, although illuminated by a transcendent light, poetry is a worldly river related to the human "deep wide sea of Misery."

15 Adonais

In *Alastor* Shelley had skeptically weighed the rewards of life against those of death and, despite his bias in favor of the Visionary, had tried to keep the question open. But all his strenuous effort in *Epipsychidion* to construct imaginatively a condition of perfect sublunary love and self-fulfillment converted itself irresistibly into a vision of the life beyond the grave. Shelley could never quite suppress the impulse to lift the veil of life, and the death of Keats provided him with occasion to devote himself exclusively to the theme of death, as though the author of *Alastor,* now persuaded that the Visionary of that poem was right, were to abandon all hopes for life and to explore the meaning of death. Keats had proved that the good, indeed, die first.

i

Shelley's decision to cast his lament for Keats in the shape of the Adonis legend and of the pastoral elegy was the result of another of those happy and precise findings by the imagination for which Shelley displayed exceptional talent in *Prometheus Unbound* and *Hellas.* The legend of a handsome mortal loved by a goddess, slain in his youth by an evil beast, and universally mourned, conformed perfectly to the conception of Keats as a poet favored by a divine spirit, slain in his early promise by malign critics, and depriving the world of a spirit of good by his absence. In its most obvious function, then, the skeletal form of the Adonis legend provided a nearly exact means of translating Keats's biography into a con-

462

ceptual pattern by assimilating the limited personal data to the archetypal myth. Moreover, since the conventions of the pastoral elegy originally grew out of the structure of such fertility myths as that of Adonis and were determined by this structure, legend and genre are nearly identical in pattern. Like the legend, the traditional artistic shape of the elegy expresses a way in which man has grasped and responded to the idea of life and death; it is an ordering that is valid because it corresponds to the laws of the mind, whether or not it corresponds to the structure of outward reality.

To these intricate elegiac conventions Shelley adhered with as much fidelity as he did to the Prometheus myth, the history of the Cenci family, and Aeschylus' *Persians*, even to the point of borrowing images, actions, and rhetorical patterns from the elegies of Bion and Moschus. Nevertheless, translating Keats into the mythic Adonis and casting the materials into the traditional elegiac form merely provided Shelley with a way of conceiving of his subject and giving it an outward shape. Since the borrowed conventions have to do with the point of view adopted in the poem rather than with its internal activities, their artistic efficacy is wholly measurable by the precision with which the Adonis myth, the elegiac genre, and Keats's biography are made consubstantial. Were the poem exhausted by revealing the presence of the myth and the elegiac form in it (a descriptive exercise taken for granted throughout this chapter), we could appraise it only as a formal construct—only, that is, for what it achieves stylistically as an adaptation of fresh substance to a given mold. Moreover, the myth and the conventions do not, in fact, constitute the whole, for both are generally abandoned by stanza 40 and do not account for the last fifteen stanzas. Consequently, efforts to read the poem solely in terms of these two controls have resulted in the stock complaint that, like most of Shelley's major poems, *Adonais* is a fractured structure, made up of a traditional elegy plus an appended quasi-Platonic commentary.[1] There is in the poem, however, a symbolic system of reference that, although operative within these traditional patterns and coexistent with them, embraces the total structure and makes *Adonais* a self-contained poem generating its own energies, a synthesized thought "containing within itself the principle of its own integrity." The value of observing how strictly it adheres to the pattern of pastoral elegy and myth lies mainly in thus discovering the economy with which Shelley manages these binding restraints so as to charge them with values that transcend their merely formal functions.

[1] Newman I. White's analysis is, as usual, fairly representative: "Shelley began, and continued half-way through the poem, under the influence of Bion and Moschus.... Though Shelley changed and elaborated with the freedom of a truly great poet and produced some beautiful stanzas based partly upon borrowed materials, the poem does not attain its full power until it becomes more fully Shelleyan" (*Shelley*, pp. 295–96). See also above, pp. 74–75n., 121.

The key to the poem's largest area of meaning—to the manner in which Keats's biography and the conventional myth become "the very image of life expressed in its eternal truth"—is to be found most readily in the significance of Shelley's decision to call Keats "Adonais" instead of "Adonis." Any relationship between Shelley's title and the Hebrew word "Adonai" has been suggested only rarely[2] and, even then, without exploring its implications. In the lexicon of the fifth-century Hesychius, the name "Adonis" is identified with the Phoenician word for "master," or "lord" ($\delta\epsilon\sigma\pi\acute{o}\tau\eta s$); and when this etymology was incorporated in the sixteenth-century *Thesaurus* of Stephanus, the information was added that perhaps the name is also related to the Hebrew word for lord, "Adonai." In the late eighteenth and early nineteenth centuries, ancient myths were being extensively re-evaluated by a large group of Casaubons intent upon finding the key to all mythologies. Although each syncretist pressed his own special thesis, all were bent on demonstrating that every myth is but a peculiar form of one archetypal myth and, consequently, that each archetypal deity appears under a variety of names. George Stanley Faber,[3] for example, borrowing from Pierre Huet, held it as "undoubted truth" that Adonis is the same as Mercury, Thamuz, Osiris, Bacchus, Vulcan, Zoroaster, Pan, Esculapius, Prometheus, Proteus, Perseus, Orpheus, Anubis, Janus, Noah, etc.[4] Many of these syncretists emphasized the archetypal nature of the name "Adonis" by pointing to its now-standard derivation from the Hebrew "Adon," or "lord," the plural form "Adonai" being used in the singular sense in the Old Testament as one of the names of God.[5] In addition, Macrobius contributed the tradition that identifies Adonis with the sun and interprets his story as a season myth.[6] "Adonis or Adonai," according to Richard Payne Knight, "was an Oriental (Phoenician and Hebrew) title of the Sun, signifying Lord."[7] "Adonis et Adonai," wrote Charles François Dupuis, "désignaient cet astre, Seigneur du Monde dans la fable orientale sur Adonis, dieu Soleil...."[8] The identity of the two names, "Adonis" and "Adonai," had been widely accepted among the mythographers and was generally drawn on to establish Adonis

[2] See *Poems of Shelley*, ed. J. Churton Collins (Edinburgh, n.d.), p. 237; and *Adonais*, ed. W. M. Rossetti (Oxford, 1903), p. 95.
[3] For Shelley's relations with Faber, see *Shelley and his Circle*, vol. II, ed. Cameron.
[4] *A Dissertation on the Mysteries of the Cabiri* (Oxford, 1803), I, p. 310n.
[5] One of the standard points of reference was Pierre Huet, *Demonstratio evangelica* (Lipsiae, 1694), p. 119.
[6] *Saturnalia* I. xxi.
[7] *The Symbolical Language of Ancient Art and Mythology* (New York, 1876; 1st ed., 1818), p. 85. Jacob Bryant is somewhat obscure, but at least implies the common origin of the two words. "Ad" he finds to be a radical meaning "king," and "On" a title of the sun; from this he concludes that from "Ad-On" "was formed... Adon, and Adonis" (*A New System: or, an Analysis of Ancient Mythology* [third ed., 1807], I, p. 27). See also John Jamieson, *Hermes Scythicus* (Edinburgh, 1814), p. 113.
[8] *Abrégé de l'origine de tous les cultes* (Paris, 1836; 1st ed., 1798), p. 288.

as the god of the season cycle, which most accepted as the basis of all myths.[9]

In telescoping the two words into the form "Adonais," Shelley, in the manner of the syncretists, was stripping the Adonis legend of its strictly Greek associations and consequently, while still able to use the details of that special legend, was raising it to the plane of archetypal symbolism. By bringing to the surface the derivation of "Adonis" from the word for divinity, he was, in effect, denying that he was employing a classical fable simply as the poetic vehicle for a lament for a particular person and was asserting that his theme was also, collectively, all those variant divinities, no matter what their special forms and names, by whom man has conceived of the godhead. But this Adonai embodied in Adonais has been variously conceived, since man has now worshipped fertility and life, and now the Power that resurrects the soul. As the Adonai, Adonais may therefore represent either of these interpretations of the presiding deity. The postulate of the following analysis of Shelley's elegy is that, like the three-stage evolution of the materials of *Epipsychidion* and the "Ode to Heaven," it progresses through three movements by means of a set of artistic controls at the core of the poem which repeatedly reshape Adonais' symbolic role as the god until he finally assumes that role which satisfies the poem's artistic requirements. In the opening section of the elegy, beneath the explicit lament for John Keats, though consubstantial with it, the imagery and the mode of expression will interpret Adonais as the fertility god—that god whom man has regarded as the power in the birth and death of Nature—in order to ask whether animation is the ultimate reality.

Given the assumption that Adonais is the season-god, the first seventeen stanzas form a coherent unit constituting the first movement, or hypothesis, of the elegy. Within the framework of this assumption, the general tentative statement being made there is that everything is nature, man as well as other forms of organized matter, and that all nature moves in time to its own annihilation, as it seems to do in the fable of *The Sensitive Plant*. Consequently, in the first movement, Adonais is not only Keats but also the tragic Lord of a religion of materialistic monism, and

[9] See, for example, N. A. Pluche, *Histoire du ciel* (Amsterdam, 1759), I, pp. 174–75. Like most of the mythographers, Pluche adds, "... Baal, ou Adonai, ou Adonis, ou Hero, tous noms qui signifient le Seigneur." Banier (*Mythology*, II, vii, 2): "...the Name of *Adonis*, which is much the same with that of *Adonai*, or Κύριος, *the Lord*, which was given to that same Prince, are [sic] all of them applicable to the Sun, who is as Master and Lord of Heaven." N. A. Boulanger (*Le Christianisme dévoilé*, in *Oeuvres*, [Amsterdam, 1794], IV, p. 24n.): Jehovah "étoit le nom ineffable du Dieu des Juifs, qui n'osoient le prononcer. Son nom vulgaire étoit *Adonai*, qui ressemble furieusement à l'Adonis des Phéniciens." *Le Christianisme dévoilé* has also been attributed to Holbach, whose *Système de la nature* played an important role in Shelley's thought. See also Augustin Calmet, *Dissertations* (Paris, 1720), II. ii. 427; [Thomas Blackwell], *Letters Concerning Mythology* (1748), p. 270; Johann Simonis, *Onomasticum Novi Testamenti* (1762), p. 186n.

the death of this divinity therefore appears for the moment to contain in itself the death of Nature. The condition that makes possible the poetic development of this tentative theme is Shelley's fusion of the various planes of reference in the name "Adonais": Keats (the particular person), Adonis (the legendary Greek who universalizes the person Keats), and Adonai–Adonis (the godhead who, as the spirit of animation, defines the protagonist as the great but perishable vitalizing power of the universe). What in turn allow this fusion are the common origin and form of both the fertility rites and the elegiac conventions. The elegiac ritual can therefore perform at the same time as biography, myth, and religious symbolism.

Because Adonais in the largest frame of reference is the sun-god, as Adonis was usually interpreted in the fertility myth—or, at any rate, is the symbol of the birth and death of nature—the quality of chill permeates the first movement. As the poem opens we learn that the dead Adonais' head is bound with frost (3); and this image reaches out in the three dimensions of reference: the frost is that of the cold corpse of Keats; the frost binds his head because frost binds (holds inert) nature in the dead winter of the year; and, by suggesting the crown of thorns, the band of frost becomes the sign of the god of animate nature, the wintry death of which is also the death of its god. This theme is then threaded through the developing movement: Adonais' heart and head are cold (80, 82), the wreath for his bier seems begemmed with frozen tears as though to emblematize his role (95), his cheek is frozen (99), and his lips are icy (105). Pierced by the shaft which flies in darkness (10–12), Adonais has perished prematurely like other great spirits, "suns" which have "sunk, extinct in their refulgent prime" (41–43).

Throughout the poem there is a recurrent opposition of two nature images which had long been part of Shelley's symbolism: light, or fire, the life symbol; and moisture, or mist, the symbol of mortality. This symbolism, derived from observation of the atmosphere and of vegetative growth, was, of course, fixed in a long tradition. In his translation of Proclus, for example, Thomas Taylor reported that "the poet calls men existing in generation ... humid, because their souls are drenched in moisture. ... souls, whether they are corporeal or incorporeal, while they attract bodies, must verge to humidity, and be incorporated with humid natures. ... But pure souls are averse from generation; on which account the same Heraclitus observes 'a dry soul is the wisest.' "[10] In this symbolic system, then, moisture is the principle of earthly existence, but if the soul is entirely deprived of light and fire, moisture becomes the death-principle. Porphyry, according to Taylor, added that the soul is collected from "the starry spheres," but that when the soul with its starry light "falls into bodies which consist of humid vapours, then a perfect ignorance of real

[10] The Philosophical and Mathematical Commentaries of Proclus (London, 1792), II, p. 291n.

being follows, together with darkness and infancy." Such a spirit "attracts moisture when it continually endeavors to associate with nature, whose operations are effected in moisture, and which are rather under than upon the earth."[11] Ultimately these notions (which are also related to belief in the transmutation of the elements) are Heraclitean and are summarized in this manner by Kathleen Freeman: the soul's "oscillation towards Fire is life in the absolute sense, the oscillation towards moisture is death; but existence in the relative sense is due to the combination of the two in this state of balance within limits."[12] Man is a vapor animated by light.

Correspondingly, the bodily life and death of Adonais are consistently expressed in imagery of moisture, and this imagery is consistent with the assumed season-myth, since the moist season is simultaneously the death of Nature and the principle for its renewed organic existence. Because the myth of Adonis told that his blood became a flower, Shelley can compare him to a pale flower "fed with true love tears, instead of dew" (48–49); and the vegetation-god, like the vegetation over which he presides, is washed in the night with "starry dew" (91). As darkness comes on, the mourning-tear of one of the Splendors falls on the dead season-god and appears "Like dew upon a sleeping flower" (86); the wreath thrown upon his bier is of "frozen tears" (95). The vegetation-god, that is, seems to be enacting the role of all vegetative nature in the early night by being covered with the dew that feeds its life. But this life-principle has become the death-principle, the moisture that emblematizes mourning, for it has proved to be tears instead of dew. The ambivalence of the image is especially evident in the comparison of Adonais' death to a "dewy sleep" (61): this could be either the sleep that refreshes life or the damp sleep of death. The funeral procession also is like "pageantry of mist on an autumnal stream" (117)—that is, a moisture that fails to rise and hovers near earth during its dying season. And later we are to learn that death itself is just such "a low mist" (391).

On the other hand, the animating power of light has been slain in the darkness; and essential vitality is embodied entirely in imagery of sun and light: Milton is one of the "sons of light," some poets are "tapers" that yet burn, and others are suns that have perished, "extinct in their refulgent prime." Correspondingly, not only the death of Adonais but also the apparent extinction of nature is conveyed by the effect of moisture on light and fire. One Splendor dulls "the barbed fire" of her arrows "against his frozen cheek" (99). Another is extinguished by "the damp death" and is eclipsed by Adonais' dead body in the same manner that a dying meteor "stains a wreath / Of moonlight vapour" (100–7). The sympathetic failure of Morning to come into being is the consequence of her failure to shake from her hair the mist of tears which should become dew and fall as

[11] *Select Works of Porphyry* (London, 1823), pp. 215–16.
[12] *Companion to the Pre-Socratic Philosophers* (Oxford, 1946), p. 123.

nourishment upon the ground; and the result is that the moist principle blots out the lights that should "kindle day" (120–23). Adonais and nature respond to the symbols of the life and death forces in exactly the same way.

The general dramatic course of the first movement is an enactment of these implicit seasonal functions of Adonais to express the first tentative hypothesis of the poem: all is matter, and the vitality it invests must inevitably be extinguished. For the moment Shelley is testing the thesis of Bion's lament for his nature-god: "all things have perished in his death." Indeed, we are told that Adonais has gone where all things "wise" (mind) and "fair" (material form) descend, never to return (24–25). The source in Bion reads merely: "O Persephone, take thou my husband...; for thou...gettest to thy share all that is beautiful." Shelley's addition of "wise" therefore seems especially significant, for its insertion erases the distinction between mind and matter, the human and the nonhuman.

What imparts to the first movement a quasi-dramatic progress is its being placed in a context of passing time, for with the death of Adonais the nature cycle begins the closing phase of its rotation. When the poem opens, it is still "blue Italian day" (59). Day yields to twilight (65) as the shadow spreads (66) and darkness comes (71–72). At length it is night, and images of moonlight (83, 107) and starriness (91) appear. Since the death of nature is also the death of its deity, the ending of day and the cessation of Adonais' life are really one. The shadow that "spreads apace" in the "twilight chamber" is that of Death slowly blotting out the life of Adonais, the sun-god; but it is also, in purely naturalistic terms, the lengthening shadow cast by the sun in its twilight sinking as it moves to its own extinction and leaves the world in the death of night. Moreover, just as Adonais has died but has not yet been destroyed physically by "Invisible Corruption," so twilight is the period after the sun has sunk below the horizon (and so is "dead") but before its light has ceased to be evident on earth. Both Adonais and the sun are gone and yet remain. Again the imagery works ambivalently so as to apply equally to Adonais and the nature whose sun, or vivifying principle, he symbolizes.

Morning now seeks to appear (120ff.), but in her sympathetic sorrow over the loss of the nature-god she cannot perform as she should. In accordance with the hyperbolic manner of elegiac personifications, she is prevented by her grief from arising in her proper radiance, for she unbinds her hair—the traditional sign of mourning—and dampens it with tears. In terms of nature, the morning moisture, which should "fall" as nourishing dew, remains in the sky as a mist because of nature's disorder and hides the sun and stars.[13] At the symbolic level, the death-principle is regnant,

---

[13] It had generally been believed that dew appears only in calm and serene weather and cannot fall when there is a "low mist" (see, for example, William Charles Wells, An Essay on Dew [1818], pp. 127–28); or, as Shelley expressed it, when, because of the death of the nature-god, "Afar the melancholy thunder moaned, / Pale Ocean in unquiet slumber lay, / And the wild Winds flew round, sobbing in their dismay" (124–26).

and it appears for the moment that in the death of the nature-god is contained the suspension of all natural processes. Thus, on the one hand, the nature-god remains suspended between death and destruction because the customary workings of "Invisible Corruption" have been postponed momentarily until "darkness, and the law / Of mortal change" are resumed. On the other hand, and in apparent sympathy, the day-cycle, now that the darkness has presumably brought with it the ravages of corruption, refuses to fulfill itself and remains suspended between a night that has passed and a morning that cannot come into being. The season-cycle also acts in seeming accord by remaining in similar suspension because of the loss of its vital power: winter (like night) has come and gone, but Spring (like Morning) grieves too greatly to act out her proper role, and, "as if she Autumn were" (137), refuses to waken the new year, sluggish in her sadness. Other natural phenomena, too, sympathize with the death of the nature-god: Echo will not reply, and the hyacinth and narcissus, which should bloom in spring, are withered.

The biographical aspects of Shelley's elegy have always been recognized clearly enough, since they are the most immediate subject and reside in the overt statements. What has not received due attention is that the theme of Nature is not merely accessory to the lament for Keats, but is the most inclusive reference of the first movement. The problems the elegy faces throughout—and not merely in the last dozen stanzas—are, What is death? and, therefore, What is the ultimate reality? The tentative (and eventually false) answer of the first movement is not overt, but is tightly folded into its normal workings as elegy; and yet the explicit, and true, answer that will evolve in the third movement will depend for its full realization upon being impelled by these earlier assertions in the same manner that the chaotic metaphors in the first movement of *Epipsychidion* generate their own subsequent reorganizations.

ii

The first movement, however, is not quite the self-contained statement this analysis has implied, for it continually tends to break out of its own boundaries and undermine its own assertions. Only imperfectly does it identify Adonais as the nature deity and state that the animation responsible for beauty and truth is destroyed; and this small residue of imperfection is restlessly pressing for a revision of the thesis. By containing in one expression both the death of Adonais and the setting of the sun, and by coordinating the fates of Adonais, the day-cycle, and the season-cycle, the movement seems to state that "all things wise and fair" descend forever to Persephone. But although Adonais is momentarily suspended between death and his annihilation, day is merely suspended between night (its death) and dawn (its rebirth), and the year is suspended between winter and spring. Hence the parallelism of Adonais and nature has only seemed to be true: the Splendor has *mistaken* the tear on Adonais for dew, and "He lies, *as if* in dewy sleep he lay" (61). This only vaguely concealed disparity between Adonais and nature will eventually force the restatement of meaning, just as in the traditional fertility rites the lamentation over the death of Adonis then gave way to the joyous celebration of his rebirth in spring. What gives impetus to that restatement—that is, the second movement of the elegy—is the temporal context, for the progress of time will reveal that nature's cessation has been only temporary.

Because of the momentary pause left by the failure of day and spring to come about, the first movement ends with a tension urging to be resolved. Now, as the next movement opens, the tension is released, and the nature-cycle is set in motion again. Winter has come and gone, such tokens of spring as the swallow reappear, and all nature is filled with a vital force. The birds whose song Echo would not repeat while nature paused in her activities (130) but whose amorousness foreshadowed the second movement, "now pair in every brake" (159). This discovery that nature does not end but forever renews herself is symbolized now by the fact that the bier of the "dead Seasons"—that is, the dead leaves and flowers, which, like a coffin, "contain" the dead Seasons—is overspread with "Fresh leaves and flowers" (158). In her inexorable cycle of death and birth nature can lament her past only by building on it a revitalized present.

But the discovery that nature ("All baser things," 169) is reborn brings with it full revelation that Adonais does not also revive: "*He* will awake no more, oh, never more!" (190). The italicized word sets up a contrast that was not relevant to the lament for Adonais in the first movement. The poem, therefore, is proceeding by a series of tentatively held hypotheses, each being pushed out of shape by the images and mode of expression that convey it, until it becomes transmuted into the succeeding hypothesis. The implied materialistic monism of the first movement has therefore evolved into a dualism of nature, which forever passes through a cycle of life, death, and rebirth, and Mind (Adonais), which terminates in decay. This antithesis of cyclical nature and perishable Mind motivates all the opening stanzas of this next stage. For example, as the "living Might" (218) Urania can pave her path to Adonais' death-chamber with "eternal flowers" (216) because vegetative life is "eternal" in its endless round. But in her efforts to revive Adonais she can, at best, cause the breath to revisit him for a brief moment and then must yield the victory to Death. Consequently the poet complains that the objects of knowledge persist, whereas the knowing power, "the intense atom," at length is extinguished. In the opening stanzas of the second movement, then, the elegiac pattern of lamentation and rejoicing reached a kind of false climax. The sluggish, agonized mourning for the season-god gives way at this point to something approximating joy in the discovery that nature is now reanimated:

> Through wood and stream and field and hill and Ocean
> A quickening life from the Earth's heart has burst
> As it has ever done, with change and motion,
> From the great morning of the world when first
> God dawned on Chaos; in its steam immersed
> The lamps of Heaven flash with a softer light;
> All baser things pant with life's sacred thirst;
> Diffuse themselves; and spend in love's delight,
> The beauty and the joy of their renewed might.   (163–71)

But the joy is at once converted into renewed and even more profound despair when it is recognized that Adonais is not identical with nature and is not renewed with the cycle of the seasons. At this point, therefore, Adonais must be divested of his illusory role of nature-god and be known as merely the perishable cognitive power, the symbol of mind hinted at even in the earlier description of him as having molded sensory qualities into "thought" (118–19).

The poem, then, is not dramatic if we take this term as descriptive of a work of art whose meaning resides in the total design marked out by the course of its materials. But it is dramatic in a manner somewhat akin to embryological growth, for it passes through discrete stages that superficially bear little resemblance to its final form and yet in which that final form organically inheres. By making only imperfect revelations, the materials of the poem, like those of *Epipsychidion*, drive forward through three successive tableaux, each being fashioned by the redistribution of the unstably ordered materials of the previous tableau; and each of the self-generated redistributions rejects the previous hypothesis concerning reality and death, and shapes itself into a new and higher hypothesis. By this means Shelley evolved a special way of proceeding that transformed his basic open-ended skepticism into a kind of poetics of assertion. The radical indeterminacy of poems like *Alastor, Julian and Maddalo*, and the hymns of Pan and Apollo, we have repeatedly seen, is his frank admission that he has no assured basis on which to arrive at truth: everything presents two contradictory faces, both of which are equally defensible and equally untenable. Lacking any grounds of assurance, he can at best arrive, beyond indeterminacy, at negative truths: a proposition is rendered probable, not on its own grounds, but because its negative proves "so difficult to conceive." Even when, in poems like *Mont Blanc* and *The Sensitive Plant*, he distinguishes between the two opposing faces of reality in terms of the senses and the imagination, and opts for the imaginative vision as the more believable, he remains honestly skeptical and acknowledges the purely speculative, or fideistic, nature of his choice, as the tentative endings of those poems suggest. In *Prometheus Unbound*, however, he fully developed a poetics of affirmation by implicit repudiation of error, akin to the processes of satire. If there are no assured first principles, at least one doctrine may be shown to be more beautiful, more aesthetically whole, harmonious, and gratifying than its contrary, and the moral and philosophic validity of *Prometheus Unbound* is relative to its aesthetic superiority to the Aeschylean drama that it reshapes and transforms. By the same token the implicit presence of Aeschylus' play is essential because its deficiency is the point of departure for, and the prime measure of, the sufficiency of Shelley's transformation. This is essentially the basis of the poetics of probabilism evolutionary to the point of unanticipated discovery that Shelley developed in *Epipsychidion*, where each successive effort to shape the original chaotic imagery is more harmonious and repudiates the previous formulation, until the sudden collapse of that aesthetic thrust is the revelation that man's aspiration to his absolute completeness and to perfect form can be fulfilled only in afterlife. But it is a revelation whose first principle is only the indeterminate possibilities in chaos—hence the significance of the fact that Shelley's heaven is a "firmament pavilioned upon chaos"[14]—and whose evolution has been brought about by the search for form. Similarly, in *Adonais* the immortality of the human soul is not a truth that can be assumed or demonstrated on its own grounds; instead, each of the first two tentative hypotheses about death and reality collapses and is rejected because the structures given the imagery that persistently embodies them, prove, like Aeschylus' drama, inadequate and incomplete. Yet, in that same imagery are the dynamic potentialities that demand that it be reshaped into a succeeding hypothesis more artistically whole and self-sustaining. The skeptic's first principle is not an axiom or a dogma but only some unassertive and disordered objects of perception; their meaning is a function of the form into which the poet's mind draws them, and his successive tentative faiths are not convictions but only aesthetic decisions. The credible "truth" the poem finally achieves is born entirely out of the errors and half-truths of aesthetic inadequacies. It is toward the final movement of the elegy, then, that all its internal force evolves in order that, by poetic logic, it may arrive at its ultimate revelation. That movement will be the fulfillment of implications latent in the first two, and the poem will complete itself artistically only when these latent factors have expended their shaping energy. Consequently, the total significance of the earlier workings of the images becomes evident only retrospectively, after the design those same images trace out in the final stage is clear.

[14] *Hellas*, 772. Cf. the so-called Prologue to *Hellas*, 2–3, where God assembles his angels in the "Senate House whose floor / Is Chaos."

At the beginning of the elegy, for example, Keats's poems are described as

> fading melodies,
> With which, like flowers that mock the corse beneath,
> He had adorned and hid the coming bulk of Death. (16–18)

The living flowers derisively defy the death above which they grow, but their gesture is pathetically futile because in the thematic context of the first movement life must eventually end in the nothingness of death. The best creations of life can only disguise and conceal temporarily Death's *coming* "bulk" (that is, the trunk of the dead body), just as the flowers cannot forever hide the fact that the corpse is the end to which they and all other things come. With the opening of the second movement these same images reappear, but in a significantly different context: when the leprous corpse is touched by the spirit of organic life, it

> Exhales itself in flowers of gentle breath;
> Like incarnations of the stars, when splendour
> Is changed to fragrance, they illumine death
> And mock the merry worm that wakes beneath. (173–76)

Now that the theme is the everlasting cycle of animate nature, the corpse which had been conceived of as lying inert beneath the living flowers and as their irreconcilable antithesis is discovered, instead, to be nurturing the growth of the flowers, and in this sense is giving itself to becoming their life. For in nature death feeds life, and life "illumines" death. The living flowers no longer defy the possibility of their own decay ("mock the corse beneath"), for they will decay, but only to become life again. Instead, the corpse-fed flowers mock a new factor—the worm which, by destroying the forms of matter, vainly hopes to play the same role as the "eternal Hunger" waiting to reduce the physical Adonais (69). That is, the materialism of the first movement is being denied because in nature's eternal cycle all things change and nothing is annihilated—the flowers scorn the worm. The stanza therefore marks the full development of a division impelled by the incompletely asserted materialistic monism of the first movement. The discrepancy between Adonais' being suspended between death and destruction and nature's being caught between death and rebirth has widened into an opposition; and consequently the poet now evaluates as ultimate realities Animation (nature) and Mind (Adonais), to find that only the first is eternal in its unbroken cyclical course.

The last movement of the elegy, opening with stanza 38, is also impelled, like the second movement, by a gradual adjustment of perspective. Having castigated the reviewers who had attacked Keats, the poet finds at least this much consolation: that through death Adonais has escaped his enemies forever. However, the poet is still caught between his double vision that nature's cycle is eternal but that mind is destroyed. From this neutral area he can look both back and forward, and the ambiguity of his position is contained in the dramatic irony of his words: "He wakes or sleeps with the enduring dead" (336). If Adonais sleeps, he has lost all being; if he wakes, he now exists in the true reality. Consequently, "enduring dead" is ambiguous: the dead may endure because in the perspective of mortality only nonexistence is everlasting; but through the excessive force in the meaning of "enduring" the words also struggle to divulge the eternity of the spirit. Urged by this intimation to the brink of his final discovery, the poet now reverses the entire perspective of the first two movements:

Thou canst not soar where he is sitting now.—
Dust to the dust! but the pure spirit shall flow
Back to the burning fountain whence it came,
A portion of the Eternal, which must glow
Through time and change, unquenchably the same.   (337–41)

The first movement implied that matter is the ultimate and enduring reality, since vitality is not: death is total extinction. The second movement distinguished vitality from spirit, or mind, the former passing through an endless circle of renewal and the latter ending in annihilation. Stanza 38 then reverts to the materialism of the first movement ("Dust to the dust") but opposes it to the revelation that it is spirit that is eternal, not because its course is cyclical, but because it is resurrected to another context of existence. This readjustment of vision that the nature of his materials has urged upon him now allows the poet to resolve his momentary doubt about the truth of death and to establish the position that the last movement will elaborate and celebrate: "Peace, peace! he is not dead, he doth not sleep—/ He hath awakened from the dream of life" (343–44). Ultimate reality is neither matter nor vitality, but spirit: death is access to eternity.

Perhaps the clearest insight into these three successive perspectives of the elegy can be gained by observing the significances of the key word "change." First, although Adonais is dead, the "eternal Hunger" dares not deface "So fair a prey, till darkness, and the law / Of mortal *change*, shall fill the grave which is her maw" (71–72). In keeping with the first hypothesis, change, to which all living things are subject, is the inexorable law that results in destruction. The second movement then opens with an account of the life-death-rebirth cycle of nature:

Through wood and stream and field and hill and Ocean
A quickening life from Earth's heart has burst

As it has ever done, with *change* and motion,
From the great morning of the world when first
God dawned on Chaos.   (163–67)

Change is now understood to be the law whereby Nature forever renews herself, rebuilding life from death. Consequently in the world of matter and motion change is the form of eternity and stands in direct opposition to the previous conception of change as destruction, represented by the contrasting passage, "*He* will awake no more." Finally, the poem reaches its resolution when this second thesis can be inverted: dust returns to dust, but the pure spirit of Adonais has become

A portion of the Eternal, which must glow
Through time and *change*, unquenchably the same.   (340–41)

Now change is only the character of sublunary perpetuity; greater than the circle of change is the enduring sameness of the spiritual eternity into which the soul of Adonais is absorbed. Both of the first two senses of "change" are at last collected and adjusted to the final interpretation in the line "The One remains, the many change and pass" (460). As matter, the Many will "pass" (change by being destroyed: first movement); as animation, they will "change" (be renewed cyclically: second movement). But the soul of man is eternal, being changeless (third movement). Adonais will awake forever.

Consequently, in the final movement Adonais drops his false role as the season-god Adonis and becomes the symbol of mind and spirit—the Adonai who is the resurrection god. The change of roles is an easy one because of the intimate connection between the resurrection pattern of Christ's career and the nature cycle that Adonis presided over. The parallelism was frequently commented on by the mythographers of Shelley's day, Dupuis, for example, noting that both Adonis and Adonai are the sun-god, "qui, comme Christ, sortait victorieux du tombeau après qu'on avait pleuré sa mort."[15] Thus the poem is built around two elegiac movements from death to rebirth, from lamentation to rejoicing. The false one progresses from the death of the season-god to the revival of nature. The other begins at the height of the first elegiac pattern in the ironic revelation that the revival of nature has not brought about the expected revival of its godhead, and so progresses from the apparent death of mind and soul ("th' intense atom glows / A moment, then is quenched in a most cold repose," 179–80) to discovery of an eternal spiritual existence ("the pure spirit shall flow / Back to the burning fountain whence it came, / A portion of the Eternal," 338–40).

Yet, these elegiac patterns are not quite the inner compulsion of

[15] *Abrégé de l'origine de tous les cultes*, p. 288.

Adonais. Still another and more important design causes the third movement to be the necessary consummation of the poem, for throughout the first two movements the elegiac conventions have been embodied in images (like that of "change") whose powers are there merely generated, not released. These images are not the surface business of the first two movements and seem no more than the normally appropriate vehicles for the elegiac machinery, but as the poem continues they become charged with energy and compel its further progress. Vehicle and tenor, that is, interchange positions: originally the vehicles for the elegiac conventions, this image complex becomes the main tenor, and the conventions become its vehicle, so that what is almost accidentally deposited in a false hypothesis about death and reality exerts a pressure for its own aesthetic fulfillment and thereby for a more probable hypothesis.

One of the most obvious of these transmutations, accompanying Adonais' exchange of roles, is the reinterpretation of the images of stanza 19 so that they come to express in stanza 43, not the perpetual cycle of nature, but the resurrection of the spirit. Stanza 19 reads:

> Through wood and stream and field and hill and Ocean
> A quickening life from the Earth's heart has burst
> As it has ever done, with change and motion,
> From the great morning of the world when first
> God dawned on Chaos; in its steam immersed
> The lamps of Heaven flash with a softer light;
> All baser things pant with life's sacred thirst;
> Diffuse themselves; and spend in love's delight,
> The beauty and the joy of their renewed might.   (163–71)

Since Shelley is here tracing the course whereby in the world of matter and motion organic life renews itself, the vital power bursts from the heart of earth itself; and organic things, thirsting for their earthly vitality, diffuse their material selves among other living things as odor, color, taste.[16] Almost precisely the same imagery reappears in the last movement:

> He is a portion of that loveliness
> Which once he made more lovely: he doth bear

---

[16] Chambers' *Cyclopaedia*, art. "Diffusion": "According to [modern scientists], there is no other *Diffusion*, but that of corporeal substance, emitted in minute effluvia, or particles, into a kind of atmosphere all around the body; which *Diffusion* of corpuscles some call *atmospherical*, as being supposed to be terminated by a circle, whereof the *diffusing* body is the centre. Every body, it is now proved, has its sphere of activity, or *Diffusion*, within which the particles, or corpuscles, torn from it, and flying away, have a sensible effect, as we see in odorous, sonorous, etc. bodies." It is consistent with their context that Shelley's words "Diffuse themselves" have this materialistic meaning; the animating force manifests itself in that material diffusion that we call sensory qualities.

His part, while the one Spirit's plastic stress
Sweeps through the dull dense world, compelling there,
All new successions to the forms they wear;
Torturing th' unwilling dross that checks it's flight
To it's own likeness, as each mass may bear;
And bursting in it's beauty and it's might

From trees and beasts and men into the Heaven's light.   (379–87)

But here the subject is the restoration of the soul to the One, not the reawakening of the vital power; and consequently the materials of stanza 19 have become reordered to reveal to us the difference. The "quickening life" has become reidentified as the plastic stress of the "one Spirit"; this force does not spring out of matter as the regenerative principle does, but is outside matter, working through it to shape it toward a likeness of its own spirituality. The "thirst" of the Many for the fire of the eternal light (485)—that "inextinguishable thirst for immortality" that impels man, as Shelley wrote in the note to *Hellas*,—is the spiritual counterpart of the "sacred thirst" of "All baser things" for organic existence. And whereas the animate power that has "burst" from the earth causes a material diffusion throughout nature, now the spiritual beauty and power of the "one Spirit's plastic stress" is "bursting" from the Many so that the One may be reflected back "into the Heaven's light" whence it came. What has been repudiated is not the original images, but the original ordering and interpretation of them, and this revision of imagistic values has brought about a revision of their contextual theses.

iii

The largest amount of the poem's energy drains into the star image that becomes explicit when Adonais is welcomed into heaven as Vesper (stanza 46), but meanwhile the image has been made part of the star-flower complex that we have already seen to be the central symbolism of *The Sensitive Plant*. Flowers, for example, are likened to "incarnations of the stars, when splendour / Is changed to fragrance" (174–75). The flower, therefore, not only is the appropriate symbol of the organic life that, in the first movement, vainly defies death and then, in the second, is renewed by the impulse death gives to life; it also is the earthly, mortal manifestation of a star, just as Keats, it will be discovered, is the mortal form of Adonais-Vesper. Keats, like the flower, is the incarnation of a star. Moreover, dew, the symbol of mortal existence, naturally associates itself with flower: the tear lies on the eyes of the dead Adonais "Like dew upon a sleeping flower" (86); and Adonais grew "Like a pale flower...fed with true love tears, instead of dew" (48–49). Thus through the relation of flower to star an analogous relation has also been established between their adjuncts, dew and light, so that there are both horizontal and vertical relations among Keats-Adonais (the nature god) and Adonais-Vesper, flower and star, dew and light; that is, the relation may also be stated as one between Adonais-flower-dew and Vesper-star-light. With this final extension, the image pattern attains its full symbolic function, the dew-moisture representing the principle of organic life and light representing absolute life. Both these last images, for example, are fittingly brought together to symbolize the paradoxical act of preserving the dead body: "One from a lucid urn of *starry dew* / Washed his light limbs as if embalming them" (91–92). Later Shelley can use the same images and the assumed metamorphic relation of flower and star to symbolize the translation from organic life to eternal life: "Thou young Dawn / Turn all thy dew to splendour" (362–63). But for the moment it is essential only to notice that in so extending his imagery Shelley is far from capricious.

The star image is also related to Urania, whom Shelley has made the mother of Adonais, instead of his lover. In her traditional astronomical role Urania's planet is Venus, one of whose appearances is Vesper, the evening star, and the other Lucifer, the morning star. Hence it is within the potentialities of the myth that Adonis-Adonais eventually become one manifestation of the star of Venus Urania: "thou Vesper of our throng" (414). That Shelley intended this metempsychosis from Keats-Adonais to Vesper to be central to the poem is evident in his having prefaced to it a verse from the *Greek Anthology* attributed to Plato and translated elsewhere by Shelley as follows:

Thou wert the morning star among the living,
Ere thy fair light had fled;
Now, having died, thou art as Hesperus, giving
New splendour to the dead.

The very tradition that the epigraph has reference to further integrates the star into the imagistic pattern of the poem, for, according to ancient belief, the soul is derived from the starry spheres, and great earthly spirits are immortalized by their translation into heavenly bodies. In the words of Thomas Maurice, "almost every nation of the ancient world united in considering [the stars] as the residence of departed spirits and the glorious receptacles of beatified virtues."[17]

Paralleling these metamorphic relationships between Adonais and Vesper and between flower and star is the ancient doctrine of the transmutation of the elements, which taught that by rarefaction earth becomes moisture, air, and then fire, or light; and a cognate belief held that the light of the stars is nourished by moist exhalations from earth. There are in the elegy, then, three intimately related symbolic systems of transmuta-

[17] *Indian Antiquities* (1794), II, p. 107.

tion: Adonais becomes the star Vesper; flower becomes star; and dew (associated with Adonais and flower) becomes light (associated with star). Hence, since flowers are embodiments of stars, or a splendor changed to fragrance, at the crucial point in the poem the poet can command Dawn to turn the dew to splendor (363). This transformation now operates at multiple levels. Descriptively, the dew glistens in the morning brightness. In terms of the transmutation of elements, moisture becomes light. Symbolically, the earth-flower becomes the heaven-star of which it has been the incarnation. At the highest plane of meaning this is the preparation for Adonais' return to his spiritual origin, Vesper. Porphyry, Thomas Taylor reports, wrote that "Whenever . . . the soul earnestly endeavours to depart from nature, then she becomes a dry splendour, without a shadow, and without a cloud, or mist. For moisture gives subsistence to a mist in the air; but dryness constitutes a dry splendour from exhalation."[18] At all these levels the statement being made is that the Many return to the One, the burning fountain, or source, whence they came.

Within the implied nature of Vesper resides a significant characteristic that cuts across all these systems of imagery and binds them together as variant forms of the same concept. As the epigraph from Plato makes clear, Vesper is only one phase of Venus. In reality Venus is always present, even though earthly man cannot see it in the daylight, and even though he calls it Lucifer in the morning and Vesper at night. As in *The Sensitive Plant*, the star is eternal, and its apparent mutability is a function of our defective senses. Lucifer and Vesper are the same, just as, according to Mary, Shelley believed that "hereafter, *as now*, he would form a portion" of the One, and just as Keats is eventually known to be eternal, the living Keats having been the morning phase of Venus' star, the dead Keats being the evening phase. In this manner the unity implicit in the star image will ultimately bind together the systems of merely apparent oppositions in the poem—the life and death of nature, the pairings of star and flower, splendor and fragrance, light and dew, morning and evening, Vesper and Adonais. When the poem reaches its climax this essential and eternal unity will supplant what appeared in the second movement as only the cyclical change of nature. These interrelations within the imagistic system do not constitute the artistry of the elegy any more than does Shelley's strict adherence to the traditional elegiac patterns; nor indeed are they explicit. Rather, they are the assumed and pre-existing interconnections with which Shelley shapes the texture that makes his artistic statement. They are the laws of the aesthetic cosmos within which *Adonais* exists as an aesthetic organism, and they determine how it goes about its business of performing artistically.

For the stellar apotheosis of Adonais and its significance the poem has

[18] *Select Works of Porphyry*, p. 216.

carefully prepared by subtle foreshadowings and gestures that make it the inevitable climax of Adonais' role. Even in the first movement, where the theme is the inevitability of decay, there had developed an almost unnoticeable contradiction: although Adonais will arise no more, the "clear Sprite" of Milton "Yet reigns o'er earth; the third among the sons of light" (36). The contradiction is hardly discernible because in their immediate setting the images of stars and sun serve only as metaphors of worldly fame. Like Keats, Milton also went "Into the gulf of death" and hence came to the same end as all other living things; but the power of his works ("his clear Sprite") persists in the mortal world ("reigns o'er earth"). It is only when we think ahead to the third movement and the transformation of Adonais into Vesper that we recognize the dramatic irony in the images and know they had been symbols masquerading for the moment as mere metaphors and that they had not yet attained the most beautiful—and true—organization that they demand. As symbol, the star image ("third among the sons of light") has been urging a statement that the first movement does not allow but that the third will confirm: although the physical Milton has been destroyed, his soul ("his clear Sprite") is immortal, and by returning to the One, that is, by becoming a reigning star, he is, like Adonais-Vesper, "a presence to be felt and known." Beneath the surface statement of the passage, it is not earthly fame, but spiritual immortality that is being measured in astronomical terms. And thus with dramatic irony the lines

> he went, unterrified,
> Into the gulf of death; but his clear Sprite
> Yet reigns o'er earth; the third among the sons of light   (34–36)

parallel and foreshadow the fate of Adonais:

> Dust to the dust! but the pure spirit shall flow
> Back to the burning fountain whence it came,
> A portion of the Eternal, which must glow
> Through time and change, unquenchably the same.   (338–41)

Yet, these astronomical images, when read symbolically, only adumbrate the final interpretation of Vesper, for they are stated with qualifications. Even the subliminal symbolic meaning does not directly assert the immortality of Milton's spirit as that of Adonais' will later be affirmed: Milton's spirit *yet* reigns, but time is still a factor. The star which is Milton's spirit has climbed to its "bright station" (38), that is, to its apogee, that highest point of its orbit when it appears to remain, caught between its direct and retrograde movements. The "station," then, is only a seeming permanence. Finally, the astronomical metaphor is applied to the earthly reputations of other poets also: some are still remembered on earth, others forgotten. But when, with hindsight, we read the metaphoric images as symbols of immortality, we find the passage has not been saying that all spirits are immortal: some are only tapers that "*yet* burn through the night of time"; others are suns that have perished utterly; still others have "sunk, extinct in their refulgent prime" (43). The veiled symbolism is only groping toward its full meaning. The word "prime," incidentally, relates both to the metaphoric (youth) and to the symbolic (dawn); and the word "refulgent," like the star imagery here, covertly foreshadows the later development of the poem's theme. Superficially it refers simply to the brightness of the planets, but it also prepares the way for the later expression of earthly life as the shining back (*re-fulgere*) of the light of the One by mortals ("as each are mirrors of / The fire for which all thirst," 484–85; "the one Spirit's plastic stress ... bursting [back] ... into the Heaven's light," 381–87).

Probably the most delicate and complex preparation for the final significance of light and star appears in the second movement when the poet complains that "th' intense atom glows / A moment, then is quenched in a most cold repose" (179–80). The context has drawn a distinction between two kinds of matter: the reality of one is dependent upon its animation, which is recurrently restored; that of the other, upon the power of knowing, which is "quenched" forever. Of the possible meanings of the word "atom" the immediate context utilizes its association with Epicurean materialism: the mind is only a glowing atom, an ultimate particle of matter having momentarily the power to know. But the passage in which the word appears also provides all the motives for a subsequent shift of context and hence a development of a wholly different sense of the word. A now obsolete meaning of "atom" is "one of the particles of dust which are rendered visible by light; a mote in the sunbeam" (*OED*); and in this sense Shelley occasionally used the word, often associating it with stars— a star, for example, is "A quenchless atom of immortal light."[19] The line says what it must in its setting: mind is matter which must ultimately lose its principle as mind. But the imagery also contains near its surface all the elements of the final truth of the poem. Mind, it will be revealed, is truly an atom in a sunbeam, for the Many are "mirrors of / The fire for which all thirst." But it will be discovered that the star-soul does not cease, nor is the light withdrawn: the soul will return to the One, which "must glow / Through time and change, *unquenchably* the same." The imagery is basically right; the interpretation is wrong, even though the imagery is gesturing toward the truth. The earthly mind will indeed prove to be a

[19] "Fragments Written for *Hellas*," 20. See also *Triumph of Life*, 445–47; *Epipsychidion*, 477–79; *Scenes from the "Magico Prodigioso"* of Calderon, III. 167; "Ode to Heaven," 18.

star, a quenchless atom of immortal light, for Adonais will prove to be Vesper, one of the "star-atoms keen."[20]

Before the full significance of the astronomical imagery can be seen clearly, it will be necessary to examine a set of companion images. For it is not sufficient to say that the world-picture controlling the poem consists of mist, or moisture (the mortal principle), light and fire (immortal, or absolute, life), and the interpenetration of the two (the condition for earthly existence). To this cosmology must be added the symbolism of the atmosphere, "that part of the air next the earth, which receives vapours and exhalations; and is terminated by the refraction of the sun's light."[21] Were it not for this vaporous atmosphere, the space outside the earth would consist only of "aether," which is distinguished from atmosphere "in that it does not make any sensible refraction of the rays of light, which air [i.e. atmosphere] does."[22] In William Nicholson's *British Encyclopedia*, which Shelley read, he would have found an account both of the necessity of atmosphere to organic life and of its role in the diffusion of light:

Atmosphere . . . is essential to the existence of all animal and vegetable life, and even to the constitution of all kinds of matter whatever . . . for by it we literally may be said to live, move, and have our being. . . . Without the atmosphere no animal could exist; vegetation would cease, and there would be neither rain nor refreshing dews to moisten the face of the ground; and though the sun and stars might be seen as bright specks, yet there would be little enjoyment of light, could we ourselves exist without it. Nature indeed, and the constitutions and principles of matter, would be totally changed if this fluid were wanting.

In this cosmology Shelley found his key symbols, the ideal spiritual condition being the sun's light undiffracted by atmospheric interference with its purity. By exploiting permutations of these symbols, a large part of the poem proceeds to its thematic tasks.

In the perspective of the first movement, we have seen, death is a mist so thick that it extinguishes light. The failure of nature to pursue its normal movement from death to rebirth is owing to the fact that the hair of Morning was "Wet with the tears which should adorn the ground" and hence "Dimmed the aerial eyes that kindle day" (122–23). The dew, which should announce the revival of the day-cycle and nourish organic life, remains the death-principle, an extraordinary heavy mist of atmosphere that obliterates the animating light. When, however, the second movement begins, the relationship of light and the moist atmosphere becomes readjusted so that the two interpenetrate to symbolize nature's organic life, which is now proposed as the ultimate reality. The "lamps of

[20] *Epipsychidion*, 505.
[21] Chambers' *Cyclopaedia*, art. "Atmosphere."
[22] *Ibid.*, art. "Air."

Heaven," by immersing themselves in earth's "steam"[23]—its atmosphere—
"flash with a softer light" (167–68), just as in *Hellas* the same interpenetration of sunlight and atmosphere symbolizes the existence of Christ on
earth. Because of the interfusion of these two principles, the vitalizing
power inherent in earth's heart bursts forth and reanimates all things.
Momentarily this appears to be the only "good" and therefore to resolve
the poet's despair over the death of the season-god, for the atmosphere
causes the harsh "flash" of the naked brilliance to become the "softer light"
responsible for organic life. But it is only a partial resolution, for the poet
has been careful to apply these values only to all "baser things." When
he finds that the mind and soul of Adonais have not returned with the
rebirth of Nature, the celestial imagery takes on yet another form and
value.

"Beyond our atmosphere," Shelley wrote, "the sun would appear a
rayless orb of fire in the midst of a black concave. The equal diffusion of
its light on earth is owing to the refraction of the rays by the atmosphere,
and their reflection from other bodies."[24] More specifically, the diffraction
of the rays by the atmosphere causes the various colors we call "sky," and
the color of other objects is the consequence of their failure to reflect all
the wave lengths of white light. This, of course, is the literal meaning of
the statement that the Many burn "bright or dim" in proportion as they
mirror the light of the One. Color, then, is the special characteristic of the
world bounded by the atmosphere. Therefore, in discovering that in the
realm where light and atmosphere interpenetrate, nature is revived in an
endless cycle, but not the soul of man, the poet now knows that

> As long as skies are *blue*, and fields are *green*,
> Evening must usher night, night urge the morrow,
> Month follow month with woe, and year wake year to sorrow.
>
> (187–89; itals. added)

In other words, the moist atmosphere is not merely the symbol of mortality
in that, alone, it is the principle of death, and, when infused with the
light of the sun, the principle of earthly existence. It is also the factor that
diffuses the white sunlight (the One) and separates it from the area where
light is only partially refracted and so becomes colors (the Many). Therefore, so long as man is confined to the sub-atmospheric world of color—
that is, of imperfection—he will find that there Nature forever turns her
wheel, but the soul of man passes, never to return. The passage is not

[23] In the posthumous edition of 1829 the word reads, "stream." But in the first
edition the word is "steam," and in the manuscript Shelley first wrote, "light," then
"vapour," and then "steam" (MS e. 20, fol. 28ᵛ). These facts, together with the
imagistic requirements of the poem, seem to make it nearly conclusive that the
reading should be "steam."
[24] *Queen Mab*, I. 242–43n.

evaluative; it simply states the poet's observation. In context, "As long as" means forever: the cycle of mutability is unending and unavoidable. But the contingency of color on the atmosphere also presses toward a recognition of a possible realm outside the atmosphere of mortality, where different physical conditions prevail and hence, symbolically, different spiritual ones. "As long as" therefore also suggests that man's limitation to the world's perpetual mutability need not be forever.

It is this implication of other physico-spiritual conditions beyond the atmosphere that the last movement of the poem then develops. By reversing directions—by replacing descent ("he is gone, where all things wise and fair / Descend," 24–25) with ascent ("He has outsoared the shadow of our night," 352), by substituting fire for the death-chill, by transmuting dew into light instead of star into flower—Shelley is exploring the area outside the atmosphere and finds there the symbol of spiritual immortality. Consequently he now calls upon Air, filled with the death-mist that had blotted out the sun and stars:

> thou Air
> Which like a mourning veil thy scarf hadst thrown
> O'er the abandoned Earth, now leave it bare
> Even to the joyous stars which smile on its despair! (366–69)

Now the atmosphere is no longer a "good" that softens the harsh glare and permits organic life; the pure brilliance has become the "good" because eternity is the "white radiance." The atmosphere is now, as it was in the first movement, the "damp Death"; and because the final theme is the immortality of the pure spirit, the poet implores that this mortal principle be removed. Since it is the atmosphere that blots out the stars in daytime by diffusing the rays of the sun, the removal of the atmosphere-mortality would allow man to perceive the immortal star-spirits despite the light of the dawning sun. Were the mourning death-principle of "Air" removed, man could perceive directly the eternity of the spirit, for the stars are ever-present, their apparent coming and going being the consequence only of the mist that surrounds the earth and causes the seeming mutability. When, in the last lines of the elegy, the poet feels himself drawn to the condition of Adonais, now returned to his spiritual source, he expresses himself in precisely the same imagery: "That Light whose smile kindles the Universe...now beams on me, / Consuming the last clouds of cold mortality" (478–86). For him, too, the light of the sun has evaporated the mourning veil of mortality and left open the path to the reunion of his soul with the One.

Taken in conjunction with the other occurrences of similar imagery, it becomes clear that the conclusion of the elegy is not the poet's weak plea for suicide, but a prayer that the limited spiritual existence on earth expand into a pure and infinite spiritual life; that in mortal life one's soul may so brightly mirror the fire of the One that this fire will burn bright and so consume "the last clouds of cold mortality." The emphasis is not upon the destruction of the mortal self, but upon the enlargement of the earthly soul until "Heaven's light," which burns bright in proportion as the earthly soul mirrors it, will remove the mortal atmosphere. The imagery makes it clear that the poet does not assume that when mortal existence ends, spiritual existence begins, but that the Many are only imperfect individualizations of the One, just as color is an imperfection of the white radiance, and that death permits the unindividualized and hence unbounded spiritual life outside mutability. It is because of the present purification of the poet's earth-bound soul that the "breath whose might I have invoked in song / Descends on me" (487–88); it is because this spirit has descended to the poet that "The massy earth and sphered skies are riven!" (491)—that is, that the atmospheric veil is partially removed and the earth left bare to the stars, or that Death is shattering the many-colored dome of the sky. And it is because of this breach the One has made in the mortal principle, not because the poet wants to destroy himself, that

> I am borne darkly, fearfully, afar;
> Whilst, burning through the inmost veil of Heaven,
> The soul of Adonais, like a star,
> Beacons from the abode where the Eternal are. (492–95)

In view of the recurrence of this complex of light (sun, star), atmosphere (mist, sky), and color, it seems curious that the passage that was most frequently condemned by the New Critics as inorganic and superimposed is the one which compares life to "a dome of many-coloured glass" that

> Stains the white radiance of Eternity,
> Until Death tramples it to fragments. . . . (463–64)

Far from being willfully overlaid upon the materials, the simile is consistent with the symbolism governing the elegy throughout. The "dome," metaphoric of the sky, or the earth-surrounding atmosphere that is the condition for mortal existence, is therefore like life. Because this atmospheric dome diffracts the sun's rays, it "stains" the radiance of eternity, which is outside the atmosphere, and thereby produces color, the quality of the world of incompleteness and mutability, where skies are blue and fields are green. In the first movement this relationship of life and the dome of atmosphere had also appeared, but in inverted order, for there the quenching of the Splendor by damp death had been compared to the dying of a meteor which "stains a wreath / Of moonlight vapour" (106–7). In a context in which the only eternal principle is death and annihilation, the light of life stains the mist of mortality. But in the third movement it is not the mortal principle that is stained by the light, as the poet had conceived of it under his initial false premise, nor do light and atmosphere form the "softer light" necessary for organic life, as he had understood it in the second movement. Instead, the atmosphere—the color-making dome—"Stains the white radiance of Eternity," for colors are to white light as the Many are to the One, as imperfection and incompleteness are to perfection. Moreover, the identification of the sky-forming atmosphere as a dome had been established at the very beginning of the poem by the reference to "the *vault* of blue Italian day," which is a "fitting charnel-*roof*" for the dead Adonais (59–60). The image, therefore, had always resided in the poem, awaiting the development of attendant symbols and shifting perspectives to gain its full symbolic power. Retrospectively, the metaphor now makes clear (what could have been sensed only vaguely in its context) why the vault of day was Adonais' "fitting" charnel-roof. What is eventually revealed is that the great chamber bounded by the roof of atmosphere, although we call it the world of life, is *the* Charnel-House. The Adonais we call dead, truly lives; "*We* decay / Like corpses in a charnel" (348–49).

The materials of the metaphor are re-ordered yet again when, in the last movement, the poet complains that, like flower, ruins, statues, music, and words, "Rome's azure sky" is too weak to reveal the glory it transfuses (466–68). Just as the diffused and partially refracted light within the atmosphere is not a faithful representation of the white radiance of the sun, so earthly life, which the poet had earlier called a "pale light" (220), is but a weak version of the immortal spiritual One. Indeed, even the command to shatter the dome of life in order that the soul may be united with a pure spiritual existence had already been anticipated by the request that Air remove the mourning veil (the "dome") it had thrown over earth and leave earth bare, even at dawn, to the spirit-light of the stars (366–69). The metaphor of life as a dome of many-colored glass therefore must be read, not as a willed assertion, but as one of the points of final revelation toward which all the previous related imagery had been driving and in which that imagery attains its most perfect form and full value.

One of the numerous functions of the comparison of life to a dome is to reinterpret a parallel imagistic complex in the first movement. For in that movement also there was a white brilliance shining through a dome. Adonais lay beneath "the vault of blue Italian day," and within this charnel-roof, this "twilight chamber" formed by the sky-atmosphere, "spreads apace / The shadow of white Death" (65–66). This is precisely the complex of images that is repeated in the later simile, but with inverted meaning corresponding to the inversion of the thematic context. In both passages the sky is the boundary of the charnel-house; but in the first, Death is the leprous whiteness whose shadow spreads and envelops mortal life. The deathly white must hint, though obscurely, at the sun, for the imagery is bound up with the "twilight chamber," the sinking sun casting the same lengthening shadow as that of the white Death that "spreads apace." The imagery works perfectly within the theme that all decays; and the description of death as "white" produces the effective horror. But in the final movement a shift of interpretive perspective has been impelled by a reorganization of the same imagery. Postmortal life now being understood to be a spiritual existence, the white and dazzling radiance is Eternity, not Death; the vault, being mortality, stains the radiance (acting against it) instead of casting into the world the shadow of Death (cooperating with it); and it is Death who now destroys the dome, allowing the soul to "outsoar the shadow of our night," instead of working inward to destroy organic existence. Conceived in its proper frame of reference, what had appeared to be physical destruction now proves to be spiritual immortality. The imagery has at last attained what in his *Essay on Christianity* Shelley called "the purest and most perfect shape which it belongs to their nature to assume." Shelley's own relation to the world of his poem is the same as the relation which, in *Adonais*, he attributes to the One Spirit and the material world:

> the one Spirit's plastic stress
> Sweeps through the dull dense world, compelling there,
> All new successions to the forms they wear;
> Torturing th' unwilling dross that checks it's flight
> To it's own likeness, as each mass may bear. (381–85)

Each of the poem's three movements is a progressively more successful formative pressure upon the materials to assume the most nearly perfect order of which they are capable and thereby to reveal successively more probable truths.

Finally, the poetic integrity of the simile of life and the dome of atmosphere can also be seen by tracing the way in which the word "spread" and its associated term "stain" operate in the poem. In the first movement it is the shadow of white Death that *spreads* to embrace Adonais as the night progresses, spreading here being the act of obliterating. In the second movement, something of this sense of spreading is contained in the words "Diffuse themselves" (170), but, in keeping with the theme that the essential reality is animation, the diffusion has to do with the spread of physical substance, as though the resulting sensory qualities—matter's only means of defining to us its existence—were the total significance of the animating force. In the third movement, however, it is found, on the one hand, that earthly existence itself, not death, is a spreading, a "slow stain" that spreads by contagion (356), since we now know that what we call "life" is a decay; therefore earthly confinement, the mortal atmosphere, *stains* the radiance of Eternity. On the other hand, it is now the resurrected soul of Adonais, incorporated in the One, not the shadow of Death or physical matter, which is discovered to be, in the true sense, "Spreading itself" throughout nature (375), for the final reality everywhere is spirit, not death or mere animation.

iv

With the poem's governing cluster of symbols in mind, we can now return to the further significance of Adonais' apotheosis. Clearly the condition to which the poet aspires is the immutability of spirit ("The One remains"); and the successive themes of the elegy have been annihilation, endlessly cyclical change, and eternity. But by the translation of Adonais' spirit into Vesper, the poet is not asserting that death is the moment of soul-making. Instead, he is identifying the earthly soul with the eternal spirituality beyond the world of decay and mutability; for Vesper not only is the star of Venus (just as the mythical Adonis is related to the mythical Venus), but is also identical with Lucifer, the morning star—the point that the epigraph from the Greek Anthology drives home. The assumption behind the third movement of *Adonais* is akin to the theme of one of the manuscript verses quoted in the previous chapter,[25] verses, incidentally, that are scattered among the drafts of *Adonais*: a "star of Heaven," a "quenchless atom of immortal light," has fallen into a human existence, "Like an Angel's spirit pent / In a form of mortal birth," until it "Shatters its charnel." Lucifer-Vesper, which repeatedly serves in Shelley's poems as variant modes of the transcendent ideal, is therefore the symbol of the eternal spirit, since its real nature is always unchangeably present behind its apparent differences. Were the atmosphere of mortality removed, man would perceive that the "One remains" and that "Heaven's light forever shines"; that day and night are one, life and death, Lucifer and Vesper, the spirit of the living Adonais and that of the dead. What is being asserted is that the ultimate reality of both earthly life and the postmortal eternity is the spiritual One. The day-night cycle and the season cycle of the first two movements, together with the life-death distinction they imply, are but earthly appearances:

> The splendours of the firmament of time
> May be eclipsed, but are extinguished not;
> Like stars to their appointed height they climb
> And death is a low mist which cannot blot
> The brightness it may veil.   (388–92)

[25] See pp. 450–51.

It is this assumption concerning the spiritual identity of mortal and post-mortal existence that finally erases the polarities running through the first two movements: life and death, vitality and mind, flower and star, dew and splendor. Because the separate identities of the two stars and the obliteration of them by diffused sunlight are only appearances, Adonais has postmortally become "a presence to be felt [in the material world] and known [in the mental world] / In *darkness* and in *light*" (373–74), just as the gleaming snow of the Power at the peak of Mont Blanc continues to fall "In the calm darkness of the moonless nights" and "In the lone glare of day." For these distinctions are not ultimately real.

Like most of the imagery of the last movement, this construct of an eternal sameness that dissolves seeming polarities has also been carefully lodged in stanza 17 of the first movement, exerting its force there just below the main level of meaning while the surface statement is performing another and more immediate task. The mourning for Bion, Moschus had written, surpassed the laments by the dolphin, nightingale, swallow, tern, ceryl, and eagle. In reproducing the mechanics of the traditional elegy Shelley imitated precisely this feature and even echoed the rhetorical structure of Moschus' lines, but he reduced the mourners to nightingale and eagle:

Thy spirit's sister, the lorn nightingale
Mourns not her mate with such melodious pain;
Not so the eagle, who like thee could scale
Heaven, and could nourish in the sun's domain
Her mighty youth with morning, doth complain. . . .
As Albion wails for thee. . . . (145–51)

For the purpose of an elegy, presumably any other mourners would serve equally well; but by making this reduction the poet has limited himself to a symbol of night (nightingale) and a symbol of morning (eagle). These, moreover, are explicitly defined as aspects of Adonais himself: "Thy spirit's sister"; "like thee could scale." In the immediate context of the first movement, they are the fitting emblems of the god of cyclical nature, who, after the passing of his night phase, nourishes "in the sun's domain" his "mighty youth with morning." But while the stanza fits perfectly into its present context both as part of the elegiac machinery of mourning and as an account of the nature-god, it is also driving by a delicate dramatic irony toward the third movement, which explicates the Hesperus-Lucifer relationship in the poem's epigraph and where the distinction between night and day is irrelevant, since the One glows "Through time and change, unquenchably the same."

Moreover, we have already noted that in *Hellas* Shelley adopted the traditional symbolism of the eagle. According to the tradition of "unnatural" natural history, in old age the eagle grows dim-sighted, flies directly toward the sun, which burns off the old feathers and removes the film over its eyes, and then dives into a spring, whose waters renew its youth; and an associated tradition attributes to the eagle the unique ability to look unblinkingly into the sun. This fable of the eagle's recovery of its youthful strength by flight into the sun had regularly been interpreted as the rebirth and resurrection of the soul by its recourse to Christ, especially in commentaries on Psalm 103: "so that thy youth is renewed like the eagle's." When we recall that in the final movement the sun will become the symbol of the One, it is apparent that, although the eagle's power to renew its vitality recurrently is immediately relevant to the season-god, Adonais' eagle-like ability to scale Heaven and nourish his youth in the "sun's domain" symbolizes, by anticipation, the third movement, where Adonais is the resurrection-god who returns immortally to the "burning fountain" whence he came. It is as though in stanza 17 the poet, while pursuing a misconception, has stumbled across a truth; but that it is a truth he has had in his grasp will not be evident until he has completely revised his mode of vision and correspondingly readjusted the complex of images he is viewing.

But if the eagle symbolizes, at one level, the soul that is resurrected, its nocturnal counterpart, the nightingale, represents the earthly poet, who sings in the "night of time." Consequently the stanza sets up the same relationship that is implicit in the poem's epigraph and that will be exploited later when we learn that Adonais-Vesper is present in both darkness and light: the nightingale, who mourns with "melodious pain," is to the eagle, the resurrected soul, as the earthly poet Keats (the morning star among the living) is to his eternal spirit, Vesper (Hesperus, giving new splendor to the dead). The relationship of nightingale and eagle, therefore, parallels that of night and day, flower and star, dew and splendor: they are the seeming polarities of the mortal world, and they are present in the poem so that they may ultimately dissolve into an overriding unity. Stanza 17, then, works simultaneously at three levels of reference: superficially it carries out the machinery of the traditional elegy; in its context it identifies the nature-god with the cycle of organic life; and there are latent within it all the symbolic factors that will bring about the poem's final revelation.

On the basis of this identity of the earthly and postmortal soul, together with the attendant star symbol, Shelley proceeds to develop the imagery and theme of stanza 47 in the third movement. Having announced that Adonais has ascended the erstwhile "kingless sphere," he turns to one who still, mistakenly, mourns the earthly Adonais, and he urges the mourner to learn the true nature not only of Adonais but also of himself:

Clasp with thy panting soul the pendulous Earth;
As from a centre, dart thy spirit's light
Beyond all worlds, until its spacious might
Satiate the void circumference. . . .   (417–20)

As elsewhere in Shelley, man is the world, since there is no real distinction between subject and object, and the world is the sum of each man's knowledge, including himself. Like the island of *Epipsychidion*, the human microcosm is animated by a star that has descended to its core, and mortal man is therefore a star—a truth anticipated by the fact that the mind is an "intense atom," a mote reflecting light. The mourner is being urged to discover the star-like nature of his own earthly self by clasping the earth and darting from its center his own "spirit's light" beyond the limits of the charnel-house world and into the realm of Eternity—just as the immortal soul of Adonais now radiates its light from Vesper in the heavens. The mourner will know himself aright when he knows that even in the mortal world his essence is a star-soul that can reach beyond the false mutability of "our day and night." In mortal life Vesper had been the star Lucifer.

v

Turning at last to the Protestant Cemetery in Rome, the poet fashions his final tableau in order to bring into summary relationship much of the poem's imagery and thereby to engage in the tableau the terminal theme of the elegy. The scene has significant structural value. First, because the cemetery is the impersonal and irrevocably final fact of death, its stillness stands in ironic contrast to the poet's previous impassioned lament. In the larger structure the scene rounds out the poem: the initial setting had been Rome, where Keats died, the final one is the cemetery in Rome where Keats was buried. Thematically the description of the cemetery gathers together, in the full development of their values, the symbols of all three hypotheses—decay, mutability, and eternity. Most important, we are promised that through the material components of the scene we will gain the final truth, for it is by observing the cemetery that the one who still mourns for Adonais is to learn the true nature of life and death. The mute and solitary symbols in this earthly otherworld have contained all the while the truth that the poet has agonized to gain.

Symbolically the area within the burial place is that of eternal spirit; and its environs—the world of "living" man—are the area of matter and mortality. In the city outside the cemetery Rome's ancient ruins figure forth the decay of matter and human endeavors; for they rise like shattered mountains, and on the cemetery's mouldering walls "dull Time / Feeds, like slow fire upon a hoary brand" (442–43). Like Adonais' poetic flowers

that vainly "adorned and hid the coming bulk of death" in the first movement, outside the cemetery the "flowering weeds, and fragrant copses
dress / The bones of Desolation's nakedness" (436–37). Here, however,
there is no suggestion that the relation between organic life and dead
matter is significant: both have been depressed into minor symbols of the
petty world that decays to nakedness and then pretends to disguise its
decay. For matter and animation are pathetically small facts in the
presence of the eternity of thought: only "the kings of thought / Who
waged contention with their time's decay, / . . . of the past are all that
cannot pass away" (430–32). Only mind is eternal, and its earthly function is to struggle against the mutability that inheres in the sublunary
realm.

But opposing this conjunction of wild vegetation and Desolation's
"bones" in the city that tell that the Many change and pass, stands one
of the most richly symbol-laden descriptions in the poem: inside the
cemetery, "like an infant's smile, over the dead, / A light of laughing
flowers along the grass is spread" (440–41). First, it is necessary to recall
the shifting, evolving significances of "spread" and of the relation of
flowers to corpse throughout the three movements. Spreading first designated the act of obliterating, then the diffusion of sensory qualities by
virtue of animation, and then the stain of mortal life on the radiance of
Eternity. Originally the flowers vainly defied the corpse and could only
disguise temporarily the annihilation they must come to (as Rome's weeds
and copses do here), and then it was found that, cyclically, the corpse
"Exhales itself in flowers of gentle breath." But meanwhile it has been
learned that it is truly the resurrected soul of Adonais that is "Spreading
itself where'er that Power may move / Which has withdrawn his being to
its own" (375–76). Consequently, in spreading their light along the grass
the flowers are now performing in this world an act parallel to that of
Adonais-Vesper and the white radiance that is everywhere a spirit to be
felt and known. No longer is flower related to corpse at all, either as a
disguise over the death that will come to it or as that which the corpse
fertilizes in nature's cycle; it is now known that dust and soul return to
their separate origins, a dualism contained in the fact that the light of the
flowers is spread "*over* the dead." The light of the flowers is like that of an
"infant's smile," not because corpse feeds the new life, but because physical death is unrelated to the pristine spiritual life symbolized by the
infant.

Finally, flower and star, the two symbols of Adonais, have been recurrently related in the poem as earthly life is related to postmortal life.
Therefore, in attributing light to the flowers, Shelley is pointing to the
spirituality that is the essence of mortal life, just as he had pointed to it
by urging the mourner to make the earth a spirit-star with his own spirit's
light. The earthly Adonais was also a "star among the living"; and since

flowers are a splendor changed to fragrance, the poet's reversal of this direction by commanding that dew be turned to splendor now reveals that the flowers also spread a spirit-light. Symbolizing earthly spirits like that of Adonais, the flowers divulge, then, that the ultimate reality of earthly life and beauty is also spiritual, not animate or material. By spreading a light they are, like great earthly souls, "mirrors of / The fire for which all thirst." Earlier, misled by the false supposition of the second movement, the poet had thought of flowers metaphorically as incarnate stars that "illumine death" (174–75); that is, that by being animate they change the darkness of death into light. What has now been discovered is that the earthly flowers are truly "incarnations of the stars," since earthly reality is embodied spirit; and that truly the flowers "illumine death"—in a symbolic sense that had not been realized when those words appeared.

It is, however, the famous memorial pyramid of Caius Cestius, standing at the center of the tableau and dominating it, that is the controlling symbol of the scene. In one sense the pyramid memorializes the earthly Cestius, praetor, man of arms, and tribune of the plebeians. He was, that is, a minister of justice and defender of the common people against the political oppression of the patricians, and therefore he would have been to Shelley one of the "kings of thought / Who waged contention with their time's decay" (430–31). Moreover, Shelley obviously thought of Cestius as a military officer: the hollow pyramid is "*Pavilioning* the dust of him who planned / This refuge for his [worldly] memory" (445–46), for it has the shape of the pyramidal pavilion, or tent, of the battlefield and therefore is a memorial of his earthly exploits. The same metaphor of the tents of the battlefield is then extended to the rest of the cemetery: below the pyramid "A field is spread, on which a newer band / Have pitched in Heaven's smile their camp of death" (447–49), other soldiers who have "waged contention with their time's decay." But that it is pitched in "Heaven's smile," or light, carries with it a strong implication of a spiritual interpretation, too great to be applicable to the graveyard as only a memorial of mortal deeds. If the camp is pitched in Heaven's light, then "That Light whose smile kindles the Universe" has joined these dead to itself—the same light that the "laughing flowers," as earthly modes of the One, spread over the dead—the same light which is the "smile" of the "joyous stars" (369).

In Shelley's day it was still generally assumed that the word "pyramid" derives from πῦρ (fire) because, according to Johnson's *Dictionary*, "fire always ascends in the figure of a cone"; and so it was accepted that a pyramid imitates the shape of a flame.[26] But before we examine the sig-

---

[26] Chambers' *Cyclopaedia*, art. "Pyramid": "Villalpandus ... derives the word from πῦρ, fire; because ending in a point like flame." Milton had written of "a Pyramid of fire" (*Paradise Lost*, II. 1013); and R. P. Knight described the Egyptian pyramids as "the symbols of that fire to which the bodies of the dead were consigned"

nificance of this etymology, it is necessary to note that in the description of the cemetery fire acts in two opposing ways, in accordance with Shelley's customary ambiguous image:

And gray walls moulder round, on which dull Time
Feeds, like slow fire upon a hoary brand;
And one keen pyramid with wedge sublime,
Pavilioning the dust of him who planned
This refuge for his memory, doth stand
Like flame transformed to marble. . . .   (442–47)

Since in the mortal world around the cemetery the Many change and pass, time is there like a fire that consumes, as the mouldering wall of the cemetery attests. But the spirit-world of the cemetery is immortal, and there Eternity displaces time. Hence the pyramid of Cestius, forming part of the wall but belonging to the graveyard, is, as the false etymology implies, "Like flame transformed to marble"—a flame fixed eternally the same. Like Shelley's Cloud, which, from below, seems to dissolve in rain but, from above, is seen to bask in heaven's smile of light, the marble flame-like pyramid, as symbol of the return of the soul to the burning fountain whence it came, stands in opposition to the surrounding mortal fire that destroys. What the tapered, aspiring shape of the pyramid reveals had been symbolized earlier by the transmutation of earthly dew into spiritual splendor and by Adonais' starry apotheosis, his outsoaring the shadow of our night. "Among the Egyptians," according to Chambers' *Cyclopaedia*, "the *pyramid* is said to have been a symbol of human life; the beginning whereof is represented by the base, and the end by the apex." The tradition summarized here had been elaborated by Pierio Valeriano in his *Hieroglyphica*, which identifies the pyramid with both fire and the human soul. The broad base, according to Valeriano, signifies matter, the stuff on which flame feeds; the remaining body, the matter ready to receive form; and the apex, the most simple, refined substance. Hence, he concludes, the pyramid signifies the human soul, which Plato stated to be of a fiery nature, the soul clinging to the body as the pyramid to its base, or as flame to the material substance on which it feeds.[27] Because this emblem perfectly corresponds to Shelley's figure of spiritual life as a flame, a descended star, or a reflected light, the reaching out of the marble flame toward a bright radiance beyond the atmosphere causes it to

---

(*Symbolic Language*, p. 117). See also, e.g., *Encyclopaedia Britannica* (Edinburgh, 1771) and *Universal History* (1779), I, p. 183.

    According to Plato (*Timaeus* 56), "the solid form of the pyramid is the original element and seed of fire."

[27] *Hieroglyphica* (Basel, 1575), p. 438. The same interpretation appears in Athanasius Kircher's *Obeliscus Pamphilius* (Rome, 1650), pp. 171–72.

be, as Chambers' *Cyclopaedia* further reports, "the symbol of immortality." The symbolic fire that, in one context, destroys and, in another, represents immortality embodies the same ambiguity expressed in the description of the kings of thought, who are "of the *past* . . . all that *cannot pass* away." Transitory time and eternity are the opposite sides of the same coin.

If we now reconsider the image of the pyramid, it proves equally ambiguous, like Shelley's Cloud: thought of as a shelter, it is a pavilion containing the mortal dust and memorializing the earthly life of the military man; thought of as an outward form, a marble flame, it bespeaks the immortality of his spirit. But the central fact of the image is that it is both tent and flame. Beneath it lie the physical remains of Cestius: "Dust to the dust!" The pyramid itself, however, is the symbol of both mortal life and immortality, and both at the same time: the pure spirit flows back to its origin, the "burning fountain." For what the poem has everywhere been leading to is that spirit is the one reality, both here and hereafter. The spirit of Caius Cestius, like that of Adonais, persists now in Eternity as part of the One, from which the earthly flame, the intensely glowing "atom," is derived.

The consequence of the poem's gradual generation of symbols is that it has transfigured all the objective features around and within the cemetery—the ruins, flowers, walls, weeds, graves, and pyramid—so that they may perform their proper roles as meaning in order to assert that although the Many change and pass, the One remains. Here in the symbol-charged cemetery the one who still mourns the death of Adonais can *see* why he should mourn no longer.

vi

It remains to examine the roles of Urania and the "Shelley" who speaks in the first person in the poem, for a fixed set of assumptions concerning them has frequently distracted from an understanding of the elegy.

Because Plato distinguished between the Uranian and Pandemian Aphrodites and because Shelley elsewhere accepted this distinction between spiritual and physical loves, it has usually seemed logical to suppose that Urania is another absolute Ideal, the One from whom all spirits come and to whom they return. But if we accept this externally imposed interpretation, insurmountable difficulties arise inside the poem. Why did Shelley choose to make this Venus the mother of Adonais instead of his lover, as in the traditional myth? Or if she is the One, why does Adonais not return to her? Why does she disappear from the poem at the point when she should be essential in this role, that is, when Adonais becomes an immortal spirit? And if she is the One, or something like Intellectual Beauty, why does she lament the death of the physical Adonais and wish to be what he now is, that is, part of the One?

Despite her various qualifying titles, the Venus of classical, extra-Platonic myth is essentially the life-giving power, the Venus Genetrix whom Lucretius invoked: *per te quoniam genus omne animantum concipitur.* Nor did the epithet "Uranian" always carry with it Plato's distinction: one chapter of Richard Payne Knight's treatise on mythology, for example, is entitled "Venus-Urania, the Mother-Goddess."[28] If, then, we put aside any Platonic interpretation and read Urania as the spirit of organic life, rather than a personification of the One, the confusion tends to disappear. An early draft of *Adonais* shows that in the original version of stanza 4 Shelley invoked, not Urania, but Poesy: "Lament anew great Poesy."[29] Presumably he then substituted for Poesy the Urania whom Milton had invoked and identified that muse with Venus Genetrix.

Shelley was quite explicit about Urania's nature. She must be the mother of Adonais instead of his lover, just as she is also the mother of Milton, because she is the "mighty Mother" (10); and she is further defined as "that living Might" (218). In her passage over the earth her "sacred blood" paved her path "with eternal flowers" (216); and so great is her strength as the "living Might" that when she entered Adonais' death-chamber, Death "Blushed to annihilation, and the breath / Revisited those lips, and life's pale light / Flashed through those limbs" (217–21). But although her blood becomes flowers that are "eternal"—because the animation they symbolize in that context ("All baser things") is preserved by the perpetual cycle of regeneration—she cannot restore Adonais to life, despite her momentary triumph, because his essence is mind, or soul, which is not reborn into the world: "Death rose and smiled, and met her vain caress" of Adonais (225), and her animating power is repulsed. Then,

[28] Banier pointed out that Herodotus had made no distinction between Urania and Aphrodite, and he derived the epithet "Urania" simply from the fact that Venus was believed to have dropped from heaven "under the Form of a Star" (*Mythology*, I, vi, 8; II, i, 11).

There is little difficulty in disposing of the theory that because Shelley thought well of *Hyperion* he was celebrating Keats as an epic poet and therefore intended Urania, the muse whom Milton invoked, as the mother of epic poets. Moschus had written of Homer and Bion: "O tunefullest of rivers, this makes thee a second grief. . . . One melodious mouthpiece of Calliope is long dead, and that is Homer . . . now thou weepest for another son. . . . Both were beloved of a water-spring, for the one drank at Pegasus' fountain and the other got him drink of Arethusa; and the one sang of the lovely daughter of Tyndareus, and of the great son of Thetis, and of Atreid Menelaus; but this other's singing was neither of wars nor tears but of Pan; as a herdsman he chanted, and kept his cattle with a song; he both fashioned pipes and milked the gentle kine; he taught the lore of kisses, he made a fosterling of love, he roused and stirred the passion of Aphrodite." This, of course, is the source of stanza 4 of *Adonais*, Shelley substituting Milton for Homer, and Keats for Bion. It is implicit in the echo of the source that Milton is to Homer as Keats is to Bion, and therefore that Keats is being celebrated as one who sang of Pan and love, not of the heroic.

[29] MS e. 9, p. 25. Cf. also MS e. 10, p. 215: "How long has Poesy, the widowed Mother / Been childless in our land [blank] he died / Blind old and lonely when [blank]."

since the poem is in process of revealing that the essence everywhere is soul, Urania disappears from the poem after the second movement because as the "living Might" she has no relevance to the theme of spiritual immortality. Urania's words to the dead Adonais, "But I am chained to Time, and cannot thence depart!" (234; Shelley's calculated variant of Bion's "I alas! live and am a Gôd and may not go after thee") now have very special significance. Clearly Shelley is not attributing to Urania a spiritual immortality. As the goddess of organic life she is "immortal" only in being chained to all of that time in which the Many change and pass. She belongs to timefulness, not timelessness. She cannot be what she wrongly conceives Adonais now to be because the animating force is perpetual, never to cease. By being yoked to Time she is opposed to, not identified with, the One, which is an Eternity outside time, an Eternity that "remains."

If, then, Urania is the earth-mother, or the "Mother of this unfathomable world" invoked by the Narrator of *Alastor*, her perspective must be different from the one the poet attains in the last movement; and her artistic duty therefore is to contribute to the ironic texture of the poem by her innocent misinterpretations. For example, she speaks as though she would willingly make a sacrifice when she says to the dead Adonais, "I would give / All that I am to be as thou now art!" (232–33), for her assumption is that he no longer has any being at all. Ignorant of a spiritual immortality, she does not see the irony of her words: that to share Adonais' present state would be to rise from her endless vital existence to an atemporal spirituality. Similarly, Urania participates in other ironic inversions. In the third movement we learn that

> the one Spirit's plastic stress
> Sweeps through the dull dense world, compelling there,
> All new successions to the forms they wear;
> Torturing th' unwilling dross that checks it's flight
> To its own likeness, as each mass may bear. (381–85)

Earlier there had appeared this account of Urania's journey to Adonais:

> Out of her secret Paradise she sped,
> Through camps and cities rough with stone, and steel,
> And human hearts, which to her aery tread
> Yielding not, wounded the invisible
> Palms of her tender feet where'er they fell:
> And barbed tongues, and thoughts more sharp than they
> Rent the soft Form they never could repel. (208–14)

The two descriptions are generally alike, but the relationships of their details are significantly inverted. The spiritual power shapes the Many toward relative likenesses of itself, although the Many resist because they cannot "bear" the full spiritual power. On the other hand, the Great Mother merely gives these successions their vital existence; and all that is material and human resists this living force and wounds it, although it cannot fully withstand it. Matter and body mutilate the beauty of the vital power; but they themselves are twisted by the One until they bear a likeness to its beauty. The true "Form" the Many wear is not Urania's, but the One's.

Urania's words, therefore, must not be read in isolation, but as forms of dramatic irony to which she is not a party. When the earth-mother laments Adonais' daring "the unpastured dragon in his den" and wishes he had "waited the full cycle, when / Thy spirit should have filled its crescent sphere" (241–42), the astronomical images are intended only as means of saying metaphorically that Adonais had not lived to earthly maturity. An astronomical symbol is appropriate since Adonais is now Vesper and had been Lucifer, the earth-phase of the same star. But as the spirit of organic life Urania can think only in terms of earthly growth and fulfillment, the evolution of the full moon from its "crescent sphere." As a burning atom of the fire for which all thirst, the human soul is always ready to return to the One from which it derives: like Adonais, the good die first, or, as Shelley expressed it in *The Triumph of Life*, "as soon / As they had touched the world with living flame / Fled back like eagles to their native noon."[30] Moreover, in imagining Adonais as the moon instead of an eternal star, Urania has chosen the essential symbol of that eternal mutability over which she reigns as the Great Mother, the moon that is the outer sphere and symbol of her realm of endlessly cyclical birth, death, and rebirth, not the superlunary symbol of eternity. It is therefore especially necessary to make an ironic reading of the following lament by Urania, which is unintelligible if read as literally consistent with the final meaning of the elegy:

> The sun comes forth, and many reptiles spawn;
> He sets, and each ephemeral insect then
> Is gathered into death without a dawn,
> And the immortal stars awake again;
> So is it in the world of living men:
> A godlike mind soars forth, in its delight
> Making earth bare and veiling heaven, and when
> It sinks, the swarms that dimmed or shared its light
> Leave to its kindred lamps the spirit's awful night.   (stanza 29)

It is significant that Urania confines her observations to "the world of living men," the only world about which the "living Might" is competent

[30] *Triumph of Life*, 129–31.

to speak. Within this limitation she divides men into three categories: the base and spiritless, who exist only briefly (ephemeral insects; the swarms that dim or share the light of the godlike mind); the lesser spirits (stars; the godlike mind's kindred lamps); and the godlike mind (the sun). In her perspective the metaphor states that when a godlike mind appears, it blots out from human attention the lesser spirits, just as the sun blots out from human sight the heavens and the stars; but that the godlike mind must eventually set, and then the lesser star-spirits must do their feeble best to illuminate the spiritual night.

But Urania's words, "immortal stars," themselves run counter to this reading. If the stars are immortal, it seems they should be the metaphor for the godlike mind rather than for lesser spirits. In its context the metaphor must mean that godlike minds are only occasional while in the world of living men there are always lesser spirits (the only way in which a time-chained goddess could understand immortality), even though they are obscured by the occasional sun-like mind. But the word "immortal" is too strong to be confined to this meaning, and it energetically points ahead to the true interpretation of the astronomical images in the spiritual and atemporal perspective. The stars, we ultimately learn, are indeed immortal, not because lesser spirits are always to be found on earth, but because stars are the symbols of the godlike mind and are outside time. The god-like mind, then, is not like the sun in coming forth and setting, but is like the stars in being ever-present; only in Urania's earthly perspective do the stars *seem* to be extinguished and then to "awake again." Nor, we learn, is it the godlike mind (the sun) that veils heaven while it illumines earth; rather, it is mortality, the atmosphere, that conceals the stars from earthly eyes by diffusing the sun's rays. Earth is not "bare" because, as Urania believes, it is flooded with sunlight while heaven is veiled; it is the removal of earth's atmosphere of mortality that leaves it "bare / Even to the joyous stars which smile on its despair!" (368–69). Finally, Urania's three categories generally correspond to the three themes of the poem: the One remains (the "immortal stars"), the many change (the godlike sun-mind) and pass (the ephemera who set "without a dawn"). But obviously her symbols for these categories, and hence her interpretation of them, are at odds with the symbols the poem finally assigns them. Briefly, Urania has used metaphors to speak an earthly truth, which is the inverse of the spiritual truth, like the outside and inside of Cestius' pyramid. When her images are inverted and then read literally, instead of metaphorically, they become the controlling symbols of the final movement.

vii

Shelley's so-called self-portrait (stanzas 31–34) has almost always proved unpleasant reading because it seems sadly marred by extravagant self-pity and unmanliness. But this human weakness is appropriate to the context, which proposes that nature is cyclical but that the soul of man is destroyed forever. The quality of the portrait is not to be divorced from its thematic context. What the poem says is that *if* we accept the thesis that man, unlike vegetative nature, is destroyed to awake no more, then Shelley is to be conceived of as "Girt round with weakness," a "frail Form, / A phantom among men," "a dying lamp, a falling shower, / A breaking billow," a flower withering in the "killing sun."

Moreover, even if we take the description in its context, it is so inconsistent with itself that it cannot be a definitive statement, but must be part of an evolving process. The thematic context is inadequate to contain the details of the self-portrait, which press for a later coherent fulfillment. What the surface of the description emphasizes is physical weakness, but subordinate elements clash with this emphasis. Shelley is a "frail *Form*," but he is also a *"phantom* among men," and the words face both ways, noting his mortal weakness but also bespeaking a spiritual strength. Certainly there is no sense of weakness in the line, "A pardlike Spirit beautiful and swift" (280), but here he is considering himself as spirit, not as form. Even the grammatical structure of the words "a Power / Girt round with weakness" (281–82) shows the restlessness of the self-description: while the ostensible theme is this frailty, the grammar gives dominant significance to the fact that the poet is a "Power." That the weakness only girds him suggests that it is not related to his essential nature.

These conflicts will eventually be resolved in the closing stanzas of the elegy, where the fire for which all thirst is described as consuming the "last clouds" of Shelley's "cold mortality." Thinking in mortal terms in the second movement, the speaker of the poem sees mainly that his mortal self is being destroyed. What has not fully revealed itself as yet is that the destruction of the poet's physical self is only the obverse of his spiritual fulfillment. Yet the unstable imagery is impelling toward the discovery that he is a "frail Form" only because his spirit now so brightly mirrors the light of the One that this light is consuming the mortal atmospheric veil and drawing him to itself. It is because this final truth of the third movement runs like an undercurrent beneath the "self-portrait" that such descriptions as "A Love in desolation masked" (281) do not ring quite true in their own setting, for the word "masked" states that Love is his true nature and that his desolation is only false-seeming. Reading the portrait in its own context makes intelligible the otherwise obscure lines:

As in the accents of an unknown land,
He sung new sorrow; sad Urania scanned
The Stranger's mien, and murmured: "who art thou?"   (301–3)

As the spirit of mortal life, Urania is unable to recognize her son because he is being absorbed into the One and withdrawn from mortality, which is only a mask over his true nature. He is therefore a "stranger," an alien, in the realm of Time, to which she is chained and which limits her knowledge; and his songs, being of the "unknown land" of spiritual eternity, are unintelligible to her.

The ironic working of the four stanzas of the portrait is especially vigorous in the following two passages:

> he, as I guess,
> Had gazed on Nature's naked loveliness,
> Actaeon-like, and now he fled astray
> With feeble steps o'er the world's wilderness,
> And his own thoughts, along that rugged way,
> Pursued, like raging hounds, their father and their prey.   (274–79)

>   On the withering flower
> The killing sun smiles brightly.   (286–87)

The reference to the myth of Actaeon is intended, of course, to suggest a penalty and physical torture, and so interpreted it is appropriate to its context. Yet, the form the allusion takes here is hardly in accord with the subsequent theme that the essence of man, the glowing atom of mind, is forever extinguished. If merely the tone of the lines were altered, they would assert, in effect, what the third movement will assert: when man looks on the One (Nature's naked loveliness), his thoughts release him from his prison of mortality. The ambiguity is precisely that of the Visionary in *Alastor*, who, having looked on the perfection he himself projects, is in one perspective pursued by, and in another drawn to, the ideal and thus progresses to death. In this sense the lines in *Adonais* parallel and anticipate the poet's statement in the third movement that the "Light whose smile kindles the Universe" (and makes evident nature's naked loveliness), which

> Burns bright or dim, as each are mirrors of
> The fire for which all thirst; now beams on me,
> Consuming the last clouds of cold mortality.

> The breath whose might I have invoked in song
> Descends on me.   (484–88)

The Actaeon myth, then, is only a slightly distorted version of the poem's final revelation and reflects the poet's momentarily mistaking spiritual resurrection for physical destruction.

The metaphor of the second passage works with equal irony. Shelley, like Adonais, is a flower, and in the perspective of mortality the sun is understood to be "killing" it. But the expression of the metaphor contains too much for its present relevance: the words "smiles brightly" carry strong overtones opposing those of "withering flower" and "killing sun," and thereby set up a discord that presses for a resolution. The bright smiles of the sun anticipate the "light of laughing flowers" like "an infant's smile" and the "Light whose smile kindles the Universe"; and they therefore contradict the harshness of "killing" and "withering," as though to tell us that the imagery is wrestling against the immediate misconception. The poem will shortly reveal that the sun is the one Spirit and that its smile kills only by consuming the mortal veil separating life from the "death" which is Eternity.

Only, then, if the four stanzas are read in isolation and not as operative elements in the total poem are they open to the charge of bathetic self-pity. For to be read as poetry they must first be integrated with their thematic context and then recognized as only a dramatic preparation for a harmonious portrait, the true contours of which will be shaped by the last three stanzas of the poem. By this process the self-portrait really becomes a preparation for the identification of Shelley with Keats. As Keats is physically dead, so Shelley, like every mortal, is physically dying; both are withered flowers on which the sun smiles; and just as Adonis-Adonais was slain by a boar, so Shelley is an Actaeon being destroyed by his own hounds, which are "his own thoughts." It is "in another's fate" that Shelley has "wept his own" (300). Shelley therefore is also an Adonai, a god-like mind. The so-called self-portrait, then, is not merely a self-portrait, but rather a means of bringing Keats and Shelley to coincide so that the subject of the poem may become neither of them alone, but the human spirit and its destiny in the "world divine" beyond the grave. Like all human souls that sufficiently mirror the One, Shelley will be

> borne darkly, fearfully, afar;
> Whilst burning through the inmost veil of Heaven,
> The soul of Adonais, like a star,
> Beacons from the abode where the Eternal are.   (492–95)

INDEX

∽

THE JOHNS HOPKINS PRESS

Designed by Arlene J. Sheer

Composed in Fairfield text
by Monotype Composition Company
Printed on 55 lb. Old Style Laid
by Universal Lithographers, Inc.
Bound in Holliston Natural Finish 31275
by Moore and Company, Inc.